INSIDE

3D STUDIO
MAX

VOLUME II:

ADVANCED MODELING AND MATERIALS

DAVE ESPINOSA-AGUILAR
JOSHUA R. ANDERSEN
STEVE BURKE
PHILLIP MILLER
ERIC C. PETERSON
MICHAEL TODD PETERSON
KEN ALLEN ROBERTSON
JONATHAN SAWYER
LEE STEEL
ANDREW VERNON

SERIES EDITOR: PHILLIP MILLER

COVER ART BY STEVE BURKE

New Riders Publishing, Indianapolis, Indiana

Contributions from KINETIX, a Division of Autodesk

Inside 3D Studio MAX, Volume II: Advanced Modeling and Materials

By dave espinosa-aguilar, Joshua R. Andersen, Steve Burke, Phillip Miller, Eric C. Peterson, Michael Todd Peterson, Ken Allen Robertson, Jonathan Sawyer, Lee Steel, and Andrew Vernon

Published by:
New Riders Publishing
201 West 103rd Street
Indianapolis, IN 46290 USA

Printed in the United States of America 1 2 3 4 5 6 7 8 9 0

Library of Congress Cataloging-in-Publication Data

```
Inside 3D studio Max / Steve D. Elliott ... [et al.].
    p.  cm.
  Includes index.
  ISBN 1-56205-679-4 (v. 2)
  1. Computer animation. 2. 3D studio.
1960-
TR897.7.I56  1997
006.6—dc20
```
96-38753

CIP

Warning and Disclaimer

This book is designed to provide information about the 3D Studio MAX computer program. Every effort has been made to make this book as complete and as accurate as possible, but no warranty or fitness is implied.

The information is provided on an "as is" basis. The authors and New Riders Publishing shall have neither liability nor responsibility to any person or entity with respect to any loss or damages arising from the information contained in this book or from the use of the discs or programs that may accompany it.

PUBLISHER	Don Fowley
PUBLISHING MANAGER	David Dwyer
MARKETING MANAGER	Mary Foote
MANAGING EDITOR	Carla Hall

PRODUCT DIRECTOR
  Alicia Buckley
ACQUISITIONS EDITOR
  Dustin Sullivan
DEVELOPMENT EDITOR
  Laura Frey
SENIOR EDITORS
  Sarah Kearns
  Suzanne Snyder
PROJECT EDITORS
  Amy Bezek
  Gina Brown
  Gail S. Burlakoff
  Karen Walsh
COPY EDITOR
  Keith Cline
TECHNICAL EDITOR
  Larry Minton
SOFTWARE SPECIALIST
  Steve Flatt
ACQUISITIONS COORDINATOR
  Stacey Beheler
ADMINISTRATIVE COORDINATOR
  Karen Opal
MANUFACTURING COORDINATOR
  Brook Farling
COVER DESIGNER
  Sandra Schroeder
COVER PRODUCTION
  Aren Howell
BOOK DESIGNER
  Anne Jones
DIRECTOR OF PRODUCTION
  Larry Klein
PRODUCTION TEAM SUPERVISORS
  Laurie Casey
  Joe Millay
GRAPHICS IMAGE SPECIALISTS
  Kevin Cliburn, Sadie Crawford, Wil Cruz, Brad Dixon, Dan Harris
PRODUCTION ANALYST
  Erich J. Richter
PRODUCTION TEAM
  Tricia Flodder, Christopher Morris, Elizabeth SanMiguel, Christy Wagner
INDEXER
  Christopher Cleveland

About the Authors

dave espinosa-aguilar is a project manager, programmer, and animator for Toxic Frog Multimedia in Reno, Nevada. A graduate in electrical engineering and physics of Gonzaga University, Dave has been training architects and engineers for 12 years on 3D modeling and visualization. Dave served as President of the Autodesk User Group International in 1996 and has been a regular faculty member of AutoCAD, Animator Pro, Animator Studio, and 3D Studio DOS and MAX courses offered at Autodesk University, A/E/C Systems, MechanCAD, and other Multimedia/CAD conferences. In his spare time, Dave also does product support for Autodesk on CompuServe's AMMEDIA, KINETIX, and ACAD forums.

Joshua R. Andersen is currently a 3D artist and animator at GlyphX, Inc. His previous experience in this field includes work as a graphic artist for a multimedia firm and as a 3D modeler at Viewpoint Datalabs, Intl. He has used 3D Studio MAX since its early beta versions and has experience with many other high-end 3D animation and modeling packages on Silicon Graphics workstations as well as on PCs.

Steve Burke is a graduate of the Business Entrepreneurship program at the University of Southern California. In addition to running his own business, Steve has worked as an artist in the game industry for six years. He is currently the Art Director at Strategic Simulations, Inc., makers of strategy, fantasy, and war games. Steve has a beautiful wife, a baby girl, a wacky brother, and a passion for creating happy, friendly artwork with a smattering of sarcasm.

Phillip Miller is the Product Manager for 3D Studio MAX at Kinetix. He is responsible for coordinating support for 3D Studio MAX from the Kinetix side, while working closely with the Yost Group to ensure that the best possible tool is created for the artists that use it. He previously managed Autodesk Multimedia's Developer Relations Program and has also led Autodesk's 3D Studio training program. Phillip is a registered architect, who before joining Autodesk was a project architect in the Midwest. He earned a masters degree in architecture from the University of Illinois.

Phillip is the co-author of *Inside 3D Studio Release 3*, *Inside 3D Studio Release 4*, and a contributor to *3D Studio Special Effects* and *Inside 3D Studio MAX Volume I*, all published by New Riders.

Michael J. Neil earned a degree in political science from Syracuse University. As Marketing Director at Mike Rosen & Associates, P.C., a national award-winning architecture, land planning, landscape architecture, and virtual reality development firm serving the commercial, industrial, and residential real estate development industries, he has garnered international media attention for the firm's work using virtual reality technology and manages the firm's computer graphics and virtual reality development projects. Michael lives in Philadelphia, is active in the community, and sits on the boards of several philanthropic organizations.

Eric C. Peterson graduated *magna cum laude* from Lehigh University, earning his B.S. in engineering mechanics (emphasis on mathematics and numerical methods). A *cum laude* graduate of the Univerity of Utah, he earned his M.S. in electrical engineering (emphasis on robotic control and simulation). Eric was Chief Mechanical Design Engineer for the Automated Wire Harness Assembly System (featured in the October/November 1994 issue of *Assembly* magazine), and Chief Mechanical Design Engineer for a 12-degree-of-freedom Compact Painting Robot for an aerospace manufacturer, designing the chassis of the 15-ton Robotic Paint Stripping System for Warner Robbin Air Force Base (featured in *Aviation Week* and *Space Technology*), and the High Speed Circuit Die Placement System for a supercomputer manufacturer. As principal engineer for Engineering Spectrum, he designed custom automation equipment for the automotive, aerospace, and semiconductor industries.

Eric is the owner of Sisyphus Graphics, which provides commercial, technical, and forensic animation contracting services. As Technical Director, Sisyphus Software, he developed algorithms for 3D Studio and 3D Studio MAX plug-ins. He and his wife Audrey, a software engineer responsible for code design and construction while he concentrates on the algorithmic and interface design, worked as consultants to Yost Group, assisting in the development of MAX 2.

Michael Todd Peterson is currently an instructor at Pellissippi State Community College, an ATC. He previously taught at the University of Tennessee College of Architecture. Todd also owns MTP Graphics, a rendering and animation firm that specializes in architectural visualization and multimedia. In addition to this book, Mr. Peterson has authored or co-authored *Inside AutoCAD for DOS*, *3D Studio for Beginners*, *AutoCAD in 3D*, and *3D Studio MAX Fundamentals*.

Ken Allen Robertson holds an M.F.A. in acting and directing from the National Theatre Conservatory and has appeared in numerous stage and film productions. Since becoming involved with computer graphics, he has created 3D models and animations for Mattel and the 1996 Summer Olympics. For the past two years, Ken has been working on next-generation real-time 3D game titles for PC and set-top gaming platforms, and prototype models and animations for interactive 3D

Internet chat environments. He has been a contributing author to *3D Studio Hollywood and Gaming Effects*. Ken teaches 3D Studio, MAX, and CGI special effects at the Computer Arts Institute in San Francisco, CA. He can be reached at aceallen@hooked.net.

Jonathan Sawyer earned a B.A. in architecture from Yale University and a Masters of Industrial Design from Pratt Institute, Brooklyn, NY. Soon after entering the building business, Sawyer started a small combined design and build firm, doing residential and light commercial projects. His continued work in architecture led to his current focus: the use of computers for imaging and presentation. A native Philadelphian, he lives there with his wife, Elizabeth.

Lee Steel spends most of his time using 3D to do prototype visualization for the electro-mechanical design industry and site visualization for civil engineering firms in the northeast. Since the release of 3D Studio Release 1, he has spent much of his free time beta-testing IPAS routines for 3DS DOS and newer plug-ins for 3DS MAX. This activity led to a regular column in the now extinct *Planet Studio* magazine, and articles for *3D Design* and *3D Artist* magazines. Lee co-founded 3D Artists & Animators, a nationwide chain of 3D users groups that cater mainly to Kinetix multimedia product users but also diversify into other packages used with 3DS.

Andrew Vernon is an animator who specializes in Character Studio. He operates Moving Figure Animation & Multimedia in San Rafael, CA. Andrew worked in Kinetix Technical Publications and was the online Help System writer for both 3D Studio MAX and Character Studio. He frequently writes articles on 3D graphics, animation, and multimedia for magazines such as *3D Design*. For information about Moving Figure, see http://www.movingfigure.com.

Trademark Acknowledgments

All terms mentioned in this book that are known to be trademarks or service marks have been appropriately capitalized. New Riders Publishing cannot attest to the accuracy of this information. Use of a term in this book should not be regarded as affecting the validity of any trademark or service mark.

Acknowledgements

New Riders would like to thank everyone who worked long and hard to put this book together. We especially would like to acknowledge Sean Hammon of Viewpoint Datalabs, REM Infografica, and Peter Watje all for their generous contributions to the book.

Contents at a Glance

	Foreword	1
	Introduction	5
Part I:	Getting Started	11
Chapter 1:	The World of Modeling and Material Techniques	13
Part II:	Advanced Modeling in 3D Studio MAX	49
Chapter 2:	Architectural Modeling and Rendering	51
Chapter 3:	Modeling for Real-Time 3D Games	103
Chapter 4:	Modeling for VR and the Web	139
Chapter 5:	Technical Modeling for Engineering Visualization	175
Part III:	Character Modeling	221
Chapter 6:	Character Modeling Basics	223
Chapter 7:	Character Modeling with Patch Tools	241
Chapter 8:	Character Modeling with Plug-Ins	271
Part IV:	Material and Texture Mapping	313
Chapter 9:	Materials Management and Manipulation	315
Chapter 10:	Designing Natural Materials	355
Chapter 11:	Designing Man-Made Materials	411
Chapter 12:	Designing Special Effects Materials	453
Chapter 13:	Animated Materials	491
Part V:	Appendix	516
Appendix A:	Integrating AutoCAD with 3D Studio MAX	517
	Index	557

Table of Contents

Foreword   1

Introduction   5

  Organization of the Book   6

  How to Read the Exercises   7

    Exercises and the CD-ROM   8

  Using the *Inside 3D Studio MAX Volume II* CD-ROM   8

    Installing the Exercise Files   8

    Registering Shareware   9

  Using CompuServe and the Web   9

  New Riders Publishing   9

Part I: Getting Started   11

1 The World of Modeling and Material Techniques   13

  The Modeling Process   14

    Conceptual Sketches   15

    Rough Models   16

    Modeling Techniques   17

    Materials in the Modeling Process   21

  The Real World   22

    Observation   23

    Attention to Detail   23

    How Much Detail Do You Need?   24

  Architectural Modeling   24

    Chartres Cathedral in Chartres, France   25

  Biped Characters   30

    The Dancing Alien   31

  Complex Character Models   34

    A Dragon   35

  Technical Modeling   36

    A Space Station   37

  Industry Modeling   38

    Modeling a Ferrari   38

  Plug-In Overview   40

    Why Plug-Ins Are Important   40

    Modeling Plug-Ins   40

    Material Plug-Ins   46

  In Practice: The Modeling Process   48

Part II: Advanced Modeling in 3D Studio MAX   **49**

2 Architectural Modeling and Rendering   **51**

    Building a 3D Architectural Model   52

    Modeling the Structure   53

        Starting out   *53*

        Extruding from Floor Plans   *54*

        Building the Walls "Lying Down"   *55*

        Boolean Modeling of Walls   *56*

        Cross-Section Lofting to Form Walls   *57*

        Combinations with Other Programs   *58*

        Some Points About Lofting   *58*

        Teetering the Shape   *70*

        Using Path Parameters to Place Scaled Shapes *74*

        Making the Columns and Cornices   *77*

        Adding Roofs   *83*

        The Doorways   *97*

    In Practice: Architectural Modeling   101

3 Modeling for Real-Time 3D Games   **103**

    2D Versus Real-Time 3D Graphics   105

    Real-Time 3D Basics   106

        The Transform   *107*

        Surface Properties   *110*

    Differences Between Real-Time and Prerendered 3D   110

        Z-Buffering   *111*

        Levels of Detail   *111*

        Shadows   *112*

        Map Size and Color Depth   *113*

        Shading Modes   *113*

    Modeling for Real Time   114

        Put the Detail in the Map, Not in the Mesh   *114*

        Don't Build What You Don't Need   *115*

        Model Convex (Whenever Possible)   *116*

        High-Res for Low-Res Modeling   *117*

    Real-Time Modeling Techniques   118

        Conscious Lofting   *118*

        Modifying Primitives for Low-Resolution Models *123*

Dealing with Texture Limitations   126
Dealing with Limited Colors   *126*
Limited Map Size   *127*
Adding "Impossible" Detail   *127*
Faking a Bump Map   *128*
Faking "Mood Lighting"   *129*
Curved Surfaces   *129*
Using Opacity for "Impossible Detail"   *134*
The Future of Real-Time   137
In Practice: Modeling for Real-Time 3D Games   137

4   Modeling for VR and the Web   139
Modeling Tools and Techniques   141
Using Tools Built into 3DS MAX   *142*
Using Tools Provided by the VRMLOUT Plug-In   *149*
Other Techniques   *151*
What VRMLOUT Can and Cannot Export   152
Creating a Virtual World with 3DS MAX
and VRMLOUT   153
General Procedure for Using VRMLOUT   *154*
Adding the VRMLOUT Helpers to a Scene   *155*
Browser Review   165
A Note on VRML 1.0 Browsers   *165*
World View, from Intervista   *166*
Community Place, from Sony   *167*
Cosmo Player, from Silicon Graphics   *168*
Live3D 2.0 from Netscape   *169*
The Best of the Web   169
Oz Inc. (www.oz.com)   *170*
The Genesis Project (www.3d-design.com/
livespace/genesis)   *170*
Intervista's VRML Circus (www.intervista.com/
products/worldview/demos/index.shtml)   *171*
Steel Studio Landscape (www.marketcentral.
com/vrml/gallery.wrl)   *171*
Construct's Stratus Gallery (www.construct.net/
stratus/)   *172*
In Practice: Modeling for VRML and the Web   172

5 Technical Modeling for Engineering Visualization   175

Characteristics and Purposes of Technical

Modeling   177

Legal Animation   *177*

Technical Documentation   *179*

Technical Promotional Illustration   *179*

Technical Proposal Illustration   *180*

The Unique Audience for Technical Animations   183

Why Technical Animation Is Unique   184

Schedule Requirements   *184*

Precision Counts   *185*

Recognition Counts   *186*

Running in Slow Motion   *186*

Typical Technical Modeling Products   *187*

Modeling for a Technical Proposal   187

Purpose of the Model   *188*

Components of the Scene   *189*

Robot Construction   192

Robot Base   *192*

Canopy Construction   202

Robot Waist Construction   215

In Practice: Technical Modeling   219

Part III: Character Modeling   221

6 Character Modeling Basics   223

Introduction to Characters   224

The Definition of Character   226

Thought Process   *226*

Emotional Life   *228*

Personality   *229*

Beginning a New Character   229

Developing the Story   *230*

Developing the Character's Personality   *234*

Defining How the Character Functions   *235*

Visual Design   *236*

In Practice: The Basics of Character Modeling   238

7 Character Modeling with Patch Tools   **241**

   Using Patches in MAX   242

     Patch Versus Mesh Considerations   243

     Modeling Issues   243

     Animation Issues   244

   Patch Limitations in MAX   246

     General Surface Control Problems   246

     Accuracy Issues   247

     Texture Mapping Issues   247

   Basic Patch Modeling Overview   248

   Modeling a Hand with the Patch Tools in MAX   249

     Needed Resources   249

     Creating a Template from an Image   250

     Creating a Spline Framework   252

     Building the Patch Surface   255

   Modeling a Torso from an Image   257

     Needed Resources   258

     Creating a Template from an Image   258

     Creating a Spline Framework   258

     Creating the Patch Surface   259

     Fine-Tuning the Surface   260

     Creating a Sharp Edge on a Patch Surface   260

   Creating a Patch Head from a Mesh Object   262

     Creating the Spline Framework with the

      Edge to Spline Plug-In   262

     Mirroring and Attaching Spline Frameworks   263

   Modeling an Arm with Cross Sections   265

     Creating Splines for Cross Sections   265

     Editing the Cross Section Splines   266

   In Practice: Modeling Characters with Patch Tools   268

8 Character Modeling with Plug-Ins   **271**

   General Principles for Character Modeling

   with Plug-Ins   272

     Start Simple and Add Detail   273

     Have References Constantly Available   274

     Work in Halves   275

     Know the Tools for "Tweaking"—One Tool Is

      Never Enough   276

Seamless Versus Segmented Modeling   281
Using Plug-Ins for Character Modeling   282
  Patch Modeling   *282*
  Metaballs Modeling   *290*
  Modeling with Skeletal Systems (Bones Pro MAX)   *298*
  Using 3D Paint to Map a Model   *304*
In Practice: Character Modeling with Plug-Ins   311

Part IV: Material and Texture Mapping   313

9 Materials Management and Manipulation   315
The Materials Lab   316
Materials Acquisition   319
  Scanners   *320*
  Prexisting Image Libraries   *321*
  Paint Programs   *322*
  3D Studio MAX and Screen Captures   *324*
  Portable Digital Cameras   *324*
  Video Cameras and Video Recorders   *326*
  Keep Your Eyes Peeled   *326*
Material Alignment Techniques   327
  Alignment by Pixel and Material ID   *328*
  Alignment by Bitmap Traces   *333*
  Alignment by Screen Capture and Grids   *338*
  Alignment by Plug-Ins (UNWRAP.DLU)   *343*
Material Management   346
Material and Bitmap Navigation   349
  Image and Material Cardfile   *349*
  Thumbnail Programs   *350*
Importing 3D Studio R4 Materials   351
  The MLI File Format   *351*
  Import Options   *352*
  Converting MLI Files to MAT Files   *352*
In Practice: Keeping Things Clean, Fast,
  and Retrievable   353

10   Designing Natural Materials   **355**

   Ground and Sky   356
     Dirt and Grass   357
     Creating a Sky   362
   Water   365
     Adding Reflection to the Water   367
     Fine-Tuning the Reflection with a Gradient 368
     Creating Other Water Effects   369
   Trees and Bamboo   370
     Trees   371
     Bamboo   374
   Stones   379
   Vegetation   386
     Bushes and Trees   386
   Other Opacity-Mapped Materials   392
     Plant Materials   393
   Tree Frog   399
   In Practice: Designing Natural Materials   408

11   Designing Man-Made Materials   **411**

   Creating Material Imperfections   412
   The Impact of Geometry on Realistic Materials   413
     Surfaces and Edge Warps   414
     Object Dents and Cracks   415
     Rounded Corners   416
     Surface Wrinkles and Folds   418
     Bulges   418
     Surface Wrinkles and Folds   418
   Material Corruption Techniques   419
     Discolorations   420
     Blurry Puddles and Smudges   422
     Scorch Marks and Dents   426
     Dust   427
     Weathering   429
   Creating Man-Made Materials   431
     Concretes   432
     Paper and Cardboard   434

Woods   *435*
Stones   *436*
Plastics   *438*
Rubber and Vinyl   *439*
Glass   *440*
Metals, Meshes, and Wires   *442*
Fabrics   *446*
Experiment!   *449*
In Practice: Creating Man-Made Materials   449

12   Designing Special Effects Materials   **453**
Explosions   454
A Bursting Meteor   *455*
An Erupting Volcano   *458*
A Shattering Window   *460*
Light Emitting and Glowing Effects   463
A Neon Sign   *464*
A Lightning Bolt   *466*
Clear and Soft Lightbulbs   *467*
A Radiant Aura   *469*
Uses of Particle Systems   475
Using Lights as Materials   479
Psychedelic Materials   481
Noise Revisited   *482*
Combustion Revisited   *484*
Mirror Tricks   *487*
In Practice: Designing Special Effects Materials   488

13   Animated Materials   **491**
Animating Color Changes   493
Creating a Simple Color Change   *494*
Blend Materials   496
Creating the Illusion of Constant Motion   500
Using Noise to Simulate Water and Sky   502
Water   *502*
Sky and Space   *504*
Fire   *508*
Third-Party Plug-Ins   510
In Practice: Animated Materials   515

Part V: Appendix   516

A Integrating AutoCAD with 3D Studio MAX   517

Why Is AutoCAD Used with 3D Studio MAX?   518
Exchanging Data Between AutoCAD and
   3D Studio MAX   519
AutoCAD Characteristics   520
   AutoCAD Organizations   521
   AutoCAD Entity Types   522
   AutoCAD Entity Properties   523
   AutoCAD Versus 3DS MAX Precision   524
Coordinating with DWG Files   525
   DWG Import Derive Options   529
   DWG Import General Options   530
   DWG Import Geometry Options   532
   DWG Import ACIS Solids Options   534
   DWG Geometry Matching   535
   DWG Export Options   537
   Entities Incapable of 3DS MAX DXF Import   541
   DXF Import in 3D Studio MAX   542
   Using AutoCAD's DXFOUT   545
   Unifying Face Normals of DXF Imports   547
   DXF Export from 3D Studio MAX   549
Coordinating with 3DS Files   551
   Using AutoCAD's 3DSOUT   551
   *3DS Export from 3D Studio MAX and
      AutoCAD's 3DSIN*   554
In Practice: Integrating AutoCAD with
   3D Studio MAX   556

Index   557

Foreword

Welcome to Inside 3D Studio MAX Volume II, *a detailed investigation into the requirements of modeling and materials. Although the official 3DS MAX manuals do an admirable job of laying the foundation for understanding the program's vast capabilities, they always leave more to explore.* Inside 3D Studio MAX Volume I *went deeper, expanding on all topics while including the adjacent information that is pertinent to the industry.* Volume II *now departs from that previous model and explores topics as they relate to specific professional applications and artistic approaches.*

This book uses *Inside 3D Studio MAX Volume I* as a foundation in much the same way that *Volume I* used the official product manuals as its base to build on. Although its predecessor went into generic depth, *Inside 3D Studio MAX Volume II* analyzes specific projects and details varying artistic perspectives for achieving professional results. This volume takes special note of what is important for modeling and texturing architectural models, characters, engineering visualization, interactive games, virtual reality, and Internet web sites.

The eventual audience and actual media most often determine a model's detail and the material's complexity. The demands of precise mechanical models are just as different from the frugal, real-time models as highly detailed film effects are from those suitable for low-resolution video. Designing models for the web means making every face count, while seeing a single facet on a magazine cover is often unacceptable. Each application has its own rigors that place unique demands on artists and the tools that they choose to use.

Most computer graphic artists agree that modeling and materials go hand-in-hand. The most critical time to apply mapping coordinates is often during the modeling process, when parts of the model may have more accessible orientations. Often, the detail of the model is dictated by what can or can not be formed in geometry. If material is creating convincing grooves, for example, then there is no need to model it, but if the groove edges are seen in distinct profile, a physical channel may need to be formed for a convincing effect.

A great deal of modeling thus progresses with evolving materials, textures, and mapping. This volume recognizes this interrelationship and concentrates on those issues as they relate to specific professions. The chapters that follow should prove a valuable resource for your own needs while aiding in the understanding of adjacent CG artists as well.

The printing of this book happens to coincide with the one-year anniversary of what has been an incredible start for an amazing program. 3D Studio MAX broke many rules, yet is well on its way to becoming a new industry standard for affordable, professional modeling, animation, and rendering. Taken literally, what 3D Studio MAX did sounded a bit crazy when first introduced. It abandoned all its former users on the DOS platform, stranded the hundreds of plug-ins developed for it, changed its interface entirely, changed nearly every paradigm, and to top it off gave away over half of its source code!

But the reality of today makes it clear why these bold steps were needed. The dedication to writing a multithreaded, Windows-compliant program was perfectly timed as Windows NT became the professional operating system of choice. The plug-in architecture of 3DS DOS was modal, limited, and difficult to program for, and the developers who seemingly had so much invested are now ecstatic to be able to "do it right" and in much less time. The interface changed to become one of the most efficient and intuitive in the industry, with traditional learning curves plummeting. The paradigms changed to enable experimentation and animation with the result being a MAX community of happier than usual animators and modelers. Artists can finally experiment, and even play, without the fear of making irrevocable mistakes. Finally, the source-code-rich SDK included with every copy of the product didn't create a trade secret disaster. Rather, it created a plug-in explosion with more plug-ins of superior quality being written within a year than in the entire life of 3DS DOS. Yeah, 3D Studio MAX was a bit crazy—crazy like a fox.

The success of 3D Studio MAX, and the many people who like to use it, has encouraged Kinetix to create a product family with more offerings for a wider audience. Kinetix is preparing to introduce a version for design professionals who do not need advanced animation capabilities or compositing, while adding features of particular interest to designers. 3D Studio MAX Apprentice is an introductory, low-cost student version (available in many college book stores) that gives those learning about computer graphics the opportunity to learn 3D modeling and animation with the 3D Studio MAX engine. Both of these products are built upon the same 3D Studio MAX platform and use the same plug-in architecture. Most of the techniques you learn in this volume will apply in those programs as well. Fluency in 3D Studio MAX will certainly become even more of an asset as these programs take hold and the flagship product continues to evolve as the professional tool of choice.

Phillip Miller
Product Manager, 3D Studio MAX
Kinetix, a division of Autodesk, Inc.

Introduction

Inside 3D Studio MAX Volume II: Advanced Modeling and Materials *is the second book in a three-volume set. Due to the robust nature of 3DS MAX, New Riders is dedicated to bringing users detailed, top-quality information on all the features and functions of the software.* Inside 3D Studio MAX Volume II *is a complete tutorial and reference on materials and modeling. It includes coverage of the many different types of modeling done in the industry, from modeling for real-time games to modeling for engineering visualization. Also included is expert coverage of MAX's powerful Material Editor. Learn how to use the Material Editor alone and with plug-ins to make natural, man-made, special effects, and animated materials.*

The next volume in the *Inside 3D Studio MAX* set is *Volume III: Animation*. Like its predecessors, it will be presented in the *Inside* style, packed full of detailed tutorials and valuable tip and techniques from industry experts. Look for *Inside 3D Studio MAX Volume III: Animation* coming soon.

Organization of the Book

Inside 3D Studio MAX Volume II: Advanced Modeling and Materials is organized around four parts followed by an appendix. These parts are as follows:

- Part I, "Getting Started," Chapter 1
- Part II, "Advanced Modeling in 3D Studio MAX," Chapters 2 through 5
- Part III, "Character Modeling," Chapters 6 through 8
- Part IV, "Material and Texture Mapping," Chapters 7 through 13
- Part V, "Appendix," Appendix A

Part I is a survey of some of the modeling and mapping techniques available and how you can make use of multiple techniques to accomplish your task. Later in this book, you will get plenty of specific examples and practice. Real-world images are disected and discussed in terms of their structure and textures.

Part II covers advanced modeling techniques in MAX. The modeling tools are not explained, rather the techniques that are best served by MAX's modeling tools and plug-ins are described. Advanced modeling tutorials take you through the steps needed to create low-polygon count models for the web, precise and highly defined models for engineering visualization, accurate models for architecture, and efficient, believable modeling for real-time games.

Part III takes you through the unique world of character modeling. From creating a character to modeling it with MAX tools and plug-ins, this section teaches the best methods of modeling for a variety of situations.

Part IV explores the world of MAX's Material Editor. These chapters cover the making and management of your material library. With just a few steps and the expert advice found in these chapters you can have your own unique library of natural, man-made, special effect, and animated materials.

Appendix A covers the integration of 3D Studio MAX with AutoCAD.

How to Read the Exercises

Unlike most tutorials that you read, the *Inside 3D Studio MAX Volume II* exercises do not rigidly dictate every step you perform to achieve the desired result. These exercises are designed to be flexible and to work with a wide range of situations. The benefits you receive from this approach include:

- A better understanding of the concepts because you must think through the example rather than blindly follow the minutiae of many steps

- A stronger ability to apply the examples to your own work

Most exercises begin with some explanatory text as shown in the following sample exercise. The text tells you what the exercise should accomplish and sets the context for the exercise.

SAMPLE EXERCISE FORMAT

You may encounter text such as this at the beginning of or in the middle of an exercise when one or more actions require an extended explanation.

1. Numbered steps identify your actions to complete the excercise.

   Indented text adds extra explanation about the previous step when it is needed.

The word *choose* in an example always indicates a menu selection. If the selection involves a pull-down menu, you will be told explicitly where to find the menu item. If the selection is from another part of the user interface, you will be told on which component to click and the location of the interface. Setting the Hemisphere option for a Sphere object, for example, requires clicking the Hemisphere check box in the Creation Parameters rollout menu (you would have been told previously whether you were accessing the rollout from the Create panel or the Modify panel). The word *select* always refers to selecting one or more objects, elements, faces, or vertices. Select never refers to menus or other user interface components.

Because this book is designed for people who already have some experience with 3DS MAX, some exercise steps are implied rather than explicitly stated. You may, for example, find yourself instructed to "Create a smooth, 20-segment Sphere with a radius of 100 units," rather than reading all the steps required to create the sphere.

Exercises and the CD-ROM

Most of the examples and exercises use files that are either included on the *Inside 3D Studio MAX Volume II* CD-ROM or shipped with 3D Studio, or they show you how to create the necessary geometry. Example files are located on the accompanying CD-ROM. Instructions on how to use the CD-ROM files or to install them on your hard drive are described in the following section.

Using the *Inside 3D Studio MAX Volume II* CD-ROM

Inside 3D Studio MAX Volume II comes with a CD-ROM packed with many megabytes of plug-ins, scenes, maps, and other sample software. The example files can be used directly from the *Inside 3D Studio MAX Volume II* CD-ROM, so "installing" them is not necessary. You may want to copy files from the CD-ROM to your hard drive or another storage device. In that case, you can use the install routines found with some of the sample programs or copy the files directly to a directory on your hard disk.

Installing the Exercise Files

All exercise files not included with 3D Studio MAX are contained in a single subdirectory on the *Inside 3D Studio MAX Volume II* CD-ROM: \I3DSMAX. You can access these files directly from the CD-ROM when you execute the examples, or you can create a directory called \I3DSMAX on your hard drive and copy the files there. Some of the example files require maps from the CD-ROM that ships with 3D Studio MAX. You will need to copy these files to a subdirectory that is referenced in the 3DS MAX Map-Paths parameter.

3D Studio MAX automatically looks for map files in the directory from which a scene file was loaded. If you copy the example files to your hard drive, make sure you keep the mesh files and map files together or at least put the map files in a directory where 3D Studio can find them at rendering time.

A number of sample scenes, animation files and maps are provided on the *Inside 3D Studio MAX Volume II* CD-ROM for your use. These are licensed free for use. You cannot, however, resell or otherwise distribute the files.

Registering Shareware

Most of the sample programs on the *Inside 3D Studio MAX Volume II* CD-ROM are either demonstration programs or shareware programs. Shareware programs are fully functioning products that you can try out prior to purchasing—they are not free. If you find a shareware program useful, you must pay a registration fee to the program's author. Each shareware program provides information about how to contact the author and register the program.

Using CompuServe and the Web

The CompuServe Information Service is an online, interactive network that you can access with a modem and special access software. The most important feature of this service (at least as far as this book is concerned) is the KINETIX forum.

The KINETIX forum is an area of CompuServe that is maintained by Kinetix for the direct support of 3D Studio MAX and other Kinetix software. Hundreds of people from all over the world visit this forum daily to share ideas, ask and answer questions, and generally promote the use of 3DS MAX. If you ask a question on the forum, you are as likely to receive an answer from one of the original programmers as you are to receive an answer from any number of other 3DS MAX artists. And every question, from the most basic to the most mind-bending puzzler, receives the same quick and courteous treatment.

Kinetix also maintains a site on the World Wide Web where you can get the latest information about 3DS MAX, future software releases, and plug-in development. You can also send questions and feedback direct to Kinetix and download software. The Kinetix web site is www.ktx.com.

New Riders Publishing

The staff of New Riders Publishing is committed to bringing you the very best in computer reference material. Each New Riders book is the result of months of work by authors and staff who research and refine the information contained within its covers.

As part of this commitment to you, New Riders invites your input. Please let us know if you enjoy this book, if you have trouble with the information and examples presented, or if you have a suggestion for the next edition.

Please note, however: New Riders staff cannot serve as a technical resource for 3D Studio MAX or for questions about software- or hardware-related problems. Please refer to the documentation that accompanies your software or to the application's Help systems.

If you have a question or comment about any New Riders book, there are several ways to contact New Riders Publishing. We will respond to as many readers as we can. Your name, address, or phone number will never become part of a mailing list or be used for any purpose other than to help us continue to bring you the best books possible.

You can write us at the following address:

New Riders Publishing
Attn: Publisher
201 W. 103rd Street
Indianapolis, IN 46290

If you prefer, you can fax New Riders Publishing at:

317-817-7448

You can also send electronic mail to New Riders at the following Internet address:

abuckley@newriders.mcp.com

New Riders Publishing is an imprint of Macmillan Computer Publishing. To obtain a catalog or information, or to purchase any Macmillan Computer Publishing book, call 800-428-5331 or visit our web site at http://www.mcp.com.

Thank you for selecting *Inside 3D Studio MAX Volume II: Advanced Modeling and Materials*.

Part I

GETTING STARTED

Chapter 1

by Todd Peterson

THE WORLD OF MODELING AND MATERIAL TECHNIQUES

Modeling and materials are two of the most difficult and challenging aspects of 3D work. The subject matter that you are trying to model will ultimately determine how difficult it will be to create the model. It is easier to model a house than an elephant, for example, but the materials can be more complex in the house than on the elephant.

To make matters even more complicated, when you model an object in 3D Studio MAX, you must choose from many different methods and approaches to modeling that object. Each method produces slightly different results and takes different amounts of time and effort to complete. You could model the elephant, for example, by using splines and lofts—but using splines is a slow and overly difficult task. Alternatively, you could model the elephant by using patch surfaces with modifiers. This method should be a little more effective and a little quicker. And in yet another method, you could use plug-ins (add-on software) for 3D Studio MAX and model the elephant quickly and efficiently by using metaballs or NURBS (non-uniform rational B-splines).

This chapter provides an overview of some of the methods you can use to model objects and create materials for them. The chapter surveys some of the techniques available and looks at how you can use multiple techniques to accomplish your task. Plenty of specific examples and practice exercises appear later in this book. This chapter, though, focuses on the following topics:

- The modeling process
- Materials in the modeling process
- Architectural modeling
- Biped modeling
- Complex character modeling
- Technical modeling
- Industrial modeling
- Plug-in overview
- Modeling plug-ins
- Material plug-ins

The Modeling Process

As a process, modeling has three main stages: conceptual sketching, rough models, and modeling techniques. Each stage helps you to define exactly how the object you are trying to model will look in the scene. The definitions that result from these different stages must be considered relative to, and in the context of, the type of use the object will have in the scene. A model of a space ship, for example, can be rather simplistic if it has good materials, whereas a model of a house or convention center needs a lot more detail in the modeling process.

The modeling process demands a full range of your skills and abilities. In the conceptual sketch stage, for example, your traditional art skills are at the forefront. In the rough model stage, however, your skills as a sculptor feature more prominently. Only in the modeling techniques stage do you use your computer skills to actually create the model.

At this point, you may be asking yourself why the first two stages of the process are necessary. The conceptual sketch and rough model stages are necessary to help you visualize the object that you are going to draw and create in MAX. Of course, not all stages are necessary for every type of object you might create. Modeling a house may require a few quick conceptual sketches, for example, but you rarely need to build a model of the house.

The following sections examine the specific stages of the modeling process in more detail.

Conceptual Sketches

Conceptual sketches are generally the first attempts to put ideas into some sort of visual form. Sketches can range from individual images drawn in pen and ink, pencil, or paint, to full-blown storyboards that illustrate modeling and animation intent. By sketching your model first, you can begin to refine the design of the object well before you actually begin modeling it. The more you know about how to build the model before you actually begin, the faster and more accurately you will be able to build the model.

Conceptual sketches are a traditional medium used time and time again to help convince clients, bosses, and others that a design vision merits the effort, before you invest a great deal of time and money in creating the CGI model.

Conceptual sketches can be created in a wide variety of formats or media. You can create conceptual sketches as pencil on paper, ink and film, paint and canvas, or even pen and napkin. Sketches also do not have to be perfect. You are trying to convey a general idea of what the object will look like, how it will move, and so on. This can be expressed through a series of quick sketches. If you need more detail, you may consider sketching a blow up of the area where you feel you may need more detail.

The conceptual sketching stage is the time to try different versions of the same object. You can quickly and easily sketch small or large changes and see the result well before you begin to model in MAX. The amount of sketching and the detail are solely up to you. Conceptual sketches enable you to explore difficult modeling and material tasks such as muscles, texture, hair, and so forth. Sketches help you to decide how much detail you need in your CGI model and how to create the model more efficiently by adding only the necessary detail. Remember, you always want to create the model with as little detail as possible. Sketching can help you decide where you can lose detail and where you cannot.

After you have finally refined your vision to your personal comfort and standards, you can move on to the next stage of the modeling process.

Rough Models

Rough models can be created in two ways: as physical models or as CGI models. Physical models are small, fairly detailed models of the object made out of a material such as clay or papier-maché. CGI models, on the other hand, are rough, low-detail, computer-generated models. Most of the time, CGI models suffice. But when a model is exceptionally complex (a dragon or a dinosaur, for example), a physical model yields more accurate results.

Physical models are made of clay or other pliable materials and are intended to be small-scale 3D representations of an object. When Draco from *Dragonheart* or the T-Rex from *Jurassic Park* were being designed, for example, several small models of each were built. These models were then used as the basis for creating the final CGI model.

For many projects, you do not need to create even a rough model. Architectural models, for example, are generally simple enough to never really need a rough model. When you create a character that you will eventually animate, however, rough models become a necessity. They not only give you a true sense of 3D scale that helps you create your model, they also give you a true representation of the actual creature.

From the CGI standpoint, building rough models is an excellent method for further refining your model. Essentially, the modeling process is one of refinement. You start with a rough model and refine any portion of that model until you have the final model you want. Best of all, you can save each revision and return to it at any time to start over or take a different approach.

Modeling Techniques

After you decide what your object will look like, you can begin the modeling process. You can use many different approaches and methods to create your model. The method you choose depends not only on how you like to model but ultimately on what you are modeling. In 3D Studio MAX, you can use any of the built-in modeling tools or a wide variety of plug-ins or other compatible software. All these options present several techniques that are quick and easy to use. These techniques include, but are not limited to, the following:

- Mesh modeling
- Spline modeling
- Patch modeling
- Solid modeling
- NURBS modeling
- Metaball modeling

Mesh Modeling

The objects used in mesh modeling comprise only 3D faces or mesh triangles. By joining many small 3D faces, you can quickly and easily create a mesh surface. Generally, mesh modeling is the most popular method. Even packages that enable you to model in a different technique eventually convert their surfaces to meshes for rendering.

In 3D Studio MAX, when you create a box, sphere, cone, or other primitive, you are creating a Mesh object. This object can then be modified into a wide variety of other, more complex objects. Mesh modeling is great for simple objects such as spheres, walls, and doors. Figure 1.1 shows two examples of mesh models.

FIGURE 1.1
*Two examples of mesh
models.*

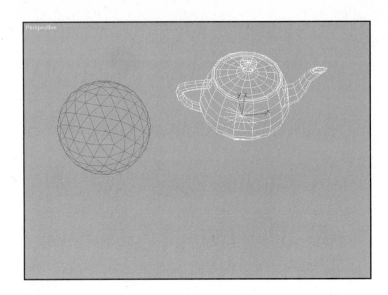

Spline Modeling

Spline modeling takes a slightly different approach to creating the object, but still produces a mesh model. A *spline* is a 3D line, arc, or circle. Spline modeling takes a spline, called a *shape*, and extrudes or lofts the shape along another spline, called the *path*. The shape can be modified as it travels along the path. Spline modeling makes creating objects such as glass bottles, wine glasses, and even bananas very easy. Spline modeling can be used also to create objects such as the walls in a house. Figure 1.2 shows an example of a spline model.

FIGURE 1.2
A spline model.

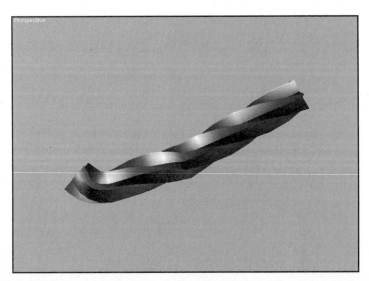

Patch Modeling

Patch modeling makes use of Bézier patches. When you work with patch modeling, you create a flat surface controlled by a lattice, or *grid,* of points. By modifying the position of the lattice points, you can create gentle curves in the surfaces. You can also create patches between splines by creating the flat surface and then adjusting the vertices of the patch to match the splines. You can use patches to quickly and easily model complex surfaces such as faces or bodies. Figure 1.3 shows an example of a patch model.

FIGURE 1.3

A patch model.

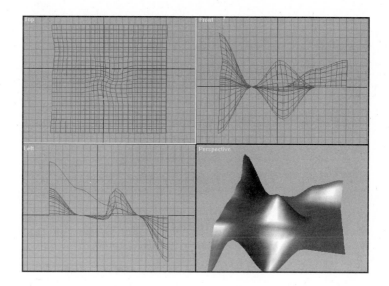

Solid Modeling

The solid modeling method also relies on mesh modeling. Unlike patch modeling, however, solid modeling creates objects by using Boolean logic to combine two or more objects. (You can subtract the volume of one object from the volume of another, for example.) Solid modeling can be used to create objects such as windows in a wall or a drill hole in a piece of wood (see fig. 1.4).

Mesh, spline, patch, and solid modeling can be implemented directly inside 3D Studio MAX. The next two methods, which require third-party plug-ins, are presented just to provide an example of how powerful third-party applications can be.

FIGURE 1.4
A solid model.

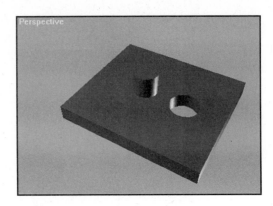

NURBS Modeling

Non-uniform rational B-spline (NURBS) modeling is similar to spline modeling but makes use of advanced mathematics to control the surfaces. Hence, NURBS surfaces are extremely accurate and precise. NURBS programs have the capability not only to create primitives and complex extruded surfaces, but also to create a blended surface between two other surfaces. This requires some work in other modeling systems. To give you an idea of how powerful NURBS modeling is, imagine trying to draw a spline directly on the curved surface of a sphere. You cannot do this in MAX, but you can with a NURBS program.

As a matter of fact, you can thank NURBS for all the slick aerodynamic cars on the road today. Car designers began using NURBS in the late '80s because the accurate surfaces could be quickly machined and created. NURBS tools are extremely powerful for modeling complex curved surfaces such as cars, faces, shoes, dinosaurs, and so on. To use NURBS with MAX, you need a third-party program such as Sculptor NT or Rhino. In either case, the files are brought into MAX as 3DS files and are converted to meshes at that point. Figure 1.5 shows an example of a NURBS model.

Metaball Modeling

The last method to mention at this point is metaball modeling, a relatively new modeling process that also requires the use of a plug-in. Metaball modeling produces a mesh surface by creating surface tension between a set of spheres. You can adjust the strength of a particular sphere to define how much it affects the surface. Metaball modeling can be used to model many complex objects such as liquid metal, faces, hands, bodies, and so forth. Figure 1.6 shows you an example of a model created with a metaball modeling program.

FIGURE 1.5
A NURBS model.

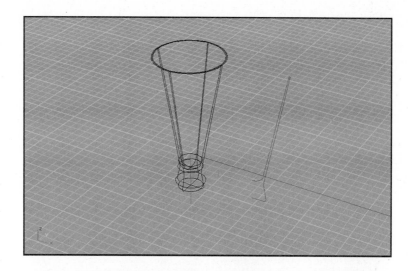

FIGURE 1.6
A hand created using Metaballs.

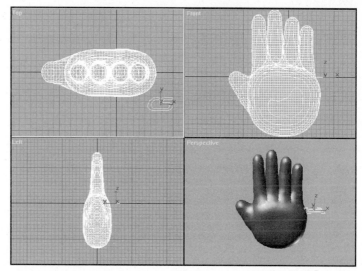

Of the many different approaches and methods for modeling, only a few are mentioned here. Other methods are being developed all the time. Later in this chapter, you explore specific examples that enable you to use one or more of these techniques.

Materials in the Modeling Process

Up to this point, this chapter has focused only on modeling. Materials, however, have a direct effect on how you model your object. Using a bump map to create the appearance of depressions in a surface, for example, is much easier than actually trying to model those depressions. When you are creating objects, especially in the conceptual sketch and rough model phases, you should give serious thought to the way you are going to use materials. They will help dictate where you add detail to a model and where you do not.

You can create a brick wall out of a box, for example, by using a brick texture map in combination with a brick bump map. This works very well in the center of the object. When you look at the edges, however, you do not see the mortar joints you would see in real life. The only way around this is to actually model each brick in the scene. This process is time-consuming (in both modeling and rendering time) and, in many instances, people who view your scene probably won't even notice the edges of the brick!

Ultimately, knowing exactly when to create the *appearance* of geometry with materials and when to actually create the geometry comes with experience. As you progress through this chapter and this book, you will get a good sense of where and when to create more detail in your models and when to rely on trickery with your materials to achieve the same effect.

The Real World

When you are creating models and materials in a CGI environment such as 3D Studio MAX, the real world surrounding you serves as your best source of guidance. If you want to create a creature such as Draco from *Dragonheart*, for example, there is no real-world image, character, or object from which to draw. But don't despair. The real world does in fact offer many images and experiences (including movement) that can influence your modeling of Draco.

Draco is a dragon with wings and four legs. When Draco flies, you can base the motion as well as the modeling on something similar (a bat, for example). When the dragon walks, you can base the motion and modeling on a cat, a horse, or even a dog. You take only what you need from the various real-world examples and combine those characteristics into your final object.

Although motion is of secondary importance in this discussion of modeling, the way a creature moves depends directly on how the creature is built. A giraffe moves differently than a horse, for example, because the giraffe's legs and neck are longer, and the front part of its body is thicker and taller than those parts of a horse, resulting in a different movement. When you model the giraffe, you must take into account the way the shape of the giraffe affects its movement. In this way, you can determine where you need to add detail in the model.

The same types of observations can be applied to materials as well as to geometry. The real world is full of examples of a wide variety of materials you can use. You can even photograph many of these materials, scan them into your system, and use them in your scenes.

When you're basing objects on real-world examples, you must develop two key skills: observation and attention to detail. Without these skills, it will be difficult for you to create objects that, when animated, look correct.

Observation

Observation is the key to determining how things act, look, and work in the real world. One of the best ways to observe how things are put together in real life is to try to draw or sketch them by hand—a bit old-fashioned, but it requires focused attention and trains your eye to be patient and specific. These days, you can take a camera and photograph anything you want so that you have a copy of the object you are observing. Although a photograph provides an accurate picture of the object, the insight you gain by sketching will enable you to more thoroughly observe what the picture shows or doesn't show—a photograph is only two-dimensional after all.

Consider a lion, for example. You most certainly can photograph a lion and try to create a model of the lion based on the photograph. This works, to an extent. When you sketch or draw the lion by hand, however, you get a better sense of scale, texture, and spatial relationship. While you sketch you also pick up many of the lion's more subtle features, such as whiskers or underlying muscular structure, that you might miss by simple observation of a photograph. The underlying muscular structure is most evident when the lion is moving. You cannot get the information you need from a photograph in this case. These details give a model the greatest sense of realism in a CGI environment. Ideally, you will always have as much information as possible available to you when you are modeling. This includes sketches, photos, or even anatomy books.

Attention to Detail

Attention to detail goes hand-in-hand with observation. The more details you pick up from real-world examples, the easier it is to eventually model the object you want to create.

Again—consider the example of a dragon. To create the wings of a dragon, you might base them on the wings of a bat. When you look closely at a bat's wings you can see how they are put together, which gives you hints for creating them in the computer environment. You can also pick up many subtle (and not so subtle) hints about materials and how you need to create them for your model. As Mies Van de Rohe, a famous architect, once said, "God is in the details!" You should, therefore, pay attention to them.

How Much Detail Do You Need?

When you observe real-world examples on which to base your objects, always try to remember where to draw the line between putting too much detail in a model versus using advanced materials to create the effect.

When you create an animation, you should always strive to keep the polygon count as low as possible so that you use less memory and the animation renders faster. Never add unnecessary detail to the model. If you can get the look you want by working a little harder on the materials, go ahead and use the materials. Don't waste time and resources trying to model it.

Again, this is an experience issue. The temptation is great to create as much detail in the model as you can, partly because doing so on the computer is easy. Some people are also skeptical about being able to achieve the same results by using less geometry and better materials. The more experience you get modeling and creating materials, the easier it is to know when you have enough detail in the model and when to start creating more advanced materials.

Now that you have had a brief overview of the modeling process, it is time to look at specific examples and how you might model them. Later in the book you are given exact exercises. The examples in this first chapter are provided to help you think about the methodology behind creating the object and how much work it will take.

Architectural Modeling

Architectural modeling is one of the more popular uses of 3D Studio MAX. Architects create their models in AutoCAD and import them into MAX or create them wholly in MAX. Architectural models are generally planar in nature and are relatively easy to model. But because they also tend to have a great deal of detail and many different materials, they are more complex than other models you will see later in this chapter and in this book.

Architectural modeling encompasses everything from conceptual design work to office buildings to houses to churches to cathedrals. Architectural modeling can also be used by artists other than architects. Many games on the market today, for example, have architectural backdrops created by architects.

Chartres Cathedral in Chartres, France

The twelfth-century cathedral at Chartres, located about an hour from Paris, France, is one of the most spectacular examples of Gothic architecture and stained glass in the world (see fig. 1.7).

FIGURE 1.7
The Chartres Cathedral near Paris.

Chartres Cathedral presents an interesting problem to the computer artist. First, it is a very complex building for an architectural model. The complexity is evident in the intricate detail of the stained-glass rose windows and the ornamentation on the outside of the cathedral. Second, the stained glass windows themselves present a challenge not only in modeling, but also in materials.

Modeling Techniques

Before you start looking at modeling techniques, you need to understand the scope of Chartres Cathedral and just how complex a modeling task it presents. Figures 1.8 through 1.11 show various views and details of the cathedral.

FIGURE 1.8

The side facade of Chartres Cathedral.

FIGURE 1.9
The buttressing details.

FIGURE 1.10
A tower detail.

FIGURE 1.11
A close-up of a tower.

As the preceding set of figures shows, the overall form of the church is not particularly difficult, but the details are extremely intricate. The first thing to decide in the modeling process is how much intricate detail you want to show. The answer depends on how close you get to the building in your animation or still. If you are a fair distance away, you can use mapped materials to create the illusion of detail. But if you are fairly close, you probably will have to model most of the details to get an accurate view of the building.

Because this is such a complex building, you must use a variety of techniques to model it. Spline modeling, for example, should be used to create the detail on the flying buttresses (see fig. 1.9). A combination of spline modeling and solid modeling should be used to create the side facade (see fig. 1.8) and the towers (see figs. 1.10 and 1.11). The main nave of the cathedral can be modeled by using standard mesh modeling, because its geometry is fairly simple.

The exterior of Chartres Cathedral is covered with many figures inspired by religious texts. You do not necessarily have to model these, but if you decide to, model only five or six different figures and use them repetitively wherever you need them. If the figure is a decent distance from the camera, use materials to imitate it.

The figures themselves can be modeled using any technique discussed in this book. Just remember that they are small and repetitive, hence they will be extremely low resolution with very little detail. You could, for example, create a few metaballs and use them as the figures. Ultimately, a box mapped with a material that is a photograph of the figures will probably yield the best result.

This approach is just one of several you can take with this model. Some of the more exotic yet effective approaches include using the photographs to generate the model from within a photo modeling program. This approach results in a low-detail building, good for a backdrop only. Another option is to build a model of the cathedral (not an easy task) and laser scan the model in through a scanning service. This technique is highly accurate, but expensive and time consuming.

Your best approach is to model the overall form of the church and then go back and add detail until you are satisfied with the model. You will use many modeling techniques to complete the model, and will end up with a fairly large, complex model. Figures 1.12 and 1.13 show you two views of the completed model inside of 3D Studio MAX, before materials are applied.

FIGURE 1.12

An Isometric View of the cathedral.

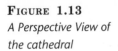

FIGURE 1.13
A Perspective View of the cathedral

Material Techniques

As for materials, Chartres Cathedral is simple in most respects. The base material in the building is limestone. You can literally scan in a photograph of the limestone and create the material based on that. The roof of the cathedral is a standard green copper. The only difficult materials on this particular building are in the stained glass windows (see figs. 1.14 and 1.15).

As you can see from figure 1.15, the stained glass is quite complex. Scanning in a photograph of the material is about the only way to portray it accurately. You must use a photo that is not distorted by perspective so that your bitmap material will be somewhat accurate.

With a great deal of work and a little ingenuity, you can eventually model the cathedral.

Biped Characters

Biped characters are objects meant to be animated by using Kinetix's Character Studio software. Biped characters are modeled with enough detail that when they are animated, the mesh transforms smoothly. Too little detail results in a blocky, faceted mesh when animated. They are also modeled with the skin as a single mesh controlled by the underlying Biped skeleton. Other parts of the body, such as hair, fingernails, and so on, are linked to the skin and move when the skin is animated.

FIGURE 1.14
Stained glass.

FIGURE 1.15
Close-up of stained glass.

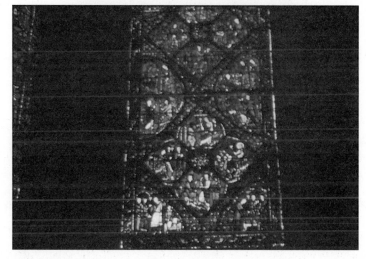

The Dancing Alien

In this example, you explore the dancing alien—a great example of a biped character—modeled by and available through Viewpoint DataLabs International, Inc. Figure 1.16 shows a wireframe of the alien.

FIGURE 1.16

The wireframe dancing alien. (3D models by Viewpoint DataLabs International, Inc.)

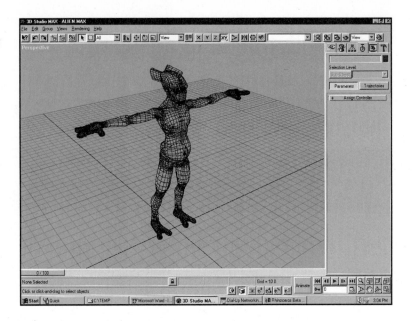

Modeling Techniques

When you are modeling a character for use with Biped, you need to model it in a specific pose. Biped characters work best when modeled with arms straight out to the sides and feet roughly shoulder width apart. This pose makes it easier to apply the skeleton and animate the model correctly. Figure 1.17 shows the correct pose for the alien.

FIGURE 1.17

The dancing alien, posed. (3D models by Viewpoint DataLabs International, Inc.)

Notice that the alien model does not have much detail and that the hands and feet have higher density meshes than the rest of the body (see fig. 1.16), which indicates that these parts of the body will be more heavily animated than the rest. There is relatively little detail in the head because facial animations generally are not applied to Biped characters. (More complex characters, discussed later in this chapter, do have facial animations.)

To model this character, you can take several different approaches. This character can easily be modeled by using metaballs. It can also be modeled with a little work by using patches. More than likely, this model was built as a clay model and laser scanned in, creating higher degrees of accuracy. Because this last approach is extremely expensive, you must rely on your own skills to create this character.

Another, more interesting, approach available in 3D Studio MAX is to create a rough outline of the character by modifying a Box object with Edit Mesh and Extrusions. Then apply the MeshSmooth modifier to smooth the object into a more natural form. A little more work beyond that, and you can quickly approximate this character.

The key thing to remember here is not to add too much detail where you don't need it. Study this model and how it is built. You can see exactly what the model is intended to be used for in an animation.

Material Techniques

The alien character presents a unique problem when it comes to materials. Because the skin is one object, the application of a material to the surface becomes much more of a problem than it would be if the skin were several objects. Also, mapping of materials is a problem because of the curved nature of the body.

One approach to this problem is to apply a bitmap, probably using the shrink-wrap mapping method, and keep adjusting the bitmap until it is correct. This works fairly well when the skin is all one material. Many characters in real life, however, have changing colors on their skin. A frog, for example, is mostly green on the backside and a very light green (almost yellow) on the underside.

Another method you might try is to use a plug-in, such as unwrap, which creates a bitmap with a diagram of the mapping layed out flat. You can then quickly and easily paint directly on the bitmap with your favorite paint program and apply it to the object.

The best method, arguably, requires the use of a plug-in such as 4D Paint or Fractal Design Detailer. These plug-ins enable you to paint directly on the 3D model, using any of a wide variety of brushes. You apply some mapping coordinates to the geometry, export it to the paint program, and then begin to literally paint your creature into life. This is the most powerful method for creating overly complex materials for objects such as this alien character. Figure 1.18 shows the alien character loaded in 4D Paint and with a little paint applied.

FIGURE 1.18

The alien being painted in 4D Paint. (3D models by Viewpoint DataLabs International, Inc.)

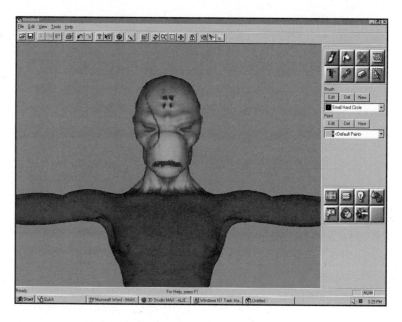

Three-dimensional object painting is extremely powerful for character models. If you are going to work much with these types of models in 3D Studio MAX, you should strongly consider picking up one of the many 3D paint programs available on the market.

Complex Character Models

A complex character model is similar to a Biped character, except that the complex model has much more detail. Complex models are generally fully animated from head to toe, including facial expressions, eyes, ears, wings, and even bulging muscles.

A Dragon

A dragon is a great example of a complex character model. A dragon has many interesting parts to model, such as wings, a tail, a body, and so on. In general, dragons have complex heads with horns, teeth, and other features. If you are going to animate the dragon blowing fire or talking, extra detail and attention to the head is necessary to model it correctly for animation. Figure 1.19 shows you a dragon that has already been modeled in 3D Studio MAX.

FIGURE 1.19

A dragon modeled in MAX. (3D models by Viewpoint DataLabs International, Inc.)

Modeling Techniques

As figure 1.19 shows, a dragon is an extremely complex and difficult character to model. This is an instance where the more time you invest in conceptual sketches and rough models, the better off you will be. Take the wings for instance. How many different ways do you think you could create the wings? Probably a lot. With sketching, you can explore these options before you spend the time trying to model them. This is especially true of other parts of the dragon, especially the head.

To model a dragon, you must use almost every modeling technique you can imagine. Because of the complexity of the shapes, a dragon really requires the use of a NURBS modeler. A dragon's head is an excellent example of a complex shape. NURBS modelers excel at creating complex surfaces and are even better at creating blends between such surfaces.

TIP

A good NURBS modeler to try is Rhino, from Robert McNeel and Associates. You can download a beta (at the time of this writing) from www.rhino3d.com. By the time this book is published, you may be able to download a demo of the final program.

The best approach to modeling a creature such as a dragon is to try and break the modeling into small tasks. You can model the wings as a separate object, for example, and then later attach them to the body. You can model the head and later attach it to the neck. This helps to keep your file sizes smaller and to make the modeling process go a little faster than if you were to model the entire creature in one fell swoop.

When you model a complex character such as this, keep in mind exactly which parts of the object will be animated more than others. You must provide enough detail in these areas so that the object can be animated smoothly. If you do your conceptual sketches correctly and create a storyboard of the character, you will know where and when to add the extra detail.

Also realize, however, that when you are working on a model as complex as a dragon, you must make a serious investment of time to complete the model. Newer modeling tools are constantly being developed and may eventually help to reduce the time involved.

Material Techniques

Dragons consist of very complex materials. Because the dragon is created as a single mesh, you are pretty much forced down the road of using a 3D paint program to correctly create a material for this type of character. Any other method will require so much trial and error in creating and placing the maps that it is worth your money to buy the appropriate program.

Other than that, pay attention to materials in nature when you create the materials for a creature such as a dragon. Base your materials on some known quantity, such as scales from a snake or wings from a bat. This makes the process of creating materials much, much easier.

Technical Modeling

A *technical model* is a model of an object that must be created precisely, to exact measurements. A space station or a car engine might be considered examples of technical models. Many technical models are created in other programs—such as AutoCAD, Mechanical Desktop, and even Pro Engineer—and brought into 3D Studio MAX for visualization purposes only.

A Space Station

A space station is a good example of a technical model. Even though only one space station exists, you have probably seen one of the many animations NASA has produced of the space shuttle docking with the International space station. Figures 1.20 and 1.21 show examples of a space station.

FIGURE 1.20

The international space station.

FIGURE 1.21

Another version of the international space station.

Modeling Techniques

Most of the forms in a technical model are fairly simple but accurate. Figure 1.21, for example, shows mostly planar or cylindrical elements. These can be modeled as simple objects and then modified to match the space station. Alternatively, the cylinders can be created as lofted splines.

Precision and detail are the keys here. Other than that, technical models should be fairly easy to create.

Material Techniques

Materials in a technical model are also fairly simple. Generally speaking, they are a collection of metallic or plastic materials that can easily be created in MAX. You might also see a set of logos that can be scanned in. Occasionally you will run into slightly more difficult materials, such as those on the solar panels of the space station, but even they can be created with just a little work in the MAX Material Editor.

Industry Modeling

Industry models are similar to technical models and are created to help sell a product. You can create models of cars, boats, jet-skis, and so on. These models should be as photorealistic as possible, to create the highest sales impact.

Modeling a Ferrari

A Ferrari is a good example of a technical model. It is a sleek, well-defined, popular car that can be easily modeled in MAX (see fig. 1.22).

Modeling Techniques

As mentioned earlier in this chapter, NURBS modelers are used to design most cars today. Hence, NURBS modelers make the most sense when you want to model this type of object. As a matter of fact, the original design models can be converted into 3D Studio MAX and rendered, if necessary.

NURBS make sense because most cars have precise curves and blends between curves. Unfortunately, because MAX does not use NURBS at this time, you have to resort to a plug-in or some other method of modeling. Of course, with a little work you can easily create a car by using patch modeling.

Like other slightly complex objects, many cars are built with plastic as physical models and then laser-scanned in. You probably have seen (or built) the many plastic car models available at any hobby store.

Material Techniques

Generally, industry models are easy to assign materials to. Most cars have one primary color, which can be either metallic or flat, and some secondary colors on the trim. Because of the fabrics or leathers on the interior, it may require a little more work to model correctly. For the most part, however, industry models are fairly straightforward and easy to create.

Regardless of the type of model you are trying to create in 3D Studio MAX, you must use one or more techniques to create the model. The following reminders are the keys to success:

- Plan before you build.

- Create sketches and rough models.

- Observe the real world for hints on modeling and materials.

- Add detail only where necessary.
- When modeling, always keep in mind the final objective.

Plug-In Overview

One of the true powers of a system such as 3D Studio MAX is the extensibility of the system—in other words, how easy it is to expand and enhance the program. You can enhance 3D Studio MAX by adding plug-ins (third-party software), adding functionality to the system without having to buy a whole new program.

Why Plug-Ins Are Important

Plug-ins are important because they give you additional ways to create objects that would be much more difficult to create with MAX alone. The fact is, you can create just about anything you want with the tools in MAX and a little work. Plug-ins just make your life easier.

Plug-ins in MAX are available in many different forms including Video Post, Bitmap I/O, File I/O, space warps, and so on. Most, however, come in the form of modeling and material plug-ins. The rest of this chapter explores some of the more popular plug-ins from these two categories.

Modeling Plug-Ins

Modeling plug-ins provide additional ways to create an object in MAX. Some of these methods are unusual; others are simply enhanced or advanced methods. You could purchase a modeling plug-in for any of a variety of reasons. Two reasons you might purchase a plug-in are: the plug-in provides you with functionality not present in MAX; or the plug-in reduces your modeling time and increases accuracy enough to justify its cost.

The next few sections cover several types of modeling methods. Specific plug-ins are mentioned for each type.

Metaballs

In *metaball modeling,* you use spheres as a modeling tool. By placing a set of spheres close to each other and assigning a tension value to them, you can create a surface based on those spheres. Figure 1.23 shows a series of spheres; figure 1.24 shows the resulting metaball surface.

FIGURE 1.23
A series of spheres.

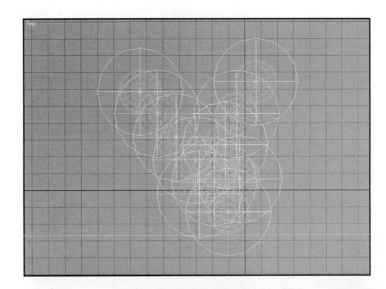

FIGURE 1.24
The metaball surface.

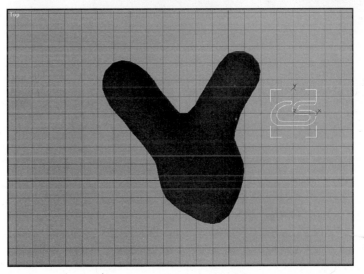

You can purchase two primary plug-ins to create metaballs: Clay Studio from Digimation, and Metareyes Metaballs from REM Infogracia. Both have a solid set of features and enable you to quickly and easily create a metaball model. Metareyes has one unique feature—metamuscle—that enables you to create creatures similar to the one shown in figure 1.25.

FIGURE 1.25
A metamuscle model and the resulting surface.

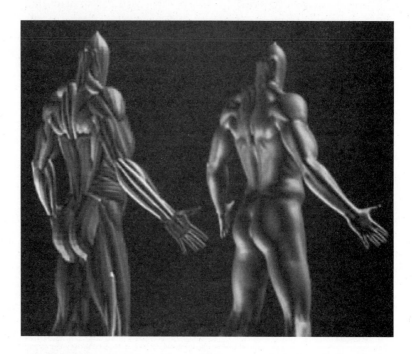

Plug-ins are integrated directly into the MAX interface. A grouping tool on the Clay Studio interface (see fig. 1.26) enables you to place metaballs next to each other without creating a surface between them and is helpful for hands and other such objects.

NURBS (Non-Uniform Rational B-Spline)

Currently, the only NURBS modelers available for use with 3D Studio MAX are stand-alone programs that export 3DS files that you can import into MAX. The best of these is Rhinoceros from Robert McNeel and associates. Figure 1.27 shows the interface for Rhino. Figure 1.28 shows a model created in Rhino and rendered in 3D Studio MAX.

FIGURE 1.26
The Clay Studio interface showing some of the controls. Note the Group Workshop Button.

FIGURE 1.27
The Rhino interface.

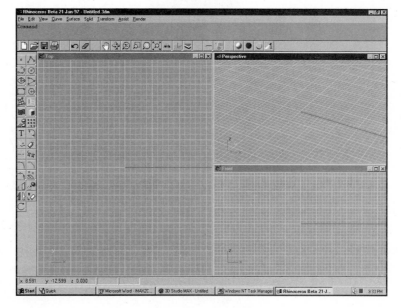

Rhino provides a complete set of NURBS tools with many, many different functions. The other NURBS modeler worth looking at is 4D Vision's Sculptor NT, another stand-alone product (see fig. 1.29). Like Rhino, it provides many NURBS modeling tools. The difference between the two lies in the way they're used, and which you should choose depends on your personality and how you like to model.

FIGURE 1.28
A model created in Rhino and rendered in MAX.

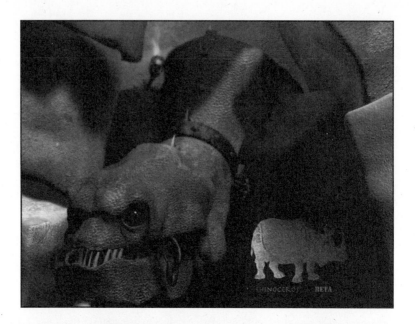

FIGURE 1.29
The Sculptor NT interface.

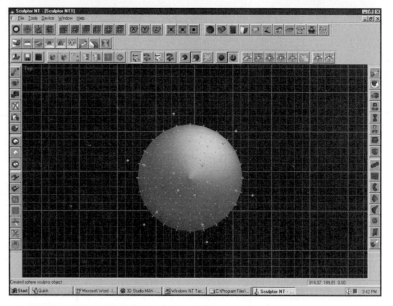

If you want to create an object with many different complex curved surfaces, one of these two products should do the trick. Yes, you can probably accomplish the same thing in MAX, but probably not as fast as with one of these programs.

Spline Tools

If you have used MAX for a while, you undoubtedly are familiar with the Lofting system in MAX for creating objects based on splines. Surface Tools, another plug-in from Digimation, makes spline modeling very easy. With Surface Tools, you can create 3D splines that approximate the contours of a surface. You can draw a spline to represent the line of a cheekbone, for example. Then, by applying Surface Tools, a surface of Bézier patches can be quickly and easily generated and manipulated. Figures 1.30 and 1.31 show examples of a set of splines and the resulting surface.

FIGURE 1.30

A set of splines.

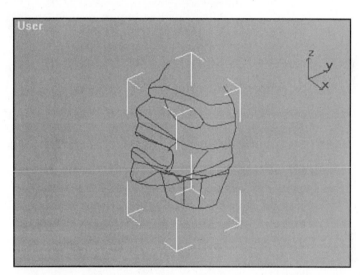

FIGURE 1.31

The resulting surface after applying Surface Tools.

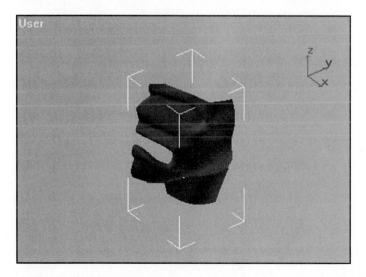

Powerful selling points for this plug-in are its ease of use and speed. With only a few hours of practice, you can begin modeling rather complex objects. As a matter of fact, with a little work, you could probably model the head of Draco from the movie *Dragonheart* in a day or two and get close to approximating the "real" head.

Using Other Plug-Ins as Modeling Tools

Through some inventive programming, developers have found ways to use other plug-ins and effects in MAX as modeling tools. If you purchase Bones Pro from Digimation, for example, you get a tool called SnapShot Plus. SnapShot enables you to use any space warp in MAX as a modeling tool. You could create a sphere and explode it with a space warp, for example. If you capture the mesh one or two frames after the explosion, you get a series of triangles that resemble leaves on a tree.

To take this a step further, other developers have produced shareware plug-ins that enable you to use particle systems as modeling tools. They work on a similar principle as SnapShot, converting the particle system over to an object at any given frame in the animation.

These are just two examples of MAX's inventive, powerful programming interface. Newer plug-ins, such as Atomizer from Digimation, enable you to create an object and do a one-to-one replacement of particles in a particle system with that object. If you use metaballs, you can create objects such as flowing water. Modeling plug-ins are exciting—and getting more so every week.

Material Plug-Ins

Material plug-ins provide additional functions to MAX's already powerful Material Editor. The two primary types of material plug-ins are paint programs and procedural textures.

3D Paint Programs

3D Paint programs are some of the most popular plug-ins for use with MAX. Some of the paint programs work with MAX; others are completely stand-alone. Of the available paint programs, 4D Vision's 4D Paint is probably the best. It works as a utility plug-in in MAX and enables you to export objects directly from MAX into 4D Paint, and vice versa. This type of integration makes it a powerful plug-in.

3D Paint programs work by enabling you to paint directly on the surface of an object. You can paint a variety of map types (such as diffuse, bump, and others) simultaneously or individually. In addition, you can create your own brushes, sprays, and so on. You can even create a brush that uses a bitmap as its paint. Figure 1.18 showed the 4D Paint interface.

3D Paint programs are the most flexible, powerful way to create complex materials for objects created as a single mesh, such as the Alien mentioned earlier in this chapter. 4D Vision has a demo of this plug-in on its web site at www.4dvision.com. Download it and give it a try. Direct experience provides the best way to gauge the power of this plug-in.

Procedural Materials

Procedural materials are generated through the use of mathematical algorithms and create some sort of real-world texture. One way to create a wood material is to use a photograph of wood. Alternatively, you can create a wood material by using a procedural noise that simulates the wood grains. Procedural materials are generally implemented as map types in Material Editor. You can apply the procedurals as diffuse maps, bump maps, or any other type of map in MAX.

A good example of a procedural plug-in is Texture Lab from Digimation. With this collection of six new material maps you can create everything from advanced noise maps to fire to electricity. The Texture Lab Fire map is loaded as a diffuse map in the MAX Material Editor.

Procedural materials are easy to use because they do not require UVW mapping coordinates. Instead, they rely on the world coordinate system to apply their textures. This means that when you cut a section out of the object to which you applied the material, the resulting object will still be mapped correctly. This is usually not the case when you use a standard bitmap-based material and UVW mapping coordinates.

Procedural materials also provide much greater control over the material's appearance. Mapped materials generally have only one look because editing the bitmap in MAX is not easy. Procedurals, however, are based on variables that can be quickly and easily manipulated to create some interesting effects. Figure 1.32 shows a rusted tin roof created with Texture Lab.

FIGURE 1.32

A rusted tin roof created through the use of a procedural material.

Image courtesy of Brandon Riza
Created using Texture Lab: Elemental Tools
available through Digimation
www.digimation.com

In Practice: The Modeling Process

- **Visualize.** Always visualize the object as much as possible before modeling it.

- **Attention to Detail.** Pay attention to things that exist in the world. You can draw a great deal of inspiration from them.

- **Just the Right Amount of Detail.** The key is details and knowing when to add detail and when not to.

- **Sketching.** Work your ideas out with hand sketches before you begin modeling. This will save you time and frustration.

- **Modeling.** If the object you are working on is overly complex, consider building a clay model as a reference.

- **Modeling Techniques.** In 3D Studio MAX, especially with the use of plug-ins, there are literally dozens of methods for modeling the same object. Select the methods you like to use the most and stick with them. Remember, whatever method you choose, the underlying process is always the same.

Part II

ADVANCED MODELING IN 3D STUDIO MAX

IMAGE BY JONATHAN SAWYER

Chapter 2

by Jonathan Sawyer
with Michael Neil

ARCHITECTURAL MODELING AND RENDERING

The last 15 years have seen the shift from hand-drafting to CAD in most architecture offices. Rarely do you find, even in small offices, construction documents still drawn by hand with parallel rule and triangle; even red-lining and mark-up is moving to the computer in many offices. In much the same way, it is very likely that the current explosion in the use of, and interest in, 3D computer visualization will force the practices of hand-rendering and model-making further and further into the background. Architects, Industrial Designers, Interior Designers—anyone who makes esthetic decisions in three dimensions—will inevitably find that 3D computer visualization is a very effective way to communicate design ideas.

In this chapter, you will use some of the techniques that enable you to make 3DS MAX do what you want it to do as an architectural modeler. You will model and render a small building, from a basic wall layout all the way through to the details that add the realism you need for a convincing presentation. This chapter deals with certain ways to use the modeling tools in 3DS MAX that are specific to architectural modeling. Accuracy is important in this context. Some topics considered include:

- Establishing the basic walls from plans
- Controlling lofts to produce architectural moldings
- Easy ways to build roofs
- Miscellaneous trim and detail

Building a 3D Architectural Model

Building a 3D model on the computer often highlights design problems and can aid in the search for a solution. On the simplest level, the process of constructing a wireframe of a building often reveals construction problems: sections and elevations that conflict, roof slopes that may not work, components that won't fit. If it does not fit together on your screen, it won't work on the jobsite either. Similarly, on a stylistic and esthetic level, a computer rendering reveals a lot—animation enables an experience of a space much more like the real experience. Eventually, full immersion in the architecture, by means of virtual reality, will likely become an important presentation and design tool.

Before any of this can happen, however, you need to build a wireframe.

In the broadest sense, a wireframe can be any of a variety of 3D computer representations. For the purposes of this chapter, a wireframe is a collection of digital entities, including lines, vertices, and faces, that make up a computer model. This model is solid in the sense that it contains surfaces, represented by collections of triangles, that define the surfaces of the object being modeled, for example, a house. This is different from true "Solid Modeling," in which additional information about the object being modeled is part of the database, information such as weight, density, and so on. In this context, you are only building a collection of "skins" that will represent the walls and other components of the building.

3DS MAX is designed to serve many different modeling, rendering, and animating applications. It was not specifically designed to model buildings. Certain strategies can make it easier to use 3DS MAX's considerable power to produce good, clean architectural models.

The building that you will model is an ornate but symmetrical poolhouse or bathhouse, a structure that might be found at a country club or on a private estate, containing changing rooms. The detailing and massing of this outbuilding are formal and have sufficient richness to enable you to explore the details of modeling techniques, but the building overall is simple enough that you will be able to complete the modeling of the exterior.

Modeling the Structure

Modeling a building for architectural presentation and analysis has very different requirements than modeling cartoon characters, aliens from a distant planet, or morphing toothpaste tubes. It's not so clear what aliens look like, at least to most people, so the modeler enjoys a little more latitude in interpretation. Almost everyone knows what buildings look like, however, and those expectations must be met.

Meeting those expectations in the digital world means building an electronic structure in steps that are not unlike the steps involved in building a real building. The walls are located and laid out and are then erected in basic form; openings are sized and located, and details are added in layers until the building is complete. Coloring and texturing the computer model is roughly analogous to painting and wallpapering an actual building, although the appearance of some surfaces is dictated by the material itself, of course, as in the case of a brick wall. Nonetheless, the broad analogy holds, and the first stages of modeling a building on the computer involve the roughing in of the walls.

Starting out

There are a few different approaches to the first step in architectural modeling—the basic layout of the walls and their various openings. Each way has advantages and disadvantages. Listed below are a few possible methods:

1. Extrude walls up from lines that you get from a floor plan, either an existing plan or one that you have drawn in a CAD program or in 3DS MAX specifically for the purpose.

2. Build the building the way real houses are actually framed—build the walls "lying down" and then stand them up and fit them together. This method may also be familiar because it is similar to the way architectural models have always been built, out of foam-core or chip board walls are cut out and then stood up and glued together.

3. Use Boolean Operations and other modifications to manipulate primitives, adding sections and cutting openings.

4. Use a wall section in its entirety as a shape and loft the entire wall of a building in one operation, along with all its various projections, cornices, and other linear details.

5. Hybrid methods where some of the initial modeling is done in a CAD program, and the result is then imported into 3DS MAX for the addition of details.

Extruding from Floor Plans

In many cases, a building to be modeled will already exist as plans. These plans can be imported into 3D Studio MAX and the walls built directly on top of them. This has the distinct advantage of ensuring that the walls will end up in the right place, assuming, of course, that the plans themselves are accurate. Plans can be drawn in 3D Studio MAX and extruded to form the walls, but in this scenario, in which all the dimensions need to be entered, it makes more sense to simply build primitives to the correct size and then modify them, which is essentially method number 3 mentioned above. The extra step of creating lines for a plan and then extruding or lofting them to form the walls hardly makes sense.

After importing the plans (a process covered elsewhere in this book), some alterations will be necessary. It is advisable to remove lines designating doors and windows, as well as most other things that do not represent the wall masses. Splines may need to be closed. Some thought will have to be given to how high to extrude or loft the various wall sections, which will in turn involve decisions about the interior modeling versus the exterior modeling, among other considerations. Other problems that will arise entail the openings, which are represented as breaks in the lines of a floor plan, and thus will become full-height, floor-to-ceiling openings when you extrude the walls, regardless of what they represent in the plan. A window, for example, will need to have wall sections added from its sill down to the floor (and to the ground, on the exterior), and above its header to the ceiling (or to the cornice, on the exterior). Keep in mind also that the various openings will need to be of a size that will allow clearance for the insertion of modeled jambs and trim in later steps. This may entail modifying the plans from which you are working before you extrude them.

If you are modeling a structure both inside and out, or one that has changes in the wall surfaces on the exterior, then polygons that span from the bottom of the wall section to the top will likely need to be redrawn and rearranged, if you want to assign different materials to different rooms. If you extrude a wall from the foundations to the top of the second floor, for example, which would be a quick and easy way to build a complete side of a house, then on the inside, all the wall surfaces will receive one material. The second floor bedroom and the family room below, for example, will share the same wall surface and hence the same material assignment. This could be rectified by erasing and redrawing faces, but that creates more steps.

One possible solution is to loft or extrude each floor separately and then stack them up. In this method, it is critical that they have the same footprint, so that they will join seamlessly. During this process, mapping coordinates can be added, saving some work down the road.

Building the Walls "Lying Down"

The second method mentioned involves drawing the walls as elevations, in the form of collections of lines and arcs, attaching the various parts to make one spline object, and then extruding it to the thickness of the wall. The window and door openings are just that—openings, sized to allow the insertion later of the miscellaneous trim pieces. The wall sections are then "stood up" and moved into place. This method is the cyber version of the way that houses are framed in the real life, in the standard stick-framing system. It has the advantage of being visually clear because you simply draw the wall the way that you want it to look in elevation. It suffers the same limitations as the previously described system, however—the need to separate wall planes for different interior rooms as well as exterior surfaces changes. It has the advantage of not having to be patched up with missing wall sections, as the previous system required. Again, size the openings to provide clearance for the trim that will be inserted later in the wall openings. In this respect, it is again analogous to the actual construction a building. Clearances are crucial.

After the walls are drawn with splines and extruded, they need to be rotated and moved into place, and the corners of the various walls need to be joined cleanly. Assuming that care and accuracy were used in the initial layout of the wall spline shapes, then joining the wall sections should be a simple matter of positioning the walls corner-to-corner and then attaching them as objects. Lastly, the vertices can be welded at the corners to complete the object.

This method may appeal to architects who are used to traditional model building methods, with the time-honored materials of foam-core, chip-board, and bass and balsa wood. You cut your openings in "sheet goods" and then glue the pieces together. Because architects are almost always at home visualizing buildings as elevations, then this method is comfortable.

Boolean Modeling of Walls

Boolean modeling is akin to carving your building out of blocks of solid material, which has an intuitive aspect of its own; architects are, in many ways, sculptors of three-dimensional space.

In this method, the building masses are defined with primitives, such as cubes. These primitives can either be built directly with the 3D Studio MAX Create Panel, which offers boxes and spheres and so on, or they can be built as lofts from shapes. Once a massing has been established, the inside can be hollowed out using Boolean Subtractions, leaving behind a shell that is the thickness of the walls. Openings are then cut in the appropriate locations by creating various solids and using Boolean Subtraction to cut holes in the walls. Always use a Hold before actually performing the Boolean operation, or do a Save. The Boolean engine in 3D Studio MAX is superior to the one in 3D Studio DOS, but it is by no means foolproof.

Here again, the mesh will probably need to be modified for the same reasons that were encountered in the other methods; different room surfaces will need to broken up, as well as separating the inside from the outside. Some of this can be accomplished by simple Multi/Sub Object mapping at the material application stage, but other problems will require rearranging the geometry.

Cross-Section Lofting to Form Walls

A possible method for making walls and some of the associated trim is to loft the entire cross-section of the wall in one operation. This method is very quick initially, but it requires the most clean-up and post-lofting manipulation of any of the methods.

In this scheme, an entire wall section is lofted around a path that follows the footprint of the wall. It will be seen that this allows the formation, in one operation, of cornices, stringcourses, crown moldings, overhangs, parapets—in short, any detail that runs parallel to the ground. After the lofting is accomplished, Boolean subtractions could be used to cut the various openings.

The strength of this method is also its weakness; it produces many elements in one operation, but often they will then need to be separated to receive their materials. Multi/Sub Object Mapping can solve much of the problem, but it does not solve the issue of what to do if it becomes necessary to edit some of the elements later—if, for example, you decide to delete a stringcourse or change its profile. In these cases, you have no choice but to edit the mesh and separate the elements. Also, this method results in a model with a greater number of polygons for the same result.

On the other hand, this method is so fast and easy for some building shapes that it might be the only choice. An example would be a curving wall with a balcony and continuous sunshade. There are some building shapes that could only be modeled, for all practical purposes, with some sort of lofting. Some examples of buildings that would be easy to loft and almost impossible to build otherwise include Wright's Guggenheim Museum in New York or the Opera House in Sydney, Australia.

Combinations with Other Programs

Another possibility is to perform initial 3D modeling in CAD to establish the basic wall volumes, and then import the model into 3D Studio MAX. Roughing in basic wall volumes in CAD in this way makes it possible to take advantage of the high degree of precision available in CAD packages. You can, therefore, start out in 3DS MAX with a perfectly accurate basic structure; each subsequent modeling operation in 3DS MAX adds small inaccuracies that have a tendency to accumulate. Thus, the more accurate your starting point, the better. 3DS MAX was never designed to match the accuracy of CAD programs.

This last method is the one that you will use in this chapter. Start by loading from the accompanying CD the file called WALLS.max. This basic model was built in AutoCAD, using a third-party parametric modeler that operates entirely inside AutoCAD. A few such front-ends are available. After importing into 3DS MAX, it is often necessary to correct some of the surface normals in the model. In the model that you are starting with, this has already been done. Also the units have already been set to U.S. Standard Fractional Inches, and the Home Grid increment set to 1", with major lines every 12".

Some Points About Lofting

In the scene, you will use a selection of shapes already made as profiles for lofting the various cornices, stringcourses, plinths, and other continuous, linear details. These shapes were created using 3DS MAX's spline creation and editing tools, described in the 3DS MAX documentation and also in *Inside 3D Studio MAX Volume I*. The shapes are next to each other on the ground plane in the middle of the main building shape and can easily be located easily by selecting them in the Select by Name dialog box and then looking for the axis tripod.

3DS MAX makes modeling linear architectural elements such as crown molding relatively painless, but there are certain demands placed on the lofting process in an architectural context. Specifically, the precision in the scaling and teetering of the shape along the length of the loft is crucial to correct lofting. In a precisely rectilinear path, such as the path followed by the baseboard, cornice, or door trim, a snag occurs when a profile that is the correct width on the straight runs of the path is pivoted by the lofter at the point where the path turns a corner. Because the profile width is unchanged, the lofted object tapers in at the corner in an undesirable fashion, unacceptable for architectural trimwork. Figure 2.1 shows such a situation exaggerated for clarity, with the corrected loft on the right where the shape has been scaled up at the corner points to compensate.

FIGURE 2.1

Uncorrected loft compresses at corners; loft with the scale-corrected shape at the corners yields uniform cross-section.

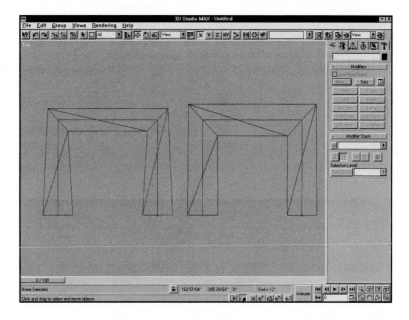

This discussion focuses primarily on the width of the shape as seen in what might be called a top view, where the path lies in a plane perpendicular to the reader's line of sight. When looking at the path from the side, which is to say edge-on, the dimension of the shape profile is constant. Such is the situation whenever the path of the loft lies entirely in one plane, as is the case with a run of door casing, or the baseboard in a room, or the crown molding that runs around a room where the ceiling is a constant height. But this scenario is not always the case in architecture; consider a run of baseboard that, for example, goes up a staircase, turns a corner at the top, goes down a hall, and then turns again and goes up more stairs. In this case, scale corrections would have to be made to both the width and the height of the shape, depending on the location and direction of the turn in the path, because the path of the loft does not lie in one plane.

Fortunately, simple formulae help to figure out how much to scale the shapes.

For a given angle θ, where θ is equal to the angle of rotation of the shape on the path (such that, one-half the angle of the change in direction of the path itself), the rotated shape must be larger than the starting shape by a factor given by

1/sineθ

This quantity is commonly expressed as

cosecantθ

and can be looked up in any table of trigonometric values or generated by a pocket calculator that has trigonometric functions. If your calculator lacks a cosecant function, take the inverse of the sine of the angle of the shape.

Multiply the original length of the shape by the quantity cosecantθ to arrive at the correct length for the shape at the point at which the angle θ occurs. In 3DS MAX, this is easy: Perform a non-uniform scale on your shape, in the desired axis, until reaching the percentage that corresponds to your factor. The following table gives some values for common angles.

TABLE 2.1

Scale Factors for Loft Shapes

Angle of turn in path (2θ)	Angle of Shape Rotation (θ)	Percentage Scale Factor for (cosecantθ)	Non-Uniform Scale
135°	67.5°	1.0824	108.24%
90°	45°	1.4142	141.38%
60°	30°	2.0000	200%
45°	22.5°	2.6131	261.31%

If the angle of the shape exceeds 90 degrees, look up the cosecant for that angle's acute complement.

LOFTING THE COLUMN BASECAPS

Start by making a simple loft to form the trim at the top of the bases that the columns will rest on. First, create a closed spline rectangle exactly the size of one of the cubes that make up the object Colbase. The object Colbase consists of eight identical boxes, part of the WALLS.max file. It does not matter which one you choose to use for the following steps.

1. Select the line tool in the Create panel, and set steps to 0 in the interpolation area of the roll-out.

2. Turn on the 3D snap tool, making certain that vertex is the #1 snap priority.

3. Snap four line segments, connecting the four top vertices of any one of the objects called Colbase (see fig. 2.2). Be sure to snap the lines in a counter-clockwise order, so that the face normals of the loft that will be made from this path will point outward.

4. Answer yes when 3DS MAX asks whether or not you want to close the spline.

5. Name the new spline **Colbasepath**, or something else that you can easily associate with this operation.

FIGURE 2.2

Rectangular spline snapped to the top vertices of one of the Colbase objects.

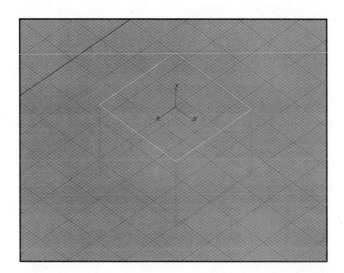

Now scale the shape, which for this loft is the shape called Stringshape. Because the corners of this loft are 90 degrees, and the shape rotation is 45 degrees, the shape needs to be scaled up by 141.38% (see table 2.1). With this particular loft, it should be scaled before being placed on the path because the path is a closed spline and the shape will be placed at a corner and thus rotated. If the path were an open spline, the shape would be placed at the first vertex, at one end of the path, and so would not be rotated. In that case, scaling for the corners would be accomplished after the shape had been placed on the path, by using the scale deformation controls. This method is used later in the chapter.

6. Select the object called Stringshape from the Select by Name button.

7. Zoom in on the shape in the top viewport and perform a Shift-clone on it, selecting Copy as the clone method. You want to keep an unscaled copy for future use. Rename the clone something like **Colbasetrim** to differentiate it from the original shape, which will be used again for another loft.

8. Apply an XForm modifier to the copy and select non-uniform scale from the transform toolbar. The axis constraint is irrelevant because you are going to use type-in. If there is a concern about this shape being instanced later, then this scaling operation should be performed on the shape after it has been assigned to the loft; in this case, however, this shape is already a copy and so will likely be used only in this loft. The original shape remains for other, later uses.

NOTE

The shape can be scaled by applying a non-uniform scale transform, rather than by applying the scale as an XForm modifier. If the scale is not applied as an XForm modifier, however, the loft ignores the scaling and uses the original, unscaled shape instead. Generally, it is a good idea to apply a scale transform as an XForm modifier, thus placing it in the stack like any other modifier, and thereby preserving your flexibility.

9. To pop up the Scale Transform Type-in dialog, right-click on the scale button in the transform toolbar.

10. In the X field of the Offset Screen column, type 141.42, and press Enter.

TIP

Use the Scale Transform Type-In dialog for accurate scaling, rather than dragging to scale. Even if you set the snap increment to less that 1", dragging the scale operation still only yields whole-inch read-outs on the status line. For greater accuracy, use the type-in method.

11. Close the dialog, turn off Sub-Object in the modify panel to deactivate the gizmo.

Now you are ready to place the shape on the path.

12. With the shape still selected, open the Hierarchy panel and select Affect Pivot Only from the Adjust Pivot roll-out.

13. Move the pivot point to the extreme lower right end of the shape. This ensures that the shape will be placed correctly on the path.

14. Select the path Colbasepath, select Loft Object from the Create panel, click on Get Shape, check Copy button below the Get Shape Button, and then click on the scaled shape. For this example, copy is chosen in case you want to use the shape again elsewhere; if not, you can always erase it at the end of the project (see fig. 2.3).

15. Open the Modify panel, expand the Skin Parameters roll-out, and check the Skin box under Display.

16. The loft appears. It bulges in the straight runs between corners because of the scale questions previously discussed above. In this case, however, it's easy to fix. Set the path steps to 0 in the Skin Parameters roll-out, and the loft becomes uniform because there are no steps between corners where the shape can reside. The lofter lofts directly from corner to corner. Setting path steps to 0 also cuts the polygon count of the loft from 2,016 to 336, as you can tell by right-clicking on the object and then choosing Properties from the pop-up menu.

17. Rotate and examine the object in a shaded view. Its profile is smooth and quite acceptable. Quick render it to see how it will look. Now check the Optimize Shapes button, and re-render. There is no visible difference, but checking the polygon count reveals that it has dropped to 176. Optimize Shapes makes intelligent decisions for you—it eliminates the steps in the segments of the shape that are straight, where steps are unnecessary anyway, and preserves them in the parts of the shape that are curved, where you want the smoothness that the steps provide.

18. Now decrease the shape steps setting one step at a time, re-rendering between each change. It is difficult to see a difference in the smoothness of the loft until you get down to 2 steps; at 1 step, it is faceted, and at 0 steps, it is no longer acceptable. But the polygon counts drop nicely: at 2 steps, 104; at 1 step, 80; at 0 steps, 56. You be the judge of the results that you need, taking into account the proposed end-usage of the model. For this exercise, settle on 2 steps as a good compromise between modeling economy and detail (see fig. 2.4).

FIGURE 2.3

The shape placed on the loft.

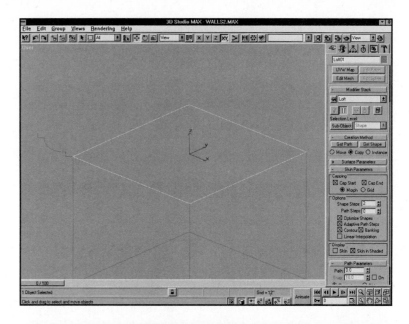

FIGURE 2.4

The loft skinned with optimize shapes checked and shape steps set to 2.

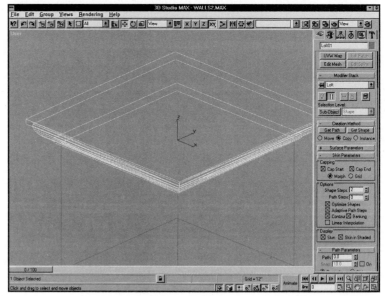

TIP

If you prefer, you can position the shape on the path by skipping the steps involving the repositioning of the pivot point, and move the shape by choosing Shape under the Sub-Object menu and moving it with the move tool, checking it in various viewports. If you were making a loft that had modifications of the same shape at different points on the path, or had many occurrences of a shape, it would be easier to set the pivot point one time and then place the shape.

The last step is to put a top on the basecap.

19. Apply an Edit Mesh modifier to the lofted object.

20. Choose Face from the Sub-Object menu, and click on Build Face in the Miscellaneous area of the roll-out.

21. Build two triangular faces by clicking on the top corner vertices of the lofted object, to make a solid top for your base. Check it in a shaded view (see fig. 2.5).

FIGURE 2.5

Drawing faces to close the top of the basecap.

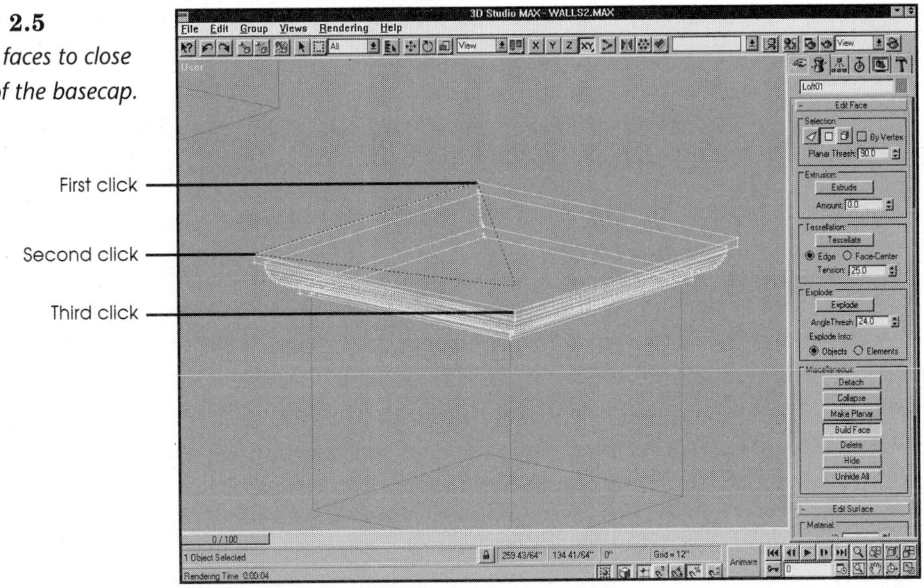

First click
Second click
Third click

NOTE

Remember that when using Build Face, the order in which you select the vertices is important. Select vertices in a counter-clockwise order if you want the surface normal of the resulting surface to face toward you (that is, be visible from your point of view). Select them in a clockwise order if you want them to be visible from the other side (that is, from a viewpoint opposite your own).

22. Finally, rename the lofted basecap something useful like **Colbasecap**, and copy it on to the tops of the other seven Colbase objects. Use Instance as the clone method, in case you want to change it later, and use snaps to position clones accurately on top of the other bases. This is probably easiest to accomplish in the top viewport. As a bookkeeping measure, it is a good idea to group all eight basecaps in a group called Colbasecap, to avoid cluttering up the object list.

LOFTING THE PLINTHS

Your next step is to make a base molding, or plinth, for these column bases. This example uses the path you have already created, in combination with another shape in your scene.

1. From the Select by Name dialog, select the object called Colbasepath.

2. Drag it down near the bottom of the Base object by using the appropriate transforms and constraints. Exactly where you put it is not important; you just need to be able to see it below the basecap. Alternatively, you can leave it where it is and simply hide the Basecap object.

3. Follow the same procedures that we used to make the Basecap object, but use the shape called XBaseshape. Copy the shape, scale it up 141.38%, move its pivot point, place it on the path called Colbasepath, and optimize it (see figs. 2.6 and 2.7).

4. Check the loft in a shaded view; the surface normals may need unifying.

5. When it's finished, rename it, move it down to the bottom of the Column Base object so it rests on the ground plane, and then copy it to the other seven Base objects.

6. Group them and name the group something like **Colbaseplinth**.

FIGURE 2.6
The shape for the plinth placed on the path.

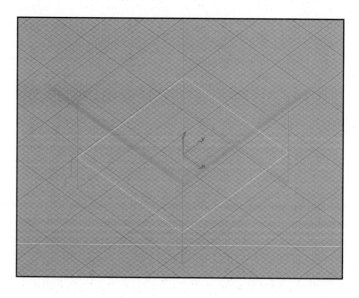

FIGURE 2.7

The completed plinth loft positioned at ground level.

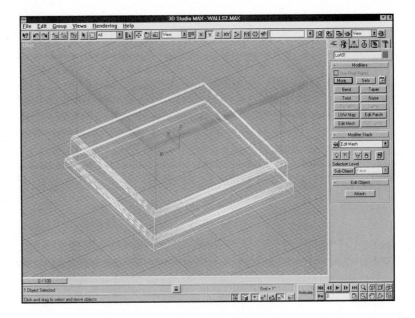

LOFTING THE STRINGCOURSE

This building has two volumes on either side of a central arcade or breezeway. On either side of this central arcade is a building mass, each containing changing rooms. Each side has two doors and a stringcourse that runs around the building about three feet above the ground; below this decorative ledge, the wall surface steps out by 3". The stringcourse that makes up this ledge is the next thing to be modeled.

First, the shape used for the previous loft needs to be slightly modified.

1. Select Stringshape from the Select by Shape dialog, and then zoom in on it in the top viewpoint. This is the original, unscaled shape from the previous exercise.

2. Turn on 2D snap and select the line tool from the Create panel. With Stringshape still selected, click on the checked box beside Start New Shape in the Object Type roll-out. This adds the line you are about to draw to Stringshape.

3. With the Home Grid on, draw a line from the upper left point of the shape to a point exactly nine inches to the right. Figure 2.8 shows the result.

4. Apply an Edit Spline Modifier, and then select the two vertices that lie at the point where you joined this new line to the existing shape. Weld them by clicking the Weld button in the Vertex Sub-Object roll-out.

5. Finally, as before, use Affect Pivot Only in the Hierarchy panel to move the pivot point to the lower right corner of the shape.

FIGURE 2.8

Stringshape modified with the addition of a line on top.

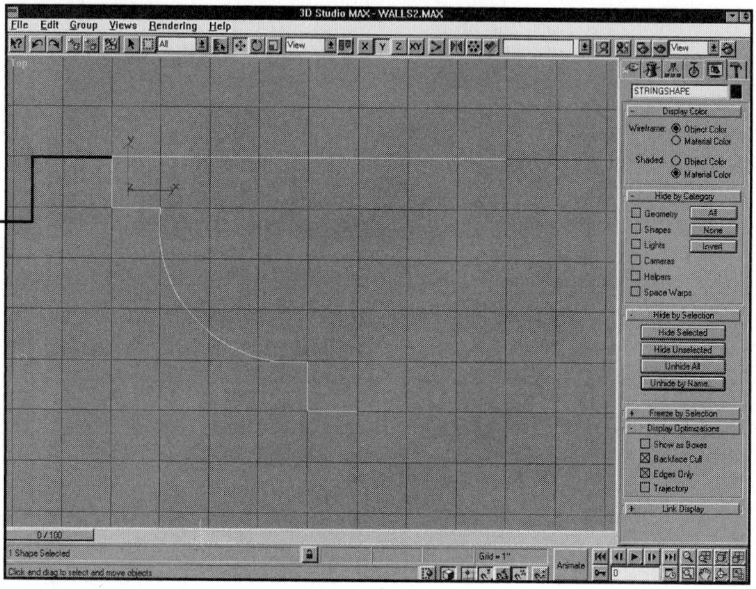

Weld these vertices ———

The next step is to create the path for this loft.

6. Select Basewall from the Select by Name dialog. This object contains four Wall objects, two of which are mirror opposites of the other two. To make it easier to see what you're doing, hide all the other objects in the scene.

7. Snap a line around the top of one of the long wall planes by using 3D snap and vertex as the #1 snap priority (see fig. 2.9). Snap the lines in a counter-clockwise order. Call it **Stringpath1**.

8. Use Stringpath1 and the new, modified version of Stringshape to create a loft, and in the Skin Parameters roll-out, set Shape Steps set to 2, Path Steps to 0 (because there are no curved sections on the path), and Contour On and Banking Off.

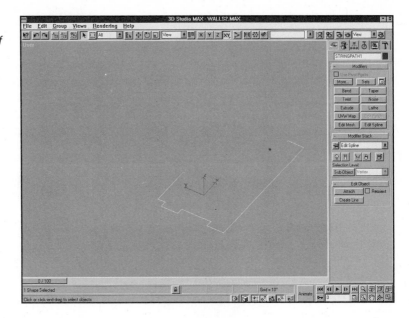

The resulting loft is distorted because the shape is both incorrectly teetered and incorrectly scaled at the vertices (see fig. 2.10).

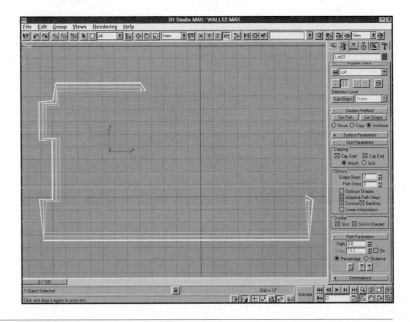

Teetering the Shape

Fixing the teetering problem will be accomplished first. For architectural moldings, you obviously want the shape profile at each vertex to lie precisely on a line that bisects the angle created by the change of direction in the path. This produces a symmetrical turn in the loft, mimicking the mitering that a carpenter would do with the actual molding. Two ways enable you to do this:

- Loft the shape and then use the Teeter Deformation controls in the Deformation roll-out at the bottom of the Modify panel to pivot the shape at the vertices to the correct angle.

- Manipulate the vertices of the path.

Both methods work well, but the second scenario is a little faster and more accurate. It takes advantage of 3DS MAX's capability to simultaneously display the lofted result while you adjust the vertices of the path generating the same loft.

MANIPULATING THE VERTICES TO TEETER THE LOFT

Following are the steps involved in correcting the vertices of the path to produce a correct loft.

1. Expand the top viewport. From the Select by Name dialog, select Stringpath1. Right-click on any vertex on the spline to display the pop-up menu, and choose Bézier from the menu, to change the vertex type. Zoom in as necessary.

   The Bézier handles will appear, and by dragging the handles, it is possible to interactively twist the tangent of the path spline at the vertex and thereby pivot the shape precisely at that vertex. Because the loft is still skinned, you get to see the result of the adjustments every time you release the handle after a drag operation. The only remaining question is how much to pivot the vertex; a reference line makes it easy. Creating one is quick with this particular loft, where the path aligns exactly with the X and Y axes.

2. Use the Home Grid and 2D snaps with grid intersections as the highest priority to draw a guide line at exactly a 45-degree angle to the path.

3. Mirror it by using the copy option with no offset, creating an X-shaped object. Use Edit Spline to attach the two together. Now you have two lines, one to use with each angle orientation. The object is visible in figure. 2.11 in position at a corner of the loft.

4. Move this X-shaped object so that the appropriate leg of the object passes exactly through the path vertex that is being adjusted. This can be accomplished by setting 2.5D or 3D snap with vertex point as top priority and dragging the intersection of the guide shape to the path vertex.

5. Reselect the path, select the vertex, and drag one of the Bézier handles until the shape at the vertex aligns with the guide line. The loft makes a symmetrical angle (see fig. 2.11).

FIGURE 2.11
Adjusting the vertex with the Bézier handles so that the corner of the loft lies on the guide line.

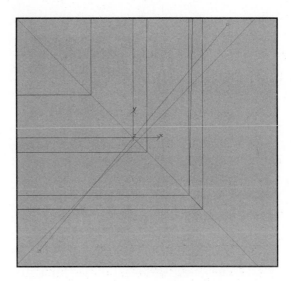

NOTE

As figure 2.11 shows, the handles do not necessarily lie precisely perpendicular to the loft angle when the shape has been correctly teetered. This results from the asymmetrical effect exerted on the vertex by the different length segments on either side of that vertex. If the segments on either side of the vertex are the same length, the handles are perpendicular to the shape at the vertex (that is, parallel to the other leg of the X-shaped Guide object).

6. Repeat the preceding steps for all the vertices on the path. Figure 2.12 shows the loft with the teetering corrected by the shapes still incorrectly scaled at the vertices. This is most evident at the ends of the loft.

FIGURE 2.12
*Loft with shapes
teetered correctly but
not scaled.*

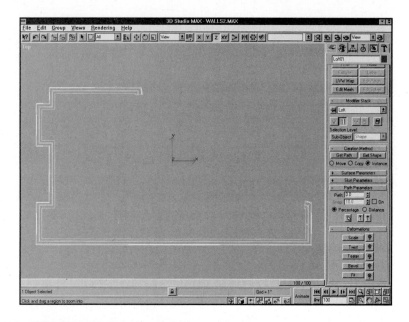

<hr>

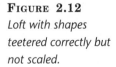

To provide more accuracy and sensitivity in the adjustment, it helps to stretch the Bézier
handles out to the edges of the view that you have zoomed in on.

Creating guide lines for any angle is easy. Use vertex and edge snaps to draw
a line segment that lies exactly on top of either of the path segments that
meet the vertex you want to adjust. Then use the Rotate Transform dialog
to enter a precise quantity to rotate the line one-half the angle that the path
forms. Then move the line into place and proceed as outlined in the preceding
exercise.

Using the Teeter Deformation Dialog

The first method previously mentioned to correct the shape teetering at the
vertices involves using the Teeter Deformation dialog found under the
Deformations roll-out at the bottom of the Modify panel. The use of this box
is covered elsewhere, but a few things should be kept in mind when using this
dialog to correct lofted architectural moldings and shapes.

- Placing control points on the curve is inherently imprecise; the snaps do not have any effect, and placing the control points accurately at the vertex locations is a matter of repeated zooming in and moving. If this is not done with reasonable care, the teetering adjustment that you want to occur at the vertex of the path will be slightly off. This tuning process can be time-consuming.

- If the Contour box is checked in the Skin Parameters roll-out, the shapes automatically teeter an amount that is difficult to measure, governed by the vertex and segment properties at each vertex. To teeter from this state to the precise angle that bisects the path angle necessitates guide lines, as used previously, and it then becomes easier to use the previous outlined method. Turning off Contour, however, produces a loft in which all the shapes at each vertex remain at zero rotation (see fig. 2.13). Then it is easy to use the Type-In option in the Teeter dialog to enter the correct rotation (45 degrees, 67.5 degrees, and so on, for example).

FIGURE 2.13
Loft with Contour unchecked and shape at each vertex at zero rotation.

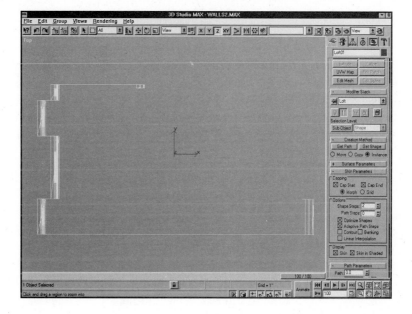

The scaling problem, fixed in the previous exercise by scaling the shape before placing it on the path, can be fixed in this case in either of two ways:

- Placing a scaled copy of the shape at the vertices (other than the end vertices, of course) by using the Path Parameters roll-out in the Modify Panel.

- Use the one, unscaled shape automatically placed at the end of the path, and then use the Scale dialog found under the Deformation roll-out to scale the shape up at the vertices.

Neither method is completely accurate.

Using Path Parameters to Place Scaled Shapes

The Path Parameters controls do not provide a way to place a shape exactly at a vertex; they only enable you to place a shape a certain distance down a path from the first vertex. Unless you know exactly what that distance is, it becomes a matter of repeated zooming in and moving. Also, you are limited by the precision of 3DS MAX and by the units that you have selected to work in, and so you may not be able to move the shape precisely the correct amount even if you know what that amount is. Fractional Inches, which you will likely be using for architectural work, is less accurate than Decimal units, but neither is useful unless you know the exact distance down the path to the vertex that you are trying to reach. It might be some nice, round number such as 3", in which case things are easier. Otherwise, you could try to determine it with the tape measure tool, but that entails the same limitations of precision.

Using the Scale Deformation controls

The Scale Deformation dialog is the easier method, although it is still not perfect.

1. Insert control points on the Deformation Curve at each vertex location (the vertical lines in the Deformation Grid). Use the X-axis for loft paths that lie in the X/Y World plane, as this one does. Set symmetry off.

2. By zooming in and adjusting, position the control points as accurately as possible at the vertex locations. Snaps are not applicable here, so it's a matter of fine-tuning.

3. Move the control points up at the vertices using move axis constraints, by selecting them one by one and typing in the appropriate scale values (as discussed previously) in the right-hand field at the bottom of the dialog. It would be handy to be able to select all the control points that you want to move the same amount and move them together, but 3DS MAX only enables you to drag the control points when multiple are selected; type-in entry is disabled. A possible strategy here is to select all the points that require similar displacements and then drag them to the correct value, using zoom to get greater and greater levels of precision. If you want to be able to enter the exact amount, however, you must do it one point at a time.

4. With this loft, the scale deformation at all the vertices is 141.38%. Figure 2.14 shows the scale-corrected loft.

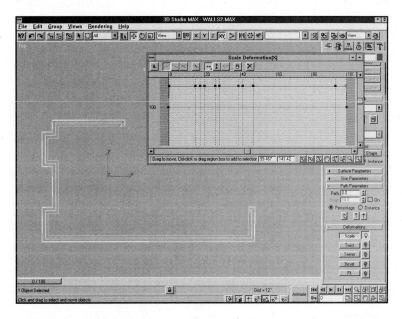

FIGURE 2.14

Scale-corrected loft and Scale Deformation dialog.

This section of Stringcourse is now lofted and corrected. The final steps follow:

1. Check surface normals and correct as necessary. Rename this loft **Stringcourse**.

2. Close the top of the ledge of this Stringcourse where the ledge bumps out and the columns are to rest (see fig. 2.15). This can be done in various ways:

- Use Sub-Object, Vertex, Collapse to bring some of the top vertices together.

- Use Sub-Object, Vertex, Weld, Target to join the vertices.

- To fill in the wider ledge top that occurs right at the corner of the building, it is necessary to either move a vertex by using move constraints or add one to the edge of the loft. You probably want to create some guide lines or boxes to help move the vertices so that the edges at the top of the shape remain perpendicular. Figure 2.15 shows this operation in progress, and figure 2.16 shows a shaded view of the finished Stringcourse in place on the building with the widened ledge sections ready for the columns that will sit on them.

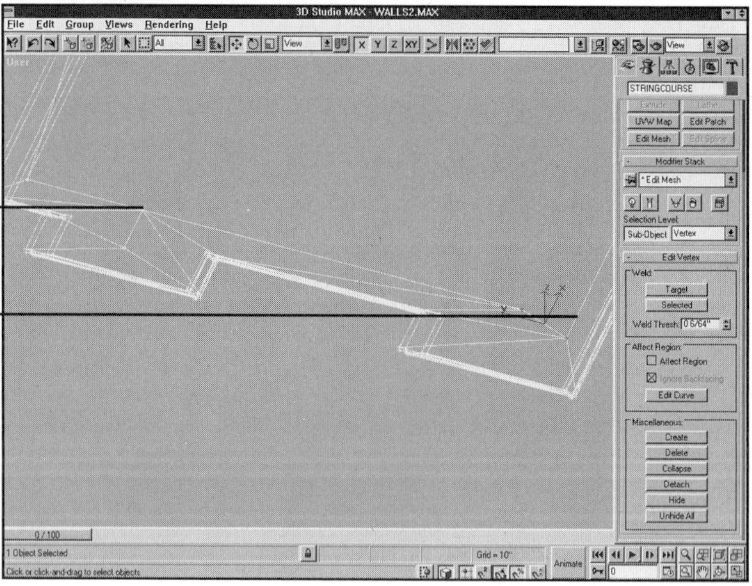

FIGURE 2.15

Filling in the top of the Stringcourse ledge to make the platform for the columns.

Collapse vertices

Create and weld vertices here

FIGURE 2.16
*The finished
Stringcourse in place
on the project to date.*

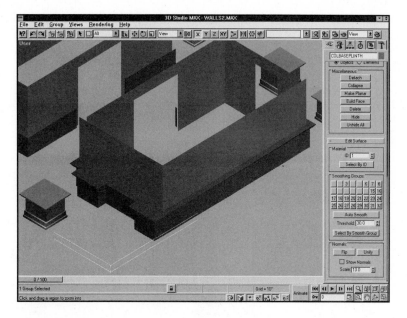

3. Use the outlined procedures to create lofts on the tops of the other three sections of Basewall, and then attach them to make one object called Stringcourse.

Making the Columns and Cornices

Forty columns surround this building. Columns are easy to make in 3DS MAX. Two methods in particular are worth mentioning:

■ Draw a spline outline for the column, and then apply a Lathe modifier to create a surface of revolution.

■ Draw a straight line and loft a circle by using the line as the path, and then create the profile of the column by manipulating the function curve in the Scale Deformation dialog.

It is also possible to build up a column shape out of primitives (cylinders, squashed spheres, and so on). This method will most likely leave you with unnecessary hidden faces, as well as being harder to modify later. Both of these mentioned methods enable you to draw the outline of the column by adjusting the Bézier handles of a spline, making it possible to tune the shape of your column quite closely. Figure 2.17 shows the base of a column lofted with a straight line and a circle, and then modified with the function curve in the Scale Deformation dialog.

FIGURE 2.17

Bottom of Column and Scale Deformation box with the function curve that generated the loft scaling.

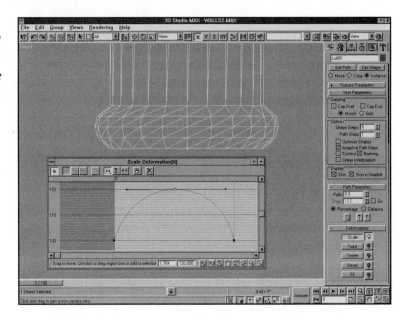

Here, the shape of the function curve is the same as the profile of the loft, a situation generally not the case in the Loft Deformation controls. Just as with a spline, you can achieve precise shaping of the curve by the use of the Bézier handles. The result here is the base of a Tuscan Order column, awaiting the addition of the abacus to complete it.

It is somewhat more difficult to control the polygon count with this method; forcing straight sections of the column to have no steps, and therefore fewer polygons, is easier to achieve with the spline-and-lathe method. If you want your columns to have entasis, they will contain no straight sections and will have much higher polygon counts. For this project, the columns are straight-sided. Follow these steps:

1. Draw a spline that outlines your column, or use the one called Columnspline supplied in the .Max file. This spline is the correct height, so if you decide to draw your own, make it the same length.

TIP

If you have straight sections in the columns, as the shape Columnspline does, it greatly reduces polygon counts. Remember to set steps to zero when drawing lines; set it higher when drawing arcs. If you use Attach to make the spline one shape, each section retains its steps. If you create a single spline by turning off the Start New Shape option, however, the results are less predictable. If you draw the line segment first with zero steps, and then uncheck Start New Shape and draw an arc with higher steps, for example, the arc is forced to have zero steps like the line segment. Maintaining control of these factors results in more efficient modeling.

2. Apply a Lathe modifier to the spline. The Direction area of the Parameters roll-out supplies options for X, Y, and Z. Pick the one that aligns the white axis line with the length of the spline. You end up with the curious object shown on the left in figure 2.18.

3. Turn on Sub-Object. Axis is the only option in the Sub-Object menu.

4. Drag the yellow axis line sideways, to generate a column similar to the one on the right in figure 2.18, the shaft of which is eight inches in diameter. If you prefer some other proportion, then drag to suit.

5. Create two boxes, at the top and bottom of the column, to form the abacuses and attach them to the column. Make them as wide and long as the decorative bulge in the column and 1-$\frac{1}{2}$ inches high, and the columns will be the correct height.

6. Copy the column to the locations shown in figure 2.19 —four on each of the Colbase objects, and two on the wide sections of the ledges that are part of the Stringcourse that was lofted in the previous exercise. Notice that the four outer Colbase objects do not have columns yet. The Columns that go there are taller and will be scaled later from a column already modeled.

FIGURE 2.18
Lathed column shape before and after Lathe Axis adjustment.

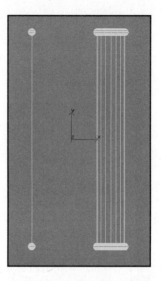

FIGURE 2.19
Columns placed on the Colbases and on the Stringcourse.

Columns on stringcourse ledge

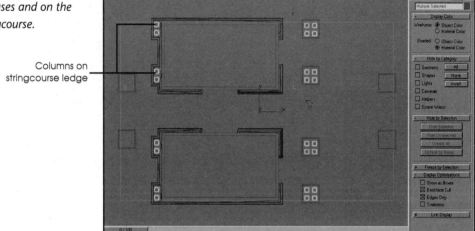

The Cornices

Two cornice lines are on this structure. One cornice line runs around the two building masses that comprise the changing rooms, and the other cornice line is higher and defines the central arcade through the building. All the cornices have the same profile, a shape included in the .Max file called Corniceshape. It can be found lying on the construction plane beside the other shapes. A path called Cornicepath1 is also in the scene; it is the path to be used to loft the cornices that run around the tops of the changing rooms. Cornicepath2 can be used to loft the cornices that run the length of the central breezeway. They all have been modeled already, using the previously described techniques, and can be unhidden if you do not wish to model them. They are called Cornice1 and Cornice2 (for the sections that go around the changing rooms) and Cornice3 and Cornice4 (for the ones that flank the central arcade). Note that on the front and the back of the building, where the cornices project out from the walls, the undersides of the lofts have to be filled in to make ceilings for these porch-like overhangs; otherwise the loft yields a floating cornice with nothing inside it when you look up underneath. This is easily done by selecting the vertices at the bottom inside corners of the cornice lofts and dragging them until they meet the exterior wall surface, filling the gap (see fig. 2.20).

FIGURE 2.20

Filling in the underside of the cornice lofts.

Drag vertices

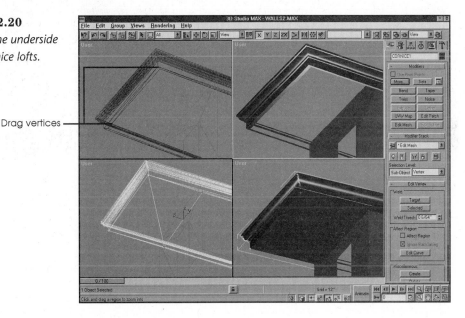

NOTE

In a fully detailed model, of course, the ceiling of these overhangs and porches would be a different material from the cornices themselves; there would also likely be a reveal where the bottom edge of the cornice projected down below the surface of this ceiling by an inch or two. The additional modeling that this involves is not central to the point of this chapter, but feel free to do it if you want.

More Columns

The next step is to place the remaining columns. The cornices that flank the arcade are supported by taller columns than the ones that surround the changing rooms. It is just a matter of copying and stretching an existing column.

---

1. In a side view, copy a group of four columns with Transform and X constraint (see fig. 2.21).

2. Select the top vertices, and stretch the columns up until they reach the underside of the arcade cornice (see fig. 2.21).

3. Position the columns on one of the unoccupied Colbase objects, and then copy them to the remaining Colbase objects under the arcade cornices (see fig. 2.22).

FIGURE 2.21
Columns copied and stretched to support the arcade cornices.

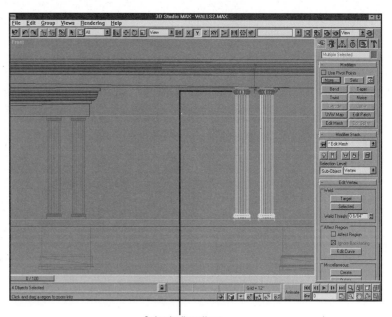

Select all vertices
at column tops

FIGURE 2.22
Columns placed on the Colbases under the arcade cornices.

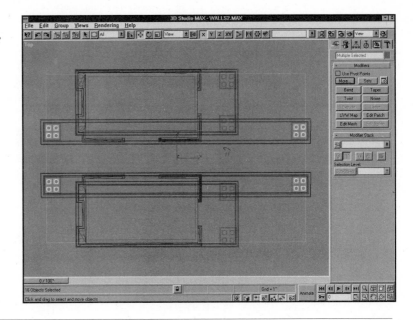

Adding Roofs

The simple hip and gable roofs on this bathhouse can be made quickly in 3DS MAX. In this model, it is not necessary to model the roofs inside and out, as would be required if the structure had cathedral ceilings, open trusswork, or a second floor with dormers. Situations like that require more complex modeling, but the basic techniques described in the following exercise will be of value in modeling any roof. For this building, you need only model primitives to achieve the shape needed, visible from the outside.

CHANGING ROOM ROOFS

The bathhouse has two hipped roofs that cover the changing rooms on either side and a gabled section that covers the central arcade. The first roofs to model are the hipped sections over the changing rooms.

1. Hide everything except either Cornice1 or Cornice2 (or whatever you called the cornices over the changing rooms, if you modeled them).

2. Create a box close to the size of the outside edge of the cornice. This can be done best in either the top viewport or in a user view. Snaps do not help you at this point; the box will be adjusted later to fit exactly. The height of the box is not important at this point. Call the box **Roof**.

3. In a side viewport, use edge snaps to move the box up or down until it rests precisely on the top edge of the cornice (see fig. 2.23).

4. In the top viewport, zoom to any corner and use edge snaps to move the box in both X and Y to align its corner exactly with the corner of the cornice.

5. Adjust the box by region-selecting vertices in the top viewport to move one entire side of the box, using the appropriate axis constraint (see fig. 2.24). Edge snap enables you to drag the sides of the box to align with the cornice edge. Do this on both sides of the box that need aligning (the other two sides having been aligned earlier when you zoomed in and aligned the corners).

FIGURE 2.23

Roof box resting on the top edge of the cornice.

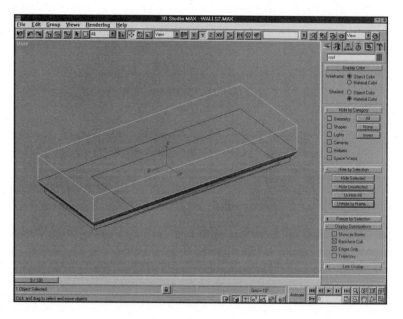

FIGURE 2.24

Adjusting the roof box by dragging the vertices by using edge snap.

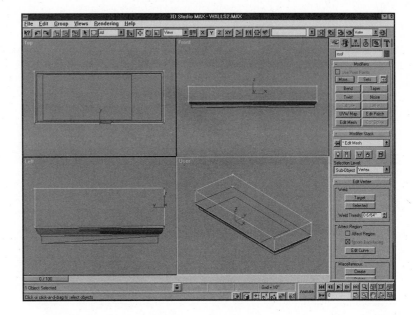

You now have a box that is exactly the length and width of the cornice. It would be more realistic, however, to have a drip-edge on the roof, a projection of an inch or two past the surface below.

6. Use the same method as before to expand the box all around by two inches. Region select vertices on one side of the box at a time and move the vertices out from the cornice by two inches. You can do this by zooming in and dragging, and watching the offset readout field in the status line. It is easier, faster, and more accurate, however, to right-click on the Move Transform button and type in your movement. You can do this without having to zoom in each time, and still achieve accuracy. Figure 2.25 shows the Move Transform Type-In dialog.

7. Select the bottom face of the roof and delete it. The roof is now a shell resting on the cornice.

NOTE

Because of this slight overhanging drip-edge, which adds a significant detail of realism with the shadow line that it casts, you must remember when assigning a material to the roof for rendering that the material should be made two-sided; otherwise, it will be possible to look up through the slight projecting edge of the roof and see the sky.

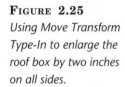

FIGURE 2.25

Using Move Transform Type-In to enlarge the roof box by two inches on all sides.

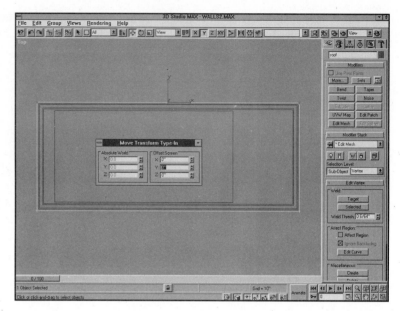

Setting the height of the ridge and pitch of the roof comes next. This building has roof pitches of 12-in-12, so the rise equals the run. The height of the ridge is therefore equal to one-half the total span of the roof. After these numbers are established, you can adjust the vertices to easily produce the roof form needed.

8. Determine the total span of the roof. This can be done by using the Tape Tool. It is, however, simpler and easier to go to the bottom of the Modifier Stack of the Roof object and read the dimension right out of the base parameters boxes.

9. While at the base parameters level, change the height of the box to equal half the box's width. The box is now precisely the height of the ridge for a 12-pitch roof.

10. Go back up to the top of the Modifier Stack and select two vertices at the top of the roof box and at one end, as shown on the left in figure 2.26.

11. Click on Collapse from the Miscellaneous section of the Edit Vertex roll-out to weld the two selected vertices together at a point exactly mid-way between their original locations. The result is visible on the right in figure 2.26.

FIGURE 2.26

Using Collapse to bring together vertices to form the gable of the roof.

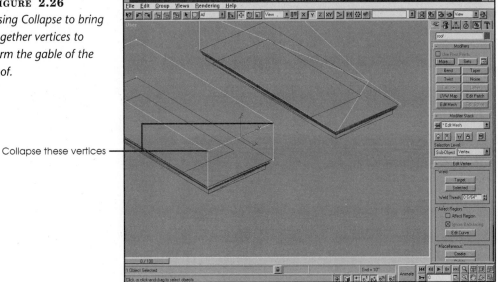

Collapse these vertices

12. Do the same for the rear set of vertices, and you have the basic shape of a 12-pitch gable roof with a two-inch drip-edge at the eaves.

These side roof sections are hips with equal pitches on all sides. You need to place a 12-in-12 pitch on what is now the front and rear gable surfaces of this roof.

13. Select the front ridge vertex, as shown on the left in figure 2.27, and use the Move Transform Type-In dialog box to move it towards the center of the roof by a distance equal to one-half the width of the roof (or the ridge height). The result is a hipped roof with 12-in-12 pitch all around, as shown on the right in figure 2.27.

14. Move the rear ridge vertex by the same method to complete the roof shape.

NOTE

These operations can also be accomplished by applying Taper modifiers, but it is more complicated and less accurate. Almost any symmetrical roof can be built with the preceding outlined steps. A roof with different pitches on all sides or different eave heights might require techniques such as Tapering, but generally this is not necessary.

FIGURE 2.27

*The front and rear hips
formed by moving the
vertices by the type-in
method.*

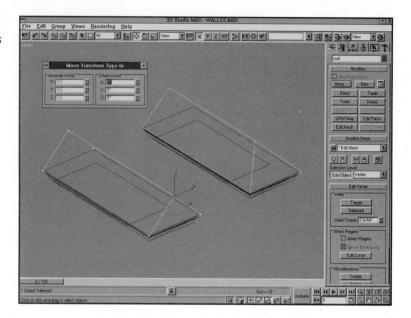

15. Use Move Transform Type-In to move the entire roof shape down one inch, to more closely represent the way the roof edge would meet the cornice.

16. Copy the roof shape to the other cornice on the other side of the building.

THE ARCADE ROOF

The central roof mass that covers the arcade can be built in the same way.

1. Hide everything except the two central cornices, called Cornice3 and Cornice4 (or whatever you named them, if you modeled them).

2. Use the same method to build a gable roof over these two cornices. This roof section is also 12-in-12 pitch but is not hipped. You should end up with a roof that looks like the one in figure 2.28.

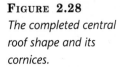

Figure 2.28

The completed central roof shape and its cornices.

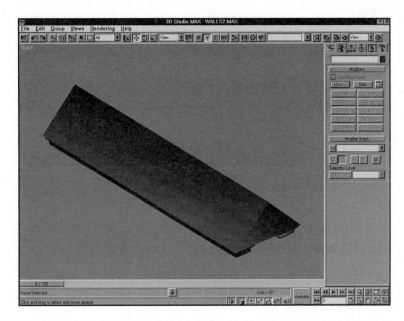

Making the Pediments over the Arcade

The central arcade has a barrelvault ceiling and a Neo-Palladian style gable treatment at each end. Some Boolean Modeling and some lofting easily produce these details.

1. Hide everything except the central roof and its two cornices.

2. Create a cylinder the long axis of which lies parallel to the central roof, with a diameter approximately equal to the distance between the cornices. The diameter will be more closely adjusted later. The length of the cylinder should be greater than the length of the central roof (see fig. 2.29).

3. Use Align to center the cylinder on the middle of the bottom edge of the gable of the roof. Figure 2.29 shows the orientation.

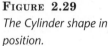

FIGURE 2.29
The Cylinder shape in position.

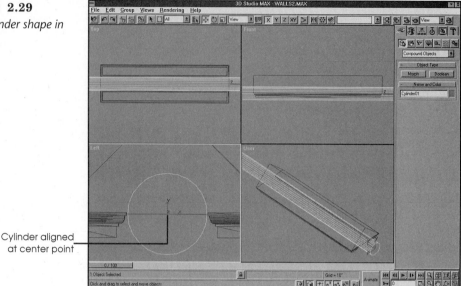

Cylinder aligned at center point

4. Adjust the base parameters of the cylinder so that the diameter is six inches greater than the diameter of the barrelvault. Compensate for minor inaccuracies, if necessary, by shifting the cylinder sideways. Absolute precision is not essential here.

5. Perform a Boolean Subtraction, subtracting the cylinder from the central roof, using the Move option in the Pick Boolean roll-out to produce the shape seen in figure 2.30.

6. Hide the cornices. Apply an Edit Mesh modifier to the roof and select the faces that make up one of the gable-ends. This is seen on the right in figure 2.31.

7. Detach the selected faces and rename them **Tympanum**.

8. Move Tympanum back from the front of the roof to get it out of the way, as on the left in figure 2.31. It will be readjusted later. Perform the same operations on the other gable at the opposite end of the central roof.

FIGURE 2.30
The barrelvault cut through the roof shape by using a Boolean Subtraction.

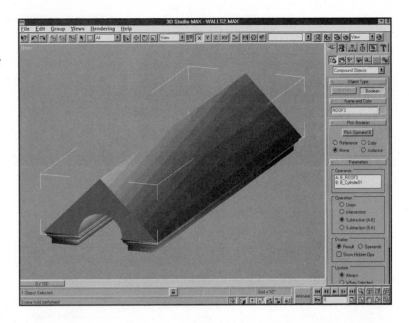

FIGURE 2.31
Creating and moving the object Tympanum.

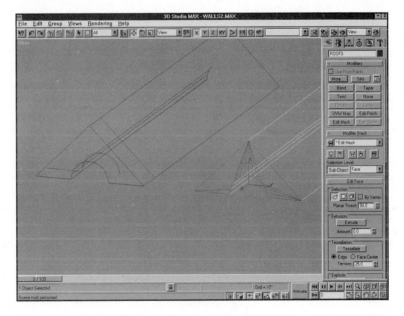

ADDING MOLDINGS TO THE PEDIMENT

To complete the pediments at each end of the central roof, various moldings are needed. The first one to model is the rake molding, the one that follows the pitch of the roof.

1. Make a copy of the shape called Stringshape, the original, unscaled shape from the first exercise. Call it **Rakeshape**.

2. Apply an XForm modifier to the copy of Rakeshape and Uniform Scale it up by 200%. Then Non-Uniform scale it on the Y-axis by a factor of 141.38%, to account for the fact that the loft path will be making 90-degree turns. This scaling is performed on the Y-axis and not the X-axis as in previous examples because of the vertical orientation of this loft path. Remember that this scaling must be accomplished by using an XForm modifier, not by directly applying the scaling; otherwise, the loft ignores the scaling and uses the unscaled version.

TIP

Don't forget that it is easy and accurate to apply these transforms by right-clicking on the Transform button and typing in the displacement.

3. In the Hierarchy, use Affect Pivot Only to move Rakeshape's pivot point to the topmost point of the shape. Figure 2.32 shows the resulting shape.

FIGURE 2.32

Rakeshape scaled up and the pivot point moved to the upper corner.

New point location ———

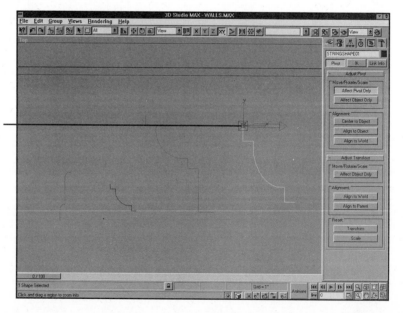

Now the path for this loft can be drawn:

4. Using 3D snap with Vertex Point as the highest priority, snap a line from one corner of the eave of the roof shape up to the ridge and down to the other corner, outlining the roof edges. Name the spline **Rakespline**.

5. Move the spline slightly inward from the roof to avoid the possibility of the edge of the lofted molding showing through the roof surface when you render. To do this, select the ridge vertex of Rakespline and using Move Transform Type-in, move it straight down ¼ or ½ inch. Select each of the vertices at the eaves in turn and move them inward a small amount in the same way so that there is a slight gap between the spline and, the roof object.

6. Create the loft by using Rakespline as the path and Rakeshape as the shape. Set path steps to 0 and shape steps to 2, and then click on Optimize Shapes. The resulting loft can be seen on the right in figure 2.33. Rename the loft **Rake1**.

7. Open the Teeter Deformation box in the Deformations roll-out at the bottom of the Modify panel. Select the existing control points at the ends of the function curve in the Teeter box one at a time and move them vertically by typing in values in the field at the bottom of the box. The left-hand control point receives a teeter of −45 degrees, the right-hand one a teeter of 45 degrees. The corrected loft is visible on the left in figure 2.33.

FIGURE 2.33

Teeter-corrected loft and Teeter Deformation box showing displacement of the function curve.

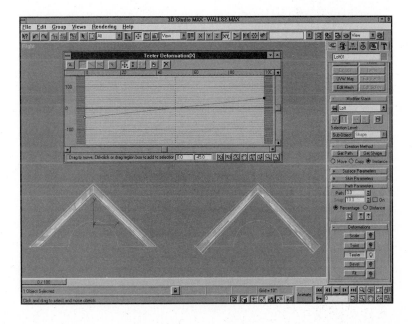

NOTE

The previous examples used vertex manipulation to teeter the shapes at the vertices of lofts; this case, however, presents a situation where it is easier to use the Teeter Deformation box. This is due to two things: First, the control points that you are adjusting are already exactly located at the vertices because they are at the ends of the path, and so the time-consuming and somewhat inaccurate process of placing control points at vertices can be skipped; Second, you know that the teeter required is exactly 45 degrees because the roof pitch is 45 degrees, being 12-in-12. Thus it is easy to type the displacement right in.

8. Correct Surface Normals as necessary.

9. Unhide the two central cornices, Cornice3 and Cornice4, and use edge snap to reposition the outermost surface of the rake molding that you just lofted to be flush with the outermost surface of the cornices.

THE BARRELVAULT MOLDING

The other molding that will be added to these pediments is a curved molding that outlines the barrelvault. First the path is generated.

1. Looking straight on at the pediment, draw a circle the diameter of which is approximately the width of the barrelvault.

2. Use Align to center the circle precisely in the middle of the barrelvault, in the same way that you aligned the cylinder to the roof shape. Use X-position and center/center in the Align dialog box.

3. Adjust the diameter of the circle to be close to the diameter of barrelvault. Absolute accuracy is unnecessary.

4. Draw a rectangle that overlaps the bottom half of the circle, the top of which aligns with the bottom edge of the barrelvault (see fig. 2.34).

5. Attach the circle and the rectangle and perform a Boolean Subtraction, leaving only the top half of the circle (see fig. 2.34).

6. Erase the bottom line segment of the circle, leaving only an arc that follows the curve of the barrelvault. This is visible on the right in figure 2.34. Rename the object **Barrelpath** and move it from the middle of the barrelvault to near the pediment. Final placement occurs after the loft is created.

FIGURE 2.34

Using Boolean operations to create the path for the molding to trim the barrelvault.

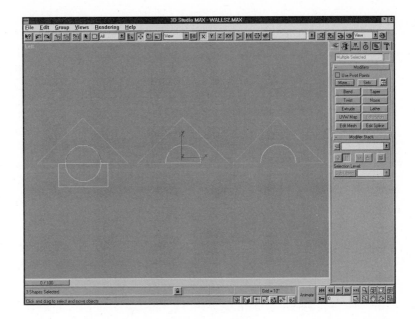

7. There is in the .max file a shape called Barrelshape; use it to create a loft with Barrelpath. It may be necessary to flip the shape as you are getting it by holding down Ctrl, and it may also be necessary to rotate the shape after it's placed on the path by using Sub-Object/Shape in the Modify panel. The correct orientation is shown in the upper left viewport of figure 2.35.

8. It will probably be necessary to set the path steps to 8 or higher to get a smooth shape; shape steps can be 2 or 3. The lower right viewport in figure 2.35 shows the loft with path steps of 10 and shape steps of 2. Polygon count is 616. Generally, it is difficult to produce good curved lofts without high face counts; when the shape also has curved sections, the problem is compounded. Rename the loft **Barrelmold**.

Now all that remains is to position the various components of the pediment and clean up some edges.

9. Use edge snap and the appropriate axis constraint to move Tympanum1 until it aligns with the inner edge of Rake1.

10. Now move Barrelmold until it wraps around the edge of the tympanum.

FIGURE 2.35

*The barrelvault
molding being lofted.*
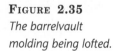

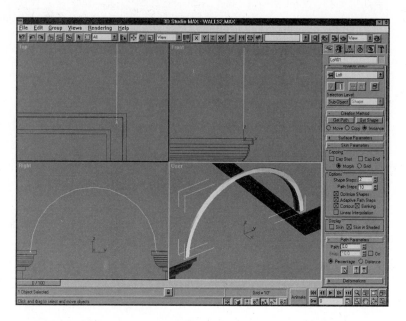

11. In the object Roof 3, the arcade roof, delete the two horizontal planes that make up the bottom of the shape on either side of the barrelvault, using Sub Object/Face to select them. This leaves only the roof planes and the actual surface of the barrelvault.

12. Select the faces that make up the barrelvault and detach them from the roof. Call the new object Barrelvault.

13. Select all the vertices at the end of the object Barrelvault, and drag them inward until the end of Barrelvault fits into Barrelmold.

14. Finally, shrink the object Tympanum slightly in the same way that you adjusted the Rakepath—select the ridge and eave vertices of Tympanum and move them slightly away from the Roof object by means of the Move Transform Type-In. This prevents the top edge of Tympanum from showing through the roof surface during rendering.

Figure 2.36 shows the finished pediment.

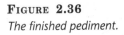

FIGURE 2.36
The finished pediment.

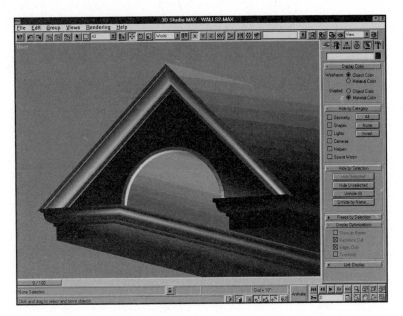

The preceding steps can now be duplicated on the other pediment at the opposite end of the building.

The Doorways

To complete the exterior of this building, you need only a few more details. The next thing to create is the door frames for the four doorways that lead in and out of the changing rooms.

1. Hide everything except the objects Wall-out and Wall-in. In the right viewport, zoom in on one of the doors.

2. Draw a box 48 inches wide, 6 inches long, and 10 inches high. Center the box on the doorway opening in the wall. The height is not important at this point.

3. Region-select the upper left vertices of this box, and using Move Trans-
    form Type-In, move the vertices two inches to the left. In the same way,
    move the upper right vertices two inches to the right.

4. Near the center of the box, create another box with a length of 10 inches,
    a width of 8 inches, and a height of 12 inches.

5. Use Align to center the second box on the first. Click on X, Y, and Z in the
    position options and center/center.

6. Region-select the lower left vertices of the center box object and use Move
    Transform Type-In to move the vertices one inch to the right. Move the
    lower right vertices of the same mass to the left one inch. The central box
    is now tapered in at the bottom.

7. Attach the two boxes and rename the resulting object **Lintel**.

8. In the top viewport, move the lintel to span equally across the Wall-in
    and the Wall-out objects, as seen in the top viewport of figure 2.37. The
    lower left viewport of figure 2.37 shows the finished lintel.

FIGURE 2.37

*The finished lintel in
position.*

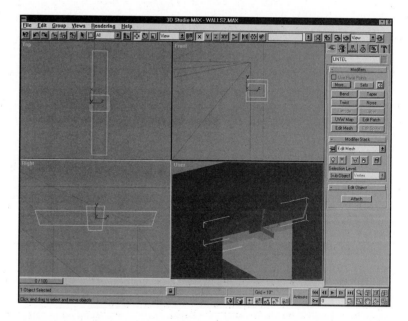

9. In the side viewport, use edge snap to move the lintel so that the bottom
    of the lintel aligns with the top of the doorway opening in the wall
    surface.

Now, create the door jambs.

10. Hide the lintel. Use 3D snap with vertex priority to draw a line around the doorway opening by snapping to the corners of the doorway. Call this line **Jambpath**.

11. Use the various loft techniques previously explored to loft a door jamb by using the shape called Jambshape included in the .Max file and the Jambpath created in the preceding step. It may be necessary to rotate Jambshape after placing it on the path so that the molded edge details face out into the doorway opening (see fig. 2.38). With the loft selected, use Sub-Object/Shape to rotate the shape. Scale and Teeter the loft as needed.

12. Center the jamb over the Wall-in and Wall-out surfaces so that it protrudes equally from each wall surface. Center it below the lintel. The finished opening should look like the one shown in figure 2.38.

FIGURE 2.38

The finished doorway in place in the wall.

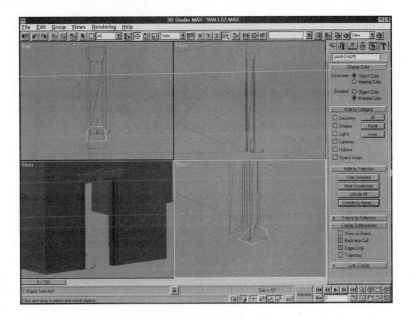

13. Copy the jamb and lintel to the other three doorways. It will be necessary to enlarge the jamb and lintel and reposition the keystone in the lintel to fit the larger doorways that face out into the arcade. Don't use a non-uniform scale for this; it stretches the width of the side jambs and the keystone in an undesirable way. Just select all the vertices on one side and pull them out to fit the doorway. Figure 2.39 shows the doorways finished.

14. Make final adjustments to the size of the jambs as necessary by unhiding the doors and doorknobs already modeled in the .max file and resizing the jambs to just fit the doors. Alternatively, you could resize the doors to fit the jambs. In either case, this should be done by selecting and moving groups of vertices.

FIGURE 2.39

The doorways and the doors and knobs.

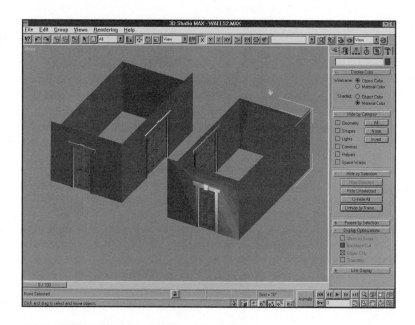

FIGURE 2.40

The finished Neo-Classical bathhouse.

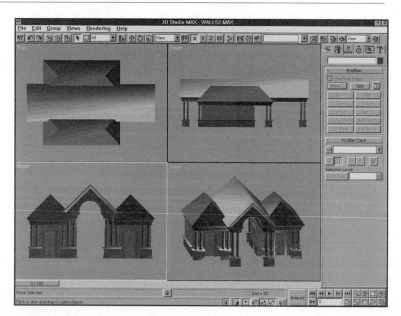

IMAGE USED WITH PERSMISSION OF GAMETEK

The exterior is now finished with a level of detail adequa
Close-ups might require more detail, depending on what y
The interior could be modeled using these procedures—ba
ways, crown moldings, and chair rails.

In Practice: Architectural Modeling

- **The Basic Walls.** Working from existing CAD documents is like
  the starting point for a lot of architectural modeling and rende
  There are advantages to roughing-out the basic walls in CAD and t
  importing them into 3DS MAX, but it is also useful to import just pla
  and extrude up from there. Be aware of how various entities import int
  3DS MAX.

- **Lofting Moldings.** A lot of the details in architectural modeling are
  lofts. Scaling and Teetering the shape correctly at the vertices is the most
  important step for good architectural lofting.

- **Polygons.** Face counts climb quickly in architectural models. Always be
  economical in modeling, keeping in mind the fact that a lot of detail and
  accuracy may never be noticeable.

- **Instancing and Referencing.** Make use of 3DS MAX's capability to
  cross-reference parameters from one object to another; architectural
  models often have repetitive elements and instancing them can make
  later changes a simple matter.

- **Overlapping Planes.** Faces need not always meet perfectly, and it is a
  waste of time to make them do so when it's unnecessary. Door trim, f
  example, can overlap the wall plane next to it. That's what it does i
  real building. Don't spend time where it's not needed.

Chapter 3

by Ken Allen Robertson

Modeling for Real-Time 3D Games

No area of 3D graphics is garnering as much attention as real-time gaming—and no other area shows as much potential for massive growth in the next few years.

Real-time 3D is only in its infancy in the consumer market. Set-top gaming systems that support real-time are in their first generation. Many real-time graphics engines (as opposed to 2D sprite graphics) are only now beginning to be widely used by PC game developers. Renderware, Brender, and Microsoft's DirectDraw (a software engine for Windows 95 graphics) are among the real-time graphics engines gaining popularity. 2D sprite graphics, however, still dominate the PC gaming market.

The massive influx of Internet games is also fueling the drive to real-time 3D games (Quake currently is the most notable). With the advent of Java and VRML 2.0, the promise of real-time Internet 3D games that can be played from any type of machine is near. 3D *MUDS* (multi-user-dungeons)— ongoing role-play worlds on the Internet—are being developed by many companies around the world.

The skills of the real-time 3D artist are broad and varied. In addition to in-depth knowledge of the software used to generate source materials (3D meshes, texture maps, animations, and so on), a real-time artist must have a firm grasp of the programmatic principles that make real-time 3D possible. This does not mean that one should be a computer programmer—far from it, in fact. The excitement of real-time games lies in the artist's creations, generated on the spot and in instant response to the user's whims, with a life and personality of their own.

Modeling is the key issue and the most critical part of creating graphics for real-time games. The myriad issues and technical details that go into making a model efficient (low-polygon count), believable, aesthetically pleasing, and poised to behave and display properly in the real-time world are issues that face the real-time artist alone; real-time engines, after all, rely on only the most basic elements of 3D graphics to create their illusion.

Fortunately, 3D Studio MAX is a dream tool for creating real-time graphics. 3D Studio MAX not only provides excellent modeling tools to control every facet of creating a model, down to the face and vertex level, but also provides fast, efficient shaded and texture-mapped views of the model being created, enabling the user to accurately preview the "look" of the finished product in the game itself.

Although all real-time game engines vary slightly in structure, capabilities, and the paradigms used to create speed, the principles behind each engine remain the same.

This chapter covers the following topics:

- 2D versus real-time 3D graphics

- The basics of real-time 3D

- The differences between real-time and prerendered 3D graphics

- Principles and techniques for using 3D Studio MAX in modeling real-time objects

- The future of real-time 3D graphics

2D Versus Real-Time 3D Graphics

You may be wondering why real-time 3D didn't appear earlier. Actually, it did. Arcade games using 3D vector graphics, such as *Tempest* and *Star Wars*, appeared in the mid-'80s. Military simulations have been using real-time 3D on high-end machines for training for quite some time. Only recently, however, could these graphics be nicely shaded and texture-mapped at a speed that could match 2D animated graphics.

To fully appreciate the speed difficulty, you need to understand the difference between 2D and 3D animation at the computational level.

2D animation relies on the principles of traditional cel animation. A huge number of pictures are created, and then captured in sequence for playback in the chosen medium—in this case, a computer of some kind (including PCs, set-top gaming systems, custom-designed arcade systems, and so forth). The computer pulls the pictures from memory and displays them on-screen as fast as necessary to give the illusion of movement. The factors critical to 2D animation are data storage space (which accounts for the rise of the CD-ROM as the preferred gaming medium), the speed at which that data can be read, and how fast that data can be displayed. The computer does not have to do much "thinking" to display 2D animation.

3D graphics require much less storage than their 2D counterparts because the 3D pictures are not predrawn (with the exception of texture maps). The "recipe" for the 3D picture (meshes and animation) is stored as a mass of formulas and called up when needed. Because the pictures are being drawn on-screen by the program as they are being seen, and not before, the computer must "think" much more and much faster than it does with 2D images.

Imagine the difference between someone pulling nicely arranged pictures from a stack and someone else trying to accurately draw, at the same speed as the person who's pulling pictures, a collection of objects that yet *another* person is moving around. Imagining such a scenario should help you easily grasp the difference in what is demanded of a machine running a real-time application. Only the current high-speed processors are capable of meeting these extreme demands. Even then, the geometry being drawn must be simple and have a low polygon count to make the process fast enough to meet acceptable display speeds.

Real-Time 3D Basics

Modeling for real-time graphics is a delicate process. One must have an accurate picture of what the result will be after the object being modeled is exported into the real-time engine. The more you know about how the average real-time engine thinks, the better your initial efforts will be, and the more time and frustration you will save yourself.

Real-time 3D and high-end, prerendered 3D graphics have many elements in common. To achieve the speed necessary for presentable game play, however, real-time must use only the most necessary elements—namely, the geometry, the transform, and the surface properties of the mesh. Most of the time, these elements are created by the export program (a third-party application that converts the source model into a language the game engine can read) and put into some kind of text file (or a "c" file, before compilation into binary code) so that they can be manually edited, if necessary. Sometimes these elements can be parceled out to a number of separate files (one for geometry, one for surface properties, and one for the transform) that are combined when the file is compiled for the game engine. Currently, there are plug-ins that enable the user to export directly from 3DS MAX into Playstation, Sega Saturn, and DirectDraw formats. More plug-ins are under construction to support the myriad of real-time formats being used in gaming. Most premade, real-time 3D Application Programming Interfaces (APIs) provide a proprietary converter that works with the 3DS or DXF format. Freeware converters for exporting OBJ and VRML files are available from several web sites on the Internet, such as 3dcafe.com and max3d.com

The geometry is exactly what you would expect: a list of numbered vertex positions in 3D space, followed by a list of how to connect these vertices into coherent polygons. The normal (or visible solid) side of the polygon is determined either by the order in which the vertices that comprise the polygon are chosen, or by a separate list of vertex normals also attached to the polygon construction list.

Most real-time engines use triangular polygons, just as 3D Studio MAX does. Some systems use quadrilateral polygons. Still other systems let you define quads and other types of polygons, but break them down into triangles at rendering time. This can be a computational expensive and unpredictable process. The best results seem to come from predefined triangular polygons. Although they require more storage than other polygons, predefined triangular polygons tend to render faster, and always display as intended. The 3DS MAX file format exports only triangles, which is why it is so widely supported among real-time engines.

A smooth export of the source model into the game engine always proves a bit tricky, and often requires a great deal of tweaking. High-powered modeling programs, such as 3DS MAX, often add unusable information to the relatively simplistic real-time game engine. Most of this information is *invisible* (it may or may not be apparent when you look at the model in 3DS MAX). This information can have drastic effects on the exported real-time model, causing it to be drawn in the wrong orientation or position, or to behave improperly when animated in the game engine. The biggest trouble areas for export are generally the transform and the surface properties.

The Transform

The *transform* is a numerical matrix that describes the orientation, position, and often the scale of an object in 3D space. This number is applied to every vertex in the object, and therefore acts as the object's center. In practice, imagine that every object you create is written as though it were centered at the global origin (0,0,0). To create this object farther off in 3D space, you could rewrite every vertex to the new location, or you could add to each vertex the distance (X, Y, and Z) the object must travel to reach the new position. Clearly, the latter method is the more efficient: Even though it takes two processes to achieve the new position, only one number is being created on the fly. The same process can be used to rotate or scale the object. This matrix may change syntax from program to program, but it will always be there because it is critical to controlling objects in 3D space.

When an object is moved in a 3D game, it is the transform that is actually affected. Prescripted animations, such as a character walking or the wheels of a car turning, are performed as if the object were standing still. To move the main object through space, the player's input is translated into a series of numbers that is combined with the transform to propel the object in the desired directions. In this way, a simple series of numbers can be generated from whatever input device is used (keyboard, joystick, and so on) to create fast, responsive action.

As mentioned earlier, the transform is usually an invisible number set in the modeling program and a numerical string in the data file(s) created by the export program. In 3DS MAX, however, the transform is also a visual tool that shows exactly how the physical geometry of the object is written.

When you select the object whose transform you want to see, and then select Reset Transform from the drop-down menu of the 3DS MAX Utilities panel, a bounding box that represents the object appears. When an object is created, it is automatically aligned to the orthographic viewports. If you rotate this object, scale it, or move it, the bounding box goes with and maintains its relative location and orientation. If, however, the object is reoriented away from its orthographic alignment, and then has its transform reset, the bounding box moves back into orthographic alignment. This effectively rewrites the object geometry and resets the axis of the object, causing the object to behave differently than expected. The results will be obvious when you animate the object in a real-time game.

Normally the transform is not something you have to worry about. When you work with primitives, 3DS MAX automatically generates them properly aligned. The only time a transform can get misaligned with primitives is when they are cloned or mirrored. When you perform these operations, always check the object's transform immediately after the modification. If a transform is off on an object that is part of a hierarchical model, to correct the transform you must detach the hierarchy, realign the object, and re-create the hierarchy. Figure 3.1 shows an object with a properly aligned transform. Figure 3.2 shows an object whose transform will cause problems when animation is applied to it.

FIGURE 3.1

An object with a correctly aligned transform.

FIGURE 3.2

*An object with an
incorrectly aligned
transform.*

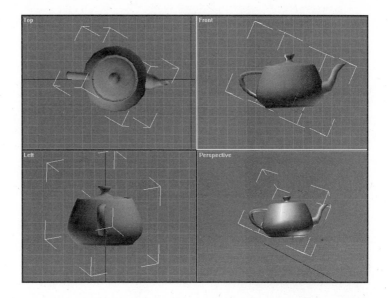

The only other time transforms can be generated differently than what you might want is when you are lofting objects that are naturally skewed. Remember that, by default, MAX automatically sets an object's local coordinates to align with those of the global coordinate system. If a Loft object is created askew to the global system, its local transform matrix will be misaligned. If an object must be created this way, manipulate it after it has been completed so that it comes as close as possible to orthographic alignment; then reset the transform and proceed with the rest of the model and animation.

You may be thinking that realigning the object center would accomplish the same thing as resetting the object's transform. That is correct when you are not exporting the object into a real-time engine. Unfortunately, most exporters are not able to use this bit of information, as it does not rewrite the actual geometry of the object as performing a "reset transform" does. In fact, to ensure that an object performs in the real-time engine in the same way it performs in MAX, make certain that the pivot point is aligned to the object. The pivot point dictates the origin of the object, but having its alignment correspond to the object ensures that rotational alignment and values will be the same in the game engine.

Surface Properties

Surface properties in a real-time engine are almost identical to those in MAX—namely, the smoothing algorithm (flat shading or Gouraud shading only for real time), the color of the polygon, the shininess, opacity, self-illumination, and the texture map applied to the polygon. These properties generally are defined after the vertex list but before the faces they apply to.

In addition, several real-time engines allow colors to be assigned to the vertices themselves, which can create the illusion of the object being lit, without direct lighting being applied to the model. Because most of the surface attributes are translated into numerical data, some strange translations can happen during the exporting process. Colors, for example, are translated from a 0 to 255 scale to a 0 to 1 scale. No hard and fast rules dictate how to minimize problems when exporting source materials from MAX. Generally, these materials must be manually adjusted in the real-time text file, unless a third-party visual exporting system is used (such as those used with most set-top gaming systems). The best approach here is to be aware that surface properties may be a trouble area during exporting, and to examine the final product closely.

Again, MAX proves to be an excellent real-time tool. It provides flat and Gouraud-shaded viewing options, enabling the artist to view an object (before the object is exported) in a manner that closely represents what the object will look like in a real-time gaming engine.

Differences Between Real-Time and Prerendered 3D

The way real-time games and prerendered 3D graphics are created differ in five major areas:

- Z-buffering
- Levels of detail (LODs)
- Shadows
- Texture map size (and color depth)
- Shading modes

The basic difference in these systems is a result of what they are intended to do: Prerendered graphics need to look as realistic as possible; Real-time needs to be as fast as possible.

Z-Buffering

Z-buffering is a computationally intensive process of determining which polygons are behind which (from the active viewpoint) so that a scene is drawn correctly with the proper depth. When you render a scene from MAX, visible portions of objects with correct mapping, shadows, and so on are produced for a near-photorealistic reproduction of the way the physical world is perceived. This process can be much too slow for real-time games. Most game engines do have the capability to perform modified Z-buffering (a faster but less accurate process than MAX). For fastest performance, however, *binary separation planes* (or BSPs) are created to give the processor a simple decision process as to what gets drawn in front of what. These planes divide concave (self-overdrawing) objects into convex pieces. These pieces, combined with the transform of the object, can be quickly evaluated by the computer to determine proper placement of objects.

Most real-time games also have a *far clipping plane*—a predetermined distance from the user's viewpoint, beyond which no objects are rendered, even though they are stored in memory. The far clipping plane can greatly increase the number of objects in a game world because the computer doesn't always have to draw everything simultaneously.

Often, far clipping planes are disguised by fog so that objects don't just "pop" into the universe, but appear to arrive out of a misty veil.

Levels of Detail

Levels of detail (LODs) also are critical in achieving the speed necessary to create an enjoyable game. In short, they are "stand-in" objects used to represent the real object at a greater distance from the user's viewpoint. When the object is close to the player, the highest-resolution model available is drawn. When the object takes up a small portion of the screen, a lower polygon count model is swapped in. Very often, at the greatest distances at which the object can still be seen, a colored box is used to represent the object. The increase in speed is dramatic because the processor does not have to calculate all the faces of the full object, but still draws the same number of pixels the object would take up on-screen. Figure 3.3 shows a model with its high, medium, and low LODs.

FIGURE 3.3
A model with high, medium, and low levels of detail (LODs).

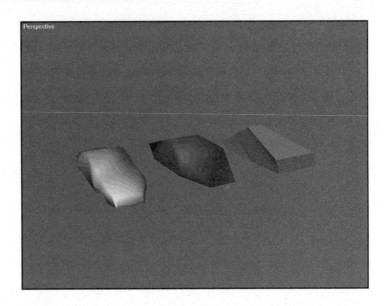

Complex objects (such as trees), which require a large number of polygons even to approximate, can be represented by an X-shaped arrangement of quads that can be mapped with a picture of a high-resolution object and an opacity map (or "cookie cutter" map) that makes everything outside the desired object invisible. This technique can also be used effectively with LODs or complex game *sprites* (2D animated objects). Figure 3.4 shows a tree model created with this cookie-cutter method for use in a real-time environment.

FIGURE 3.4
A real-time tree model.

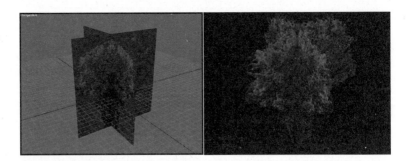

Shadows

Although shadows add a great deal of realism to any 3D scene, they require far too much calculation time to be feasible in a real-time engine. Instead, shadows are generally created by mapping a silhouette onto a semitransparent polygon positioned parallel to the ground plane of the game world. The same cookie-cutter technique mentioned earlier can be used for simulating shadows. Figure 3.5 shows an object with its real-time shadow plane attached.

FIGURE 3.5
An object with a shadow plane attached.

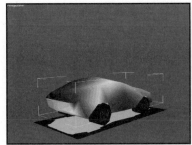

Map Size and Color Depth

Because of active memory limitations (RAM) and the processor demands of calculating TrueColor (24-bit) images, most real-time engines utilize smaller texture maps at a smaller color depth (usually 8-bit). Most systems use texture maps sized from 16-by-16 pixels up to 128-by-128 pixels. As a result, texture maps can be stored in RAM for quickest access whenever necessary (depending on the platform, up to 60 times a second).

Although some set-top gaming platforms can use 24-color maps, most systems use 8-bit color for texture maps. On many PCs, 8-bit color is the average display color depth. Because this is 3D, however, remember that light sampling is still calculated, in some form, and colors will vary. On systems that can display higher color modes, your 8-bit map can reach TrueColor levels when different lighting is applied.

Shading Modes

Real-time engines currently support only two shading modes: Flat shading (which makes an object look faceted) and Gouraud shading (which smoothes out most edges). Phong shading is too processor-intensive to be fast enough for real-time games.

Modeling for Real Time

With all the limitations of real-time games, modeling for real time involves a great deal of thought and precision. Real-time models must achieve the right balance of detail and low geometric complexity to make them fast, recognizable, and believable elements of the gaming experience.

Although modeling varies some from platform to platform, several basic principles should always be considered at the start of a gaming project:

- Put the detail in the map, not the mesh.
- Don't build what you don't need.
- Model convex whenever possible.
- High-res for low-res modeling.

Put the Detail in the Map, Not in the Mesh

Every polygon added to a real-time mesh takes a certain amount of time to render. Even if it is less than 1000th of a second, that time adds up and diminishes the possible frame rate during game play. To be effective, however, an object's texture maps must be able to fit into RAM. And the texture maps will be drawn much faster than the polygons needed to create the details that could be "painted" into the texture map. Therefore, any detail that can be effectively simulated by adding it to the texture map should be mapped, not modeled—as should any detail that is too mesh-intensive to be effective (such as the "cookie cutter" trees discussed earlier).

A great example of when to map instead of modeling is the muscle tone in a character. Nice, rounded muscle structure is far too polygon-intensive to accomplish in real-time. When muscles are added to a texture map, however, a similar effect can be achieved through careful use of simulated highlights and shadows, with almost no cost in frame rate.

A helpful process when you create real-time models is to create a fully detailed, high-face-count model first. Then construct the low-resolution model over the high-resolution model, using the latter as a template. You can then take individual orthographic renderings from the high-count model, tweak them in a paint program, and then use them as texture maps for the low-res model. This process is discussed in more detail in the "Dealing with Texture Limitations" section later in this chapter.

Another related process is to load two images (preferably scanned pictures) of the object you're creating, seen from the side and the front, as a texture map to be placed on a two-quad "tree" in MAX. This tree can then be displayed as a shaded template to be built over. This technique can be very handy as a reference for building real-time characters.

Don't Build What You Don't Need

This (the heading for this section) may seem obvious, but it should be a principle you return to often to ensure that your objects maintain the lowest possible polygon count.

Real-time game environments are more akin to Hollywood movie sets than they are to real-life environments. Like a movie set, they are seen only from limited viewpoints. Specific knowledge of where your objects and environments will and will not be seen by the player is critical to efficient modeling. Figure 3.6 shows a real-time environment from a top-down view (a view the player would never be able to see) that illustrates set-like construction.

FIGURE 3.6

"God's eye" view of a real-time set.

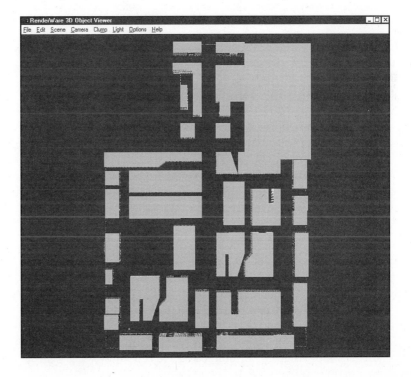

If you were building the cars for a racing game, for example, you would need to know whether the cars would ever flip over, exposing the undercarriage. If not, you could eliminate that part of the mesh and add detail (if necessary) to the parts of the vehicles that would be seen most often.

Segmented real-time characters offer another example. Normally the segments are modeled solid at the joints so that no holes appear in the mesh throughout a full range of motion. In a game setting, your model may not need a full range of motion, or different versions of the model may be swapped in depending on the action, damage to the character, and so forth. By eliminating the "capping" polygons inside the joints (which are never seen) you lower the total face count of the model, and make rendering more efficient.

Model Convex (Whenever Possible)

The differences between Z-buffering and using BSPs in real-time gaming systems were discussed earlier in this chapter. *BSPs* are a system by which game designers can "pre-make" decisions for the game hardware as to which objects (or parts of an object) will be drawn on-screen last (over the other screen objects) to create the illusion of depth. The use of BSPs creates a dramatic speed increase over Z-buffering, which not only has to keep the movement of the game going but also must determine object placement on-screen based on the position of every polygon in the scene.

For BSPs to be effective, they must divide objects into pieces that can be drawn correctly on their own, without any sort of depth information. This means that you must make convex pieces—where all the face normals of the object face away from the center of the object and do not point to each other. Convex pieces are absolutely critical to real-time game engines because they can be rendered at the maximum speed possible and still display correctly. Figure 3.7 shows a model with its BSPs visible. The data would be invisible in the real-time game engine.

The best test of convexity is to look at the object in a shaded, perspective view (smooth or faceted), hide the faces on opposing sides of the object (top and bottom, left and right, or front and back), and rotate the object in multiple directions. If you can see a solid face through an empty space in the model (where the normals are facing away, making the polygons invisible), the object is not convex and will need modifications (or more dividing) before it can be used effectively in a BSP sorting engine. Repeat the process for each opposing pair of sides. Figure 3.8 shows the visible differences between a convex and a concave object.

FIGURE 3.7
A model with visible BSPs inserted.

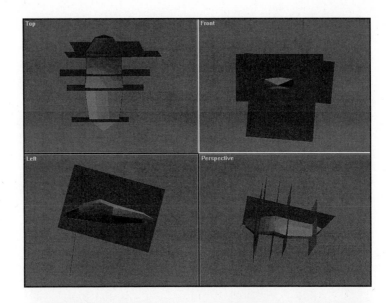

FIGURE 3.8
A convex object section and a concave object section.

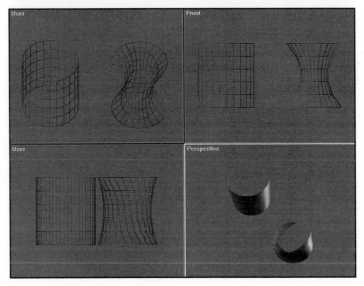

High-Res for Low-Res Modeling

When you're working with low polygon counts, it can be extremely difficult to see whether a proper level of detail has been accomplished to make the object clearly recognizable and distinguishable from other similar objects. It can be extremely helpful, therefore, to build a high poly-count "template" object, with as much detail modeled as possible, over which to construct a low-count model. This process clarifies where detail is needed in the low-count object, and where it can be omitted and placed in the texture map. And, as mentioned before, the high-detail model can be used to generate intricate texture maps for the low-count model later on.

Note that trying to use the Optimize modifier in MAX to lower the polygon count of the high-detail mesh to acceptable real-time levels is highly unadvisable. The Optimize modifier is an excellent tool for making a complex mesh more efficient, and even for using on a real-time model just to make certain that there are no unnecessary polygons, but it can easily create unpredictable losses in detail when you're trying to drastically reduce a high-count model. The Optimize modifier works by eliminating faces that are determined to be coplanar, based on the entered face and edge threshold angles. The Optimize modifier has no intelligence as to which details are important and which are not; it just uses a straight numerical algorithm. When a parameter high enough to bring drastic face count reductions is entered, the Optimize modifier also eliminates most of the nice smooth areas that have been created to round out certain edges.

Real-Time Modeling Techniques

The best way to ensure that your model has appropriate detail where it's needed and the lowest possible polygon count is to create the model with a low polygon count to begin with, and then to add detail and subtract faces only where necessary. The sub-object editing tools of the Edit Mesh modifier will become your best friends when you finalize a real-time model.

For object creation, however, the best options fall into the following two categories:

- "Conscious" lofting
- Modifying primitives

Conscious Lofting

Lofting Mesh objects has long been a mainstay for creating complex shapes in 3D Studio, and continues to be a critical MAX tool for the real-time artist. Lofting with deform-fit creates beautifully detailed meshes by adding interpolative steps between vertices on both the fit shapes and the shape(s) being lofted. Unfortunately, this can add a tremendous number of polygons very quickly. But by lofting with no added steps, and by using multiple shapes on the loft path, you can generate extremely detailed models with predictable face counts and detail. Also, lofting objects this way creates clean cross-sections that can then be divided by BSPs, if necessary.

The following exercise demonstrates this process by using a staple of real-time games—a car. Instead of a boxy NASCAR type of vehicle, however, you create something more organic and smooth—a high-tech sports car.

1. On the *Inside 3D Studio MAX Volume II* CD, open the file named CAR01.max. You will see a high-res sports car model, frozen, for use as a template. You will also see a spline outlining the top of the vehicle, a cross-section shape (derived from the most complex area of the vehicle—the hood, centered above the wheel wells), and a straight line to be used as a preliminary loft path. Figure 3.9 shows these objects.

FIGURE 3.9

The objects in the exercise file CAR01.MAX.

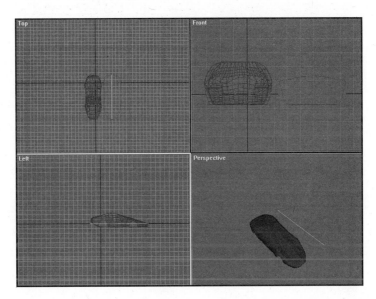

2. Select the top outline shape in the Front viewport, hold down the Shift key, and rotate the shape 90° around the viewport's Z axis, so that you create a new shape aligned to the side view of the frozen car. Name this new shape **side outline** (see fig. 3.10).

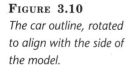

FIGURE 3.10

The car outline, rotated to align with the side of the model.

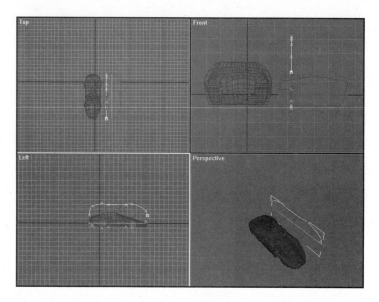

Deform fit creates a path that derives its shape from the vertices of the two fit shapes. Wherever a vertex is present, a path step will be inserted. If the two fit shapes share the same vertices in the same alignment, a minimum number of path steps will be created, therefore creating the minimum amount of geometry in the Loft object. To ensure the fit shapes contain the same vertex alignment, you just clone the more complex of the two shapes. In the next step you adjust the clone to match the profile of the car from the side, by using the vertices present in the top outline, keeping them in their original alignment.

3. Select the new spline, and go to the Modify panel. Click on the Edit Spline button, and turn on the Sub-Object button, and select Segment from the rollout menu. Select all the segments on the bottom half of the shape (in the Left viewport) and delete them.

4. Turn off the Sub-Object button, and move the entire spline close to the top of the car in the Left viewport.

5. Turn the Sub-Object button back on, but select the Vertex Sub-Object this time. Still in the Left viewport, start moving the vertices so that they form a tight outline of the top of the car. Be certain to move the vertices on the viewport's Y axis *only*. You can adjust the Bézier handles of the vertices by using both the X and Y viewport axes to make the outline tighter.

6. Mirror this spline across the Y axis, and make a copy. Attach the bottom spline to the top, and continue the outline process with the bottom vertices adhering to the same rules of vertex manipulation as in step 5. Both the front and back vertex pairs need to be welded together. Don't worry about modeling the wheel wells at this stage. You can also delete any vertices that you don't need for straight segments—but don't *add* any.

The final outline should look something like the one in figure 3.11

FIGURE 3.11

The final modified side outline.

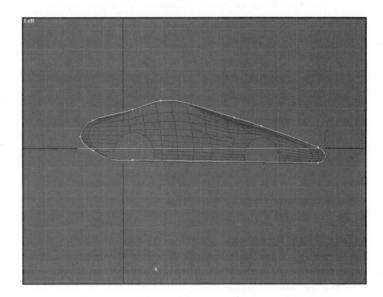

You now have all the elements you need to create the deform-fit loft.

NOTE

The loft will be created by lofting the general shape from the nose to the tail. You could also loft from one side of the car to the other, or from the top to the bottom, but this method gives you the simplest loft shape to work with and keeps the rounding on the sides of the vehicle. The other options would not give you the nice clean cross-sections you can use later for possible BSPs.

7. Select the cross-section shape, and click on the Create panel. Click on the Geometry button, and then select Loft Object from the drop-down menu.

8. Click on the Loft button, select Get Path as the creation method, and then click on the path01 line. This should give you a long loaf-of-bread-type

shape. Uncheck the Cap-Start and Cap-End options. Check both the Skin and Skin-in-Shaded options in the Skin Parameters area. For now, leave Shape Steps and Path Steps at the default setting of 5. Figure 3.12 shows the shape you should have just created.

9. Go to the Modify panel and, with the Loft object still selected, click on the Deformation rollout panel. Click on the Fit button. The Deformation Fit window pops up.

10. In the Deformation Fit window, uncheck the Make Symmetrical button (the first button on the upper-left side of the window). Then click on the Display X Axis button, immediately to the right.

11. Click on the Get Shape button (second to the last on the top menu bar), and then click on the Top-Outline shape. It should appear in the Deformation Fit window, and your loft should now become a strange blobby shape (don't worry about this for now). Repeat the process for getting the Y axis fit shape.

NOTE

3D Studio MAX depends on the alignment of the axes of all shapes, those being lofted and those being used for deformation. For this reason, if the axes on the shapes are not aligned properly, the first Loft object will appear blobby and not as you intended. This problem can be solved by reorienting the axes of the original shapes. Because the Deformation Fit window gives you options to manipulate the shapes, however, it is often more helpful to adjust the parameters there, so that you get immediate visual feedback when the object is correctly created. The mesh itself can then be oriented visually, after it is created, to match the Template object.

12. Click on the Display XY Axes button, and view both shapes in the Deformation Fit window.

13. Click on the Rotate 90° CCW button. The fit shapes will look squashed, but the object will be rendered correctly, only backward.

14. Rotate the new object 180° from the top view so that it lines up with the Template object.

15. In the Surface Parameters of the Loft rollout, set the Path and Shape Steps to zero. Figure 3.12 shows the final model.

FIGURE 3.12
The final low-res model.

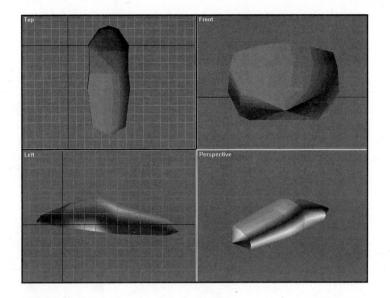

You now have a low-res car that closely approximates the original object. You could add modifications to the original loft shape and place them on your loft path to further enhance the detail of the vehicle without adding more faces. The level of detail can be taken as far as necessary, however, by manipulating the vertices of multiple cross-section shapes and placing them into the existing path steps.

The other primary way of creating an efficient real-time mesh, which usually creates lower face counts but is not as BSP-friendly, is to start with a primitive (preferably a multisegmented cylinder or box) and manipulate the individual vertices to match the Template object.

Modifying Primitives for Low-Resolution Models

The following exercise will demonstrate this modeling process.

1. Open the file CAR02.max on the accompanying CD. You should see only the car Template object from the preceding exercise.

2. Create an eight-sided cylinder, centered on top of the car template, and extend the cylinder's height to match the car's length. Leave the Height and Cap Segment settings at their default level for now. You should have something similar to the objects shown in figure 3.13.

FIGURE 3.13

The cylinder covering the template model.

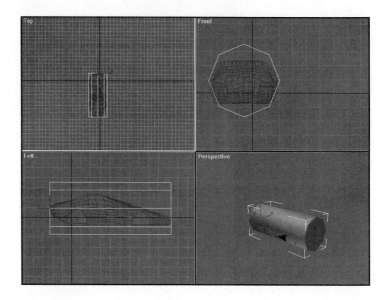

The car should now be almost completely concealed by the newly created cylinder. Next you need to set the segments of the cylinder to approximate the linear changes in the side and top profiles of your template.

3. Set the Height segments to 8 to approximate the number of linear changes in the side profile of the car. (Because the top profile should be quite a bit less, this number will create adequate geometry for you to work with and be accurate to all views of the car.)

4. Click on the Edit Mesh modifier, activate the Sub-Object menu, and select Vertex from the drop-down menu. In the Front viewport, begin selecting vertex groups down the length of the cylinder, moving them to line up with the front view of the template car. Figure 3.14 shows what the modified cylinder should look like now.

5. Go to the Left viewport and begin lining up the cross-section lines with the linear changes in the side view of the template car. Then begin moving vertices on the top and bottom of the cylinder to closely match the template profile (see fig. 3.14). You can also begin moving the vertices (in the middle of the cylinder's length) to line up with the wheel wells.

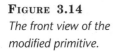

FIGURE 3.14
The front view of the modified primitive.

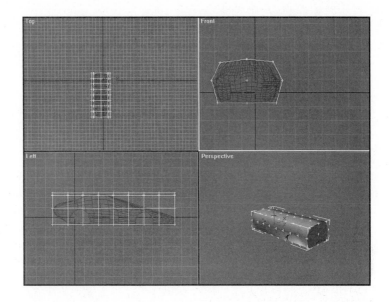

6. Now go to the Top viewport and continue the process with any vertices that are out of alignment with the template's profile. You may find that rotating small groups of closely placed vertices gives more rounded corners on the front and the back.

While modeling this way, it's always a good idea to keep a shaded Perspective viewport active, checking it often to make certain that a vertex has gone where you intended. If it did not, use the Undo feature until it reaches the place where the error occurred. (The more often you check, the less you have to undo in case of an error.)

You have almost completed this model. Clearly, you can add more detail by hiding selected faces and modeling more interior detail (such as the fenders or the hood cowling), but for the purposes of this example, you should move on to the last large bit of detail.

7. Switch to Face Sub-Object mode, and select the faces that were created earlier for the wheel-well area. Select only the wheel wells on one side of the car.

8. Click on the Extrude button, and extrude these faces –7.0 units. This creates the wheel-well inlets, and adds only six polygons per wheel well. Repeat the procedure with the other side. Go to the Display panel and click on Hide Unselected to hide the Template object and see the final real-time car.

As you can see, you have created a vehicle with as much detail as the preceding version, but saved over 80 polygons in the process. You can easily see by the cross-section alignment, however, that this would be a difficult model to separate with BSPs if you had to. The best way to make this model would depend entirely on the game engine being used.

Dealing with Texture Limitations

As you have already seen, quite a bit of detail can be accomplished with limited meshes. To get the most out of limited geometry, however, you must rely on texture maps. Maps have their own limitations—either limited size, limited color depth (usually 8-bit), or both. Fortunately, you can work around these limitations and still produce excellent results.

Dealing with Limited Colors

Opinions abound on the subject of how to create a real-time environment by using 256 colors. Many people favor starting with a limited palette (prepicking the colors that will be used) and making all texture maps from those colors. Others believe that better results derive from creating the maps with the full 16.7 million colors available, and then using another program to evaluate the texture maps and remap them into the 256 most-used colors.

Generally, however, when you create texture maps with 16.7 million colors, you don't use them all (or even a significant percentage of them). To achieve a happy medium between the two previously mentioned methods, first decide on a general scheme (based on the scene, time of day, mood, and so on), and then paint in 24-bit color, focusing on the selected color scheme. This method also provides a better distillation to 256 colors when you create the final game palette, while still keeping the scene focused toward the visual goals identified with the color scheme.

If you don't have access to a program capable of distilling a 256 palette from multiple images (and remapping the colors in those images to the new palette), your best choice is to start with a predetermined 8-bit palette.

Limited Map Size

All gaming platforms today use small texture maps, ranging from 16-by-16 pixels to 128-by-128. Although this may be intimidating for those whose smallest maps are 320-by-240 (one quarter the size of the average monitor display at low resolution), after a bit of practice you will discover how much detail you can achieve in a very small area. You may even find that texture mapping with small maps opens new techniques for creating larger maps when you're creating prerendered 3D images.

A great temptation is to create a texture map at a high resolution and then scale it down to the parameters of whatever real-time engine you are working with. This seldom works well. Scaling, in most paint programs, is done by a mathematical elimination of pixels based on the percentage of down-scaling. When you reach real-time limits, where every pixel counts, this process can make quite a mess of an originally great texture map— filling it with scattered, color-cycling pixels and making an otherwise smooth map look rocky or rough.

Your best bet for making certain that the exact detail you want (and nothing else) appears on-screen during game-play is to start with the same size texture map that will be in the game. This technique leaves no room for extraneous information, and enables you to be very precise as to what amounts of detail go where. And you can use multiple maps (or a large map carved into real-time sizes) on an object with very little impact on the speed of the game.

Adding "Impossible" Detail

As you might have gathered from everything discussed in this chapter so far, real-time is mostly a matter of creating the best illusion with what is technologically possible. Most of the model-creation process, so far, has been accomplished by using limited versions of what is already available in 3DS MAX, and using simple planning and efficiency to achieve results. Some things, however, cannot be done in real time. Certain mapping types (bump mapping, shininess, and specular mapping), specific lighting design, and many other techniques are beyond the limitations of real-time games at this point, because of the bare-bones shading limitations needed to create speed. These more complex maps require the computationally expensive Phong Shading mode, and must simply be "faked." Here again, a little planning can go a long way.

Faking a Bump Map

Bump maps, in prerendered 3D, are a way to create the illusion of limited surface relief on an object. Artists have been doing this in flat images for thousands of years by creating highlights and shadows in still images. The same techniques work very well for creating "fake" bump maps. Determine the angle of your light source (high and right always creates a believable, recognizable source), and paint in the highlights and shadows. The only difference is that your shadows will not move in response to the real-time light source, and the "bumps" will not be visible from the edge of the faces to which they are applied. Figure 3.15 shows a "faked" bump map.

FIGURE 3.15
A "faked" bump map.

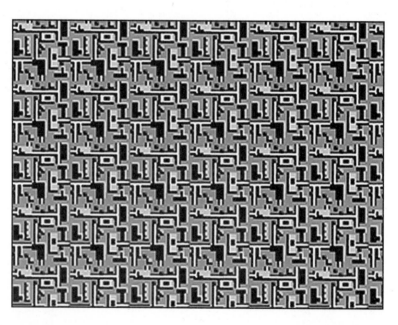

If creating bumps through painting seems a bit intimidating, you can create your bump-mapped material, apply it to a flat plane in 3DS MAX, add lighting, and render the image out to a file for use on your real-time mesh. But remember the earlier comment about map sizes: Render the image to the size it will be in the game, instead of rendering the image larger and scaling it down later.

Faking "Mood Lighting"

To create spot-light effects (such as under-lighting or light pooling), you can repeat the preceding "create it in MAX" technique or use the lighting filters available in many image-editing packages (such as Photoshop or Painter) to get similar results. Moving a MAX light around in 3D space can give you a much more specific effect than using a light fixed to a two-dimensional plane.

Curved Surfaces

Creating a curved surface with geometry is an almost impossible accomplishment in real time because curves require a high number of polygons.

Fortunately, creating the illusion of a curved surface in a texture map is not difficult. It can be painted into the map using a highlight for the highest point on the surface, and blending that into half-tone at the sides of the curve, with shadows reacting to the light source. Again, rendering a fully mapped, highly detailed curved surface in MAX and then using it as a texture map for the flat-surfaced real-time object yields great results.

The following exercise demonstrates most of the previously mentioned concerns when texture mapping.

REAL-TIME TEXTURE MAPPING

1. From the accompanying CD, open the file called Wheel01.max. This is a sporty mag-wheel (see fig. 3.16) that would add a nice bit of detail to your real-time sports car. It was modeled in high detail, and is obviously much too complex to be used in real-time, especially when you consider that it would have to be multiplied by four. The chrome reflection map on the spokes of the wheel would also be impossible in real-time, but renders very nicely in MAX.

FIGURE 3.16
*The high-detail wheel
mesh in MAX.*

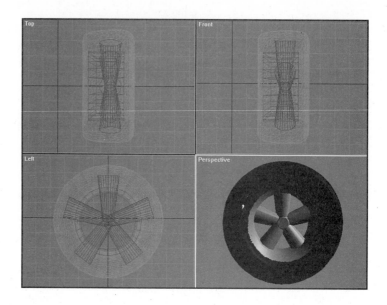

2.   Change the Left viewport display method to Bounding Box mode. With
     the Zoom Region tool, go into the Left viewport and scale the view very
     close to the wheel's bounding box, leaving a small space around the
     outside for cropping later (see fig. 3.17). In the Environment settings, set
     the background color to a bright yellow (red –255, green –255, blue –0).
     This makes cropping and manipulation in your paint package much
     easier later on.

FIGURE 3.17

*The cropping area of
the bounding-boxed
wheel.*

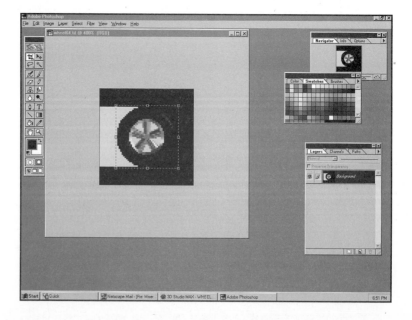

3. Render the Left viewport, at a size of 64 by 64 pixels (an average real-time texture map size), with anti-aliasing turned off. Save the file as a 32-bit Targa filecolor with alpha channel, and name it wheel_src.tga. This is the source file for your texture map.

4. In your favorite image editing program open wheel_src.tga.

5. First, crop the image down to only the pixels you want, leaving no border around the wheel. With the Cropping tool, create an outline that fits exactly to the outside edge of the tire. Crop the image. Resize the image back to 64 by 64 pixels.

6. Now, with the Magic Wand tool, select the yellow pixels that are left. If you are using Photoshop, select one of the yellow corners around the wheel, and then choose Similar under the Select drop-down menu. This should select all the yellow pixels, including the ones between the spokes of the wheel.

NOTE

Rendering the image from MAX with anti-aliasing turned off provides a clean edge around the wheel. By setting the background to an extremely bright color, not found anywhere else in the image, you can create a map in which you can easily replace the background color. Additionally, you can add other colors if your map does not easily fit exactly onto the real-time object (and might leave undesired edges). If you see strange edges when the map is applied, you can go back to the image and "tweak" it to make certain that you get a clean texture map.

7. Choose pure black as your foreground color, and fill the yellow area. If any partly yellow pixels remain at the selection line, stroke the selection line with a two-pixel line of black, centered on the selection line.

8. In the Channels panel, go to the alpha channel (channel 4 in Photoshop), select all the image, and cut it.

9. Go back to the RGB channel, and select Blur from the filters drop-down menu. This adds back the anti-aliasing you removed from the rendered image. Set Color mode to 8-bit (256), and save the image as wheel64.tga (see fig. 3.18). This is your color texture map.

FIGURE 3.18
*The wheel64.tga
image.*

10. Under the File menu, select New. The setting should automatically be 64 by 64 pixels because this was the size of the alpha channel you cut to the Clipboard. Paste the alpha channel into the new file, and set Color mode to grayscale. Select white as your foreground color. This time, fill in just the black corners around the edge of the wheel; this ensures that the edges of your wheel are solid all the way around. Save the image as wheel64o.tga (see fig. 3.19). This is your opacity map.

FIGURE 3.19
*The wheel64o.tga
image.*

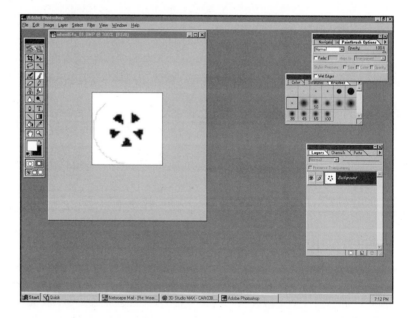

11. Go back into MAX, but this time open the file called CAR03.max (your real-time car from the last modeling exercise). At one of the wheel-wells create an eight-sided cylinder with one height segment, to be used as a

wheel for your car. Make the depth and radius roughly the appropriate size for your vehicle (see fig. 3.20). Keep the new Wheel object selected, and choose the UVW modifier from the Modify panel. Make certain that the mapping type is planar, that the top is aligned with the top of your newly created wheel, and then choose the Fit option to fit the mapping coordinates to the bounding box of your wheel.

FIGURE 3.20

The real-time car, with one wheel added.

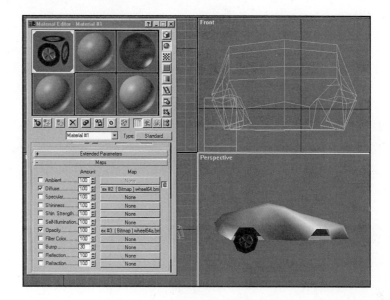

12. Open the Material Editor and create a new material that has constant shading, no shininess, and no shininess strength. Apply the material to the wheel.

13. In the maps area of the Material rollout, load wheel64.tga into the Diffuse channel, and wheel64o.tga into the Opacity channel. Change the material sample type from a sphere to a cube so that you can see exactly what the map looks like on the wheel. In the Alpha Source section of the Map Parameters panel, set the Alpha Source to none (opaque).

14. Render a clean view of the newly mapped wheel, and adjust it until it has a nice rounded feel on the edge of the tire and you can see through the spokes. Clone this object three times, and place the copies into the other wheel wells (see fig. 3.21).

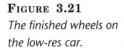

FIGURE 3.21
The finished wheels on the low-res car.

Using Opacity for "Impossible Detail"

Sometimes an object is far too complex to be modeled convincingly in a low-polygon fashion. When you are using 3DS MAX to create models of objects with holes and complex edges—objects so detailed that you cannot make them recognizable—you can use a simple opacity map to create the effect.

Fortunately, almost all real-time systems have some capacity for using opacity maps—whether they are 8-bit grayscale maps or just 1-bit black-and-white, cookie-cutter type maps. This capability enables the model maker to add detail that would otherwise be impossible. The effect is not quite as clean as it would be in 3D Studio MAX, but the result is still quite effective. The following exercise shows how opacity can be used to create the illusion of hair on a real-time character.

1. In the Chapter 3 directory on the accompanying CD, open the file called hair01.max. You will see the head of a real-time humanoid character.

2. Click on the Create panel, and create a box with three segments for height, length, and width. The specific size does not matter, just make certain that the top of the box is bigger than the top of the head.

3. With the box still selected, go into the Modify panel, select Edit Mesh, click on the Sub-Object button, and then select Face from the drop-down menu. Select all the faces except those on the top of the box, and delete them.

4. Open Material Editor, and click on the Get Material button. Click on the Material Library radio button on the top left of the editor, and load hair.max from the accompanying CD. This library has only two materials for this scene: the Phong skins material on the head (which should already be in place), and the hair material in the second material slot (which consists of a comic-book type hair map and a black-and-white opacity\shininess map). Click on the Hair window, and assign the material to the top plane of the box.

5. Minimize the Material Editor, go back to the Modify panel, and click on the UVW Map button. Click on the Sub-Object button, and rotate the mapping gizmo so that the top aligns with the top edge of the box-top in the Top view. Click on the Fit button.

If you have not already done so, configure one of your active viewports to display in Smooth with Highlights mode. You should be able to see the hair map on the Box object now, which makes the next few steps much easier.

6. Click on the Edit Mesh modifier again, and select the Sub-Object button, but select Vertex this time. Begin moving the vertices of the box top down around the head so that it starts to form a sort of shower cap shape, moving the hair where it should be on the head. Don't worry if the lines start to go through the top faces on the head. Render a view occasionally to see how the opacity mapping is making the complex shape of the hair look molded onto the head. Figure 3.22 shows the model after this step, and figure 3.23 shows the rendered version.

7. Click off the Sub-Object button, select the Head object. Select Edit Mesh, and choose the Vertex sub-object. Begin to move the vertices of the top of the head to "tuck" them under the hair. You may find it useful to alternate between editing the hair and the head vertices until you find the best combination.

FIGURE 3.22
*The head with the hair
molded around it.*

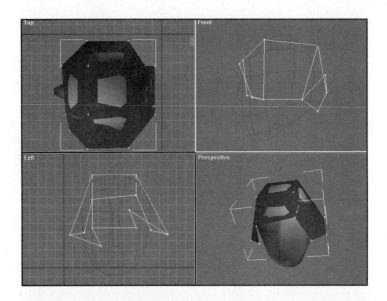

FIGURE 3.23
*The rendered version of
the head, with the hair
molded around it.*

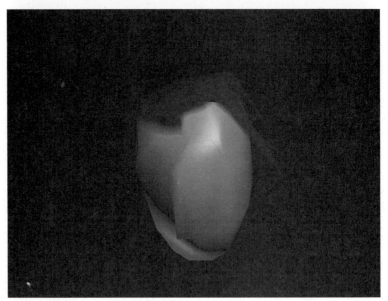

8. Now for the final step. Because this is a real-time model, you want to eliminate any geometry that will not be seen. Select the Head object, click on Edit Mesh, turn on the Sub-Object button, and select Face. Now delete from the head any faces that are completely covered by the Hair object, or that protrude slightly through the hair (do frequent renderings with this step to ensure that you haven't created any visible holes in the head).

The Future of Real-Time

With technology rapidly expanding, real-time 3D is certain to grow past its current limitations, but so will prerendered 3D graphics. Real-time 3D will always be the domain of those who use their imagination to create the illusion of reality, instead of relying only on the latest tools. 3DS MAX will always be a tremendous asset to the real-time artist, however, because of its vast (and continually expanding) tool set and its capability to use these at the most basic levels of a 3D object.

With the introduction of real-time 3D to a mass consumer market, 3D gaming is here to stay. When the technology becomes available, gamers will almost certainly be able to create their own personalized stand-in 3D representatives (or avatars) to take into battle, tackling international opponents across the Internet, or on their own in ever-expanding, increasingly detailed worlds. In the future, real-time gaming will almost certainly become less like a computer game and more like stepping into a new world, filled with personalities, characters, and adventure. The promise of virtual reality will finally be fulfilled.

In Practice: Modeling for Real-Time 3D Games

- Real-time 3D gaming relies on speed and must use only the bare basics of 3D to accommodate the extensive calculations necessary. These basics include limited geometry, limited texture map sizes and color depths, and often, the use of Binary Separation Planes (BSPs) rather than slower Z-buffering calculations for depth.

- Modeling is the most critical process in real-time 3D because everything depends on the alignment and efficiency of the object being created.

- Creating a 3D template over which to model is a useful procedure for creating real-time objects with enough detail in the right places.

- The basic procedures in creating a real-time model are "conscious lofting" and modifying primitives.

- Detail that cannot be accomplished with mesh can be created with texture maps, using opacity, "faked" bump maps, and rendered images of high-detail meshes manipulated for real-time use.

IMAGE BY ANDREW VERNON

Chapter 4

by Andrew Vernon

MODELING FOR VR AND THE WEB

The World Wide Web's unexpected emergence and hectic growth has been one of the phenomena of the '90s. Although exact figures are not available, it's generally believed that the number of people accessing the web will grow from about 20 million today to about 200 million by the year 2000. During this same time period, computer processing power is expected to continue to double every 18 months, coupled with an enormous expansion of line bandwidth and modem speed. Barring some disaster, the future of the web is very bright indeed. It's no wonder, therefore, that so much creative talent—and money—is being invested in it. Virtual Reality Markup Language (VRML, usually pronounced vermal) is one of the best ways that 3D artists and animators can take advantage of the tremendous opportunity presented by the web's growth.

VRML, as conceived by its creators, is much more than a method of displaying 3D models. It's a conceptual system that might ultimately enable you to navigate the web as one continuous 3D space, in the same way that HTML enables you to navigate the web as one giant hypertext document. This is the real potential of "cyberspace." In the future, web addresses will map to the interiors of personal or corporate 3D spaces within the context of a borderless virtual world. This world continuously will be extended but will always be coherent and consistently navigable because it is implemented in a common language—VRML.

This chapter helps you keep up with the fast-paced world of 3D on the web. It covers the following topics:

- Modeling tools and techniques

- Summary of what is and is not exported by VRMLOUT

- Creating a virtual world with 3DS MAX and VRMLOUT

- VRML browser reviews

- The best of the web

NOTE

If you want to find out more about the goals and potential of VRML, go to Mark Pesce's site at www.hyperreal.com/~mpesce/. The latest VRML specification is available at vrml.sgi.com/moving-worlds/spec/index.html. All the web addresses mentioned in this chapter are included in a bookmarks file (Ch4bkmk.htm) provided on the *Inside 3D Studio MAX Volume II* CD-ROM.

VRML is an *"open" standard*—a specification openly published that does not contain code owned by any corporation. VRML was created and is maintained by individuals who have a vision of 3D on the web and want to make it possible for anyone to use it freely. Naturally, the open philosophy of VRML is endangered in this age of megacorporations. If a company such as Microsoft, for example, were to develop a proprietary VRML specification—one that added Microsoft's own "extensions" to the VRML specification—many people would doubtless be tempted to use it. The result would be that models created by using this version of VRML would not display, or would not display properly, on browsers that support the original VRML specification, and vice-versa. This is not to suggest that Microsoft, or any other company, is about to do so. Rather, it is an illustration of the potential that exists in cyberspace, as in any other world, to descend from order and civilization into chaos and anarchy. Good citizens of cyberspace can, and should, remain aware of the freedom of speech issues involved in the maintenance of an open standard, and avoid using proprietary versions of the language (should any appear).

Having said that, the outlook today is very positive. The VRML Consortium, formed December 1996, has taken over responsibility for the development of the language from the VRML Architecture Group. Hopefully, all those companies that might otherwise have gone their separate ways will now come together and make VRML the single, solid standard it needs to be.

Modeling Tools and Techniques

As with all files destined for display on the World Wide Web, smaller is better with VRML. On a standard 28.8 kbs modem, with average network traffic, a VRML file of 150 KB downloads in about 120 seconds. To that time, you must add extra time for downloading any texture map files. Download performance, then, is the first issue: How long does it take to download the file from the web server and load it into memory? This is a function of file size. The only time file size might not be an issue is when you are creating VRML worlds for access over an intranet in a particular organization.

The second issue is navigation speed or performance after the file loads into memory, a function of model complexity. This relates to file size, of course, because the more complex the model and the more faces it has, the larger the file. The main bottleneck here, however, is in the video display: How many pixels does the video display card have to process and put out to the screen? When you navigate within a VRML world, the browser interprets the VRML code and passes it to your PC hardware, which actually renders it in real time.

NOTE

The term *browser*, as used here, refers to the VRML-viewer software that plugs into your web browser (Netscape or Internet Explorer). Available VRML browsers are reviewed later in the chapter.

Keep in mind that performance that depends on file size is a more subjective measure. What seems an unacceptably long download time to one person may seem quite acceptable to another. Download time is the lesser of the two limitations. Generally speaking, you won't want to miss out on the vitality that texture maps bring to your model for the sake of the extra time needed to download them. What you definitely want to avoid is creating models with so many faces that the computer gets bogged down trying to display them.

This section introduces tools and techniques you can use to work with both these limitations and produce VRML files optimized for download and navigation performance on the web.

Using Tools Built into 3DS MAX

You can reduce file size and speed performance in several ways, just by careful management of the objects you create. Before you begin modeling a scene for the web set a face (polygon) "budget" appropriate for the complexity of the scene and then roughly portion out the number of faces for the different objects. The Polygon Counter (a utility that comes with the VRMLOUT plug-in for 3DS MAX) helps you stay within your budget.

The sample world used throughout this chapter (City.wrl), for example, has about 2750 faces. Its file size is about 150 KB (the compressed size is less than 30 KB)—still a large file.

Reducing the Number of Segments

The simplest thing you can do to cut your face count is to reduce the number of segments in any primitive you create. The default segment settings for 3DS MAX primitives give you more faces than you want for a VRML world. When you create a primitive in a scene destined for export to VRML, therefore, go immediately to the Modify panel and use the spinners to reduce the number of segments.

Figure 4.1 shows two rows of primitives rendered in 3DS MAX. The upper row shows the primitives with the default number of segments. The lower row shows the same set of primitives after segment reduction. How much you reduce depends on how the primitive will be viewed in the scene. Objects that remain in the background can be reduced much more than objects intended to be viewed up close. This illustration shows how you can easily cut the face count in half (or more) without losing an enormous amount of quality. Table 4.1 summarizes the face savings between these two sets of primitives.

FIGURE 4.1
*3DS MAX primitives,
before and after
reducing the number of
segments.*

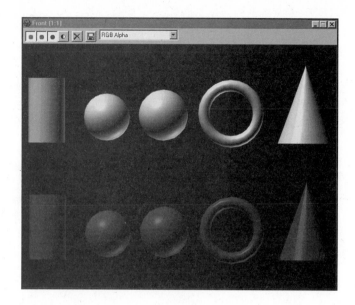

TABLE 4.1

Summary of Face Savings Earned by Segment Reduction

Primitive	Default Segments	Face Count	Reduced Segments	Face Count
Cylinder	24	96	12	48
Sphere	24	528	16	224
Geosphere	4	320	3	180
Torus	24/12 sides	576	16/6	192
Cone	24/5 height	288	12/1	48
TOTAL		1808		692

Deleting and Hiding Faces

Another very simple thing you can do is delete from the objects in your scene any faces that will never be visible. In the scene of an ancient city in this chapter, for example, deleting the faces on the underside of the landscape object cuts the number of faces from 1072 to 709 (see fig. 4.2). This particular object is a box with 14 segments each way, which was molded with the

Freeform Deformation modifier to create slopes and hills. If you were happy with a completely flat landscape, you could reduce the face count to 12 by using a simple box.

Actually, you don't have to use a base object to create an effect of the ground under your buildings. VRML 2.0 provides a Ground Color option for the Background helper, which enables you to set the color of the viewport below the horizon (this helper is described later in the chapter).

FIGURE 4.2

Hiding faces that will never be visible.

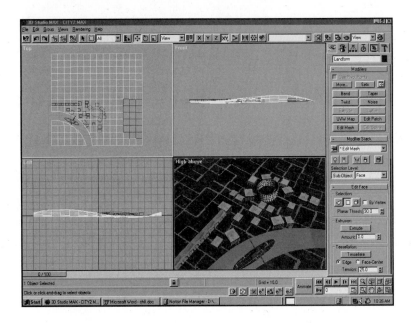

Another option is to hide the faces you don't want instead of deleting them. Because the VRMLOUT plug-in doesn't export hidden faces, those faces will not be part of the eventual download file size. 3DS MAX still counts the hidden faces, however, and you will not have a completely accurate face count during the modeling process. Whether you delete or hide faces is up to you. You may find it more convenient to delete them if your model is intended solely to be viewed in a VRML browser.

Using the Optimize Modifier

You're doubtless already familiar with the Optimize modifier; it's hardly necessary to point out its advantages for creating low-face-count models for VRML worlds. Perhaps the most useful thing at this point is to look at some examples of objects optimized with this modifier at different levels of severity. Figure 4.3 shows what happens to a palm-tree mesh with successive increases in the Face Threshold setting.

FIGURE 4.3

Different settings for the Optimize modifier.

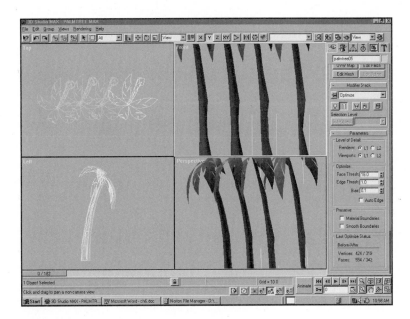

- The tree on the left is not optimized and has 554 faces.

- The second tree has the Face Threshold set to 8 and has 538 faces.

- The third tree has the Face Threshold set to 12 and has 420 faces.

- The fourth tree has the Face Threshold set to 18 and has 342 faces.

From experiments like this, you may conclude that you can turn up the Face Threshold to 12 and still get acceptable results for objects that stay in the middle distance, but that a setting of 18 distorts the mesh too much. Generally, the more complex the mesh, the more dramatic the savings you get by using the Optimize modifier. You need to experiment to find what works best for your scene.

Using Instances

An *instance* is an interdependent copy of a 3DS MAX object; when you make a change to any of the instances, all the other copies change also. Instances are useful in creating smaller-size files for the web; when you use an instance, the set of faces that make up the instance object has to be defined only once in the VRML code. Consequently, you can use the same piece of geometry many times without any increase in the download time for the file. Figure 4.4 shows an example of the use of instances in a VRML world. All the rectangular buildings in the scene are instances, derived from a single box primitive.

FIGURE 4.4

Using instances for multiple occurrences of the same geometry.

Texture Mapping Versus Geometry

Figure 4.4 also shows another easy way to reduce the amount of geometry that needs to be described in the VRML file—use texture mapping instead! The buildings in this scene are mostly plain boxes, as mentioned earlier. By applying different texture maps to the boxes, however, and changing the scale and orientation of the buildings, you make the scene look much more varied than it really is. Although texture maps increase the download time as well as the speed of screen redraws, the extra time incurred is a small price to pay compared to what it would cost to model the doors, windows, and columns of all the buildings.

When you upload texture maps, remember that the Unix system your web server is most likely running is case-sensitive, and will not find the map files unless the case is exact. If you specified a map called bridge.gif in the

Material Editor, for example, but the file you upload to the web server is called Bridge.gif, the map will not display.

Texture maps look strange but not unattractive when you zoom in close enough to see the pattern of the colored pixels. This is becoming part of the "style" of VRML models, as you'll see if you look at some of the web sites listed later in this chapter. One way to work with this limitation rather than against it is to design texture maps that make no attempt to look realistic, but look as though they were painted on, like stage scenery.

You might have noticed in figure 4.4 that the buildings appear to have different maps on their different sides. You can apply the same map to all sides of a box by using the Box option of the UVW Map modifier in 3DS MAX. To get different maps on different sides, however, you have to use different maps. The mapping in this scene was done using a feature of the 3D paint program, Fractal Design Detailer. This feature, called *implicit mapping,* enables you to use a single texture map to paint on all six sides of a box (see fig. 4.5). You can do the same thing without a 3D paint program by using a freeware plug-in for 3DS MAX called Unwrap (available on the accompanying CD-ROM).

FIGURE 4.5
Box-mapping technique in Fractal Design Detailer.

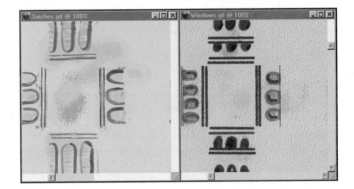

Creating Camera Views

Placing cameras in the scene is not, of course, a modeling technique per se, but it needs to be mentioned here because cameras are so useful in making a successful VRML world. The different cameras you create in your scene are listed by the VRML browser, usually in the menu that pops-up when you right-click in the browser's viewport. Users can navigate within the scene by selecting one camera view after another; be sure to provide plenty of them and name them descriptively. Even very large worlds that navigate painfully slowly in the browser can be viewed pleasurably from a series of camera views.

Use the cameras you create to show off the best views of the scene—to point out unusual perspectives or to provide close-ups of the parts of the scene over which you lavished the most care. If you leave it to the user to navigate through the scene, you have no control over what he or she will look at. With a good selection of camera views, on the other hand, you can control this to a large extent. Because selecting cameras is simpler than manually navigating with the mouse and because the browser makes an elegant transition from one camera to another, if you make an interesting and original sequence of camera views, they will be used.

Types of Animation

VRML 2.0 provides animation support for the VRML worlds you export from 3DS MAX. The following list identifies a fairly wide variety of animation methods that you can use:

- Simple transforms (move, rotate, and scale)
- Animated hierarchies and inverse kinematics
- Coordinate interpolation animation, such as animated modifiers (Bend, Taper, and so on)
- Morphing
- Character Studio animation

You can do any kind of animation that doesn't involve changing the number of vertices. If the animation requires use of the Modifier stack, you need to turn on the Coordinate Interpolation option when you export the scene.

It's easy to exceed your file-size budget quickly when you start using animation, especially with coordinate interpolation. With this last type of animation, the VRMLOUT exporter has to track the position of every vertex over time, requiring the generation of a lot of code in the VRML file. Simple transform animation, on the other hand, is not nearly so demanding. Use it whenever possible.

It's useful to think of animation as a moving accent in an otherwise-still VRML world; in the current climate of the web, a little goes a long way.

Some animation examples follow in the project section, "Creating a Virtual World with 3DS MAX and VRMLOUT."

Using Tools Provided by the VRMLOUT Plug-In

The VRMLOUT plug-in provides some special tools for managing your scene. These include the Polygon Counter, the Level of Detail helper, and the Export dialog box. The next sections discuss these tools in detail.

The Polygon Counter

The *Polygon Counter* is an excellent little gadget that keeps count of the number of faces in the scene as a whole, as well as in the selected object or objects. You can set a budget for the number of faces in the scene or for each object; the counter displays a colored "thermometer" when you approach the limit or go over the top. This utility is invaluable when modeling for VRML export. You soon get a sense of how many faces should be in various objects, according to their relative importance in the scene, and the Polygon Counter helps keep you on target. Use it in conjunction with the Optimize modifier for a real-time graphic display of the optimization process; as you change the modifier values by using the spinners, the Polygon Counter changes also. Figure 4.6 shows the Polygon Counter in use with the Optimize modifier.

FIGURE 4.6
Using the Polygon Counter utility.

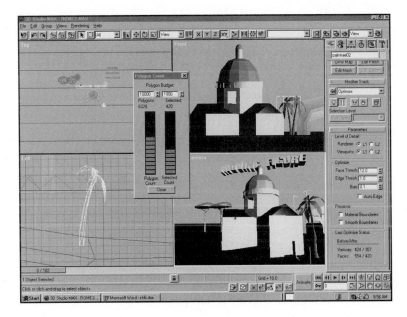

The Level of Detail Helper

The *Level of Detail* helper (LOD) is one of the VRML Helper objects you can place in your scene. It speeds up navigation in the viewport by displaying different objects, depending on their distance from the viewer. You can have the browser display a detailed version of a building, for example, when the viewer comes within 100 units. As soon as the viewer moves farther away, the browser can display a less detailed version of the same building, with fewer faces.

You don't have to use different versions of the same objects. By substituting completely different objects, you can do a kind of simple morphing.

LOD objects are covered in the project section of the chapter, "Creating a Virtual World with 3DS MAX and VRMLOUT."

Settings in the Export Dialog

The VRMLOUT plug-in's Export dialog has a number of settings that affect file size.

Always leave the Primitives option checked when primitives are in the scene. This parameter tells the exporter to convert 3DS MAX primitives to VRML primitives, which require less code in the VRML file. The 3DS MAX scene with the two rows of primitives shown in figure 4.1, for example, exported to 45 KB with this option checked but increased to 85 KB when it was unchecked.

If you never need to look at the VRML code generated by the exporter, you can uncheck the Indentation parameter. Indentation makes the VRML code easier to read. Unchecking this parameter reduced the 45 KB file just mentioned to 38 KB.

The Digits of Precision option controls the accuracy with which dimensions are calculated. Reducing the Digits of Precision from the default 4 to 3 is probably acceptable unless you have an architectural model or some other scene in which measurements need to be precise. Decrementing this parameter reduced the size of the test file to just under 36 KB.

It's probably not worth reducing the value of the Sample Rate parameter for transform animation. Doing so doesn't save you much in terms of file size, but it does rapidly start to make the animation play back less smoothly. You might want to experiment with the sample rates if you have coordinate-interpolation animation in the scene. Reducing the value in this case can make a significant difference in file size.

Other Techniques

You can use a couple of other techniques to speed things up: one to help control screen-update performance, and the other to help reduce download time.

The EMBED HTML Statement

The *EMBED statement* is a technique for constraining the size of the viewport occupied by the browser on the web page. By controlling the size of the browser, you can ensure, for example, that the user will not try to display the scene maximized on a 17-inch monitor or otherwise on such a large scale that the computer cannot properly process the number of pixels that must be rendered.

The HTML format for the statement follows:

```
<EMBED SRC=filename.WRL WIDTH=300 HEIGHT=200>
```

Figure 4.7 shows the Cosmo browser constrained to an area of the screen with the EMBED statement (from the Kinetix site at www.ktx.com).

FIGURE 4.7

Use of the EMBED HTML statement to constrain the size of the browser viewport.

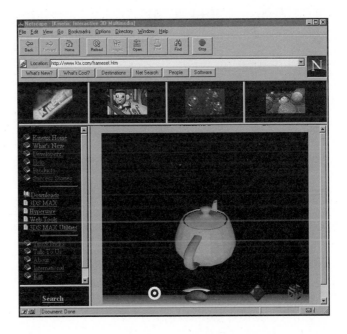

GZIP File Compression

The good news about file compression is that it works well, greatly reducing the size of the VRML (WRL) file. The bad news is that you probably have to use a Unix command to do it. If your web site is on a Unix web server, as most of them are, you are probably already familiar with the Telnet-type commands needed to create directories, set access rights, and so on. To compress a VRML file, change to the directory where the file resides and type:

gzip *filename*.wrl

This creates a gzipped (compressed) file with the name:

filename.wrl.gz

When you attempt to view a gzipped file from your web page, the message `Warning: Unrecognized encoding: x-gzip` appears. This is not a problem because when you click on OK, the file opens as usual. Browsers may some day be smart enough not to display pointless messages. Until then, the inconvenience is minor; don't let it stop you from compressing your files.

What VRMLOUT Can and Cannot Export

Before you create a scene for export to VRML, you should be aware that not everything you can model or animate in 3DS MAX is supported by the VRML 2.0 standard. Table 4.2 lists the elements of the 3DS MAX scene that can be exported to a VRML 2.0-format file, as well as some notable elements that cannot be. If you're not sure whether something will or will not export, you can always make a simple test scene, export it, and load it in your VRML browser.

TABLE **4.2**

Summary of Exportable and Nonexportable Elements

Can Be Exported	*Cannot Be Exported*
Geometry	Smoothing groups
Hidden objects (Export option)	Hidden faces
Transform animation	
Coordinate interpolation animation	

Can Be Exported	Cannot Be Exported
Inverse kinematics	Inherit links
Animated cameras	
Light color	Volumetric lights
Standard materials and multi/sub-object materials (see the following indented list)	Other types of materials
Ambient, diffuse, and specular color	All other aspects of the material not listed in the first column
1 map (in diffuse channel)	
Shininess	
Opacity	
Wire frame	

Creating a Virtual World with 3DS MAX and VRMLOUT

This section explains how to create a virtual world for the web, using 3D Studio MAX and the VRMLOUT plug-in. You can access a web page that displays the completed sample world used in this chapter at www.jps.net/avernon/worlds.html. The page also contains instructions for viewing the various VRMLOUT features in the sample world. You should view this web page in your web browser, both to see what you will be doing if you work through the rest of this chapter and to get the real-world experience of the way a large VRML file actually performs.

If this is not possible, the same VRML file (CITY.WRL) is included on the accompanying CD-ROM. You can open it locally by using your web browser's Open File menu option. Whether you view the file live on the web or locally, you need to have a VRML 2.0 browser installed, and, as discussed in the Browser Review section of this chapter, Live3D 2.0 is recommended. New Riders has included Live3D 2.0 on the accompanying CD to save you the download time.

The CITY.WRL sample world is designed to demonstrate most of the helpers of the VRMLOUT plug-in (also included on the accompanying CD-ROM; see the Kinetix web site, www.ktx.com, for updates). This section steps you through the process of adding each helper to a partially complete version of the sample scene (City.max). It describes the procedure used and indicates what you then need to do to see that helper in action in the browser (navigation, clicking on objects, and so on).

General Procedure for Using VRMLOUT

The following list summarizes the general procedure for adding the individual helpers. This should prove helpful before you begin because the procedure is the same or very similar for all of them.

1. Create your scene in the usual way with lighting, materials, and animation. Pay special attention to creating and naming cameras; they are listed in the VRML browser and are an important means of navigation. (In the 3DS MAX file you start with, the cameras are already defined.)

2. Go to the Create panel and choose Helpers. Then select the VRML option from the drop-down list. Select VRML 2.0 for all the features described in this section unless otherwise noted.

3. Click on the button for the helper you want (TimeSensor, for example), and then click and drag in the Top viewport to place the helper icon. (Figure 4.8 shows some of the helper icons used in the sample file.) Most of the helper icons can go anywhere in the scene. Some, such as the Level of Detail helper, must be placed next to the objects they affect.

4. Link the helper to the objects in the scene that it affects. You usually do this by picking the objects, as described in the procedure for each helper.

5. Export the file in WRL format. Select VRML 2.0 for all the features described in this section. If you have a static scene with no animation, you probably don't need VRML 2.0 export and can export the file in VRML 1.0 format instead. This means that your file will also be viewable in browsers not yet VRML 2.0 compliant. Check the VRMLOUT plug-in help file for a list of which features belong to VRML 2.0 and which are included in VRML 1.0.

FIGURE 4.8

VRMLOUT helpers in the 3DS MAX scene.

Anchor

NavInfo

Background

Sound

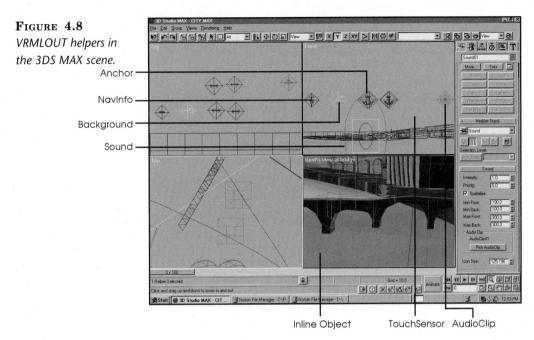

Inline Object   TouchSensor AudioClip

6. Test the file in your VRML browser. To test the file, open it from your hard disk first to make sure that the helper works as expected. Then upload the file to the web server and test the world live on the web.

Adding the VRMLOUT Helpers to a Scene

You don't need to add the helpers to the sample scene in any particular order. There's no right order to placing them, although starting with the background seems logical.

This chapter does not attempt to describe all the many parameters for these helpers; that is done adequately in the VRMLOUT help file and elsewhere. Instead, this chapter focuses on the parameters you should be especially aware of and those that need to be changed from the default values.

Background

The *Background* helper defines the colors for a sky or ground backdrop to the world. This can be a plain color or a gradation made of two or three colors. If you define both sky and ground, you get a horizon line. The Background helper also provides options to set a bitmap image for the sky and ground (however, no browsers support this feature yet.)

You should place a Background helper in your scene whenever you want to control the colors of the Browser viewport. In daylight scenes, for example, you want a sky-colored background. (Cosmo and Sony Community Place both display a black background by default.)

In this procedure, you use a Background helper to create a blue-sky backdrop for the scene:

1. Open the City.max file on the accompanying CD-ROM.

2. Select the Background helper from the VRML 2.0 helpers in the 3DS MAX Create panel. No linking is required; just place the icon in the Top viewport and adjust the settings. Figure 4.9 shows the settings to use (the blue in the sample file has an RGB value of 40,140,220).

3. From the File menu, choose Export, and then choose VRML from the list of export formats.

4. In the Export dialog, select VRML 2.0 from the list. You can leave the other settings as they are.

5. Open the VRML file in your web browser (in Netscape, choose Open File from the File menu).

The colored-sky background should be visible as the file loads.

FIGURE 4.9

Settings for the Background helper.

NavInfo

The *NavInfo* helper enables you to control some of the characteristics of the browser display, such as navigation type and speed, whether a headlight is on, and so on. The default browser settings are generally acceptable, so a NavInfo helper is not essential. You may want to place one to increase the speed setting from 1.0 to about 5.0, however, if navigation seems slow when you test the file on the web.

In this procedure, you use a NavInfo helper to speed up the navigation slightly:

1. Continue with the City.max file.

2. Select the NavInfo helper under VRML 2.0 helpers in the 3DS MAX Create panel. No linking is required; just place the icon in the Top viewport and adjust the settings. Figure 4.10 shows the settings to use.

3. From the File menu, choose Export, and then choose VRML from the list of export formats.

4. In the Export dialog, select VRML 2.0 from the list. You can leave the other settings as they are.

5. Open the VRML file in your web browser (in Netscape, choose Open File from the File menu).

The NavInfo settings take effect when you load the file.

FIGURE 4.10

Settings for the NavInfo helper.

TimeSensor

The *TimeSensor* helper controls animation settings such as Start and End Frames and Looping. By adding a number of TimeSensors to the objects in your scene, you can play segments of the scene's animation out of sequence— something you cannot do in 3DS MAX. Suppose, for example, that you have two boats rowing down the river with exactly the same animated stroke of the oars. By using a separate TimeSensor for each boat, and selecting a different range of frames, you can have the stroke of the oars different for each.

In this procedure, you place a TimeSensor to loop an animation and to start the animation when the file is loaded. Figure 4.11 shows the settings to use.

1. Open the Galley.max file. This file already has an animation for the movement of the oars.

2. Select the TimeSensor helper under VRML 2.0 helpers in the 3DS MAX Create panel.

3. Place the icon in the Top viewport.

4. Click on the Pick Objects button, and then click on each of the oars individually. Make certain that you select all the animated objects to be controlled by the TimeSensor.

5. Turn on the Loop and Start on World Load options.

6. Export and test the file.

FIGURE 4.11
Settings for the TimeSensor helper.

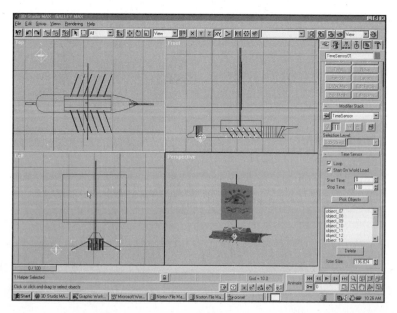

Inline Object

The *Inline Object* helper inserts another WRL file into the world in place of the Inline helper icon. This is useful for the following reasons.

- Because inline files start to load at the same time as the "host" file, the scene as a whole builds faster.

- By instancing one inline file, you can quickly insert more than one copy of an object.

- You can include objects created by someone else.

In this procedure, you place two Inline objects to insert two copies of the galley model into the scene.

---

1. Open the City.max file.

2. Select the Inline helper under VRML 1.0/2.0/VRBL helpers in the 3DS MAX Create panel.

3. Place the icon in the Top viewport at coordinates 480X, 430Y and enter Galley.wrl, the name of the WRL file to insert.

4. Hold down the Shift key and drag the Inline icon to create a second Inline object. Make it an instance of the first, and place it at coordinates 472X, 400Y.

5. Export and test the file.

When you use an Inline object, always make certain that the helper icon is positioned and rotated correctly relative to the other objects in the scene. The object or objects to be inserted must have been created at the same scale as the host scene. The inline file must be in the same folder as the host file.

Notes on viewing this feature in the browser: The two galleys (boats) on the river are the Inline objects (see fig. 4.12). The initial camera view's setting for the world gives the best view of these objects. Note that the two boats start loading almost immediately when you load the exported file (see fig. 4.13).

FIGURE 4.12
Inline objects as they appear in the 3DS MAX scene.

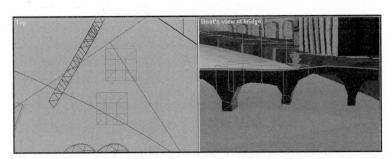

Level of Detail (LOD)

The *LOD* helper speeds redraw time by substituting different versions of an object. The more detailed, complex object is loaded when the viewer is close; the less detailed, less complex object is loaded as the viewer moves away.

Unfortunately, a bug in the current VRMLOUT plug-in prevents the export of LOD objects to the VRML 2.0 format. They are exported to VRML 1.0, however. Consequently, a separate version of the sample world includes the LOD helper and the other VRML 1.0 helpers, but not the VRML 2.0 helpers.

FIGURE 4.13

Inline objects as they appear in the VRML world.

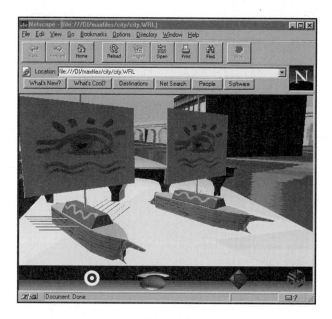

To add a LOD object to a scene, choose VRML 1.0/2.0/VRBL from the list in the Create panel to display the LOD helper. Follow the procedure in the VRMLOUT help file to create the LOD objects. Because you need to place the objects at the same coordinates, you cannot see them all simultaneously. The best way to handle them is to hide and unhide them as necessary. Figure 4.14 shows the settings used for the LOD objects in the sample file.

To see this feature in the sample file, open the Lodcity.wrl file in your browser. The initial camera view's setting for the world gives you a view of the LOD objects. Navigate forward in the viewport toward the building immediately in front of you. As you draw near, the plain texture-mapped-box building changes to a fully modeled version.

FIGURE 4.14
*Settings for the LOD
helper.*

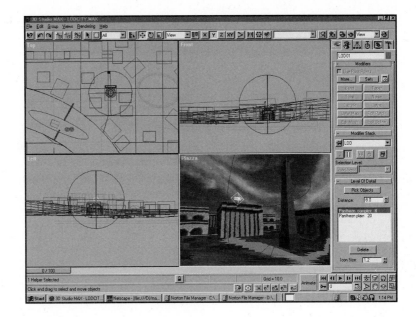

Anchor

The *Anchor* helper creates a link from an object in the VRML world to another URL (WRL or HTML file) or to another camera viewpoint in the same world.

In this procedure, you add several Anchor objects to set up jumps to different cameras in the scene. The viewer can then click on four objects to go to close-up camera views: the Colosseum, the Island, the Aqueduct, and the River.

1. Open the City.max file. The different camera views are already defined.

2. Select the Anchor helper under VRML 2.0 helpers in the 3DS MAX Create panel.

3. Place the icon in the Top viewport.

4. Click on the Pick Trigger Object button, and then click on the Colosseum Building object.

5. In the Description field, enter **Go to Colosseum camera**. Some browsers (such as Live3D 2.0, for example) display this text in the Browser viewport to guide the user.

6. Select Set Camera, and then choose the Colosseum camera from the list.

7. Repeat steps 3 through 6 to add three more Anchors to the scene. The trigger objects are the Island (**Go to Island view camera**), the Aqueduct Structure (**Go to Aqueduct camera**), and the River (**Go to Downriver camera**).

8. Export and test the file.

Notes on viewing this feature in the browser: Select the Map View with Anchors camera viewpoint from the list in the browser. You should then be able to click on the four objects—the Colosseum, the Island, the Aqueduct, and the River—to go to close-up camera views. In Cosmo, the pointer in the Browser viewport changes to a cross to indicate that you are over an object for which an anchor has been defined (see fig. 4.15).

FIGURE 4.15

Selecting an anchor link.

TouchSensor

The *TouchSensor* helper starts an animation or sound file when the user clicks on the linked object.

In this procedure, you add a TouchSensor helper to open the Colosseum door:

1. Continue with the City.max file.

2. Select the TouchSensor helper under VRML 2.0 helpers in the 3DS MAX Create panel.

3. Place the icon in the Top viewport.

4. Set one of the 3DS MAX viewports to show the Colosseum camera view.

5. Click on the Pick Trigger Object button, and then click on the right door (Door2) to the Colosseum. The name of the object appears in the Control panel.

6. Click on the Pick Action Objects button, and then on the left door (Door 1).

7. Export and test the file.

When you place a TouchSensor, first pick the *trigger object* (the object to be clicked on). Then pick the *target object* or objects (the object(s) animated or the Sound helper activated). Figure 4.16 shows the settings used in the sample file.

Notes on viewing this feature in the browser: Select the Colosseum camera viewpoint from the list in the browser, and click on the right door to open the door.

FIGURE 4.16

Settings for the TouchSensor helper.

AudioClip and Sound

The *AudioClip and Sound* helpers work together to provide 3D, spatialized sound in the world. *Spatialized sound* is sound that increases in volume as you approach its source.

In this procedure, you add an AudioClip helper and a Sound helper to create the 3D sound of oars splashing in the water:

1. Continue with the City.max file.

2. Select the AudioClip helper under VRML 2.0 helpers in the 3DS MAX Create panel.

3. Place the icon in the Top viewport.

4. For URL, enter **splash.wav**.

5. Add a text description (optional); this text does not appear in the browser).

6. Check the Loop box and the Start on World load box.

7. Select the Sound helper under VRML 2.0 helpers in the 3DS MAX Create panel.

8. Place the Sound helper in the Top viewport, close to the Inline objects on the river.

9. Click on the Pick AudioClip button, and then click on the AudioClip helper you just added. The name of the AudioClip appears in the Control panel.

10. Use the Min/Max spinners to adjust the blue and red ellipsoids. These two ellipsoids show the distances within which the sound is at full volume and still audible, respectively. Figure 4.17 shows the settings to use.

FIGURE 4.17

Settings for the Sound helper.

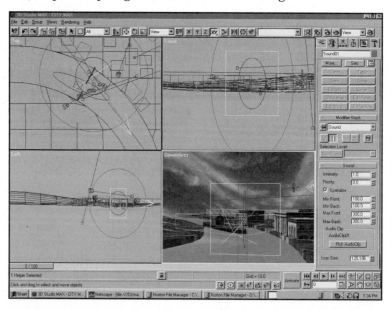

11. Export and test the file.

Notes on hearing this feature in the browser: Navigate toward the ships on the river. As you get closer, you should hear the oars splashing in the water. As you go farther away, the sound fades out.

This completes the construction of the ancient city world. If you've followed the steps in this section, you now know how to use all the helpers provided by the VRMLOUT plug-in, except for Fog and Billboard. Fog is not supported by any browsers yet, and Billboard doesn't seem to work as specified, so at this point you have all the tools you need to take your 3DS MAX scenes into the wonderful world of VRML and the web.

Browser Review

Several VRML browsers are available that do a fine job of implementing the VRML specification. As this book is being written, *VRML* means VRML 2.0. The VRML 2.0 spec was approved in mid-1996, and the best browsers already support it. Not all VRML 2.0 browsers are equal, however. This section looks at some of them, comparing them specifically in terms of how well they handle VRML files exported from 3DS MAX with the VRMLOUT plug-in.

A Note on VRML 1.0 Browsers

Things change very quickly on the web, and what is true today may not be true—or be only relatively true—tomorrow. Other browsers may appear that are superior to the ones discussed here. These browsers are the best available today, however; they are likely to continue to evolve along with the VRML specification itself.

On the other hand, some browsers have not evolved fast enough to be included in this review. The most notable of these is the Topper browser from Kinetix, which still supports only VRML 1.0. Topper adds some extra functionality (called *VRBL*) that is not in the VRML 1.0 specification, but these extra functions (which are for basic animation) have been superseded by the new functionality in VRML 2.0. Also, Topper does not seem to be maintained by anyone at Kinetix and is therefore not recommended.

Changing VRML browsers is a simple task: Download the new browser and run the setup program. In most cases, this automatically installs the new browser over the old one. The next time you access a VRML world, the new browser should run (exceptions are noted in the following browser description sections).

World View, from Intervista

Intervista's World View is a handsome browser with excellent navigation tools—a genuine and very fast VRML 2.0-compliant browser. Intervista does not display the lights and texture maps of the MAX model very well, however, having obviously sacrificed some display quality to speed. Figure 4.18 shows the sample WRL file in the World View browser. Even in black and white, you should be able to see the pixelation of the textures and the absence of shadows (compare this with figs. 4.19 and 4.20, in the next two sections). World View is recommended as a primary browser only if navigation speed is much more important to you than appearance.

FIGURE 4.18

A sample VRML file in Intervista's World View.

TIP

World View has a Pointer tool that enables you to click on an object to zoom in on it. Another tool, Stand-Up Straight, puts you in an upright position relative to the horizon.

Download the browser at www.intervista.com. World View automatically installs itself over Live3D in Netscape without stopping to inform you that it has renamed the Live3D DLL. It has an uninstall program in case you want to get Live3D or another browser back again.

Community Place, from Sony

Community Place, a recently released browser from Sony in Japan, is promising but has some peculiarities. In particular, the navigation tools are difficult to use and don't seem to do what you expect (not easily zooming directly forward in the viewport, for example). This browser also has the odd characteristic of unexpectedly animating the model, moving it slowly upward in the vertical axis as soon as it has loaded. With collision detection on, it does provide a suitably unpleasant thudding sound effect when you walk into something. As for the display of lights and textures, Community Place generally is somewhat better than Intervista's browser (compare fig. 4.19 with fig. 4.18), and it (Community Place) loads and navigates a file almost as quickly as the Intervista browser. This browser rates third place (this author's view).

FIGURE 4.19

Sample VRML file in Sony's Community Place.

Download the browser from www.sony.com. Community Place does not install automatically over Live3D in Netscape. You must manually remove or rename the Live3D DLL file in the Netscape\Navigator\plug-ins folder after Community Place is installed. It has no uninstall program; if you want to get Live3D or another browser back again, you must manually restore what you removed or renamed.

Cosmo Player, from Silicon Graphics

The VRMLOUT plug-in was originally developed and tested with the Cosmo browser in mind. Cosmo's capability to display 3DS MAX lights and textures is much better than that of the other browsers reviewed here. The drawbacks to Cosmo are its speed—it can be extremely slow—and its navigation tools, which are quite primitive compared to those that come with World View and Community Place. You must navigate by manipulating the navigation control in the dashboard rather than moving the mouse in the viewport itself. The display quality is so much more faithful to the original, however, that Cosmo receives a qualified number one recommendation from this author.

Download the browser at www.sgi.com. Cosmo automatically installs itself over Live3D in Netscape.

FIGURE 4.20

Sample VRML file in Silicon Graphics' Cosmo Player.

Live3D 2.0 from Netscape

As this book is being written, Netscape 3.0 still ships with Live3D 1.0, which is strictly a VRML 1.0 browser. In January 1997, however, you could download a new version—Live3D 2.0—that does support VRML 2.0. Future releases of Netscape will have Live3D 2.0 built in.

Live3D is a very attractive, very fast browser with good light- and texture-display capabilities (see fig. 4.21). This is really the browser to use for general-purpose web surfing, although you might want to try Cosmo to see whether you prefer it. This browser also receives the number one recommendation from the author.

Download Live3D 2.0 at www.netscape.com.

FIGURE 4.21

Sample VRML file in Netscape's Live 3D 2.0.

The Best of the Web

What makes a great VRML world, given the limitations of today's technology? This section points you to some of today's best VRML web sites and discusses some general characteristics of these top-flight VRML implementations.

Oz Inc. (*www.oz.com*)

The Oz site worlds show what can be done with simple geometry and complex texture maps—a theme covered earlier in this chapter. Figure 4.22 shows the excellent use of lighting in one of the worlds from this site.

NOTE

The Oz site has the best VRML worlds the author has found so far.

FIGURE 4.22

Stage world from the Oz Inc. site.

Unfortunately, the Oz worlds were not modeled in 3DS MAX. They are exported for VRML 1.0 and are best viewed with Live3D. If you use Cosmo Player to open some of these worlds, an error results because of the incompatible sound systems.

The Genesis Project (*www.3d-design.com/livespace/ genesis*)

The Genesis Project, an ongoing demonstration site for VRML features, operates under the auspices of *3D Design* magazine. It provides a good example of a world created with 3DS MAX and VRMLOUT, showing simple but effective use of animation and texture mapping. At present, this world can only be browsed with Intervista's World View.

Intervista's VRML Circus (*www.intervista.com/products/worldview/demos/index.shtml*)

This site has some nice character animation, probably done with the Character Studio plug-in (see fig. 4.23).

FIGURE 4.23

Animated juggler from Intervista's site.

Steel Studio Landscape (*www.marketcentral.com/vrml/gallery.wrl*)

This world provides a great example of the use of scale. Try zooming back from the initial camera view (see fig. 4.24) to see the real extent of the objects that make up the scene.

FIGURE 4.24

The Steel Studio landscape.

Construct's Stratus Gallery (*www.construct.net/stratus/*)

The Stratus gallery is an elegant way of displaying 2D artwork in a 3D world (see fig. 4.25). The gallery shows good use of many different camera viewpoints (one for each canvas hung in the gallery).

FIGURE 4.25

Artwork hanging in the Stratus gallery.

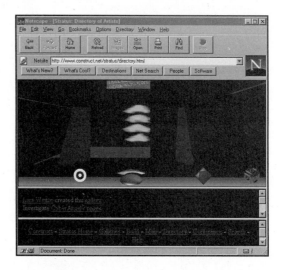

For a list of other notable VRML sites, refer to the Ch4bkmk.htm bookmarks file on the *Inside 3D Studio MAX Volume II* CD-ROM.

In Practice: Modeling for VRML and the Web

- **VRML's bright future.** VRML is an open standard that provides an evolving framework for 3D artists. The combination of 3DS MAX, the VRMLOUT plug-in, and VRML 2.0 browsers such as Cosmo and Live3D makes it possible for you to create truly interactive environments you can share with others through the medium of the World Wide Web. If you are an architect, for example, you can point potential clients to models they can walk through. If you are a game designer, you can set up spaces where users can play against one another online. VRML has tremendous potential for many applications.

- **Modeling techniques.** You can use many simple techniques to keep down the size of your scenes so that when you export them to VRML format, they load quickly and perform well. These techniques include: reducing the number of segments in primitives, deleting unnecessary faces, optimizing objects, and using instances.

- **The VRMLOUT plug-in.** The VRMLOUT plug-in enables you to export VRML 2.0-compatible worlds from 3DS MAX scenes. It even supports some VRML 2.0 features not yet available in any browser. Adding the VRMLOUT helpers is a simple process, but you can create some powerful effects with them (multiple clickable trigger objects and 3D sound, for example).

- **Think VRML.** Creating scenes for display and interaction on the World Wide Web is essentially different from creating scenes for film and video or CD-ROM. You always have to think about the limitations of the medium and how to make the most of them. "Thinking VRML" also means trying to visualize how people will relate to the worlds you create, and how they will experience them and navigate through them, all of which implies cooperation and sharing—and that's what the Web is all about.

Please contact the author via his web site and let him know about the new VRML sites you have enjoyed exploring or, especially, those you have created yourself.

IMAGE BY ERIC C. PETERSON

Chapter 5

by Eric C. Peterson

TECHNICAL MODELING FOR ENGINEERING VISUALIZATION

What constitutes "technical" modeling? That question, presented

to a dozen different animators, may well elicit a dozen different

answers. In a general sense, technical modeling describes any

number of animation and rendering disciplines more concerned

with the quantitatively accurate representation or duplication of

an event than with the artistic or interpretive elements.

Computer Aided Design (CAD) tools such as AutoCAD and Cadkey are designed as technical modeling packages. They also incorporate specialized tools—dimensioning engines, symbol libraries, and plotter drivers, for example—optimized for the technical drawing and illustration task. CAD tools, however, often don't provide the high-end rendering capabilities typical of dedicated rendering packages, and few provide the animation capabilities increasingly in demand in technical presentations and documentation.

Toward that end, the technical illustrator has two options: to use rendering and animation plug-ins or add-ons for the modeling and drafting software; or to use purpose-built rendering and animation software, separate and distinct from the design and drafting system. Because add-ons for the drafting software frequently cost as much as a purpose-built package by itself—and are often limited in capability as well—turning to tools designed specifically for the rendering and animation task often makes more sense.

3D Studio MAX for Windows NT is the successor to the four iterations of 3D Studio for DOS. MAX doesn't incorporate every last feature of 3D Studio Release 4, whose CAD-like interface presented a gentle learning curve to many engineers, architects, and drafters, but MAX still provides a formidable array of modeling tools that supports precision work. In conjunction with MAX's vast array of animation and rendering tools directed toward supporting the artist, it presents an environment with few equals (or none).

This chapter covers the following technical modeling topics, especially as they apply to 3D Studio MAX:

- Technical modeling characteristics

- Purposes of technical modeling

- Why the intended audience for technical animations is unique

- Why technical animation is unique

- Typical technical modeling products

- A large technical proposal animation illustration project revealed

Characteristics and Purposes of Technical Modeling

Some aspects of technical modeling, rendering, or animation chores are common to the different applications in the genre. That is, some identifiable characteristics are associated with all technical applications. Others may be present in some applications, but not all. These characteristics include the following:

- The presentation of events in a specific and rigorous time sequence

- The duplication of the appearances of objects or locations with high quantitative accuracy

- The retention or simulation of the precise relationship between events or objects

- The presentation of information in a manner to facilitate instruction

- The presentation of information in a manner to facilitate immediate recognition of a particular and specific object, event, location, or relationship

- The use of Computer Aided Design system-generated data at any point in the development of the animation

Clearly, some of these characteristics describe other, nontechnical applications as well, especially some advertising efforts. A better job must be done of defining applications and audience. The next sections go into these areas in more detail.

The next few paragraphs present some very specific groups of applications that exhibit the characteristics just listed.

Legal Animation

The term *legal animation* usually evokes images of automobile accident reconstructions prepared for courtroom presentation. Although common, this is only one application of legal animation. Auto accident animations fall into a larger class of legal animation products whose purpose is to present the conclusions of the "expert witness"—usually an accident reconstructionist or forensic scientist skilled in the simulation and reconstruction of events, based on evidence.

Some experienced animators at this point will wonder at this chapter's use of the term "legal animation," when the trades usually term it "forensic animation." The distinction is this: the latter category does not include patent law animation, which is almost a purely educational tool and rarely reconstructive or interpretive.

A common misconception on the part of animators and legal representatives who have never used legal animation is that the animator becomes the expert witness or that the animator performs the services of the forensic scientist or reconstructionist. This position is both dangerous and untenable, and the animator trying to enter this field is well advised to understand the relationship between the parties involved. In most cases, the animator works closely with the forensic scientist to implement the expert's opinion of just exactly how a specific sequence of events transpired. The degree to which the animation product accurately and precisely matches what the expert witness believes to have happened is a measure of the animation product's usefulness in the courtroom.

The animator, unless he or she is also the reconstructionist or forensic scientist, usually never sees the courtroom.

A second and growing application for legal animation is the use of animation products in patent litigation. Because the jury system cannot pick and choose members specifically suited for a particular trial, rarely is the jury chosen to sit in judgment for a complex technical patent litigation case well versed in the technical issues involved. In these cases, the expert witnesses for each side—usually engineers or scientists—may work closely with animators to construct graphic representations of processes or mechanisms to demonstrate in the simplest possible fashion why the processes at issue are alike or different. When the parties to the litigation present complex technical issues to the jury in this way, the jurors are able to reach an informed decision without necessarily understanding the intricacies of the underlying technology.

Technical Documentation

In the design and construction of complex equipment and systems, the creation of the documentation may precede the actual existence of the equipment by weeks, months, or even years. Particularly in the delivery of specialized equipment to the government, milestones for deliverable documentation products can be before any hardware has been built. Even in relatively small projects, for example, in which the total system cost barely reaches seven figures, the government may require preliminary technical documentation four to six months before the hardware is actually assembled. Today, animation and rendering products derived from the CAD design data frequently take the place of the photographs and hand-drawn line drawings of old.

Concurrent engineering describes a process in which all phases of a design effort—design, design for manufacturing, documentation, and tooling design—occur simultaneously. In support of these accelerated efforts, facilitated in part by advanced software design tools, other advanced software tools have appeared.

Syndesis Corporation, for example, publishes a range of products, collectively called Interchange, that translate modeling data formats. Many of the formats are CAD-based, and others support animation software. Newer products from other developers support very difficult translations, such as that between Parametric Technologies' Pro/Engineer and 3D Studio MAX. Given these tools, it is possible to isolate subassemblies of a product and proceed with documentation many months before tooling-up and manufacturing has even begun—by moving data from the design tool to the rendering tool. Given the quality of the output of modern rendering tools such as 3D Studio MAX, the result frequently costs even less than studio photography.

Technical Promotional Illustration

A related application of technical modeling involves rendering images of a product or piece of equipment for press release or advertisement even before a prototype exists. Marketing specialists may even recognize that a prototype may not be photogenic and may choose a rendering of the "production version" over costly construction of nonoperational stand-ins, once the standard for this sort of requirement.

NOTE

The author's experience is more closely aligned with one-off systems or systems destined for only a very limited production run. In such cases, the marketing effort is very highly directed and not truly comparable to that associated with a mass-market product. When industrial designers get involved, as is inevitable—and prudent—for products intended for larger production runs, the process is much more involved and more dependent on a cooperative effort between system designers, industrial designers, and marketers.

The computer model has the advantage of being much less costly than an actual nonworking prototype to modify as the design evolves. An additional advantage of computer models is that they are inherently easier—as digital products—to graft into artwork or advertising copy.

Technical Proposal Illustration

Perhaps the widest use of technical animation and rendering is in the document known as the *technical proposal*. Throughout the defense and government research complex, and through much of commercial industry, the allocation of resources in support of new and original capital equipment depends in large part on the success of technical proposals.

The process works like this: Organization A decides it needs a multimillion dollar SuperWidget to do a particular job. The job might be cleaning nuclear waste tanks, removing the paint from aircraft as a prelude to overhaul, applying sealant to the seams in automobile bodies on the assembly line, sorting documents, or assembling terminals and the connected wiring into wiring harnesses. Whether organization A is private or government, it probably will first survey potential suppliers, perhaps prequalify a subset of those, and finally solicit quotes from those it determines are qualified to bid.

The quoting process is much more than faxing a price figure to the solicitor. A primary component of the bidding process is to convince the solicitor that the bidding firm has the know-how and experience to design, build, test, and deliver a successful design. This process usually includes detailed cost estimates broken down to the level of major components in the equipment, preliminary designs, detailed designs of critical subassemblies, resumes of critical development and test personnel, development schedules, and quite possibly an animated portrayal of the equipment in operation.

Bidders quite often invest hundreds (or even thousands) of man-hours in a large technical proposal. Compared to that, the effort involved in generating a technical rendering or animation seems trivial.

Figures 5.1 through 5.4 depict illustrations prepared for or from technical proposal animations. Figure 5.1 represents a set of equipment modules selected to perform a testing operation. At the time this image was created, some of these components did not yet exist, and yet the potential client was interested in the appearance of them.

FIGURE 5.1

This is modular testing equipment, some of which does not yet exist.

Figure 5.2 depicts a modular testing system for automobile components. Note the safety covers in various positions, the storage position for the keyboard, and the detailed computer housing whose manufacturer is identifiable based on case characteristics alone. These features were essential because the soliciting firm for this system uses an approved vendor list and only a limited number of computer suppliers, and because the request for quotes specifically mandated some operational features.

FIGURE 5.2

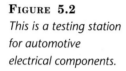

*This is a testing station
for automotive
electrical components.*

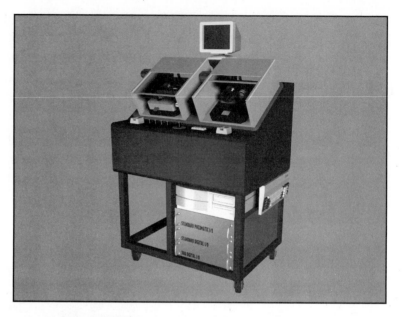

Figure 5.3 represents the final iteration of an avionics test set delivered to
the United States Air Force. This illustration, also part of an animation, is
actually the fourth iteration of the design—yet was still prepared months
before the system was assembled. The system designers used earlier versions of this rendering prepared during the proposal phase to present control
layouts and to address safety issues.

FIGURE 5.3

*This is an avionics test
set for fighter aircraft
line replaceable units.*

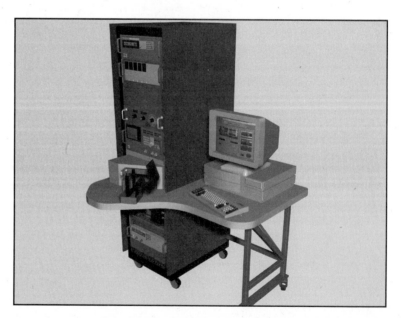

Figure 5.4 represents a lunar soil sampler, a concept for a study project that would have compared various approaches to this application.

FIGURE 5.4

A proposed deployable lunar soil sampler rests on a simulated lunar surface.

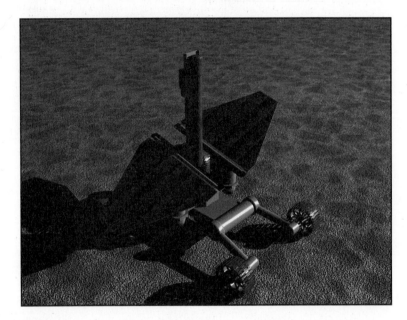

The Unique Audience for Technical Animations

The unusual thing about technical renderings is that the audience most likely contains experts who are more than happy to tear the work apart. Thus, the illustrations and animations must convey not only the appearance of a particular system, but also that the system is well thought-out and solidly designed. This also holds true for legal animation, in which opponent experts do everything possible to discredit your work—the manner in which it adheres to the reconstructionist's timing schedule, and the degree to which the vehicles or mechanisms resemble the real things.

When used as a documentation tool, the work is probably part of an evaluated deliverable that must satisfy the client in terms of accuracy, completeness, and ease-of-understanding. Often, a defense client evaluates an illustrated technical manual by providing the manual and the system described to a competent, but unprepared, technician. The efficiency with which the technician tears down, repairs, or reassembles the hardware is taken to be a measure of the completeness of your illustrations.

When used as a sales tool, the technical animation is reviewed by technical and management experts whose job is to compare your work with other work aimed at the same high-quality target. Any shortcoming or inconsistency stands out and could cost your employer millions of dollars.

This scrutiny differs completely from that faced by the entertainment industries that use computer animation. Not surprisingly, therefore, the ranks of technical illustrators derive in part from drafters and engineers rather than from artists and sculptors. Yet the tools used are the same and the end product, to the uninitiated, is similar. The purpose of this chapter is to describe some typical but advanced aspects to the construction of a technical model, providing an example to engineers and sculptors alike.

Why Technical Animation Is Unique

The foregoing discussions presented some qualitative, loosely example-driven reasons why technical animation is different from entertainment applications. Loose examples and general discussions are fine, but all the arm-waving in the world cannot adequately describe precisely the reasons that technical animation represents a separate discipline, unless it's possible to somehow classify and categorize the differences in techniques and applications. These differences fall into identifiable categories:

- Schedule requirements
- Precision
- Recognition
- Running in slow motion
- Typical technical modeling products

Schedule Requirements

Most animators would cringe at the requirement that a model have millimeter-level accuracy. Taken in the context of a large defense project, that is not a handicap. It isn't unusual for an animation or still image created in support of a multimillion dollar proposal to itself cost hundreds of man hours. Models frequently begin in CAD systems, and animators may actually have precise geometry they transform into renderable models.

A related consideration is that a technical animation may cost many, many times what a similar entertainment animation costs, not only because of the direct labor involved but also because of the labor spent defining and verifying requirements. Into this category also fall site surveys, library models laboriously digitized by service bureaus, and tedious conversion or construction of new models.

During the preliminary design of a nuclear reactor containment vessel refurbishment device, for example, one bidder devoted approximately 120 hours of engineering labor—at loaded rates approaching $100 an hour—converting one complex set of drawings into a single renderable model for use in proposal illustrations. A single illustration wound up in the proposal. Thus, the generation of one illustration from one complex model cost almost $12,000. In a gaming application, such expensive models may be crucial to gameplay, used over and over again in many scenes or used in vital plot-driven animations. For the purposes of one technical proposal, the single illustration presented a design—already laid out in detail in both text and schematic—so that the nontechnical evaluators would better understand the presentation.

Precision Counts

It isn't unusual for an accident reconstructionist to work not in frames not in fields, but in increments of tenths or even thousandths of a single second. No game animator ever set keys in increments of .001 second, but an accident reconstructionist who stands up in court and swears to this level of accuracy requires his animators to implement precisely the motion his calculations determine to be most likely.

NOTE

This is a vitally important point not only for animators who may not be closely familiar with MAX's advanced timekeeping features, but also for plug-in developers (or any potential plug-in developers) perusing this text. Plug-ins, especially plug-ins that can *ever* be used in forensic animation, absolutely must be subframe aware. That is, the plug-in must provide for those cases in which the animator attempts subframe keying with the plug-in. This isn't idle speculation. The author developed the algorithmic elements for Make Tracks for 3D Studio Release 4 and for MAXTrax for MAX. The original algorithm called for frame-specific keying, or for the creation of as many as 30 steps in the procedural trail per second. For applications using this

continues

plug-in, such as the electronics superstore gift-wrapping animation seen in the southwestern U.S. during the 1995 Christmas season, frame-keying is fine because no close-up, no slow-motion, and no subframe examination of the effect is ever important. A customer reported late in 1996 that MAXTrax would not satisfy his reconstructionist client, however, because a close-up of a skid mark generated with the utility failed to depict the marks accurately to the nearest .010 second. Because of the extremely high speeds involved in the accident, and because of the stakes involved in the lawsuit, the reconstructionist wanted to see skid marks accurate to the nearest four to six inches—a requirement at odds with the .033 second resolution of a plug-in designed to update only at integral field counts. The MAXTrax algorithm was modified to accommodate updates at nonintegral value keyframes.

One could argue that this makes MAX a better technical tool in one respect than 3D Studio Release 4 because no subframe keying was possible with the DOS versions—*and* the argument would be correct.

Recognition Counts

In a game animation, it is frequently important that an object resemble a class of objects, or that it implement an art director's vision of how a particular object must appear. In technical animation, each model must often be CAD-accurate so that no question whatsoever exists about accuracy or operation. A visual difference, no matter how slight, that interferes with apparent viability or causes the slightest doubt on the part of witnesses, can be fatal to the goal of the animation product.

Running in Slow Motion

Unlike entertainment products, in which a single frame with a glitch may be left in the final cut because no single viewer will catch it, a technical animation will be run in slow motion over and over and over again. And this will happen, repeatedly, in front of expert witnesses scouring your work for problems, usually on a projection big-screen television. Each field artifact has to be cleaned up. Each impulsive motion with no physical analog has to be smoothed. No transient visibility or smoothing artifacts are permitted— vastly different than the scrutiny directed at a product that might wind up as a 320-by-200 pixel lossy compressed AVI.

Typical Technical Modeling Products

Legal animation is almost always just that—technical modeling and precision keyframing in support of full animations. Technical proposal illustrations, on the other hand, are almost always still images and— if the project is large enough—animations as well. In support of consistency and the highest possible quality, the models used for both products are usually the same, resulting in uncharacteristically (for other genres) detailed animations. Still images, the animator may be certain, will be blown up by presenters into overhead transparencies, posters, report covers, and at the very least 8½-by-11 inch glossies. No detail remains hidden.

Modeling for a Technical Proposal

Figure 5.5 depicts the illustration effort accompanying a relatively large ($1,000,000 range) technical proposal effort. The rendered output of the models pictured was presented on everything from giveaway mousepads to overhead transparencies to 11-by-17 inch report covers. Additionally, a full animation of the robotic workcell using precise timing and actual motion programming was required by the solicitation, supplied in high-quality video format for distribution by the client within his organization.

NOTE

The term *workcell* may be a new term to some readers. It will not be a new term to the large percentage of programmers and developers, however, who derive in no small part from the ranks of roboticsts and animation engineers. The mathematics of 3D graphics are the same as the mathematics of robotic motion control. Workcell describes a frequently modular, or *cellular*, work space in which a robot and its closely related tooling is installed in a production environment.

Figure 5.5 depicts a complex robotic system whose function is to remanufacture fighter aircraft canopies. The system shown here is the basis for the technical portion of this chapter.

FIGURE 5.5

A canopy processing system consisting of industrial robot and custom-engineered components is shown as its designers intend that it be installed.

Unfortunately, for reasons of confidentiality, a discussion of the precise function of the workcell cannot be included here. The workcell facilitates the remanufacturing of fighter aircraft canopies damaged by any of a variety of events. Toward that end, equipment in the workcell moves the canopy around and the robot moves a tool over the components of the canopy. Fortunately, any additional information is irrelevant to the discussion of this scene's creation.

Purpose of the Model

Figure 5.5 depicts the third iteration of the model. A preliminary model, created during early discussions with the client, served as a reference point from which both the client and the designers could build. The need for safety equipment was the first to surface, and the preliminary model served as a base into which the safety features of the client's choice could be incorporated. Note the vertical optical interrupt towers at each corner of the equipment pit. Details, such as the collocated control station and operator chair, came later to provide a visual indication of the system's user-friendliness and of the relative comfort in which the (unionized) operator would work.

System design consultants also recommended placing the system in a pit to minimize the visual impact of the large, powerful central robot (in fact, quite a frightening piece of equipment). Interestingly enough, the elevation of the control and observation deck with respect to the machinery has significant psychological implications for management reviewers, not technically educated, who might have seen demonstrations of this same robot at another facility.

Note the lettering visible on the robot arm. This was vital to the system concept because research indicated that this brand name was favored by the client as an equipment supplier. It was also known that a competitor had advanced the use of a different robot arm less suited to the application and with logistical support requirements far less convenient to the end user. Thus, the detail visible in the rendering is a subtle indicator to the reviewers—even those cost and logistical support management types who would recognize the *name* of the equipment if not the *shape* of the model—that this supplier had done more and better planning in the preliminary design of the workcell.

The renderings, as they evolve in keeping with actual design changes, will likely be used in end-user training manuals and videos as well. Given the cost of such a system, using available computer simulations to provide training and orientation tools makes far more sense than taking downtime to present or film the actual hardware.

Components of the Scene

This is a complex robotic workcell. It accurately represents the actual design. It lacks, however, visually distracting but mechanically trivial features such as cable management hardware and pneumatic and hydraulic plumbing. Fortunately, these elements are as unnecessary as they are unsightly and tedious to model.

Robot

The robot is a large standard industrial unit typical of heavy-duty welding, lifting, and general-purpose process machines available in Europe and Japan. No U.S. firm manufactures comparable machines. The machine illustrated is a Staubli Automation RX-170L, the heaviest, largest unit offered by the firm that some years ago purchased Unimation from Westinghouse. Fortunately for the animators, this is a simple kinematic linkage with no closed four-bar structures that—until 3D Studio Releases 4 and MAX—were the bane of modelers and animators alike. Furthermore, the links of the machine are closed and solid, formed from relatively simple primitives and loft/surfrev shapes in combination. Note that detailed drawings of this machine were available to the modeler, but CAD models were not.

Its appearance was critical to the success of the renderings because technical evaluators for the customer would recognize it instantly. Thus, a large effort ensured the accuracy of both the dimensions and materials used in the construction of the robot model.

The robot model makes heavy use of primitives, extended primitives, and custom lofts.

Robot Tool

The tool wielded by the robot is an accurate representation of an existing tool employed by similar systems in the field. Its design features are significant to process operation and critically important to the quality of the presentation. The level of detail is sufficient to support close-ups that would lose much of the remainder of the scene. The robot tool employs mostly primitives and surfrevs.

Aircraft Canopy

Even more important than the robot, the aircraft canopy is unique because of its size. In fact, it was the size of this canopy that dictated the use of the Staubli RX-170L because no other industrial machine of comparable configuration would reach the entire canopy. Note that both the canopy glass and frame are present, and that *both* surfaces of the glass are required to support close-ups and particle special effects added to the animation.

Although detailed drawings of the canopy were not available, a very large high-quality plastic model of the entire aircraft yielded a canopy digitized at critical points to provide the required geometry.

The aircraft canopy is a complex mesh formed from custom loft planning, Boolean operations, and multiple extrusions and reorganizations.

Support Hardware

The framework holding the canopy is an element of the design proposed by the supplier. It needs to be accurate to the extent that it is practical to build, does not interfere with robot motion, and attaches to the canopy at the mounting points specified by the client. The support hardware represents components fabricated from simple welded steel stock.

The hardware below the mounting frame is an accurate portrayal of similar hardware that exists in similar systems. There are large semicustom linear drives, notable because the only visible drive hardware is the accordioned flexible cover over each linear shaft and screw. There are also large rotary table drives, notable because the orientation of the motor is critical to system clearances.

Environment

Various design considerations suggested that the system be mounted in a pit. For the concrete enclosure, aesthetics and practical considerations mandated chamfering the upper edge of the pit to reduce generation of debris and to facilitate sealing the concrete with a paint. The safety railing is more than simple welded pipe because similar systems have become showpieces for other end users, with visitors constantly moving through for demonstrations. The safety systems mandated by law and prudence are built into heavy structural supports designed to integrate visually with the appearance of the robot and canopy handler.

The desk and chair are library components from the Kinetix Commercial Props Compact Disk. Because these meshes are copyrighted, they are omitted from the scene file on the *Inside 3D Studio MAX Volume II* CD. The chair was not modified. The desk was heavily modified to improve smoothing group consistency and to eliminate unnecessary faces. The materials of the desk also were changed.

The computer and associated peripherals were created by the modeler for another project and are, in fact, the same components depicted in figures 5.2 and 5.3. Remember that the shape of the computer had special significance for figure 5.2; here, it is just another computer.

Robot Construction

The robot exists as a linkage of six objects, each of which has unique construction requirements and features. Each represents a separate exercise in technical modeling. These objects are—in order from the base to the tool—the Robot Base, Waist, Upper Arm, Lower Arm, Main Wrist Link, Wrist Pitch Link, and Tool/Roll Link.

Robot Base

One of the most recognizable elements of the robot, and therefore one of the most critical to the success of the model, is the base. Figure 5.6 shows the base in the MAX interactive display's viewports. Note that this project's default viewports are not the standard default viewports; they are more closely akin to a CAD configuration in which the three orthographic views align properly in the American style.

FIGURE 5.6

The robot base mesh looks like this in the interactive display.

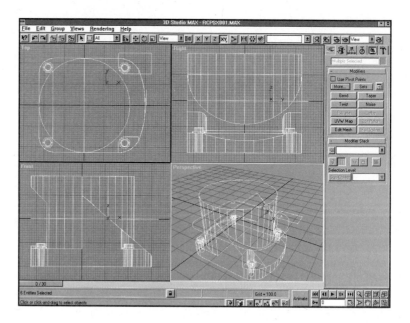

BUILDING THE ROBOT BASE

You build the base in several steps. Figure 5.7 shows the base shape imported from a CAD drawing.

NOTE

This robot, environment, and support system hardware has one common minimal dimension: five millimeters. Generally, five millimeters serves as a good basic value—a minimum resolution—for all the existing hardware and new design. Certainly the actual detailed design of the system employs a greater precision, but the value of five first came up because all the quoted robot dimensions were in multiples of five. From there, preliminary design of the support equipment moved along with the same resolution.

This is also a convenient unit because convenient snap grid sizes are in multiples of ten units.

Note that the projects do *not* redefine the basic units in the MAX setup to millimeters. There is no need to do this unless these meshes will be merged with other meshes built to scale later on. Changing MAX's system units setup is risky and something to be avoided. Using a *consistent* set of units is all that's necessary.

FIGURE 5.7
The robot base shapes look like this when the file loads.

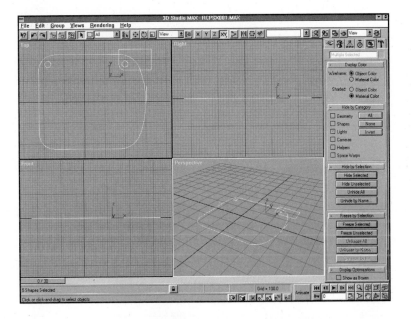

The robot base and source shapes are contained in the file RCPSX001.MAX on the accompanying CD. This is *not* the actual file taken from the complete scene, but rather a file built up specifically to illustrate the creation of the mesh from the component splines. Note that many of the modifiers applied will destroy the splines or incorporate them into a mesh. The sample file, as all other sample files in this chapter do, contains copies of the splines used and the finished object, frozen, so that you can follow along and use the complete object as a template.

1. Select the main shape only. Apply an Extrude modifier with a distance of 75 to the base cross section.

2. Apply an Optimize to the Extruded shape, with values of 10 for Face Threshold, 5 for Edge Threshold, and .25 for Bias. Turning on Auto Edge within the Optimize results in a faster regenerating base with no loss of resolution and is generally preferable, unless you want the edges delineating the sides of the base to remain visible. Figure 5.8 depicts the base at this point in its construction.

FIGURE 5.8

The robot base extrusion looks like this after step 2.

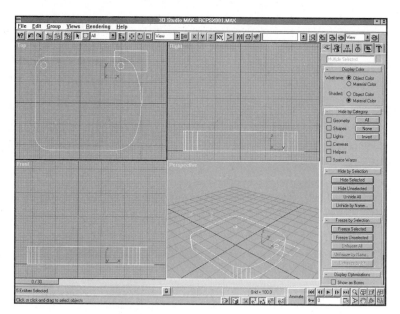

NOTE

Many regard what the exercise does next as unnecessary, undesirable, and poorly considered. MAX is a fantastic modeling tool and an even better animation tool. After the animator gets a shape in MAX to a point at which it is verifiably correct for a technical model, however, there is no reason to retain the history of the solid unless it is likely to be used elsewhere. Because subsequent operations include Edit Mesh steps and Booleans, a Collapse at this point loses little information but improves the stability of subsequent steps. You can use the Editable Mesh feature directly to bypass the overhead required by the use of Edit Mesh, but it *is* wise to retain all the history you might need until a part is complete and verifiably correct or until the part has passed a major milestone.

3. If you want, edit the object stack and do a Collapse All. Note that a Collapse All changes the object into an Editable Mesh type object. Editable Meshes give the animator full access to the tools formally available only under Edit Mesh, but without the overhead required by the Edit Mesh modifier.

4. Select the robot base object and use Display to turn off Edges Only.

5. Apply an Edit Mesh modifier to the robot base object, turn on Sub-Object, and select Edge. Then reconfigure the edges on the upper surface by using Divide and Turn until the result resembles figure 5.9. Some selections and the use of Visible and Invisible are also required. Note that the configuration of edges along the side is mirrored for the other side, which is not visible.

FIGURE 5.9
Edited robot base edges subsequent to step 5.

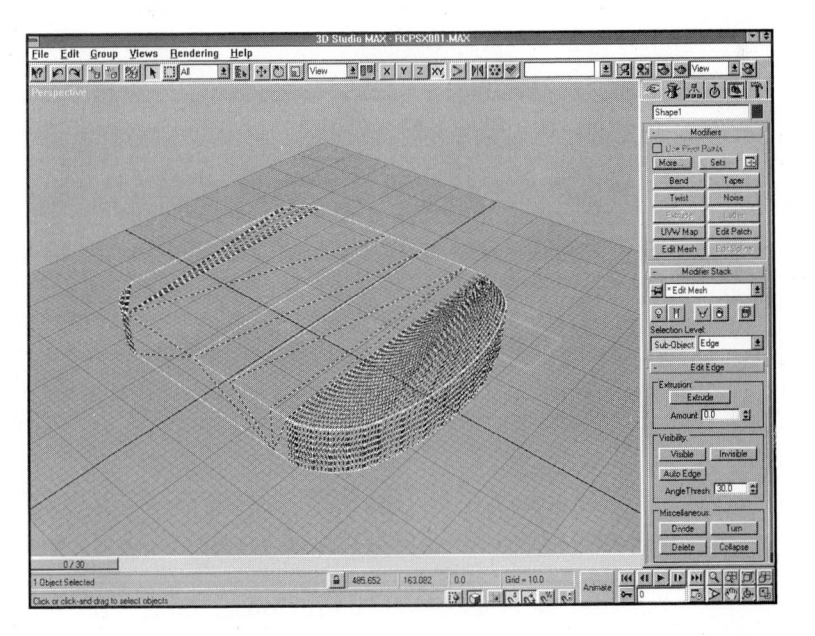

6. Select Sub-Object Vertex. From the Front view, use Selection Sets, Rotate, and Move to change the profile to that depicted in figure 5.10. Liberal use of Absolute Snap here on a grid of 10 units in each direction is very useful for placing the vertices correctly.

A Skew applied to the upper vertices of the rounded end, with a value of 117.5 at a direction of 0.0 along X, goes a long way toward shifting them properly. An Edit Stack here followed by a Collapse All speeds up evaluation somewhat, but be absolutely certain that the base is correct so far. Examine the Template object in the sample file for verification.

FIGURE 5.10

Edited robot base vertices after step 6.

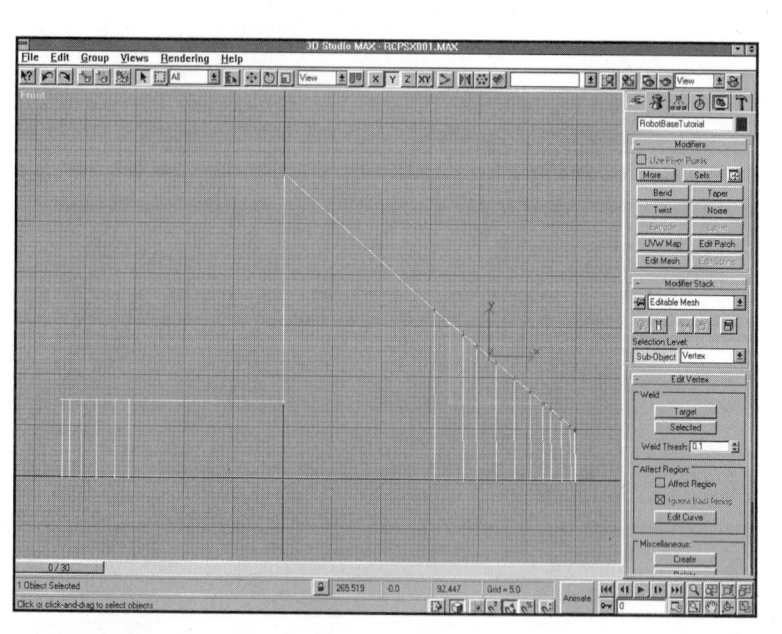

7. Use Absolute Snap to create a cylinder of radius 225 and height 305 with 36 sides, and place it over the frozen template. These dimensions are the same as those of the partial cylinder incorporated into the base. Note that you may have to create the cylinder and then modify it to get the exact dimensions. You may also have to rearrange your Snap priorities to get the cylinder to settle properly, or choose a particular edge when you move it. Using the top edge with High Snap Priority assigned to Grid works well and enables you to keep the 10-unit grid at this time.

8. Collapse the cylinder into an Editable Mesh and delete the faces of the bottom surface. They serve no useful purpose and consume unnecessary resources. A Cylinder does consume fewer resources than an Editable Mesh, but that point will soon be moot. The precise sequence here is, of course: Select, Modify, Edit Mesh, Sub-Object: Face, Crossing Off, Select Faces, Delete, Edit Stack, Collapse All.

9. Select the shape labeled BaseCutout and apply an Extrude modifier with a value of 400, using both end caps on and a single segment. Note that BaseCutout is a simple linear shape created by using Create Spline with a segmentation of 0. Move the resulting solid so that the midplane aligns approximately with the midplane of the base-in-progress. Use the Y-Axis Only button on the Move panel to move the cutout object in the Top viewport, thus preserving the precise relationship of the cutout to the cylinder.

NOTE

No, the cutout did *not* come from a CAD package. The cutout represents a cast-in feature of low precision. Because appearance and ease of construction are more important than precision for this particular feature, the cutout was constructed in MAX, using the base as a reference.

At this point, the interactive display should resemble figure 5.11.

FIGURE 5.11
This is the cutout in place after Step 9.

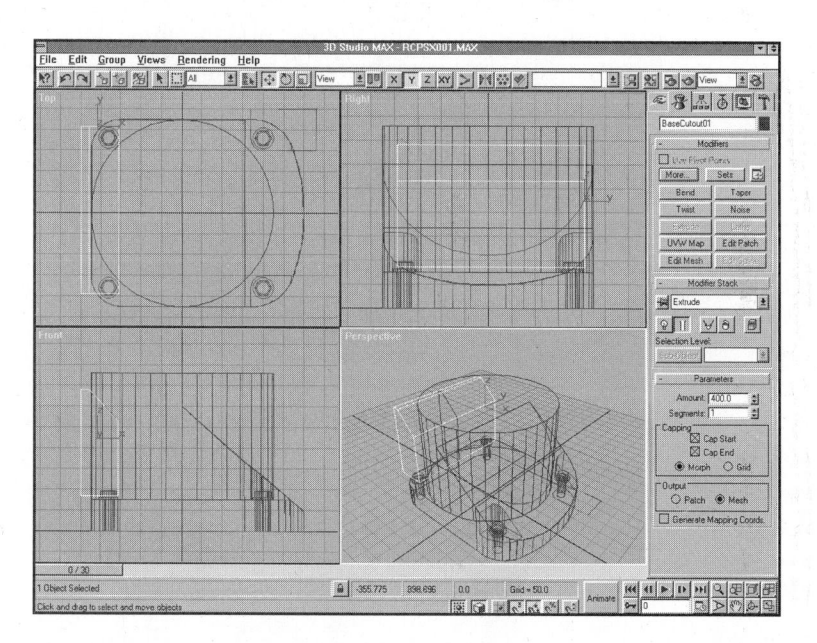

10. Select the cylinder. Use Create, Geometry, Compound Objects, Boolean to subtract the Cutout object from the cylinder. Then, having verified that the result is correct by comparing it against the template, use Modify, Edit Mesh, Edit Stack, Collapse All to reduce the Boolean to an Editable Mesh again. Note that in the absence of a template, you compare features to grid lines or use a ruler helper.

11. Most modelers skip this step or attempt to use a Boolean. A Boolean *fails*, however, because the bottom of the cylinder no longer exists. Use Modify, Editable Mesh, Sub-Object Edges to divide the edges of the cylinder coincident with the vertical edges of the wedge-shaped portion of the base object you've created so far. Move the two new vertices up in line with the top of the wedge, and then use Edge, Turn; Vertex, Move; or Vertex, Select; Skew; or Face, Delete to clean up the object so that it resembles figure 5.12. This is not necessarily the precise sequence required because the editing sequence can be iterative.

Generally speaking, the modeler needs to balance the complexity of the model with the prospect of having hidden portions of faces. Hidden faces—even partially hidden faces—increase rendering time. However, subdividing faces—either with the use of a Boolean operation or at the edge/vertex level—in order to reduce overlap and hidden surface area can overly complicate the mesh by creating a multiplicity of faces. In this case, move the edges of the cylinder up because it results in minimal increase in face count while reducing overlap. Modifying the faces of the sloped portion, however, is both unnecessary and undesirable because doing so only increases complexity while not reducing face overlap. Also, note that placing the cylinder vertices coincident with the back of the slope is critical for correct smoothing.

NOTE

Balancing face complexity with face overlap could be a quantitative problem, but the problem is far too complex to evaluate in a deterministic fashion in order to find the best solution to each modeling choice. Over time, the animator/modeler develops a "feeling" for what becomes worthwhile and for what isn't.

FIGURE 5.12
This is the modified cylinder Editable Mesh after step 11.

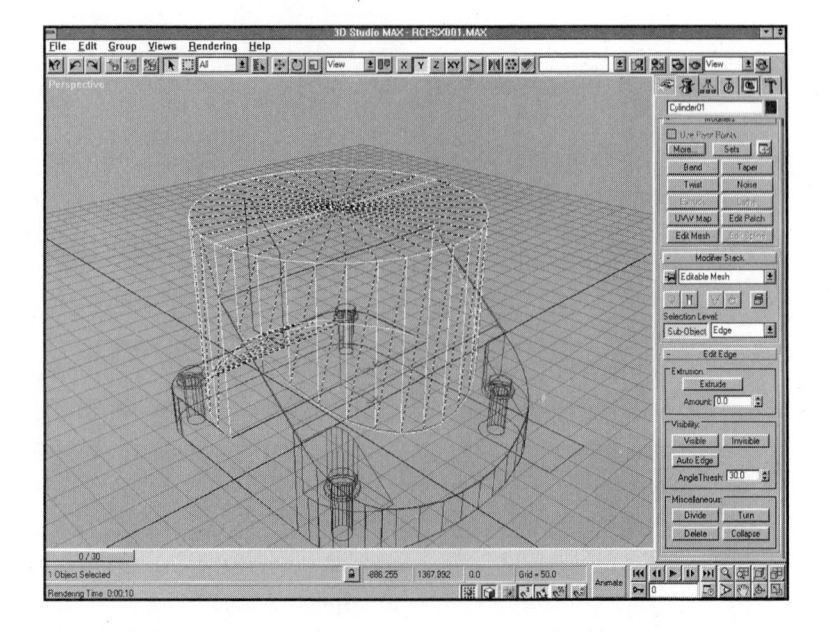

12. Attach the modified cylinder to the sloped base and select and weld the eight vertices—four from the cylinder, four from the wedge, at the four corners of the old upright, vertical surface of the wedge—by using a threshold of approximately .8 to 1. Select and delete the faces on the

back, vertical portion of the slope. Apply a Smooth modifier to the object with a default threshold, collapse the stack, hide the frozen template object, and do a sample render to verify the object so far. The important thing to look for is the lack of a visible break between the sides of the wedge and the cylinder. If breaks are visible in the curved forward lower edge of the base, make visible a few critical edges, and use Sub-Object: Face and MeshSmooth modifiers until the edge renders smoothly. This is also a good time to go over the mesh, using Vertex, Weld, Target to get rid of slivers of unnecessary geometry, and to clean up the object in general. Compare it to the template and collapse the stack.

At the two front corners of the sloped base are flats where installation bolts can tighten against a flat surface.

NOTE

There are two ways to install the hollows and the bolt holes that pierce the base. In the first method—the one used to create the template object—the animator must use Edge, Divide and Edge, Turn to split the model along the midplane. The Boolean operations necessary to form the holes and hollows are then performed on one half, and the finished half is mirrored to create a second finished half. The two finished halves are then attached and welded. This method results in a perfectly symmetrical model.

The other method is to mirror the smaller Boolean objects and to perform twice as many Boolean operations on the single whole object. This method is often faster than the first but has the following drawbacks:

- The model is not symmetrical.

- If the Boolean fails on one side, the animator must revert to the first method.

- If the Boolean doesn't fail, but generates unsightly mesh or smoothing artifacts, twice as many faces, edges, and vertices may need to be cleaned up manually.

The first drawback is often not truly a problem, but the more detail-minded may consider it a serious source of frustration if the mesh has to be modified later. Note that this tutorial could have instructed you (the animator) to split the robot base earlier in its construction if the first drawback were of paramount importance, but in most cases it's more a matter of preference than anything else.

13. Apply an Extrude modifier to the shape labeled NutPad. The value of 400, used for the last Extrude, serves here as well. Note that because this is another CAD-generated shape, substantial segmentation exists along the "straight" edges. This isn't a problem for now; read the following tips on Booleans to understand why.

TIP

Booleans fail for a number of reasons. The most serious problems associated with Boolean operations, or those that are most likely to cause failures, are as follows:

■ Coincident, unwelded vertices

■ Any edge belonging to only a single face that participates in the Boolean intersection

■ Normals of adjacent, essentially parallel faces that are opposed in direction

■ Multiple, re-entrant intersections (the intersection of a pincushion with the collection of all pins assembled into one object, for example)

Generally speaking, a Boolean operation between two objects—both well-constructed, with complete, enclosed volumes, uniform normal direction, and welded vertices, where the intersection between the surfaces of the two can be described as a single, closed curve—is least likely to cause a Boolean failure.

TIP

Generally speaking, welding all the vertices of the two operands prior to performing a Boolean considerably improves the chances that the Boolean will succeed.

TIP

The Boolean algorithm implemented in 3D Studio MAX has certain fundamental limitations. By planning ahead, however, you can avoid problems with these limitations. Ordinarily, subtracting a simple object from a complex object may cause an undesirable loss of mesh resolution at the intersection under certain circumstances. That is, cutting a box with no segmentation into a convoluted surface may distort the surface of the convoluted surface along the edges of the intersection with the box. The problem is very difficult to duplicate reliably and, interestingly, is generally not a problem with default objects like GSpheres. The problem seems more common when the surface of higher resolution is open (even though the open edges are not involved in the Boolean) or when the surface of higher resolution has substantially higher mesh segmentation in one direction than the other.

14. Move the extruded cutout into position in the Front viewport by using only the Y-Axis Only button. Note that, at this point, the template should be Frozen again to avoid selecting it unnecessarily.

15. In the Top viewport, make a mirrored copy of the extruded cutout symmetrically about the midplane of the base so that the second cutout aligns with the finished cutout on the other side of the template.

TIP

When you prepare shapes and splines specifically to be extruded into Boolean operands, use Snap liberally on the vertices that will have no part in the final operations. In the cutout just extruded, for example, the outer and forward edges are both well clear of the base geometry and are both aligned with the snap grid. Thus, placement of the cutout object prior to the Boolean is simplified because at least two of the edges align with the snap grid.

This is an important point: Boolean operations frequently remove temporary features. Any temporary feature can be built and placed to make the process as convenient as possible for the animator. Edges and bounding dimensions that need not appear in the final model can be placed as alignment tools.

16. Select the Robot Base object and Boolean it with the two cutout objects in succession, selecting "subtract" from the option roll-up in the compound object/Boolean menu. Collapse the final object into an Editable Mesh after you verify the dimensions and placement against the template master.

17. Note that the intersections of the cutouts with the base have created numerous vertices around the fillets in the cutout. Applying a MeshSmooth at Face level to eliminate hidden lines cleans up this excess resolution. Collapsing the object again after using Display to unhide the hidden lines, and examining the mesh minimizes the resulting overhead of the Base Mesh. Render a sample image after unfreezing and hiding the Template object. Some manual cleanup of edge visibility, coincident vertex welding, and edge orientation is probably unavoidable. Be prepared to spend a little time here cleaning up the mesh, especially around the two Booleaned cutouts.

18. Optional steps: If the robot will never appear without its mounting bolts, the mounting holes don't need to be cut into the base. Two circular splines, RobotHole1 and 2, are already in the sample file, ready to Extrude, Move, Mirror, and Boolean into the base. It's important to move the resulting cylinders below the plane of the bottom of the base and to make them long enough to pierce the base completely, but otherwise there should be few problems.

19. The bolts are simple lofts between hexagonal and circular curves of identical vertex counts. The washers are cylinders. A simple goldish metallic material duplicates the alodyned finish of very high-grade structural bolts.

Figure 5.13 depicts the finished robot base with mounting bolts. Note that you don't have to cut the mounting holes into the base because the bolt heads and washers, of course, cover the bolt holes.

FIGURE 5.13
This is the finished robot base.

Canopy Construction

The aircraft canopy is one of the most difficult, complex technical models an animator might ever have to create. Not only is it essential that the canopy assembly flow in smooth curves, it must also resemble as closely as possible an actual canopy with precise dimensional constraints. Worse, because the object is mostly transparent, the detail of the inner surface shows through in many views. This object requires complex loft, deformation fit, Boolean, and vertex and edge-level manipulation.

1. Load the file RCPSX002.MAX from the *Inside 3D Studio MAX Volume II* CD. Note that this file follows the same format as the others: A frozen Template object resides in the file for reference, and all the necessary shapes are present as well. In the case of the canopy, the shapes derived from CAD data and moved from there to 3D Studio Release 4 via a DXF import for minor cleanup, and from there to 3D Studio MAX. Figure 5.14 shows the interactive display immediately after this file is loaded.

FIGURE 5.14

Canopy shapes in interactive display look like this.

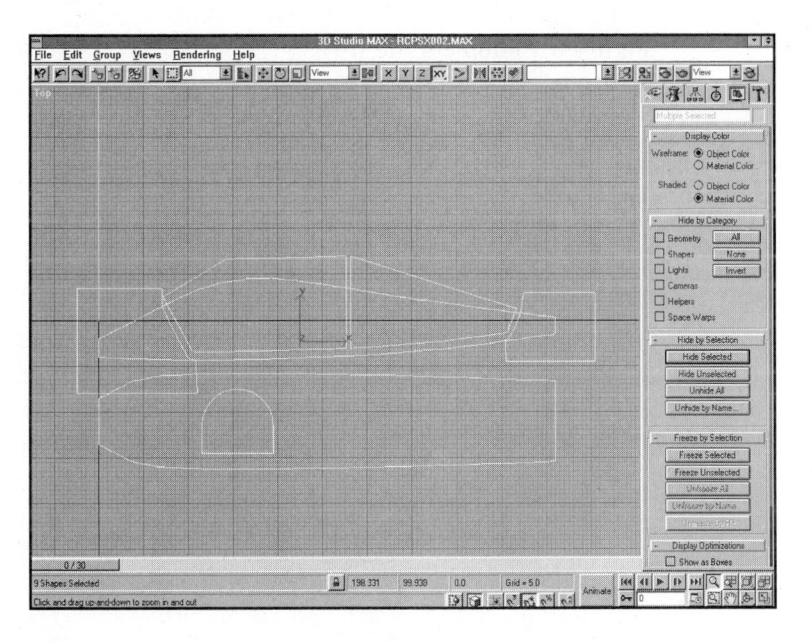

2. Use Select by Name in the toolbar to select CanopySideActual. This is the actual CAD-derived profile of the aircraft canopy assembly, the frame of the windscreen, and the transparent material together. Note the difficult fit shape inherent in this profile: the fillets at the bottom corners, the sharp edges at the upper corners. The requirements are further complicated by the need for a varying cross-section that, more than anything else, resembles sections taken from the same curve as it traverses the length of the canopy. Note most especially that the side profile is the only shape that represents the true profile of a required object in this file.

TIP

One of the biggest and most frequent mistakes a modeler can make is to try to build a complex or difficult shape in too few steps. MAX possesses incredible modeling features, but trying to use one or another to implement too many features in great, sweeping operations is predestined to fail. Trying to loft the canopy section shown within fit curves identical to true top and side profiles, for example, would squeeze the section at the ends into unnatural, contorted shapes. Laboriously building multiple sections gets better— but still not correct— results. *Never* be afraid to take three, four, five, or more steps to get a solid near a finished step. Plan for the operations ahead of time and they will not seem so great a burden.

One such plan-ahead operation is *overlofting*, or extending the Loft object on either end of the required geometry in preparation for later Booleans or editing. That technique is presented here in the second technical exercise of this chapter.

3. Select and examine the shape called CanopySideExtended. Note that this shape is derived from the true CAD-based side profile, with a few critical modifications. First, the fillets and sharp edges have been merged into smoothly flowing lines that terminate at either end at blunt segments with sharp corners, top and bottom. The precise dimensions of the blunt ends are unimportant. In fact, by creating the ends along grid lines and fixing the corners at grid intersections, the animator can move and reposition the shape easily, using the Snap system.

4. Select and examine the shape called CanopyTopExtended. Note that no "Actual" version exists in this file because it is unnecessary to the exercise. If the section and the cuts made later with Boolean operations are correct, there is no need for one because a comparison of the final solid and the actual side view is enough to verify a correct build. As with the extended side profile, the CanopyTopExtended spline derives from actual CAD data derived from the digitized model and extended into smoothly flowing lines beyond the actual top profile, terminating at blunt ends with sharp corners on either side. The CAD drawings of the top and side profiles began aligned. As the top profile was modified and as the revised side profile grew in length, the original segments of the splines remained unchanged, and hence, aligned. The CanopyTopExtended spline extends precisely the length of the CanopySideExtended spline, and the ends of each are aligned at the same grid lines.

5. Create a line segment as long as the extended profiles in a convenient position.

6. Select the CanopySection spline and use Create, Geometry, Loft Object. Use the Get Path button and select the line segment. Use the default options, but turn on Skin in the Display roll-up area so that the Loft object is visible.

7. Select Modify while the Loft object is selected and open the Deformations roll-up, an area available only in the Modify branch. Select Fit, turn Symmetry Off, unlock Aspect Ratio, and use Get Shape to select the extended top profile.

8. Switch deformation fit curves and use Get Shape to select the extended side profile.

9. Use the Generate Path button. At this point, you may want to switch to a Shaded viewport to preview the canopy. Your Loft object should look something like the one in figure 5.15.

FIGURE 5.15
This is how the preliminary canopy loft appears after step 9.

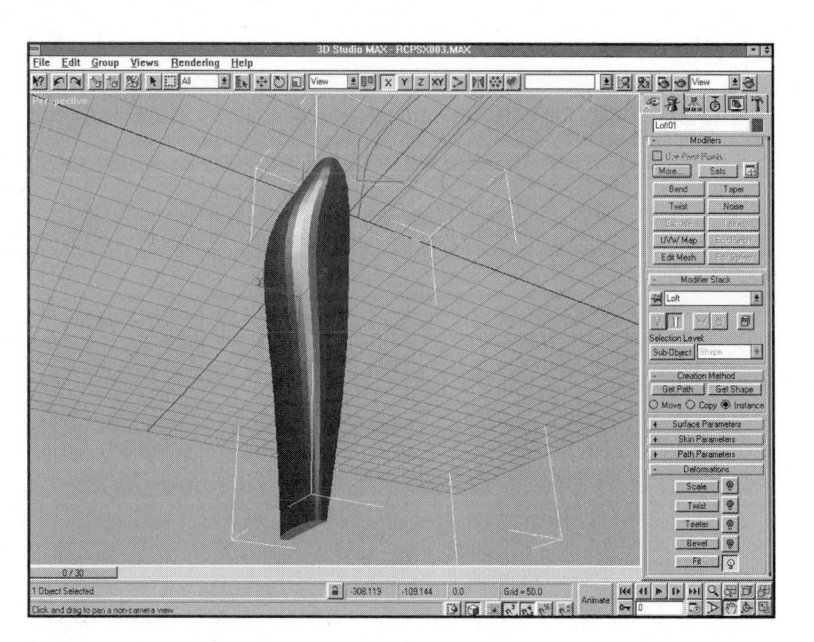

10. Much of the extra resolution in this object represents a carryover from the CAD-generated splines that imported as Bézier objects. Unfortunately, this Canopy object at this point is so complex that adding modifiers slows the evaluation pipeline to such a degree that the scene becomes unwieldy. Apply an Edit Mesh modifier after verifying that the loft matches the profiles from the CAD data, and Collapse the object by using Edit Stack. This may take a few minutes on slower machines.

11. Apply an Optimize modifier with values of 1, 1, and .1, and then a Smooth with a default value of 30 degrees and Auto Smooth checked. Collapse the mesh again when the Shaded viewport shows a good, clean mesh.

12. Notice that the mesh is asymmetrical. This is both a handicap and a blessing. It is a handicap because the animator should correct the asymmetry in this highly technical mesh, and a blessing in that subsequent Boolean operations will produce slightly different results on the two halves, enabling the modeler to pick and choose parts of the mesh based on their appearance and Boolean solutions.

13. Hide the deformation fit curves and the section; they are no longer necessary to the construction of the canopy. Leave the trim splines and the extended side view visible.

14. Numerous Booleans are required. First, use Edit, Clone to make a copy of the canopy object, select both the original and the copy, and move both into place in the Top view so that they are aligned with the CanopySideExtended spline. You must be creative with Snap priorities to align the solids with the deformation curve. Now deselect one copy and hide the other. From now on, always be sure to have two copies of the canopy, one of which is protected and unmodified. Booleans destroy the separable histories of meshes and are difficult to undo; always make backup objects before proceeding.

15. One after another, select and Extrude the two glass cutouts and the fore and aft trim splines. Select the set of four extrusions and move them into place in the Right view so that they straddle the canopy. One by one, use Edit Mesh and Edit Stack to collapse the four extrusions into Editable Meshes. At this point, the scene should look like that shown in figure 5.16.

FIGURE 5.16

Canopy solids are aligned with splines in this view of the display subsequent to step 15.

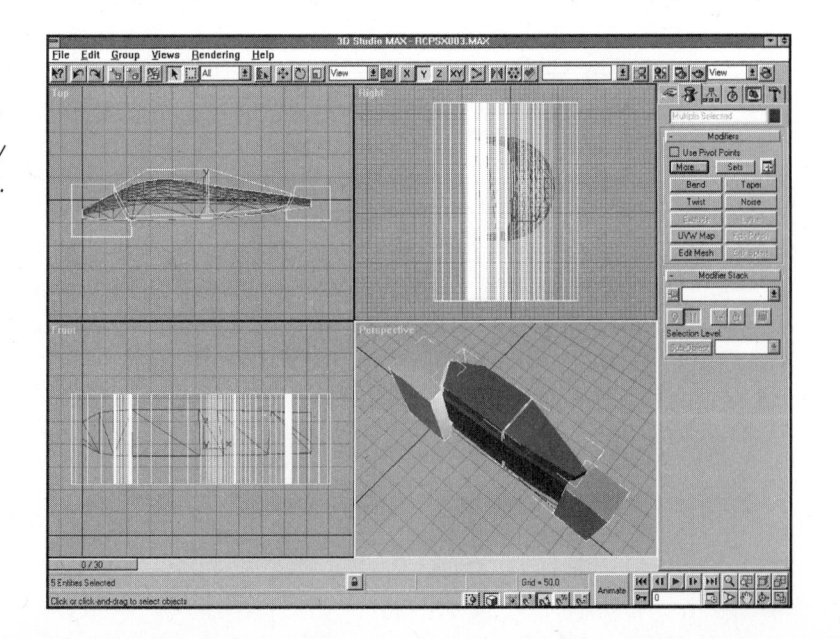

16. Although you could use creative mapping techniques to achieve the transparency of the canopy assembly over the two windows, by using Booleans you not only can achieve greater realism with simpler maps, but also have the glass and frame appear in the scene independent of one another. Begin the complex construction of the separate canopy glass areas by using Edit, Clone to make copies of the two glass cutout extrusions now collapsed into Editable Meshes. Hide the two copies. Hide also the extended side profile spline, which is no longer necessary for construction.

17. Use Boolean subtract to remove, one after another, the four cutouts visible from the canopy copy. The result will look something like figure 5.17. The operations may be more reliable if the mesh is collapsed after every Boolean.

Figure 5.17

The canopy appears here minus ends and glass.

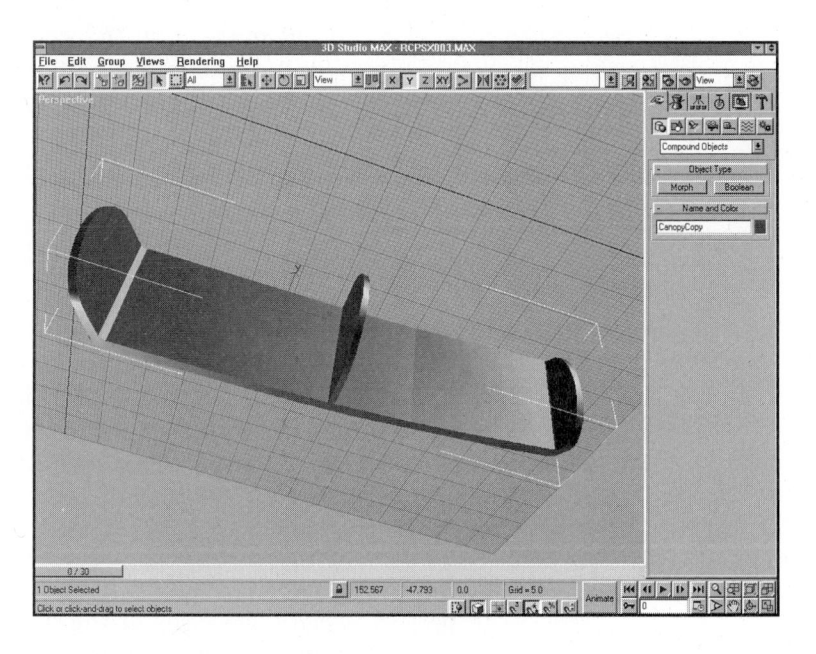

18. Apply a Smooth modifier and collapse the canopy mesh.

Tip

It is possible to use a Smooth modifier with Autosmooth on to locate the "bad" faces from a nonrobust Boolean operation. That is, when autosmoothed, a mesh with single reversed faces has unique smoothing groups assigned to the "bad" faces. Extra faces whose edges represent a discontinuity cause breaks in the smoothing groups and the assignment of additional groups.

TIP

Many modelers have difficulty isolating and remapping the sections of an object formed by a Boolean operation. If hundreds of windows are cut into the sides of a ship's hull by subtracting the cylinders from the hull loft, for example, it is very tedious to select the faces corresponding to the window glass, after the Booleans are complete, for retexturing. 3D Studio Release 4 provided an incredibly powerful tool for organizing Boolean result geometry by assigning materials to the operands *prior* to performing the operations. Then, Show Material would select the faces corresponding to the operands with the material specified. MAX unfortunately reassigns the material of one operand to the faces of both subsequent to Booleans, but the Face ID Numbers *are* unique for the geometry derived from the two operands. Thus, an Edit Mesh used to pick selection sets based on Face Material ID Number will isolate the faces corresponding to one operand or the other, even if the material itself is not retained.

Use the smoothing groups to locate reversed and extra faces. Select all vertices at the Sub-Object level, and weld them by using a threshold of .5 to 1 millimeter. Weld target vertices manually, as necessary. Expect to spend some time cleaning up the canopy mesh at this time. Be careful not to change the overall dimensions or appearance of the frame.

Use Edge, Turn; Vertex, Weld; and Autosmooth as necessary until an Autosmooth with a relatively small threshold—on the order of 10 degrees or less—reliably separates the cutouts, bottom, ends, and framework exterior into separate smoothing groups. There will be 10 smoothing groups when you achieve success: three for each window cutout, three for the outside bottom and ends of the canopy, and one for the surface of the "frame" corresponding to the outer skin. Select faces by smoothing groups to select only the bottom, ends, and two cutout areas. Delete these faces to leave only the exterior of the frame. At this point, the mesh should resemble figures 5.18 and 5.19.

19. Carefully compare the right and left sides of the exterior surface and find the side that is more precise or that has greater resolution and can be made more precise. Delete the faces of the discard half, mirror the remaining faces, attach the two objects, and re-weld. Collapse the mesh. The purpose of this operation is to restore symmetry and improve the predictable nature of the extrusions and scaling operations to follow.

Be certain during the face selection part of this operation that Select Face is in "single face" mode, probably with crossing Off.

FIGURE 5.18

The canopy frame exterior surface should look like this.

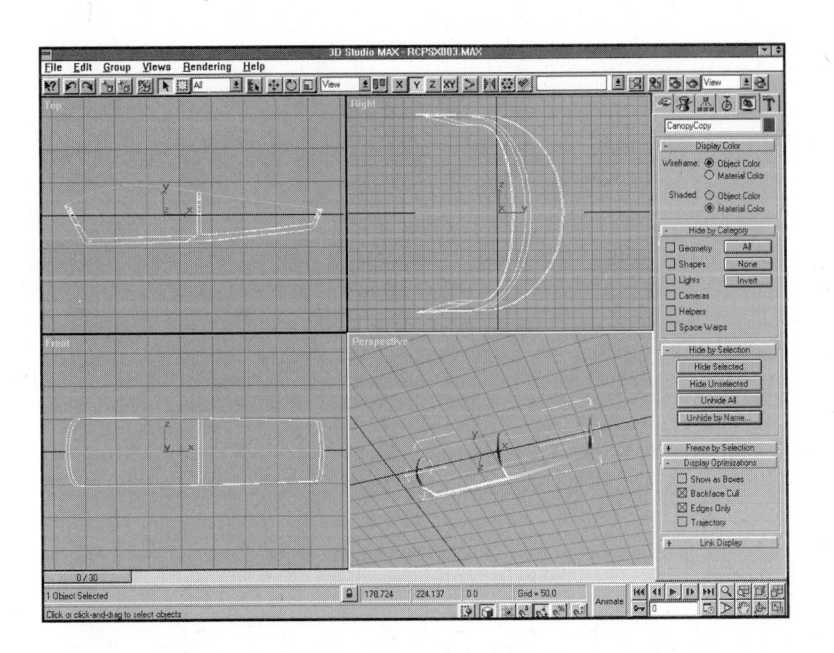

FIGURE 5.19

The canopy frame exterior surface should also look like this.

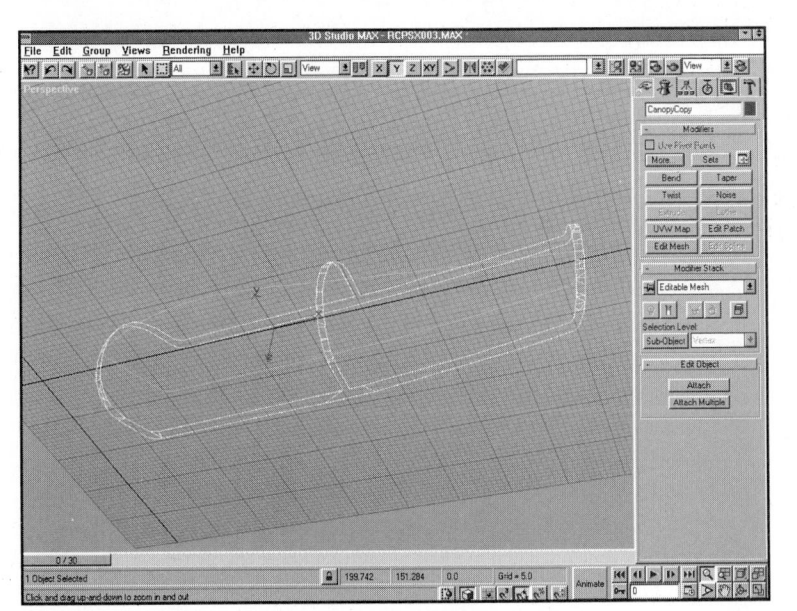

20. Use Edit, Clone to make a copy of the exterior surface of the canopy frame, and then hide it. Use Editable Mesh, Sub-Object: Face mode to select the entire frame, and then type a value of −5 in the Extrude section of the rollout.

WARNING

A bug exists in MAX 1.0 and 1.1 that may cause a failure or crash during the next step. It is advisable to Save or Hold your scene here.

21. *Without deselecting the extruded faces,* use scale and move transforms on the face selection set to produce a "lining" of faces with respect to the original exterior framework. Generally, this is possible in the Right or Left viewport in the following sequence:

   - Non-uniform scale in viewport Y, only until the framework thickness is approximately equal all around

   - Nonuniform scale in viewport X, only to shrink the thickness of the uppermost rib and to reduce the protrusion of the bottom edges below the outer surfaces

   - Motion of the selected faces in viewport X, only to restore the thickness of the uppermost web and to move the bottom inner edges even with the bottom outer edges

At this point, your incomplete, inside-out canopy frame missing an outer skin now will resemble the image of figure 5.20.

FIGURE 5.20

Make the canopy frame ribbing extrusion look like this.

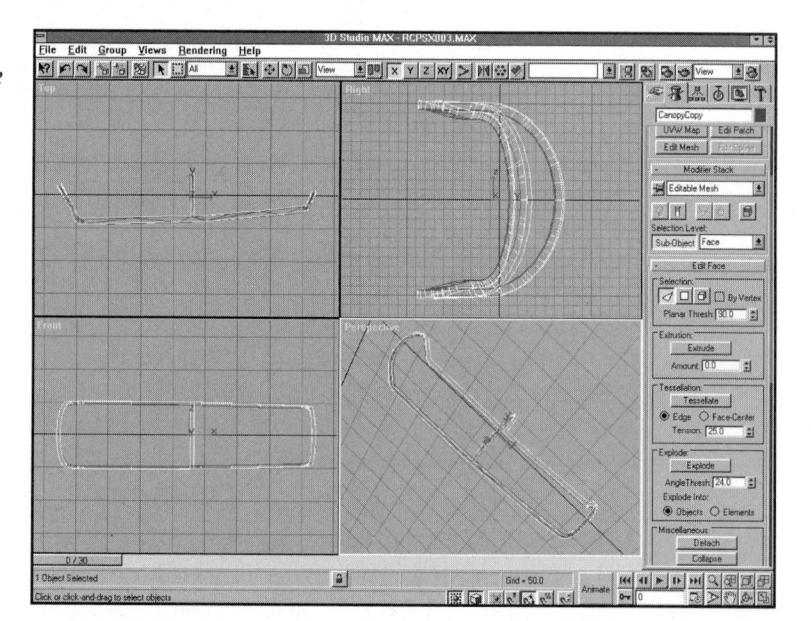

22. Note that, at this point, two problems exist with the ribbing surfaces. First, the normals are reversed because the extruded surfaces derived from faces directed outward with a negative extrusion value. Second, extruded surfaces have the same smoothing group as the parent faces. Thus, it is necessary to select all the faces of the ribbing, invert the normals, and then resmooth the ribbing with a Smooth modifier. Unhide the original exterior framework surface mesh and shade the viewport. Note that the two meshes represent a complete formed support frame with thickness and correct smoothing. Attach the two, weld all vertices, and resmooth to simplify the database. Then collapse the mesh (see fig. 5.21).

FIGURE 5.21

This is the finished canopy framework.

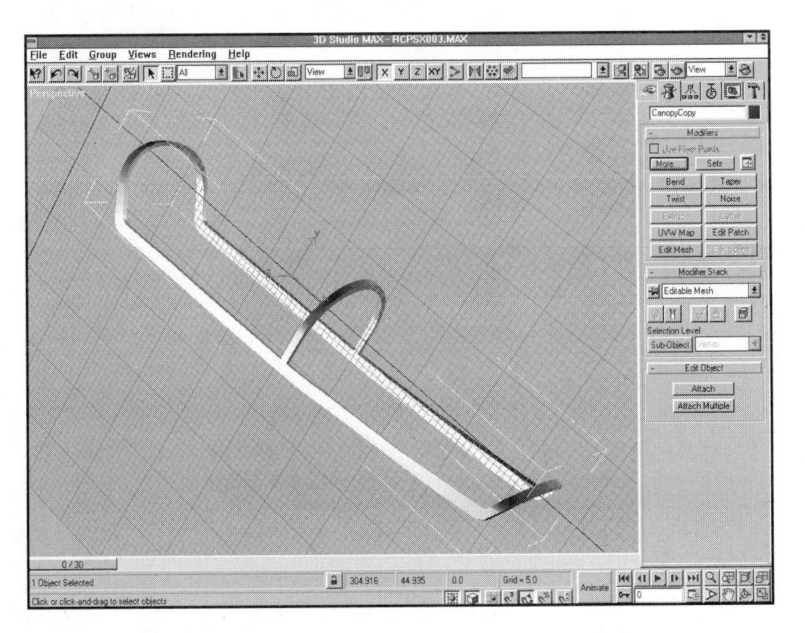

23. Hide the canopy framework.

24. Unhide the original copy of the canopy loft, collapsed into an Editable Mesh along with the two Glass cutout objects (see fig. 5.22).

25. Use Select and Edit, Clone to make another copy of the lofted Canopy object.

26. Use Boolean Intersections twice to create, in turn, the intersections of each glass cutout with one of the Canopy Loft Meshes each. Note that this is the last copy of the Canopy Loft Mesh if you follow instructions precisely. You may want to make another backup copy in case something goes wrong. The result is two collapsed meshes, each of which represents one segment of the transparent portion of the canopy (see fig. 5.23).

FIGURE 5.22

This is the scene prior to preparing to build the glass.

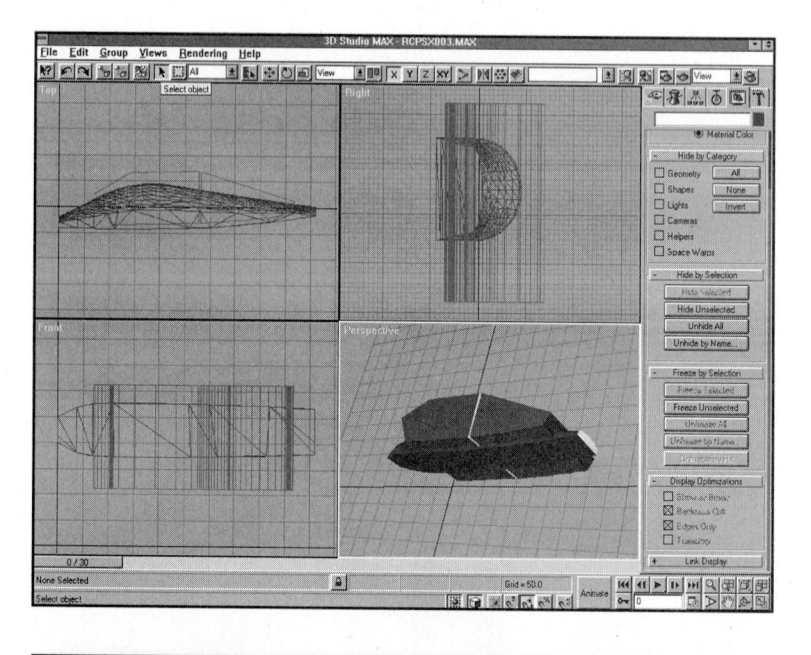

FIGURE 5.23

Preliminary canopy transparencies after Boolean intersections look solid, like these.

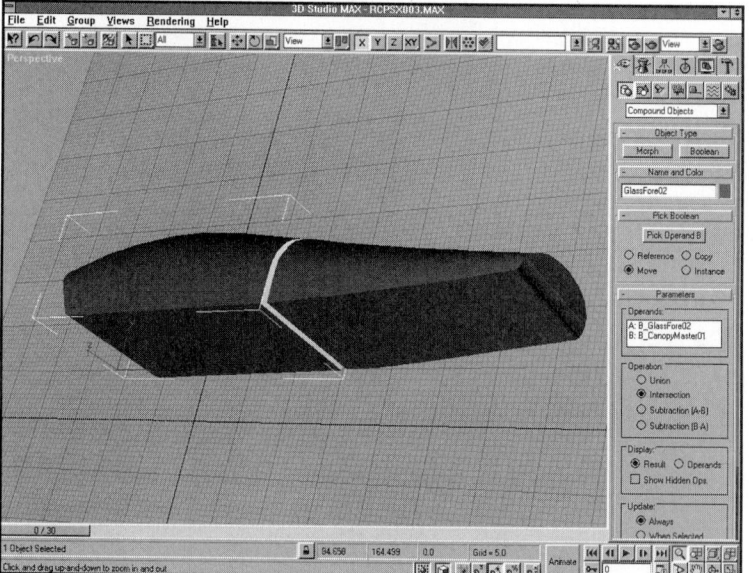

27. Edit the two Canopy Transparency objects, as follows:

   ■ Clean up the results of the Boolean operations, eliminating loose edges, loose vertices, jagged edges, and flipped normals.

- Use Smooth modifiers and smoothing groups in the Sub-Object: Face branch of Editable Mesh to locate and eliminate any remaining flipped or loose faces.

- Use Edge, Turn and Vertex, Weld, or Optimize modifiers to improve the appearance of the outer surfaces.

- Use Smoothing modifiers and Selection sets to isolate and delete the inner and end surfaces.

- Choose the side that has the fewest undesirable face artifacts and the best mesh resolution. Delete the other halves and then mirror, attach, and weld duplicates of the retained halves. Resmooth and collapse the finished surfaces.

Figure 5.24 shows the finished outer transparency surfaces.

FIGURE 5.24
These are finished canopy glass exterior surfaces.

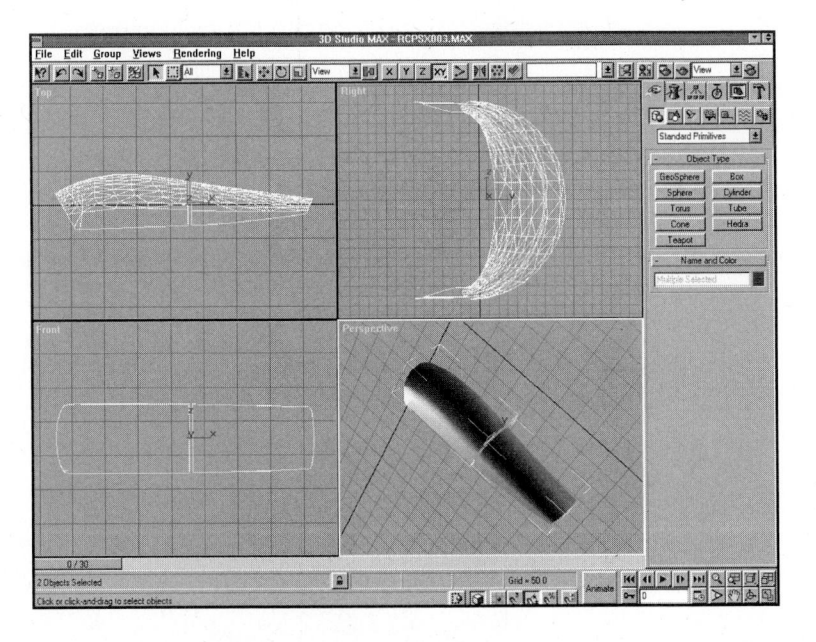

28. As with the framework, use Select, and Edit, Clone in turn to make copies of the outer glass surfaces. Hide both copies of one glass segment and one copy of the other.

29. In this order, do the following:

- Editable Mesh, Sub-Object: Face, select all. Enter an extrude value of –3.5, and choose Extrude in the Face menu.

- In the Right viewport, without changing the Face Selection set, use a nonuniform scale in viewport Y only to reduce the overall dimension of the inner surface until the width of the extruded edges is nearly constant.

- Use a nonuniform scale with the Face Selection set in the viewport X-only direction, and then use an X-only move to reduce the overall span of the inner surface and to move it back up near the (now missing) outer surface. The bottom edges, both inner and outer, should be roughly even.

- Select all faces. Flip Normals.

- Unhide the corresponding outer surface and then attach, weld, resmooth, and collapse. Figure 5.25 shows the Aft canopy transparency at this point in the process.

- Repeat all steps for the Forward canopy transparency.

The result of this complex operation is roughly equivalent to a Pro/Engineer "shell" operation on the solid and selected outer surface. The result, if the steps are done correctly, is a solid object of near-constant thickness with square, separately smoothable edges. As noted previously, this is essential here because the glass needs to look as realistic as possible and because the glass and frame may be rendered separately in some applications of the model. Figure 5.25 shows the finished transparency meshes.

FIGURE 5.25

The finished transparency solids have two sides.

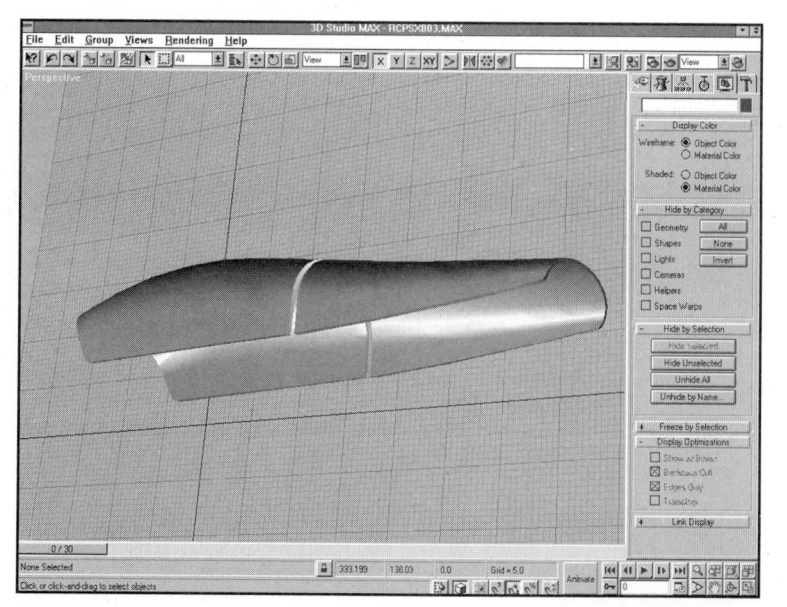

Construction of materials is omitted from this chapter; the reader is free to examine the finished sample file to analyze the materials used in the canopy frame and glass.

Robot Waist Construction

The robot waist is important because it represents a combination of Loft objects with primitives and because it uses detailed mesh elements in lieu of texture mapping to achieve extremely realistic and detailed specific appearances.

1. Load the file RCPSX003.MAX from the *Inside 3D Studio MAX Volume II* CD. Figure 5.26 depicts the contents of the file immediately after loading. Note that this file contains most of the source geometry as well as a finished version, currently frozen and usable as a reference template for the exercise.

FIGURE 5.26

The robot waist file just after loading.

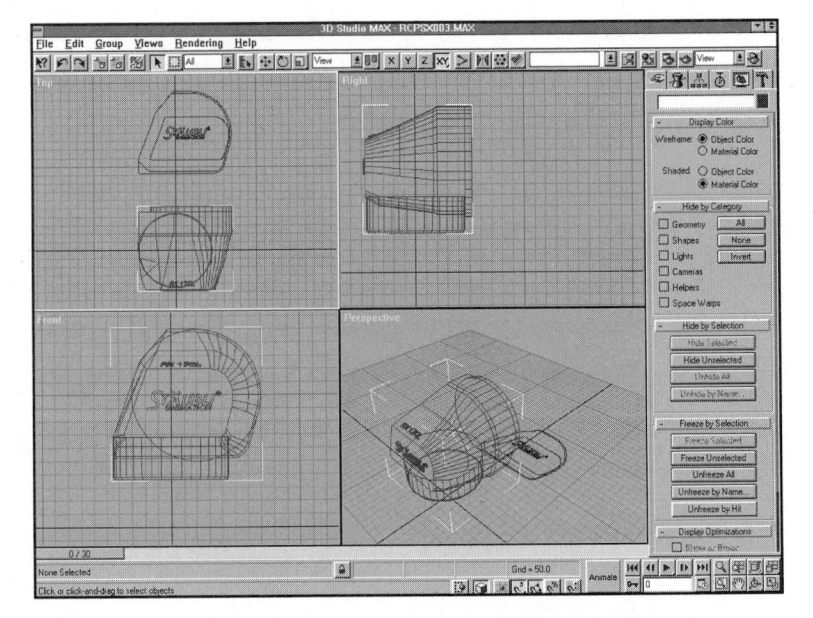

2. The file does not contain the loft path. Construct the loft path by using the frozen geometry as a reference in the Top viewport, building a path with vertices at the levels of the various cross sections. Ignore the geometry belonging to the lettering and shoulder hub at the back of the object.

3. Select the WaistEnd spline shape and then use Create, Geometry, Loft Objects, Loft. Click on the Get Path button and select the linear path created in step 2.

4. Using the Modify panel, change Path Steps to 0 and Shape Steps to zero. This is possible because the imported CAD splines have a great deal of detail that needs to be optimized out later or minimized now.

5. The first vertex occurs at 32.5 percent of path length. No additional shape is required here, however. Turn off Adaptive Path Steps.

6. The second vertex occurs at a distance of about 320 units along the path length. Move to that level on the path and use Get Shape to select the WaistMiddle spline.

7. Move to a level of 335 on the path and use Get Shape to Copy WaistLarge into the Loft. Do the same at a distance of 465, a percentage of 100. At this point, the Loft object should resemble the geometry of figure 5.27.

FIGURE 5.27

The preliminary waist object looks like this next to its template master.

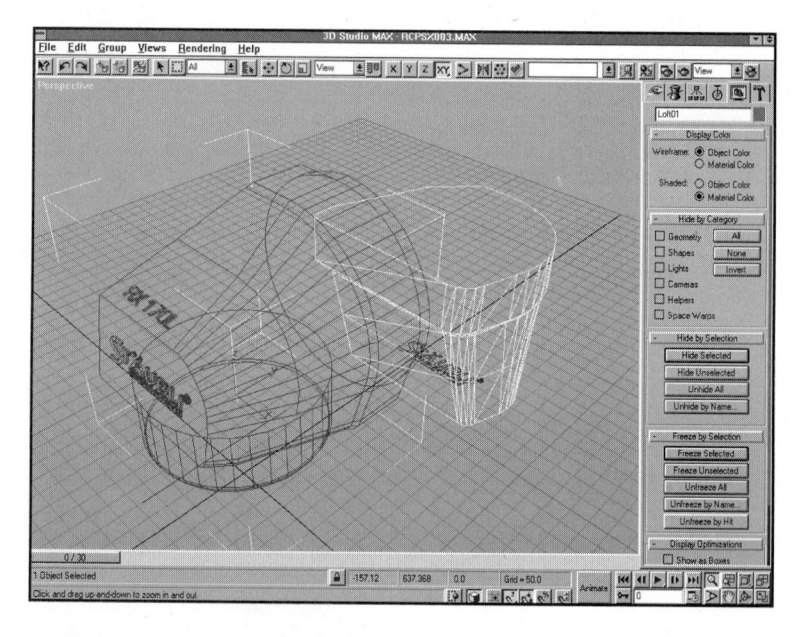

8. Optionally, collapse the mesh now.

9. Using Snap and grid lines, move the Loft object into a position where it corresponds with the frozen template. If this object were being built in conjunction with the other robot segments, the overall CAD layouts or

the completed modules would form similar references. Use combinations of Snap priorities with Absolute Snap to align the two objects to the 5 millimeter grid. You may need to do a mirror depending on the direction in which you drew your path.

10. Note that the objects don't match exactly. Use Edit Mesh or Editable Mesh in Sub-Object: Vertex mode with selection sets and Move to warp the Loft object into correspondence with the finished object. The finished object was aligned with a photograph in the Top view; because the photo cannot be distributed, the finished object will have to do here. The finished object should look like the one in figure 5.28.

FIGURE 5.28

The finished robot waist main housing was built against a photo reference.

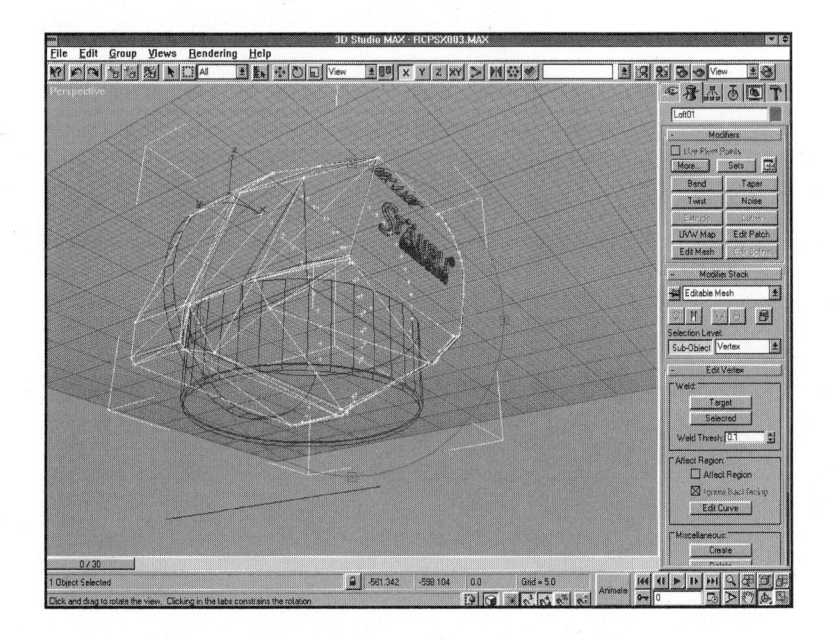

11. Note that the object, even after all the vertices have been moved around, does not correspond with the finished object. The object represents a casting. The casting possesses some complex transitions between sections that are difficult to duplicate by using the sections only. Use combinations of Sub-Object: Edge, and Divide and Turn to realign the lower-left edges with the finished transition. This level of editing is, in some cases, the only way to achieve the final result.

This step may require numerous jumps between selection sets and viewports. Be prepared to spend 10 minutes to an hour sculpting the surface into the desired profile. Most of the changes are concentrated along the one lower edge. Figure 5.29 depicts the edited object.

FIGURE 5.29

The completed robot waist main housing looks like this after sculpting is complete.

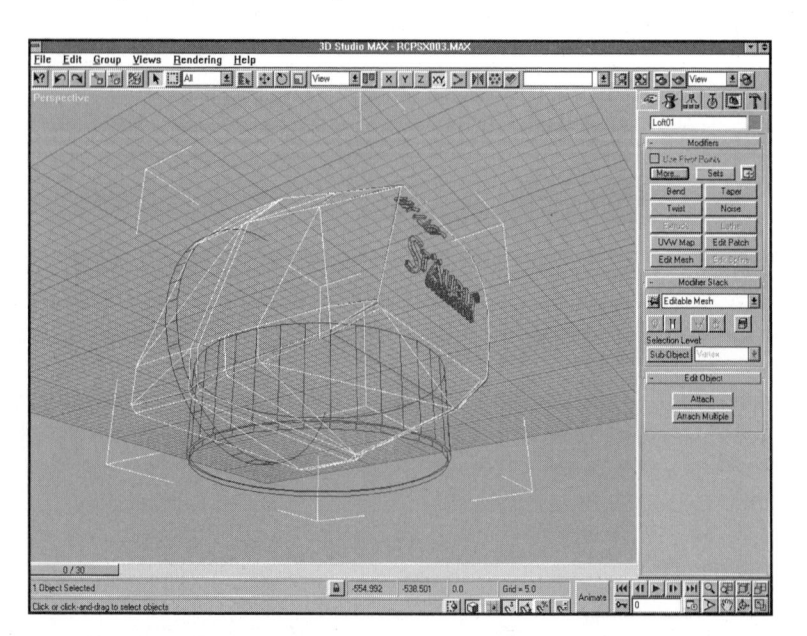

12. Smooth using Autosmooth with a threshold of around 20 degrees. It may be necessary to smooth the transition between the bulk of the object and the larger section manually to make the transition sharp.

13. Construct three cylinders to match the profiles of the three cylinders attached to the complete template. The larger cylinder at the bottom has parameters of radius, 225; height, 150; with 36 sides. The smaller bottom cylinder has parameters of 220, 10, and 36. The shoulder root has parameters of 250, 30, and 36. Because the waist root and shoulder root mate with circles of larger diameter or with other geometry, neither cylinder needs end caps. The larger cylinder below the Loft Mesh needs only the lower end cap.

14. Unhide the NameText spline—already collapsed into a single Bézier Spline—and apply an Extrude modifier with a distance of 5. Turn off the Start end cap and apply a Smooth modifier with Autosmooth. Collapse the mesh but do not attach it to the main casting object. Use Rotate and Move to align the new solid cast text with the text on the original object.

15. Use Create, Shapes, Text with an "Arial" font or near equivalent to create the text RX 170L. Using the Front viewport with a text size of 40 to 45 will get you closest to the final result with a minimum effort. Extrude five units with only the front end cap, then resmooth, skew, scale, and collapse this mesh to most closely match the text on the top of the casting. Attach this lettering to the top slanted portion of the casting, aligned approximately with the finished work.

16. Assign a safety orange plastic material to the casting and a gloss black to the loose lettering. Attach the two objects. Figure 5.30 shows a rendering of the finished mesh.

FIGURE 5.30

The finished robot waist mesh should resemble this after the lettering is positioned.

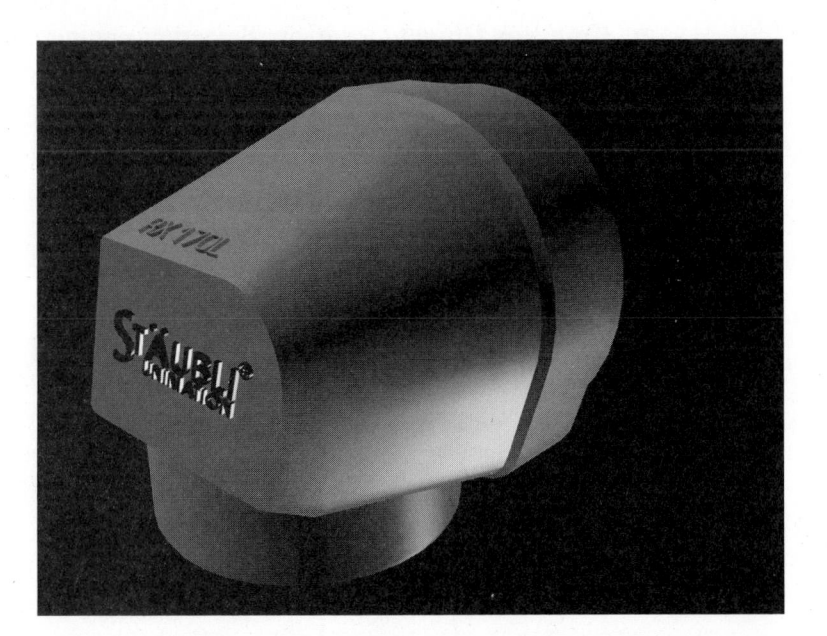

Note that the linkage and arrangement of the robot modules are straightforward applications of hierarchical linking and pivot-point control.

In Practice: Technical Modeling

- **Technical Applications.** Technical Application Modeling is used in support of animation and rendering chores that require very high degrees of precision and accuracy. The degree to which accuracy and precision is required may be unfamiliar to entertainment animators.

- **Modeling Methods.** In creating a technical model, be prepared to spend a great deal of time integrating CAD data into the MAX environment, tweaking Snap priorities and settings, and editing objects at the edge and vertex level.

- **Object Oriented Mesh Building.** Although MAX supports an incredible array of history-sensitive, fully editable object stack operations, the demands of technical modeling, the number of steps involved in an object's construction, and the ease with which an object can be verified objectively against the source data call for a different mode of modeling where Collapse is far more popular than in general use.

- **Complex Object Creation.** Sometimes numerous steps contribute to the creation of a single complex part. Never try to accomplish too much in too few steps. Be creative in the application of Boolean, Extrude, and Edit Mesh operations and in their combinations.

Part III

CHARACTER MODELING

IMAGE BY KEN ALLEN ROBERTSON

Chapter 6

by Ken Allen Robertson

CHARACTER MODELING BASICS

Creating animated characters is a multifaceted and complex process. Traditionally, most attention has been focused on making characters move in an exciting and illuminating way. But animation is the last step in the process of character creation. This chapter—indeed, this book—does not delve into the technical process or evaluations involved in creating great character animation. Fortunately, the process of animation is well-covered in both Inside 3D Studio MAX Volume III, *and in George Maestri's wonderful book,* Digital Character Animation, *also published by New Riders. Rather than cover the animation process, this chapter focuses on the creation process necessary to facilitate the animation process.*

Before you begin to model the character, you must know how the character will look, behave, and move. You must also know what part the character plays in moving the story forward, and what tasks the character must perform within the context of the story you are telling. Without knowing at least this amount of information, you will likely reach an impasse at some point, in which the modeling of the character inhibits it from performing as it should. Defining your character, therefore, becomes the critical first step in creating the illusion of a living being.

Characters must look as though they belong to the world of the story. Otherwise, they will be ineffective storytellers. A perfectly still character that already conveys life, personality, and emotion can serve as a blueprint for that character's qualities of motion when the animation process begins. Your audience will immediately identify with such a character the moment it appears.

Before examining the technical software aspects that make it possible to create characters (aspects covered extensively in the next two chapters) and before you touch the keyboard, it is important to review some principles that will give your characters life before you ever create them:

- Introduction to characters
- The definition of character
- Developing the story
- Developing the character's personality
- Defining how the character needs to function
- Defining the visual design of the character

Introduction to Characters

When humankind first began communicating with pictures, characters instantly became a critical and popular part of storytelling. From Cro-Magnon cave paintings to the high-tech, computer-generated beings of today, images that mirror humanity intrigue and fascinate us. These images have become omnipresent in modern society. Characters are used to teach, sell, entertain, and enlighten.

Characters have gone through an extraordinary evolution from their humble beginnings. Every time a new medium is created and made available to the public, characters are among the first creations presented. They are pushed and pulled by their creators to test the strengths and weaknesses of the medium in which they find themselves. Computer-generated characters are no exception.

Computer-generated characters have come a long way in a very short time. From the stained-glass knight in 1985's *Young Sherlock Holmes* to the myriad personalities of 1995's *Toy Story*, computer artists have consistently pushed their equipment, software, and imagination to the very edge in an attempt to capture every aspect of life's endless possibilities. Fortunately, hardware and software companies have been willing to meet the challenge alongside the artists.

Until recently, truly astounding computer characters were relegated to high-end workstations running high-priced software. But as consumer-level PCs grow in speed and capability, "character power" is now becoming available to a wider group of artists. 3D Studio MAX has put the powerful tools formerly available only in high-priced animation packages, as well as tools unique in the software industry, into the hands of those artists.

Unfortunately, however, the millennia-old skills of story-telling have not been made as widely available to computer artists. Only in recent years have the principles of animated story-telling, tried and tested for more than 60 years, become available to the average computer artist. Many books on the subject of animation, which had gone out of print, are only now coming back on the retail market, most notably *The Illusion of Life* by Disney animators Ollie Johnston and Frank Thomas and *Cartoon Animation* by Preston Blair.

No amount of power or tools by themselves can create a character. It takes a creator who is part artist, part storyteller, part actor, part director—all under the guidance of a dreamer—to breathe life into an inanimate collection of computer data. Most artists, when first faced with having to create a character, may feel a bit like Dr. Frankenstein. The task of creating a living being can be daunting and overwhelming, and the need to see whether it *can* be done may easily exceed the need to design the way it *should* be done. The mysteries of giving the illusion of life to an object of your own creation are very rarely covered in software manuals.

Remember, a character is a device used to tell a story, and a story will vary a little with each medium in which it is told. 3D graphics have the capability to mimic two different mediums: live-action film and hand-drawn animation. For the first time, a medium can almost perfectly imitate reality—

albeit, a reality not bound by "real-world" physics. This is a critical distinction that makes 3D computer characters unique from their relatives in any other medium, and that can provide countless variations of style. Your characters, to accomplish their roles in their respective stories, must be responsive not only to the story itself but to the medium and to the style in which the story is being told. Hamlet would look terribly out of place in a shoot-em-up action film, and Daffy Duck would probably not be taken seriously as a pivotal part of an historical drama (even if he did not move or talk). Without a knowledge of your particular story, the style being used to tell the story, and the medium in which it will be told, you set up your characters to fail—from the start.

The Definition of Character

What distinguishes a character from any other object in a 3D world? Characters do have several properties: movement, voices, faces, and so on. But other objects that are not considered characters can have these properties also. For a definition to be of any use in the character-creation process, it must identify the bare minimum attributes that distinguish a character from a noncharacter.

In that light, the following definition should prove helpful:

> A *character* is any object to which a thought process, emotional life, and distinguishable personality may be attributed, and which "acts" of its own accord.

With this definition, you can easily distinguish a character from a noncharacter, whether the character is an animal, a humanoid, a robot, or a household item. As the preceding definition makes clear, character comprises four major attributes. These attributes create a blueprint of the questions that need to be answered before your character can begin to take on a life of its own.

Thought Process

What constitutes a thought process? Human beings are constantly thinking (see fig. 6.1). "About what?" you ask. The answer: "About events—those that have happened or are going to happen, whether imaginary, real, or perceived as imaginary or real." Almost every human thought chain begins with the recollection or awareness of some sort of event, and then expands into the interpretation of it. The basic thought string "If x happens, what will it mean?" is familiar to all. Likewise, as something is happening, the normal human thought process is to evaluate the event and determine our personal response to it (including no response). Notice that this is a precursor to the fourth character attribute—the ability to take action.

FIGURE 6.1
What constitutes a thought process?

Is your character a quick thinker or slow? Does the thought process flow easily through the character's brain, or is it as thick as molasses in winter? Does the character evaluate each event that happens for its niceness, its potential harm, its money-making potential, or its potential for a great practical joke?

Different characters will think differently, some sliding through enormous chains of evaluations with grace and speed—whereas for others, remembering their own name would bring on a hemorrhage. Considering how your character thinks is a great step toward making your character come to life, even if you never show the character just "thinking."

The thought process can be developed with the personality, by itself, or as a springboard from which you can jump back and forth between the personality and emotional life as well as the thought process. The important thing to remember is that thought process should be considered, at some point, a critical aspect in the "life" of the character.

Emotional Life

Emotions also can be a by-product of the thought process, or a result of the events that spark the thought process (see fig. 6.2). Emotions are the character's reaction to its interpretation of the events it is experiencing or has experienced.

FIGURE 6.2

Emotions can be the
result of an event that
sparks the thought
process.

Consider the difference between two characters being slapped in the face. One might react with outrage, viciously attacking the slapper. The other might take it as a sign of great affection and fall madly in love with the slapper. Imagine that the two characters are identical twins. Now notice the difference in the way you picture the two characters—the subtle differences in how they stand, the expression on their faces, and so forth—and you can easily see that having a clear idea of a character's emotional life benefits the design and modeling process.

Personality

Personality is most simply defined as a predisposition to certain patterns of emotion and thought. A character that always expects other characters to take advantage of him, for example, will always be grouchy, untrusting, and wary. Whenever another character appears to do something nice, the mistrusting character will examine that character's motives and actions for any sign of trickery.

Knowing a character's personality smoothes out many decisions about how the character will look and move. An exercise later in this chapter will help to simplify and enhance the process of defining a character's personality.

Beginning a New Character

The process of creating a character can begin in many places: with the character itself, that has inspired the story you are going to tell; with the story, in which the character plays a part in moving the story to its conclusion; or with the world of the story, from which the characters and the story are born. Whatever your starting point, all character design must go through the following steps:

- Developing the story

- Developing the character's personality

- Completing a definition of how the character needs to function (physically and as a story device)

- Visually designing the character

The first three steps are pretty much interchangeable and can be accomplished in any order. But the final step should always be the visual design of the character (from which the character will be modeled). Rough sketch ideas can certainly accompany any of the early steps, but final visual design should be done only after the story, personality, and character function have been completely fleshed out. Otherwise, the character will not be able to perform the tasks set for it.

As you read the following paragraphs, think about a character you are currently working on (even if you believe that character is almost totally complete) or begin to create a new character in your mind. Ask the questions being posed (and any others that might arise in the process) and begin to get an idea of the answers, keeping in mind that the answers are likely to modify themselves a bit as you consider each new aspect of your character's life.

Developing the Story

Besides being a simple linear narrative, a story must have four other elements to make it interesting, attractive, and alive: mood, stylization, setting, and multiple characters. Other elements may come into play, but these four must be present to bring the story to a life beyond mere words.

Mood

Every story has an overall mood or feel to it. That mood may be spooky, warm, cheerful, funny, frightening, somber, tragic, and so forth (see figs. 6.4 and 6.5). Stories, as they progress, go through many mood changes, but every story has a prevalent mood to which it returns again and again. This is the mood you want your audience to remember long after your story is over.

FIGURE 6.4

Compare the mood of this figure with figure 6.5.

A great tool for defining mood is the ever-popular, low-tech thesaurus. After you have approximated the overall mood you want to achieve, crack open your thesaurus and see whether other words mean approximately the same thing. Those other words might strike you as being juicier or more precise or appropriate to the story you wish to tell. Often, this can add an immediate spark of even greater life to your story, making obvious the little details you may have yet to discover.

When you know the overall mood of the story, ask how the particular character you are examining adds to that mood. Does the character drive the mood of other characters or strive against the mood you have set? The answer to this question will be a great beginning to your definition of the character's emotional.

Stylization

Stylization is the prevalent visual style you use to tell the story. A circus-like atmosphere of bright, saturated primary colors says something very different about your world and its characters than a shadowy, stark, film-noir style palette says.

Some stories automatically lend themselves to one style or another. Taking a story from its obvious stylization and forcing it into another will result in your story and characters being seen as a spoof on the new style. A Mother Goose fairy tale stylized to resemble a 1930s monster movie will most likely be perceived as a send-up of the material being presented. Characters, too, can be counter-stylized, but they will probably suffer the same fate.

With the current state of 3D graphics, "near-photoreality" is a frequent choice. Understand that this too is a choice, and that reality, when put under the microscope of a presentational medium, rarely looks real. Think about the visual differences between an action-adventure movie and the average man-on-the-street documentary. Both present pictures that have the appearance of reality, but the action-adventure film has been carefully tailored into a heightened and focused reality. Its limited focus and carefully placed lighting and camera angles create a reality that appears more real than reality itself, which is vital to the pulse-pounding, sweaty-palm mood it needs to be effective. Just choosing "reality" as the overall stylization is not enough. You must decide what kind of reality you want to present.

Clearly, stylization has a major impact on the visual presentation of your character.

Setting

What is the world of your story? Characters that inhabit a medieval kingdom of magic would look terribly uncomfortable in an urban ghetto, even though characters in both worlds might have similar personality traits. Remember, stories are devices of limited focus. Just as most planets in science fiction stories are dominated by one topographical setting (forests, deserts, ice, and so forth), a focused story takes place primarily in one world. That world can be psychological as well as physical, springing from the imagination of a child or an oppressive world of tyrannical overlords (see figs. 6.6 and 6.7).

Keep in mind your intended audience's view of the world. Will they see a child's imaginary world through the eyes of a child or those of a disapproving parent? Will the oppressiveness be seen from the overlord's point of view, or from that of the oppressed?

After you nail down the setting, examine your character. Is the character an outcropping of the world or a foreign element in it? From which viewpoint does the character see this world? Does the character share the viewpoint of the audience or have one completely contradictory to that of the audience? This provides a base for the thought process that goes on within this character.

FIGURE 6.6
Your story's world can spring from the imagination of a child.

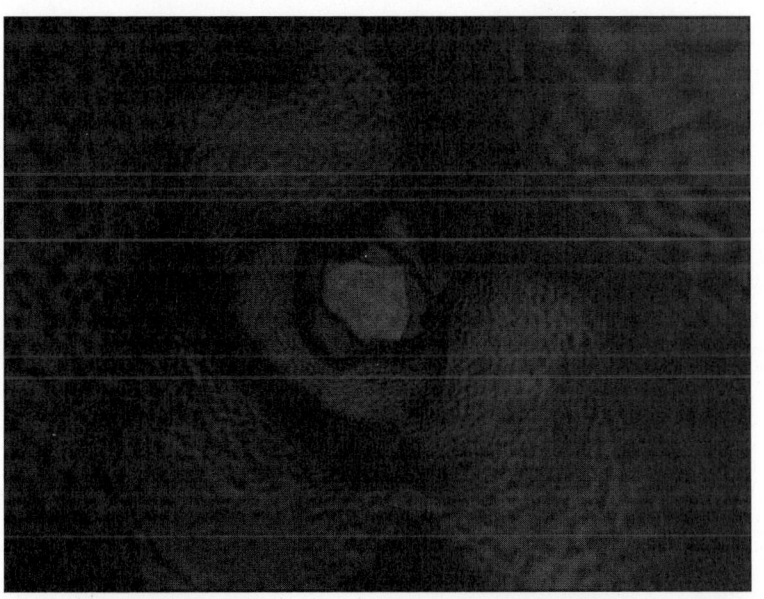

FIGURE 6.7
Your story's world can spring from an oppressive world of tyrannical overlords.

Multiple Characters

Stories grow out of the interaction between characters. Even if only one moving character is in the scene you are creating, everything that affects the character in such a way as to move the story forward should be treated as another character. This includes the audience itself, if your character breaks the fourth wall (the invisible barrier through which the character watches the story) and becomes aware of the audience through asides or direct reaction to the audience's presence.

By considering the character's reaction to all the other characters in the scene, you will gain a clear picture of the breadth of emotion a character must be able to express. You will also gain a clear picture of where the character model must accommodate these expressions by having the supporting geometrical construction with which to achieve them.

Developing the Character's Personality

The previous steps of clarifying the story and how it will be told should create a fairly complete blueprint of the character's personality in the context of the story. But what if the character has to go through multiple stories? If actions or events are added to the story, or you discover new events while you're animating, how will you determine how the character will react? What you have seen before will be a clue to the total personality of the character, but it will not be the complete picture. You need to make a conscious definition of the character's overall disposition toward the world. By doing this, you can create a physical posture, expression, and an idea of how the character moves that can make it more readily identifiable and easily accessible to your intended audience. The following exercise will provide an simple, effective, and reusable tool that will help you in nailing down a tight definition of your character's personality.

THE PERSONALITY PARAGRAPH

Write a paragraph (or two) describing your character's attitude toward its world. Avoid any physical description of the character, just focus on emotions and emotionally charged adjectives and adverbs (for example, he looks angrily on the playfulness of the little fuzzy creatures). When you have finished, go back to the trusty thesaurus, look up the adjectives and adverbs you have written down, and see whether any synonyms give you a better or more powerful idea of your character's overriding personality.

Does the character see the world as a great big playground? A massive opportunity for playing jokes? A world of ravenous predators, waiting and watching? The world's largest salad bar? Or a place filled with money that should belong to your character (but, unjustly, doesn't)?

What opportunity does each new day bring to your character? Does the character greet each day angrily, fearfully, cheerfully, greedily, or snidely? Adverbs make great catalysts to the discovery and refinement of personality. Use them often in your paragraph.

Defining How the Character Functions

Characters function in many ways, both physically within the story and as a plot device to move the story forward. By defining the tasks set out for your character in both areas you will gain a deeper understanding of the way the animated character must move, and what its physical structure must be to accomplish the movement.

Functioning as a Plot Device

Is your character the protagonist, whose actions drive the story forward? Is the character the hero that saves the day? Is the character the antagonist, determined to thwart the hero at all costs? Or is the character a representative of the world of the story, expressing the concerns and cares of the unseen masses? No matter who or what the character is, it will have some critical part to play in the telling of the story. Even crowds of nameless, faceless characters have a function—adding drama, ridiculing the main character, or helping to create the mood. Identifying this function will be of great benefit in identifying the physical appearance and personality of your character.

Physical Functions

Does your character need to run and jump to escape the villain (see fig. 6.8)? Lift impossibly heavy objects (see fig. 6.9)? Swallow dynamite and contain the explosion in its stomach? Or does your character collapse with exhaustion at the mere mention of physical labor?

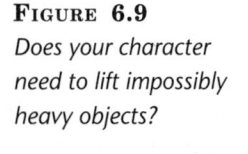

FIGURE 6.8
*Does your character
need to run and jump
to escape the villain?*

FIGURE 6.9
*Does your character
need to lift impossibly
heavy objects?*

You must know what tasks await your character to know what sort of physical structure the character model must have. And if you know how the character responds to physical tasks, you have another part of the picture of the character's outward appearance.

Visual Design

If you have been reading with a particular character in mind, notice whether these suggestions have changed your ideas for the character's outward appearance. If you have been reading and mentally creating a prototype for a new character, how clear a picture do you have now of the character's outward appearance? You can see why visual design of a character is the last step—the outside of a character must express its inner life.

Now that the life of the character has been pretty much defined (but feel free to explore further), you can bring the character into a physical (computer-generated) existence.

Before you begin modeling, you should be aware of three elements that can be of tremendous help in the process:

- References
- Sketches
- Maquettes

Use one or all of these elements to finalize the visual design of the model before you begin modeling in the computer.

References

Almost all character creators, whether make-up artists, sculptors, actors, painters, or animators, have found quick and easy access to character references. These references can be videotapes, photographs, books, magazines, whatever. But having visual references can fill out the details that make a character unique.

What sort of references should you seek? Pictures that express the personality you have defined serve as excellent references. What profession or archetype would you classify your character as having? Find pictures of those professions or traditional representations of those archetypes. Find pictures of whatever is unique to your character, its nationality, time period, social status, and definable psychosis. These pictures will show what these attributes actually look like, or how they have been represented in the past.

Sketches

Even if you and pencils have maintained a mutually respectful distance for most of your life, rough sketches of a character further flesh out its outward appearance. The sketches do not have to be major works of art, and they don't have to be absolutely accurate. Instead, they serve as visual aids in focusing the direction of your model. You should strive to create at least a top, side, and front sketch of your character. With these in hand, you can more readily see where the character needs to go, what is lacking, and what is correct. And remember, nobody else ever has to see the sketches. Even a final sketch, however, does not preclude a last-minute change of mind (due to a flash of brilliant inspiration) when the modeling process begins.

Maquettes

Maquettes are sculpted models that give you a 3D representation of your character. Even with orthographic sketches of you character, you will not have a completely accurate picture of what the model will look like in 3D. Use whatever materials you have handy—clay, papier-maché, Sculpey, whatever—but having a reference that you can pick up and rotate around is invaluable. And again, you don't need to be Michelangelo, and no one else needs to see the final product. As long as it helps your creation process, do it!

3D computer graphics are a relatively new medium. As such, new aesthetics will be tried, accepted, and rejected for a long time to come. New techniques and tools are being invented every day. But the ability to create an interesting story full of vibrant and passionate characters, and the skill to tell that story well, are talents that have been prized since the very dawn of mankind. Those talents will be treasured until the end of the human race; stories, and the characters that make them possible, help human beings to reflect, relax, learn, and dream. The characters you create today may be passed down from generation to generation to generation and medium to medium. Create them on strong foundations—they might be around for a while.

In Practice: The Basics of Character Modeling

- A character is any object that "acts" of its own accord, and to which a thought process, emotional life, and distinguishable personality may be attributed. Defining these aspects of your character will create a life for the character, a life that suggests patterns of movement, and therefore, construction techniques and requirements.

- Before creating the character, define the story in which it must act and define how that story will be told.

- Define the personality of the character, comprising the patterns of emotion and thought your character most often experiences and the disposition of the character toward the world.

- Define how the character functions in the story, both physically (accomplishing certain tasks) and as a plot device.

- The last step in creating a character (before modeling) is the visual design of the character.

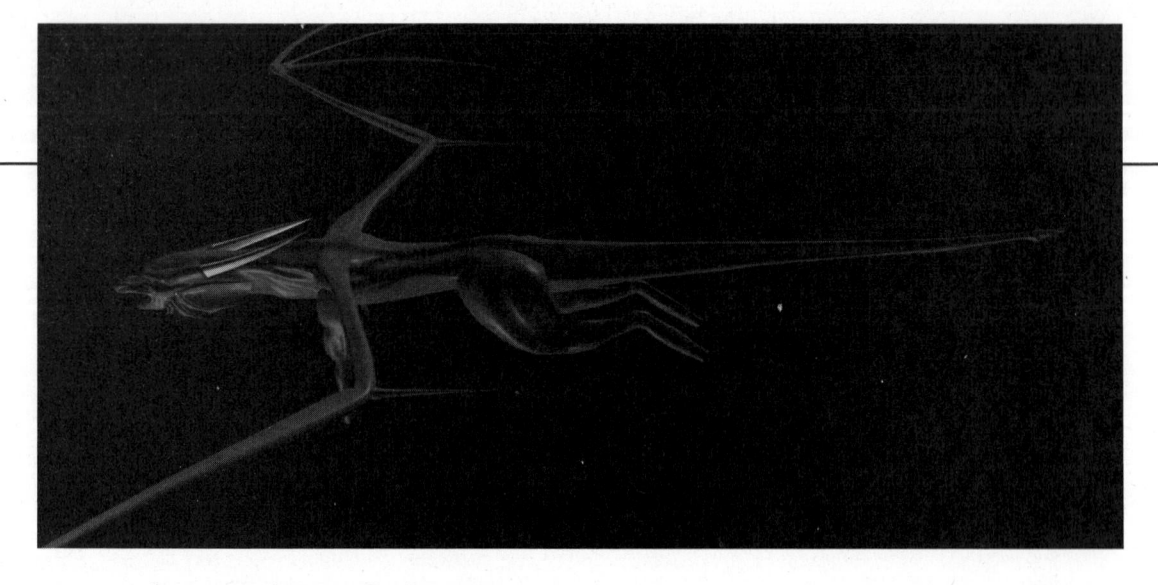

IMAGE BY JOSHUA R. ANDERSON

Chapter 7

by Joshua R. Anderson

CHARACTER MODELING WITH PATCH TOOLS

Patch modeling is a fairly new feature to 3D Studio users, and few methods for creating models from patches have been developed or shared. The patch tools in 3D Studio MAX enable you to create simple patch models with relative ease. If you need more information on the basics of patch editing and modeling, Chapter 14 in Inside 3D Studio MAX Volume I *is an excellent reference. Complex surfaces require advanced techniques to achieve the look you want. This chapter not only demonstrates advanced patch modeling techniques, it also shows you many techniques used to model great looking characters by using MAX patches. This chapter has two major objectives: to show how to model complex* surface objects by using both the patch tools in MAX and plug-ins, and to show character modeling techniques by doing the following:

- Showing the benefits of patch surfaces over mesh objects in character modeling

- Describing in detail the limitations of patches so that you can decide whether they suit your project

- Teaching new techniques in patch modeling that use the tools provided with MAX

- Introducing plug-ins, which greatly expand the patch modeling potential of MAX

- Stepping through the process of creating a complex character

- Showing important techniques to use when modeling single-skinned characters for animation

Using Patches in MAX

Working with patches in MAX is different from most other programs. Although it is true that patches are controlled in much the same way as splines, the surface appears to be made of polygons (just like a mesh object). This can be confusing at first, but when you approach patches as a completely separate entity—a balanced mixture of both spline and polygonal geometry—you should begin to understand the power behind patch modeling. Patch modeling requires a different thought process than that required when working with mesh objects or splines. Although techniques for patch modeling vary, the planning of the model is crucial. The planning can dramatically affect both the quality of the model and the time it takes to create it. Many plug-ins, both free and commercial, exist to make patch modeling easier. Not all of the available plug-ins are used in this chapter, but they are listed here.

- Surface Tools

- Edit Spline 2

- Interpolate Spline

- Reverse Spline

- Edge2Spline

- Mesh2Spline

- Patch MatID and PatchOut

Patch Versus Mesh Considerations

When choosing between using a patch model or mesh model, remember the following important facts:

- Patches are parametric like primitives, meaning their resolution—or poly count—is dynamic.

- Patch surfaces are ideal for flexible, organic surfaces, but can run into trouble when hard edges are needed.

- Patch models generally have higher hardware requirements than mesh models of similar complexity.

- Patch models and mesh models work fine together in the same scene.

You may choose to use patch models for the organic objects in your scene and mesh models for architectural and mechanical objects. You may have some objects organic in some parts and mechanical in others. In any event, patch objects should not be left out of the planning process for a project.

When working with a large amount of splines and patches, the RAM requirements can greatly exceed those required by mesh objects. This problem can be reduced or eliminated altogether by collapsing the edit modifiers in the Modifier Stack and re-applying them as needed. This is because MAX stores the edits of each spline and patch vertex, and collapsing the modifier clears all of that storage. This can even reduce the file and RAM size to below that of a mesh object.

Modeling Issues

Creating good-looking patch models with only the tools provided with MAX can be a daunting task, although it is definitely possible. If you have the right tools and techniques, however, patch modeling can be the easiest way to create complex models, especially characters. The dragon shown at the opening of this chapter (and used in the tutorials later in this chapter) was modeled from scratch in about three working days. Your mileage may vary, but this gives you a reasonable idea of what you can expect after you become accustomed to patch modeling.

In reality, patch modeling is much more straightforward than mesh modeling. You deal more with the shape of the model than with its structure. This makes modeling easier to learn and more fun to do.

Animation Issues

Patch models carry several distinct advantages over mesh models when it comes time to animate them:

- The dynamic resolution of patch models ensures optimal rendering times and better detail and smoothing for close-up shots (see fig. 7.1).

FIGURE 7.1
Identical surfaces with different step values.

Patch steps set at 1 ——

Patch steps set at 3 ——

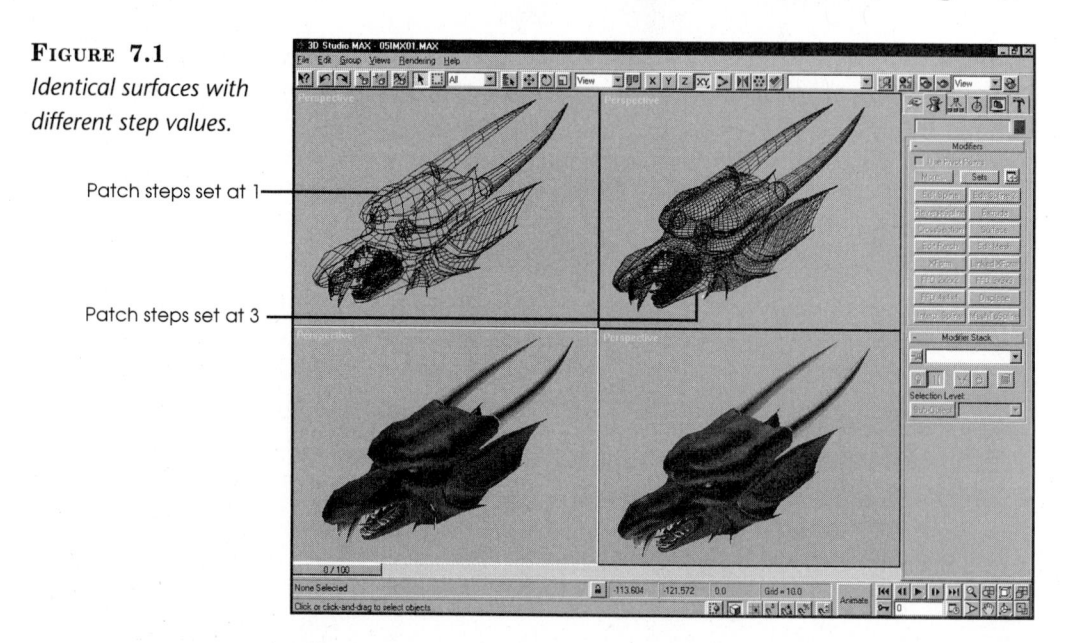

- Patch surfaces can be smoothly bent and stretched without the aid of a skin plug-in (see fig. 7.2).

FIGURE 7.2

An arm with Linked Xform from the arm to the bones.

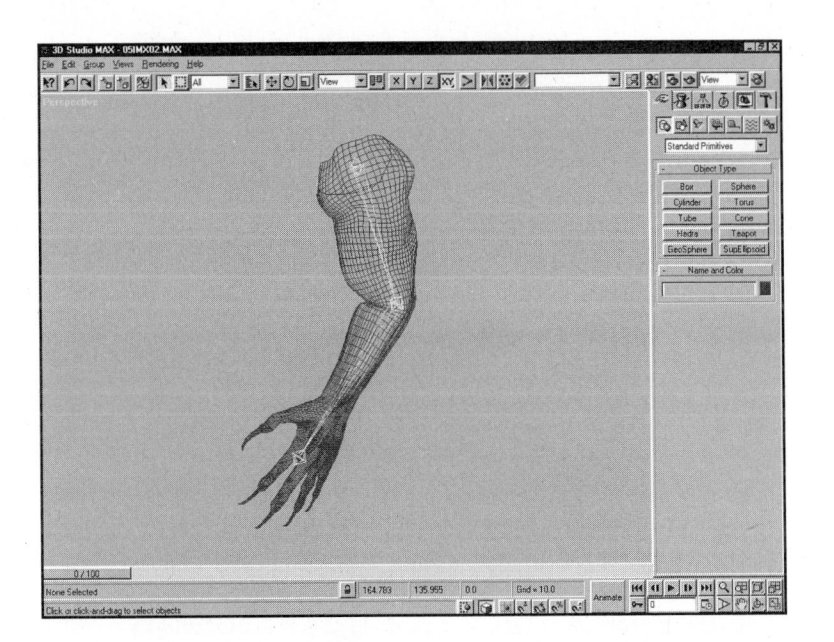

- If you are working with Morph Targets and using Surface Tools, you can easily pose the model by returning to the spline level in the Modifier Stack and setting its pose. The vertex count remains the same, and the surfaces are smoothly transformed to their new pose (see fig. 7.3).

FIGURE 7.3

A head with mouth open and closed.

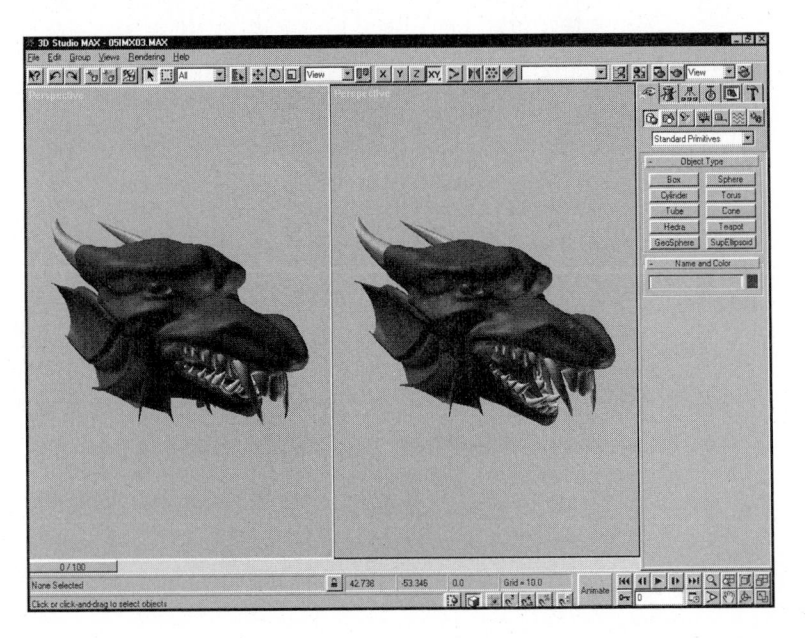

Animating patch models can be a great relief from rigid mesh models. Patch models' flexibility extends well beyond their easy bending and stretching—beyond even the dynamic resolution. The Modifier Stack enables you to go back and to easily make large or small changes to any part of your object and still have the surface come out looking just as good.

Patch Limitations in MAX

Although patch surfaces are versatile and easy to work with, it is important to know what you cannot do with them. Many of the seeming drawbacks of patches shown in this section should not actually be regarded as limitations, but rather as aspects of patch modeling that need to be known (just as the aspects of mesh modeling should be).

General Surface Control Problems

Patch surfaces, by nature, are rendered smoothly. They are not composed of faces, edges, and vertices as are mesh models, and they cannot be edited at that level. With this in mind, you can understand some of the problems you would face if you approached patch surfaces and thought you could use the same techniques as used on mesh models.

Smoothing groups do not exist where patch models are concerned. Because of this, creating a sharp edge in the middle of a patch surface requires the special technique shown in the section of this chapter entitled "Fine-Tuning the Surface."

Normals are another tricky problem with patches, as they are controlled by the direction of the splines used to create the patch. No *Flip Normals* feature for patches is built into MAX. You can, however, apply a two-sided map to the patch surface if needed or turn off Back Face Cull. Both sides are displayed in such a case.

T I P

You may want to assign a keyboard shortcut to toggle Back Face Cull on and off if you model with patches a lot.

Accuracy Issues

Although precise surface curvature is not generally required for the majority of the work done in MAX, for some projects it may be necessary. It is important to note that although it is easy to adjust the curves of the splines that control a patch surface, the patch surfaces themselves can be quite difficult to match with another. The difficulty arises because you are essentially dealing with what could be seen as a broad-tipped brush for laying out a surface. Even with Manual Interior turned on, you are moving a region of the surface rather than directly manipulating its structure. For this reason, you may want either to opt for mesh objects altogether for such a project, or to use patches to create the initial surface and then convert it to a mesh for more precise control.

Texture Mapping Issues

Of all the limitations of patch surfaces, texture mapping may be the most serious for one critical reason: Patch surfaces can hold only one material. If you attach two mesh objects they retain both their mapping coordinates and their assigned materials. If you attach two patch objects, they retain their mapping coordinates but inherit the material of the parent patch. If you are dealing with jointed characters, this is not a problem. If you plan to use Bones Pro or some other skin plug-in, however, you need to change your patch object into a mesh. This is not too drastic because the mesh object looks just like the patch object. You just can't adjust the topology steps any more, and you lose the patch lattice.

TIP

Physique in Character Studio seems to be the exception to this problem, as it can be applied to a selection of objects. Just select all the patch surfaces, then apply Physique to them.

A pair of free plug-ins is available that overcomes this problem altogether. Patch MatID and PatchOut enable you to use Multi/Sub-Object materials on patch objects. Another free plug-in, Face Map 2, enables you to use face maps on triangular patches and meshes. Peter Watje made all three of these, and they enhance other plug-ins he has made.

Basic Patch Modeling Overview

Patch models can be created from just about anything in MAX. Primitives provide a quick base if you are building a less complex patch object; extrusions and lathes can provide more complex starting points. (Primitives or extrusions do not need to be turned into patch objects unless you need the attributes of a patch to model the object.)

Applying the Edit Patch modifier affects primitives differently. Generally, it conforms optimally for the primitive to which you apply it. You should understand, however, the way in which MAX constructs its patches from mesh and primitive objects.

Overall, patch primitives are more limited in function than their mesh counterparts. Unless you need a specific feature that can be found only in patches, it is best to stick with standard primitives.

You will probably find creating patches from extruded splines to be the most useful of the basic patch creation methods. It gives the most control over patch layout and overall form. If you want a patch cylinder, for example, it is better to extrude a circle as a patch rather than to apply the Edit Patch modifier to a cylinder primitive (see fig. 7.4).

FIGURE 7.4

An example of a primitive patch and an extruded patch.

Primitive cylinder with Edit Patch applied

Extruded circle with Patch option selected

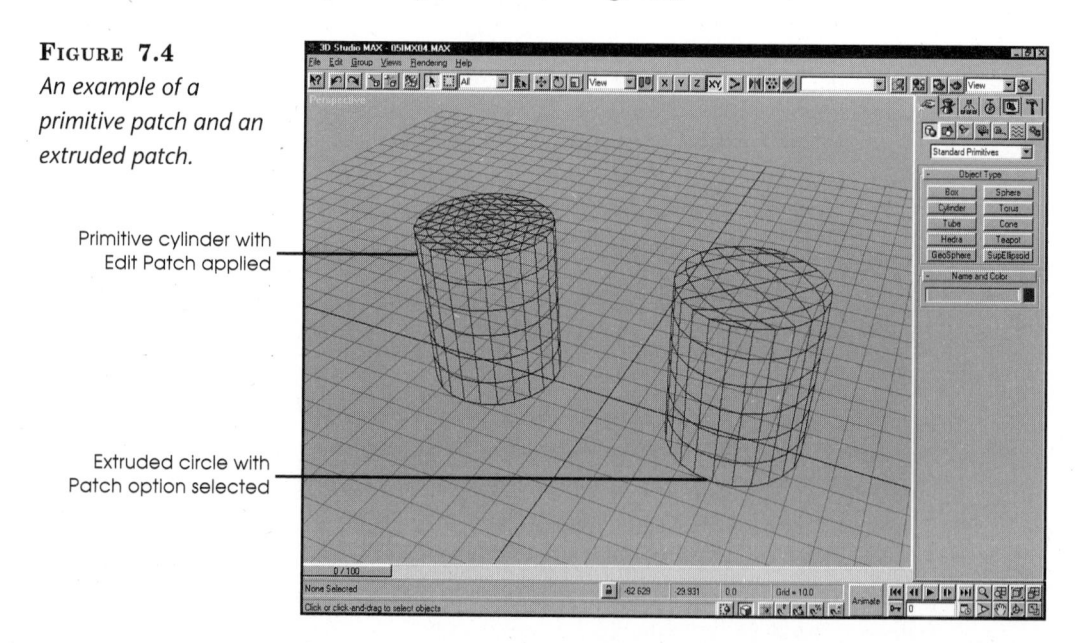

You have much more control over how many patches the cylinder will be composed of and how the patches are laid out. The patches on the extruded cylinder are divided by the control vertices on the circle used to create it and the number of segments. The patches on the primitive cylinder are always in the same arbitrary layout. You cannot add more patches to it without subdividing it or deleting a patch, selecting an edge, and adding a patch.

Modeling a Hand with the Patch Tools in MAX

The power that the splines give you in manipulating complex surfaces makes them an excellent tool for creating cars, characters, food, and designer furniture and architecture. Remember that the entire surface is controlled by splines, and that the Bézier splines give you full control over the surface curvature. Because of this, you can lay out a complete framework by using Bézier splines. You can then apply patches to the framework and align them to it by using the same methods used to create it. Not only do you have the patch modeling tools with which to work, but also some of the tools in MAX usually only associated with meshes. Booleans can add a great deal of functionality to patches, enabling you not only to trim surfaces but to add incredible detail.

Needed Resources

One of the most important aspects of patch modeling is source material use and management. Without quality source materials, professional results are difficult to achieve (if not impossible). Depending on the shape of the object you are creating, images of different views are required. For a hand, the most important views are of the top and bottom. Although you can get away without using a side view, it is highly recommended that you use one to achieve correct proportions. Access to a scanner is important, although not vital in many cases. A good image editor is almost always needed to make adjustments to the images and to create a wireframe template over them. Other things can make patch modeling easier as well, but they are not required. A digitizer to create a basic mesh to which to snap your splines can increase speed as well as improve accuracy. A vector-based drawing program that can export to DXF can make creating the initial 2D template a lot easier. In this exercise, sketches of a hand have been scanned and imported into Adobe Photoshop.

Creating a Template from an Image

When modeling a hand that will be animated, it is crucial to apply certain structural attributes. This is not only because the hand is a complex mechanical system, but because slip-ups in hand mechanics can cause this easily recognized appendage to appear fake and unprofessional. Joints must have more patch density than the areas between them. The point at which the finger meet the base of the hand should be meticulously sculpted because of the multiple directions of stretching that occur there. The palm of the hand has defined lines along which folding of the skin occurs, and that wrinkle considerably when the hand closes even partially. Before attempting to model a hand, study your own closely. No anatomy books, videos, or images can compare with first-hand experience. It seems like a funny pun, but it's actually the best way to describe the process. Locate the points of rotation. Observe the overall structure. Hands are not static objects. Their internal bone structure enables the base of the hand to conform to a surface while still retaining a great deal of strength. The first thing you need is to have your source material in digital form so that it can be loaded into an image editor.

FIGURE 7.5

A sketch of the top view of a hand.

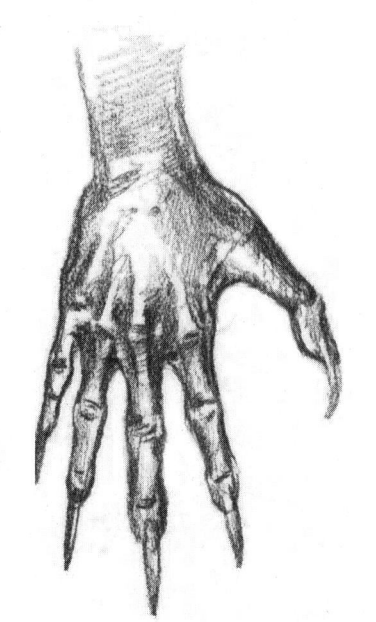

FIGURE 7.6

*A spline layout derived
from a sketch of the
top view of a hand.*

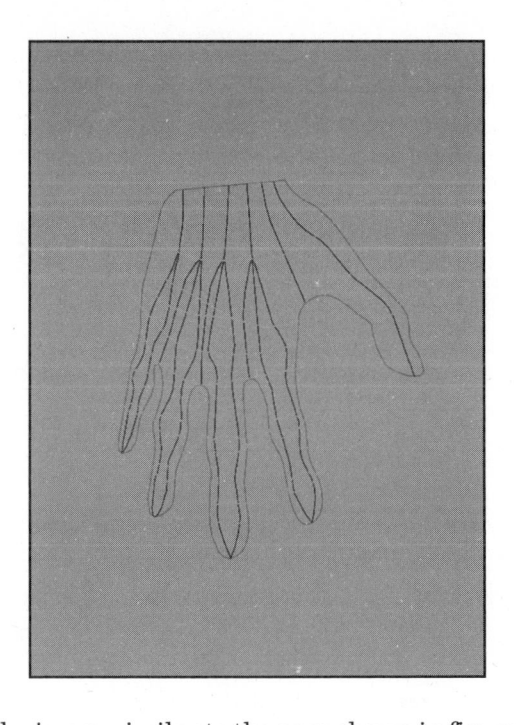

Draw the template on the image similar to the ones shown in figures 7.5 and 7.6. Afterward, if your image is on a white background, fill it in with gray. This makes working on it in MAX much easier.

TIP

In Photoshop, you can draw the lines on separate layers and place them on a gray layer after you are finished.

After you have a viable template of the top view on which to build your framework, make a template of the palm. The palm image should be exactly the same size. The lines for the palm need to be drawn to match the lines where the skin folds. The easiest way to start the palm template is to overlay the top-view template on the image of the palm. Use the same outline as the top image and continue the lines running the length of the hand around the palm. Be careful to line up the palm folds correctly. If your estimation of the end point locations of the palm folds is a little off, put the line where it should be on the palm and it can be fixed when the framework is made. If it is off by too much, you should fix it in the template. You may find it easier to start with the palm and then do the back of the hand.

If you choose to make a side view of the hand, it should consist only of an outline and a horizontal line representing the top outline as viewed from the side.

NOTE

You may be wondering why you need to go through this process. After all, you could load the image into MAX and draw the splines over the image. Creating a gridwork on the image is necessary, however, because it would be very difficult to lay out a proper spline framework without it. By laying out all the lines beforehand, you can see where every spline will intersect, which is where the control vertices must be placed.

Creating a Spline Framework

A spline framework is not the same as a wireframe; it does not represent the actual surface. A spline framework works at a different level, as more of a foundation supporting the surface. Remember that patch edges operate like splines. You will be using the framework to conform the patch edges to the shape you create with it.

TIP

Much of the work in this section can be accomplished more easily in a vector drawing program or an image editing package that can export paths in a format that MAX can read. In Photoshop, for instance, you can trace the template with paths and then export the paths in Adobe Illustrator format, which MAX can read in as Bézier splines. After importing, use the InterSpl plug-in to adjust the smoothness of the spline curves. Not only is this easier, it's also faster and usually more accurate.

1. Start MAX. Set the top template as the background image and make the background image visible in a Top viewport.

2. Using the Line tool in Create Shapes, trace the outline of the template first, placing a control vertex wherever it intersects another spline.

3. Turn off Start New Shape, and trace the lines that run the length of the hand, (again) placing control vertices at every intersection.

4. Clean up the trace, using the Edit Spline modifier. Use a combination of vertex types to create an accurate trace.

5. Freeze all the splines except for the outline.

6. Set the palm template as the background image and make the background image visible in a bottom view.

7. In the bottom view, trace the outline of the template.

8. Trace the lines running the length of the hand, (again) placing the control vertices at each intersection, and snapping the endpoints of the splines to the outline.

9. Lock axis movement so that you will only be moving vertices perpendicular to the grid. This varies depending on which reference coordinate system you use. (I recommend switching to the World coordinate system for this process and locking movement to the Z axis.)

10. Create a viewport layout so that you have one top view and one side view. This gives you the maximum viewable area.

11. Use the top view to select control vertices and the side view to move the vertices up and down.

12. Unfreeze the splines for the top of the hand and freeze the palm splines.

13. Perform the same procedure for the top of the hand (see fig. 7.7).

FIGURE 7.7

Lengthwise splines for the top of a hand after they've been raised.

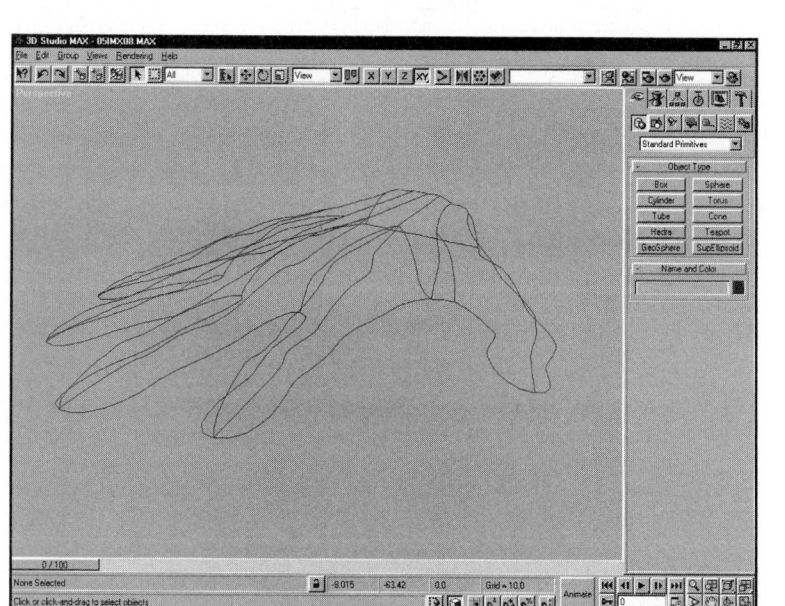

Inspect the layout of the splines closely. Use 3D snap to position the control vertices at intersecting splines on top of each other, and adjust any curves that are not aligned correctly. The result should be a fairly nice, yet simplified contour of the hand. The last process of creating the spline framework is fairly easy.

14. From the top view, with 3D Snap turned on and only Vertex Snap active, draw the lines that run the width of the hand. As you are drawing the new lines, make certain that the cursor is snapping to the vertices on the horizontal lines.

TIP

Notice the "V" shape of the splines on the knuckle joints. The extra spline gives the joint more faces so that when it bends and stretches, the surface remains smooth.

15. Lock axis movement to Y/Z.

16. In a User or Perspective viewport, adjust the curves of the vertical lines to match the curve of the hand as closely as possible.

17. With the Edit Spline modifier active, but not in SubObject mode, use the Attach command to attach all the splines together (see fig. 7.8).

FIGURE 7.8

Completed spline framework for the hand.

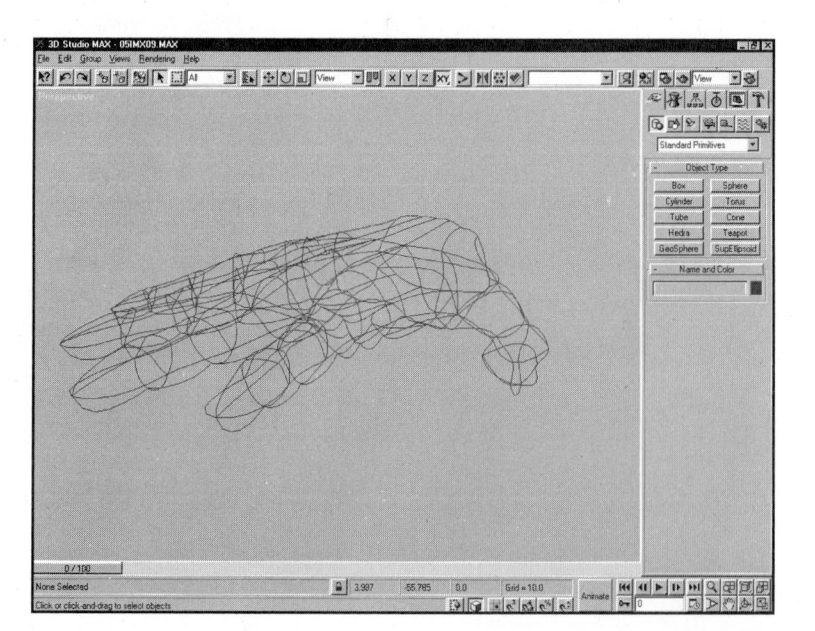

That's it. The spline framework is complete. You probably want to collapse the stack and re-apply Edit Spline at this point. This optimizes the stack. After you have done this, save the file and a copy of the splines; they can be used for other things later.

Building the Patch Surface

Creating a patch surface by hand in MAX can be a time-consuming process at first. After you gain some experience with patch placement and alignment, however, your modeling speed increases dramatically. The hard part is already done after you have a well-designed spline framework. A poorly constructed framework can make creating the patch surface take much longer, if it can be constructed at all.

1. Open the file 07imx09.max on the CD, hide the palm splines, and freeze the top splines.

2. Create a quad patch, move it to the base of the hand, and align it as closely as possible to a square along the bottom of the outline.

3. Apply Edit Patch and place the patch vertices on their respective spline vertices. Don't worry too much about accuracy for this model, just place them as closely as you can.

4. Go to the Edge sub-object level and select the top edge of the patch.

5. Click Add Quad Patch and align the new patch to the patch framework.

6. Repeat step 5 until you reach the top extent of the hand, replacing quad patches with tri patches if triangles are in the framework.

7. Add patches to the left edges of the patches you created. You can do this to multiple patches at a time. Just select all the edges that require quad patches, then click on Add Quad Patch, and then do the same for tri patches with Add Tri Patch.

8. Weld each new pair of patch vertices together and snap them to the framework.

9. Repeat steps 7 and 8 until the top of the hand is covered with patches (see fig. 7.9).

FIGURE 7.9
A hand with patches added to the top.

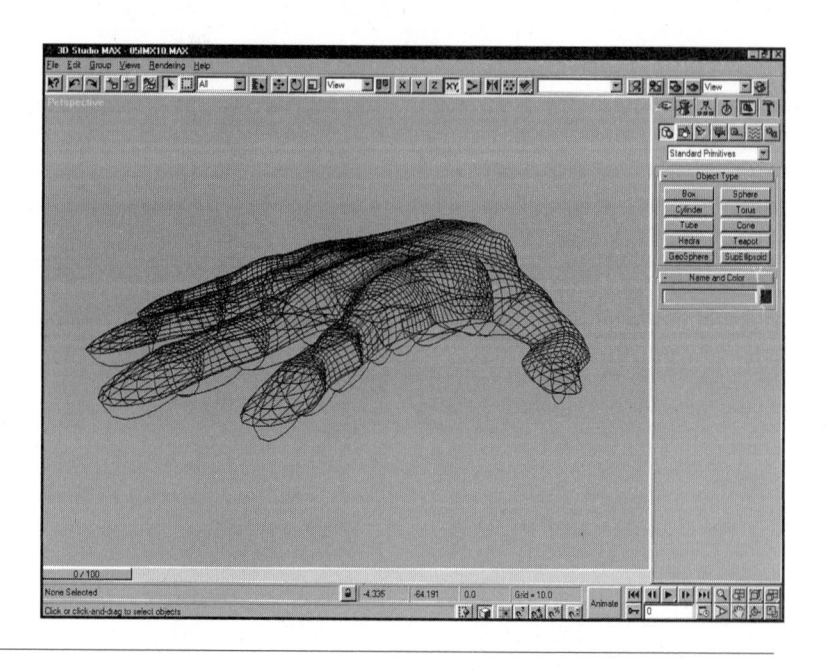

After this process is finished, perform a similar process for the palm. When the entire surface is created, examine it closely in both shaded and wireframe mode. Align the patch edges with the splines in the framework as closely as possible, and try to keep a smooth continuity to the surface (see fig. 7.10).

FIGURE 7.10
A completed hand shown both in wireframe and shaded mode.

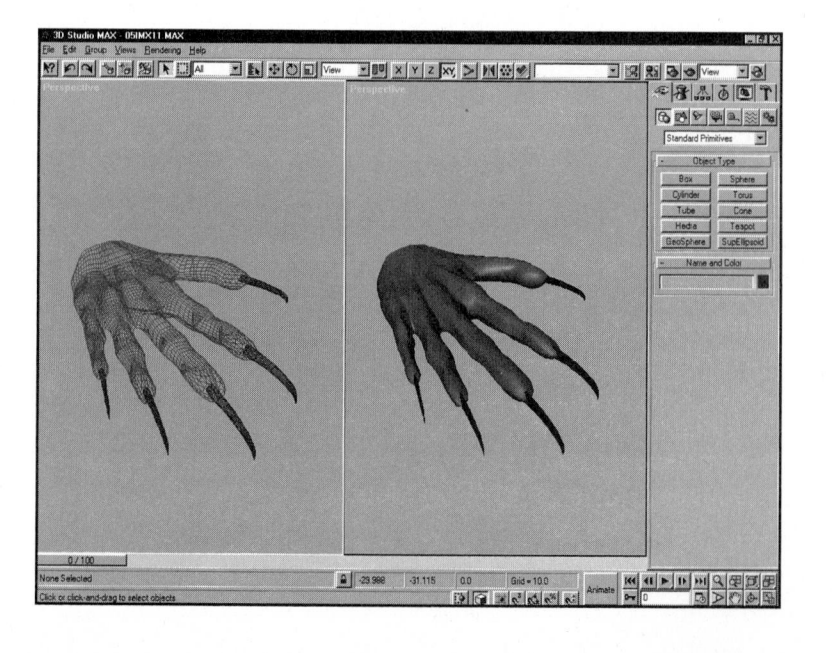

When working with patches, apply a two-sided material to them. This aids greatly when working in shaded mode because you can see the surface from both sides and catch surface problems very difficult to see from just one side.

When working with patch surfaces, it is important to remember that they are surfaces not solid models. You can add detail much more easily by adding more surfaces rather than by trying to build the details into the existing surface.

Now the hand is finished, and should look like figure 07imx11.tif. The claws are very simple objects that can be added later.

Modeling a Torso from an Image

The subtle variations in curves and proportion make modeling a torso seem deceptively easy. All too often, however, these subtleties are missed. This is partially because most traditional modeling methods make it difficult to create a mesh structure that supports the complex curvature of the torso. The exercises in this section help take the guesswork out of modeling the torso. Although the torso could be modeled using methods similar to those used to create the hand, the Surface Tools plug-in is demonstrated to show how much faster it makes patch modeling.

The Surface Tools plug-in, created by Peter Watje and distributed by Digimation, removes a great deal of the work from creating patch models and can actually help make much better models as well. Combined with several free plug-ins also created by Peter Watje for patch and spline editing, patch modeling becomes an even more powerful method for creating many complex surface types.

Surface Tools is composed of two modifiers: Cross Section and Surface. Most of their basic usage is described in the manual that accompanies the product, so the following sections focus on actually creating a full character by using Surface Tools and combining the functionality given by the other plug-ins with it. In the following tutorials, several methods are used to generate the spline framework of different parts of the body. Note that the optimal methods for creating spline frameworks for different shapes and detail levels vary. You may find yourself mixing and matching the different methods based on your resources and the type of model you are building.

Needed Resources

Naturally, the more source material you have on the modeling subject the better; certain types work better for different objects. For a less detailed model, you may only need images of the side and top. For more accuracy, you may want to use photographs of a marked-up object. For optimal accuracy and detail, you should start with digitized data. For this first tutorial involving the creation of the dragon's body, only a pair of sketches were used: one of a top view, and one of a side view (see fig. 7.11). This is a fast way to create a spline framework, although not very accurate. The peaks and valleys of the surface are fairly well defined in the sketches, however, and this should make it easy to create something similar.

FIGURE 7.11

A side view sketch of a dragon.

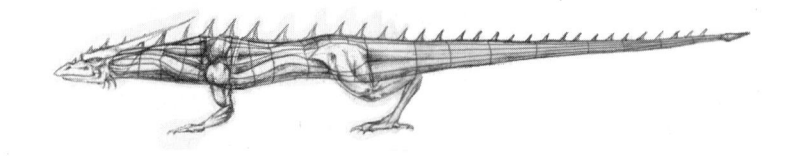

Creating a Template from an Image

The steps involved in creating a template from an image for a Surface Tools model are identical to those used in creating the template for the hand—with an emphasis on form, however, rather than on mechanics. Keep in mind that splines can do a lot of the work for you. Many times, you won't need a spline for both the peak and the valley because the spline control handles can be used to make a rounded peak fairly easily. This reduces the number of splines required and gives you a wider range of polygon count adjustment.

Creating a Spline Framework

Surface Tools gives you some leniency when creating the spline framework; it welds control vertices for you at a tolerance you specify. This can speed things up somewhat for some models, but on a model like this one—with such a large difference in patch sizes—it is best to use 3D Snap and be exact. Otherwise, it welds together vertices of multiple smaller patches. Other than that, create the spline framework for the dragon body by using the same steps used on the hand (see fig. 7.12).

FIGURE 7.12
*A completed spline
framework for half of
the dragon's body.*

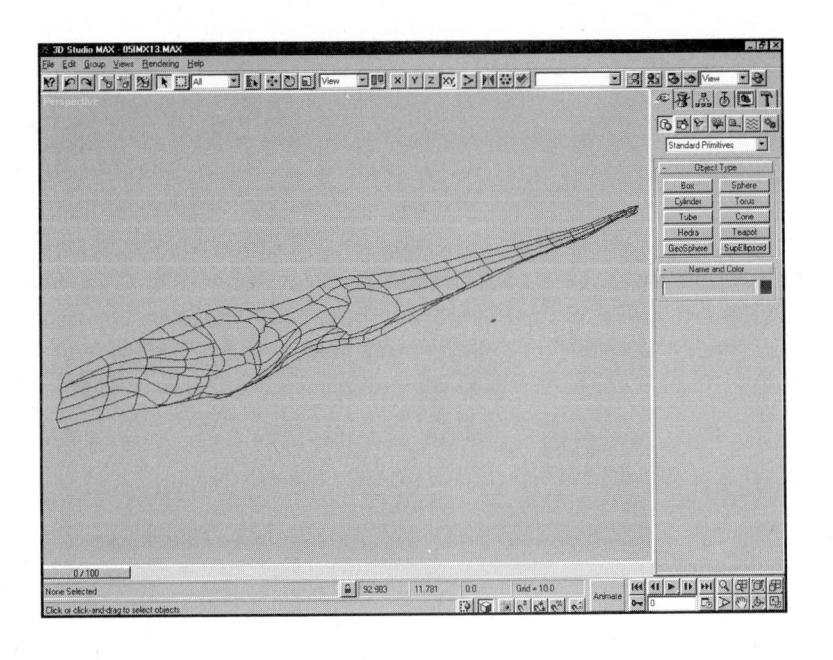

WARNING

Vertices of splines that have been attached to each other do not snap to each other. Leave all the splines unattached until you have finished creating the spline framework. If you have already attached them, you can select independent splines and segments and detach them. After you are finished modifying the splines, remember to reattach the splines.

Creating the Patch Surface

To create the patch surface, apply the Surface modifier to the spline framework. Because the spline control vertices rest on each other at the intersections, you can set the weld threshold very low. For this example, set the weld threshold to .01. The following symptoms indicate that your weld threshold is too high:

- Patches with edges that don't follow the spline framework

- Visible lines or seams on the back side of the patch surface

- Holes in the patch surface

Many times, the normals of the patches wind up reversed. If this is the case, choose the Reverse Normals option in the Surface modifier. On some occasions, some of the patches along the edge of the surface are flipped. This is because the starting points of the splines are mismatched. Try to keep all the starting points in the spline framework on the same end.

Another problem erupts when the spline framework has sections with more than four control vertices. Because five-sided patches do not exist, Surface Tools cannot fill these in. You must either weld two of the points together or add another spline inside the section. This can be a useful tool for adding holes to your surface as well.

The Surface modifier's steps operate like those for the Edit Patch modifier and translate directly over if you apply an Edit Patch modifier to the surface. Lowering the steps to 1 or 0 dramatically speeds up redraw times while you are working. Setting the steps up to 5 or higher gives you crisp, smooth detail for rendering output.

Fine-Tuning the Surface

Many times, after the patch surface is created, you get something close to what you want. Rarely, however, does it turn out exactly the way you want it. This is especially the case where tri patches are joined with quad patches. This often causes a variation in shading or puts small wrinkles on the surface. Most of the time, this only occurs in tight curves; try, therefore, to keep tri patches on broad, flat areas.

The internal layout of the patch surface is controlled not only by the position of the edges but by the length of the control handles as well. Normally, you will want to keep an even spread of patch density, but in some situations, you can sacrifice faces in one area and add them in another without adding more splines. The steps or faces of a patch will gather to where the control handles push or pull them.

Creating a Sharp Edge on a Patch Surface

A common problem associated with patches is the difficulty of getting a sharp edge along a surface. This is made even more difficult by the fact that patches do not have smoothing groups. The first thing to remember is that you should plan the sharp edges before you create the surface; it is really only possible to obtain one along the patch edges. That means you need to have a spline running along wherever you need a sharp edge. After your surface follows this guideline, follow these steps:

1. Make certain that the lattice is visible, and go to the Vertex sub-object level of the Edit Patch modifier.

2. Convert all the vertices that run the length of the intended sharp edge into Corner vertices, and adjust them to meet your angle requirements.

3. Select all the patches that run the length of the sharp edge on one side of it and detach them.

4. Get out of sub-object mode and reattach the patches (see fig. 7.13).

FIGURE 7.13

An example of the difference between smooth and sharp edges.

Torso with smooth muscles —

Torso with sharp-edged muscles —

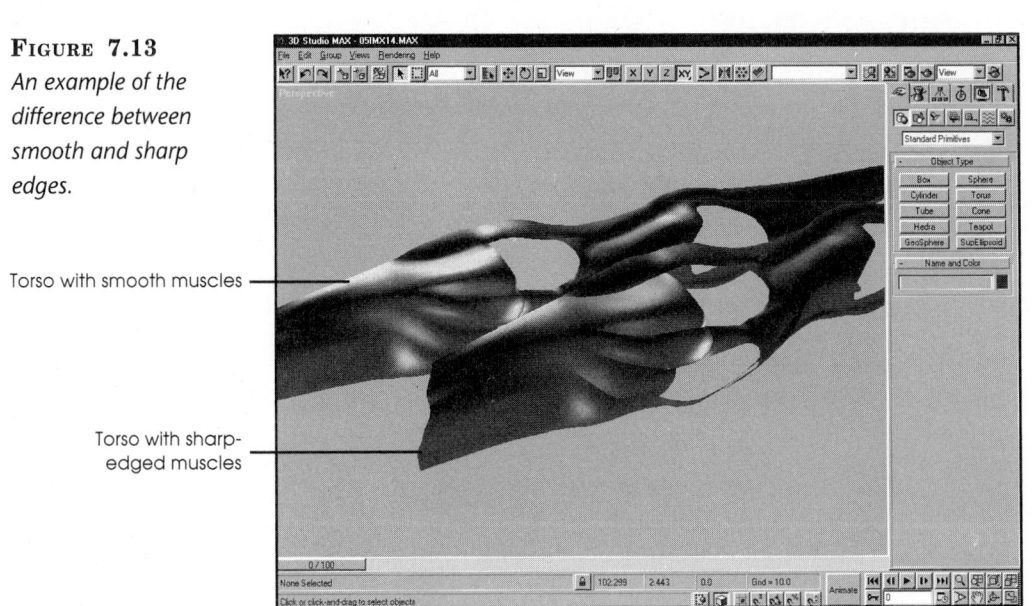

This is currently the only way to create a controlled sharp edge along a patch surface. Some flaws exist with it, however. The vertices along the sharp edge are no longer welded. If you do weld them, it smooths the surface, and if you move them one at a time, it creates a break in the surface. When you need to adjust those vertices, always select both vertices.

Creating a Patch Head from a Mesh Object

The most accurate way to create a detailed patch object is to derive its splines from a mesh object. This can actually save a great deal of work both in preparation and in touchup—you can use a low-detail mesh to create the splines. The head created in this exercise was originally sculpted in clay, marked up with only the amount of lines required to get its surface detail, and then digitized. The process should be planned carefully to use as few triangles as possible. After you have the mesh object, you can use a free plug-in called Edge to Spline to create the splines.

Creating the Spline Framework with the Edge to Spline Plug-In

The process involved in creating a framework from a mesh is different, and in some ways, more involved than the previous methods shown in this chapter. These ways, however, almost always lead to a more accurate, detailed end product more quickly. The reason for this is that not only do you have exact locations for each vertex, but you also have the spline layout created by the mesh.

T I P

When selecting edges to convert to splines, selecting multiple sets of edges speeds things greatly. As you select them, make certain that none of them cross or attach to any of the other selected edges in any way.

1. Open file 07imx15.max from the CD. This is the mesh of the dragon's head.

2. Select a series of edges, following the contour of the object.

3. Select the Utilities command panel and then select Edge to Spline from the drop-down list.

4. Click on Pick Object and then click on the head (see fig. 7.14).

FIGURE 7.14
A continuous selection of edges changed into a spline.

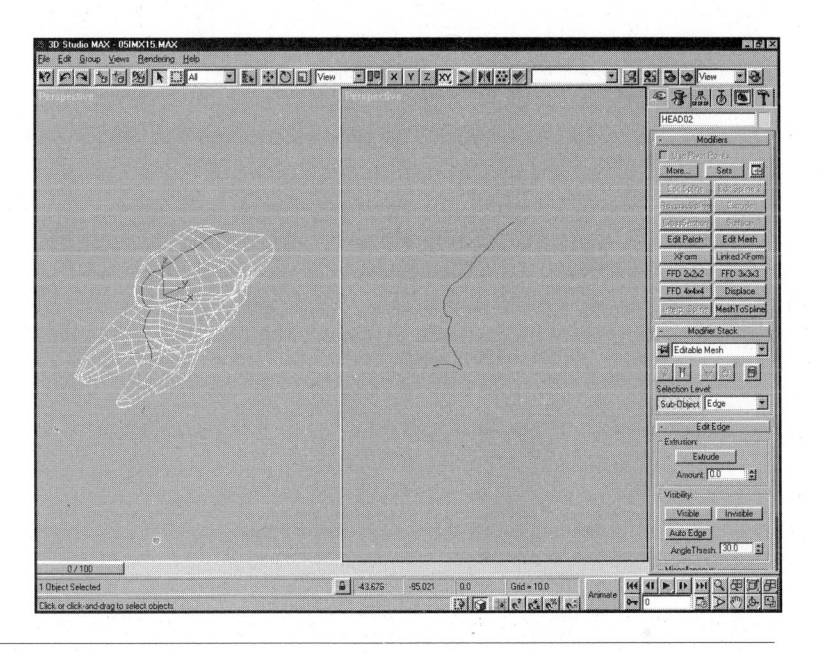

The edges selected in sub-object mode are converted into a spline. The spline's control vertices are left as corner vertices. It is useful to convert them into smooth or Bézier vertices as you go along; this separates their segments from the mesh slightly, enabling you to see what you have accomplished. Repeat the process until all the edges have been converted into splines, and then attach all of them together.

You probably need to edit the splines somewhat to get accurate curves across the object. Use the four types of control vertices as required. If the mesh object was planned out correctly, it should not require an excessive amount of editing.

Mirroring and Attaching Spline Frameworks

It is fairly standard practice to model half of a symmetrical object and then mirror it. This cuts modeling time in half and helps keep proportions accurate. The same holds true for patch modeling, but some differences exist when working with splines. Make certain that all the end-control vertices along the edge are exactly aligned along one axis at 0 in the World coordinate system. If they are not, apply a non-uniform scale on them along that axis.

WARNING

Do not scale vertices that are either Bézier, Bézier corner, or smooth. This scales their handles and curves as well, creating a nightmare of cleanup work. Change the end handles to Corner before scaling them. You can always change them back later.

After the object meets these parameters, follow these steps:

1. Open file 07imx16.max from the CD.

2. Detach the spline that runs along the edge on which the object will be mirrored.

3. Change the coordinate reference system to World, and the pivot point to Use Transform Coordinate Center.

4. Click Mirror, set Y as the Mirror Axis, select Copy, and then click on OK.

5. Exit Sub-object mode, attach the mirrored splines, and open Sub-object mode again.

6. Go to the Vertex sub-object level and weld all the vertices that run down the center.

7. Get out of sub-object level and reattach the center spline (see fig. 7.15).

FIGURE 7.15
Dragon head splines mirrored.

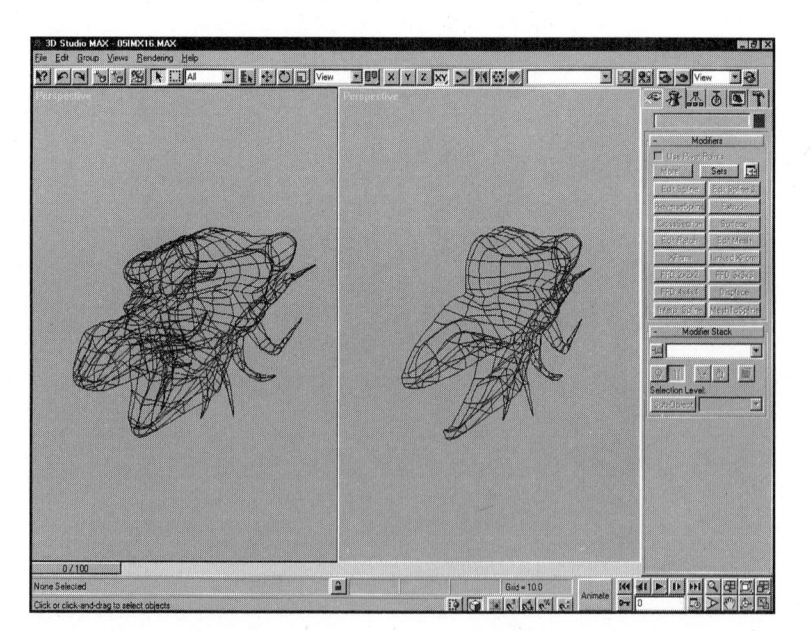

Inspect the mirrored edge, checking for any vertices that were not welded or which were welded improperly. Remember that you can only have three- and four-sided patches. You may need to adjust the curves of some of the center vertices to create a smooth transition.

After the framework is in order, apply the Surface modifier to it with a low-weld threshold, and then look over the object again. Check for surface irregularities and holes. If holes exist, it is usually the result of either a section with more than four vertices or a place where two vertices lie outside the weld threshold. You can fix the former problem by adding new splines to the sections and the latter problem by uniformly scaling the vertices together or raising the weld threshold slightly.

Modeling an Arm with Cross Sections

One of the easiest ways to model a narrow and fairly simple appendage is to just use cross sections. This enables you to keep the joint where arm and torso meet exact, while creating a consistent, flexible surface for the arm. This section shows how to create the cross sections to create the arm and introduces the Cross Section modifier. The Cross Section modifier creates for you all the lines that run the length of the cross sections.

Creating Splines for Cross Sections

The first thing to remember when creating cross sections is that left as they are, they offer limited control. Think of cross sections as a quick start for creating the base shape of your object. Keep that in mind as you plan the layout of the object and you usually wind up with much better models when finished. Notice that in the torso, holes were left where the arm, wing, and leg can extend from. These are used to create the initial cross section and are what the subsequent cross sections are based on.

1. Open file 07imx17.max from the CD.

2. Select the spline segments that make up the hole for the arm and detach them as a copy.

3. Apply an Edit Spline modifier to the new spline and weld the vertices to make it a single spline.

4. At the spline sub-object level, clone the spline by holding down the Shift key and moving it to the right.

5. Select all its vertices and then apply a non-uniform scale on them to 0 percent. This flattens the cross section, making it much easier to work with.

6. Now edit the vertices of the cross section, conforming it to the shape you need for the shoulder. Then rotate it and position it below and to the right of the first cross section (see fig. 7.16).

FIGURE 7.16

Arm cross section splines created by cloning the edges of the hole left in the torso framework.

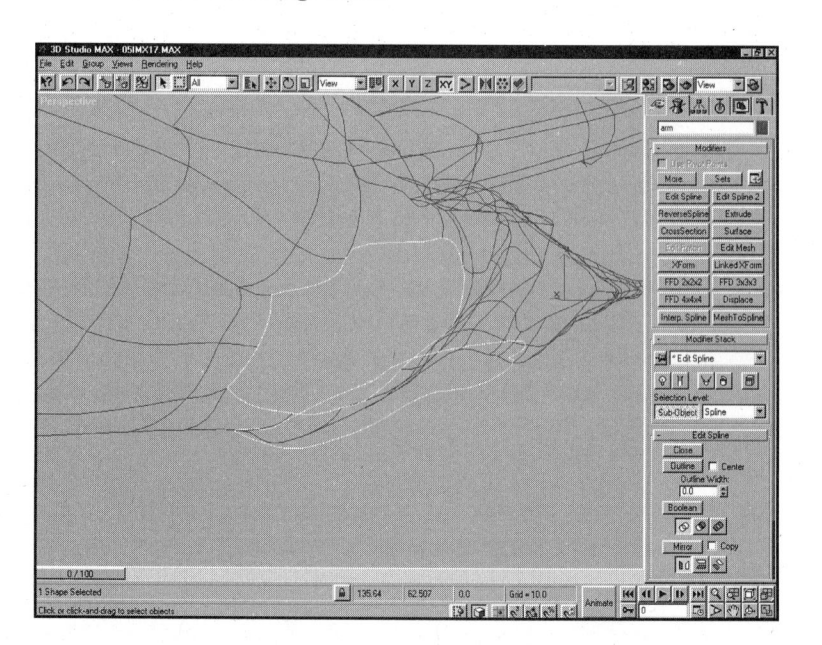

Repeat this process until you have all the cross sections needed for the arm. This step should not take too much effort because you won't have a good idea of what it will look like until the lengthwise splines are added. At that point, most of the modeling is done.

Editing the Cross Section Splines

After all the cross sections are complete, apply the Cross Section modifier with Smooth selected, and then apply an Edit Spline modifier to the entire new set of splines. To get a solid idea of what really needs to be done to it to make it look like an arm, apply the Surface modifier with a low-weld threshold to it.

Although the general shape of the arm is okay, leaving the framework as it is results in poor muscle arrangement. The vertices must be edited to get the proper shape of the arm. This is why the second Edit Spline modifier was applied.

1. Open file 07imx18.max from the CD.

2. Leave the Surface modifier in the stack, but go back to the second Edit Spline modifier.

3. Go to the Vertex sub-object level and then modify the vertices—both in placement and in curvature—until you have what you think is much closer to the actual arm.

4. Remaining in sub-object mode, click on and hold the Show End Result button (see fig. 7.17).

FIGURE 7.17
Seeing the effects of your editing.

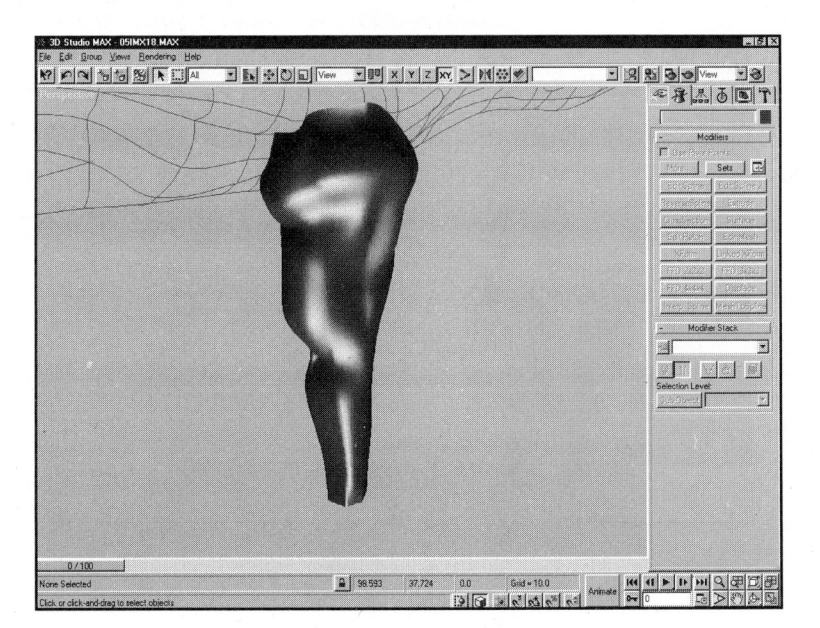

By using Show End Result, you can see the effects of your editing quickly, without ever leaving the Edit Spline modifier. This makes for faster modeling times and better models. Use the same procedure to model the leg and wing, the horns, and the ear bones.

In Practice: Modeling Characters with Patch Tools

- **Patches versus meshes.** Patches lend themselves to creating complex surfaces much more easily than meshes. This makes them well-suited for modeling single-skinned characters.

- **Patch limitations.** Modifiers that require the mesh structure of faces, edges, and vertices convert a patch into a mesh. If there is no way to avoid using one of these modifiers, finish making any changes you need to the model in patches, save a copy, and then convert it to a mesh.

- **Basic patch models.** Creating patches from primitives or extruded or lathed splines can be a good starting point for simple patch objects. There is no need to convert a primitive into a patch object unless you need patch attributes to edit the primitive.

- **Planning for a patch character.** Planning out a model beforehand is much more important when creating a patch model. Good source materials and a sound knowledge of Bézier splines are vital assets to creating a good model.

- **Modeling with only the patch tools in MAX.** Creating complex patch models with only the patch tools in MAX is definitely possible. It just takes a lot more work than when plug-ins are used.

- **Spline frameworks.** The spline framework is the structure on which a good patch model is based. It provides an easily editable infrastructure and enables you to make large changes by just moving the spline vertices.

- **Plug-ins.** Several plug-ins are available that greatly enhance patch modeling in MAX. Most of them are free and add functionality ranging from spline editing to texture mapping.

IMAGE BY KEN ALLEN ROBERTSON

Chapter 8

by Ken Allen Robertson

CHARACTER MODELING WITH PLUG-INS

To understand the paradigm inherent in the design of MAX, imagine that the program is like your closet. You have certain types of clothing, shirts, jeans, and shoes arranged to mix and match in any way you see fit. In addition, you have special pieces for special occasions—jackets, dress shirts, and ties. You can add to this collection at any time. The new pieces take their place alongside the others, no different than the others (only newer). You don't have to go to a different closet to get the newer pieces, or perform some special procedure to insert them into the closet in the first place. In addition, you can use these new pieces with the older pieces to create entirely new combinations (why not a tuxedo jacket with sneakers and jeans?).

MAX takes advantage of the latest thinking in object-oriented programs, providing a vast array of elementary (and not-so-elementary) 3D processes. By providing every user with the MAX Software Developer's Kit, Kinetix gives any user with the knowledge (or the desire to learn) access to almost all these functions—to be arranged in new combinations as the developer sees fit. As another benefit, development in the 32-bit Windows environment (either Windows 95 or NT) provides access to an even greater library of functions called the Microsoft Foundation Class library. This library consists of the most basic elements of windowed programming and graphics. MAX provides the developer with the world's greatest collection of building blocks to stack and arrange (and rearrange) to create new and exciting combinations with ease and stability.

Character modeling—an exacting and multifaceted process—will certainly reap the greatest rewards from this new paradigm. Already, amazing packages such as Surface Tools, Bones Pro, and Metareyes 4.0 are making incredible leaps, enabling artists to create characters recently possible to create only in 3D packages that cost at least three times what MAX costs. New plug-ins are also being generated almost daily, a number of them available for limited or no cost to the end user. With animation packages such as Morph Magic, Hypermatter, and Metacloth on the horizon, 3DS MAX has proved itself to be a world class professional tool for character creators.

This chapter covers the following topics:

- General principles for character modeling with plug-ins
- Seamless versus segmented modeling
- Using plug-ins for character modeling

General Principles for Character Modeling with Plug-Ins

Although every new plug-in will vary a little in how it utilizes the power of MAX, some general rules make character modeling a much simpler and effective process, no matter which techniques are used. The following general rules should be observed:

- Start simple and add detail.

- Have references constantly available.

- Work in halves.

- Know the tools for "tweaking"—one tool is never enough.

Start Simple and Add Detail

When you have a beautiful character design that just begs for an artist to build it, you can easily get caught up in the massive details involved in fully realizing a stunning model. You might focus on one part of the model until it is complete, and then move on to the other parts. Often, however, this method leads to creating detail that conflicts with parts of the model created later in the process. These conflicts can result in frustrating, tedious manipulations of the model to tweak it into a workable form.

You should instead try to envision the modeling process more along the lines of sculpting: Building the basic proportions of the model in a simplistic form, aligning them to their proper locations, and then adding detail as needed. All the current modeling tools lend themselves easily to this process, and the MAX modifier stack is an incredibly useful tool to go back over your steps if you take a wrong turn during the modeling process. This process also enables you to see where detail is (and is not) needed.

A helpful technique is to build a *mock-up*—a stand-in character made up of simple primitives, boxes, and spheres—as a prototype of your character, similar to figure 8.1. A mock-up provides you with a simple, proportionally accurate model that can be frozen and used in the background, and over which to sculpt the detailed model. If you are planning to use Bones Pro to animate the model, this framework can also serve as the beginnings of your skeleton. If you are using Character Studio for your animation, creating a biped for your mock-up proves quick and effective.

FIGURE 8.1
A character mock-up.

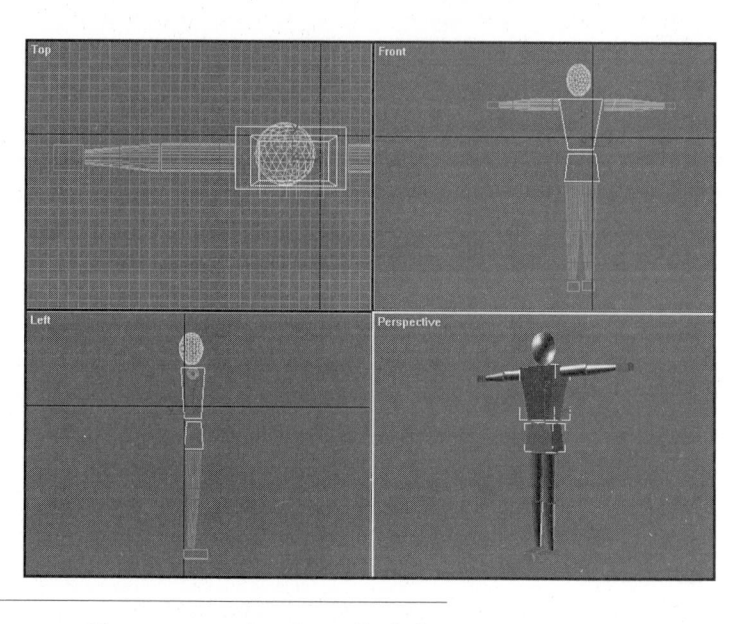

Have References Constantly Available

Characters can have their beginnings in any number of places—an idea sparked by a picture, a song, a story idea, or any combination of these are only a few examples. If you start the character-modeling process in the computer without a clear visual idea of what the final character should look like, however, you are bound to go through an exercise of trial and error that dramatically increases the time required to create the character. Before you start modeling, create visual references, such as sketches and *maquettes* (small sculptures). If you are building a previously created character, you should have multiple pictures of the character at hand.

If you have the time, it is highly recommended that you create a maquette for the character. Two-dimensional information available through sketches, even if extensive *turn-arounds* (various views of the character) are created, can be deceptive and misleading when translated into three dimensions. By having a three-dimensional reference available, however, you can easily focus on any part of the character with which you are having trouble. You can actually pick up the maquette and rotate it to get a clearer picture of the modeling requirements.

With your visual references for the character at hand, you have ready access to the essential blueprint of the character. Better yet, you can load your visual references for the character (whether preexisting or created for your current project) into MAX as a texture map on two crossing planes. You then have the critical information for the character on-screen, accessible without your having to divert your attention from the modeling process on your monitor. If you have created a maquette of your character, take pictures of the side and front views of the maquette, scan them, and use these as texture maps. Remember, though, to always keep the maquette nearby.

As you progressively add detail to your character, other available kinds of references come into play. Excellent resources for detailing a character include books on human anatomy and proportion, pictures of various types of animal anatomy, and pictures of humans and animals in motion. You should consult these resources when you add muscle tone, creases, folds, and bumps to characters. The detail you add will make a character look more alive.

Work in Halves

The look of all organic characters benefits from having some *asymmetry* (one side different than the other); the asymmetry makes them appear more "real." You can save a great deal of time, however, by initially creating only half the character. This "halving" also makes it easier for you to focus as you detail the model. To realize the benefits of halving, create half the model and add all the necessary detail. Then make a mirror clone of the model. Attach this mirrored clone to the piece you originally created. This results in an exact symmetry that you can then tweak to create the asymmetry discussed earlier.

One danger in creating half-models is the possibility of leaving a seam down the middle where the halves are joined. To avoid this problem, be certain to test the mirroring process often. To so test, create the mirror clone, take a look at how the halves match up, and then delete the clone and go back to working the original piece. After the model is completed and joined, use any of the smoothing tools available (Relax, MeshSmooth, or Bones Pro Smooth, for example). Make certain to use these tools on the vertices that run down (or very near) the seam *only*. In this way you can make the seam invisible.

Know the Tools for "Tweaking"—One Tool Is Never Enough

Character modeling is a process of finesse. As mentioned earlier, it is generally advisable to start with simpler forms and add detail as you progress. Fortunately, MAX provides a bevy of tools to do just that. You should familiarize yourself with these tools. They can, after all, be the difference between an average model and a spectacular character.

3DS MAX includes the following tools that enable you to add detail to characters as you progress through your modeling:

- Sub-object controls of the Edit Mesh Modifier (face, vertex, and edge editing)
- Relax
- MeshSmooth
- Free-form deformation

The following sections review the simple ways in which these tools can be applied to a model. For an explanation of the exact parameters of these tools, refer to *Inside 3D Studio MAX Volume I*.

Sub-Object Controls of the Edit Mesh Modifier

Being familiar and confident with sub-objects and their controls is critical to the process of finessing a model. The capability to access the model at its most basic level has always been an excellent part of 3D Studio, and MAX has pushed this capability even further.

Even if you are just selecting sub-objects within the Edit Mesh modifier, to be adjusted with other modifiers, you can save time and produce much greater results by knowing how to maneuver through the sub-object panels and also knowing which sub-objects to select for which modifiers.

Face Controls

The following face controls are those most often used in character modeling (in addition to selecting).

- Extrude

- Tessellate

- Build face

Extruding a face (or a group of faces) is critical to adding large features to the surface of a mesh. Extrude is, therefore, an extremely important tool. You can start modeling a head by modifying a sphere, stretching it longer, and sculpting the basic skull shape with free-form deformation. To add the nose to the model, you can create a separate nose model and perform a Boolean union to attach the two pieces. Boolean operations are often unpredictable, however, and can leave tiny gaps or odd smoothing and can drastically increase geometric intensity.

By selecting the polygons on the face that would correspond to the placement of the nose and then extruding them, your positioning can be exact. The geometry stays extremely close to its original density, and the face remains in one solid piece. The nose faces can then be manipulated into the desired position. Then, with MeshSmooth and Relax, a smooth and organic feature is created.

Tessellating and building go hand-in-hand with extruding faces. If you don't have the proper geometry to extrude a complete smooth feature, performing a simple tessellation of the desired faces can often provide the desired geometry. Generally, it is a good idea to also tessellate the faces around the ones you want to extrude. This gives you a cleaner base from which to perform the extrusion.

If adding faces is not the problem, or if the geometry is too dense to get a clean selection, building faces is often an excellent option. Delete the dense faces in the area from which you want to extrude, and then build new faces attached to the surrounding points in a way that makes the desired area for modification easier to see and better supports the extrusion process.

TIP

When creating faces, always be certain to select the vertices in a *counter-clockwise* order. Otherwise, the normal of the newly created face will face away from you and the polygon will appear to be invisible.

Vertex Controls

In addition to moving vertices to sculpt the model, the most helpful tool in the Vertex Sub-object panel is the Affect Region button. By adjusting the Falloff, Pinch, and Bubble settings, you make it a rather simple matter to pull small organic protrusions from the mesh objects. Used in this way, the vertex controls are the best tools for adding bump-like detail to a character; face controls are better suited for larger, flatter features.

Edge Controls

Two controls in the Edge Sub-object panel are often used for tweaking a character mesh. These controls—Dividing and Turning—enable you to use the vertex and face controls with great efficiency and precision.

Dividing an edge is an excellent way to add pinpoint detail to a mesh. By selecting an edge and dividing it, you provide another vertex for manipulation and create two more faces exactly where you need them for extrusion. Before you begin an edge division process, it is helpful to select all the edges near the area where you will be working and click on the Visible button in the Visibility section of the Edit Edge rollout menu. This will make all the edges in the proximity visible, so that you will get immediate feedback on your division operation.

Turning an edge is also highly useful, especially if the edge operations are going to support a vertex manipulation later. By turning an edge, you choose the way the polygons line up with existing geometry and where you will see the results of the final vertex\face operations. Again, it is helpful to make all edges in the proximity of your work area visible before turning an edge.

Relax

The Relax modifier is a dream tool for the character modeler. By selecting the desired faces or edges and applying a Relax modifier, you can turn hard edges into rounded, organic ones.

A particulary useful way to use Relax is after you model in simple forms and then use sub-object tools to add simple detail. By using the Relax modifier you can change sharp forms to organic ones.

Although you can get similar results by using the Relax settings in the MeshSmooth modifier, performing a separate relax operation before you use MeshSmooth is highly recommended—it leaves a very clear picture of what the precise relax results are and where the MeshSmooth modifier is required.

Relax can also be used with patch models without converting them into mesh objects (as many other modifiers, including MeshSmooth, will do).

MeshSmooth

If the Relax modifier is a dream tool, the MeshSmooth modifier is beyond dreams for the character modeler.

MeshSmooth combines a Relax control with a modifier that creates the geometry necessary to make a completely organic mesh from even the most hard-edged objects. This is an amazingly powerful feature.

By using a MeshSmooth modifier, you can model organic characters by starting with extremely simple figures, as shown in figure 8.2. Such simple features can provide clarity, proportion, and ease of manipulation. You can then move on to organic forms as a final step, without being bogged down with dense geometry during the initial creation process. In addition, MeshSmooth works on sub-objects (faces) with just as much accuracy, making it simple to add detail with sub-object tools and then smooth that detail into organic features at any point in the modeling process.

MeshSmooth should definitely be a major part of your character mesh-modeling process.

Free-Form Deformation

Free-form Deformation builds a simple lattice cage around an object or any selected group of sub-objects. By pushing and pulling the control points of the lattice, you can gently mold mesh surfaces into curved forms without the harshness of manipulating the sub-objects directly.

FIGURE 8.2
A simple hand created from simple geometry using MeshSmooth.

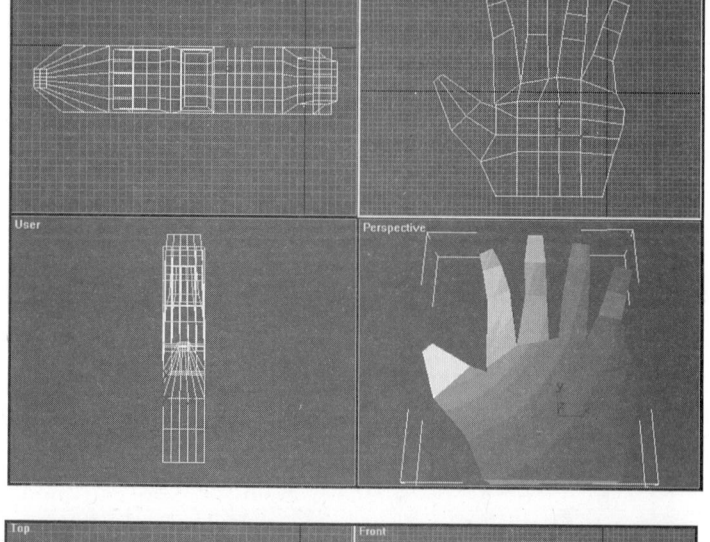
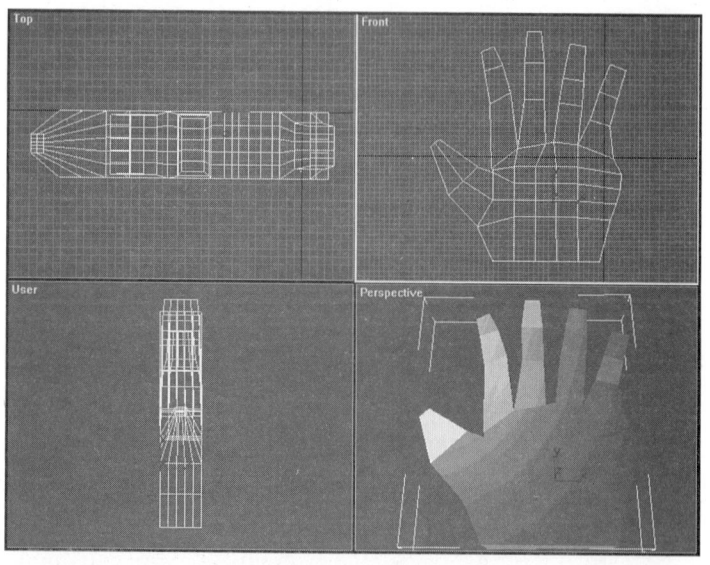

Free-form Deformation proves especially useful for adding finesse to a model. If you are creating a face, for example, it is fairly easy to select the polygons you want to make up the nose and extrude them from the face itself. By adding a Free-form Deformation modifier to the nose polygons, you can create a nose that would make a plastic surgeon proud. Certain tasks are very difficult to perform with simple sub-object tools, especially if you want to keep the modifications rounded and organic. These difficult tasks include adding the correct curvature on the tip of the nose, making the tip a bit back-tilted to give the illusion of snootiness, and stretching the nostrils to make them bulbous. With Free-form Deformation, however, the process becomes more like sculpting clay than dealing with stiff and unforgiving polygons.

In addition, Free-form Deformation serves as a wonderful alternative to modifying patch models with the vertices of the patch itself—all this without converting the model to polygons.

As a general rule, look to Free-form Deformation whenever you need to pull detail from the surface of a model or add a curve to the existing polygon surface.

Seamless Versus Segmented Modeling

In the not-too-distant past, seamless versus segmented modeling was not an issue. At first, if you were not using a high-end 3D package, you had little choice but to animate a segmented model and hide the seams as best you could. After skeletal deformation became an option for 3D Studio users, an animated segmented model looked clunky in comparison to the smooth-skinned animated models. Segmented models were almost abandoned in most circles. With the advent of real-time 3D, however, interest in creating effective segmented models has revived. (See Chapter 3, "Modeling for Real-Time 3D Games," for more about real-time 3D.)

Modeling segmented characters is not drastically different from creating seamless meshes. When you begin a model, you should know whether it will be animated with a skeletal deformation system (Character Studio or Bones Pro) or by rotating the various parts of the body itself. The method of animation and the amount of detail needed in the animation will determine whether the mesh can be created with patches or polygons alone. If you are creating a character that uses detailed facial expression (or is lip-synched with prerecorded speech), you probably want to use patches to get the smoothest animation from the finite details of the face without having to worry about hard polygonal lines appearing in the face during the animation. If you are creating a model that uses only bodily animation, even if you are creating tummy-wobbles or muscle bulges, it probably is in your best interest to use polygons because they are easier to control on a large scale (especially with skeletal animation systems) and have many more tools available for the mesh-modeling process than patches (at this time).

If you are dealing with patches, and especially if you are using Surface Tools, it is best to create the model in as few pieces as possible so that they can be easily "stitched" together.

If you are working in polygons that will later be joined (through Boolean operations and smoothing), try to create the largest segments possible. If you are creating a humanoid character, for example, create the arm in one piece (if possible) instead of creating a separate lower and upper arm. This will enable you to perform fewer joining operations, resulting in fewer areas to smooth over (a process that can be time-consuming). If you create half the body—welding only the arm, leg, and neck—and then mirror the model after the smoothing is completed, you save yourself six operations and realize an exact symmetry.

If you are working on a model to be animated by using the model's segments, the requirements of the animation determine the size of the segments. You should never, however, have multiple segments between the joints themselves.

Using Plug-Ins for Character Modeling

Three types of character-modeling plug-ins are:

- Patch modelers
- Metaballs modelers
- Skeletal systems

The only existing modeling paradigm not currently supported under MAX is the use of NURBS to model characters. It is highly probable, however, that this omission will be well-addressed in the near future. This section discusses the currently supported systems only.

Skeletal systems, although widely known for their animation capabilities, also have unique modeling properties. When used with a little foresight and cleverness, they can create quite stunning and unique effects.

Patch Modeling

As this book was being written, Surface Tools was the only plug-in available that aids in modeling with patches (discussed in great detail in the preceding chapter). Because patch modeling in general is very new to previous 3D

Studio users, however, and because patches are tremendously powerful tools for character creation and animation, other plug-ins are almost certain to surface in the not-so-distant future.

With that in mind, it is worth taking another brief foray into modeling with the Surface Tools plug-in. This discussion of Surface Tools is limited to examining a slightly different technique more applicable to creating animated cartoonesque characters than to the creation of realistic characters.

The following exercise does not detail the various supporting plug-ins that have been created for Surface Tools. It does, however, show a fast and effective procedure for modeling. For in-depth descriptions of the Surface Tools plug-ins, refer to Chapter 7, "Character Modeling with Patch Tools." For a technical look at the parameters of patches in general, refer to *Inside 3D Studio MAX Volume I.*

With plug-ins, you are never limited by one technique. You are limited only by your creativity and knowledge of the tools at hand.

NOTE

To perform the following exercise, you must have the Surface Tools plug-in installed. No other supporting plug-ins are required. The Edit Spline 2 and Edge-to-Spline plug-ins will be very useful, however, and are referred to in the exercise.

CREATING A CARTOON HEAD WITH SURFACE TOOLS

Because this is a cartoon character, exact precision to the line is less critical than the look and feel of the character in 3D space. Instead of tracing a sketch that has been loaded into a MAX background, therefore, you will just refer often to the sketch. This gives you the freedom to mold and sculpt the character—when you see the character actually realized in 3D space—as you see fit.

1. Go to the Create panel and click on Splines. Select the NGon object type and, in the Parameters rollout, set Sides to 12 and turn on Circular. In the Front viewport, create an n-gon.

2. Go to the Modify panel, and click on Edit Spline (or Edit Spline 2 if you have it installed). Click on the Sub-Objects button, and choose Spline from the drop-down menu.

3. Select the spline in the Left viewport. Hold down the Shift key and clone the spline by moving a new copy a little to the left of the original spline. The new spline will serve as the mouth of the character.

4. Choose the Uniform Scale transform from the top toolbar, and scale the original spline down very small so that it is only barely recognizable as a circle. This will be the back of the characters mouth, visible only when the character opens wide.

5. Select the new spline and perform another clone by holding down the Shift key and moving the copy to the right this time at a position roughly half-way between the back of the mouth and the mouth splines. Scale this spline a little bigger than the mouth so that it is easily visible and distinguishable from the mouth spline in the Front viewport.

6. Perform the clone operation six more times, moving the new copy to the right each time to a position easy to see (and select) from the Left viewport. Scale the new shape so that it is easily visible and selectable from the Front viewport. Scale the first two clones up and the last four down, so that the splines form a roughly ellipsoidal shape when seen from the Left viewport (see fig. 8.3).

FIGURE 8.3

The final spline objects before adding the Cross-section modifier.

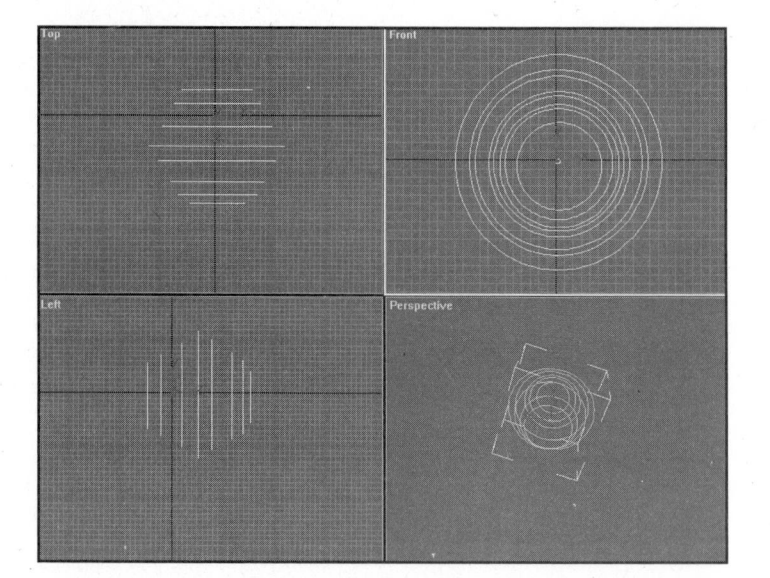

7. After all the splines are in place, deselect all the spline sub-objects and select the Cross-section modifier. Choose Bézier as the Spline Option parameter. This creates splines that turn our spline cross-sections into a single-piece 3D spline model.

8. Apply the Surface modifier to the cross-sectioned object. Make certain that none of the spline options are checked and that Threshold is set to 1.0. You should now have a smooth shape that looks similar to a vase tipped on its side (see fig. 8.4).

FIGURE 8.4
The surfaced spline object.

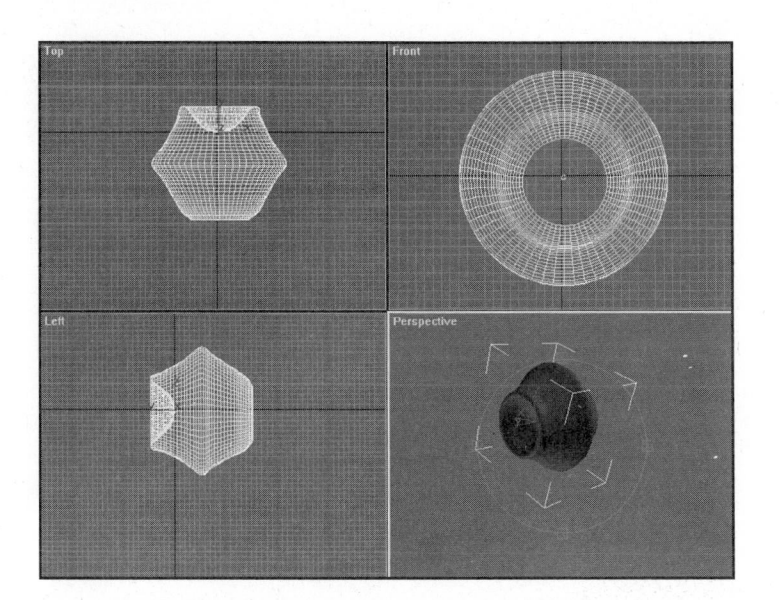

9. Go to the Modifier Stack rollout and click on the arrow to the right of the stack display window to drop-down the stack list. Click on the Cross-Section modifier to make it active. Then immediately click on the Edit Spline (or Edit Spline 2) button, adding a second spline editing operation. This enables you to use the splines created by the Cross-Section modifier. By clicking on the Show End Result toggle button, you can immediately see whether an operation has produced the desired results.

NOTE

If the Edit Spline modifier is grayed out after dropping down the modifier stack, go down one more level to the first Edit Spline and then back to the Cross-Section modifier. This re-identifies the object to MAX as a spline object.

10. You can now begin sculpting the shape of the character's head. Start by selecting the vertices on what should be the upper lip, pressing the spacebar to lock down the selection set. Move them forward, effectively "folding" the lip into place and then rotate this set into an alignment

more representative of the angle of the lip. Repeat this procedure with the vertices that should comprise the lower lip (see fig. 8.5).

FIGURE 8.5

The model with lips in place.

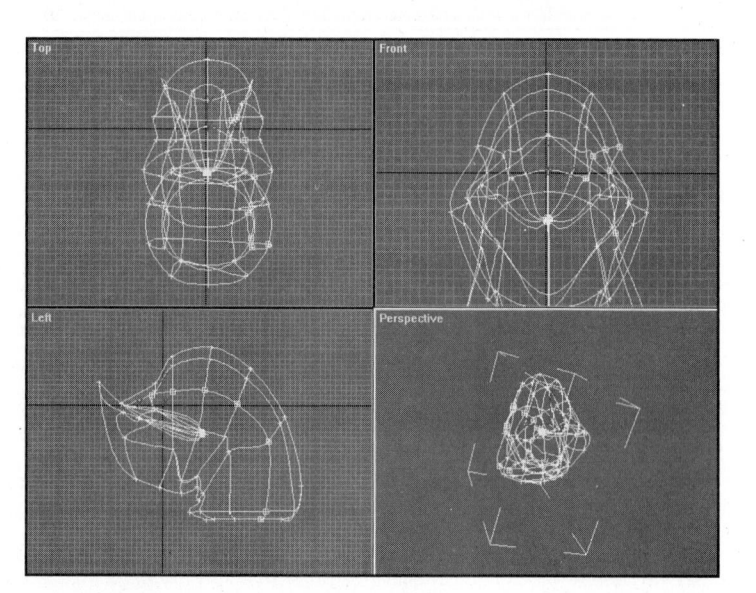

11. Now you will create the character's neck (which can later be "stitched" onto a spline body) by moving the last two splines you created. Select these splines with the Spline sub-object, move them down below the main part of the head, and then rotate them 90° (clockwise, in the Left viewport) from their original position.

12. Now you can begin to fully flesh out the character by pushing and pulling individual vertices, as though you were molding the character with clay. Continue sculpting until you have a three-dimensional representation of the spirit of the character in the sketch.

13. Now create the horns. Create a five-sided circular n-gon and move it close to the position where it will sit on the head. After the original spline is in position, you perform the same edit spline/clone procedure you used for the head. This time, however, you will create only three copies, each new copy scaling down to a tapered point for the horn. The copies should be rotated as shown in figure 8.6.

FIGURE 8.6
The position of the horn splines.

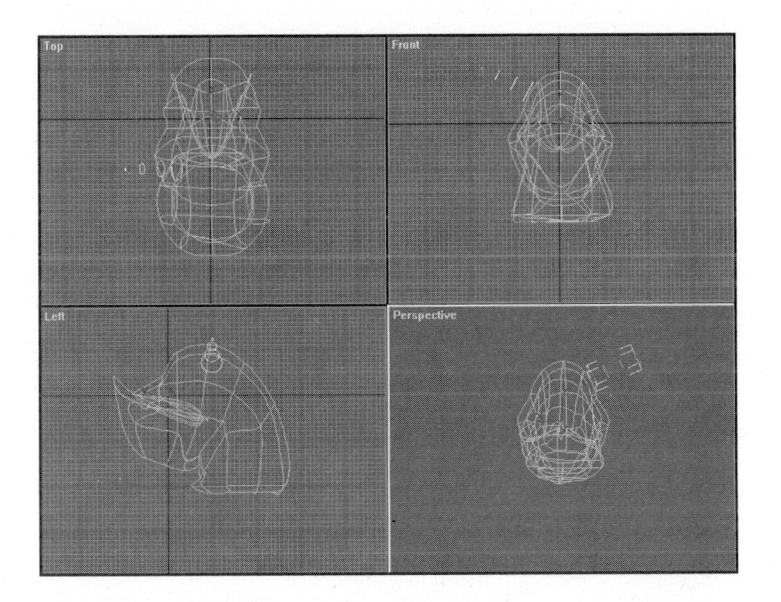

14. Add the Cross-Section modifier to the horn splines, and then add another Edit Spline modifier. Scale the vertices on the last horn spline down to a single point. Perform a Mirror transform on the horn, and make a copy of the object on the other side of the head. The copy will not be used in construction, but as a visual reference of what the result will be.

NOTE

MAX might ask if you want to weld co-incident endpoints when scaling a cross-sectioned model, or when moving vertices closer to other vertices, such as in the horn. This is because MAX does not currently support branching splines (splines that have more than one line passing through a single vertex). Surface Tools creates the illusion of branching splines by moving the vertices of non-branching splines virtually on top of the coinciding vertices of other non branching splines. Often, welding co-incident endpoints results in collapsing the "virtual" branching spline into a single spline, making it impossible for Surface Tools to add a patch to an area of the spline model. If you choose to weld co-incident end-points, immediately push the "display end-result" button in the Modifier Stack panel to ensure that no surface patches have been eliminated. If they have, undo the weld, then continue with the next step in creating your model.

15. Select the main Head object. In its modifier stack, go back to the last Edit Spline modifier, and make it active. Deactivate the Sub-Object button. Click on the Attach button in the Main panel, and select the horn on the left side of the head (as seen from the front).

At this point, you are going to attach the head and horn spline objects by "stitching" them together. If you have the Edit Spline 2 modifier, this is a fairly easy procedure. Be certain to set up your snap settings so that Vertex Snap receives first priority and all other geometry is turned off (see fig. 8.7). Set the snap strength to 20 and click on the 3D radio button.

Note

The Edit Spline 2 modifier is more helpful when using Surface Tools than the original Edit Spline modifier because it enables you to see the vertices of the spline object at all times in all the other sub-object modes.

FIGURE 8.7
The Snap Settings for the attachment procedure.

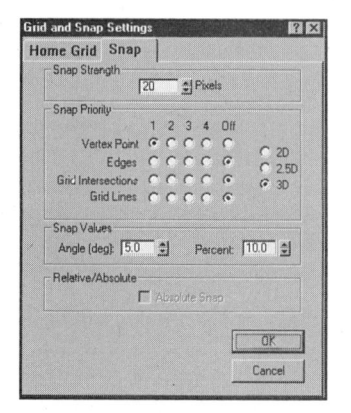

16. Now click on the Create Line button. Click on any of the vertices at the base of the horn, draw a line to the nearest corresponding vertex on the head, and click again. Finish the operation with a right-click. Continue the procedure until all the vertices at the base of the horn are stitched to the head. You most likely will have to rotate the view around the head to see clearly where to align the vertices on the horn side. Click on the Show end result toggle in the Modifier Stack panel to make certain that the process hasn't created any holes in the final surfaced model. If they have, try welding the new vertex groups (where the horn lines have been attached to the head) by selecting two corresponding vertices only and using a low weld threshold setting. Often this immediately solves the problem.

17. You are now ready for the final steps to complete the head. In the Modifier Stack, go to the Surface modifier and delete it. This reduces the head to a spline cage only. In the Edit Spline modifier (which should be at the top of the stack now), go to the segment Sub-Object level. Select all the segments on the side of the head opposite the one to which you just attached the horn. Delete these segments, leaving only half the head. Look carefully at the object and adjust any vertices that look out of place or that are not what you expected.

18. Deselect the Sub-Object button and mirror the head, creating a copy that lines up exactly with this half. Back in the Edit Spline modifier, click on the Attach button and select the unselected half. Apply a Surface modifier to the newly attached halves.

19. Go back to the last Edit Spline modifier, and then go the vertex Sub-Object level and select all the vertices down the middle of the object. Then deselect the small circle of vertices that make up the back of the throat. Weld the selected vertices at a low threshold (1.0 should do), and then press the Show End Result toggle button to check whether welding has created any holes. If any seams appear in the model, select the vertices along the seam and reweld them at a slightly higher threshold, repeating the process until the seam disappears. The final model should look something like figure 8.8.

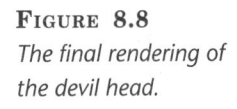

FIGURE 8.8
The final rendering of the devil head.

Metaballs Modeling

To create polygonal models, metaball modelers first create reference spheres. Each reference sphere is surrounded by a field that either attracts (positive) or repels (negative) other metaball geometry. This field also has a finite distance and a fall-off of intensity as the distance from the center of the sphere increases.

When two metaballs with attraction fields are placed close together, they suck together like drops of water in outer space. The closer together they are the more they are sucked into each other. When two metaballs with repelling fields are placed close together, they will not generate any surface. If a metaball with a repelling field is pushed *near* a sphere with an attraction field, the attracting sphere will generate a surface resembling a sphere with a dent in it. If a metaball with a repelling field is pushed *into* a sphere with an attraction field, the attracting sphere is split into two kidney shapes around the repelling field of the first sphere. This effect can only be seen when an *isosurface* (a mesh object that is generated based on these fields and the position of the metaballs) is created. Metaballs, however, can be animated in this stage to create convincing fluid effects, leaving the isosurface to be generated during the rendering process.

When several metaballs of varying positive and negative fields are grouped together, they result in an extremely smoothly curved surface. This technique is especially useful for creating characters because the modeler can use it to build rolling surfaces with great amounts of organic detail for muscle tone or facial features.

As with almost all plug-in technologies that were used with 3D Studio, metaballs modeling has taken a massive leap forward with its integration into MAX. This leap comes in the form of Metareyes 3.0 from InfoGrafica, a major developer of MAX plug-ins.

The latest paradigm leap involves not just metaballs, but *meta-muscles*—chains of metaballs along a spline curve that create a sausage-like surface. What once took several metaballs to create can now be done with a single meta-muscle. In addition, meta-muscles can be used in conjunction with other meta-muscles of varying positive and negative field intensities in the same ways that single metaballs could be used before. This paradigm creates a massive increase in the detail that can be achieved with metaballs modeling and a tremendous reduction in the amount of time necessary to complete a detailed model.

As if this weren't enough, meta-muscles come in two varieties: static and dynamic. Actually, all meta-muscles have dynamic properties, namely, contraction and oscillation levels, as well as some inertia control. This discussion so far has dealt with static metaballs modeling to create a mesh surface. Dynamic meta-muscles are created initially as sort of barbell shapes—two metaballs connected by a single straight spline. This shape is then generated into an object that bulges between the two initial spheres, like a biceps muscle, changing its thickness in reaction to the animation. The end spheres can now be linked to parent objects (most likely bones), and the bulging area between the two initial spheres will expand and contract almost exactly as a real muscle reacts to movement. This muscle also has a definable inertia level that will control how much the muscle wobbles in reaction to the movement of the parent objects. At long last, creating and animating jello arms is now possible!

This section, however, does not deal with dynamic meta-muscles (because they depend on animation). Instead, this section focuses on creating detailed organic surfaces from static meta-muscles. Note, however, that the modeling process of both dynamic and static meta-muscles is almost identical, with minor exceptions (such as the linking of the dynamic reference spheres).

For the following exercise, you must have Metareyes 3.0. If you have another metaballs modeler available, you can achieve similar results, but the meta-muscle structure is unique to Metareyes 3.0.

For reference material, any number of "Anatomy for the Artist" books contain excellent visual diagrams of muscles. In addition, any weight-lifting magazine has excellent pictures of arm structure and detail from many different viewpoints. Because this is a super-hero arm, you need to take liberties and use your imagination as you embellish the model.

Creating a Meta-Muscle Super-Hero Arm

1. Go to the Create panel, click on the Systems tab, and click on the Bones button. Create a bone in the Front viewport, starting at the top of the viewport and dragging toward the bottom. Select the entire bone by drawing a rectangular fence around it. Hold down the Shift key and clone the bone by moving it directly beneath the first bone. Link the bottom bone to the topmost bone (bone01, unless you have chosen different names). Freeze both of these objects; they will serve as templates to

ensure that the scale and proportion of the upper arm and lower arm are accurate and as the link that holds the model together for the generation of the fusion surface at the end of the exercise.

2. To begin the meta-muscle structure, go back to the Geometry tab in the Create panel and click on the Metareyes button. Make certain that the muscle type is static and the fusion type is soft positive. Over the top bone in the Front viewport, create one meta-muscle that consists of three spheres—smaller spheres at the ends with a slightly bigger sphere in the middle. This meta-muscle will serve as a blank fusion surface, covering the little areas not covered by the major muscles.

3. Clone the first meta-muscle and move it over the bottom bone. You should now have something resembling two sausage shapes (see fig. 8.9).

FIGURE 8.9

The two meta-muscle blanks.

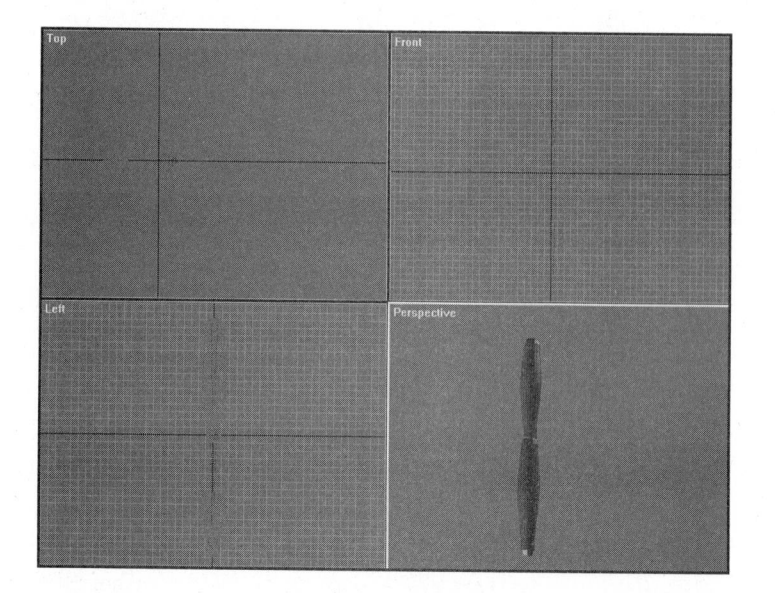

4. Now you can begin building the major muscle groups. Go back to the Create panel and click on the Metareyes button, leaving the muscle type as static. This time, however, change the fusion to medium hard positive (light green). The muscles will squish down less when you generate a fusion surface for the mesh, creating greater muscle definition. Begin by creating the deltoid (the shoulder cap). In the Left viewport, create a meta-muscle at the top of the arm, ending just above the halfway point of the upper arm. This meta-muscle should consist of two spheres—the first just

over twice the diameter of the arm blanks, and the last about half the diameter of the arm blank. This should result in a reverse pyramid shape (see fig. 8.10). In the Front viewport, move this object over to the right so that its left edge lines up closely with the left edge of the arm blank.

FIGURE 8.10

The deltoid shape.

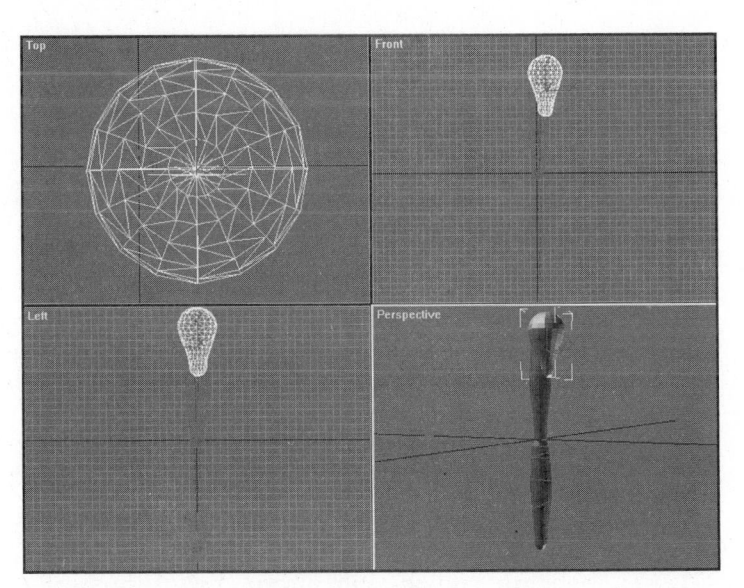

5. In the Left viewport, create the bicep by creating another three-sphere meta-muscle just to the right of the arm blank. This time, use a small sphere at the top of the arm (under the deltoid), a large sphere at about the middle of the arm—this is a super-hero's arm, don't be afraid to go for the big guns—and another small sphere at the base of the upper arm. The spline that links them together should curve out slightly from the arm blank.

6. For the triceps, select the biceps muscle in the Left viewport and make a mirror copy of it across the X axis, offsetting it about –30 units. In the Modify panel, choose Muscle Edit, click on the Sub-Object button, select Move, and move the middle and bottom muscles up (one at a time), aligning them just below the spaces between the spheres on the biceps muscle. The result should resemble figure 8.11. Scale down the middle sphere of the triceps to your liking, using the Muscle Edit modifier.

Now you can begin to create the major muscles of the forearm. You can also begin to see the advantage of meta-muscles over metaballs.

FIGURE 8.11

The biceps and triceps added to the model.

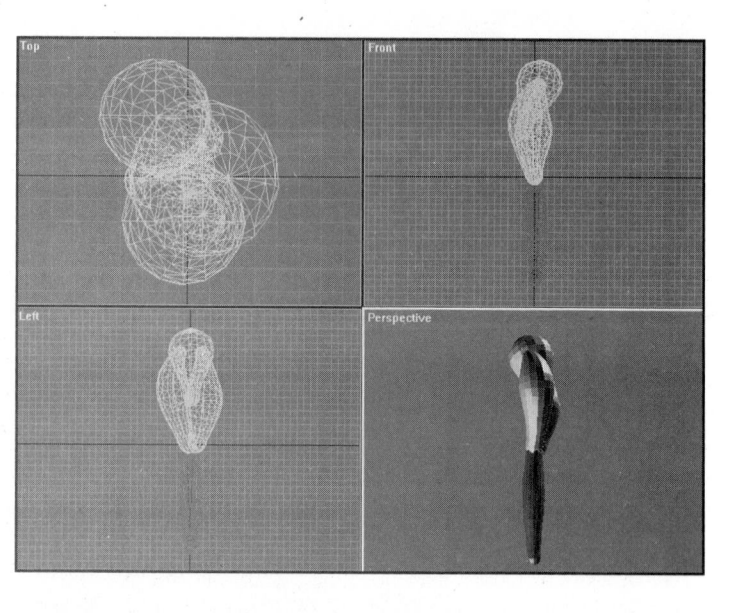

7. Create a four-sphere meta-muscle, starting at the base of the triceps with a small sphere, moving about one-third of the way down the lower arm, and creating a much larger sphere (which will be the major forearm muscle). Then move about another third of the way down, and create a slightly smaller sphere. Finally, at the base of the lower arm, create another small sphere (approximately the same size as the first sphere).

8. In the Modify panel, choose the Muscle Edit modifier. Click on the Sub-Object button and begin to move the lower three spheres of the last meta-muscle so that they wrap around the lower arm (see fig. 8.12). Make certain that the large sphere remains about halfway between the triceps and biceps muscles in the Left viewport, and only about a third of the way down the lower arm blank.

9. Now create the last muscle for the forearm—another three-sphere muscle, similar to the biceps but with a much smaller scale variation—along the side of the forearm opposite the major forearm muscle bulge.

10. The last thing you need to create is the elbow. Go into the Create panel and click on the Metareyes button. This time, switch the fusion to hard positive (light blue). Create a three-sphere meta-muscle, starting within the base of the triceps, close to the blank. The first muscle should be completely inside the triceps. Create the second muscle at the joint of the two blanks (scaled up a tiny bit), and create the third sphere inside the muscle at the back of the forearm, again—well inside and close to the

blank. Then create another single-sphere meta-muscle, just to the left of the muscle you last created. To finish it off and shape it more like an elbow, create two single-sphere meta-muscles with medium-hard negative fusion (emerald green) to the left and right of the elbow sphere. Move them just to the left of the elbow sphere in the Left viewport. You should end up with a complete mesh that resembles figure 8.13.

FIGURE 8.12
The arm with two forearm muscles added.

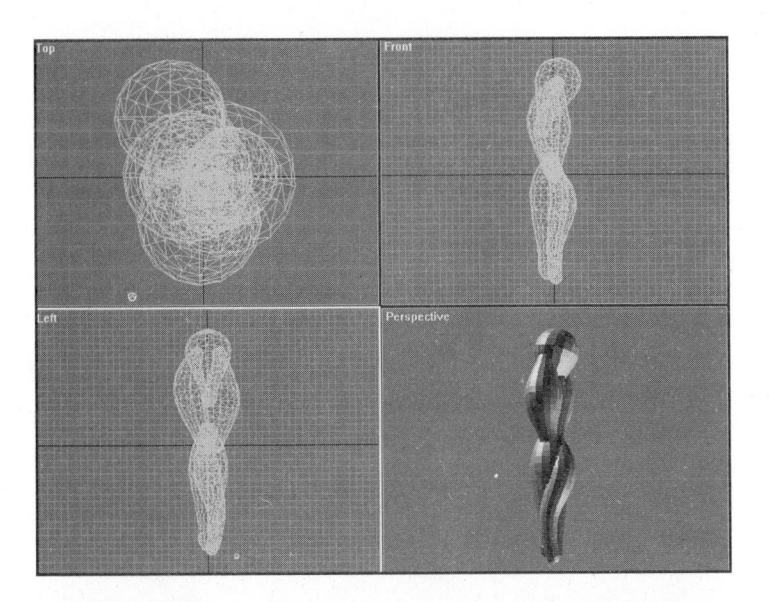

FIGURE 8.13
The finished meta-muscles.

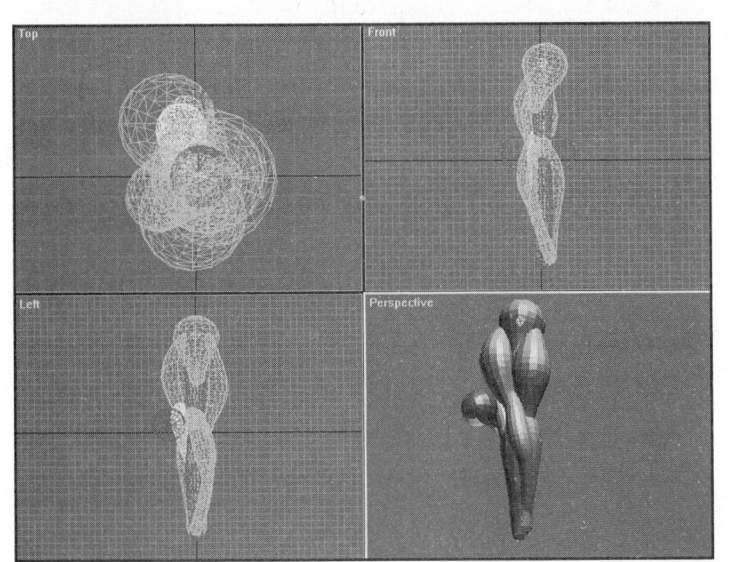

If you are not quite satisfied with the overall shape and placement of the muscles, now is the time to adjust them—before you generate the final surface. You have already seen how the Muscle Edit modifier works. To move, rotate, or otherwise transform entire meta-muscles, however, you must disable the dynamic properties of the muscle being worked on; otherwise the transform operation may not work at all, or may have results that affect the other meta-muscles in ways you did not intend. Remember that all meta-muscles have dynamic attributes, such as inertia levels, contraction, and oscillation, which react to animation. The specifics of these functions are beyond the scope of this discussion; they apply only when you are animating a meta-muscle model, not when you're modeling.

If you need to move, rotate, or scale an entire meta-muscle, go to the Utilities panel and select Metareyes from the drop-down menu. Select the specific muscle(s) on which you want to perform gross adjustments, go to the Tools rollout of the Metareyes panel (see fig. 8.14), and click on the button labeled Selected Din. No. This sets the dynamic status of the muscle to off and enables you to transform the selected muscles. After you complete the transform(s), go back to the Metareyes Utilities panel, select the adjusted meta-muscles, and click on the Selected Din. Yes button. This reactivates the dynamic status of the meta-muscles before you generate the fusion surface.

FIGURE 8.14

The Metareyes Utility Tools panel.

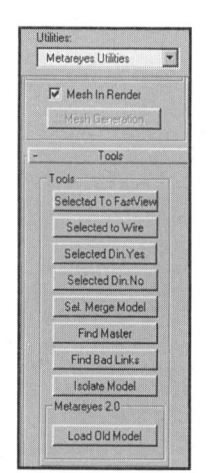

Metareyes has very advanced features for generating a fusion surface for a complex model, such as an entire humanoid. The way in which these surfaces are generated depends on the hierarchy and grouping set up in the Metareyes utilities. For the purposes here, the arm, which belongs to one hierarchical chain, should be fused as one group, and the elbow as a separate group that shares only the elbow "muscle" as a common element. If you were working on a more complex chain, however, you could use the option of creating more groups based on the sub-hierarchies you have built into the model. Note, however, that although meta-muscles can be linked to each other, the fusion works much better when they are linked to separate objects such as bones or dummy objects.

11. Now you can generate the final fusion surface for the forearm. Unfreeze the bones and link all the meta-muscles to the top of the bone hierarchy. In the Utilities panel, choose Metareyes from the drop-down menu.

12. In the Metareyes Utilities panel, press the Select Model button, and select a meta-muscle (any one of them); they should all be selected now, if they have been properly linked to the bone chain.

13. In the dialog under the Make Groups panel, enter the name **arm**, and then select all the meta-muscles in the arm except the two negative spheres at the elbow and the elbow sphere itself. Press the Make Group button.

14. Now select the elbow muscle, the elbow sphere, and the two negative spheres. Enter the name **elbow** in the Groups dialog, and press the Make Group button.

Your model should now have two fusion groups: the main muscles of the arm that will not be affected by the negative spheres; and the elbow group in which the negative spheres will interact to shape the elbow sphere and elbow muscle, with the common fusing muscle of both groups being the elbow muscle. This is a major advantage over standard metaballs modeling. With standard metaballs, all metaballs act on all other metaballs, without the capability to choose which groups are not affected by other groups, and still have them fuse together into a single mesh object.

At this point, the model is technically complete. You could animate the bones you have created and the mesh object would appear in the rendering. If you want to create a mesh object that can be used with other mesh surfaces, and that you can see the final result of before rendering, however, you need to generate the mesh from the Metareyes Utilities panel.

15. In the Mesh Generation dialog, enter the name **arm** again, and then click on the Mesh Generation button. This produces the final fusion surface of the model (see fig. 8.15).

FIGURE 8.15
The final mesh arm.

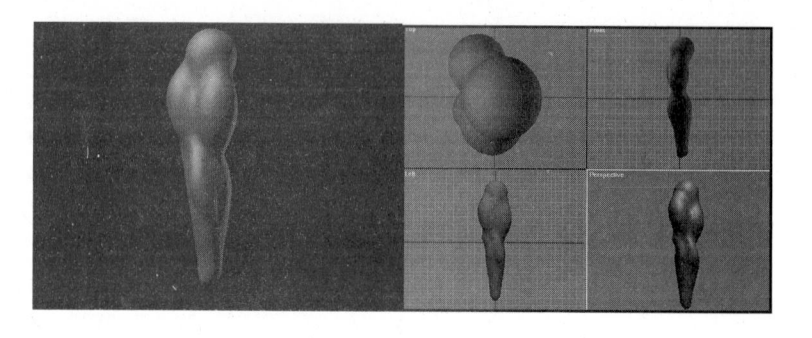

You could go on to add quite a bit of detail, creating very small muscle groups that would render as veins bulging on the surface of the arm, for example, or recreating some of the larger muscles (such as the deltoid) with smaller muscle segments, to add striation for an even more buffed look. The only limit is time and imagination.

Modeling with Skeletal Systems (Bones Pro MAX)

Although skeletal deformation systems are known primarily for their capability to animate seamless meshes for lifelike results, certain systems have tools that enable you to use them for modeling as well. Bones Pro MAX is one such system that provides tools for amazing results, especially when you're detailing a model.

You begin the process by creating a basic model (in this case, a head). Then you apply a specific set of bones to produce cosmetic results, bumps, or crevices in the mesh. In this way, the process closely resembles that of sculpting prosthetic makeup features on an actor. The same results can be achieved by using Displace modifiers or space warps. With Bones, however, you do not have to create the various sub-object selection sets necessary to creating the effects with displacement. With Bones, you also have an active visual tool that enables you to make modifications interactively, without having to adjust an external bitmap. The next exercise demonstrates this process by turning an average-looking head into a humanoid alien similar to those seen in many popular television shows.

You must have Bones Pro MAX installed for the next exercise.

DETAILING A HEAD WITH BONES PRO MAX

1. Open the file named Bonehead.max on the accompanying CD. This is a basic no-frills humanoid head mesh, which has been frozen for the first part of the exercise. This is the basic model to which you will add alien features. Select the head mesh and freeze it.

   The first bones you create will be the active detail bones. When you have an entire set of them, you will link them to a common object and then create the retaining bones—the bones that will hold the mesh in place while you use the detail bones to modify the face.

2. In the Create panel, select the Systems tab. Click on the Bones button. On the left half of the model, create three bone segments, which will actually be four bones, starting at the center and dragging to the left (see fig. 8.16).

FIGURE 8.16

The position of the first bone chain.

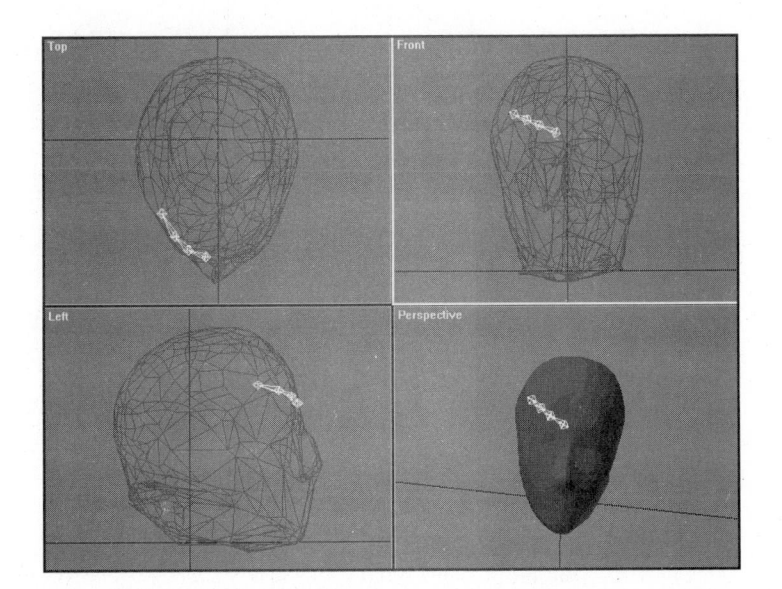

3. Clone this bone set three more times by rotating around the parent bone—two above the current set and one below. Do this by setting the transform center to the parent bone, holding down the Shift key, and rotating about the Y axis. This will be half the bone set for the forehead details.

4. Now create some bone for the nose detail. Create one bone, angle it so that it lines up with the nose, and align it on the nose bridge. Then hold down the Shift key and clone the bone by moving it down. Do this two times, until the entire bone set looks like that shown in figure 8.17.

FIGURE 8.17

The facial bone set.

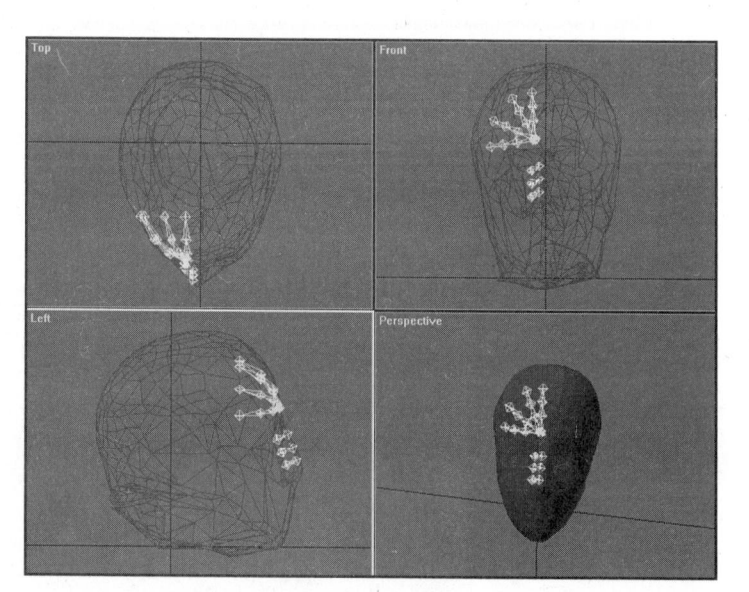

5. The last cosmetic bones you need to add are those for the cranial bumps. To do this, create a single bone, drawing from the bottom to the top, approximately the same length as the nose bones. Clone this bone five times to get a good dispersal of cranial bumps across the top of the skull.

6. Now select all the facial bones (all the bones except the ones created in the last step), and perform a mirror copy operation in the Front viewport to create symmetrical detail on the other side of the face. Offset the new bones about 2.8 units.

7. Select all the bones, and create a named selection set for these bones called **Cosmetic Bones**, in the Named Selection Set box in the top toolbar.

8. On the Hierarchy panel, with all the bones still selected, click on the Affect Pivot Only button in the Move/Rotate/Scale sub-panel, and click on the Align to World button in the Alignment sub-panel. Now freeze all the selected bones.

Now you need to create the retaining bones that hold the geometry you don't want to modify.

9. Find the original forehead detail bones (the first set created), unfreeze them, hold down the Shift key, and move and clone these bones up in a space unoccupied by the cosmetic bones. Copy these bones in the same way that the cosmetic bones were created. These will be used to create negative or "retaining bones," for areas where the mesh should not change shape drastically.

10. Continue the copying operation by creating bone copies that go between all the original bones on the nose and on the cranium, unfreezing the desired sets of frozen cosmetic bones as needed. When you have finished, create the mirror copies of these bones as well. Name these bones **Negative Bones** in the Selection Set box, and realign their pivots with the world in the IK panel (just as you did with the cosmetic bones). Freeze this set also.

11. The last bones you need to create are the retaining bones at the sides of the head and the base of the cranium (at the back). Because simple large bones will do for this, create one bone at each side of the head (going bottom to top) and one lateral bone at the back of the head, below the last cranial ridge bone. Name this set **Retaining Bones**. Reset their pivots, and freeze them as well. You should now have something resembling the setup shown in figure 8.18.

FIGURE 8.18
The final bones setup.

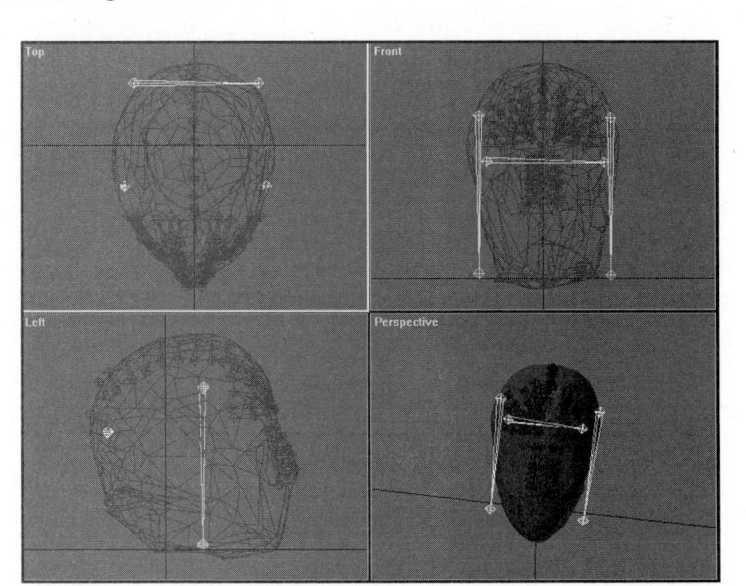

12. Unfreeze the head and all the bone sets. Then, on the Utilities panel, choose the Skeleton utility from the drop-down menu.

13. Select each of the named sets, starting with the Cosmetic Bones set. Click on the Generate Boxes button. In the dialog, enter **cos** in the Name prefix slot (see fig. 8.19). Leave the default Box width setting as it is. Repeat the procedure for the Negative Bone set (with the prefix **neg**) and the Retaining Bones set (with the prefix **ret**). Set the Box width of the retaining bones to 0.75.

FIGURE 8.19

The setup for generating the cosmetic bones.

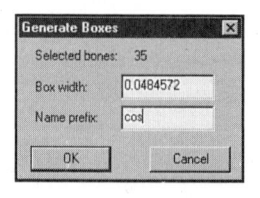

14. Delete all the original Bones objects, and go to the Create panel. Select the Space Warps tab. Create the Bones warp icon, somewhere easy to select from the head. Bind the head to the space-warp by clicking on the Bind to Space Warp button in the top toolbar, clicking on the head and holding, and dragging over to the Bones Pro space warp icon you just created.

15. Select the Bones space-warp. Then, in the Modify panel's Bound Node sub-panel, click on the None button. Choose the head from the pop-up list.

16. In the Bones sub-panel, click on the Assign button and choose all the Bones objects (with the prefixes cos, neg, and ret).

17. In the main selection toolbar (on the top of the screen), click on Select by Name and select all the cos objects. Then click on the Animate button and advance to frame 1.

18. With the coordinate system set to local, and all the cos objects still selected, uniform scale all the objects until you can see large protrusions from the head object (see fig. 8.20).

19. Click on the Bones space-warp, and go back to the Modify panel. Click on the Influence Editor button. You should see all the Bones objects. Click on the Select bones from list button, and select all the cos objects. Then click on the Exclude unlinked bones from selected bones button.

FIGURE 8.20

The Bones scale effect on the head.

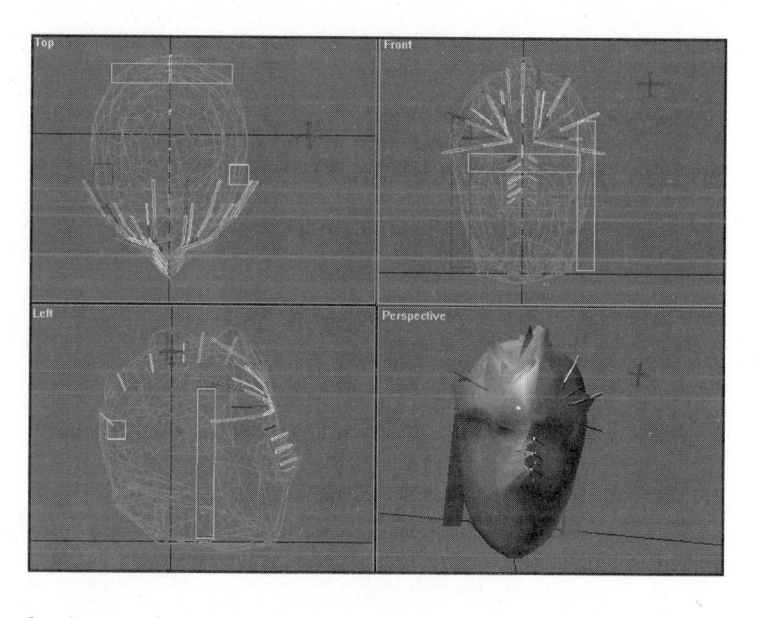

20. Click on the Invert bones' selection button in the Influence Editor, selecting all the neg and ret bones. Click on the Exclude unlinked from selected bones button. This ensures that the areas you don't want to move will not move.

21. Now close the Influence Editor, and begin to move the cosmetic bones around to make the model suit your taste. All aliens are different—feel free to customize this one a bit.

22. When you have completed your adjustments of the cosmetic bones, click on the Utilities panel, and find the Snapshot Plus utility.

23. Select the head mesh, and click on the Snapshot button. Make certain that your snapshot settings are for only one copy (see fig. 8.21).

FIGURE 8.21

The Snapshot settings dialog.

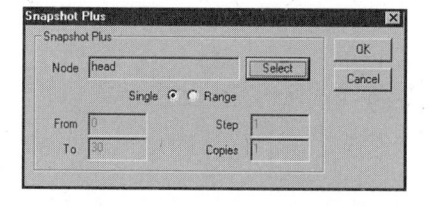

24. Select everything except the new head mesh, and hide those pieces.

25. To finish, perform a MeshSmooth modifier operation on the new head, adjusting the settings until the model looks like a nice organic humanoid (see fig. 8.22).

FIGURE 8.22
The final alien head.

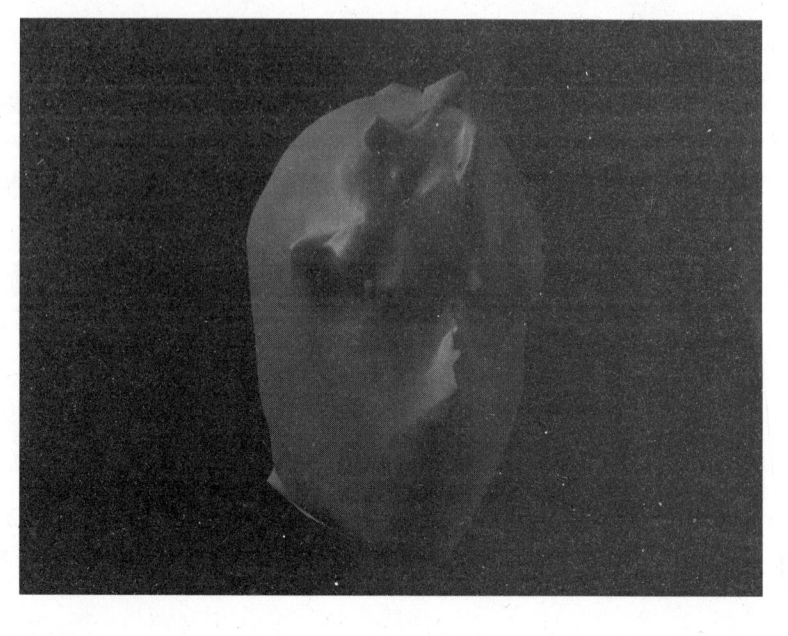

With this process, you can perform multiple iterations on your snapshot models, stacking various levels of detail on top of previous details (again, very similar to adding prosthetic makeup to a character).

Using 3D Paint to Map a Model

3D paint packages are a relatively new invention in the world of 3D graphics, and even newer to the PC. These packages can be quite a benefit to texture mapping, especially if you are familiar with certain techniques used to paint traditional (plastic, polyvinyl, or resin) models.

3D paint packages do, however, have limitations. It is very difficult to create intricately detailed bitmaps of repeat minute detail (such as lizard skin or scratched metal). In principle, if you have an overall complex map that must be present on the model, create it in a traditional paint package (such as Photoshop), apply it to the model, and use the 3D paint package to add the details on top of the map.

Currently, three 3D paint packages are available, two of which support exported 3DS files, and one that works as a seamless plug-in with MAX.

The two packages that support exported 3DS files are Fractal Design's Detailer and 3D Paint.

Detailer has some excellent features, one of the best being its very affordable price. You have access to most of the natural media tools available in Fractal Design's Painter, including the *image hose* (a paint device that enables you to "pump" an image onto a selected area of a mesh). The only drawbacks to this program are its speed (quite slow, even on a very fast machine) and the fact that you have to convert any patch or meta-objects to mesh, export them through the 3DS format, and reimport them. Therefore, if you are creating anything besides a diffuse color map (opacity, specular, self-illumination), you will also have to reimport it into the objects material when you reload the mesh.

3D Paint has been the only 3D paint program available to 3D Studio users since 3D Paint became available on the PC. The new NT version is a good stand-alone product that, although it still suffers from the 3DS export problems mentioned earlier, is fairly fast and reliable.

The last package, and the only package that functions as a MAX plug-in, is 4D Paint. In addition to its capability to keep patch models as patches while painting, 4D Paint reads the MAX material in its entirety, and automatically creates layers for opacity, bump maps, self illumination, you name it—a feature that is not available in the other packages. The only MAX material function that 4D Paint does not currently support is sub-object materials.

Granted, you are definitely going to pay for this functionality (the current cost of 4D Paint is almost twice that of its closest competitor), but you are going to get quite a bit for your money.

The following exercise offers a brief foray into 3D painting, using 4D Paint.

You must have 4D Paint to do the following exercise. You may be able to achieve similar results with another 3D paint package, but the process and specific steps will vary.

USING 4D PAINT TO TEXTURE-MAP A HEAD

1. Open the file named Bonehead02.max on the accompanying CD. This is the head mesh created in the last exercise, separated into two objects: the back of the head and the face. The face already has a texture applied to it—a grassy green alien skin, complete with a bump map (see fig. 8.23). Shrink-wrap mapping also has been applied to this mesh.

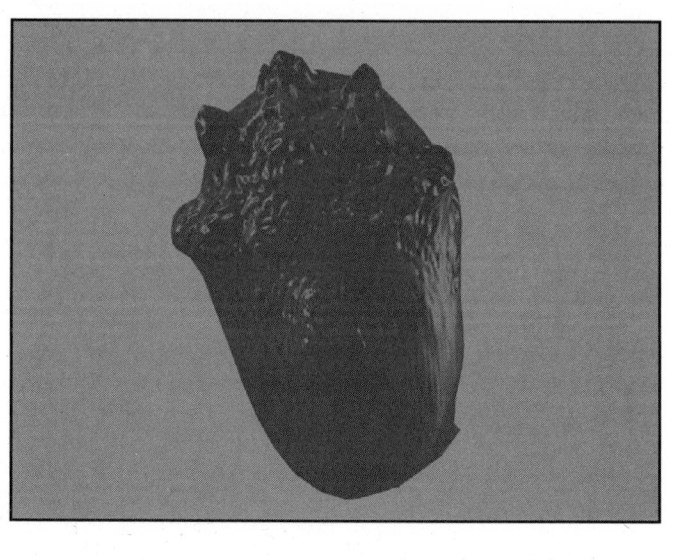

2. Select the Face object. Then on the Utilities panel, choose the 4D Paint utility from the drop-down menu. Click on the Paint! button; 4D Paint will start up and automatically load the maps that comprise the face material.

3. Click on the Layers Window button in the bottom-right corner of the 4D Paint window. Select Color Map from the tabs on the pop-up display. You will see a queue of color entries, including Color Base Layer and Renderer Layer. Click on the New button and create a new color layer, which will go into place at the top of the stack (see fig. 8.24). This is the layer you will modify, so as not to modify your original bitmap texture.

   To take full advantage of the capabilities of a 3D paint package and what it can do for a character, start by adding some subtle shadows and highlights to the face (like putting makeup on an actor). Then you will customize your lizard-skinned alien by adding stripe details and spots to make it look a little more tribal and unique.

4. Click on the Brush Tool button in the upper-right tool panel, and then click on the Brush drop-down list and highlight Default Brush. Right-click on the highlighted name, and the Edit options will appear. Choose Edit Brush. In the Brush Settings dialog, click on the General tab, and rename the brush **Shadow**, leaving the rest of the settings at their default levels. Click on the Brush Head tab, and create a long thin brush with a high fall-off that matches the settings in figure 8.25. When you finish, close the Brush Editor and say Yes to create a new brush.

FIGURE 8.24

The Color Layer dialog in 4D Paint.

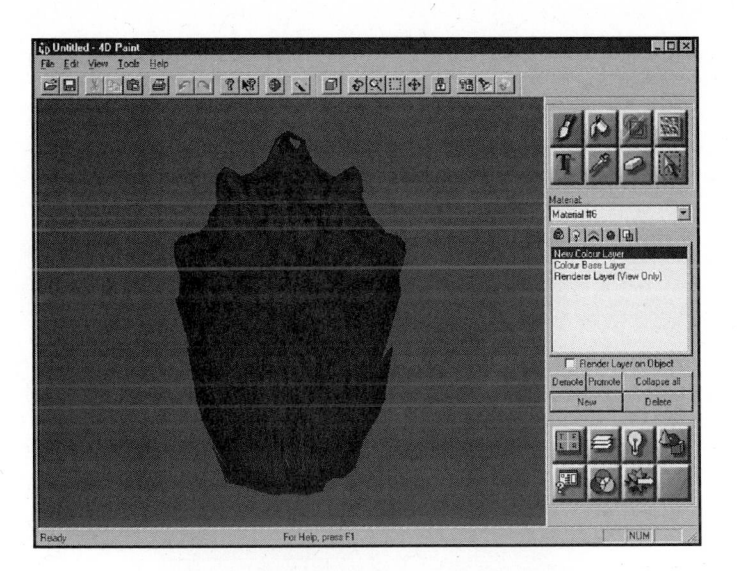

FIGURE 8.25

The Brush Settings for the first brush.

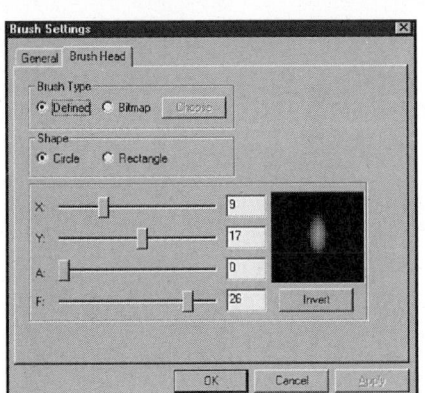

5. Click on the Color Picker button from the bottom-right panel, and select the Fore box. Create a darkish brown color that is about 50 percent transparent. This will be your shadow color. Minimize the Color Picker; you will use it quite a bit in this exercise.

6. Leave the paint choice at default for the moment, and begin painting in some shadows. These shadows should be subtle; they are more like makeup than a bump map or modeled detail. Punch in shadows around the forehead bones, under the chin and brow ridges, and even around the muzzle. Remember that Undo is available, and you can paint with a free hand. If something is not to your liking, you can undo it immediately, or go through a series of Undo operations, or use the eraser in the upper-right Tool panel to erase just a portion. Indulge yourself, but keep it subtle (see fig. 8.26).

FIGURE 8.26

*The final shadow-
painted face.*

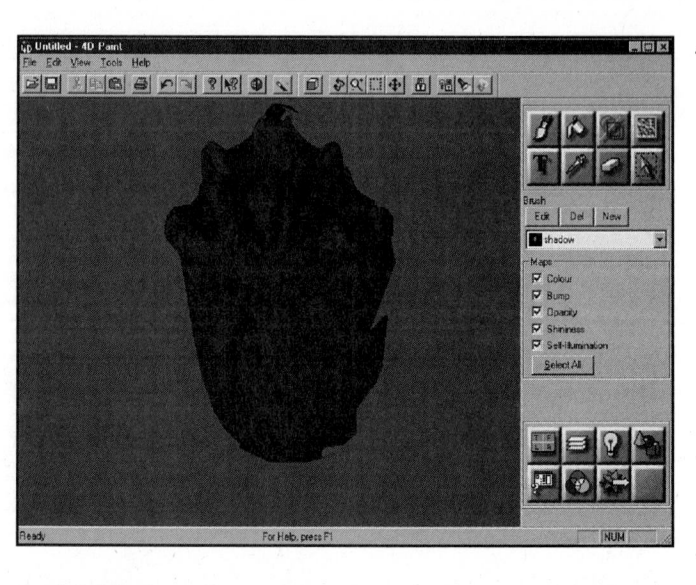

7. Now add some highlights. Go back and create a new color layer in the Layer Editor. Edit your brush so that it is only five pixels wide (X setting). This time, however, instead of using the default paint, go to the Paint drop-down list and choose Drybrush. With Drybrush selected, right-click on the Paint drop-down list and choose Edit Paint for the Editor menu. Set the Drybrush Paint settings to match those in figure 8.27. Rename this paint **Highlight**, and save it.

One of the great features in almost all 3D paint packages is the variety of paints available for creating different effects. 4D Paint, in keeping with the concepts used by plastic kit modelers, includes several unique paints whose effects vary according to information from the different maps that make up the material on an object. Drybrushing looks at the level of light in the bump map and applies more paint in areas that have a high luminosity value, creating a streaked, spotty, organic look that is excellent for subtle effects.

8. Open the color picker, lighten your paint to a medium amber color, and begin punching in the highlights. Again, the sky's the limit. Have fun but keep it subtle; that subtlety will pay off.

9. Now for the last bit of color detail. Create another color layer called **Stripes**. Add some war-paint type details in different colors (yellows and reds will probably work best on this green background) and with various brushes, using a default paint. You should end up with something resembling figure 8.28.

FIGURE 8.27
*The Drybrush Paint
Settings.*

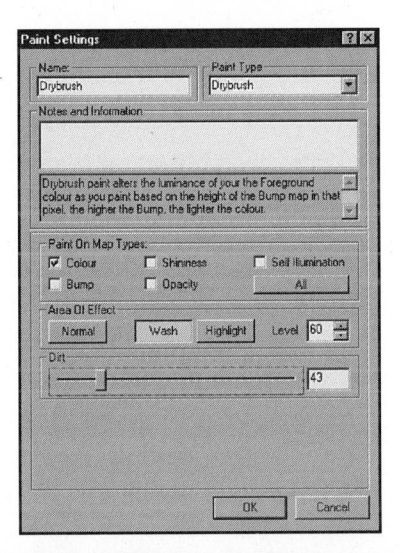

FIGURE 8.28
The final color maps.

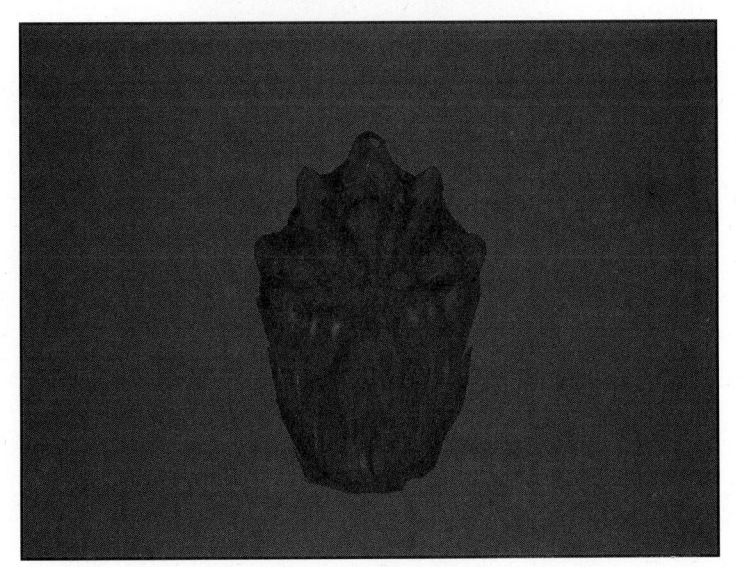

10. For the final bit of detail, go back to the Layers Window and create a new bump layer called **Added Bumps**. Finish the model by actively painting a bump map under the color layer. Create a 10-by-10 brush with no fall-off, name it **Added**, and save it. Click on the Paint drop-down list and select the Bump paint. With this option selected you will paint on the bump layers only, and will not add color variations to the diffuse maps. Open the Color Picker and slide the Bump Paint Slider all the way up. Create some raised detail dabs (these work very well under the

war-paint colors) and some long strokes, to add more detail to the bone forehead and all over the face. Finish by changing the bump paint to its lowest setting in the color-picker.

11. When you have completed the bump details, press the MAX Out button in the lower-right of the Tool panel. For the map export method, choose Generate New Bitmaps, enter **alien** as the prefix, and name the new files when 4D Paint asks you to. These new files will automatically replace the images you had as bump and diffuse maps in the Material Editor hot spot for the material applied to your character.

The final image should look something like that shown in figure 8.29. Compare this with the first alien image, figure 8.23. Notice how the subtle changes have made a drastic difference in creating the feeling of a living being.

FIGURE 8.29

The final texture mapped alien head.

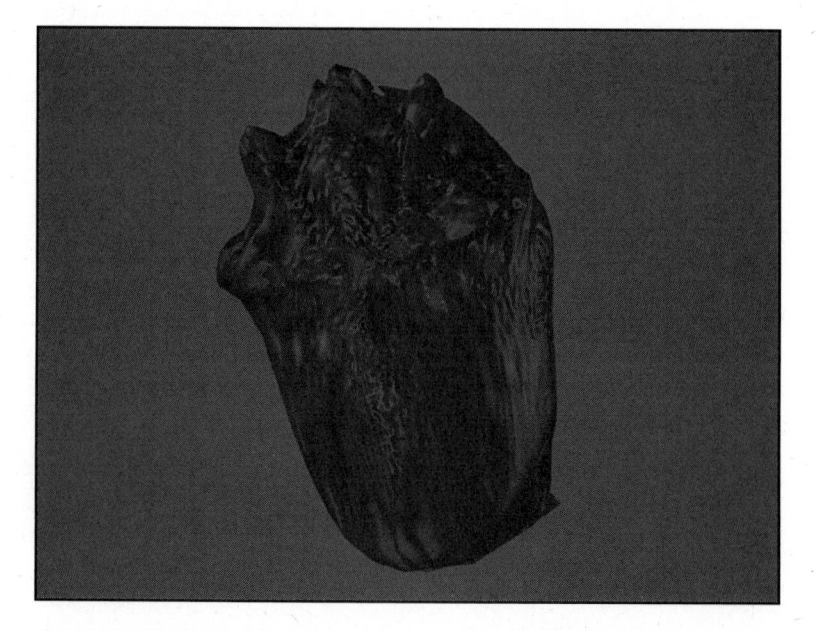

The technological leap in power and paradigm from 3D Studio release 4 to 3DS MAX has opened entire worlds of character power previously unavailable to the PC-based 3D artist and to plug-in developers. Plug-ins for MAX are becoming available at break-neck speed (including free, low-cost, and premier packages). The majority are either aimed directly at, or have tremendous benefit to, character creators. Keep you eyes and ears ever vigilant and your mind flexible. New techniques present themselves with every new addition to the ever-expanding power of MAX plug-ins.

In Practice: Character Modeling with Plug-Ins

- The object-oriented design of MAX makes plug-in integration seamless and easier to create.

- When creating a character model, start simple then add detail.

- Always have sketches, maquettes, or photographic references available when creating a character.

- Create the model in halves that can later be mirror-copied and tweaked to create a more natural asymmetry.

- One creation tool is never enough when building a character. Be very familiar with the Edit Mesh sub-object tools, Relax, MeshSmooth, and FFD modifiers.

- The process for creating seamless and segmented models is mostly identical. But you need to know how the model will be animated, how much detailed animation (such as facial expression) will be used, and if you need to use patches or polygons to suit the animation techniques and details.

- Plug-ins for character modeling currently extend from only three types of plug-ins: Patch modelers, Metaballs modelers, and Skeletal systems.

- Metaballs are reference spheres that have an attracting or repelling field around them, that are combined to create a very smooth, very organic "isosurface."

- Meta-muscles are a new paradigm in metaballs modeling that uses metaballs created along a spline path to construct sausage-like shapes that resemble muscles, and can be combined like metaballs to generate detailed isosurfaces that resemble musculature.

- Skeletal systems, such as Bones Pro Max, can be used in conjunction with a Snapshot tool to add organic detail to a model before animation.

- 3D paint packages are best used to detail general detail texture maps created in a 2D paint package, rather than creating entirely new surface textures from scratch.

Part IV

MATERIAL AND TEXTURE MAPPING

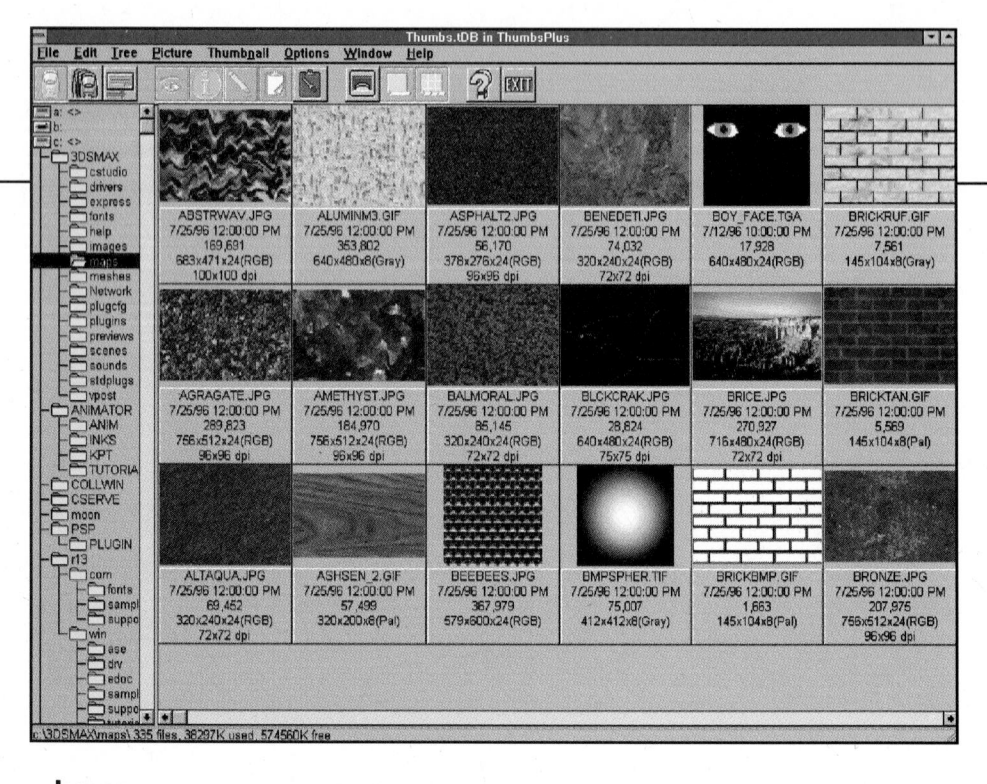

IMAGE BY DAVE ESPINOSA-AGUILAR

Chapter 9

by dave espinosa-aguilar

MATERIALS MANAGEMENT AND MANIPULATION

One of the more challenging aspects to becoming more productive and proficient with 3D Studio MAX is learning how to acquire, manage, and manipulate materials and how to align them effectively to geometry. Very little information is available on sources for material maps; on how to organize a project's materials internally and externally so that they can easily be manipulated, referenced, imported into, or exported from any other project; how to manipulate complex materials within a scene; how to apply materials in an accurate and predictable manner onto any geometry;

and how to take advantage of materials previously generated in 3D Studio DOS R4. This chapter covers all these essential aspects of MAX material usage—aspects that all serious materials designers need to know and understand.

Although the manuals for 3D Studio MAX do a superb job of outlining each tool and setting in the program functions, and although the tutorials cover many concepts and techniques in a limited amount of space, very little information is available to new users about how to design materials quickly and accurately, how to·align them perfectly with any object (or create objects perfectly from the materials), how to acquire and manage materials and material files, how to navigate materials quickly, and how to convert older 3D Studio R4 DOS materials to a usable format for 3DS MAX. This chapter addresses all these concerns and presents discussions on the following topics:

- Strategies for optimizing the design of materials
- Material acquisition
- Material alignment techniques
- Material management philosophies
- Material and bitmap navigation
- Importing material files from 3D Studio DOS

The Materials Lab

3DS MAX will never run faster on your machine than it does the moment you launch a new session. With no objects in your scene to calculate, every control, every dialog, and every viewport updates as fast as it ever will unless you increase your system's resources. For this reason, many developers and designers of materials use fresh new sessions—*materials lab sessions* dedicated solely to constructing materials—to do their materials design, instead of trying to design within the scenes where the materials eventually will be used. Although there are numerous ways in 3DS MAX to disable the viewing of objects, to minimize the calculations of surfaces and speed up rendering times, nothing can compare to minimizing the size of your session. Put another way, MAX always runs faster working with nothing than it runs working with something.

Realistic scenes can get complicated very fast, and the use of many elaborate materials in a scene can get unwieldy if the materials are not designed and organized ahead of time. With the capability to save materials out to external files, it becomes practical to keep similar materials together in their own material libraries and to edit and maintain them away from the scenes that will eventually use them. Another good reason for keeping your materials separate from scenes is that they can be used with any scene instead of being limited to the scene in which they were designed.

A materials lab also enables the designer to subject a material to a wide range of different geometries and lighting considerations without making any changes to the scene in which the material eventually will be used. Any object onto which a material will be applied can be imported individually into a fresh session. Its geometry can be varied to optimize the number of surfaces needed to accommodate the material being designed. Lights can be created from any angle to experiment with the levels of brightness, shininess, and opacity in a material. Deformations and corruptions to the bitmaps themselves, used for the mapping channels, can be toyed with and applied for fast renders on objects. Changes in mapping models can also be experimented with. These things and more can all be done without affecting the final complicated scene. The perfected material can then be saved to a material category file, imported into complicated scenes, and applied to objects with a minimum of tweaking.

Following is a list of typical questions and concerns for any material being designed in a materials lab:

1. **What essential bitmaps are needed for the material?**

   For the vast majority of man-made materials you will ever create, you need a bitmap (or series of bitmaps) of the actual material. Although paint packages can assist in creating helpful masks, patterns, and a variety of random imperfections for materials, realistic textures usually depend to a large degree on realistic images. You can acquire these images in numerous ways, not the least of which is to use a portable raster-image camera and literally take planar snapshots of the materials as they occur in the real world. The resolution of these bitmaps should vary with the level of detail in the material. Be certain that you have enough pixels to accommodate the smallest, narrowest features (such as a spider web). Keep in mind that the resolution and brightness of the bitmap itself has a profound impact on the appearance of the materials that use it.

2. What geometry will the material be applied to?

The number of surfaces an object has greatly determines the appearance of any material applied to it. If need be, import the object(s) from the complicated scenes that will use them so that their vertex counts can be optimized for the material to be applied. If further tessellation of faces is necessary to get a reasonable deformation or smoothness to the geometry, you can easily and quickly experiment with and render values for this process without any overhead from the complicated scene.

3. What lighting will the material receive, and from where?

The realism of a material is only as effective as the lighting it receives. Put another way, displayed in a room with no lighting, the most sophisticated material ever designed will appear black. It is recommended, therefore, that you create a "lighting studio" as part of your materials lab. In this way, you can design materials with whatever experimental lighting you need to use to see how they hold up under any lighting conditions, without having to modify the existing lighting settings in the final scene and without having to render the final scene.

4. How far will the camera be from the objects with the material?

This is a crucial issue for any project. If an object is far enough away from the camera, with more complicated objects targeted in the foreground, the distant object may not require intense detail. It won't matter how much attention to detail you spend on an 8×4×4 inch brick if the brick is viewed from a mile away. By the same token, the closer you get to an object, the more important detail in a material becomes. If the resolution of the bitmaps used in a material is not high enough, pixels and "jaggies" may actually become visible as you near an object. Motion studies and storyboards can help tremendously with this phase of materials design.

Have an idea ahead of time of where your camera will go and what it will target, before you start tweaking the objects and materials that will appear in front of it.

5. **How long will the material actually be in view of the camera?**

Trickiest of all is deciding how much attention to detail one should give, based on the amount of time an object will appear in front of the camera. Objects that are seen for only a few seconds, or are seen only as a blur for a second or two as a camera pans quickly past them, may not require intense detail. Make the time in front of your camera a consideration when you design these materials.

The considerations for creating impressive materials are certainly not limited to these five aspects of material design, but they do have a profound impact on anyone's productivity with 3DS MAX. One of the most common factors reducing MAX's productivity is ineffective time management with materials design.

No clear-cut formulas exist for this aspect of 3DS MAX. Every material you design must be based on the objects and scenes being created and the way in which you decide to view them. Sweetspots for the most part are found through trial-and-error rendering, which is why having a dedicated materials lab session that optimizes editing refreshes and rendering-time calculations can be so helpful.

Materials Acquisition

This section treats sources for images that can be used to design materials, and how to use them to create seamless tileable materials. 3DS MAX comes with a large set of predefined default materials that can be used for production work or as examples of how to design your own materials. Where do the bitmaps for these materials come from, though? How were they edited to tile perfectly, and how can you acquire bitmaps of the same level of quality for specialized materials and create tileable materials from them?

The following sections discuss several examples of hardware and software in light of using them to acquire images for designing your own materials. Keep in mind that price of the solution should always be a consideration.

Scanners

For acquiring photorealistic colored or grayscaled images from old magazines, photographs, and practically anything you can roll a mouse over or set down on a glass surface, scanners can be well worth the investment if you plan to design many of your own materials. Depending on the types of images you work with, you may decide to look into hand-scanners, desktop scanners, or large-format scanners.

Key considerations in the purchase of any scanner include:

- What resolutions can the scanner provide (often referred to as the DPI or *dots per inch*)?

- At what color depths can it scan (monochrome, grayscale, 8-bit, TrueColor, and so on)?

- What file formats does it output, and are they compatible with your bitmap editing and conversion software?

- How large will the scanned images need to be?

- Does the scanner need to be portable or shared by other users?

- What kind of warranty does it come with? Is there local repair support for it if something breaks down?

- Are special drivers or software necessary to run it? Are the drivers and software compatible with the operating system and software you currently use?

- How much memory does the scanner require to accommodate the images and process them?

- How long has the scanner manufacturer been in business, and how often do they update their equipment and drivers? What is the typical longevity of their products and support for their products?

As an alternative to purchasing a scanner, you might want to use the scanning services available at many business office supply warehouses, copy/print houses, and reprographics and blueprinting companies. Such a service may be a far more economical way to get the raw bitmaps you need for your first few projects so that you can later invest in your own equipment.

Preexisting Image Libraries

Many companies today provide CD-ROM libraries of textures and materials, complete with optimized browsers and well-thought-out material categories. Navigating these collections and dumping what you need into your mapping project directories is such a simple, fast process that you can get right to work. An example of such a library resource is Autodesk's own Texture Universe collection (see fig. 9.1). This kind of low-cost resource can be an incredible time-saver for people who need to integrate images with high-quality materials, photographic backgrounds, or complex texture maps into their productions. An obvious benefit of this type of a resource is that most of the materials have already been carefully edited to ensure that the bitmaps are perfectly seamless and, if necessary, tileable.

FIGURE 9.1

Texture Universe's Windows Browser utility—the Metals category offers a variety of instantly usable, seamless, and tileable metal TrueColor bitmaps.

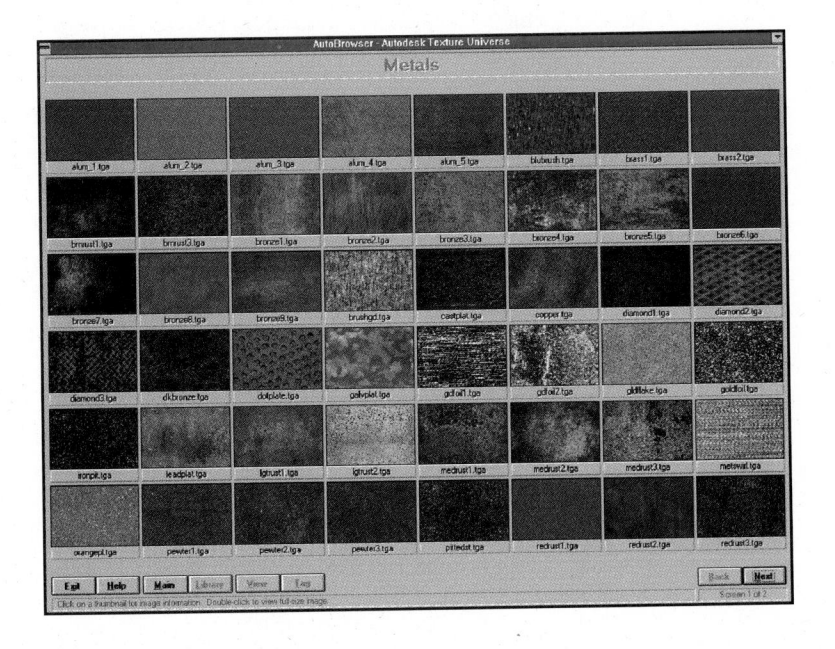

NOTE

A collection that keeps its file resources off your system, whose browser uses a minimum of RAM, and that restores memory after its browser is exited can make a tremendously positive impact on the performance of applications running in the background—such as 3DS MAX.

Key considerations in the purchase of any materials library collection include:

- What is your time worth? Compared to the time and money involved in creating equivalent materials, is the price of the collection reasonable?

- What file formats are used in the collection? Do they have a high enough resolution to be useful for your work?

- Have the images been edited to be seamless and tileable, if necessary?

- Does the collection come with an optimized browsing tool to help you navigate quickly through the collection?

- Are the materials well-organized, with names that make finding what you need easy?

- Does the collection require installation of its own software or drivers? If so, are they compatible with your software?

- Do you have the necessary system resources to accommodate the collection? Does it operate from the CD? Or do you have to spend hard drive space and precious RAM installing and running it while you work in 3DS MAX?

- What is the product support like for the product(s), and how often does the manufacturer update and maintain the library?

An astonishing number of 3D Studio DOS users have never examined either the full World Creating Toolkit that shipped with 3D Studio Release 4 or the full library of materials shipped with 3DS MAX. Also, many Animator Pro users are not aware that the latest version (1.3a) shipped with a CD packed with material images. Before you shop for new material collections, examine *every* material collection you have already purchased. Take the time to go through them all—it is time well-spent—and take notes, if necessary, to remind yourself later where to find what you need.

Paint Programs

Although the detail and believability of many materials depend on raw photorealistic images, the value of a painting program and the capacity to manually design and edit material images cannot be stressed enough.

Typical functions reserved for paint programs include the capability to change the level of brightness or darkness in an image; the capability to mirror an image and edit it to create a tileable version of the image; and the capability to change an image's color depth, resolution, gamma correction, colorization, and file format. Although 3DS MAX provides powerful compositing tools in its Video Post dialog, many paint programs are optimized for mixing, matching, and compositing still images and animations with full palette control and file attribute control. These in turn are often used as materials themselves (such as a television screen material that is an animation of a TV show). In addition to the editing tools available for work on preexistent movies and stills, a wide range of painting tools and ink types, image area selection tools and onionskinning tools, and specialized plug-in filters lend invaluable control over the design of materials, texture maps, and background images. Paint programs can often be the ideal environment for creating masks and grid-aligned patterns and for controlling alpha information in an image.

Key considerations in the purchase of any painting program include:

- Does the program run under your current operating system with your current system's resources and drivers? Does it conflict with any previously installed software resources or drivers?

- Does the program offer the types of tools and inks you need for your image or animation editing?

- Does the program have an open-ended architecture to accommodate specialized third-party plug-ins and filter inks?

- Does the program use a minimum of system resources while running so that it can be used as a sidekick to 3DS MAX, if necessary, without significantly degrading MAX's performance?

- Does the program come with adequate tutorial and reference documentation, and product support from the manufacturer?

- Is the program fast? Can it handle a wide variety of file formats, including still image and animation file formats?

- Does it offer control over color depth and image resolution?

- Does it offer batch image processing, if necessary?

- Do the program's features focus on treating animations, still images, or both?

───────────────────────────────────

Because 3DS MAX does not ship at this time with a powerful 2D-dedicated bitmap browser, you may also want to verify that the paint package you're purchasing comes with one (many do). Test it out on the MAPS directory of 3DS MAX; see how fast the bitmaps load and how much information is reported back for each image. Numerous powerful shareware (and even freeware) utilities are available also on many online forums.

3D Studio MAX and Screen Captures

One of the more obvious sources for creating materials is 3DS MAX itself. Through the use of the program's many tools and features, an unlimited amount of materials can be generated from texture maps, dent maps, noise maps, and geometrical patterns and objects (see Chapter 12, "Designing Special Effects Materials," for examples). You can also create materials from any Windows screen on your computer's monitor by using screen captures. Techniques to do this are outlined in the "Alignment by Screen Capture and Grids" section of this chapter.

Portable Digital Cameras

In recent years, a vast array of portable digital cameras has appeared on the market. Many of them are incredibly affordable. Depending on the number of images you need stored at a time, the file types you need, the color depths and resolutions you need, and the unending accessories that can be added to a camera, these devices can be the "portable scanner" of choice for serious materials designers.

Key considerations on the purchase of any portable digital camera:

- Is it manufactured by a nondigital camera manufacturer (this often determines the accessories available)?

- What is the camera's battery life, and how expensive are its replaceable batteries?

- How many images can the camera accommodate at one time?

- At what resolution and color depths can the images be taken?

- Does the camera have a flash, and does it offer reasonable control and reporting features for addressing lighting considerations?

- Does it require its own specialized software or drivers to interface with your system, and do these conflict with your existing configuration?

- Does the camera come with its own image browser (a surprising number of them don't)?

- What kind of repair, product support, and warranty are available for the camera? (These pieces of equipment are not cheap to fix.)

Remember that a nondigital camera used with a high-quality scanner or a high-quality scanning service may be a low-cost alternative to a digital camera. A key issue here is how fast of a turnaround you need from the time an image is snapped until you start using it to design your materials. If you can afford to wait for film to be processed, and if the quality, brightness, and resolution of the film are adequate to accommodate the resolution of the images scanned from the photographs, this approach may work fine.

Another key issue is the need for immediate verification and control over an image. Many cameras enable you to view an image immediately after it has been taken. There are no surprises. If the image is smudged, unbalanced, off-center, ineffectively lit, obscured by unexpected objects, or for any reason requires retaking, you can immediately replace the current shot with a new shot until you are satisfied. Finally, you have far more control over an image at the editing level if the image is originally digital. The graininess, brightness level, and clarity of photo images are highly dependent on the skill of the photo-processing staff and their equipment: You are at the mercy of someone else's work. If you take a superb shot of a material, and the photo-processing business produces a lousy image from it, all the digital scanning and editing tools in the world may not be able to save it. For this reason alone, many MAX users have made the leap to taking complete control over their image acquisitions.

Video Cameras and Video Recorders

From high-end to low-end, video cameras and video recording equipment remain a powerful material and background acquisition technology. The considerations for purchasing video equipment vary tremendously with the specific equipment itself. Consulting a multimedia dealership that has experience with the equipment, its installation, and its use is highly recommended. Such a dealership may also have demo units in stock that you can test-drive with real-world examples.

For many peple, entering the world of multimedia is also the beginning of a journey into the universe of broadcast technologies. A low-end solution such as the Intel Personal Video Recorder (comprising a single card, cable, and home video camera) may be all that is necessary for some users' applications. It is simple enough to install and use without any training or technical background. By the same token, high-end cameras and recorders that use specialized recording media are rarely plug-and-play. They usually require skilled technical expertise to install properly, and a significant amount of training on the equipment's use, limitations, and industry standards.

One general recommendation can be offered for any video solution: Get your hands on it, or see a real-world demonstration of it before you purchase it! Many users buy equipment that is overkill for their applications, and others buy equipment that doesn't have enough power to do what they need it to do. Some people make a living by installing, tweaking, consulting, and training on video equipment. Generally, an investment in their time is well worth what you pay.

Keep Your Eyes Peeled

Every year new technologies arrive on the scene to make image acquisition simpler, more affordable, and more accessible to the MAX user. Many users attend national conferences to see these new solutions in action. At the same time, the number of schemes and approaches that users who didn't have the budget for expensive hardware have come up is a surprisingly large number of schemes and approaches to get quality work done.

Here's one example of the way one user managed—on a shoestring budget—to acquire images for designing his materials. First, he used a copy machine to create a hard-copy image of whatever object or material he needed to create. He would then fax this sheet of paper to his own system, which has a fax broadcasting software program. This program would convert the faxed document to a 300 DPI PCX or TIF file that could then be imported into a paint program for cropping or editing, and applied as a material map in MAX. His work was surprisingly impressive at the time, and his first set of projects later paid for more elaborate image-acquiring technologies.

Material Alignment Techniques

One of the first essential techniques that you need to have under your belt for creating any materials accurately is the ability to perfectly align bitmaps and their map modifiers with geometry. No matter what map type you use and no matter how sophisticated it gets, most material maps must have mapping coordinates assigned to them for the objects to which they are applied. Although a great deal of work can be accomplished by eyeballing the fitting of maps to geometry, realistic materials have realistic dimensions: Brick bitmaps accommodate realistic brick sizes, and labels on jars accommodate realistic surface areas of the jars. Should a bitmap have an edge that needs to be perfectly aligned with the edges of geometry, the techniques described here can ensure predictable alignment.

Four methods for aligning bitmaps to geometry are outlined in this section. All four use Paintbrush, a common Windows utility in the Accessories Group, to demonstrate how a bitmap can be manipulated and applied accurately to geometry. Note, however, that any paint package can be used in a similar or more sophisticated manner to accomplish the same types of alignments. The first technique uses the actual bitmap resolution in pixels to control the fitting of a map to geometry with known dimensions. The second technique uses existing bitmaps to create map-accommodating traces for lofted fit-deformed objects. The third uses screen captures of existing objects directly from MAX's viewports to create guides for perfectly fitting painted maps. Finally, the fourth technique uses a nifty freeware utility developed by Peter Watje (nice work Peter!) to create a planar grid representation of any object's texture map coordinates. Perfect alignments are not limited to these four techniques, but these techniques give you several ways to accomplish the task.

Alignment by Pixel and Material ID

Suppose that you have a block of material (any material) whose dimensions are 80 units by 40 units by 20 units, and that each side of this block needs a unique and perfectly matched material. You can do the job by creating three bitmaps with resolutions of 80-by-40, 80-by-20, and 40-by-20 pixels, assuming that 80 pixels, 40 pixels, and 20 pixels are enough to accommodate the necessary resolution of each material on each side of the object.

This unity ratio (1 pixel per unit) can be used as a helpful starting point for any material you design using this technique. After the material is created and aligned with the object, the ratio of pixels per unit can easily be scaled up to create more detailed materials with the same perfect alignment on the object, because bitmaps can be reloaded easily within the Material Editor. Any of the three resolutions used for this tutorial, for example, can be multiplied by any common value if higher or lower resolutions are needed to accommodate the material's detail. The resolutions of all bitmaps could be multiplied by a value of 20.0, so that the bitmap resolutions would be 1600-by-800, 1600-by-400, and 800-by-400, respectively. For this tutorial, values of 80, 40, and 20 are used to control a unity alignment.

1. Start a new session in 3DS MAX. On the Create panel, click on the Geometry button, and create a Box with a length of 80, a width of 40, and a height of 20. Segment values for each dimension can be set to 1. Toggle on Generate Mapping Coordinates. Center the block in the screen, and use the Arc Rotate and Pan tools in the Perspective viewport to get a good look at the block so that your session looks like figure 9.2.

2. Launch Paintbrush (Paint in NT 4.0), and use the Options/Image Attributes (Image, Attributes in NT 4.0) pull-down menu option to set the image attributes. Set the Units to Pels, set the Width to 80, and set the Height to 40. Toggle the Colors to Colors mode. The Image viewport shrinks to an 80-by-40 pixel size.

FIGURE 9.2
An 80×40×20-unit block is created.

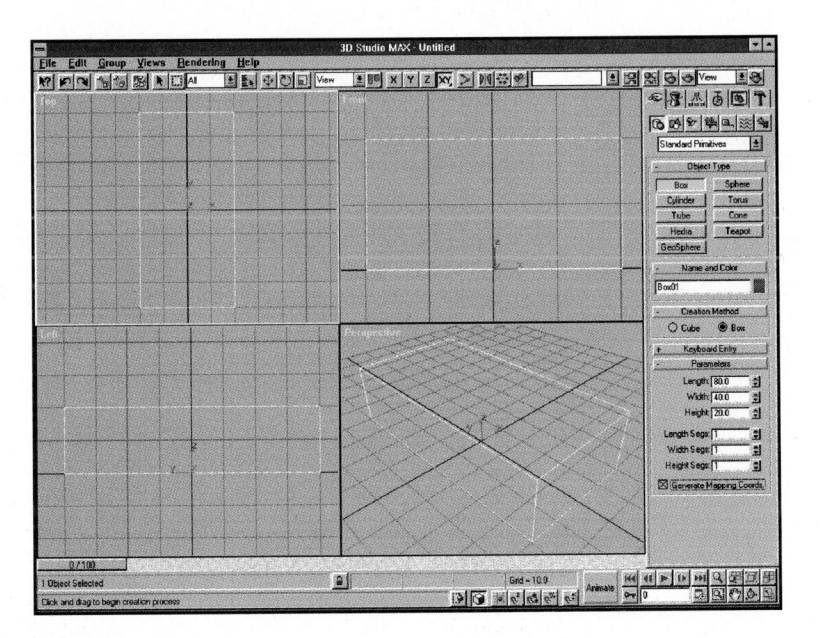

3. Use the View/Zoom In (in NT 4.0 use View, Zoom, Large Size and View, Zoom, Show Grid) pull-down menu option(s), and pick anywhere in the viewport. A large grid of 80-by-40 squares, with each square representing one pixel, appears. Using the mouse pick buttons, create a single pixel border around the entire window and create black squares of 5-by-5 pixels in each corner. Use the View/Zoom Out (in NT 4.0 use View, Zoom, Normal Size) pull-down menu option to return to Full View mode, and use the Text tool to write **80×40** in the center of the bitmap. Zoomed in, your bitmap should look like figure 9.3.

4. Save the file as 80X40.BMP in the \3DSMAX\MAPS directory.

5. Use the Options/Image Attributes pull-down menu option to set the image attributes. Set the Units to Pels, set the Width to 80, and set the Height to 20. Toggle the Colors to Colors mode. The Image viewport shrinks to an 80-by-20-pixel size. Repeat step 3 and save the image as file 80X20.BMP in the \3DSMAX\MAPS directory.

6. Repeat step 5 to create a third bitmap of 40-by-20 units. After all three of these pixel-accurate bitmaps are saved, you are ready to begin creating a perfectly aligned material.

FIGURE 9.3

A pixel-accurate bitmap is created to perfectly fit the 80×40-unit surface of the block.

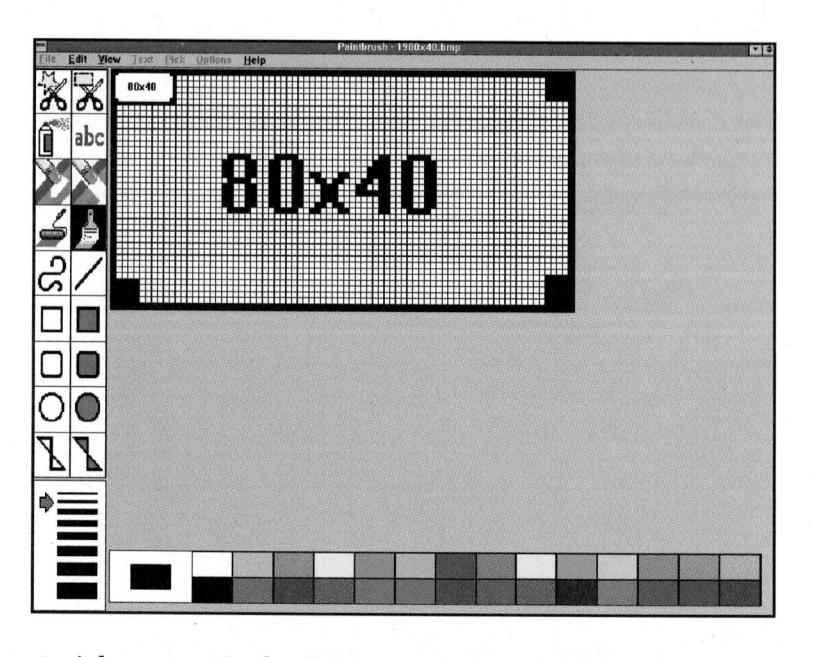

7. Begin material construction by clicking on the Material Editor button on the main toolbar. Select the upper-left sample slot in the Material Editor. Enter **PixelMap** for the name of the material. Click on the Type button, and set the type to Multi/Sub-Object. This material type enables you to apply multiple materials to a single object, with each material corresponding to a material ID assigned to surfaces on the object.

8. In the Basic Parameters rollout menu, click on the Set Number button, set the number of materials to 3, and then click on OK. Three Material buttons appear, with Material #1 corresponding with whatever surfaces are assigned to Material ID #1, Material #2 corresponding with whatever surfaces are assigned to Material ID #2, and so forth. Click on the Standard button to the right of Material #1. Open the Maps rollout menu.

9. Click on the Diffuse button. Select Bitmap from the Material/Map Navigator browser, and click on OK. In the Bitmap Parameters rollout menu, set the Bitmap to \3DSMAX\80X40.BMP. Click on the Show Map in Viewport button beneath the sample slots so that the 80×40 material will eventually be shown in the viewport after Material IDs have been assigned. Also click on the Assign Material to Selection button below the sample slots to assign Pixelmap to the block. Make certain that the block is highlighted when you do this.

10. Click on the Go To Parent button beneath the sample slots to return to the Maps rollout. Enter the name **80×40** in the Material Name edit box. Click on the Go to Sibling button beneath the sample slots to move to the Map parameters for the second material in your Multi/Sub-Object material.

11. Repeat step 9, but select \3DSMAX\80X20.BMP for the Bitmap and name the material **80×20**. Repeat step 9 again, but select \3DSMAX\40X20.BMP for the Bitmap and name the material **40×20**. When you have finished, click on the Material/Map Navigator to see the overall construction of the Pixelmap material. It should look like figure 9.4.

FIGURE 9.4

The Material/Map Navigator shows the internal structure of the Pixelmap material.

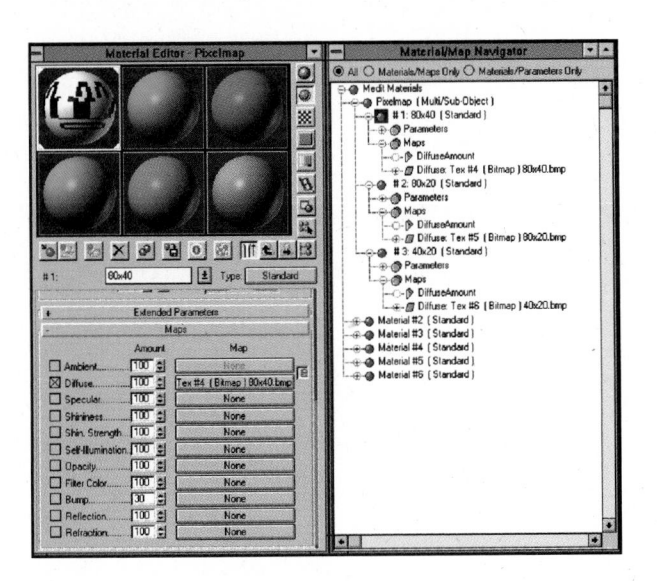

Now that the material is completely defined, begin assigning material IDs to the block surfaces.

12. Close the Material Editor and Material/Map Navigator dialogs. Make certain that the block is selected. Go to the Modify panel and apply an Edit Mesh modifier to the block. Set the selection button at the bottom center of the screen to Window Selection mode. Click on the Select Objects button in the main toolbar. In the Modify panel, set the Selection Level to Face, and click on the Polygon button in the Selection area.

13. In the Front viewport, pick a point to the upper-left of the top of the block, and draw the mouse across the top surface. The top face turns red. Hold down the Ctrl key and drag a window over the bottom surface to add the bottom surface to the currently highlighted set of faces to be treated.

14. In the Modify panel, scroll down until you reach the Edit Surface rollout menu. Type **1** in the ID edit box and press Enter. This assigns the Material ID #1 to the top and bottom surfaces of the block.

15. Right-click over the word *Perspective* in the Perspective viewport, and set the Viewport mode to Smooth+Highlight. Materials now appear on the block in the viewport. They may need to be rotated (this will be done shortly).

16. In the Top viewport, pick a point to the upper-left of the left side of the block and draw the mouse across the left surface. The left face turns red. Hold down the Ctrl key and drag a window over the right surface to add the right surface to the currently highlighted set of faces to be treated.

17. In the Modify panel, type **2** in the ID edit box and press Enter. This assigns the Material ID #2 to the left and right surfaces of the block.

18. In the Top viewport, pick a point to the upper-left of the front side of the block, and draw the mouse across the front surface. The front face turns red. Hold down the Ctrl key and drag a window over the back surface to add it to the currently highlighted set of faces to be treated. In the Modify panel, type **3** in the ID edit box and press Enter. This assigns the Material ID #3 to the front and back surfaces of the block.

Now that all three materials have been assigned correctly to each side of the block, all that remains to be done are rotations of the bitmaps, if necessary. To change the rotation of any of the three bitmaps, click on the Material Editor button in the main toolbar; then, in the Basic Parameters rollout menu, click on one of the three material buttons, and then click on the Diffuse button in the Maps rollout menu. In the Coordinates rollout menu, look for the Angle parameter. Set this to 0, 90, 180, or 270, as appropriate. The bitmap rotates in the viewport. Rotate each diffuse map, as necessary, until your block looks like that shown in figure 9.5

FIGURE 9.5
Each sub-object material is fitted perfectly to each assigned side of the block.

This technique relies on knowing the exact dimensions of the surfaces to which a material will be applied. Figure 9.5 shows the actual pixels in the letters on each material. To make the text appear less pixelated you need a higher resolution for each bitmap, and a smoother font must be used. File 9PIXMAP.MAX can be used as a reference for this technique.

Alignment by Bitmap Traces

In some cases, you may have photographs or bitmaps of something, which need to be used to somehow create an object in 3DS MAX—with the photographs or bitmaps used as a map for the applied material. By setting the viewport background feature to the image, using 2D tracing tools in the Create panel to generate top and side profiles, and generating a fit-deformed Loft object from the profiles, you can crop and apply the same photograph or bitmap to the object as an almost perfectly aligned material.

For this example, a bitmap called 9BIRD.BMP is used (see fig. 9.6). This simple black-and-white, 100-by-60, very low-resolution image is used as a viewport background image to create traced profiles of a bird. The profiles are then used to create a fit-deformed Lofted object of a bird. Finally, the bitmap is used to create a bird material that is applied as a planar map to the side of the bird.

FIGURE 9.6

More elaborate maps can be used in the same way to create traces of profiles.

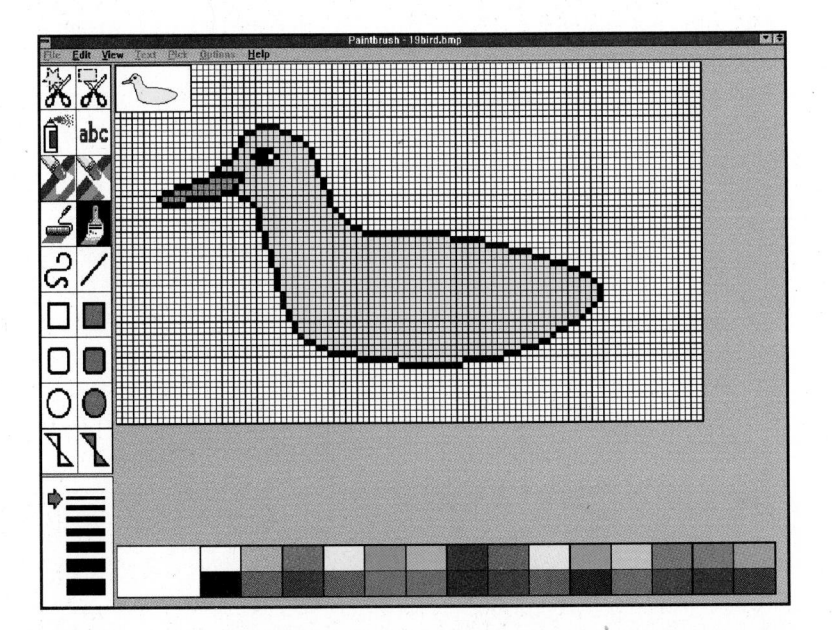

1. Start a new session of 3DS MAX.

2. Right-click in the left viewport. Select the Views, Background Image pull-down menu option. In the Viewport Background dialog, click on the Files button and load 9BIRD.BMP from a legal maps directory to set the Current Background Source (you may need to move this file to \3DSMAX\MAPS). Set the Aspect Ratio to Match Bitmap. Toggle Display Background to On, and then click on OK. Click on the Min/Max Toggle to maximize the Left viewport.

3. In the Create panel, click on the Shapes button, and then click on the Line button. In the Create Method rollout menu, set the Initial Type toggle to Smooth. Pick a point at the tip of the beak in the image background, and then pick points along the edge of the bird's profile until you have traced the entire image. When prompted, close the spline. Use the Views, Background Image pull-down menu option, toggle Display Background to Off, and then click on OK. You can now see the profile you have created from the background image.

4. Using the profile spline as a guide, create a new spline that represents half the top of the bird's profile. Mirror it to produce a perfectly symmetrical other half, and use the spline editing Vertex tools to attach the two shapes and weld together perfectly the vertices at the tip of the beak and tail.

NOTE

If only one bitmap image is available to create a side profile, eyeballing a top profile can take some experimentation. Fortunately, MAX makes it very easy to edit splines and update the resulting Loft objects until you are happy with the results.

5. Create a circle for the Loft object shape and create a straight spline for the Loft object path by using several points to accommodate the curvature of the bird's top and side profiles. The more points you use, the better the fit deformation appears. Use the length of the profiles as a guide for the length of the Loft object path spline. Your profiles, circle, and loft path spline should resemble those shown in figure 9.7.

FIGURE 9.7
Aligning the top profile and the Loft path spline with the side profile makes their construction easier and more accurate.

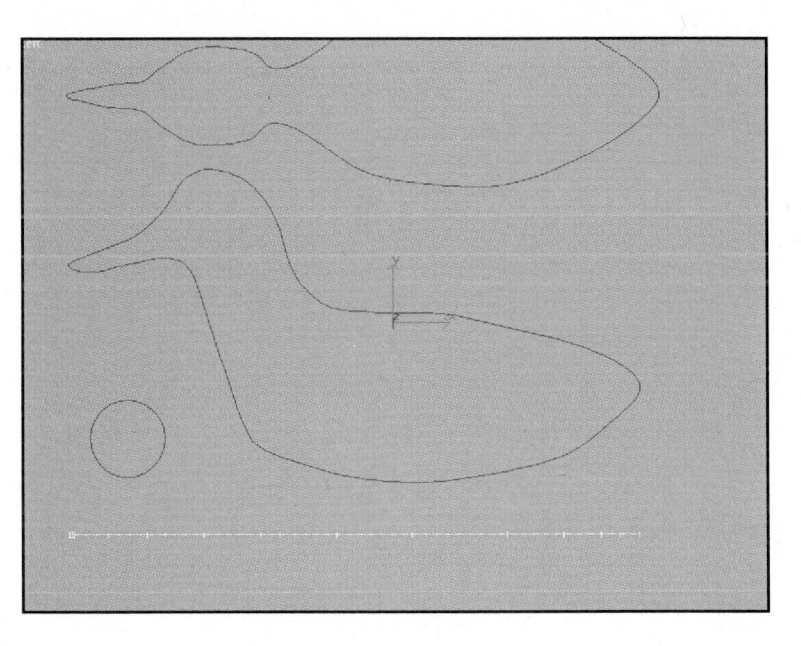

6. Select the Loft object path spline. In the Create panel, click on the Geometry button, and in the combo box click on Loft Object. Click on the Loft button, and then click on the Get Shape button and select the circle. By selecting the loft path spline first and then selecting the Loft object shape, you make the resulting Loft object align itself with the Loft path. In the Skin Parameters rollout menu, toggle Skin to on in the Display area. A cylindrical skin appears in the viewport.

7. In the Modify panel, open the Deformations rollout menu and click on the Fit button. The Fit Deformation dialog appears. Click on the Make Symmetrical button to turn this mode to Off because you will be using different top and side profiles. Click on the Display X Axis button, click on the Get Shape button, and select the original side profile spline you created from the background image. Click on the Fit Deformation dialog's Zoom Extents button, and stretch the dialog to get a good view of the X axis deformation profile. Click on the Display Y Axis button, make certain that the Get Shape button is still active, and select the top profile spline of the bird. Click on the Display XY Axis button to see both deformation profiles (see fig. 9.8).

FIGURE 9.8

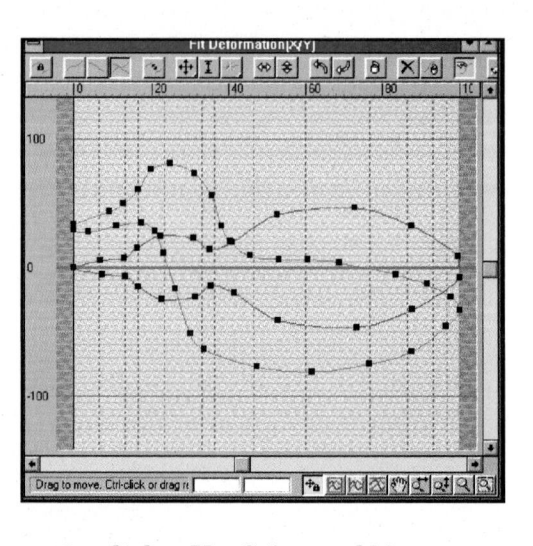

The fit deformation profiles immediately update the Loft object in the viewport.

8. Close the Fit Deformation dialog. Use Select and Move to move the Loft object so that it fits perfectly inside the original side profile spline. Click on the Views/Background Image pull-down menu option, and toggle Display Background to On. You are now ready to create the bird material.

9. Click on the Material Editor button in the main toolbar, select the upper-left sample slot, and open the Maps rollout menu. Click on the Diffuse button, click on Bitmap in the Material/Map browser, and click on OK. In the Bitmap Parameters rollout menu, click on the Large Bitmap button and load the file 9BIRD.BMP. Making certain that the Loft object is selected, click on the Assign Material to Selection button under the sample slots. Close the Material Editor dialog.

10. In the Modify panel, apply a UVW Map modifier to the Loft object. Make certain that the Mapping toggle is set to Planar mode. In the Parameters rollout, click on the Bitmap Fit button in the Alignment area and select 9BIRD.BMP as the file to set the dimensions of the modifier's gizmo. Click on Sub-Object to edit the gizmo. Then, using Select and Move and the Select and Uniform Scale transforms, position and scale the gizmo so that it perfectly aligns horizontally with the bitmap shown in the viewport's background image. After this is set, click on the Sub-Object button.

11. Click on the Min/Max Toggle to view all four viewports again. Right-click in the Perspective viewport; then, using the Arc Rotate, Pan, and Zoom buttons, set a good view of the bird Loft object. Right-click over the word *Perspective* in the Perspective viewport, and set the Viewport mode to Smooth+Highlight.

12. Click on the Material Editor button on the main toolbar. You should still be at the Bitmap parameters level of the bird material. Click on the Show Map in Viewport button; the material appears on the bird. You may need to rotate the material by setting the Angle parameter to 180 in the Coordinates rollout menu. (Alternatively, you can do this by rotating the gizmo.) Figure 9.9 shows the material's perfect fit on the bird Loft object.

FIGURE 9.9

By activating the Show Map in Viewport button in the Material Editor, you can experiment in real time with a material's parameters.

Show Map in Viewport

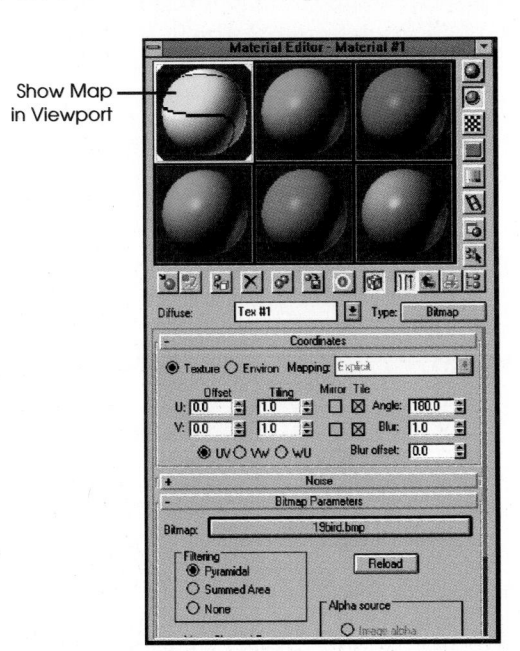

The extremely low resolution of the bitmap is responsible for the chunky black outlines on the bird object's material. This has been done on purpose so that you can see the exact lineup effect of your map with the Loft object. The higher the resolution of the image used for traces and the material, the more cleanly the material aligns itself with the object. The smoothness of the lofted object's geometry also impacts the map's alignment limitations. To ensure that areas of the image outside the object do not appear on the Loft object's material, it is helpful to trace the profiles a short distance "inside" the background image perimeter so that the lofted object is created a fraction smaller than the map image applied to it.

Alignment by Screen Capture and Grids

In some cases, you may have an object in MAX that needs to have bitmaps created from its surfaces to generate its material(s). By using Windows' internal screen-capturing capabilities and by using helpful viewport views and grids, you can create bitmaps that can be used to create perfectly fitted materials. For this example, the file 9BIRD2.MAX (see fig. 9.10) is used as the starting geometry for creating a fitted bird material.

FIGURE 9.10

The geometry for this bird was created through processes outlined in the preceding technique.

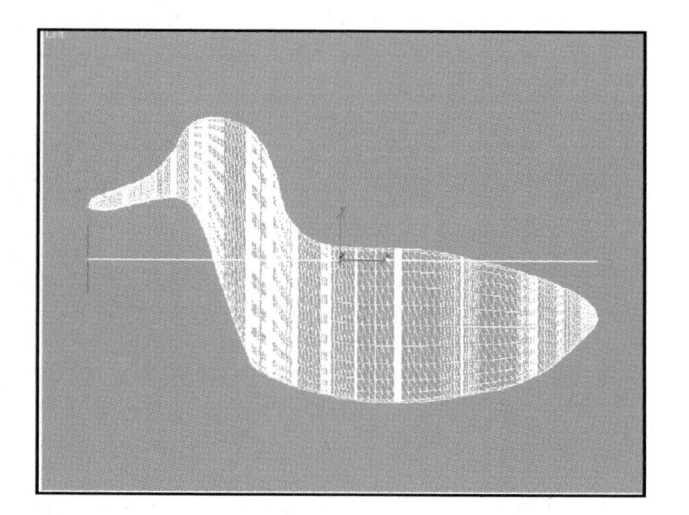

1. Start by opening file 9BIRD2.MAX. The Min/Max Toggle has been used to make the Left viewport fill the screen. The bird has been created from a Loft object whose path is perfectly aligned with the home grid. All other objects in the scene have been hidden, and Zoom Extents has been used to maximize the bird object in the viewport. All work to generate the map relies on not moving the bird and on using Zoom Extents to fit the bird object into the viewport.

2. With the bird maximized in the Left viewport, press the Print Screen button on your keyboard to capture the current screen to the Windows Clipboard. Minimize the 3DS MAX window.

3. Open Paint or Paintbrush from your Accessories group, and maximize its window. Use the Options/Image Attribute (in NT 4.0 use Image, Attributes) pull-down option to set the image pels to your current full-screen resolution. If your screen resolution is set to 1024×768, set the pel values to a width and height of 1024 and 768, respectively. The resolution of the initial bitmap is determined by your full-screen resolution set in Windows.

4. Use the View/Zoom Out pull-down menu option to show the entire graphic area's boundaries. Use the Edit/Paste pull-down menu option to import the image placement, and then use Edit/Paste a second time to paste the contents into the graphic area.

NOTE

In Paintbrush, you must use the Edit/Paste option twice to completely transfer the Clipboard contents to the graphic. In many paint packages, an option enables you to use the current Clipboard contents to create a new image.

Use the View/Zoom In pull-down menu option to verify the integrity of the Clipboard image transfer and to return you to Editing mode (see fig. 9.11).

FIGURE 9.11

After the image has been transferred to the graphic area, you can also control the image's color depth by saving out to any of the permitted file types and then reloading it.

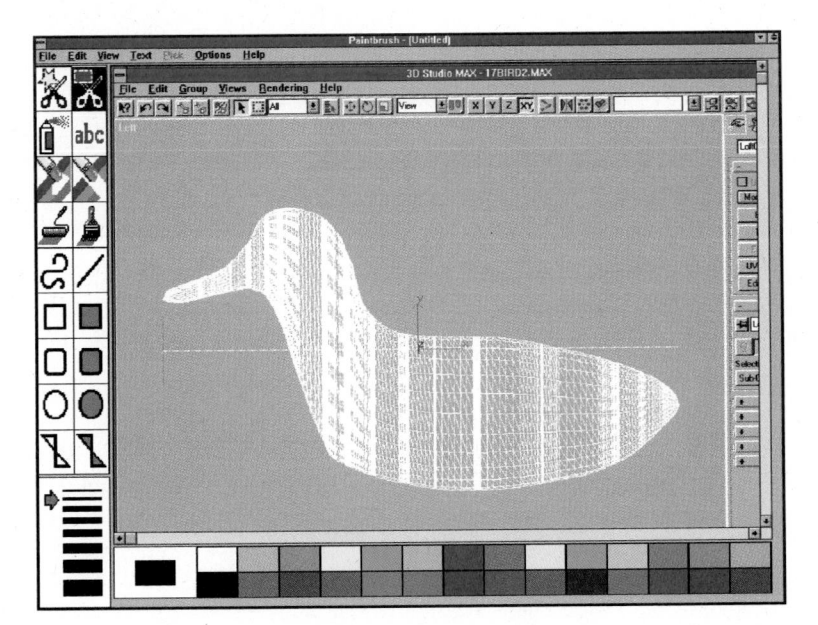

5. Because the next steps make changes to this image, save the image to a file in case you make changes and then decide to start over. Use the available paint tools to paint the image as you want. An example of how you might paint the image is shown in figure 9.12. Having a photograph of the real object nearby can really help when you paint manually. Use the View/Zoom In pull-down menu option, if necessary, to make certain that the borders of the mesh are completely painted.

A quick way to paint an image like this is to create accurate borders without "leaks," and then use fill tools to fill the interiors quickly.

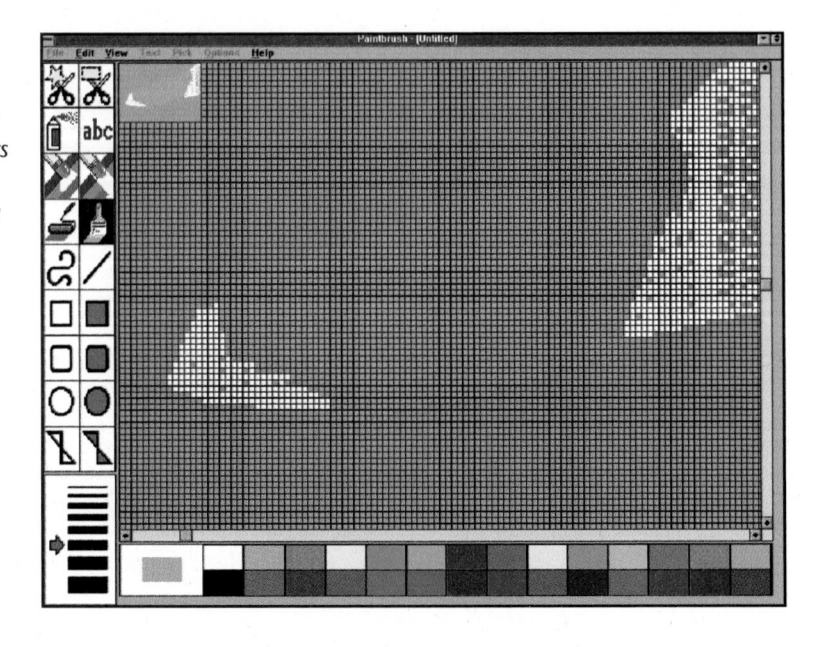

NOTE

Overextending the painted colors beyond the mesh boundaries ensures that all areas of the object's surface receive a nonmesh color when the map is applied. Make one exception to this rule, however: Paint to the exact borders of the topmost, bottommost, leftmost, and rightmost points on the bird so that you can accurately copy the map in later steps.

Figure 9.13 shows one way the bird can be painted. The more time you spend on the detail and blending of colors in the image, the more alive the material appears when applied to the object. Many paint packages also enable you to uniformly scale the image to a higher or lower resolution. If a lower-resolution bitmap will suffice for the material, use it—to reduce rendering times and the use of system resources while you edit. Some paint packages also enable you to use photorealistic images as fill-pattern inks; with this capability, you can hollow out areas of the image and then fill those areas with realistic feather images from real photos.

6. In Paintbrush, use the rectangular Scissors tool to create a cutting border of the bird. If you need to, reselect the borders by repicking the diagonally opposite corners of the rectangle until the bird fits perfectly inside them. Use the View/Cursor Position pull-down menu option to view the pixel X and Y positions of the cursor at the upper-left and bottom-right corners of the scissor rectangle border. Record these numbers and use them to determine the width and height of this area in pixels. In this example, the upper-left corner reports (64,185) and the

bottom-right corner reports (782,582), which means that the image inside the cutting border has a resolution of 718×397. Figure 9.14 shows the cutting boundary.

FIGURE 9.13

This paint job took about five minutes.

FIGURE 9.14

Make certain that your cutting boundary approximates the top and bottom and left and right edges of the mesh as closely as possible.

7. In Paintbrush, use the Edit/Copy pull-down menu option to copy the contents of the border to the clipboard. Use the File/New pull-down menu option to start a new session in Paintbrush. Use the Options/Image Attributes pull-down menu option and set the image pels to the clipboard content's width and height (in this example, set width to 718 and height to 397). Be certain to enable Color mode if your clipboard uses color. Use the Edit/Paste pull-down menu option to paste the clipboard contents into the new graphic area, save the file as \3DSMAX\MAPS\BIRD.BMP, and minimize Paintbrush.

8. Maximize 3DS MAX. Click on the Material Editor from the main toolbar, and select the upper-left sample slot. The Type is already set to Standard. Enter **Duck** as the name of the material. Open the Maps rollout menu and click on the Diffuse button. Select Bitmap from the Material/Map browser and click on OK. In the Bitmap Parameters rollout menu, click on the Bitmap button and load the file \3DSMAX\ MAPS\ BIRD.BMP. Make certain that the Loft object is selected, and click on the Assign Material to Selection button beneath the sample slots. Click on the Show Map in Viewport button under the sample slots, and close the Material Editor dialog.

9. Right-click over the word *Left* in the viewport, and set the Viewport mode to Smooth+Highlight. In the Modify panel, apply a UVW modifier to the bird object. Make certain that the Mapping mode is set to Planar. The UVW gizmo is already fitted to the Mesh object's boundaries. Flip the U and V tiles as necessary so that the material map is oriented properly to the object. (Alternatively, you could do this by entering an angle value in the Coordinates rollout menu in the Material Editor.) Your bitmap is applied perfectly to the object (see fig. 9.15).

FIGURE 9.15

After a basic bitmap is fitted, you can use it as a guide to create other bitmaps such as bump maps, shininess maps, or opacity maps.

Alignment by Plug-Ins (UNWRAP.DLU)

The technique described in this section demonstrates how to paint literally every surface of an object as you want, with precise control, by using a free plug-in designed by Peter Watje (and available on the *Inside 3D Studio MAX Volume II* CD-ROM). After you place the plug-in, UNWRAP.DLU, in your \3DSMAX\PLUGINS directory, it can be loaded from the Utilities panel by picking on the Utilities combo box and selecting Unwrap Object Texture.

The plug-in depends on the object to be unwrapped already having its map coordinates assigned. This can be done either by applying a UVW modifier to an object, or by toggling an object's Map Coordinates at the time of creation, or from the Modify panel. This example uses a file called 9WRAP.MAX for reference.

1. Make certain that UNWRAP.DLU has been moved or copied to your \3DSMAX\PLUGINS directory. In the Utilities panel, select Unwrap Object Texture from the Utilities combo box. Set the Width to 640 and the Height to 480. Click on the Pick Object button and then on the Loft object. Save the file out to \3DSMAX\MAPS\UNWRAP.BMP.

2. Start by opening the file 9WRAP.MAX. Three shapes and a lofting path spline have been created to generate a lofted object that transitions (changes) its skin from a circle to a hexagon to a star. In the Control panel, click on the Geometry button and select Loft Object from the combo box. Select the open-ended loft spline path. Click on the Loft button; then, on the Creation Method rollout menu, click on the Get Shape button.

3. Click on the circle. A circle shape appears at the beginning of the loft path spline. In the Path Parameters rollout menu, set the Path value to 50 in Percentage mode, and click on the hexagon. A hexagon shape appears in the middle of the loft path spline. Set the Path value to 100, and pick the star. A star shape appears at the end of the loft path spline. In the Skin Parameters rollout menu, toggle Skin On in the Display area. The loft object skin appears. In the Surface Parameters rollout menu, toggle Apply Mapping On in the Mapping area. This is similar to applying a UVW modifier to the object, except that the mapping coordinates are aligned along the spline path.

N OTE

The higher the resolution you save to, the more precise the texture coordinates represented in the unwrapped bitmap.

4. Minimize 3DS MAX, launch Paintbrush or Paint, and load UNWRAP.BMP. Your image should resemble the one shown in figure 9.16.

   At the top of the image is the unwrapped map near the star, and at the bottom of the image is the unwrapped map near the circle. The horizontal seam running through the exact middle of the image is the unwrapped map at the hexagon. You are now staring at every surface on the object, and you can paint every surface on the object precisely.

5. Using the paint tools in Paintbrush, use the texture grid bitmap to create red stripes perfectly aligned with the alternating sides of the surfaces near the star end of the Loft object, and to create yellow bands of color at the ends and the precise middle of the Loft object (see fig. 9.17).

FIGURE 9.16

Depending on the object's geometry, it may be more advantageous at times to reverse the values in the plug-in for height and width, to better represent the texture surfaces.

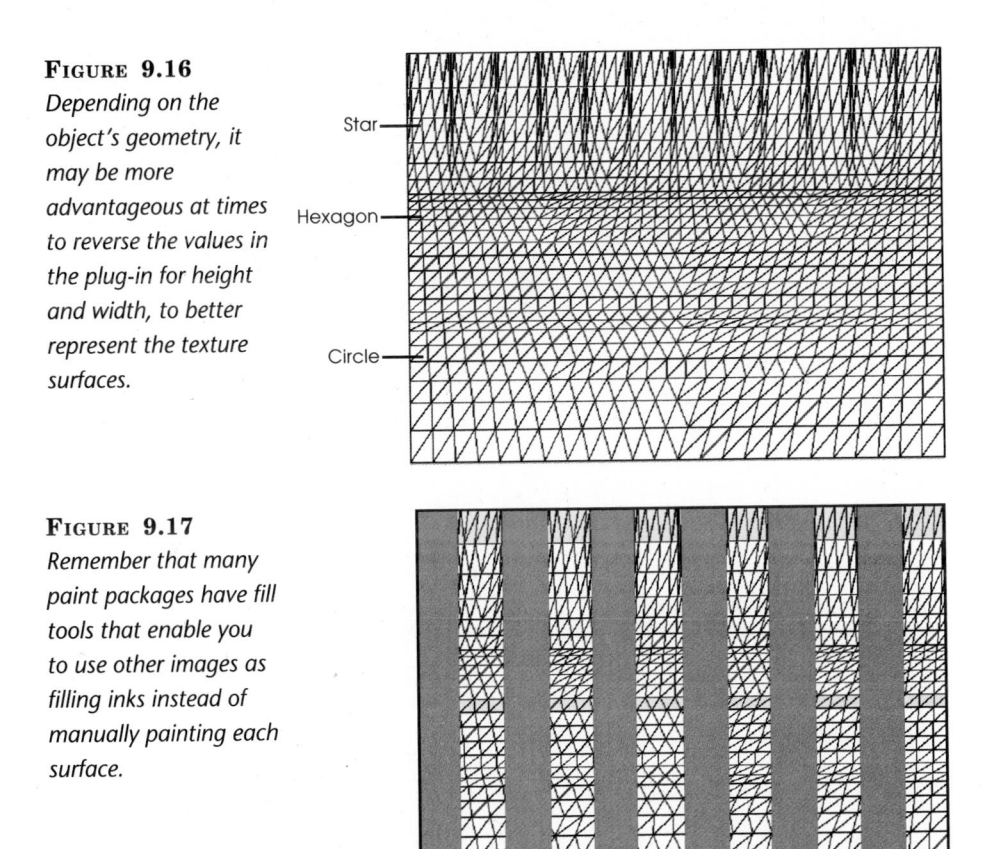

FIGURE 9.17

Remember that many paint packages have fill tools that enable you to use other images as filling inks instead of manually painting each surface.

6. Save the file as \3DSMAX\MAPS\UNWRAP.BMP. Minimize Paint-brush and Maximize 3DS MAX. Click on the Material Editor button on the main toolbar and select the upper-left sample slot. Open the Maps rollout menu and click on the Diffuse button. Select Bitmap as the type and click on OK. Click on the Bitmap button in the Bitmap Parameters rollout menu and select \3DSMAX\MAPS\UNWRAP.BMP. Click on the Show Map in Viewport button under the sample slots. The material appears perfectly aligned on the Loft object (see fig. 9.18).

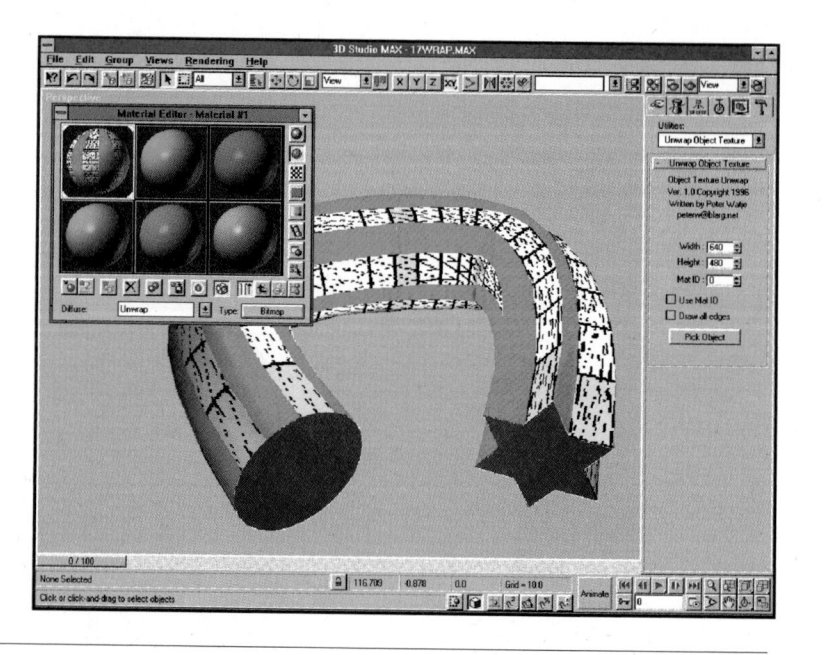

Material Management

Depending on the complexity of the scenes you're creating, a tremendous number of files may be involved in creating and managing your materials. Many users get off to a dangerous start by pooling all the bitmaps for any project into a single support directory. When the next project comes along, searching for and finding the bitmaps they need can take twice as long as it should. If they rely on bitmaps from external sources such as CD collections, their browsing time can increase even more, making the task of building bitmap resources for any project a nightmare. Here are some basic file-management techniques that can keep your material design (and your project) running smoothly and efficiently:

- **Organize all the files you need for a given project into a dedicated project directory structure.** Do not use 3DS MAX's own directories for your work. Doing so can get you into a lot of trouble when you need to start separating out your files from the program's. If a project requires its own meshes, its own bitmaps for materials, its own notes, its own system and MAX configuration files, or any of the resources supplied with 3DS MAX, all of them can be kept together in a separate project directory, isolated from 3DS MAX and other projects. In this way, an entire project can be completely archived or distributed without any missing files, and you always keep 3DS MAX's directories clean.

- **Move external resource files to your project directories.** When you rely on external resources for a project (such as mesh and material file collections off a CD-ROM library), move the necessary resource files to your dedicated project directory so that you know where to find them. Although it may seem redundant and wasteful to have bitmaps common to several projects stored in a unique place for each project, you always know where to find a project's bitmaps regardless of the project you're in. When a project is archived, you won't have to spend time figuring out which maps from a general all-purpose bitmap bin were used.

- **Create intelligent project subdirectories to keep files organized.** In the same way that a project directory can help to manage all the files used and generated in a project, project subdirectories can help to manage the function of the files used in a project. Bitmaps used for materials can be separated from bitmaps used for backgrounds and environment; template meshes (such as floorplans) can be separated from furnishing meshes, in the event that they need to be imported separated into other projects; area lots and streets can be separated from landscaping features, and so forth. Although it may seem a bit cumbersome to organize your files in this manner, it can make life much easier for someone new coming into a project and needing to find something. It can also keep hair on your head if you ever need to revisit an old project and have forgotten how things were organized and used back then.

- **Never abandon anything you have generated until the project is completed.** Clients often change their minds in the middle of a project. It isn't unusual for a client to request that you make modifications to your current work, and then later request that you scratch the modifications and continue with the original plan. This can be devastating if you have overwritten the original work with your modifications. When modifications come into play, do not continue working with the scene by overwriting the prior work. Save the current work at that stage in case you need to come back to it. Create a complete copy of all files in use, and use these to begin working on the modifications. Hard drive space is incredibly cheap these days, and there are numerous large-file–format saving devices you can use to move your current work off your hard disk if you need the space.

- **Use practical file names.** It pays to spend a little time thinking about the names you give to the files you create. Using file names such as WOOD.BMP may work fine for your first and only project, but after a few projects you will not remember whether the wood is maple, ash, cork, or pine. File names such as WOOD01.BMP won't help much either, unless you're using a powerful bitmap browser and don't mind sifting through hundreds of files. One of the great things about today's operating systems is that they enable you to go beyond the eight-character file name limitation. Take advantage of this. The same philosophy can be applied to material library files. LIBRARY.MAT will not remind you of a library's contents unless it is the only library you will ever use. By naming library files after projects or after the types of materials contained in them, you have a far better idea at the File Manager level of where to find what you're looking for.

- **Take advantage of material library files.** It is tempting to keep every material you ever create in 3DSMAX.MAT. After creating your first 100 materials in this file, however, waiting for the Material Browser to display all the materials contained in the file can take a lifetime. There's a reason the program enables you to create your own material library files. Don't hesitate to create a library for each project. In this way, the library file can also travel with the project, if necessary. By keeping library files small and organized, you can sift through their contents faster. It's not unreasonable to use more than one library file for a project either, especially if major changes come along in the middle of the project. Before making modifications to your current materials, save them out to a backup library file in case you need them back some day.

- **Name every level of the material.** 3DS MAX has made it easier than ever to name the materials and their sub-levels. Don't just name the top level of a material. If your material uses several levels of map channels, take a moment to describe the purpose of the material level. This takes some getting used to, but get into the habit of describing what you are doing. This applies not only to material design but to modifiers, objects, selection groups, and coordinate systems. You may know what's going on *today* with a material, but six months down the road you may forget why you designed the material the way you did. Never leave those name fields blank. Explain what you are doing (even if it's only to yourself) as you go along through the material design.

- **Keep notes.** It doesn't take long for a project to get complicated. If you were to try to write out from memory every bitmap file you used in your last project, do you think you could do it? How about from the project before that? Many thumbnail programs have the capability to create hard-copy catalogues of bitmaps in selected directories. If you plan to generate hundreds of custom materials, it can be to your advantage to log everything you use in case you ever need to find it again. This helpful technique can also be applied to any series of techniques you run across, any resource contact information you depended on, any problems that cropped up during the project with your system's hardware, software, drivers, or peripherals—*and how you resolved them.*

Material and Bitmap Navigation

The Material/Map browser in 3DS MAX has come a long way from the material browsing capabilities in 3D Studio DOS. An entire screen of materials in TrueColor can be viewed at one time. Depending on the kind of system you have 3DS MAX running on and the number of materials in your materials libraries, however, it may take some time for all the materials to be calculated and shown in the Material/Map browser's View Large Icons mode. And 3DS MAX has no tool with which to quickly and easily find, report, and graphically show all the information associated with any bitmap on your system. For this reason, it pays to examine some bitmap referencing techniques and utilities.

Image and Material Cardfile

One alternative to waiting for the browser to calculate and show all available materials in a materials library file each time you open the browser to find a material is to create a series of image files from screen captures of all the materials represented in the browser. If the image files are named cleverly to reflect the groups of materials displayed at one time in the browser, the materials in each image can be viewed very quickly by using the File/View File pull-down menu option and selecting the appropriate file. It may take a half hour or so to generate an image for each group of materials, but after they're created, you can reference them with lightning speed.

Even faster than using 3DS MAX's File/View File option is to use a bitmap browser such as PaintShop Pro to view the reference files simultaneously. Screen captures of browser images in other materials collections on external CDs can also be created to help find materials not loaded on your system. It might take you a day to assemble screen captures of all the materials resources you have, but after you create them, all these screen capture images can be opened simultaneously and treated like Rolodex cards. Using minimal system resources, you can view the images instantly without having to load a CD-ROM. Some bitmap browsers can even automate the process of opening all the images for reference, through scripts or batch processing features.

Thumbnail Programs

Finding bitmaps on your system can be a tedious and time-consuming task. When you use a series of still images to create an animated material, or for Video Post editing, converting these files from one file format to another can waste a great deal of time. Fortunately, some powerful bitmap browsers are available to speed along these tasks and make them painless.

Another alternative to navigating materials and the bitmaps associated with them in 3DS MAX is to invest in a dedicated thumbnails program such as Thumbnails Plus. These types of programs are optimized to search entire directories and report back not only a visual of the bitmaps found, but all the detailed information you might need about each bitmap, including its date of creation, resolution and color depth, DPI, and file size. Figure 9.19 shows an example of the way Thumbnails Plus reports its findings in the \3DSMAX\MAPS directory.

Thumbnails Plus and other programs like it are graphic file viewers, locators, and organizers that simplify the process of finding and maintaining graphics, clip-art files, fonts, and animations. They display a small image, called a *thumbnail*, of each file in a directory you specify. You can use these types of programs to search, view, edit, or crop images, launch external editors, and copy the images to the Windows Clipboard. They can be used also to organize graphics files by moving them to appropriate directories. Some can create slide shows from the image files in specified directories, print the files individually, or print bitmap catalogs from all files in a directory. Many can convert images to several formats, either one at a time or in batch mode.

FIGURE 9.19
Programs such as ThumbsPlus can display hundreds of bitmaps in a matter of seconds.

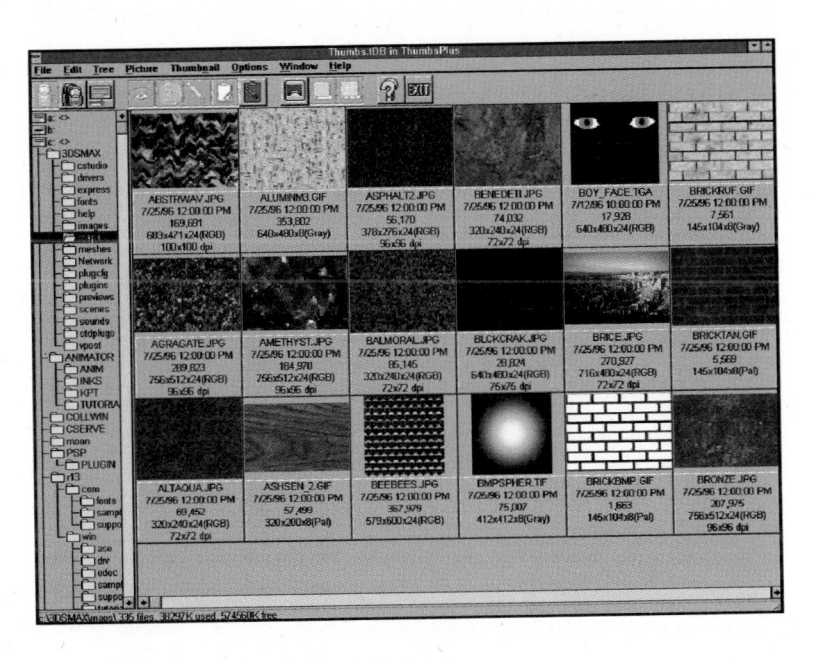

Importing 3D Studio R4 Materials

Recently, an MLI Import plug-in was created and made available to the public. It is not officially supported by Kinetix or the Yost Group, but was supplied as a service to the many users who have asked for a way to import material libraries created in DOS releases of 3D Studio. The file MLIIMP.DLI, provided on the accompanying CD, needs to be placed in the \3DSMAX\PLUGINS directory. Then, on the next session of 3DS MAX, you will be able to import MLI files.

The MLI File Format

The MLI file is the material library format for the DOS releases of 3D Studio. Each material library can store more than 255 material definitions in 3D Studio Release 4 format. The MLIIMP.DLI plug-in translates these earlier libraries directly into 3DS MAX; you don't need to assign them in a 3DS file.

Import Options

After the MLIIMP.DLI file is included on your plug-in path, the MLI extension is listed as a choice from the 3DS MAX File/Import dialog. The MLI Import dialog has two Import Options:

- **Import into Scene.** This option creates an object for every material in the material library (255 maximum). Each object is a single texture-mapped face with a unique material from the library, and shares the name of the assigned material. All objects created by MLI Import are placed in a "fan" configuration, centered at the world origin. To make the fan easier to manipulate, a parental dummy object is placed in the center of the fan with the name of the imported MLI file. The triangles are then attached as children to the dummy object.

- **Import into Material Editor.** This option merges the materials in the material library with the current material library present in the 3DS MAX Material Editor. To see the newly merged materials, enter the Material Editor's Material/Map browser and choose Browse From Material Library.

Converting MLI Files to MAT Files

The Save As function in the Material/Map browser enables you to create a 3DS MAX material library (MAT file) from everything in the scene or from just what is currently selected. When you import an MLI file to the scene by using the MLIIMP plug-in, the fan of material objects is selected. Enter the browser, choose the Browse From: Selected option, and the material definitions that you just imported appear. You can save this list to a MAT file by choosing the Save As option and entering a name for the new library in 3DS MAX format.

NOTE

The MLI Import plug-in does not translate procedural textures (SXPs). To import these materials, you need to assign them to an object in 3D Studio R4, save the 3DS file, and then import the file into 3DS MAX. *3DS MAX does not support the 3D Studio Save Selected option.*

In Practice: Keeping Things Clean, Fast, and Retrievable

- **Minimize the required resources when designing.** One basic truth about 3DS MAX is this: It will never run faster than the moment you start a new session. The fewer objects, lights, and materials in a scene, the faster MAX performs. Therefore, it makes sense that at every level of design, you minimize the number of objects, lights, and materials to only what you need to keep the program fast.

- **Keep design elements modular.** By designing materials in dedicated sessions, you enable yourself to subject new materials to a wide range of lighting and geometric mapping tortures without jeopardizing the status of (or being at the rendering mercy of) the final scene in which they will eventually be used. This strategy of modularizing development of materials also makes future development modifications easier to experiment with. Keep track not only of your projects but of your experiments.

- **Stay on top of new design and development resources.** New material development resources are created almost every week, and it can be highly profitable and powerful to regularly explore the Kinetix forums and see what's come out of the oven lately. With the advent of 3DS MAX's capability to use other filters, the same can be said for any compatible manufacturer's resources.

IMAGE BY STEVE BURKE

Chapter 10

by Steve Burke

Designing Natural Materials

Natural materials such as grass, water, and rock are often challenging to create on the computer. 3D Studio MAX, however, affords many ways to achieve convincing results. This chapter demonstrates how to build natural materials for a tropical forest scene, replete with pond and tree frog. The materials discussed in this chapter are useful for many types of scenes. In addition, the techniques described are universal and can be used to build any type of natural material.

This chapter describes the creation of several natural materials that are then used to create a realistic tropical forest scene. Further, you build the materials in a logical order, much as an artist would paint a landscape, starting with the sky and ground plane and adding elements one at a time. The primary objective is to present useful techniques for designing natural materials. The secondary objective is to demonstrate a practical method of working that eliminates rework and achieves good results.

The techniques in this chapter include methods to achieve realistic color and texture, and ways to simulate natural variation; these are the two most important considerations when you design natural materials.

This chapter covers the following material types, in order:

- Ground and sky
- Water
- Trees and bamboo
- Stones
- Vegetation
- Plant leaves
- Tree frog

Ground and Sky

Designing the ground and sky materials is the first step because they provide both the backdrop for the scene and a reference for each new material. Many natural materials rely on subtle coloring for their effect. These materials could not be created without first establishing the background of the scene. When finished, if the colors in the scene look natural, and each material looks as though it fits into the scene, the image will be believable.

TIP

When you design natural materials it is often necessary to do test renderings of the scene. Never do test renderings against a black background. A black background makes it very difficult to judge color relationships. Changing the background color to a neutral gray or representative scene color is always a better choice. The best solution is to make test renderings against the actual background you will be using in your scene.

Dirt and Grass

Load file GROUND.MAX from the accompanying CD. The scene in this file consists of a single mesh object that will serve as the ground plane for the scene you are building. A Multi/Sub-Object material containing two sub-materials, Dirt and Grass, has been applied to the object. The Grass material is represented by the green color, and brown represents the Dirt material (see fig. 10.1).

FIGURE 10.1

The terrain mesh with a Multi/Sub-Object material applied.

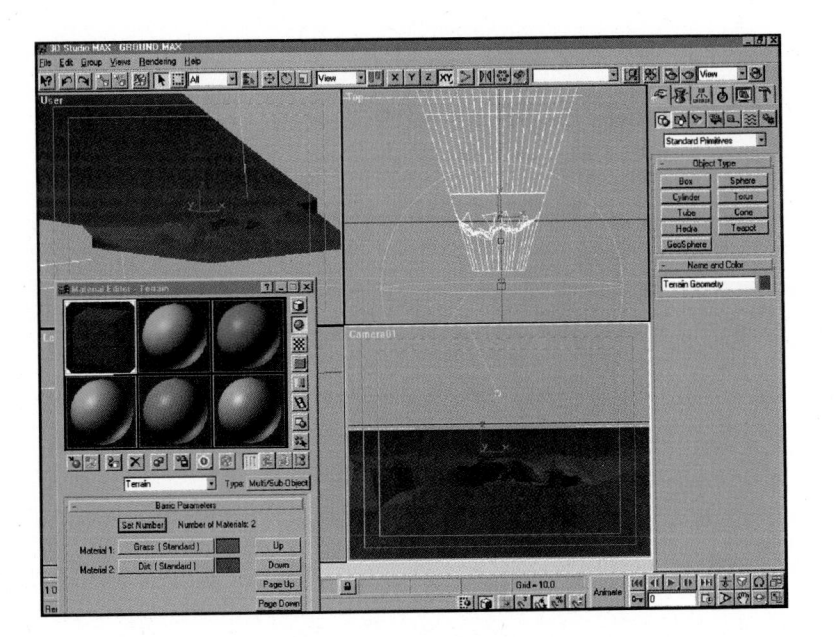

In the Material Editor, examine the Dirt and Grass materials in Slot #1. Both materials are standard. Neither would be very convincing up close, but because they will be covered with other objects and viewed at a sharp angle, great detail is not needed. As long as the diffuse maps used consist of realistic earth tones and a natural-looking pattern, the effect will be successful.

TIP

When bitmapped materials are viewed at a sharp angle, the bitmaps used should not tile more than a few times across the object; otherwise, obvious patterns are unavoidable. One quick solution is to stretch a small bitmap across the object to provide subtle color fluctuations rather than to create an obvious, unnatural tiling pattern.

Both materials are comprised of a color bitmap used as a diffuse map. Additionally, the dirt material uses a grayscale bitmap instanced for both Bump and Shin. Strength, as well as an RGB Tint to alter the color of the diffuse map (see fig. 10.2). RGB Tint is a great way to fine-tune the appearance of a bitmap in the 3DS MAX environment. It is an important tool because lighting, atmosphere, and geometry all affect the rendered color of a material. Notice also that the diffuse map on the dirt material is not applied at full strength. Lessening the effect of the diffuse map pushes the color of the object toward the diffuse color. This technique can be used to lighten or darken a material. In either case, it always reduces the contrast of a material.

FIGURE 10.2

The definition of the dirt material maps in the Material Editor.

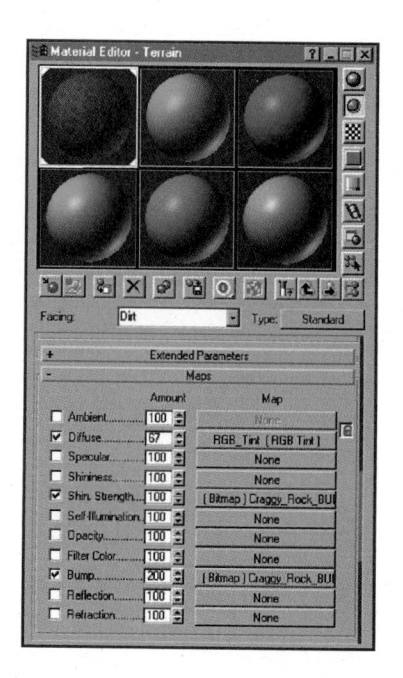

Return to the scene and look at the Terrain object in a shaded viewport. An abrupt break occurs where the dirt and grass materials meet on the Terrain object. This is intentional. The area that is now grass will remain unchanged. The dirt material will be replaced with a Blend material that will form an organic transition from grass to dirt, and then a transition from dirt to mud. The mud material will be placed in the recessed area of the geometry to form the bottom of a pond.

In each Blend material a bitmapped mask will determine how the transition from one material to the other occurs. To define how the mask is applied, the terrain mesh has been given a Planar UVW Mapping modifier (see fig. 10.3). The bitmaps to be used to define the blends that have been built to fit inside the Planar UVW Mapping gizmo. Because the gizmo is smaller than the terrain mesh, the bitmaps used can also be smaller. This saves both memory and rendering time. If you were to apply a blend to the entire object, rather than to just a small portion, you would need an enormous bitmap—and the results would be no better.

Figure 10.3

The terrain mesh with a Planar UVW Mapping modifier applied.

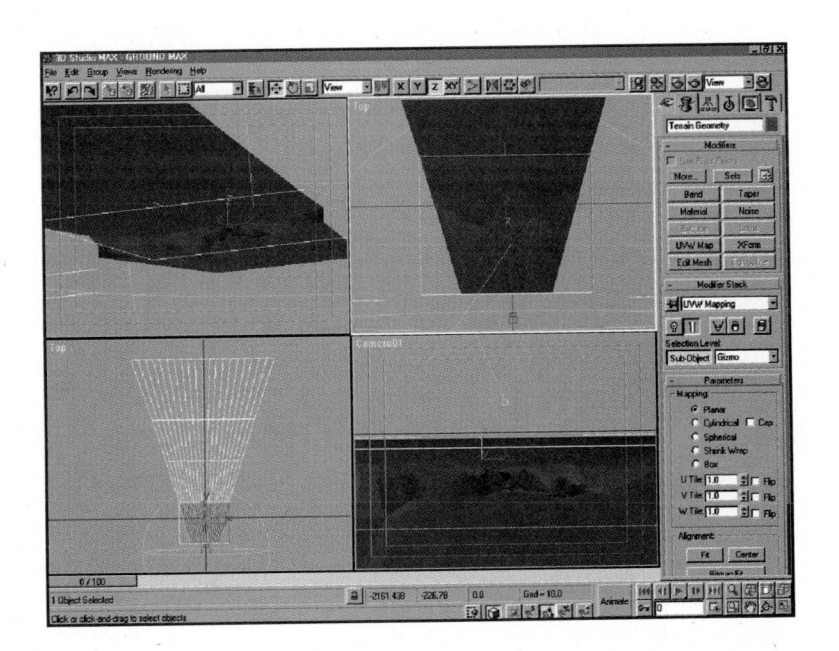

The following tutorials describe how to blend one material into another, using a bitmap as a mask. If you haven't already done so, open file GROUND.MAX from the Chapter 10 Files directory on the *Inside 3D Studio MAX Volume II* CD.

BLENDING GRASS AND DIRT

1. In the Material Editor, select the Multi/Sub-Object material in Slot #1.

2. Click on the Material 2 button to edit the Dirt material.

3. Click on the Type button to bring up the Material/Map Browser. Choose Browse From New, select material type Blend, and then click on OK.

From the Replace Material dialog, select the Keep Old Material as Sub-material option, and click on OK. This will make the Dirt material the first component of a Blend material.

4. Name this material **Blend_Grass&Dirt**.

5. From the Basic Parameters of the Blend material, click on the Material 2 button to edit the second material.

6. Click on the Type button to bring up the Material/Map Browser. Choose Browse From Material Editor, select the Grass material, and click on OK.

7. Name this material **Grass**.

8. Click on Go to Parent to return to the Blend material. Click on the Mask button to bring up the Material/Map Browser. Choose Browse From New, select material type Bitmap, and click on OK. Load Terrain_Mask_01.TGA from the accompanying CD. Set U and V Offset to 0.1 and −0.07, respectively. Set U and V Tiling to 2 and 0.9, respectively.

The grass and dirt should now blend seamlessly into each other (see fig. 10.4). The next step is to create a smooth transition from dirt to a mud material suitable for the bottom of a pond. The mud material does not need to be detailed because water and reflection will obscure most of it.

FIGURE 10.4
The terrain mesh on the left was done without blend. The mesh in the middle was done with blend. The image on the right is the mask used to create the Blend.

Notice seam

BLENDING DIRT AND MUD

1. In the Material Editor, select the Terrain material in Slot #1.

2. Click on the Material 2 button to edit the first Blend material.

3. Click on the Material 1 button to edit the Dirt material. Click on Type to bring up the Material/Map Browser. Choose Browse From New, select material type Blend, and click on OK (see fig. 10.5). In the Replace Material dialog, choose Keep Old Material as Sub-material and click on OK.

FIGURE 10.5

The Material/Map Browser.

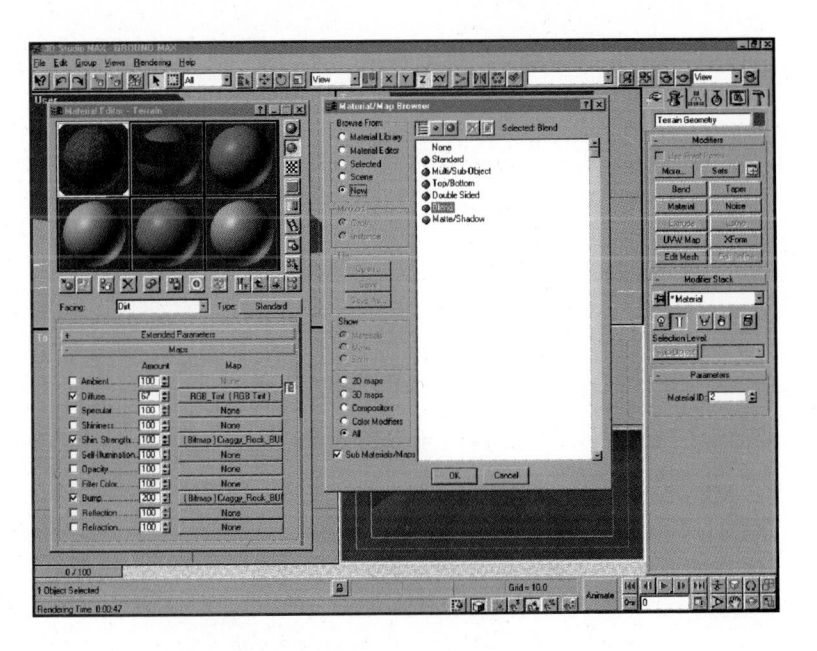

4. Name this material **Blend_Dirt&Mud**.

5. Click on the Material 2 button to edit the second material. Click on the Type button to bring up the Material/Map Browser. Choose Browse From Material Editor. Choose the Dirt (Standard) material and click on OK. The dirt will be the starting point for mud.

6. Rename this material **Mud**.

7. From the Maps rollout of the new Mud material, remove the Bump and Shin. Strength maps by copying one of the empty map slots onto each unwanted map. By removing these maps you make render times faster. Because the mud will be obscured, these maps are not needed.

8. In the Basic Parameters section of the rollout, set the Diffuse color to RGB 62, 53, 42.

9. In the Maps rollout, change the Diffuse amount to 60.

10. In the Maps rollout, click on the Diffuse map to display the RGB Tint applied to the Diffuse map. Set each component of the RGB Tint as follows:

   ■ Set the R component to RGB 141, 0, 0.

   ■ Set the G component to RGB 0, 152, 0.

   ■ Set the B component to RGB 0, 0, 91.

11. Click on the Go to Parent button twice to return to the Blend material.

12. Click on the Mask button to display the Material/Map Browser. Choose Browse From New, select material type Bitmap, and click on OK. Load Water_Line_MASK.TGA from the accompanying CD. Set V Offset to −0,014. This small offset is essential to getting the map into the correct position.

After you complete the preceding steps, the dirt will blend into mud in a very natural way (see fig. 10.6). The mud itself is not a very convincing material, but you don't need to spend a great deal of energy perfecting it because it will not show much in the final scene.

FIGURE 10.6
On the left is the terrain with the transition from dirt to mud; the bitmap used for the Blend is on the right.

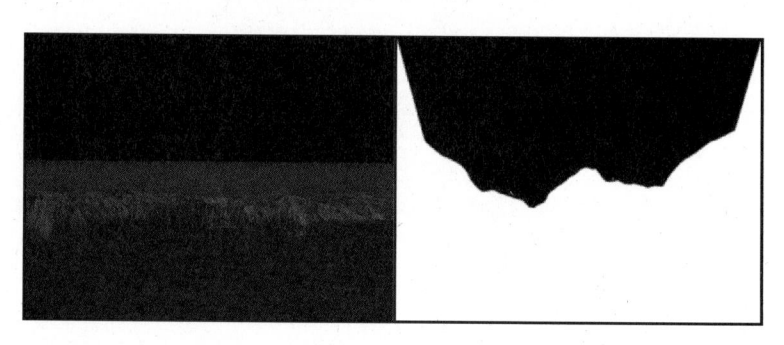

Creating a Sky

A sky does not have to be complicated to be convincing. A realistic sky can be made from a gradient material and assigned as either a background image or a fog map. Because assigning the gradient as a fog map has the added advantage of giving the scene atmosphere, that is the method to use. To create a sky, follow these steps:

USING A GRADIENT TO CREATE A SKY

1. In the Material Editor, select the material in Slot #2.

2. Click on Get Material to display the Material/Map Browser. Choose Browse From New, select material type Gradient, and click on OK.

3. Name the Material **Sky_Gradient**. Set the gradient colors as follows:

   ■ Set Color #1 to RGB 178, 199, 227.

   ■ Set Color #2 to RGB 228, 238, 245.

- Set Color #3 to RGB 255, 255, 255.

- Set Color 2 Position to 0.69.

4. Under the Coordinates portion of the command panel, select Environ (Environment) and choose Screen for the Mapping type (see fig. 10.7). This sets the mapping coordinates of the gradient so that it will always appear full-screen; the top of the gradient will appear at the top of the image when rendered, and the bottom of the gradient at the bottom.

The gradient for the sky is completed, but it needs to be assigned in the Rendering Environment dialog for it to appear when rendering.

FIGURE 10.7

The Gradient command panel.

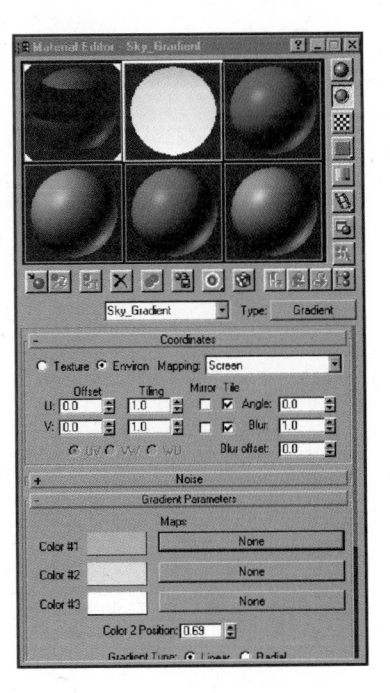

5. Open the Render Environment dialog and click on the Add button in the Atmosphere portion of the dialog. In the Add Atmospheric Effect dialog, select Fog and click on OK. This will add fog to the scene, and you can now assign the gradient to the fog.

6. In the Environment Color Map section of the Fog parameters dialog, click on the Assign button (see fig. 10.8). This displays the Material/Map Browser. Choose Browse From Material Editor, select Sky_Gradient, and click on OK. The gradient will now define the color of the fog.

FIGURE 10.8

The Fog parameters dialog.

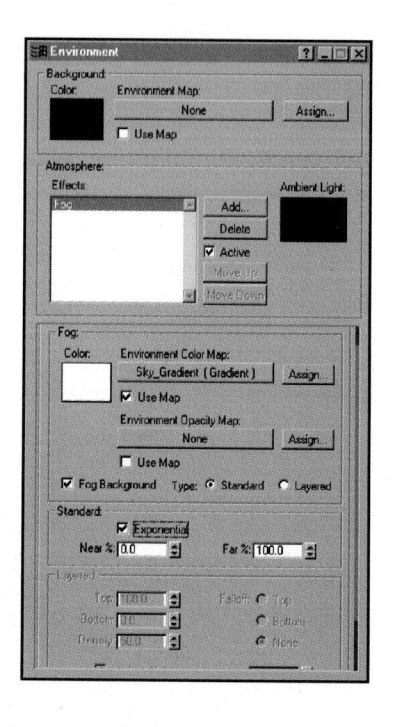

7. Enable the Exponential option. This produces more accurate results when Opacity mapped objects are inside the fog. Many of the objects you will create later depend on opacity mapping for their effect.

8. Render from the Camera viewport to see how the sky gradient affects the scene (see fig. 10.9). The sky is plain but provides a nice backdrop.

    Adding atmospheric effects slows down rendering times. If you want to speed up test renderings, you can disable the fog and assign Sky_Gradient as a background image. This will enable you to view your materials against the correct background, but without having to wait for the fog effect to render.

FIGURE 10.9
The terrain with a
bitmapped fog effect
added.

Water

Water adds a great deal of realism to a scene. The best advice with computer-generated water is probably to keep it simple and understated. You will create a water material from scratch and apply it to a simple plane intersecting the terrain geometry. Reflection and transparency form the basic illusion. A gradient used as a mask can add that extra touch of realism by fading the reflection as the water's surface nears the camera.

Open the file WATER.MAX from the Chapter 10 Files directory on the accompanying CD (see fig. 10.10). This scene contains a planar object intersecting a terrain mesh. This planar object will become the surface of the water.

FIGURE 10.10
*A simple plane will
form the basis of a
water material.*

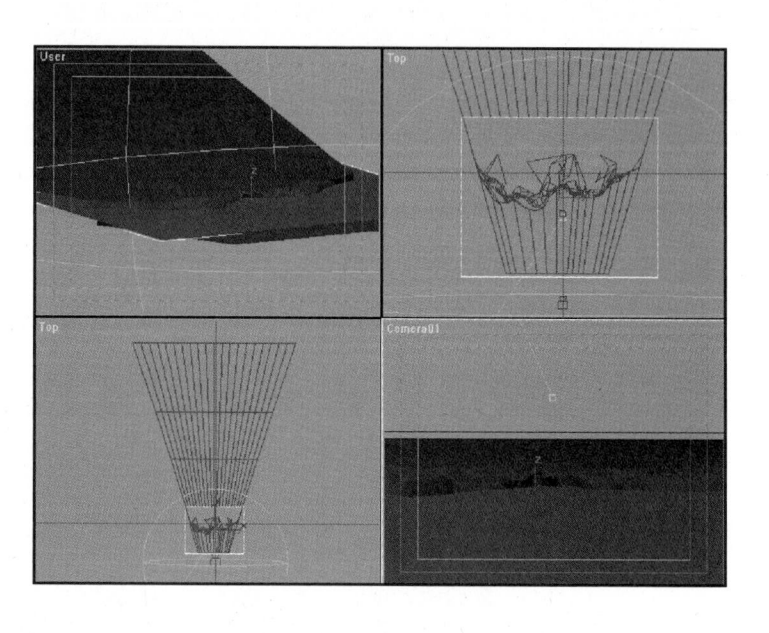

CREATING THE BASIC WATER MATERIAL

1. In the Material Editor, select the material in Slot #1. This material has already been applied to the Water Surface object.

2. Rename the material **Water**.

3. Set the Diffuse color to RGB 81, 73, 60. This is a dark brown color.

4. Drag the Diffuse color onto the Filter color swatch, and select Copy from the Copy or Swap Colors dialog.

5. Set the Ambient color to RGB 26, 26, 26. This is a dark gray color.

6. Set the Opacity amount to 59.

Render the scene to check the new material (see fig. 10.11). Although the effect is still not a convincing one, it is important that you check the color and basic look before proceeding. Remember two important considerations when you create water effects. First, the water is usually darker than the terrain around it. Notice that the water color is similar to the dark colors in the dirt material. Second, the color of the water's surface should be similar to the color of the material under the water. By keeping the colors close in value, the effect of a solid body of water is enhanced. If the water color is too light, it will look like a plastic sheet draped over the terrain.

FIGURE 10.11
The basic water material with no reflection.

NOTE

Dark water colors also provide better reflections. The closer the diffuse color is to black, the more accurate the reflections.

Adding Reflection to the Water

One of the advantages to using a planar object as the water surface is the capability to use a flat mirror reflection on the surface material. This generates an accurate reflection relatively quickly. Follow these steps to add a flat mirror to the water's surface:

1. From the Water material in the Material Editor, open the Maps rollout and click on Reflection map to bring up the Material/Map Browser.

2. Choose Browse From New, select material type Flat Mirror, and click on OK.

3. Click on the Go to Parent button to return to the Maps rollout. Set Reflection Amount to 50 percent.

4. Render the scene to see how the Reflection map has added depth and realism (see fig. 10.12).

FIGURE 10.12
The Water material with a Flat Mirror reflection.

Fine-Tuning the Reflection with a Gradient

Now, having established the basic look of the water and having added some reflection, it is time to finish the illusion. Next you add a mask to the Reflection map to decrease the amount of reflection as the water nears the camera.

Fading a reflection as it nears the camera is a subtle touch of realism that adds gobs of credibility to a scene.

1. From the Maps rollout of the Water material, click on the Reflection map button.

2. Click on the Type button to bring up the Material/Map Browser. Choose Browse From New, select material type Mask, and click on OK. In the Replace Map dialog, select Keep old map as sub-map, and click on OK.

3. Click on the Mask button to bring up the Material/Map Browser. Choose Browse From New, select material type Gradient, and click on OK. Adjust the gradient colors as follows:

■ Set Color #1 to RGB 255, 255, 255.

■ Set Color #2 to RGB 255, 255, 255.

■ Set Color #3 to RGB 13, 13, 13.

■ Set Color 2 Position to 0.56.

4. Render the Camera viewport so that you can see the impact of the mask (see fig. 10.13). The effect is much more realistic than it was.

FIGURE 10.13
Water with graduated reflection.

Creating Other Water Effects

Bitmaps and masks can be used in other ways to enhance the realism of water effects. A Shininess Strength map could be applied to the water's surface to give the look of particles and debris on the surface. Also, small geometry such as leaves and sticks can be added to the top surface of the water. Gentle currents could be intimated by animating the debris, and moving it across the surface of the water. This would provide a subtle but realistic effect.

In addition, animated bump maps can be used to simulate ripples and movement in the water. As a last resort, the water itself can be animated, although the density of the water mesh would make this a very costly effect.

Trees and Bamboo

The trees are large and prominently positioned in the scene. For this reason, it is important to do them well but not make them overbearing. The tree texture maps use the same colors as the earth around them, which helps them to blend into the scene.

Open the file TREES.MAX from the accompanying CD (see fig. 10.14). This file contains the scene from the first tutorials, with two trees and several bamboo stalks added. The big tree was modeled in 3D Studio MAX and given a cylindrical U/V Mapping modifier and a Bend modifier. The distant tree was made by copying the first tree, rotating it, and then changing the parameters of the Bend modifier. This is a quick way to create two different-looking versions of one object. By placing cylindrical UVW Mapping coordinates on the objects before any of them were deformed, you ensure that the bitmaps stick to the objects and look correct.

TIP

When you build models of natural objects, design them to look different from every angle. Doing so enables you to reuse an object several times in a scene without foregoing a look of natural randomness. One end of a rock could be sharp, for example, and the other rounded; tall at one end, short at the other. When cloned and rotated into different positions in a scene, each clone will look unique and natural.

FIGURE 10.14

The Scene file with the tree and bamboo objects in place.

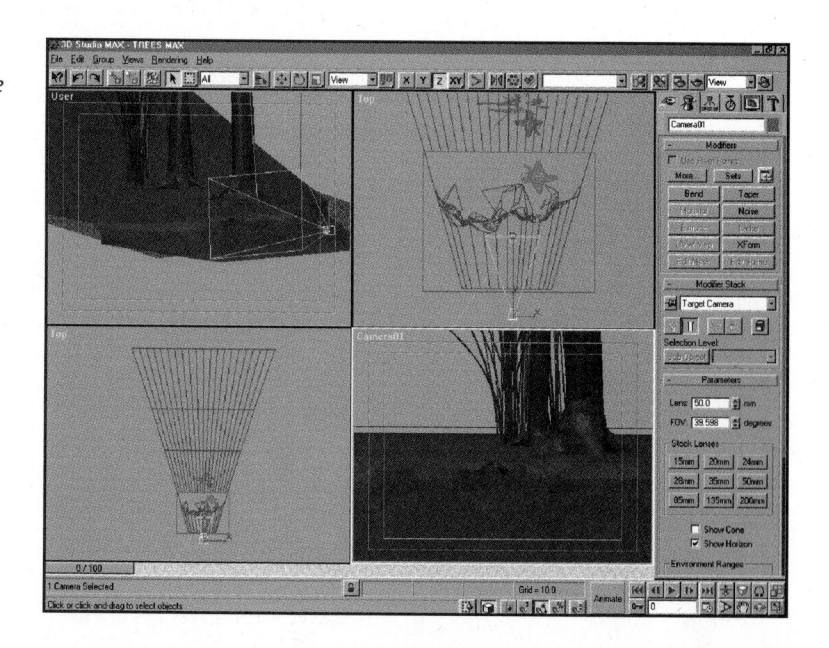

It is important that materials work in combination with models. Creating efficient models gives you the freedom to make better materials. If you create a scene that's overloaded with polygons, waiting for renders may be so laborious that you do not experiment as much as you should to achieve the effect you want.

Sometimes simple geometry can accomplish realism that materials alone cannot. To add credibility to the scene, the bamboo was created as geometry. This bamboo has highlights and depth that Opacity Mapped objects would not have. All shrubbery and foliage for this scene is built with opacity-mapped materials. Combining faked geometry with real geometry makes the faked geometry harder to detect.

The bamboo objects in the scene all started as three-sided cylinders with varying numbers of height segments. The most detailed bamboo pieces appear toward the front of the scene, with the least-detailed ones toward the back. The polygon count of the bamboo was kept to a minimum, and excess faces were deleted to ensure that the objects could be copied several times without greatly increasing rendering times. In addition, each cylinder was given cylindrical U/V Mapping and Bend modifiers. Some of the bamboo objects were assigned material IDs at the face level, others have material modifiers assigned to enable quick changes from one Multi/Sub-Object material to another.

Trees

The most difficult aspect of designing the tree material is keeping the bitmap from smearing across the roots of the tree. The trees are mapped with a cylindrical UVW mapping coordinate, which works well for the trunk, but not for the roots (that project out and are almost perpendicular to the mapping coordinate at certain points). The trees require two separate materials: one for the trunk and one for the roots. A Blend material is used to combine both materials on the Tree objects. This method can be used to blend the tree colors smoothly into the colors of the earth under the tree. This subtle touch of realism adds believability to your scene.

DESIGNING A TREE MATERIAL

1. Load file TREES.MAX from the Chapter 10 Files directory on the accompanying CD.

2. Select Bamboo in the Named Selection Sets pop-up menu. In the Display panel, select Hide Selected.

3. In the Material Editor, examine the Tree_Exotic material in Slot #1. This basic tree material has already been applied to the trees in the scene.

    The material contains a Diffuse map, as well as a grayscale image used as both a Bump and Shininess Strength map. Both maps have been set to 2 and 5 for U and V Tiling, respectively. Note that Shininess is set very low. The Ambient and Specular colors have been tweaked slightly, and the Diffuse color is replaced by the Diffuse map.

4. Click on the Type button to bring up the Material/Map Browser. Choose Browse From New, select material type Blend, and click on OK. In the Replace Material dialog, select the Keep old material as Sub-Material option, and then click on OK. You now have a Blend material with one sub-material already defined. Now for the root material.

5. Click on the Material 2 button to go down in the material hierarchy to the second material.

6. Name this material **Tree_Exotic_Noise**.

7. From the Maps rollout, click on the Diffuse Map button. From the Material/Map Browser, select Browse From New, select material type Noise, and click on OK.

8. Set Noise Type to Turbulence. Set Size to 19.5, and Noise Threshold Low to 0.02. Set Color #1 to RGB 56, 46, 40, a dark brown. Instead of using a second color for the noise, you will use the bitmap from the trunk material, to ensure that the root material blends well with the trunk material (see fig. 10.15).

9. Click on the Color #2 Map button to display the Material/Map Browser. Choose Browse From Material Editor, and select Tree_Exotic_DIFF.

10. Click on the Go to Parent button twice to return to the Blend material. Next you will create the mask bitmap that defines where the two materials appear on the tree objects.

FIGURE 10.15

*The Noise material for
the tree.*

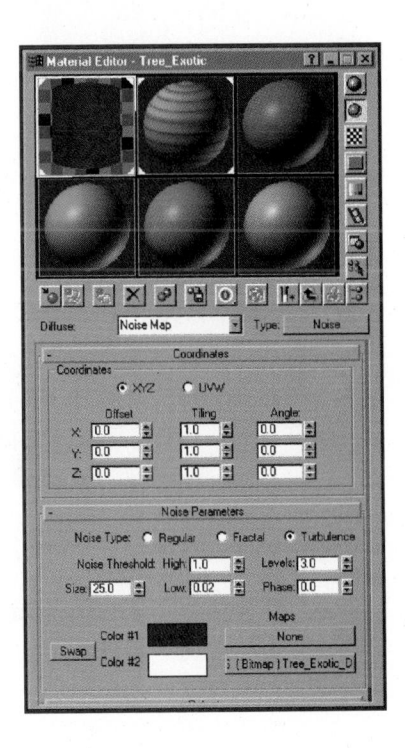

11. Click on the Mask button to bring up the Material/Map Browser. Choose Browse From New, select material type Gradient, and click on OK. Set the gradient colors as follows:

- Set Color #1 and Color #2 to RGB 0, 0, 0.

- Set Color #3 to RGB 255, 255, 255.

- Set Color 2 Position to 0.07.

- Set Noise to Fractal, Amount to 0.09, and Size to 0.17.

12. Render the Camera viewport to see the finished trees (see fig. 10.16). You may want to experiment with the different Blend, Noise, and Gradient settings to achieve different results.

T I P

Blending between bitmapped and procedural textures is a very powerful technique. Consider using it when you want to map odd-shaped objects with a procedural texture, but also want to use bitmaps for added detail and realism.

Figure 10.16
The finished trees.

Figure 10.16
The finished trees.

Bamboo

The bamboo material is simple, but you need to establish variation from one bamboo stalk to another. Two ways to do this are: by altering the objects in the scene so that each looks different, or by creating more than one bamboo material. This scene takes advantage of both methods to make the final image more realistic.

The bamboo stalks in the scene were all created from four original objects, each with a slightly different circumference. They were then cloned and positioned throughout the scene. The copies were rotated, moved, and given unique Bend modifier settings until each stalk faced a different direction, looked unique, and related well to the scene. Then several stalks were grouped, and this group was cloned throughout the scene. By creating the bamboo in this way, you eliminate much of the hard work involved in making each stalk look unique.

Next, you create a Multi/Sub-Object material for the bamboo and apply it to the bamboo objects. Because this material will consist of one light and one dark bamboo material, you can choose whether a bamboo stalk is light or dark by changing the number its Material ID. This makes fine-tuning a scene very easy. The Material IDs for these objects have already been set, but you can change them.

DESIGNING THE FIRST BAMBOO MATERIAL

1. Use the previous file, TREES.MAX, and click on Unhide All from the Display panel.

2. In the Material Editor, examine the Bamboo material in Slot #2. This basic bamboo material contains a Diffuse map and a grayscale image that's used as both a Bump and Shininess Strength map.

   Both maps have been set to 1 and 3 for U and V Tiling, respectively. Also note the Shininess, Ambient, and Specular values. The material looks good as is, but you need to make it brighter, change the material type to Multi/Sub-Object, and then create a second bamboo material, which you will make darker than the first.

3. Navigate to the Diffuse map layer of the Bamboo material. Select the Type button to bring up the Material/Map Browser. Select Browse From New, select material type RGB Tint, and click on OK. In the Replace Map dialog, select Keep Old Map as Sub-map, and click on OK.

4. To brighten the material, you need to add red and green to the bitmap, and decrease the blue. Change each component of the RGB Tint as follows:

   - Set the R component to RGB 255, 73, 0.
   - Set the G component to RGB 113, 255, 20.
   - Set the B component to RGB 0, 0, 209.

   You now have a bright bamboo material. When it's rendered, notice that all the stalks are about the same height and that they are all the same color (see fig. 10.17). Some differentiation still exists because the light is hitting all these objects differently. All the stalks are facing in different directions, and all are placed differently in the scene.

FIGURE 10.17
*A single material,
applied to all bamboo
objects.*

Next, you can add some variety by converting this material to a Multi/Sub-Object material and adding a second bamboo material (by copying the first material and altering some of its parameters).

DESIGNING A SECOND BAMBOO MATERIAL

1. From the top level of the Bamboo material, click on the Type button to bring up the Material/Map Browser. Click on Browse From New, select material type Multi/Sub-Object, and click on OK. In the Replace Material dialog, select Keep Old Material as Sub-material, and click on OK.

2. Rename Material 1 **Bamboo_Yellow**. Now you need to define the second material.

3. Click on the button next to Material 2 to edit its parameters. You are going to replace this material with the first bamboo material.

4. Click on the Type button, select Browse From Material Editor, select the Bamboo_Yellow material, and click on OK.

5. Rename this material **Bamboo_Brown**. At this point, both materials are identical except for their names.

6. Click on the *M* next to the Diffuse color swatch of the new material. This takes you to the RGB Tint map. Change each component of the RGB Tint as follows:

- Set the R component to 255, 0, 0.
- Set the G component to 0, 238, 0.
- Set the B component to 0, 0, 234.

These settings will darken the bitmap.

Finally, you need to make sure that this material tiles differently than the first so that the different stalks don't line up in an ordered, unrealistic way.

7. Select the Map button next to the RGB Tint color swatches. This takes you to the Diffuse map. Change the U and V Offset to 0.2 and 0.3, respectively.

8. Click on the Go to Parent button and then on the Go to Sibling button, to display the Shininess Strength map settings. The offset for this map needs to be the same as for the Diffuse map.

9. Change the U and V Offset to 0.2 and 0.3, respectively. Because the Shininess Strength and Bump maps are instances of each other, this change affects both maps.

10. Render the scene to see the results so far (see fig. 10.18).

FIGURE 10.18
A Multi/Sub-Object material applied to the bamboo objects.

You should see a random assortment of light and dark bamboo stalks growing in different directions. The bamboo is now fairly convincing, but there is one more thing to do. The yellow bamboo looks very nice on top, but is much too bright where it grows out of the earth. It looks unnatural, and not connected to the ground. Also, the bright yellow color is distracting against the dark brown of the tree, focusing attention on a rather unimportant part of the image. You can make the yellow bamboo more convincing by adding a mask to the Diffuse map.

1. Navigate to the Bamboo_Yellow material. From the Bamboo_Yellow material, click on the *M* next to the Diffuse color swatch, to display the RGB Tint map.

2. Select the Type button, select Browse From New, and select material type Mask from the Material/Map Browser. Click on OK. In the Replace Map dialog, select the Keep old map as Sub-map option, and then click on OK.

3. Click on the button next to Mask to add a gradient. From the Material/Map Browser, choose Browse From New, and select material type Gradient. Click on OK. Set the gradient colors as follows:

   ■ Set Color #1 to RGB 255, 255, 255.

   ■ Set Color #2 to RGB 255, 255, 255.

   ■ Set Color #3 to RGB 0, 0, 0.

   ■ Set Color 2 Position to 0.35.

   The mask limits the Diffuse map to only white areas of the gradient. As the gradient fades to black toward the bottom of the bamboo, the Diffuse map becomes less prominent as it is replaced by the Diffuse color.

4. Render the scene again to see the difference (see fig. 10.19).

The yellow bamboo gets darker as it nears the ground. By using a mask, you are able to keep the bamboo color bright and still have it look realistic.

FIGURE **10.19**
The finished bamboo material.

Stones

Load file STONES.MAX from the Chapter 10 Files directory of the accompanying CD. New stone objects have been added to the scene (see fig. 10.20).

FIGURE **10.20**
The STONES.MAX file.

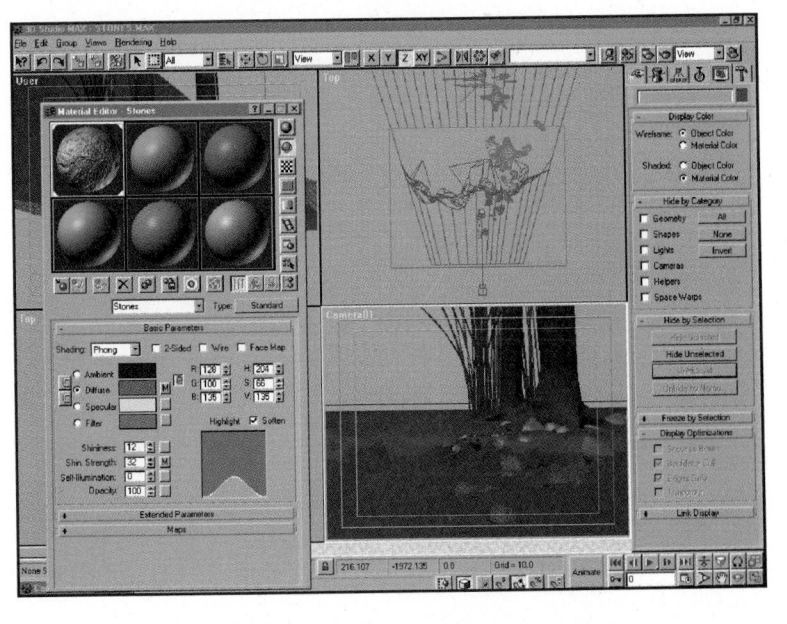

The rocks have all been given spherical or shrink-wrap UVW mapping coordinates. The rocks themselves are clones of about four original rock objects. All were created with as few polygons as possible, and all have had their bottom faces deleted.

The rocks are more than just decoration. They serve three major functions: they provide depth and greater realism to the terrain; they break up the shoreline and hide flaws in the terrain mesh; and they add a small bit of color, texture, and realism to the scene.

The terrain object is not very detailed, compared to a real slice of earth. The Diffuse and Bump maps do provide an illusion of detail, but this effect alone cannot provide true realism. Another way to increase the resolution of the terrain is to use a very high-density mesh, but that requires tremendous rendering time. The solution here is to use low-polygon stone objects that blend seamlessly with the dirt material and add resolution to the terrain.

The second function of the rocks is to break up the shoreline and hide flaws in the terrain mesh. Without the rocks, the shoreline looks too perfect and linear. The rock in the water and the rocks along the edge of the water help to break up this edge and give it a more realistic look. Also, spots appear on the terrain object where the bitmap is smeared or doesn't look quite right. Rather than alter the terrain mesh, it is easier to cover up these spots with rock objects. Generally speaking, hiding imperfections in this way is a bad idea because it often entails cluttering a scene or foregoing aesthetic concerns just to hide sloppy work. In this case, the offense is less egregious because the rocks blend well with the dirt material and also add depth to the ground.

Last, the rocks in the scene add a small bit of color, texture, and realism to the scene without being overbearing. The rock breaking through the surface of the water provides an opportunity to contrast a different texture against both the water and the dirt. The rocks under the water add subtle realism and break up the repetitive pattern of the lake bottom.

DESIGNING A ROCK MATERIAL

1. Load file Stones.MAX from the Chapter 10 Files directory on the accompanying CD.

2. In the Material Editor, examine the Stones material in Slot #1. This, the basic stone material, contains a Diffuse map, and a grayscale image used as both a Bump and Shininess Strength map. Note the Shininess, Ambient, and Specular values in the Basic Parameters section of the rollout.

   An RGB Tint has been applied to the Diffuse map for this material. You will use it to fine-tune the color of the stone material and to ensure that the material blends well with the surrounding terrain. Later, you will change the material type to Multi/Sub-Object and make four versions of the stone material. The first three versions will be used for the rocks on the ground; the fourth, for the stones on the lake bottom.

3. Render the Camera viewport to get an idea of how the stone material looks without the aid of an RGB Tint (see fig. 10.21). The Diffuse map was made from a scanned photo of rock. Although it is a realistic texture, it is much too bright for this scene, and the stones do not blend at all with the surrounding terrain.

FIGURE 10.21
The original stone material, before color correction.

TIP

If rendering the entire scene is too slow on your machine, try turning off Auto Reflect/Refract Maps in the Render Scene dialog. This speeds things up considerably. Rendering by Region or by Selected also saves time.

4. From the Basic Parameters section of the stones material, click on the *M* next to the Diffuse color swatch to display the RGB Tint map. Set each component of the RGB Tint as follows:

    ■ Set the R component to RGB 144, 0, 0.

    ■ Set the G component to RGB 0, 154, 0.

    ■ Set the B component to RGB 0, 0, 154.

Make another test render of the scene to see how the material is affected (see fig. 10.22). Notice that the stones are much more natural now. This example illustrates the paramount importance of color when you design natural materials.

FIGURE 10.22
The stone material after color correction.

DESIGNING MORE ROCK MATERIALS

1. Return to the top level of the Stones material. Click on the Type button to bring up the Material/Map Browser. Click on Browse From New, select material type Multi/Sub-Object, and click on OK. In the Replace Material dialog, select the Keep old material as sub-material option, and then click on OK. Now that you have a Multi/Sub-Object material, you need to create different versions of the original material.

2. Rename Material 1 **Stone_Purple**. Next you need to copy this material; it will serve as a basis for your other rock materials.

3. Click on the Material 2 button. Then click on the Type button and select Browse From Material Editor in the Material/Map Browser. Select the Stone_Purple material and click on OK. Rename this material **Stone_Green**.

4. Click on the *M* next to the Diffuse color swatch to navigate to the RGB Tint map. Set each component of the RGB Tint as follows:

- Set the R component to RGB 122, 0, 0.
- Set the G component to RGB 0, 128, 0.
- Set the B component to RGB 0, 0, 119.

5. Select the Map button next to the RGB Tint color swatches. This displays the texture map being tinted. Change the U and V Tiling to 2 and 2, respectively.

6. Click on the Go to Parent button, and then on the Go to Sibling button to display the Shininess Strength map settings. The tiling for this map needs to be the same as that for the Diffuse map. Change the U and V Tiling to 2 and 2, respectively. Because the Shininess Strength and Bump maps are instances of each other, this change affects both maps.

7. In the Maps rollout of the Stone_Green material, change the Shininess Strength to 100 and the Bump Strength to 400. In the Basic Parameters section, set the Shininess to 30.

   You now have two finished materials. You can retrieve a third material from the scene and place it in the Material 3 Slot.

8. From the top of the Stones Multi/Sub-Object material, click on the Material 3 button. Click on the Type button, select Browse From Scene, select the Stone_Dark_Rough material, and click on OK.

9. Name this material **Stone_Dark_Rough**.

NOTE

This material was applied to a hidden object. By Browsing From Scene, it can be retrieved.

This third stone material is similar to the other two but differs in a couple of important ways. First, it uses different Diffuse, Bump, and Shininess Strength maps than the first two stone materials. The bitmaps it uses are the same ones used to create the dirt material. Because these bitmaps are already used elsewhere in the scene, they do not require extra memory at rendering time. Second, the Diffuse map is not applied at full strength. This means that the Diffuse color is used to calculate the final look of the material. This was done because the Diffuse map was overpowering when applied at full strength and detracted from the overall scene. Examine the material parameters and maps used, and compare them to those used for the other two materials.

Render the scene to see how the additional rock materials add to the scene. As you can see from figure 10.23, the scene is much more realistic.

FIGURE 10.23
Three different stone materials are used in the scene.

Finally, you need to create an underwater stone material.

CREATING AN UNDERWATER STONE MATERIAL

1. From the Stones material in Slot #1, click on the Material 4 button to edit the fourth material. Click on Type to open the Material/Map Browser. Choose Browse From Scene, select Stone_Mossy, and click on OK.

2. Name this material **Stone_Mossy**, and examine it to see how it is built.

   Render the scene to see the new rock material with the water (see fig. 10.24). The rocks look rather mossy, but you can achieve a better result by using a Top/Bottom material to blend the two rocks with the mud. Top/Bottom materials are great for static objects, but because they are calculated in world space, they are not well suited to most animation.

3. Make certain that you are at the top of the Stone_Mossy material. Select Type to display the Material/Map Browser, select Browse From New, select material type Top/Bottom, and click on OK. In the Replace Material dialog, select the Keep old Material as Sub-material option, and then click on OK. You now have a Top/Bottom material with Stone_Mossy as the top material.

4. Click on the button next to Bottom Material and select Type to display the Material/Map Browser. Select Browse From Scene, select the Mud material used in the terrain material, and click on OK.

5. Rename this material **Mud**. Click on Go to Parent to return to the Top/Bottom material parameters.

FIGURE 10.24
The underwater rocks do not blend well into the scene.

FIGURE 10.24

The underwater rocks do not blend well into the scene.

6. Set the Position to 84 and the Blend to 9. This gives you a nice blend between the mud and rock.

7. Click on Render Last to see how the material has been affected. The stones now blend more naturally into the scene (see fig. 10.25).

FIGURE 10.25

The underwater rocks blend well into the scene.

Vegetation

An important element of any outdoor scene is vegetation. Opacity-mapped plants, weeds, and shrubs not only add realism but also serve to hide and soften the hard edges exhibited by computer-generated objects. Strategically placed plants can add subtle touches of realism. They are not actual 3D objects, however; placed too close to the camera, they can ruin an otherwise good scene. Flat or nearly flat objects such as leaves and palm fronds can be convincing at close range, but objects that are not inherently 2D, such as vines and bushes, do not look good up close.

Bushes and Trees

Bushes and trees are very difficult to model. They also require many polygons, and therefore take a long time to render. Filling a scene with polygonal bush or tree models is impractical. Bushes and trees, viewed from a distance, can be simulated quite easily. The basic method is to apply an opacity map to a set of intersecting planes. If the planes are crossed to form an X (viewed from above), the object will appear solid when viewed from most directions. More detail can be achieved by crossing four planes in a double-X pattern. You can enhance the realism of this effect by using masks and gradients in addition to opacity maps.

Load the file FOLIAGE.max from the Files directory on the accompanying CD, and examine the geometry used to display the bush material. Four planes intersect to form a double-X or asterisk pattern when viewed from the Top viewport (see fig. 10.26). The basic concept is that these four planes act as projection screens. Their only job is to provide a surface for displaying the tree material. The material therefore needs to look as much like a tree or shrubbery as possible. Sometimes this effect is done with noise, but noise will never give you the realism that using a well-drawn bitmap will.

FIGURE 10.26

The forest project file with opacity-mapped bush objects.

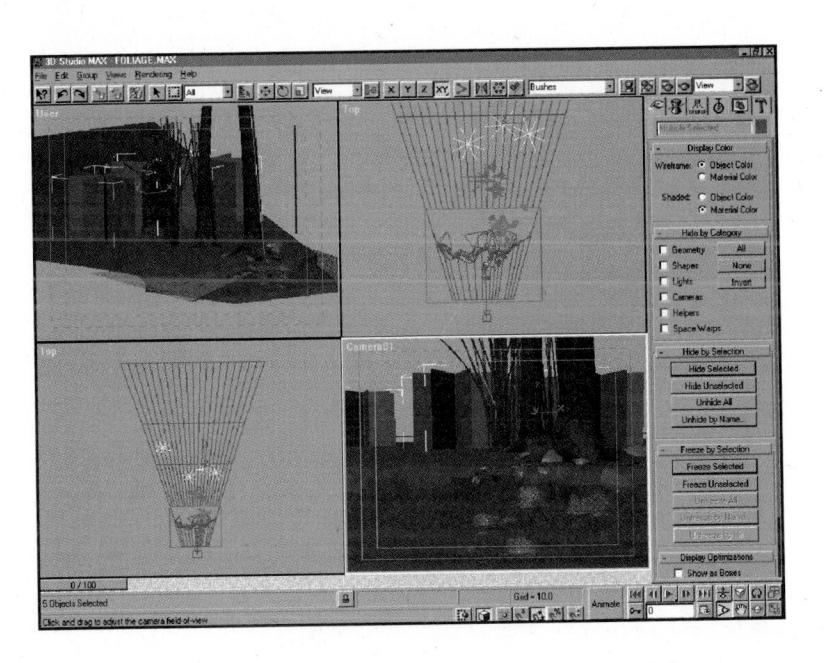

Use the following steps to build an opacity-mapped bush material.

DESIGNING A BUSH MATERIAL

1. With the FOLIAGE.max file loaded, open the Material Editor.

   You will create this material from scratch.

2. Select the material in Slot #1. Click on the Type button to display the Material/Map Browser. Select Browse From New, select material type Multi/Sub-Object, and click on OK. Select Discard Old Material from the Replace Material dialog, and click on OK.

3. Rename the material **Shrubs_and_Plants**. This material has already been applied to the mesh objects in the scene.

4. Click on Material 1 to edit it. Rename this material **Shrubs_01**. Naming materials as you build them will help to keep your project organized.

5. Set the Basic Parameters of the material as follows: set the Ambient color to RGB 9, 23, 11; set the Specular color to RGB 229, 229, 229; set Shininess to 40, and make sure that 2-Sided is checked.

6. Open the Maps rollout and click on the button next to Opacity. This brings you to the Material/Map Browser. Select Browse From New, select material type Bitmap, and click on OK.

7. Select the button next to Bitmap to assign an image. Choose the file Shrub_OPAC02.TGA (from the Chapter 10 Maps directory). Set both U and V Tiling to 1.7.

This gives you the basic Opacity map. The bitmap is a black-and-white painting of indecipherable leaves and twigs. By default, the opacity map will tile across the entire surface of the planar objects to which it is applied. The effect, however, does not look very realistic. The solution is to limit the effect of the Opacity map by adding a mask.

NOTE

View the bitmap Shrub_OPAC02.TGA used in the preceding step 7. This bitmap is tileable in all directions. It is also purposefully ambiguous. This material is meant to provide leafy filler at the back of the scene. If the leaves were too orderly and defined, it might prove distracting. In addition, an orderly pattern, even a well-drawn one, would be easier to recognize and would not look as realistic. The goal is for the viewer not to be able to discern one leaf from another, but to get the impression of a great deal of foliage. Also note that plenty of stems and lines are in the bitmap. The lines are important because they connect the leaves and make the bitmap more realistic.

8. Click on the Type button to display the Material/Map Browser. Select Browse From New, select material type Mask, and click on OK. In the Replace Map dialog, select Keep Old Map as Sub-map, and click on OK.

9. Click on the button next to Mask to assign an image. Select Browse From New, select material type Bitmap from the Material/Map Browser, and then click on OK. Click on the Bitmap button, and assign Shrub_01_MASK.TGA (from the Chapter 10 Maps directory). Set the Blur to .1, the lowest value.

By reducing the Blur value of the mask bitmap you can ensure that parts of the mask do not bleed into other parts of the mask.

NOTE

Combining a mask with different tiling textures and also combining each material with several different masks allows for a great deal of variation without the memory overhead of creating new maps for every situation.

10. Click on the Go to Parent button twice, and return to the Maps rollout. Drag a copy of the Opacity map to the Shininess Strength slot. Select Instance from the Copy Map dialog, and click on OK.

11. Click on the Map slot next to Diffuse. Select Browse From New, select material type Gradient from the Material/Map Browser, and set the gradient colors as follows:

   ■ Set Color #1 and Color #2 to RGB 128, 183, 53.

   ■ Set Color #3 to RGB 82, 109, 69.

   ■ Set the Color 2 Position to 0.76.

These settings create a nice blend from a bright yellow-green to a warm muted green—a nice effect of depth and sunlit foliage.

At present, you have only half a bush material. You still need to create a second bush material. Each bush object requires two materials to keep the objects from looking too symmetrical.

FINISHING THE SHRUB MATERIAL

1. Return to the Basic Parameters section of the Shrubs_and_Plants material. Click on the button next to Material 2 to edit that material. Click on the Type button to display the Material/Map Browser, and select Browse From Material Editor. Select the Shrubs_01 material, and click on OK.

2. Rename the material **Shrubs_02**.

3. Select the Opacity Map button from the Maps rollout, and then select the Map button to edit its parameters. Set both the U and V Offset to 0.4, to ensure that this material and the previous material do not tile in exactly the same way.

4. Click on the Go to Parent button to return to the Mask level, and then select the Mask button to edit the map. Replace the current opacity map with Shrub_02_MASK.TGA.

5. Now that you have finished Material 2, you can render the scene (see fig. 10.27).

FIGURE 10.27
The shape of the bushes was created by combining an opacity map and two different mask bitmaps.

NOTE

The subtlety of the foliage gradient exemplifies why it is important to establish your background imagery first. This effect relies entirely on accurate color choices to be convincing.

This is the basic technique for creating opacity-mapped materials. It can be modified to create a number of different effects. With this method, you could create grass, plants, leaves, and so on. In the next tutorial, you use the technique to create tall grass material.

DESIGNING A TALL GRASS MATERIAL

1. Continuing with the file FOLIAGE.max (from the Chapter 10 files directory). Select Unhide by Name from the Display panel, and click on OK. From the Selection Sets pop-up, choose Grass. Click on Unhide to make all the grass objects visible.

2. In the Material Editor, select the Multi/Sub-Object material in Slot #1. Select Material 4 to edit its parameters.

   Because the grass material is similar to the shrub material, the easiest way to begin is to copy the shrub material and edit it to suit the grass material.

3. Click on the Type button to bring up the Material/Map Browser. Select Browse From Material Editor, select the Shrub_01 material, and click on OK.

4. Name this material **Grass_Clump_Dark**.

5. From the Maps rollout, copy one of the empty map slots onto the Opacity and the Shininess Strength maps. It is easier to recreate these maps than to adjust them.

6. Select the Opacity Map button to bring up the Material/Map Browser. Select Browse From New, select material type Bitmap, and click on OK. Load Grass_OPAC.TGA (from the Chapter 10 Maps directory on the accompanying CD) as the bitmap. Set the Blur to 0.53.

7. Click on Go to Parent to return to the Maps rollout. Copy the Opacity map onto the Shininess Strength map as an instance.

8. Select the Diffuse Map button to edit the gradient. Set the gradient colors as follows:

   ■ Set Color #1 to RGB 117, 172, 53.

   ■ Set Color #2 to RGB 111, 132, 53.

   ■ Set Color #3 to RGB 63, 82, 49.

This new material needs to be applied to the grass objects in the scene.

9. From the Named Selection Sets dialog in the toolbar, select Grass. All the grass objects should now be selected. From the Material Editor, click on the Assign Material to Selection button. The grass objects will now display the Grass material. (The grass objects have already been given the appropriate Material IDs.)

Render the scene to see the new grass material (see fig. 10.28).

FIGURE 10.28
Tall grass created with an Opacity map.

Other Opacity-Mapped Materials

Load the file FOLIAGE2.max from the Chapter 10 Files directory on the *Inside 3D Studio MAX Volume II* CD. This file contains more bush objects and materials. They were all created in the same way as the shrub and grass materials that you have been building—only the bitmaps have changed.

The rendered scene is starting to look quite natural (see fig. 10.29). You can see how opacity-mapped materials can add depth to a scene that geometry alone cannot provide.

FIGURE 10.29
The final background foliage is added to the scene.

Plant Materials

Plant leaves are not difficult to simulate. To create the plant materials for this scene you combine a simple leaf texture with a bright, mottled plant texture, using Mix, RGB Tint, and Opacity maps to alter the appearance and proportions of each texture. The effects created in this way look very natural and organic.

The mesh for the plant leaves was created from a single plane that was modified into its current shape. Several leaves were then copied, and two of them were created with greater resolution (to hold the bitmap better and also to prevent edges).

Leaves could be made from a simple plane, with the outlines created with opacity maps. This is not a bad method. Your image will be more realistic, however, if you place a texture map on an object that has actual dimension and curves. The leaves in this scene bend and curve, which adds to their realism. A planar mapping coordinate was applied to the objects before they were modified so that the texture would stick to the surface of the leaves without excessive blurring. Because they are foreground objects, it is important that their edges are crisp and that their texture is not blurry.

TIP

Every bitmap in MAX is blurred to a certain degree. The best way to ensure a crisp texture map is to apply a Sharpen filter to your bitmap before you bring it into 3D Studio MAX. This can be done in most paint programs.

DESIGNING A SIMPLE PLANT MATERIAL

1. Load file PLANTS.MAX from the Chapter 10 Files directory on the accompanying CD. Foreground leaves have been added to the scene (see fig. 10.30).

FIGURE 10.30
Plants have been added to the scene's foreground.

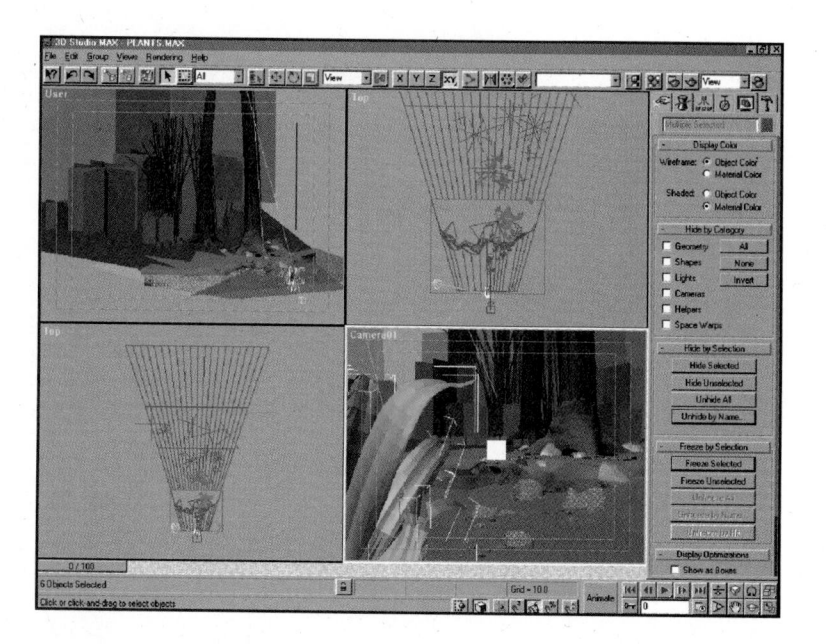

2. In the Material Editor, select the material in Slot #1.

3. Name the material **Leaves**. This material has already been applied to the leaf objects in the foreground of the image.

4. Check 2-Sided.

5. Open the Maps rollout and select the Diffuse Map button. Select Browse From New, and select material type Bitmap from the Material/Map Browser. Load Plant_01_DIFF.TGA as the bitmap file. Set U and V Tiling to 2 and 3, respectively. Set Angle to 25. Click on Go to Parent to return to the Maps rollout.

6. Click on the Bump Map button. Select Browse From New, select material type Bitmap from the Material/Maps Browser, and click on OK. Load Leaf_01_BUMP.TGA as the bitmap. Click on Go to Parent to return to the Maps rollout. Set Bump amount to 61.

7. From the Maps rollout, drag the bump map onto the shininess strength map. Select Instance from the Copy Map dialog, and click on OK.

The first leaf material is complete. Render the scene to view the material. The leaves look realistic, but they are all very similar (see fig. 10.31). Next you will create different versions of the same leaf material and place them on the leaf objects.

FIGURE 10.31
Realistic plants are only seconds away.

CREATING VARIATIONS OF THE PLANT MATERIAL

1. Select the Leaves material. Click on the Type button to open the Material/Map Browser. Choose Browse From New, select material Multi/Sub-Object, and click on OK. From the Replace Material dialog, select Keep Old Material as Sub-material, and click on OK.

2. Rename Material 1 **Leaf_Green**.

3. Select the Material 2 button.

4. Select the Type button to bring up the Material/Map Browser. Select Browse From Material Editor, select the Leaf_Green material, and click on OK.

5. Name this material **Leaf_Red_Yellow**. You can now edit this material to add variety.

6. In the Maps rollout, select the Diffuse map to edit it. Select the Type button to bring up the Material/Map Browser. Select Browse From New, select map type Mix, and click on OK. In the Replace Map dialog, select Keep Old Map as Sub-map, and click on OK.

7. Click on the Color #2 Map button to bring up the Material/Map Browser. Select Browse From New, select map type Bitmap, and click on OK. Load Plant_Spots_DIFF.TGA from the Chapter 10 Maps directory. Set U and V Tiling to 2 and 4, respectively.

8. Click on the Type button to bring up the Material/Map Browser, select Browse From New, select map type RGB Tint, and click on OK. In the Replace Map dialog, select Keep Old Map as Sub-map, and click on OK. Set each component of the RGB Tint as follows:

   - Set the R component to RGB 255, 66, 51.

   - Set the G component to RGB 58, 255, 0.

   - Set the B component to RGB 0, 0, 255.

9. Click on the Go to Parent button to return to the Mix map parameters.

10. Click on the Mix Amount map button, select Browse From New, select map type Bitmap, and then click on OK. Load Leaf_01_MASK.TGA from the Chapter 10 Maps directory. This map places the brightly colored plant material around the edges of the leaf material.

So far, you're simply varying the leaf material. You can achieve even greater realism by adding an opacity map to the material to simulate the effect of ravenous insects.

11. Return to the top level of material Leaf_Red_Yellow. From the Maps rollout, click on the Opacity Map button to bring up the Material/Map Browser. Select Browse From New, select map type Bitmap, and click on OK. Load Leaf_01_OPAC.TGA from the Chapter 10 Maps directory. Set Blur to 0.1.

This puts a series of holes on one side of the leaf and a ragged edge on the other. The next step is to ensure that no highlights appear on top of the holes. This can be done by applying a mask to the Shininess Strength map. You can use the same bitmap you used to define opacity.

12. Return to the top level of material Leaf_Red_Yellow. From the Maps rollout, click on the Bump Map button to edit its parameters. Click on the Type button to bring up the Material/Map Browser, select Browse From New, and select map type Mask. Click on OK. In the Replace Map dialog, select Keep Old Map as Sub-map, and click on OK.

13. Click on the Mask button, select Browse From New, select map type Bitmap, and click on OK. Load Leaf_01_OPAC.TGA from the Chapter 10 Maps directory. Set Blur to 0.1.

The material for the first two leaves is finished, and you can render the scene to see the extra realism the opacity map has added (see fig. 10.32).

FIGURE 10.32
*The final leaf is
mapped with two
Diffuse maps, a Bump
map, an Opacity map,
and a Mix Mask.*

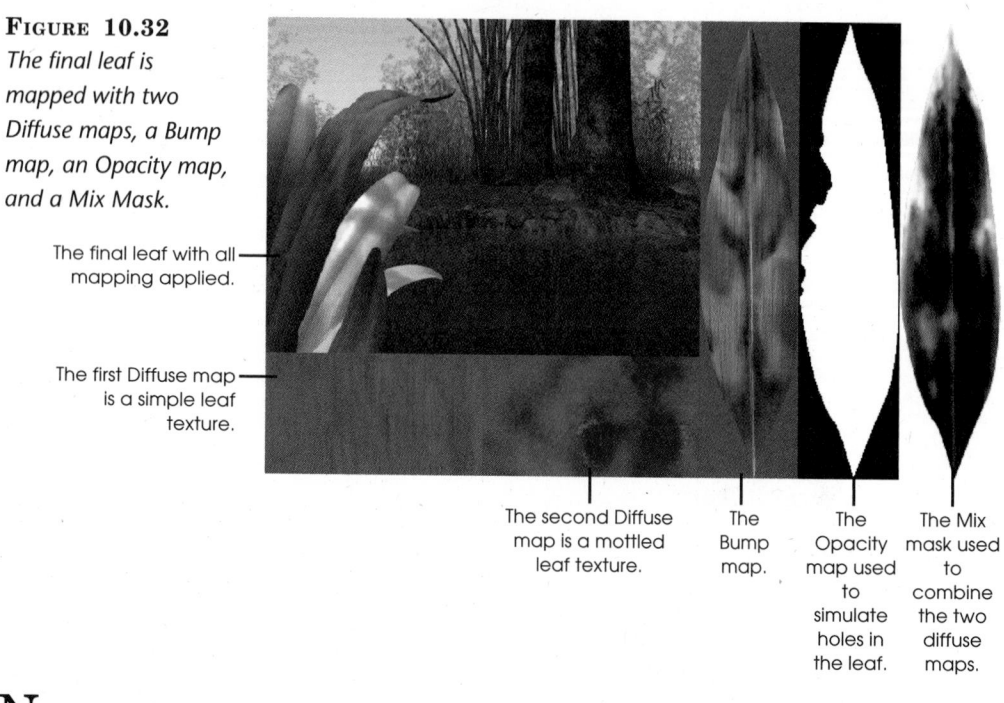

The final leaf with all mapping applied.

The first Diffuse map is a simple leaf texture.

The second Diffuse map is a mottled leaf texture.

The Bump map.

The Opacity map used to simulate holes in the leaf.

The Mix mask used to combine the two diffuse maps.

NOTE

Switching from a Standard material to a Multi/Sub-Object material has caused some of the leaves to lose their textures. This occurs because the Material IDs assigned to those leaves are currently filled with the default texture, and the actual materials have not yet been created.

To see other ways of combining maps to create realistic plant textures, load PLANTS2.MAX from the Chapter 10 Files directory of the accompanying CD (see fig. 10.33). This file contains all the objects with full mapping. The Leaves material in this file contains three additional leaf types. All were created with the same few maps but combined in different ways with different settings. Take some time to examine the materials and maps to get an idea of how they were made.

Most of the materials for the forest scene are now complete. The finishing touch in this scene, however, is an ornery tree frog. The next section describes techniques to texture map a tree frog.

FIGURE 10.33
The finished leaves.

Tree Frog

Mapping oddly shaped objects is difficult in any 3D program. The most important aspect to making texture maps look natural is to apply the correct mapping coordinates. Designing the actual material is the second most important consideration. The texture maps should be designed only after the object has been given appropriate mapping coordinates.

Although most oddly shaped objects can be given spherical, shrink-wrap, or box mapping coordinates, these methods have very distinct disadvantages. First, all these mapping methods will cause distortion and/or seams to appear on your object. Second, these methods are imprecise. They might work fine for rocks and amorphous organic items, but they don't give you the control you need to ensure that each pixel in your texture maps is applied to the appropriate part of an object. Three-dimensional paint programs give you the ability to paint on a mesh, and are one way to apply paint accurately to a mesh. Another effective method is to use Planar and Cylindrical mapping coordinates.

Both cylindrical and planar mapping can be applied without noticeable distortion. Certain caveats apply, however, to using planar mapping on an oddly shaped object. Specifically, smearing occurs when planar mapping is applied to faces perpendicular to the Planar Mapping gizmo.

This streaking can be minimized by reducing the detail of bitmaps where they are likely to hit perpendicular faces and therefore streak through an object.

NOTE

When you create materials for a realistic organic object, the texture maps are critical to the success of the material. Many of the tools and combination map types have little practical impact when maps need to be of the precision necessary for a complicated organic object.

DESIGNING MATERIAL FOR A FROG'S TOPSIDE

1. Load file TFROG.MAX from the Chapter 10 Files directory (see fig. 10.34). This file contains a frog ready to be mapped. Examine the model to become familiar with it.

FIGURE 10.34
The tree frog model, ready for mapping. Notice how the planar mapping coordinate is applied to the object.

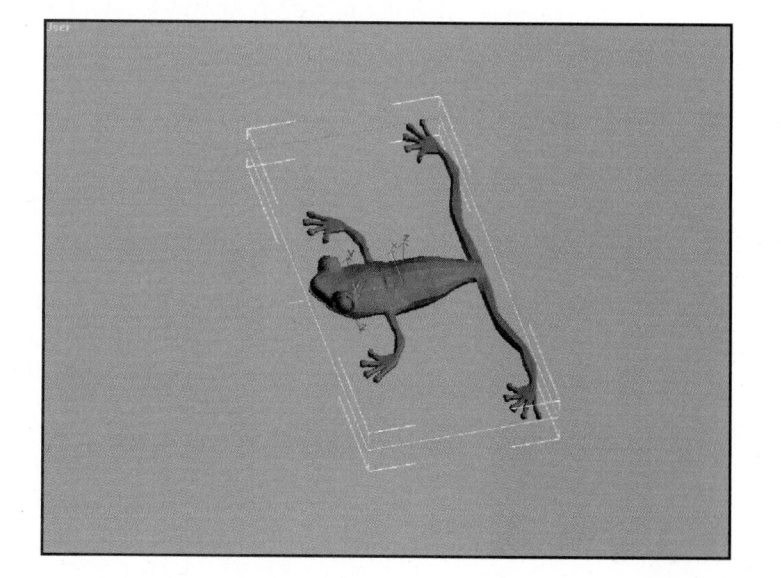

NOTE
_____

Both the model and the bitmaps for the frog are of relatively low resolution. The frog will look very good when viewed at a size of no more than one-third that of the screen. Up close, it doesn't hold up well. Both the frog model and the bitmaps were built specifically for this scene and were kept small to conserve memory. How close should one get to a tree frog anyway?

2. In the Material Editor, select the Material in Slot #1. This material has already been assigned to the frog mesh. The next step is to make it a Multi/Sub-Object material. Then you can assign the different materials to the frog mesh by assigning designated faces to an appropriate Material ID.

3. Click on the Type button to bring up the Material/Map Browser, select Browse From New, and select material type Multi/Sub-Object. Click on OK. In the Replace Material dialog, select Discard Old Material, and click on OK.

4. Name the Material **Tree_Frog**.

5. Click on the Material 1 slot to edit the first material. Name this material **TFrog_Top**. Set the Shininess to 31, and check Soften.

6. Open the Maps rollout and click on the Diffuse Map button to bring up the Material/Map Browser. Select Browse From New, select map type Bitmap, and click on OK. Load TFrog_Top_DIFF.TGA (from the Chapter 10 Maps directory). Click on the Go to Parent button.

7. From the Maps rollout, click on the Bump Map button to bring up the Material/Map Browser. Select Browse From New, select map type Bitmap, and click on OK. Load TFrog_Top_BUMP.TGA (from the Chapter 10 Maps directory). Click on the Go to Parent button.

8. Drag the bump map to the Shininess Strength button. In the Copy Map dialog, select Instance, and click on OK.

9. From the Maps rollout, click on the Opacity Map button to bring up the Material/Map Browser. Select Browse From New, select map type Bitmap, and click on OK. Load TFrog_OPAC.TGA (from the Chapter 10 Maps directory). Click on the Go to Parent button.

Next you will render the frog to see how the material is progressing. First, the modifier stack of the frog model needs to be adjusted. Two UVW mapping modifiers are applied to the frog model. The first is a UVW planar mapping coordinate encompassing the whole model and applied from the top viewport. The second UVW planar mapping coordinate is applied from a side view and is used to map the sides of the frog. This UVW map modifier is applied to only a small number of faces. The face selection is defined with an Edit Mesh modifier placed after the first UVW Mapping modifier and left in Sub-Object mode.

10. Return to the scene. Select the Tree_frog mesh by clicking on one of the legs. In the modify command panel, return the modifier stack to the topmost level. The second UVW Mapping modifier, applied to the side faces of the frog, should now be active. Leave all other settings intact.

NOTE

When applying UVW Mapping Coordinates to Sub-Object selections, always apply a UVW Map modifier to the entire object first. Applying a UVW Mapping modifier to only part of an object, without first having given the entire object UVW Mapping Coordinates, can produce unpredictable results.

The material for the top of the frog is finished. Note that many of the presets (such as Blur, Ambient color, and Specular color) were left untouched. It is best to leave the settings as they are until all your maps are in place. Often these items do not have a big impact on the look of your materials and do not need to be altered from their presets.

Render the User view to see the results so far (see fig. 10.35). Notice that the top of the frog already looks finished. Also notice that there is little evidence of the bitmap smearing on the sides of the model. Some streaks are noticeable, but they are minor. If necessary, streaks can be removed by opening the bitmap in a paint program and adding a solid colored border to the outside edge of a bitmap.

Also notice that very little texture is near the edges of the bitmaps. The detail in a bitmap should be decreased in areas where you can reasonably expect the bitmap will hit perpendicular or near perpendicular faces. This takes a bit of guesswork and experimentation, but it is not that difficult to do.

FIGURE 10.35
The tree frog with top
material in place.

Several faces on the frog model appear white rather than green. These faces are mapped with the same material as the rest of the object; they look different because they have been given a different mapping coordinate. They are mapped from the side with a planar mapping coordinate.

In the next tutorial, you continue to build the frog material. This time you create the material for the underside of the frog.

DESIGNING THE MATERIAL FOR THE BELLY OF THE FROG

1. Click on the Material 2 slot to edit the second material. Name this material **TFrog_Belly**. Set the Shininess to 4.

2. Open the Maps rollout and click on the Diffuse Map button to bring up the Material/Map Browser. Select Browse From New, select Bitmap, and click on OK. Load TFrog_Belly_DIFF.tga from the Chapter 10 Maps directory. Click on the Go to Parent button.

3. From the Maps rollout, click on the Bump Map button to bring up the Material/Map Browser. Select Browse From New, select Bitmap, and click on OK. Load TFrog_Belly_BUMP.tga from the Chapter 10 Maps directory. Click on the Go to Parent button.

4. Drag the bump map to the Shininess Strength button. In the Copy Map dialog, select Instance and click on OK.

5. From the Maps rollout, click on the Opacity Map button to bring up the Material/Map Browser. Select Browse From New, select Bitmap, and click on OK. Load TFrog_OPAC.tga from the Chapter 10 Maps directory. Click on the Go to Parent button.

That is all it takes to create the material for the underside of the frog. The only task left is to assign Material ID 2 to the bottom faces of the frog.

6. Select the Tree_Frog object in the User window. In the Modify panel, select the Edit Mesh modifier. This modifier is currently defining an active selection. You will also use this Edit Mesh modifier to change the Material IDs of some of the faces of the frog. After you are done assigning Material IDs, you will return the Edit Mesh modifier to its present state.

7. Select TFrog_Belly from the Named Selection Sets drop-down list. This will select all the faces on the underside of the frog that should receive the TFrog_Belly material.

8. Assign these faces Material ID 2 in the Edit Surface portion of the Command panel.

9. Select TFrog_Sides from the Named Selection Sets drop-down list. This returns the selection to its former state. Leave the Edit Mesh modifier in Sub-Object mode.

10. Rotate the User view so that you can see the underside of the frog model, and render the object again (see fig. 10.36).

FIGURE 10.36
Frog model with bottom faces selected and when rendered.

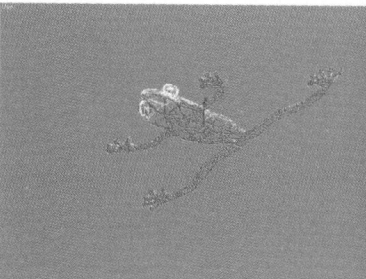

The sides of the frog require a separate material. This material will help to blend both of the top and bottom materials together.

DESIGNING THE MATERIAL FOR THE SIDES OF THE FROG

1. In the Material Editor, click on the Material 3 slot to edit the third material. Name this material **TFrog_Side**.

2. Open the Maps rollout and click on the Diffuse Map button to bring up the Material/Map Browser. Select Browse From New, select material Bitmap, and click on OK. Load TFrog_Side_DIFF.tga from the Chapter 10 Maps directory on the accompanying CD. Set Angle to 90. Click on Go to Parent to return to the Maps rollout.

3. From the Maps rollout, click on the Bump Map button to bring up the Material/Map Browser. Select Browse From New, select material Bitmap, and click on OK. Load TFrog_Side_BUMP.tga from the Chapter 10 Maps directory on the accompanying CD. Click on Go to Parent to return to the Maps rollout. Set Amount to 81.

   This material will provide a nice blend from the top material to the bottom material. First, the side faces that require this material need to be selected and assigned Material ID 3.

4. Make certain that Sub-Object and Face are both still active in the Modify panel and that the side faces of the frog are selected. If not select TFrog_Sides from the Named Selection Sets drop-down list, to select all the faces on the sides of the frog. These faces will receive the TFrog_Side material.

5. Set the Material ID to 3 in the Edit Surface portion of the Modify panel.

6. Rotate the User view to display the sides of the frog model, and render the object again (see fig. 10.37).

You have only three more materials to create. The first is the eye, and the other two materials provide the colored rings around the eye.

FIGURE 10.37
The frog's top, bottom, and sides are mapped.

DESIGNING THE EYE MATERIALS

1. In the Material Editor, click on the Material 4 slot to edit the fourth material. Name this material **TFrog_YellowRings**. Set the Diffuse color to RGB 197, 194, 116. This material provides the cream-colored ring around the eye of the frog.

2. Click on the Material 5 slot to edit the fifth material. Name this material **TFrog_BlackRings**. Set the Diffuse color to RGB 26, 26, 26. This material provides the dark colored ring around the eye of the frog.

3. Click on the Material 6 slot to edit the sixth material. Name this material **TFrog_Eye**. Set Shininess to 48, and Shininess Strength to 91.

4. From the Maps rollout, click on the Diffuse Map button to bring up the Material/Map Browser. Select Browse From New, select material Bitmap, and click on OK. Load TFrog_Eye_DIFF.TGA from the Chapter 10 Maps directory of the accompanying CD.

    This is the last of the frog materials. Next, you assign these three eye materials to the correct faces.

5. Make certain that Sub-Object and Face are both still active in the Modify panel. Select TFrog_Yellow_Rings from the Named Selection Sets drop-down list. This selects a ring of faces around the eye sockets.

6. Set the Material ID to 4 in the Edit Surface portion of the Modify panel.

7. Select TFrog_Black_Rings from the Named Selection Sets drop-down list. This selects a ring of faces around the base of the eyeballs.

8. Set the Material ID to 5 in the Edit Surface portion of the Modify panel.

9. Exit Sub-object mode.

10. Select Eyeballs from the Named Selection Sets drop-down list. This selects both of the frog's eyeballs. These are separate objects; because they are not attached to the frog, they cannot be selected in Sub-object mode.

11. Apply a Material modifier to both objects. Set the Material ID to 6. This assigns the eyeball material to the two spheres.

That's how to to make materials for a tree frog. When rendered, your image should resemble figure 10.38. The key to success when you create an organic object like a tree frog is to paint the texture maps with care. The entire illusion rests on whether the combination of model and material is convincing. For that reason, as much care should be taken when you design materials for an object as you would take when you model an object.

FIGURE 10.38
The finished tree frog.

The last exercise is to put the tree frog in the scene and animate him—or perhaps her—it's hard to tell with amphibians. A finished version of the scene is shown in figure 10.39. Some new models and materials have been added—all using the techniques described in this chapter. The tree frog is relaxing on a leaf and appreciating all the hard work that went into building his/her pond. There aren't any steps for making the final image, so you are on your own. Good luck!

FIGURE 10.39
Palani's Pond
by Steve Burke.

In Practice: Designing Natural Materials

- **Ground and sky.** These two items often form the foundation of an image or scene. Whenever possible, the background should be established first because it has perhaps the greatest influence on the "look" of a scene.

- **Natural colors and textures.** Perhaps the most important aspect of designing natural materials is the use of realistic colors and textures. RGB Tints are great for perfecting colors and balancing the colors of a scene.

- **Water.** The best, most convincing water effect is sometimes the simplest. Reflection masks can add realism to reflections by fading reflections near the camera.

- **Opacity maps.** Making good use of opacity-mapped materials can add new depth to your work. Opacity maps can achieve results not possible with regular geometry. The best opacity mapping effects are those that are difficult to decipher.

- **Variation.** Natural materials should have imperfections and natural variation. Multi/Sub-Object materials are good for this because they enable you to work with several materials at one time and are quick and easy to use.

IMAGE BY DAVE ESPINOSA-AGUILAR

Chapter 11

by dave espinosa-aguilar

DESIGNING MAN-MADE MATERIALS

3D Studio MAX makes it possible to create extremely realistic man-made materials if you have an eye for detail and imperfections. Often, the "perfect" man-made material is an "imperfect" man-made material. Look around you. Most man-made objects have noticeable flaws—stains or discolorations; uneven warps, wrinkles or folds along their surfaces; chips, cracks, tears, or dents along their edges; patches of unexpected dullness or shininess; dirty smudges, streaks, dust, or some form of deterioration. Very few things remain unaffected by the elements, handling, or accidents. The key to creating realistic man-made materials is to subject them to entropy.

Man-made materials such as concretes and ceramics, paper and other processed woods, carved or unnaturally shaped stones, plastics and rubbers, glass, metals, and fabrics can all be created with realism if you have effective bitmaps and geometry for each material and if you have material and geometry corruption skills under your belt. This chapter examines essential techniques for creating a wide variety of common man-made materials and corrupting them into believable man-made materials. The following topics are discussed:

- The impact of geometry on realistic materials

- Techniques for corrupting geometry

- Techniques for creating corruption materials such as smears, discolorations, blurry puddles and smudges, scorch marks, dents, dust, and weathering

- Considerations for creating concretes, papers, woods, plastics, rubber, vinyl, glass, metals, wires, fabrics, carpet, and stones (translucent, polished, and dull)

Creating Material Imperfections

Look around the room. Is there a book nearby that you refer to quite often (see fig. 11.1)? Pick it up and look it over for a minute with a careful eye. Don't rush now. Take your time. This kind of close scrutiny is the essence of this chapter. Ask yourself, "How does this book deviate from a box primitive?"

Look for perfectly straight edges and perfectly aligned page grooves. Do they occur? Look for areas of the cover where the paper material shows through. If the cover is shiny, can you see your fingerprints on it? Are the edges of the cover dented, ripped, or worn? Look at the exposed edges of the pages when the book is closed. Are they pure white or do you see dirt along the sides and at the corners? Are there streaks of grime on any of the sides? Set the book down flat on the table or desk and look at its rectilinearity. If you follow the edges of the book, is it a perfect box, or are any of the edges warped? Is the binding of the book perfectly flat, or is it bent and cracked? Does the cover press firmly against the pages when left alone or does it stick up a bit?

FIGURE 11.1

If your 3DS MAX Reference and Tutorial manuals do not make great examples of wear and tear on an object, this may be a bad sign.

It would be easy to create perfect books in 3D Studio MAX. You could create boxes with the dimensions of the books and apply six bitmaps to the sides of each box, representing the cover and pages. But to make a book look realistic, the types of flaws described earlier would have to be incorporated somehow. It would also be easy to create a wooden table by applying a bitmap of wood to the top of a table object. But to give the wood any realism, you would have to consider what can happen to a wooden table after it has been used for a while—discolorations or stains from spilled drinks, chips and dents from things banged against its surfaces, smudges from the oils in people's hands if its surface is polished, dust settled on its surface from lack of use, and perhaps unevenness from years of moisture. All these imperfections have the potential to wage war on your perfect wood bitmap. But these "imperfections" that change "primitives" into "real things" make your scenes look more believable, more "in the world." In many ways, therefore, the study of man-made materials is the study of material and geometry corruption.

The Impact of Geometry on Realistic Materials

No matter how skillfully crafted a material you create in 3DS MAX, its believability is always at the mercy of the geometry it is applied to. If you create a fantastic denim fabric material and you apply it to a box, no one is going to believe that box is a pair of jeans. This chapter does not focus on creating elaborate material-suiting geometries, but it cannot be emphasized enough that your materials are only as realistic as the objects to which they are applied. The following sections provide just a few examples of techniques used to corrupt geometry.

Surfaces and Edge Warps

As figure 11.1 shows, many man-made objects such as books do not have perfectly flat surfaces. On books you might find pen or pencil indentations, scrapes and tears, bends or wrinkles in the paper, warped or frayed edges, and cracked seams from handling. These kinds of geometry imperfections can be created through a variety of techniques. Here are a few:

- **Warped edges.** Separate surfaces that need to be warped from the object, if necessary (for example, to create a separate surface for the top cover of a book) so that they can be treated as separate meshes. Select the vertices along the outer edges of these surfaces and apply subtle Noise modifiers to them.

- **Warped surfaces.** Try applying space warps to or using Affect Region Edit Mesh modifiers on different areas of the surface. Vary the values for different areas of the surface. Avoid symmetry to your corruption. Applying subtle Noise modifiers can also do a good job of warping surfaces.

- **Torn or bent edges.** Increase the number of mesh vertices (tessellation) to improve a surface area's capability to be bent, torn, tapered, or warped. Modifiers are only as effective as the density of vertices they treat. You can also edit faces by adding and subtracting vertices to and from a surface to create tears and seams in it.

- **Objects that only need the edges warped.** Create Trim objects around the original objects and apply Noise modifiers, warps, and mesh vertex editing, as necessary, to these much smaller objects, rather than to the larger ones. Figure 11.2 shows an example of the way smaller objects at the perimeter of larger ones can eliminate the need to distort in great detail the high segment values of those larger objects.

FIGURE 11.2

Instead of applying Noise modifiers to large objects with huge vertex counts, use Trim objects to corrupt a large object's edges.

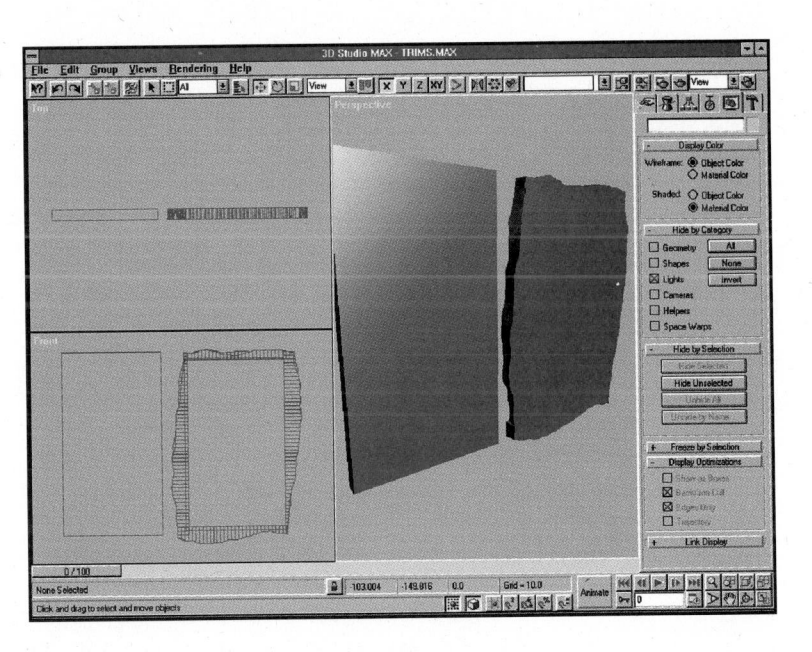

This use of Trim objects can save incredible refresh time and rendering time. Also, instead of increasing segment values for very large objects, you can increase to workable detailed corruption values the length, width, and height segments of Trim objects. This works beautifully as long as the Trim objects and the original objects have perfectly matching seams.

Object Dents and Cracks

Examine figure 11.3. Notice that the bricks are chipped and cracked in several places. Even brand-new materials (such as bricks) may have these types of imperfections. A new material is not necessarily a flawless material. Flaws often lend the desired character to a material.

Here are some techniques to create these types of corruptions at the geometry level:

■ **Chips on flat surfaces.** Create objects with high fractal (spiked) noise values and use them as Subtraction objects to take chunks and chips out of flat surfaces. Collapse the stack, if necessary, to keep the resulting object frugal with memory.

- **Splits and seams.** When you're using Loft objects, use open-ended shapes along the path to create splits and seams. On existing Mesh objects, try deleting a few vertices and moving vertices that surround the gap closer together to "almost close the hole."

- **Dents.** After a dent or chip has been carved out of an object, try applying a regional Noise modifier to the dented area by using a Volume Select modifier.

FIGURE 11.3
Brand new bricks for a fireplace often have cracks and chips in them.

Rounded Corners

Two of the most important corruptions you can create in materials are smoothings and rounded edges. Even if an object came with rigid corners, after a time of use its perfect edges may have been worn down to more rounded edges. It is easy to draw loft profile shapes without taking time to create small rounded fillets, but these tiny time-consuming edits are the very things that allow light to dance more realistically off an object and its material. The shower rail in figure 11.4 could easily be drawn with a sharp-cornered profile, but the thin reflective streaks along it are the result of very small rounded edges.

FIGURE 11.4
Although the rounded fillets of this rail are tiny, the reflection they cause is significant.

Shown in figure 11.5 is how the corners of a shower rail loft shape profile were refined to create rounded corners. This type of small refinement can impact even the simplest material's ability to reflect light more realistically.

FIGURE 11.5
Three vertices per corner were used to create these rounded fillets.

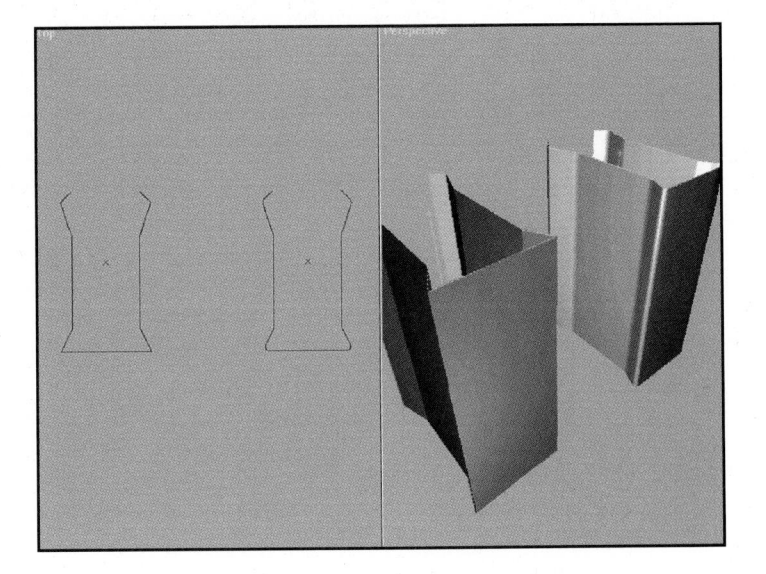

Bulges

Bulges are one of the easiest corruptions you can make to geometry. By applying Bend and Taper modifiers to the surfaces of objects, you can give a surface more character. Grab your favorite thin cardboard tea box or a milk carton and examine to see how the cardboard paper is folded and glued so that the material overlaps and bulges. Notice that the paper material has a visible thickness, and that the lid and the sides cave in or outward to accommodate the folding, leaving gaps everywhere that reveal more of the material maps applied than a "perfect" box primitive would. Figure 11.6 shows how such a tea box might be created with successive Edit Mesh and Bend modifiers applied to the sides of a box-shaped Loft object to bulge its sides. The lid is created with a separate tessellated mesh surface.

FIGURE 11.6

Cartons and packaging rarely look like perfectly orthogonal geometry.

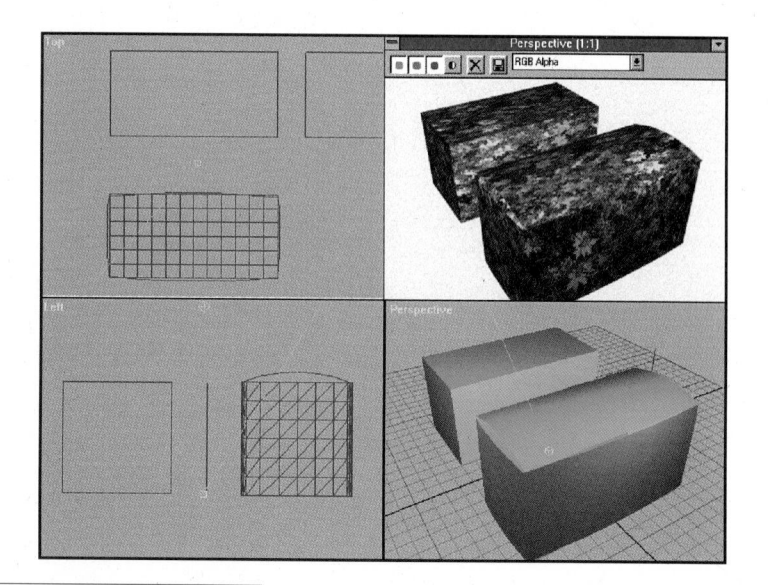

Surface Wrinkles and Folds

Many materials, especially fabrics, get most of their believability from the way the geometry to which they are applied undulates in random directions. Unless you want all your 3DS MAX fabrics to look as though they were soaked in starch for a year, crinkling, wrinkling, and folding geometry are crucial meshworking techniques. Figure 11.7 shows two rectangular meshes to which the same planar acrylic material has been applied. The rectangular mesh on the left was treated with successive applications of Edit Mesh modifiers and Noise modifiers using different Z axis strengths and applied over different areas of the mesh, and by applying a MeshSmooth modifier with "relaxing" over the final mesh.

FIGURE 11.7
Billowy acrylic fabric created from billowy geometry.

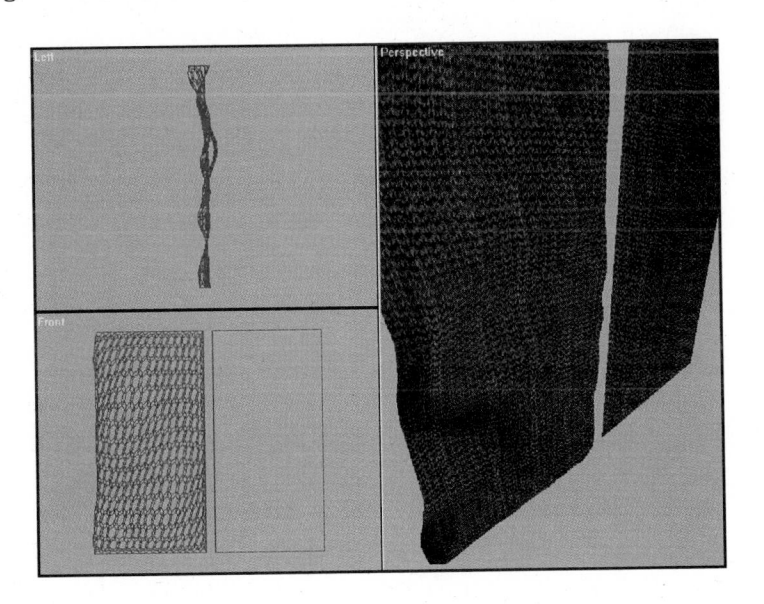

NOTE

The more you look at a material in the real world, the more its imperfect details become apparent. Take a digital camera out to a site where the objects you are trying to create are located. Take close-up photographs of them and view these images as you create the geometry for them. This can have as profound an impact on the resulting image as any bitmap you might apply to the object. When possible, have an example of the material in front of you.

Material Corruption Techniques

This portion of the chapter provides several tutorials to show how to create smears on shiny surfaces, discolorations in a material, puddles of liquid on a material, dusty materials, and dented and warped materials. These techniques can also be modified to create other types of material corruptions such as rot, rust, cracks, and streaks. The tutorials use the two bitmaps shown in figure 11.8 to create all corruptions treated. These types of bitmaps can be generated with any paint program that can export Truevision Targa (.TGA) files with alpha channel.

FIGURE 11.8
These two corruption bitmaps were generated with an airbrush tool in Animator Studio.

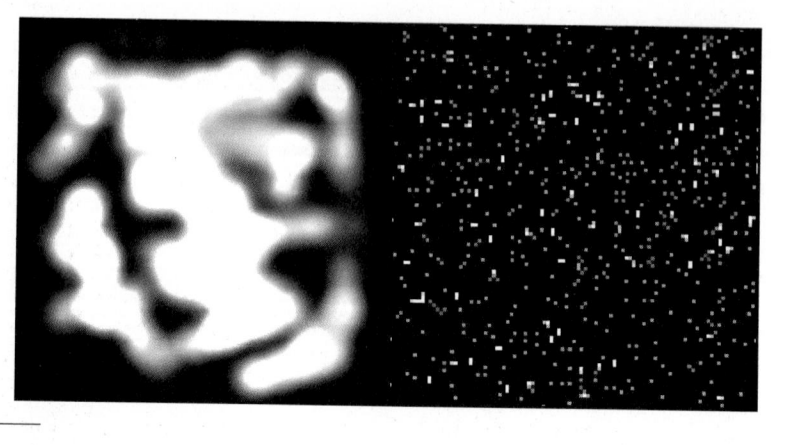

Discolorations

Discolorations in your materials can be the result of prolonged exposure to heat or moisture, defects in the material itself, or other materials resting on it. This technique creates stains, abrasions, spills, and other effects through variations in the RGB levels of bitmaps and the use of masks. Two blocks are used for these tutorials. The vertical wall block has the Kinetix logo on it, and the horizontal floor block is used for the corrupted materials. The floor block starts with a gray material.

CREATING DISCOLORATION

1. Open file 11CORRUP.MAX from the *Inside 3D Studio MAX Volume II* CD. Right-click on the Camera viewport to make it active. Then, on the main toolbar, click on the Render Scene button and then on the Material Editor button.

2. Make certain that the second sample slot (top middle) is selected. In the Maps rollout menu, click on the Diffuse button, select Composite from the Material/Map Browser, and then click on OK. In the Composite Parameters rollout menu, click on the Set Number button and set the value to 2.

3. Click on the Map 1 button, select Mask from the Material/Map Browser, and then click on OK.

4. In the Parameters rollout menu, click on the Map button; select Bitmap from the Material/Map Browser, and click on OK. In the Bitmap Parameters rollout menu, click on the Bitmap button and select the file \3DSMAX\MAPS\ASHSEN_2.GIF. This is a bitmap supplied with 3DS MAX.

5. Click on the Go To Parent button beneath the sample slots. Click on the Mask button, select Bitmap from the Material/Map Browser, and click on OK. In the Bitmap Parameters rollout menu, click on the Bitmap button and select the file 11IMX08A.BMP from the accompanying CD. Make certain that this file is in a legal Maps directory.

NOTE

You can disable the Show End Result button beneath the sample slots to see how the material is behaving as you construct it, level by level.

6. Click on the Go To Parent button beneath the sample slots. If Show End Result is disabled, an area of the sample slot now displays dark wood. Click on the Go To Parent button again. This takes you back to the Composite Parameters rollout menu, where you define the other half of the material.

7. Click on the Map 2 button, select Mask from the Material/Map Browser, and then click on OK. In the Parameters rollout menu, click on the Map button, select Bitmap from the Material/Map Browser, and then click on OK.

8. In the Bitmap Parameters rollout menu, click on the Bitmap button and select the file \3DSMAX\MAPS\ASHSEN_2.GIF. Open the Output rollout menu beneath the Bitmap Parameters rollout menu and set the RGB Level to a value of 2.0.

9. Click on the Go To Parent button beneath the sample slots. Click on the Mask button, select Bitmap from the Material/Map Browser, and then click on OK.

10. In the Bitmap Parameters rollout menu, click on the Bitmap button and select the file 11IMX08A.BMP. Open the Output rollout menu beneath the Bitmap Parameters rollout menu, and toggle Invert on.

11. Double-click on the Go To Parent button beneath the sample slots. You can now see streaks of brighter wood in the sample slot.

12. Make certain that the floor box is selected. Click on the Assign Material to Selection button beneath the sample slots, and render the Camera viewport. Figure 11.9 shows the discoloration.

FIGURE 11.9

By using masked areas of the same material with different RGB levels of the material, you can create discolorations in the material.

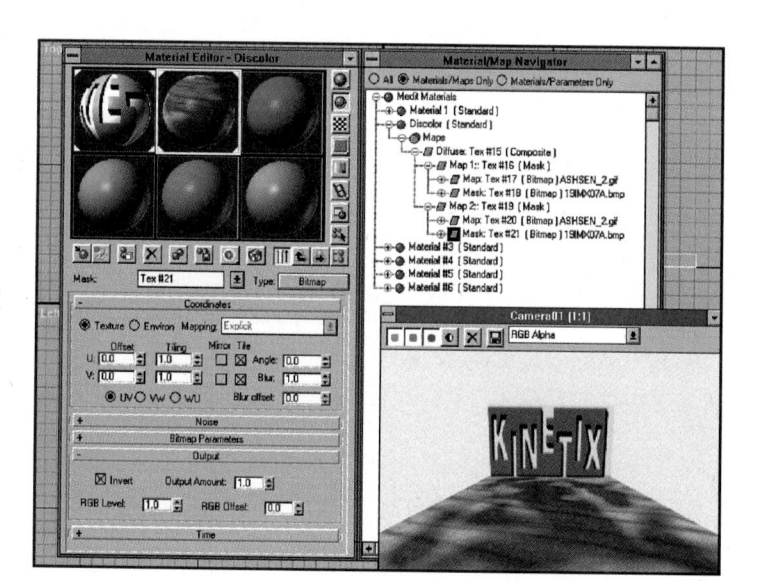

NOTE

For a variation on this technique to create stains, try setting the RGB level to a value between 0.0 and 1.0 instead of increasing the RGB level of the wood bitmap in the Output rollout menu.

Blurry Puddles and Smudges

Whether you are trying to create puddles of water, blurry smudges on polished surfaces, or varying levels of reflectivity in a material, the following technique, which uses a flat mirror and masks, serves a variety of purposes. Because this technique uses a flat mirror for regional reflection control, the entire material must be created not as a Standard material but as a Multi/Sub-Object material.

CREATING PUDDLES

1. Open file 11CORRUP.MAX from the accompanying CD. Right-click on the Camera viewport. Click on the Material Editor button on the main toolbar. Make certain that the second sample slot (top middle) is selected, and click on the Get Material button beneath the sample slots.

2. Select Multi/Sub-Object from the Material/Map Browser, and click on OK. In the basic Parameters rollout menu, click on the Set Number button and set the value to 1.

3. Click on the Material 1 button. In the Maps rollout menu, click on the Diffuse button, click on Mask, and then click on OK in the Material/Map Browser.

NOTE

You can disable the Show End Result button beneath the sample slots to see how the material is behaving as you construct it level by level.

4. In the Parameters rollout menu, click on the Map button, click on Bitmap, and then click on OK in the Material/Map Browser.

5. In the Bitmap Parameters rollout menu, click on the Bitmap button and select the file \3DSMAX\MAPS\CONCGREN.JPG. This is a bitmap supplied with 3DS MAX.

6. Click on the Go To Parent button beneath the sample slots. Click on the Mask button, click on Bitmap, and then click on OK in the Material/Map Browser.

7. In the Bitmap Parameters rollout menu, click on the Bitmap button and select the file 11IMX08A.BMP. In the Output rollout menu beneath the Bitmap Parameters rollout menu, toggle on Invert. Click on the Go To Parent button. If Show End Result is turned off, you can now see where the concrete material will show through.

8. Click on the Go To Parent button again. The main Maps rollout menu is displayed.

9. Click on the Diffuse button; then hold down the Pick button, drag until the boundary of the button is over the Bump Map button, and release. At the prompt, create an Instance of the Diffuse material so that values that change in the Diffuse channel will change also in the Bump channel. Set the value of the bump map to 100.

NOTE
Remember that the top limit for a bump map value is 999, not 100.

10. Make certain that the floor block is selected. Click on the Assign Material to Selected button under the sample slots, and render the Camera viewport. The gray areas define the puddles of water.

11. In the Maps rollout menu, click on the Reflection button, then on Mask, and then on OK in the Material/Map Browser.

12. In the Parameters rollout menu, click on the Map button, on Flat Mirror, and then on OK in the Material/Map Browser. The Blur value will be changed later to control the clarity of the reflection.

13. Click on the Go To Parent button. Click on the Mask button, on Bitmap, and then click on OK in the Material/Map Browser. In the Bitmap Parameters rollout menu, click on the Bitmap button and select the file 11IMX08A.BMP.

14. Double-click on the Go To Parent button to display the main Maps rollout menu.

15. Right-click on the Camera viewport, and click on Render Scene on the main toolbar. Now the white puddles on the concrete perfectly reflect the Kinetix logo. To change the color of the water reflecting the logo, decrease the value of the reflection map from 100 to 20. This reveals more of the material's main diffuse color (gray). To change the murkiness of the water, increase the Blur value of the flat mirror. Click on the Reflection Map button, click on the Map button, and change the Blur value to 10.0.

16. Double-click on the Go To Parent button, and render the Camera viewport. Your scene should resemble the one in figure 11.10.

The technique used to create smudges is similar to the puddle technique. The only difference is that the diffuse map uses a bitmap material rather than a masked material. By decreasing the value of the reflection map, therefore, the material bitmap shows through rather than the global diffuse color. To create oil stains on a wooden table, make the following changes to the current material:

FIGURE 11.10

The global diffuse color of the material determines the color of the reflecting material when the reflection map value is decreased.

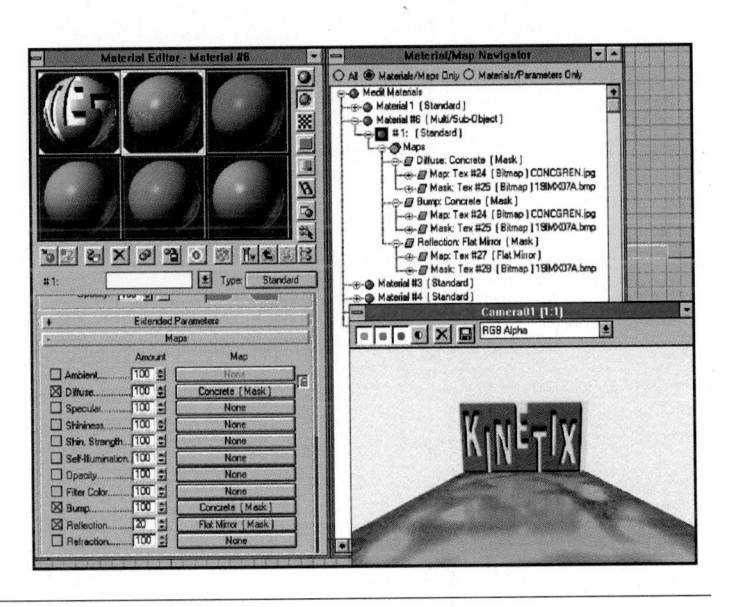

CREATING OIL STAINS

1. Click on the Diffuse Map button, and then click on the Type button. Select Bitmap and click on OK in the Material/Map Browser. In the Bitmap Parameters rollout menu, select the wood bitmap file you used earlier (named \3DSMAX\MAPS\ASHSEN_2.GIF). Click on the Go To Parent button.

2. Pick on any map button labeled with the word None, and drag the button boundary over the Bump Map button, thereby setting *it* to None. This will make the wooden surface smooth.

3. Set the Reflection Map Value to 30, and render the Camera viewport. The reflective areas of the surface now give the illusion of oily or polished spots on the wood (see fig. 11.11).

FIGURE 11.11

Variations in the flat mirror's blur value and the value of the reflection map can create a wide range of material blemishes.

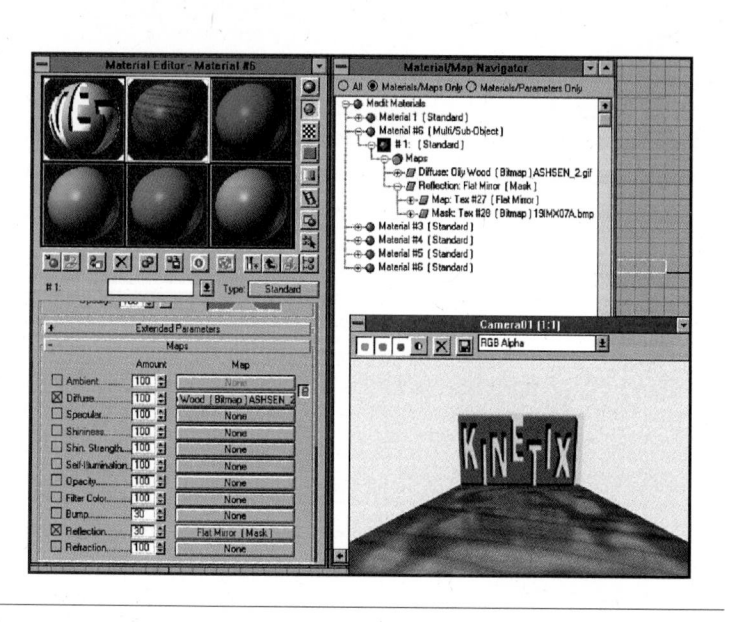

Scorch Marks and Dents

Chips and dents in the geometry can determine in a crucial manner the believability of some materials, especially when those chips and dents occur along the edges of an object. You can achieve a surprising degree of realism also by taking advantage of the Dent map type.

DENTS

1. Open file 11CORRUP.MAX from the accompanying CD. Right-click on the Camera viewport. Make certain that the second sample slot (top middle) is selected, and click on the Get Material button beneath the sample slots. Select Standard from the Material/Map Browser, and click on OK.

2. In the Maps rollout menu, click on the Diffuse button, click on Dent, and then click on OK in the Material/Map Browser. In the Dent Parameters rollout menu, set Size to a value of 1000, set Strength to a value of 5, and set Iterations to a value of 10.

3. Click on the Swap button to switch the white and black colors of the Dent map. Click on the Color 1 Maps button, click on Bitmap, and then click on OK in the Material/Map Browser. In the Bitmap Parameters rollout menu, select the wood bitmap file you used before (named \3DSMAX\MAPS\ASHSEN_2.GIF).

4. Double-click on the Go To Parent button to return to the main Maps rollout menu. Make certain that the floor box is selected, and then click on the Assign Material to Selection button beneath the sample slots.

5. Click on the Render Scene button of the main toolbar. The Dent map adds "scorch marks" to the wood material. To really get the effect of an indentation, you can recycle the diffuse map as a bump map and take chunks out of the object's edges (see fig. 11.12).

FIGURE 11.12

Actual nonrectilinear dents in the geometry edges and surfaces can be achieved easily by creating subtraction objects from severely deformed Noise-modified spheres.

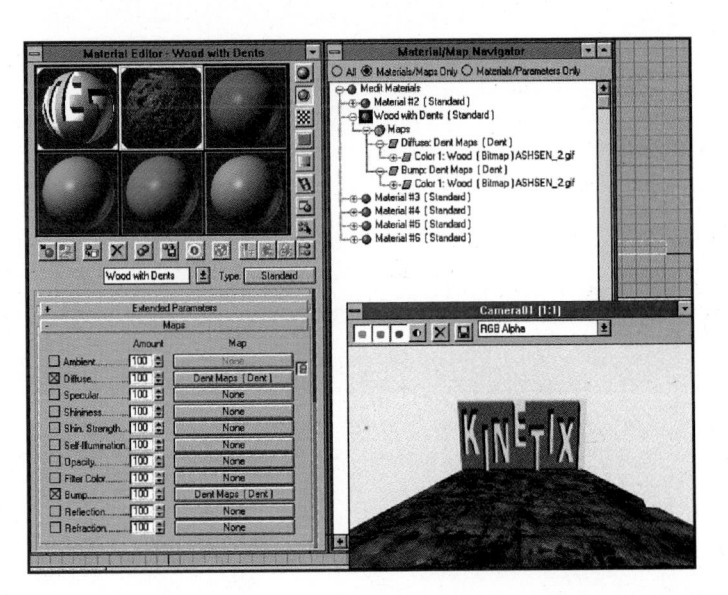

6. Click on the Diffuse button, hold down the Pick button, drag until the boundary of the button is over the bump map button, and then release.

7. At the prompt, create an Instance of the Diffuse material so that values which change in the Diffuse channel change in the Bump channel also. Set the value of the bump map to 100. Render the Camera viewport.

Dust

Creating dust and debris on materials is easy to do with composite materials that use maps with alpha channel information. If a corruption map is a Targa (.TGA) file with alpha information, it can be applied in the same way a decal is applied (but, in this case, to dirty up a surface).

DUST

1. Open file 11CORRUP.MAX from the accompanying CD. Right-click over the Camera viewport. Make certain that the second sample slot (top middle) is selected. Click on the Get Material button beneath the sample slots. Select Standard from the Material/Map Browser, and click on OK.

2. In the Maps rollout menu, click on the Diffuse button, click on Composite, and then click on OK in the Material/Map Browser. In the Composite Parameters rollout menu, click on the Set Number button, and set the value to 2. In Composite maps, higher-numbered maps overlay lower-numbered maps; the dusty material will take the Map 2 slot and the wooden material will take the Map 1 slot.

3. Click on the Map 1 button, select Bitmap from the Material/Map Browser, and click on OK. In the Bitmap Parameters rollout menu, click on the Bitmap button, and select the wooden bitmap file named \3DSMAX\MAPS\ASHSEN_2.GIF.

4. Click on the Go To Parent button beneath the sample slots. Then click on the Map 2 button, select Bitmap from the Material/Map Browser, and click on OK. In the Bitmap Parameters rollout menu, click on the Bitmap button and select the file 11IMX08B.TGA. Make certain that this file is in a legal Maps directory.

NOTE

To verify the alpha channel data in file 11IMX08B.TGA, use the File, View File pull-down menu option and pick on the file 11IMX08B.TGA. When the image is displayed, use the Display Alpha Channel button to show the white-to-black levels of opacity in the image. In purely white areas, nothing will show through. In purely black areas, any materials underneath will show through completely. Gray areas are areas of partial opacity. Close the image window.

5. Make certain that the floor box is selected. Click on the Assign Material to Selection button beneath the sample slots, and render the Camera viewport. This image demonstrates the way basic decals are applied to materials. If the desired effect is a crisp clean image of the corruption map, the corrupting map must account for areas in the image in which edges meet the underlying material. By softening and anti-aliasing the opaque areas in the corruption map, you can avoid sharp, jagged edges where the overlapping material meets the underlying material. To create the illusion of a thin veil of dust, however, tiling, dimming, and blurring of the corruption map are necessary.

6. In the Coordinates rollout menu, set the U and V tiling values to 3.0, and set the Blur Offset value to 0.1. In the Output rollout menu, set the RGB Level to 0.9. Render the Camera viewport. The specks in the corruption map have been blurred by the expanded tiling, and the RGB Level change has reduced each speck's density (see fig. 11.13). Save this file for use in the weathering tutorial to follow.

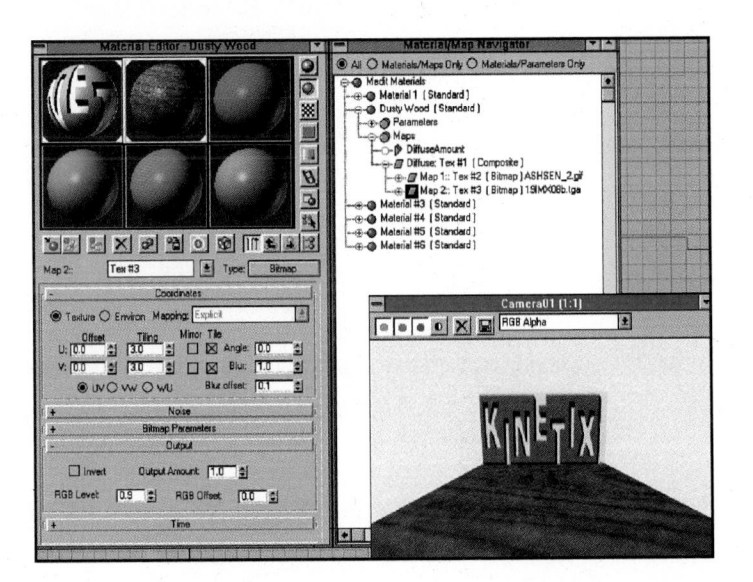

FIGURE 11.13

Varying densities in the alpha channel of the corruption map can create very different effects, from dust to large snowflakes.

NOTE

The Blur Offset value should be used like Tabasco sauce in cooking: go easy on the amount you use to get the right effect. If you were to change the Blur Offset value from 0.0 to 0.2 rather than 0.1 in this example, the dust effect would be lost.

Weathering

One of the great challenges faced by many 3DS MAX users who want to create realistic scenes is learning how to keep from giving the scenes an overwhelming sense of newness. In the same way you can apply dust and soot (try values between 0.0 and 1.0 for the RGB Level value in the corruption map of the preceding example), you can also make a material look weathered and worn. One such effect is a sort of bleaching out or fading of a material's character. To easily accomplish this effect, take advantage of a Noise map. The next set of steps builds on the preceding tutorial, picking up where it ended.

AGING OBJECTS

1. Click on the Go To Parent button to return to the Composite Parameters rollout menu. Click on the Map 2 button, and then on the Type button. Select Noise, discard the map, and click on OK in the Material/Map Browser. In the Noise Parameters rollout menu, set the Noise Type to Fractal, and set the Size to 50. In the Output rollout menu, set the Output Amount to 0.5.

2. Render the Camera viewport. The effect, shown in figure 11.14, is a bleaching or fading of the material. The two colors specified in the noise map determine the weathering color, and the Output Level determines the severity of the weathering. With values close to 1.0, you can hardly make out wood at all. This also can be a neat corruption. Increasing the size parameter creates larger patches of weathering distortion.

FIGURE 11.14

Values near 1.0 for Noise Levels create wide sweeps of weathering. Values near 5.0 create concentrated splotches of weathering.

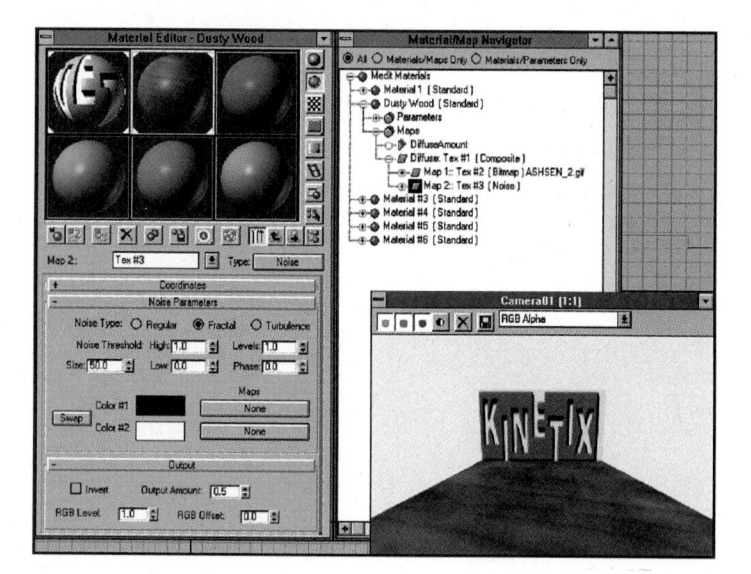

For a variation on this technique, try experimenting with different Noise types and Size values. Try a different color for Color #2, or use a bitmap for Color #2. Set global Shininess Strength to 0 to achieve a thoroughly faded material.

These are just a few examples of ways to give your man-made materials some character. Although creating these types of corruptions may seem time-consuming, paying attention to these types of details can have a huge impact on the mood of your scenes. It doesn't take long to build up a library of corruption maps that can be slapped on top of other materials for "instant grime." The real challenge is to keep notes on variable settings. Trying to remember all the possible effects that different numeric values have, applied to a given corruption map, is next to impossible. Experiment with the settings, and when you get the effect you want, take notes!

Creating Man-Made Materials

One very helpful technique for keeping track of the man-made materials you create is to use the material category as the first word of the material's name. By calling a material Concrete Gray rather than Gray Concrete, you can view the entire group of concrete materials in a scene or in a library, if necessary. Users seldom need to look at "all the red stuff" in a library, but often need to look at all the woods, all the concretes, all the glass, or all the plastic materials. Using a consistent set of properties in the material names (such as the material's color and texture) also proves helpful. Having Concrete Gray Grooved, Concrete Gray Smooth, and Concrete Gray Grainy together in a list of materials for a scene or in a library materials can save a great deal of time when you try to find them by color or texture. Some users take this approach to the next level by creating copies of their libraries organized by material category, by color, and by texture. The same material might be named Concrete Gray Grooved in one library, Gray Concrete Grooved in another, and Grooved Concrete Gray in a third. In this way, you can find a material if you know any one of its three main properties.

One of the easiest ways to get your hands dirty with man-made materials is to examine the materials supplied with 3DS MAX in the default materials library. From metals to woods to ceramic tiles, wonderful examples are already assembled on your hard drive. These materials can show you how map types, settings and parameters, and bitmaps can be combined to give surfaces the appearance you want. This section outlines techniques (and variations on those techniques) for creating a variety of man-made materials. Each material category includes examples of diverse material types, a few techniques, and some examples (including corruption considerations) of how to create the material.

NOTE

Frequently, you will need bitmaps of the materials you want to create. For suggestions on how to acquire bitmaps, refer to Chapter 9, "Materials Management and Manipulation."

Concretes

Concretes are one of the quickest man-made materials to create. The 3DS MAX library provides some good examples of concrete, and many architectural material libraries have a collection of different concretes with common textures; Autodesk's Texture Universe (see fig. 11.15) is an example. Some examples of concrete textures include smooth walls, porous CMU block, raked pavement, and sidewalks with tarred seams.

FIGURE 11.15
Concretes come in many different colors. The key consideration for realism is texture, controlled primarily by bump maps.

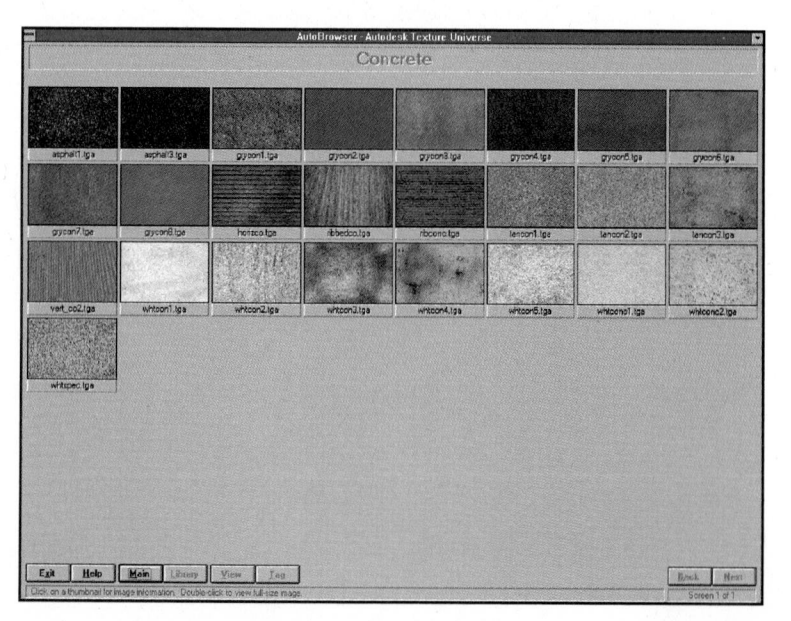

Creation Techniques

Concrete can be created quickly by using a bitmap of the concrete texture for a diffuse map, and recycling it for a bump map to control the texture. Slippery or smooth concrete can be shiny. You can apply a Noise map or a concentrated Dent map for different concrete textures. This works especially well for long strips or wide surfaces of concrete. For CMU and other grainy concrete, a fibrous bitmap used as a bump map works very well and can be generated in minutes with Noise maps of small size values (see fig. 11.16). File CMU.MAX is provided on the accompanying CD for a quick example. For raked driveways, sidewalks, and porches, tileable grooved bump maps work well; seams and cracks can easily be draped over as decal-style materials.

FIGURE 11.16
An example of a fibrous bump map used to create a grainy concrete masonry unit.

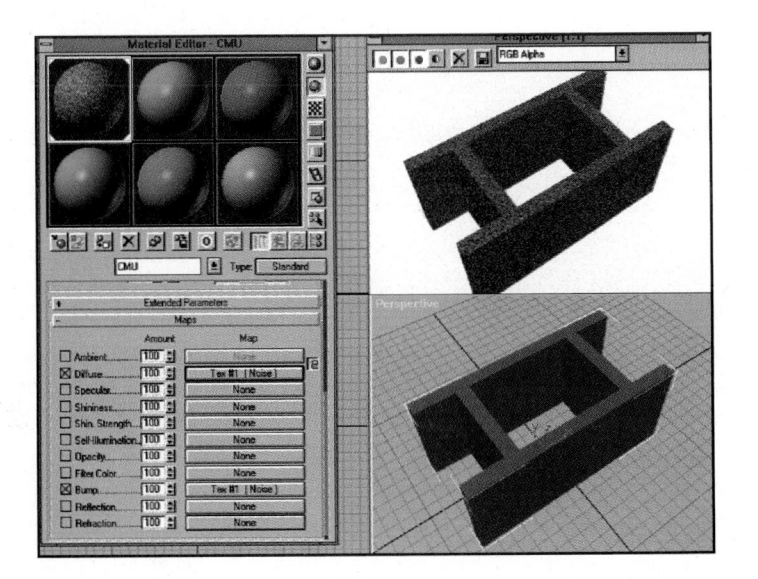

Corruptions

Concrete often has water or oil stains, cracks, chips, or uneven expansion slots. Concrete also collects puddles. It may be covered with debris and have discolorations from heavily used areas. Concrete textures also vary widely from smooth to porous.

Paper and Cardboard

One of the trickiest things about creating paper materials is addressing the material's thickness. For thin paper materials such as bond, a 0.0 height patch grid will usually work with an applied subtle bond texture. For thicker paper materials such as milk cartons and cardboard packaging, however, the geometry gets more complicated.

Creation Techniques

Creating a sheet of paper can be as simple as creating a flat patch grid with a bitmap of what is on the paper. On the other hand, the process is more complicated when you create "sturdier" paper, such as the corrugated packaging cardboard used for heavy shipments. For sheets or reams of paper, use patch grid connected at the seams. This gives you the ability to bend, fold, or bulge edges or areas on the sheet, if necessary. Subtle Noise modifiers can add a hint of realism to sheets sitting on flat surfaces. One way to make cardboard geometry is to create the cardboard profile as a shape and generate a lofted object for the sheet (see fig. 11.17). File CARDBORD.MAX on the accompanying CD provides a simple guide to this method. Widely spaced, subtle dents lend believability to cardboard.

FIGURE 11.17
Cardboard surfaces rarely stay flat. The key to realism in a paper material is the way its geometry sits on truly flat surfaces.

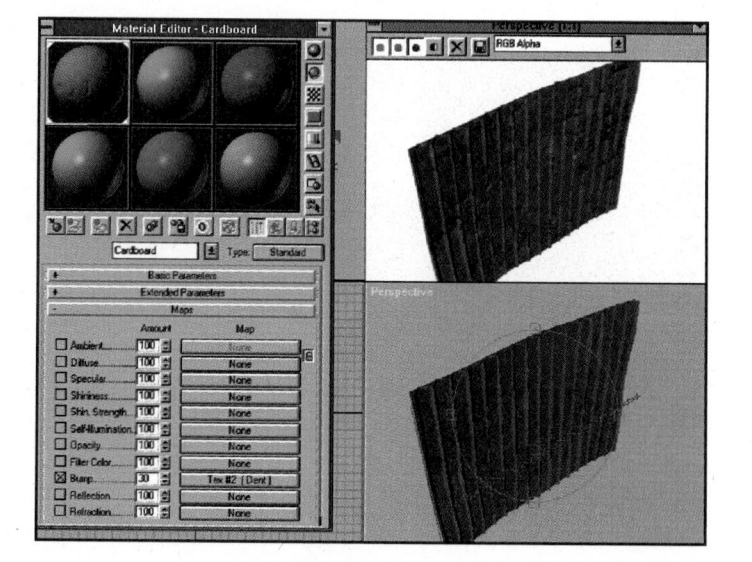

Corruptions

Paper-type materials can be stained, waterlogged, indented, punctured, folded, wrinkled, smudged, and rolled. Surfaces can range from shiny lamination to dull packaging. On some paper objects, especially those used for packaging, rounded corners and subtle bulging can make all the difference in the world. Try to avoid perfectly orthogonal surfaces; most paper materials are not metal-stiff. Widely spread-out dents and bended edges are classic corruptions.

Woods

Half the challenge of getting a wooden material to look right is having the right bitmap. Wood, being an organic material, can be an extremely difficult pattern to tile seamlessly. Many users will use a high-resolution bitmap to cover an entire object rather than try to use a low-resolution bitmap that is tiled. By purchasing a collection of seamless tileable wooden materials such as those shown in figure 11.18, you can expand significantly your ability to create and work with wooden materials, because creating tileable and seamless wood bitmaps yourself can be very time-consuming.

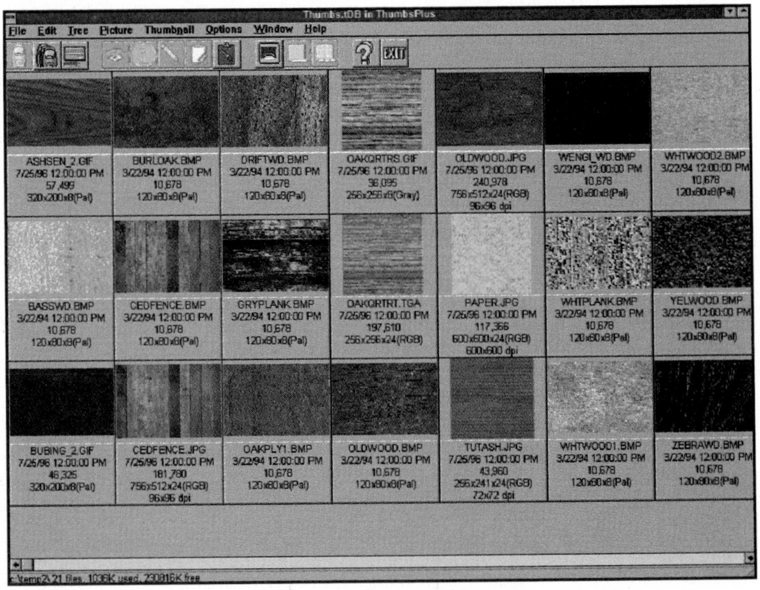

FIGURE 11.18

If you intend to do much work with woods, a collection of tileable wood bitmaps is an excellent investment.

Examples of wood materials include smooth maple desktops, rain-weathered knotted pine fences, punctured cork, patterned floor tiles, dull oak, fake wood laminate, unpolished balsa, chopped logs, sawdust, and grainy plywood.

Creation Techniques

The 3DS MAX default library contains a wide assortment of wooden materials you can look at for examples. If you cannot get a tileable wood bitmap, try to work with wood bitmaps large enough to accommodate the entire object, so as to avoid seams that don't match seams. To apply a wooden planar map to an object with a minimum of streaking, an old trick is to apply the bitmap UVW modifier at an oblique angle to all flat sides of the object. Wood tiling works quite well on floors, walls, and other horizontal surfaces. For unusually shaped wooden objects, use of the Wood map type also can be helpful. To create wood laminates, apply raw wood bitmaps to perfectly flat surfaces; this effect looks intentionally fake.

Corruptions

Woods are easy materials to corrupt. Wood corruptions can include smudges, warps, stains, discolorations, weathering, scratches, chips, dents, scorchings, rough or oily patches, and dust. Examples of these corruptions are discussed in this chapter's tutorials.

Stones

The ability to creating man-made stone materials that have been polished or cut depends in large part on the stone bitmap's detail. For stone types with thin veins of different colors, higher resolutions are a must. Stone materials of stones arranged in patterns pose the same types of challenges that wooden materials do—both materials are difficult to seam and tile realistically. Again, the purchase of a stone materials collection can save you a tremendous amount of time.

Examples of stone materials include translucent and refractive diamonds, metallic and shiny marbles, grainy and dull pebbles, streaked basalts and sharp-cornered crystals, fine sand and sandstones, and petrified wood.

Creation Technique

You can create diamonds of different colors by using lathing diamond profiles and applying reflection or refraction maps (see fig. 11.19). The material requires strong shininess and opacity values, and the filter color determines the color of the "glass." Geometry for believable stones, rocks, and even asteroids can be generated easily by applying strong Noise modifiers along all three axes to a sphere (see fig. 11.20). Grainy stone materials and marbles also can be achieved through the use of Noise and Marble map types. Sand bitmaps work well applied as diffuse maps and bump maps.

FIGURE 11.19

The more facets the diamond geometry has, the more it can play with spectral reflections.

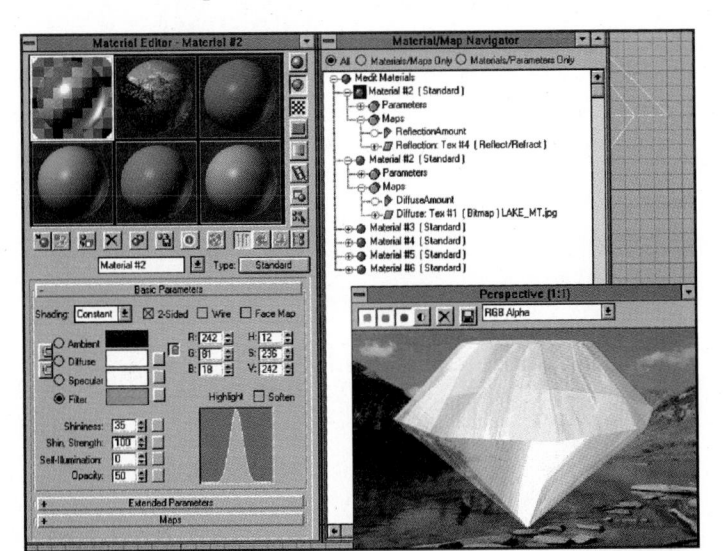

FIGURE 11.20

By using different colors for the Noise diffuse map, you can create very different stone textures.

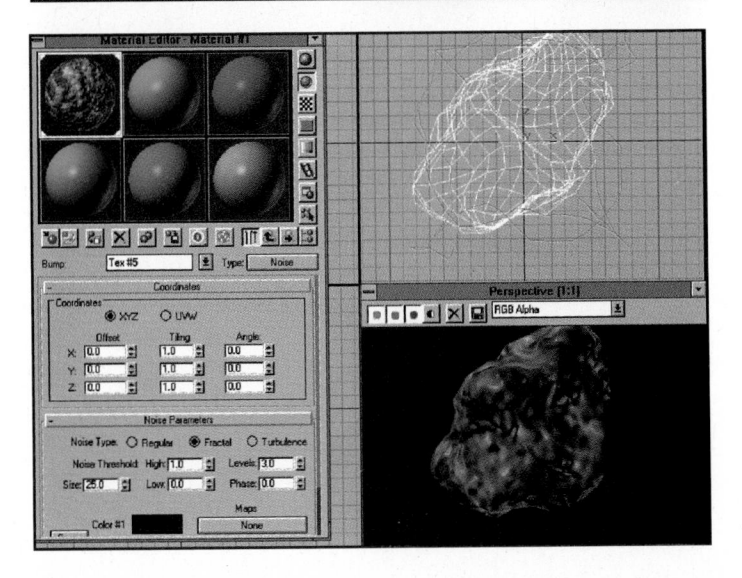

Corruptions

Stones, like woods, are easy materials to corrupt. Corruptions can include smudges, warps, stains, discolorations, weathering, scratches, chips, scorchings, rough or oily patches, and dust. Examples of these corruptions are discussed in this chapter's tutorials.

Plastics

Shininess and opacity play major roles in determining a material's plasticity. The 3DS MAX default library contains several examples of plastics (including shiny, dull, and mottled). Because plastics typically absorb a great deal of light, a hint of ambient light in a scene can dramatically enhance a plastic material's appearance.

Examples of plastic materials include the shiny solid plastic of telephones; the dull, textured, semitransparent plastic of milk jugs; crinkled clear plastic, such as that used for "zippered" storage bags; the tinted plastics used in small accessories for offices; and the mottled, blurry, semitransparent plastic of shower doors.

Creation Techniques

Solid plastics are fairly easy to create using full opacity. When you create plastic lights, rely on the material's self-illumination settings. Blur values are more important that any other factor in making semitransparent and clear plastics believable, and the plastic's geometry can make or break its realism. Figure 11.21 shows an example of how a Patch grid object, tessellated repeatedly with tri and quad patches and corrupted with Noise and Bend modifiers, can be used with a transparent, highly reflective material to create plastic wrap. Note how crucial the materials and backdrop color behind the wrap are to giving it a sense of transparency. File PLASWRAP.MAX on the accompanying CD can be used as a reference for creating crinkly materials such as plastic wrap and aluminum!

Corruptions

Corruptions can include rips and rough edges, crinkles, cuts and dents, stains, blurred textures, and streaks. The weathering techniques outlined earlier in this chapter can be used very effectively on plastics.

FIGURE 11.21

If you intend to work often with plastics, purchasing a collection of tileable plastic bitmaps is a good idea.

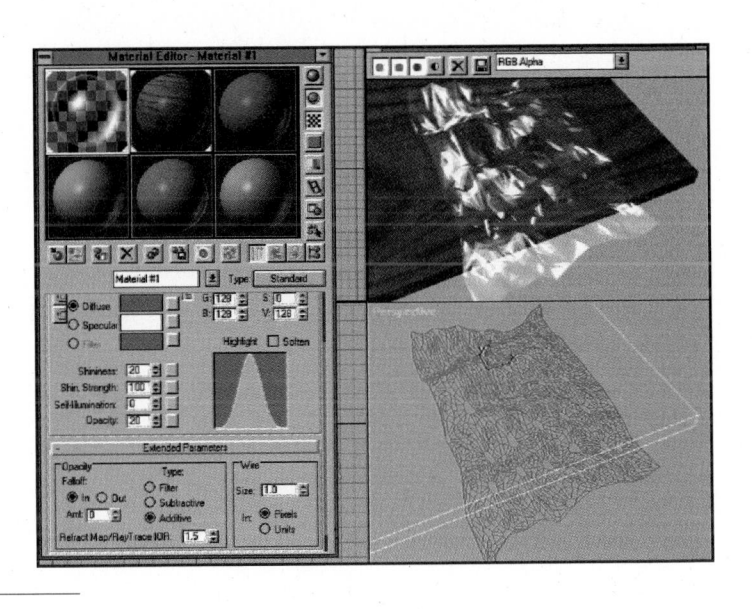

Rubber and Vinyl

Among the easiest types of materials to create are matte materials, such as rubber and vinyl. These can be generated by using small Shininess Strength values with wide spectral areas. Rubber and vinyl objects are more likely to have punctures and tears in them than folds or wrinkles, and rarely are these materials perfectly flat.

Examples of rubber and vinyl materials include tires, furniture coverings, tabletop surfaces, floor stripping, and cartridges.

Creation Techniques

To create a typical rubber material, you can use the default materials in the sample slots with a smaller value for Shininess. Experiment with this value; it can make the difference between a vinyl and a plastic. In the file VINYL.MAX on the accompanying CD, each of the sample slot materials has had its Shininess value set to 20 in the Material Editor. By applying subtle Checker maps, Dent maps, or Noise maps, you can add a grid of graininess or ribbon of wear-and-tear to the surfaces to which the material is applied. Figure 11.22 shows a vinyl shield collar whose rounded edges and bulged surfaces enable the material's dull specular highlights to stand out.

FIGURE 11.22
By using different Material IDs assigned to different faces of mesh objects, you can control which areas of the vinyl are smooth and which are bumpy.

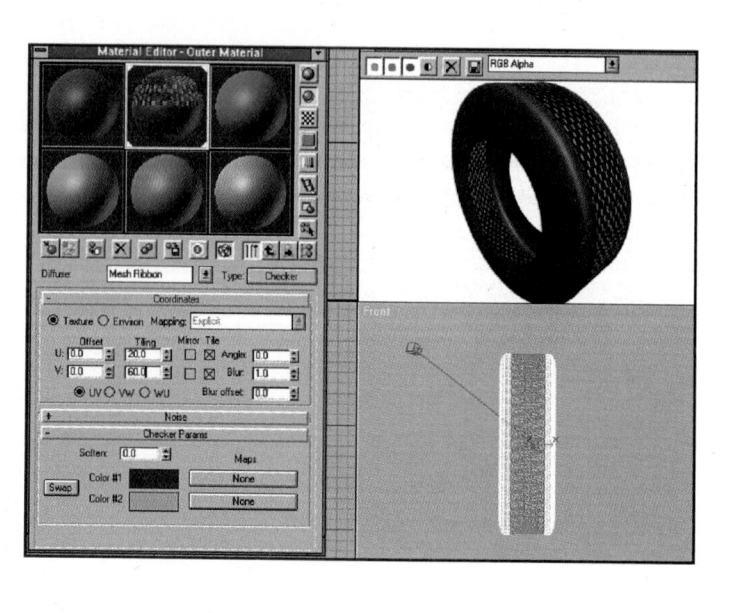

Corruptions

Corruptions include streaks, slashes, punctures, dents, cuts, oily spots, and abrasions. Again, the weathering techniques outlined previously in this chapter work very effectively on vinyls and rubbers.

Glass

Many examples of glass materials are provided in the 3DS MAX default library. The tutorials in the middle of this chapter also treat refraction techniques. Typical challenges a user faces to creating glasswork are obtaining believable refraction of materials behind glass, creating a glass thickness at edges of the object, blurring of images through glass, and glass corruptions.

Examples of glass materials include warped jars, tinted and leaded oven window glass, dot-matrixed textured glass, ceramics, frosted crystal, opaque mixing bowls, textured shower doors, and stained-glass windows.

Creation Techniques

Typical glass materials use mid to low Opacity settings, a two-sided material to create specular highlights through the material, and mid to high levels of Shininess. The Extended Parameters rollout menu has crucial settings that control a glass material's tinting, refraction, and opacity fall-off. A thorough examination of these values is provided in Chapter 21 of *Inside 3D Studio MAX Volume I*, under "Opacity Parameters." Used with subtlety, composite materials (decals) are an easy way to frost, texture, smudge, and blur glass materials. For static scenes, you can get away with murder by using 2D paint programs to create post-processed glass effects. Do not underestimate these types of techniques! They are fast and effective.

One old trick often used to create the illusion of a textured blurry glass material is to render the scene without the glass and use a 2D paint program's brightening, jumbling, tinting, and softening tools in the "glass area" (see fig. 11.23). Autodesk's Animator Studio makes successive applications of different inks to the same areas a cinch with its Repeat Ink application feature. Many refraction and reflection filter inks are also available for these types of raster-editing programs. File CERAMICS.MAX on the accompanying CD shows how the default Glass material can be varied to create a ceramic glass material (see fig. 11.24). IOR values between 0.5 and 1.0 work well for refraction and reflection maps used this way. Loading the default Glass material and experimenting with its values is a great way to discover new types of glass materials.

FIGURE 11.23
Painting glass effects into a static scene can be quick and powerful.

FIGURE 11.24
By using refraction and reflection maps in a glass material, you can create the illusion of textured or opaque glass materials, such as polished ceramics.

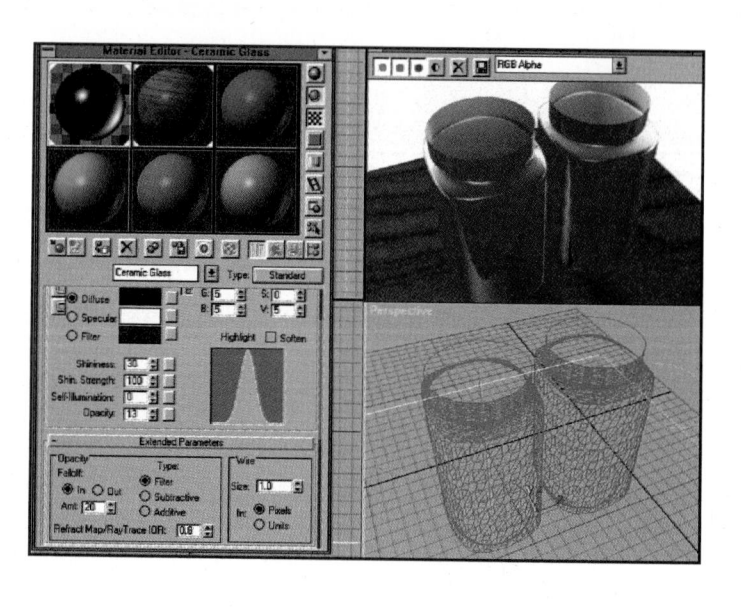

Corruptions

Corruptions include cracks, stains, condensation, oily smears and streaks, dust and rain marks, warping, bulges, and blurs. Bitmaps such as those used to create puddles, dull spots, discolorations, and dust can be applied mildly to glass surfaces to create these types of corruptions.

Metals, Meshes, and Wires

The 3DS MAX default library includes many examples that show how environment and scenery bitmaps can be manipulated to create gold, silver, chromes, and brushed and mottled metallic materials. Crumpling techniques such as the one outlined in the plastics section of this chapter can be used to create foils and crumpled metal sheets. Creating curvilinear metals is relatively easy, but creating believable flat metallic materials can be tricky.

Examples of metal, mesh, and wire materials include tin and aluminum foil, brushed metals, polished brass, dull gold, aluminum siding, stainless steel, woven metallic fabric, chromes, and rusted panels.

Creation Techniques

Materials for many of the metal, mesh, and wire examples exist in the MAX library. Many bitmap material collections contain wide assortments of metallic bitmaps, such as those shown in figure 11.25. When these bitmaps are used as diffuse maps, bump maps, and shininess maps, they make very realistic metals.

FIGURE 11.25

Metals have unlimited textures. By brightening, tinting, or smoothing existing metallic bitmaps, you can create radically new metallic-looking materials.

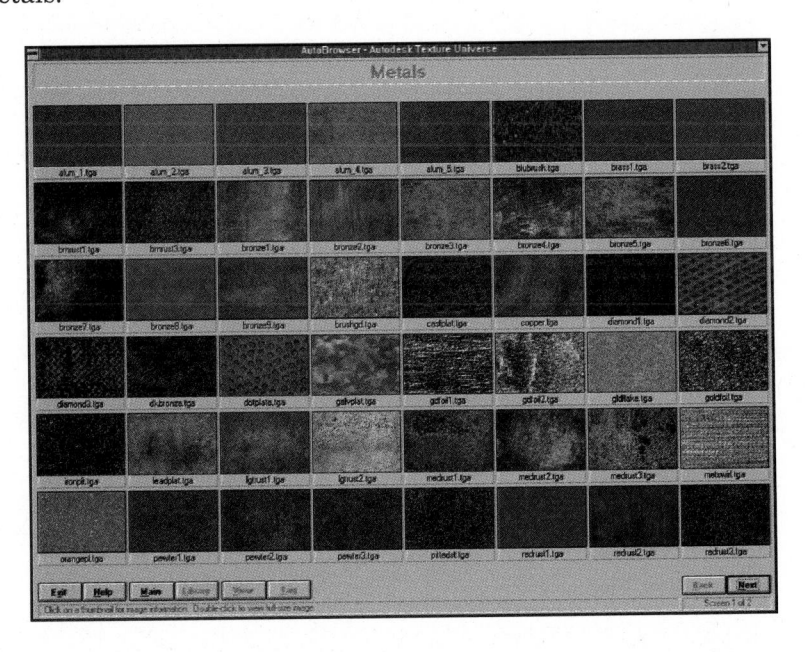

Reflective metals are easiest to create on curved surfaces because those surfaces distort the reflected environment objects and maps more drastically than flat surfaces do. To create reflective flat metals, you need "busy maps" such as the files CHRMWARP.JPG and CHROMIC.JPG in your \3DSMAX\MAPS directory. By themselves, these maps seem like chaotic swirls of black and white. Applied to a flat surface with the right material settings, however, they produce stunning flat metals. To see how this works, follow these steps:

FLAT METALS

1. Open the file 11FLTMET.MAX from the accompanying CD. Two boxes that represent slabs of metal appear. Click on the Material Editor off the main toolbar and examine the materials in sample slots 1 and 2.

2. Notice that a busy map has been applied for the Reflection Map channel. The Coordinate rollout menu uses Spherical Environment mapping mode, double tiling values to spread the bitmap wider across the surface, and a dab of Blur Offset to distort the raw bitmap pattern. Notice also that the Box objects have only one segment in each axis. Render the Perspective viewport to get two very different metallic materials (see fig. 11.26). Concentrated noise maps, dent maps, wood maps, and marble maps can also create these kinds of busy maps.

FIGURE 11.26

"Busy maps," applied with wide tiling and effective blurring, give flat surfaces the appearance of metal.

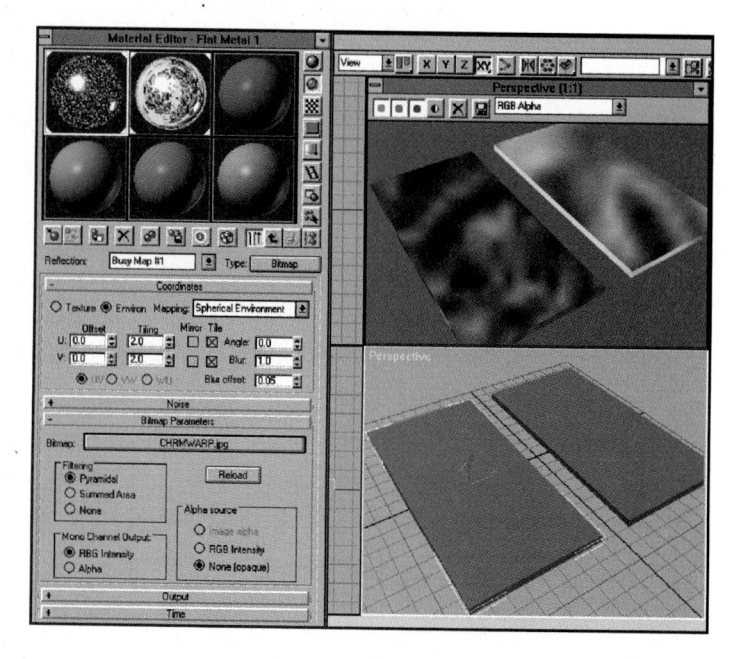

NOTE

For a variation on this technique, change values for the U and V Offsets, change Tiling values, and vary the Blur Offset ever so slightly. The smallest change in this setting has a profound impact on the resulting material.

Woven metal fabric, such as wire screens, can be created in the same way, except that the Wire toggle is activated in the Basic Parameters rollout of the material, the number of segments of the object must be increased to create the wire density of the mesh, the wire thickness must be set in the Extended Parameters rollout, and the thickness of the object needs to be reduced to 0.0. File 11MSHMET.MAX on the accompanying CD can be used as a reference for these settings. In addition, like most fabrics, wire mesh looks more believable when it is wrinkled a bit. This can be achieved by applying a subtle Noise modifier (see fig. 11.27).

FIGURE 11.27
Different Noise modifier seed values can make the wire mesh look very different.

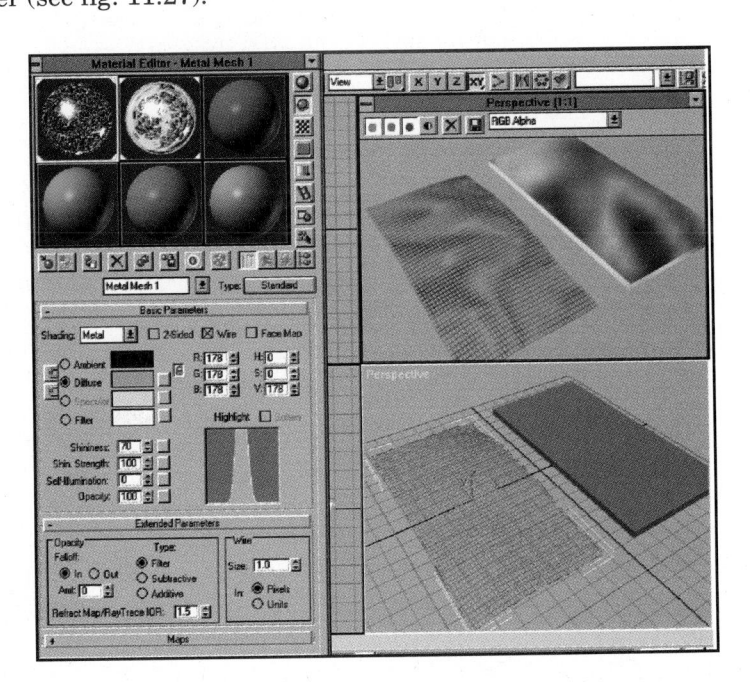

The simplest way to create the geometry for wire is to create a spline for the wire path and use a large circle as a beginning Loft object shape. After the Loft object tube is created and the metallic material has been applied to it, go back to the circle shape; in the Modify panel, decrease the radius value to something very small. To be effective, this value will vary according to the material's distance from the camera. Figure 11.28 shows an example of wire created with this technique. Examine the file 11WIRE.MAX from the accompanying CD for a closer look at the material applied to the Loft object.

FIGURE 11.28
Wire for coat hangers, for wiring between circuits, and for antennas is easy to create with a splined Loft object.

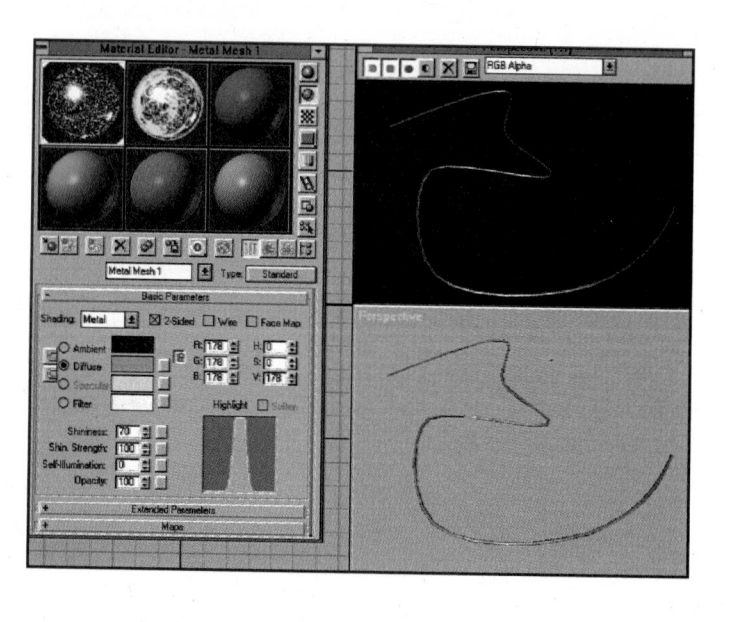

> **NOTE**
>
> This technique can be used also for creating string and rope. For rope, apply a bump map that recycles the rope bitmap used for the diffuse map.

Corruptions

Corruptions include rust, crumples, dents and bends, smears, abrasions, tears, and corrosion. Rust and corrosions that appear in metallic diffuse maps can be greatly enhanced by applying bump maps that only treat the areas of rust and corrosion. This can be done by using any 2D paint program to make a copy of the original metallic bitmap, by brightening those areas of rust and corrosion in the bitmap and changing all non-areas of rust and corrosion to a black color value, and finally by applying this resulting bitmap as a perfectly superimposed bump map.

Fabrics

The realism of fabrics depends almost entirely on the resolution of the fabric bitmap to accommodate the fabric's detail and on the suitability of the geometry onto which the fabric material is mapped. Of all the man-made materials treated in this chapter, fabrics require the greatest attention to detail, for their geometry. Figure 11.29 shows two bolts of fabric, similar to those you might find at a fabric warehouse. The front bolt holds a denim, and the one in the rear holds a rayon.

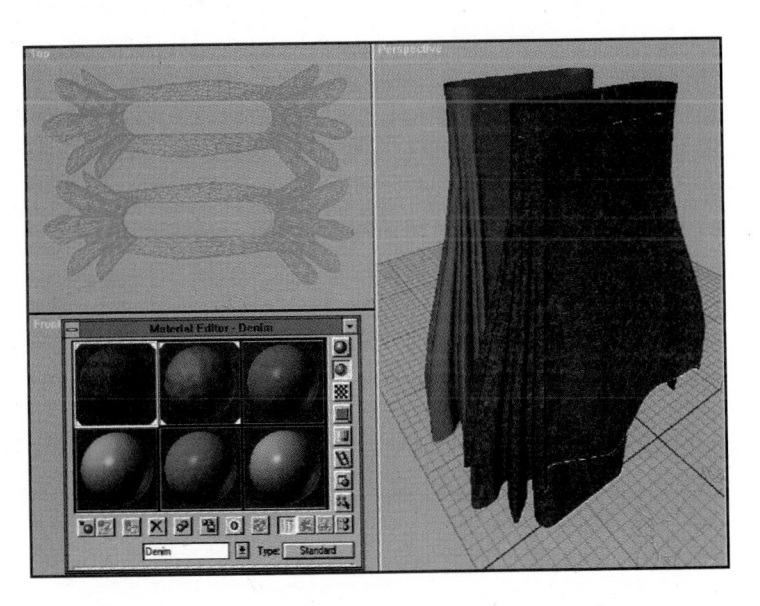

FIGURE 11.29
3D Studio MAX's capability to view materials in the viewport saves time when you're setting effective bitmap tiling values. To accelerate the viewport refresh rates of the material currently being worked on, disable the viewing of other objects in a scene.

Examples of fabric materials include linens (easily wrinkled fabrics), denim, leather, velvet, corduroy, synthetics (acrylics), terrycloth, flannel, wool, satin, silk, lace, and carpet.

Creation Techniques

The geometry of "folds" of fabric draped over the edges of a horizontal surface can be achieved rather easily through the use of the horizontal surface as a loft shape at 0 percent of the loft path, and a vertical Noise-modified "folds shape" as a loft shape at 100 percent of the loft path. Fabrics with frayed edges can be achieved through the use of fabric bitmaps with alpha channel gaps where the material is frayed, and through the recycling of these bitmaps used for opacity maps. Wrinkling can be achieved through the combined use of space warp transforms and Noise modifiers.

Pay close attention to a fabric's thickness. Silks and satins should be paper thin. Acrylic and wool fabrics, on the other hand, usually have a noticeable thickness when viewed from the side. After using multiple transforms and modifiers to deform an object so that it's the way you want it, you can minimize that object's use of memory by collapsing the stack of the object. Most fabric bitmaps can be used as bump maps to complement their use as diffuse maps, but they can also be used as shininess maps and spectral maps to give highlights to a material.

Creating seamless and tileable fabric materials such as those shown in figure 11.30 can take a great deal of time, and a fabrics bitmap collection is a good investment. One of the greatest challenges for many fabrics is to avoid giving a look of stiffness to the fabric's surfaces and orthogonality to the fabric's boundaries. MeshSmooth and Relax modifiers can help tremendously with abrupt Noise modifiers applied to surfaces. Likewise, by increasing the number of mesh vertices along the perimeter of a fabric object, you are better able to corrupt its unnatural linearity. Metallic materials actually work quite well for satins and silks.

FIGURE 11.30

These fabrics are only as effective as the light cast on them. When fabrics are used in a scene, make certain that Ambient Lighting is set to a value other than zero to brighten their highlights in all areas of the scene.

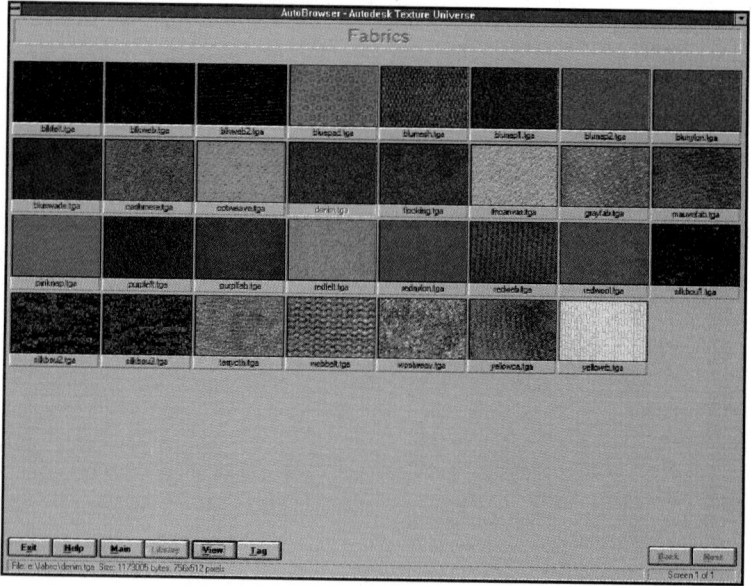

Corruptions

Corruptions include seams, stains, frays, wrinkles, blemishes, and fades. The edges of many fabrics can be corrupted effectively by using flat trim objects, as discussed earlier in this chapter.

Experiment!

The unlimited potential of man-made material bitmaps to create new materials when applied in unorthodox ways is staggering. Fabric materials can create new metals, concretes, and interior wall surfaces—and concretes can create new fabrics. Toy with a bitmap's Tiling and Blur settings to see what other possibilities the bitmap has. Remember that material bitmaps need not be used "as provided" or "as captured." If you have a 2D paint program at your disposal, try corrupting these raw bitmaps with various inks, such as Brightness, Jumble, Soften, and Emboss. Save the new materials with new names.

When possible, place a sample of the material where you can look at it while you are designing the material in MAX. Use a bitmap viewer at full-screen, with photo-captures of the objects or scenes you are reproducing. Toggle back and forth between MAX and the viewer by using Alt+Tab. In this way you can make man-made material design a royal pleasure.

Many companies that produce man-made materials also provide catalogs and samples. Architectural offices are typically swamped with laminate and tile samples, material catalogs, and color-guides. Trips with a digital camera to your local fabric warehouse or home-building supply warehouse can help you create quick libraries of woods, plastics, glass, and fabric materials in a few days. Balance the cost of a digital camera against the cost of premade material bitmap collections and the value of the time you would have to spend to create seamless and tileable versions of your bitmaps.

Finally, remember to keep a sense of the material's "time and place onstage" when you dedicate hours to material design. It is easy to get caught up in creating masterfully detailed materials, but this is not profitable if your materials will be in front of the camera for only a few seconds or are applied to objects too far in the scene's background to be appreciated.

In Practice: Creating Man-Made Materials

- **Age.** Consider the age of the elements in your scene. Unless everything you intend to visualize is brand-spanking new, you can achieve more dramatic scenes by aging their elements. When you create materials, give thought to how time acts upon them. The white paper pages of an old book fade or yellow. The high-traffic areas of a carpet or wooden floor reveal trails.

- **Lighting.** Consider how imperfection lighting can accentuate imperfect materials in a scene. In the case of a lamp, if the lampshade is tilted or worn, the light emitted from it may be dulled or projected against a nearby wall slightly off-center. The level of brightness above the lamp may be different than the level of brightness below the lamp due to discoloration of the shade. The glow behind the lampshade may have cracks of brightness revealed where the interior plastic lampshade shield has been overheated. Imperfect lighting results from imperfect light source materials.

- **Location.** Consider the imperfect locations of elements in your scene. In the case of a house interior scene, tilting one of several chairs at a dining room table, leaving a pen or book resting at a non-symmetrical non-orthogonal angle to the edges of a table surface, leaving curtains half-opened, a lampshade slightly tilted, or patches on the rug where more traffic occurs can all suggest in subtle ways that these places and items are used and therefore their materials are real.

IMAGE BY DAVE ESPINOSA-AGUILAR

Chapter 12

by dave espinosa-aguilar

DESIGNING SPECIAL EFFECTS MATERIALS

Many ordinary features in 3D Studio MAX can be used in extra-ordinary ways to produce wild and unexpected variations in material properties. Through the use of Video Post Filters, Light Objects, Environmental Atmospheres, and unusual geometries, you can generate a vast array of special effects materials. The techniques for designing these materials can vary with static and dynamic images because the believability of a material may or may not be dependent on an object's motion or behavior. This chapter and the following chapter examine several ways to create special effects materials in static and dynamic images, respectively.

Special effects materials can be created in 3D Studio MAX by using tools you may already be familiar with in new ways: by corrupting existing materials with exaggerated settings, by viewing ordinary effects from unusual angles, and by experimenting with some of the program's internal special effects capabilities. This chapter covers the following effects:

- Explosions

- Lighting and Glowing Effects

- Psychedelic Materials

Each of the topics in this chapter outline ways in which these common tools can be combined to produce very different images.

Explosions

The first example shows how two Combustion apparatuses can be combined seamlessly to create the Combustion Atmospheric Effect of a flaming fireball. When Combustion apparatuses overlap, a very noticeable boundary is created by the last apparatus listed in the effects list. It is by tweaking the seed values for the apparatuses and the characteristics of the effect, and by placing the engulfed geometry within the apparatuses that this seam is avoided.

The second example shows how Atmosphere Effect characteristics can be exploited to create explosive shapes other than flames. Through careful placement of the Combustion apparatus, you can limit the concentration of thin flames to create spurts. By using an elongated Combustion apparatus, you can create bands of flames that can be used as tiled materials to produce lava flows and streams of fire.

The third example shows how the combined use of overlapping Particle Systems and Combustion Atmospheric Effects can create shattered glass, blast effects, and smoke. The Combustion Atmospheric Effect has an Explosion capability built right into it. By setting ranges of values for the Phase of the explosion, you an produce smokeless flames, smokey flames, or flameless smoke. Particle Systems can use varying flake or drop sizes to produce a more convincing debris.

A Bursting Meteor

Meteors burst into flames when they enter the atmosphere. At the front of the meteor is a superheated flame generated from the air friction, and at the rear of the meteor is a trailing flame. Producing flames with the Combustion Atmospheric Effect and Combustion apparatus is not a difficult thing to do after you know the basic steps, but combining these effects without creating ugly flame boundaries is quite a trickier task.

When two of more apparatuses are positioned close together in a scene, the order in which the effects are listed in the Atmosphere Effects listbox has a profound impact on the final image. If any of the effects have a high enough density to hide effects behind them, a very noticeable seam appears at the flame boundaries.

To dissolve this seam with high-density effects requires two things—tweaking the seed values for each Combustion apparatus so that the flame boundaries match up, and geometry that can disrupt the seam between the two Combustion apparatuses. Open file 12METEOR.MAX (see fig. 12.1). Use the Rendering/Environment pull-down, and select either of the Combustion items listed in the Effects listbox to examine the shapes and settings of each Combustion Atmospheric Effect. Select the Combustion apparatuses and click on the Modify panel to see the settings for each apparatus.

The meteor object was created by applying a Noise Modifier with varying strengths in the X, Y, and Z axis to a 16-segment sphere. The Meteor material applied to the meteor is a basic Noise Map applied as a diffuse map and a bump map by using default values. The two Combustion apparatuses have been placed in a way to create the effect of the flames at the front and rear of the meteor.

FIGURE 12.1

A meteor object with two aligned Combustion apparatuses.

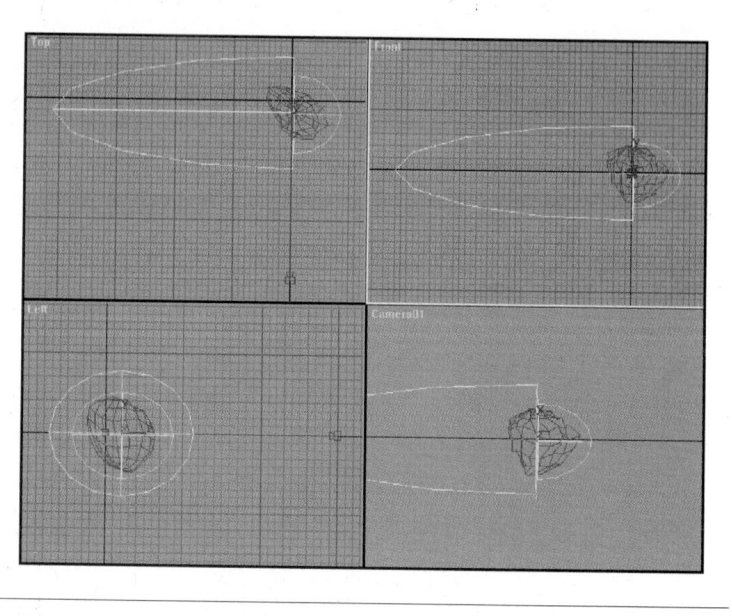

To create a Combustion apparatus, follow these steps:

1. In the Create panel, click on the Helpers button.

2. Click on the object subcategory drop-down and select Atmospheric Apparatus.

3. Click on the Combustion button.

4. Pick a point in a viewscreen and drag to set the radius of the apparatus. A toggle is provided to create spherical or hemispherical boundaries for the object.

You can non-uniformly scale spherical and hemispherical apparatuses to control the shape of the combustion boundary area. After an apparatus is created, you need to attach an Atmospheric Environment Effect to it. To so attach, follow these steps:

1. Choose Rendering, Environment. The Environment dialog appears.

2. In the Atmosphere area of the dialog, click on the Add button. Select Combustion from the Add Atmospheric Effect dialog and click on OK. Combustion now appears in the Effects list.

3. In the Combustion Parameters area, in the Source Apparatus panel, click on the Pick Object button and select the apparatus in the viewscreen. The name of the apparatus now appears in the field to the right of the button.

After an apparatus has been created and attached to an Environment Effect, you can render and view the combustion effect (see fig. 12.2). In this example, a fireball flame type is used at the front of the meteor, and a tendril flame type is used near the rear of the meteor with a wider apparatus radius to match the flame boundaries of the fireball. By selecting an apparatus and entering the Modify panel, you can vary the shape of the flames by setting different seed values in the Combustion Parameters rollout.

FIGURE 12.2

The meteor explodes into flames as it enters an atmosphere.

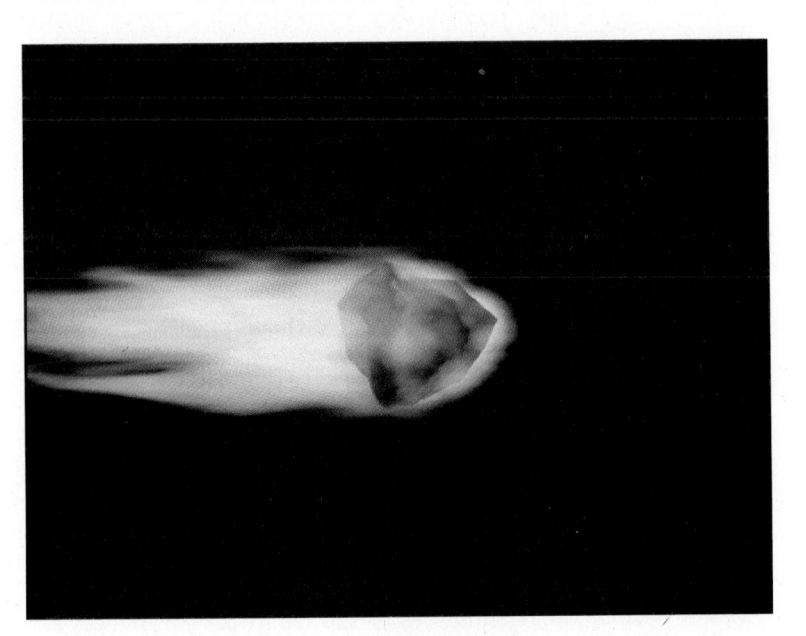

The meteor does not have to be centered on the hemispherical apparatuses. Depending on how much of the object you want revealed through the flames, you can move the object farther from or closer to the camera. You can also move the meteor completely in front of the apparatuses to create a glowing burn that completely reveals the entire meteor rather than a consuming burn that envelopes it.

TIP

Try several different apparatus seeds to get the cleanest flame match at the seam.

Render this scene with the meteor object hidden to get a better idea of how combustion flames match up. The order in which atmospheric effects are listed makes a blatant impact on the appearance of the *seam* between the flame types. In this example, the fireball is rendered after the tendril so that a clean vertical seam is created. It is the geometry of the meteor that destroys the appearance of the seam.

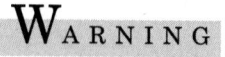

WARNING

Be aware that fireballs traveling in nonvertical directions can appear to burn *upward* with certain Combustion Parameter settings. You can blur the appearance of fireball flames to avoid giving the flames a direction.

An Erupting Volcano

Volcanoes produce a wide array of different exploding and combusting material effects, from lava spurting from the mouth of the volcano to fiery streams of lava flowing down the side of the volcano. By using tendril flame shapes with thin flame sizes and concealing the core of an attached Combustion apparatus beneath geometry, you can isolate the tips of flame tendrils to produce hot spurts. By using over-elongated apparatuses and rendering an perpendicular view of a Combustion Atmospheric Effect out to a Targa file (which includes alpha information), you can create a lava river material that can be draped over other materials to produce rivers and streams of lava.

Experimenting with the colors, shapes, characteristics, motions, and explosion parameters of the Combustion Atmospheric Effect can be time-consuming, but rewarding; the tool's settings can produce radically different results. Open file 12VOLCANO.MAX (see fig. 12.3). In this model, the landscape is generated with a 0.0 height box that uses a Noise Modifier and an Edit Mesh Modifier's Affect Region function to bulge the object into a volcano.

Examine the settings of the Combustion Atmospheric Effects and the Combustion apparatus to see how the smaller flame sizes and other characteristics create spurts. To create the lava material, open file 12LAVMAP.MAX and render the Camera viewport. After this image is saved out to a Targa file, alpha channel information is saved wherever the flame does not show (see fig. 12.4). An elongated fireball creates a band of fire that can be draped across surfaces. The more elongated the apparatus is, the straighter the band of flames will be.

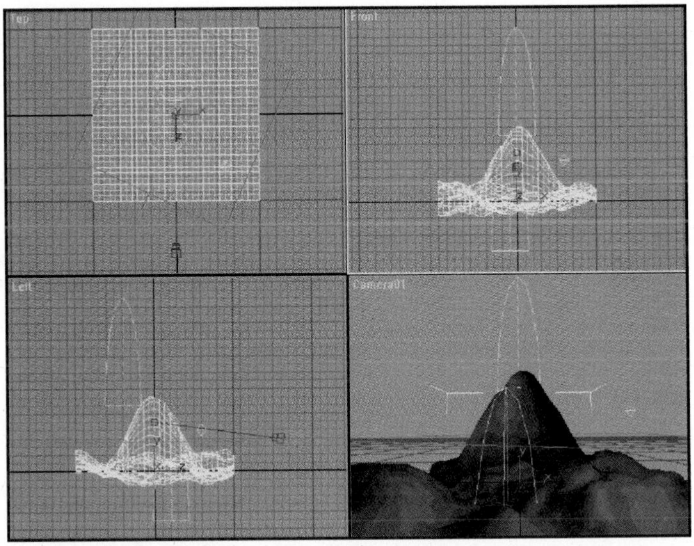

FIGURE 12.3
Two combustion apparatuses are used to create flames within the volcano and lava splashing against the landscape in the foreground.

FIGURE 12.4
A band of flames is created from an elongated fireball.

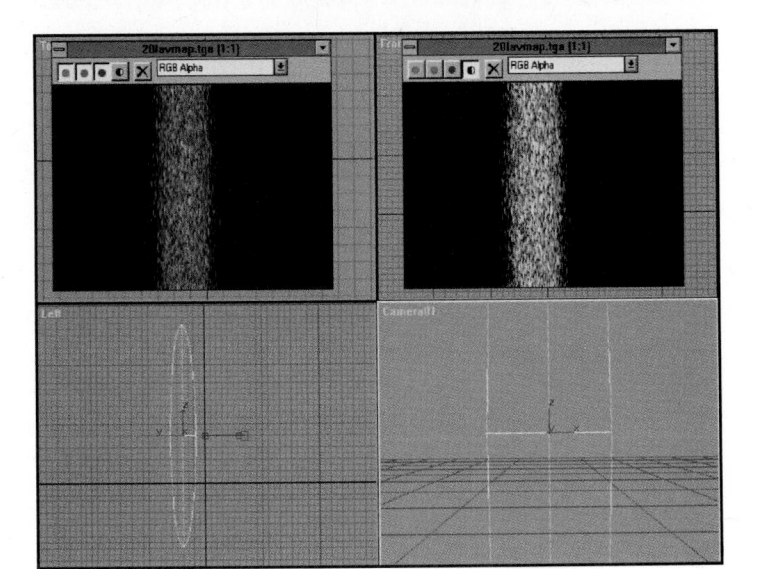

Reopen the file 12VOLCANO.MAX and examine the materials used in the scene to see how the composited maps were tweaked to create a deep-glowing, red-mountainous material with a stream of lava. Notice that the tile settings of the material can have a profound impact on the appearance of the material. You can increase or decrease these settings to change the overall character of the flowing lava.

An Omni light is placed to light the landscape and the lava river material mapped to it. The placement of the Omni light determines the lava's brightness and detail. You can control which areas of the lava flow are brightest by moving the Omni light or adding new Omni lights. As the Omni light is moved forward, the stream of lava flowing down the mountain fades while the stream flowing over land brightens (see fig. 12.5).

FIGURE 12.5

A volcano with a lava flow comes to life.

TIP

By decreasing the smoothness of the geography, applying noise modifiers to the mapping materials, and experimenting with different flame settings, the lava river becomes even more lively. Numerous lava splashes can also be placed along the lava river with varying sizes to simulate rapids and heat pools.

A Shattering Window

Explosions can make a great impact in the dark, but creating realistic explosions in daylight is a little more involved. For one thing, the effect of flames is reduced, and motion plays a big part in the believability of an explosion. Looking at still images of real explosions can help tremendously in the modeling of explosions. Depending on the material being exploded, blasts and flames are often shrouded in darker clouds of smoke or debris. The Combustion Atmospheric Effect can create smoke and fog through the uses of its internal Explode capability and by changing the colors of the flames.

Open the file 12WINDOW.MAX. This scene includes a window frame without any glass materials in it (see fig. 12.6). Move the frame slider to about frame 30 to see the Snow Particle Effects objects in the scene. Select each Particle Effect and view its settings in the Modify panel.

Each Particle System uses a different flake size and triangular particles to create the illusion of shattered glass and blast debris.

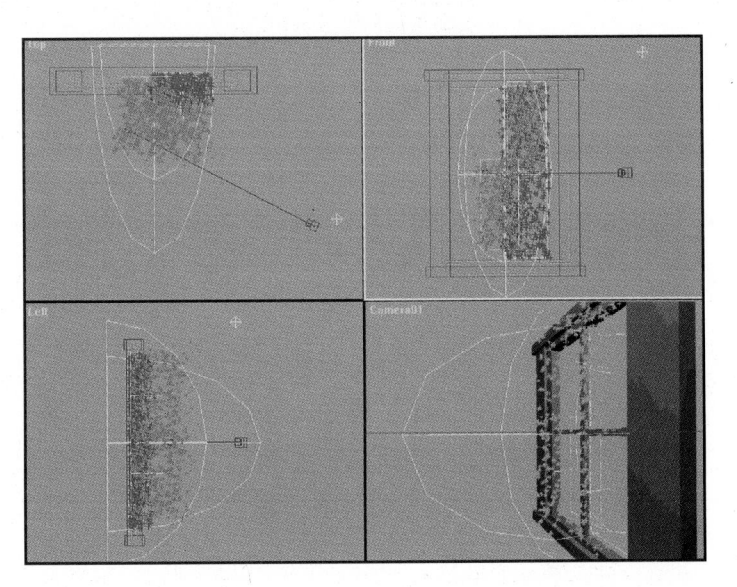

Particle Systems can often render more clearly than Combustion Atmospheric Effects in bright settings. To enable the effects to have a stronger impact at the back of the explosion, no Particle Systems are placed over the farthest glass areas. The Combustion apparatuses have been positioned far behind the window frame to ensure a thicker blast effect at the glass area borders.

Click on the Rendering/Environment pull-down option and examine the two Combustion Atmosphere Effect settings.

The first effect, which uses the larger Combustion apparatus, takes advantage of the Explosion capability built into the effect. By toggling Explosion on in the Explosion area of the Combustion parameters and setting the phase to a value between 100 and 200, smokey flames or flameless smoke can be created (see fig. 12.7).

FIGURE 12.7
A smokey flame bursts from inside the window frame.

Try using various Phase settings between 100 and 200 and re-render the scene. The differences are quite dramatic. The closer you set the Phase value to 100, the more flames you see. The closer you set the Phase to 200, the more smoke you create.

TIP

Finding the right Phase value for a still image is worth taking the time for.

The second effect does not use the internal Explosion capability, but does use a white and black flame color combination to create a blasting *cloud*. The density of the flame is set to a higher value to give the flame a tight fogging effect around the frame area (see fig. 12.8).

Play with the settings of the Combustion Atmosphere Effects and Particle Systems to create very different types of blasts. Particle Systems were used to simulate glass in this example, but more sophisticated glass can be generated with the use of bomb space warps applied to semi-transparent glass objects with high segment values and noise modifiers.

FIGURE 12.8
*A foggy smoke hugs
the window frame.*

Light Emitting and Glowing Effects

Numerous ways enable you to create objects and effects that give the illusion of emitting light in your scenes. Video Post filters such as Glow can be applied to self-illuminated materials to create thick or thin ribbons of light that imitate neon, lightning bolts, lasers, and bright filaments. Volumetric Lighting can be used from different angles and with different noise levels to create color-banded Volumetric Lighting. Particle Systems can be used to create an unlimited array of sparkles and highlights.

The first example outlines the basic use of the Glow filter in Video Post to create a neon sign. This includes the use of Object Channels and Material Channels to assign effects to unique objects in your scene or all objects that use a common material.

The second example shows how using different geometry with the Glow filter can produce lightning. A number of lightning-specific utilities are currently in development for 3D Studio MAX, but the technique used in this exercise lends itself to any type of glow that requires streaking or forking.

The third example overcomes a limitation of the Glow filter, namely that it does not behave the same way when the material it is applied to rests behind another semi-transparent material. Through multiple rendering passes in Video Post or through carefully positioned geometry, this problem can be corrected.

The fourth example is an extensive look at how volumetric lights can be superimposed to create gradient and color-banded Volumetric Lighting, and how surrounding or engulfing auras can be created about objects by viewing volumetric lights from different angles.

The fifth example is a study in the use of mapped Particle Systems to create flares, sparkles, and mixed highlights. The sixth example briefly touches on how Projector Spotlights can be used to create *geometry-independent materials*, *attenuated materials*, and *non-axial materials*.

A Neon Sign

Creating a neon sign is a perfect introduction to the Glow filter in Video Post. After you understand this powerful tool and how it uses Material Channels and Object Channels to create basic glows, you can create new material effects with it which simulate lightning, lasers, and other streams of energy.

Open the file 12NEON.MAX and render the Perspective view. The word NEON has been created using lofting techniques, and a self-illuminated material has been created and applied to each letter boundary (see fig. 12.9).

FIGURE 12.9

The self-illuminated material appears to glow.

Although self-illumination can create quick and impressive glowing effects on its own, it does not soften or blur the glowing about the edges of the geometry. The glow filter adds a more realistic boundary to the light.

To create and use a glow filter, follow these steps:

1. In the Material Editor, click on the Material Effects Channel button and set it to Channel 5. You can use any one of the channels for this glow effect. Close the Material Editor.

2. Select the Rendering/Video Post pull-down menu option to bring up the Video Post dialog. Click on the Add Scene Event button. Set the View to Perspective, and make certain that the Enabled check box is active in the Video Post Parameters panel. Click on OK. The Queue now displays a scene event.

3. Select the Perspective scene event by clicking on the word Perspective in the Queue. The track to the right turns red.

4. Click on the Add Image Filter Event button. Set the Filter Plug-In to Glow (frame only). Click on the Setup button. In the Glow Control dialog, set the Source to Material Effects Channel mode and set the field to the right of the toggle to a value of 5. Set the Color to User mode and click on the color swatch to the right of the toggle. Set the color to a bright red (around RGB 255, 0, 0). Set the Size to 10 and click on OK. Make certain that the Enabled check box is active in the Video Post Parameters panel, and then click on OK.

5. Click on the Execute Sequence button of the Video Post main toolbar. Set Time Output to Single mode, the Output Size to 640×480, and click on the Render button (see fig. 12.10).

NOTE

When you use the combination of a self-illuminated materials and a glow filter, the colors of the overall neon tubing are a combination of the self-illuminated diffuse color and the Glow filter color.

For a glass-tubing effect, go to the self-illuminated material Basic Parameters rollout and try setting a bright white color for the Specular color swatch, a shininess value of 50, a shininess strength value of 100, and an opacity value of 50. Place one or more Omni lights in front of the neon objects. Experiment with different values for Opacity and Opacity Falloff when varying the Self-Illumination value of the material.

FIGURE 12.10
A subtle glow gives the neon material added realism.

A Lightning Bolt

With effective geometry and a few tweaked settings, similar techniques used to create neon can be used to create sizzling bolts of lightning. This tutorial examines the Glow filter as a function of the Object Channel rather than a Material Effects Channel. Open the file 12BOLT.MAX and render the Perspective viewport. The bolt turns gray from an applied self-illuminated material.

To apply a glow filter by using an Object Channel, follow these steps:

1. Select and right-click on the Bolt object and select Properties to bring up the Object Properties dialog. In the G-Buffer panel, set the value of the Object Channel to 25. Click on OK.

2. Pick the Rendering/Video Post pull-down menu to bring up the Video Post dialog. The Queue still reports a Glow Filter event and the Perspective Scene event. Double-click on the Glow track to bring up the Edit Filter Event dialog. Click on the Setup button. Set the Source to Object Channel rather than Material Effects Channel, and set the Object Channel spinner to 25. Click on OK twice to return to the Video Post dialog.

3. Click on the Execute Sequence button of the Video Post main toolbar. Set Time Output to Single mode, the Output Size to 640×480, and then click on the Render button (see fig. 12.11).

FIGURE 12.11

The smaller the radius of the circle, the cleaner the lightning appears.

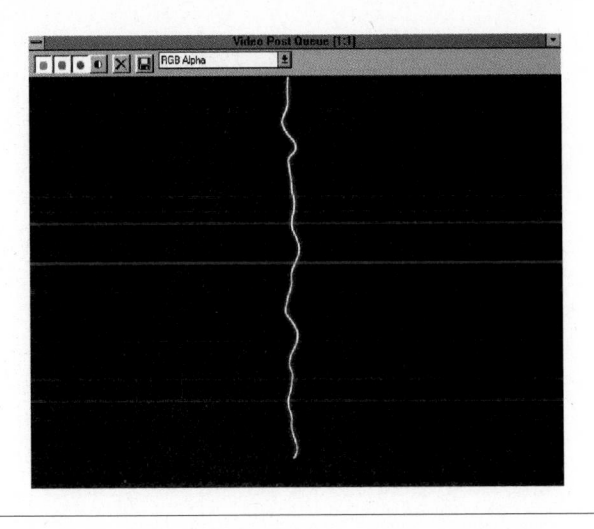

Realistic lightning has many different looks. Forked bolts during a thunderstorm appear very differently than the static discharges of heat lightning softened by clouds. Using the techniques outlined in the previous section on explosions, you can create very thin tendrils of blue-white lightening. Try using multiple lofts of varying radii together for a stringy lightning effect. By using a photo of a lightning bolt as a background in the Front viewport, you can also trace a bolt lofting path easily.

The same techniques for lightning can be used on slender, straight, lofted objects with high values for the Glow size to create sizzling laser bolts and laser bullets. Try using bright greens and reds for the Glow color and vary the size of the Glow filter to achieve the desired effect.

Clear and Soft Lightbulbs

Self-illuminated materials and Glow filters can be used to create lightbulbs. The Glow filter behaves quite differently, however, when it is applied to an object within or behind another object. Open the file 12BULB.MAX and render the Perspective viewport.

To set up Video Post to handle this scene, follow these steps:

1. Pick the Rendering/Video Post pull-down menu to bring up the Video Post dialog.

2. Click on the Add Scene Event button, and set the View to Perspective. Click on OK.

3. Pick on the Perspective track. The track turns red.

4. Click on the Add Image Filter Event button. Set the Filter Plug-In to Glow (frame only), and click on the Setup button. Set the Source to Material Effects Channel with a spinner value of 1, set the color to User and the User color swatch to bright white (RBG 255, 255, 255). Set Size to 30. Click on OK twice to return to the Video Post dialog.

For the glow to appear *inside* the glass sphere, the filaments are moved out in front of the glass spheres. You can verify this by moving the filaments inside the spheres and out in front of the spheres.

1. Move the filaments inside the glass spheres.

2. Click on the Execute Sequence button of the Video Post main toolbar. Set Time Output to Single mode, the Output Size to 320×240, and click on the Render button. The glass bulb sphere on the left and the filament inside it render, but without a glow. Select the left bulb glass sphere.

3. In the Display panel, click on the Hide Selected button. Click on the Execute Sequence button of the Video Post main toolbar, and click on the Render button. Without the glass bulb showing, the filament renders with a glow.

4. In the Display control panel, click on the Unhide All button. Click on the Select by Name button from the main toolbar, click on the Loft01 object in the Select Objects dialog, and click on the Select button. Using the Perspective viewport as a guide, move the filament in front of the Sphere.

5. Click on the Execute Sequence button of the Video Post main toolbar and click on the Render button. The glass sphere renders with a glow in front of it, appearing *inside* of it. Figure 12.12 shows two bulbs using this technique. A semi-opaque, self-illuminated, shiny white material is used for the soft white bulb on the right (see fig. 12.12).

The geometry of the lightbulbs can obviously be enhanced, but the example shows the basic workaround to produce glows *within* other materials.

FIGURE 12.12
Placing Glow-filtered objects in front of other objects can give the illusion of glows within objects.

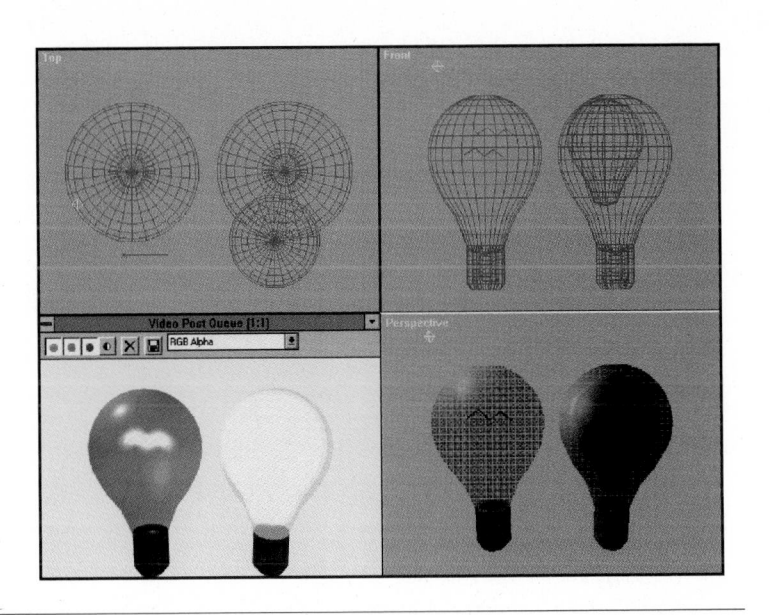

A Radiant Aura

Through the use of superimposed volumetric lights, and by viewing these lights from different angles, you can create a wild assortment of multicolored and multipatterned auras that frame or engulf objects. This can give them the effect of being gaseous, glowing, or radiant. In the examples that follow, techniques to create rays, bursts, auras, and streams of energy are shown. The files 12AURA1.MAX and 12AURA2.MAX can be used as a reference for following these examples.

By setting the camera angle so that it stares directly into a volumetric light, you can create basic ray patterns. The Filter Shadows mode set too high can prevent light banding. The following steps show how this can be done:

1. Use the File/Reset pull-down menu function to start a new session.

2. In the Create panel, click on the Lights button and click on the Target Spot button. Pick a point near the top center of the Front viewport to place the camera, hold the pick button down and drag downward about 200 units, and release the pick button to place the camera target.

3. In the Modify rollout, find the Spotlight Parameters panel and activate the Show Cone check box. In the Shadow Parameters rollout, activate the Cast Shadows check box.

4. Use the Rendering/Environment pull-down menu function to bring up the Environment dialog. In the Atmosphere panel, click on the Add button, select Volume Light, and then click on OK.

5. In the Volume Light Parameters rollout, click on the Pick Light button, move the cursor over the spotlight icon in the Front viewport, and select it. The name Spot01 appears in the Lights edit field. Close the Environment dialog.

6. Use Zoom Extents All. Right-click on an area in the Perspective viewport to make it active. Use Zoom and Pan to zoom in and center in on the spotlight cone.

7. Click on the Render Scene button from the main toolbar. Set Time Output to Single mode, set the Output Size to 320×240, and click on Render. A volumetric light appears, shining past the bottom of the screen.

8. Click on the Modify Panel. In the Attenuation area of the panel, set the Start Range and the End Range to 200, and activate the Use and Show check boxes.

9. Click the Render Last button from the main toolbar. The volumetric light fills only the cone area.

10. In the Create panel, click on the Geometry button, click on the Hedra button, select Star1 from the Parameters Family panel, pick a point in the general center of the spotlight cone shown in the Front viewport, and drag the cursor to create an object that fits entirely inside the cone boundary. Set the Star's radius to 40.

11. Click on the Render Last button from the main toolbar. The spotlight casts shadows from the Star.

12. In the Create panel, click on the Cameras button, click on the Target button in the Object Type panel, and in the same way you created the spotlight, pick points in the Front viewport so that the camera looks directly up from underneath the spotlight cone and the Star. Pick a distance from the Camera to the Camera target of about 100 units, and position the camera's target directly under the spotlight target icon.

13. Right-click on an area in the Left viewport and press C to change the viewport to Camera view. Click on the Render Scene button from main toolbar, and click on Render.

    Although the banding of the light is a neat effect in itself, it can be dithered by controls in the Environment dialog. Also notice that the Star is completely unlit.

14. Use the Rendering/Environment pull-down menu to bring up the Environment dialog. Pick on Volume Light in the Atmosphere Effects listbox to bring up the Volume Light Parameters rollout. In the Volume panel, pick High mode for Filter Shadows. Close the Environment dialog.

15. In the Create panel, click on the Lights button, click on the Omni button, and pick a point in the Front viewport directly beneath your camera icon. Right-click on an area over the word *Camera* in the Camera01 viewport, and set the viewport mode to Smooth + Highlight.

16. Click on the Render Scene button from the main toolbar, and click on Render. A series of radial streaks shine from behind the lit Star.

TIP

Using High mode for Filter Shadows increases rendering time significantly. Alternate between high and low mode as needed while you work to get the effect you want.

You can assign a projector image to the spotlight to get colored streaks. You can also use other objects between the Star and the spotlight to create streaks that do not fit the Star's geometry.

To create multicolored volumetric lights:

1. Use the Rendering/Environment pull-down menu to bring up the Environment dialog. Pick on Volume Light in the Atmosphere Effects listbox to bring up the Volume Light Parameters rollout. In the Volume panel, set the Volume Fog Color swatch to red (RGB 255, 0, 0). In the Attenuation panel, set the End % to 50.

2. Right-click on an area in the Perspective viewport. Click on the Render Scene button from the main toolbar, and click on Render. Red light only extends halfway from the spotlight source.

3. Click on the Select Move button from the main toolbar. Holding the Shift key, pick on the spotlight icon and release. This brings up the Clone options dialog. Set Copy for the Object mode and click on OK. You now have two spotlights, superimposed on each other.

4. Use the Rendering/Environment pull-down menu to bring up the Environment dialog. In the Atmosphere panel, click on the Add button, select Volume Light, and then click on OK.

You now have two volume lights listed in the Effects listbox.

5. Pick on the second Volume Light entry in the listbox. In the Volume Light Parameters rollout, set the Volume Fog Color swatch to yellow (RGB 255, 255, 0). Click on the Pick Light button. Selecting the second Volume Light by clicking on it can be difficult in this scene. Press the "H" key instead to bring up the Pick Object dialog and select the second Volume Light. The name Spot02 appears in the Lights edit field. Close the Environment dialog.

TIP

If you have difficulty picking Spot02, move one of the spotlights temporarily and select it. Make certain to move the spotlight back to its original position so that both spotlights superimpose.

6. Right-click on an area in the Perspective viewport. Click on the Render Scene button from the main toolbar, and click on Render. The red light from the first spotlight is tinted orange. This is how volumetric lights can be colorbanded. Many volume settings can be used to blend, sharpen, intensify, or thin the blending effect (see fig. 12.13).

FIGURE 12.13
After you know how to overlap attenuated volumetric lights, colorbanding is possible.

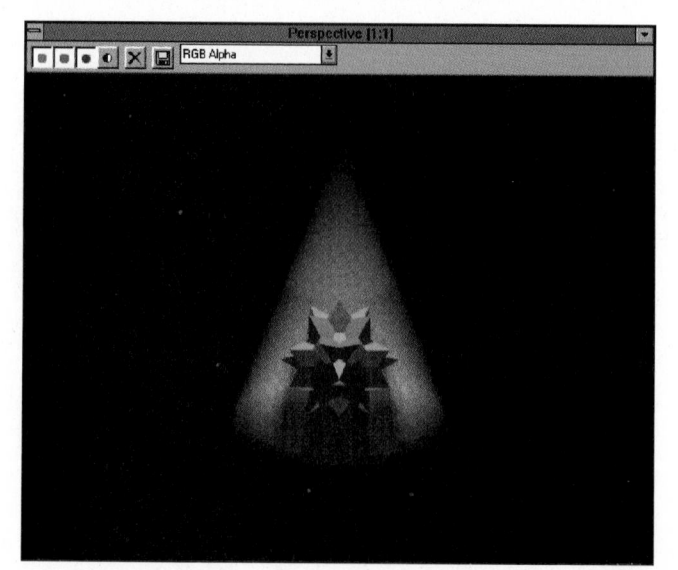

Now that you know how to blend two volumetric spotlights, noise will be added to one, then both, to achieve some remarkable auras around the Star object. The following steps show a possible approach to this technique:

1. Pick on the first Volume Light in the Effects listbox of the Environment dialog. In the Noise panel of the Volume Light Parameters rollout, enable Noise by picking on the Noise On check box. Set Amount to 1.

2. In the Attenuation panel, set End % back to 100. In the Volume Panel, set the Density to 50.

3. Right-click on an area in the Perspective viewport. Click on the Render Scene button from the main toolbar, and click on Render.

   The volumetric lighting appears like a matrix! Variations on this theme can produce some surprising energy fields (see fig. 12.14).

FIGURE 12.14
By combining volumetric lights with noise, you can create multipatterned lighting.

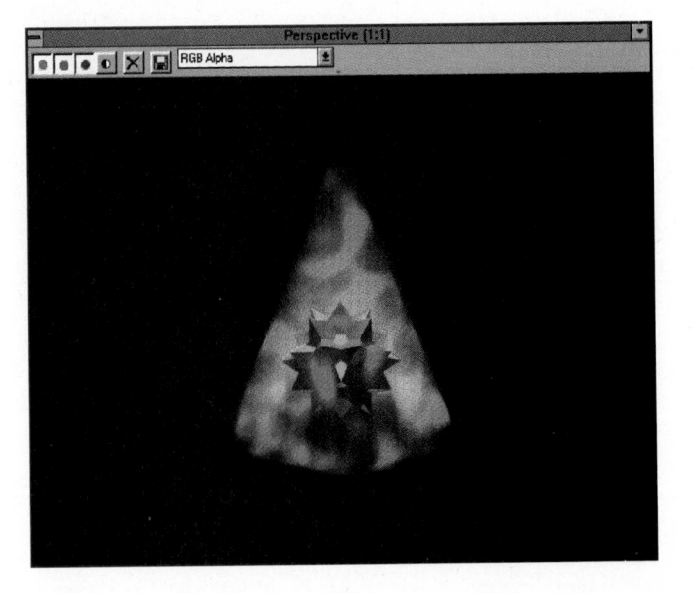

4. Right-click on an area in the Camera viewport. Click on the Render Scene button from the main toolbar, and click on Render. The Star object is surrounded by a misty swirling glow. Try rerendering this scene by setting the Filter Shadows toggle to High mode for the second volume light to see the improved effect.

5. Pick on the second Volume Light in the Effects listbox of the Environment dialog. In the Volume panel, set Density to 20. In the Noise panel, toggle Noise on, set the Amount to 0.8, set Size to 15, and set Phase to 0.5.

TIP

In the Modify panel, you can select each spotlight and disable the Cast Shadows check box. This enables the Star object to be engulfed in the aura. If you allow the spotlights to cast shadows, the Star object appears clearly in the camera view, but is surrounded by the aura.

6. Click on the Render Last button from the main toolbar. A sphere of almost gaseous light surrounds the Star object (see fig. 12.15).

FIGURE 12.15

Seen from above or below, volumetric lighting creates unlimited auras.

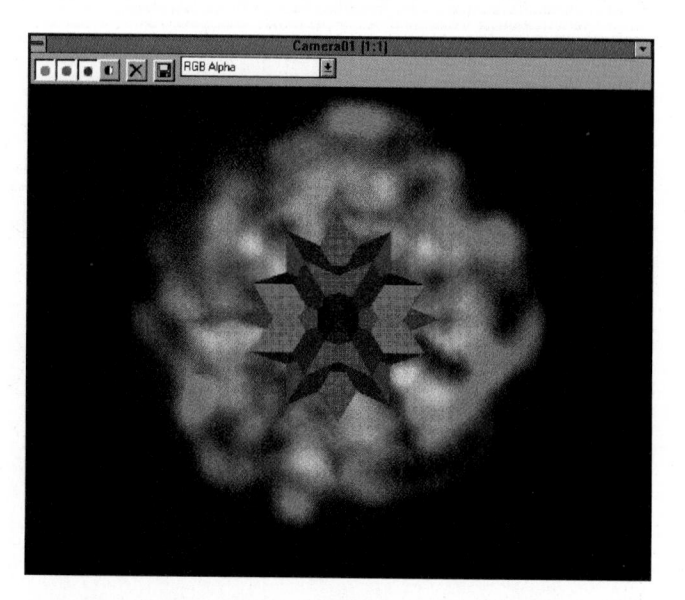

From here on out, things can get downright weird. There seems no limit to the number of lights or shapes that can be achieved by combining different light models with different volumetric light settings. Lights can travel with objects in animations, and wind effects can be applied to animated volumetric light noise values.

You can try to vary these effects in a number of ways, such as:

■ Experiment with different values for the Noise of each spotlight.

■ Try using three or four spotlights together to create four bands of color or four swirls of different densities.

- Remember that volumetric lighting can be applied to other light models. Try using Omni lights or Direct lights. Superimpose Omni lights and Direct lights similar to the way spotlights were used in this tutorial. Streams of volumetric light can be achieved by using Direct lights with small radii.

- Remember that Spotlight cones can be non-uniformly scaled. Limit motion in the X or Y axis and see what happens when you non-uniformly scale one of the two spotlights used in this tutorial.

- Combine projected images with the spotlights.

- Try a camera inside the spotlight cone. Close-up shots from this angle, which fill the screen, can produce some fantastic gaseous materials.

- View the Star object and Volumetric spotlight from above or from slightly off-center to the zenith.

Uses of Particle Systems

Particle Systems can be used along with Space Warps such as Gravity to generate unlimited sparkles and highlights. Because any particle can have a material mapped to it, clouds of objects can be quickly and easily generated. The one trick that must be played to achieve the follow effects is that the border of each face of each particle must be transparent. This can be accomplished by either mapping a material with transparent (0 opacity) borders or by mapping a material with alpha channel borders. If the material mapped has opaque borders, the square faces of the particles can be seen.

Open file 12SPARK.MAX and move the frames slider to about frame 30. The particles in the Camera01 viewport may not be clearly visible due to the diffuse color being used for them. Select Spray from the modifier stack. In the Parameters rollout are shown the particle models including drops, dots, and ticks. Ticks should be selected.

Click on the Materials Editor button in the main toolbar. Six materials appear. These are created by using a Gradient map applied as a diffuse map and an opacity map. When they are applied to a particle system, they generate radically different images (see fig. 12.16).

FIGURE 12.16
The opacity map prevents the square boundaries of the particle faces from being seen.

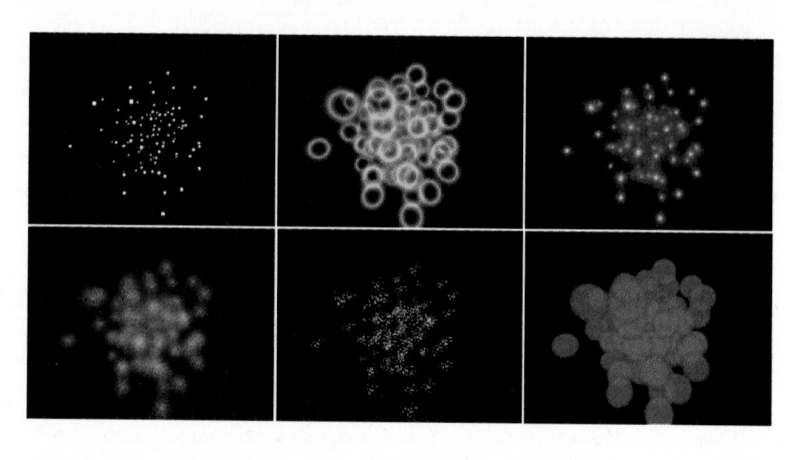

In the same way that opacity maps can be mixed with basic materials to create transparent boundaries, images rendered as Targa files (which include alpha transparency information) can also be used to create clouds and sprays of glowing objects. A basic bubble shape was rendered to a Targa file and applied as a material to the particle system to create this image (see fig. 12.17).

FIGURE 12.17
These bubbles take less time to render as a particle system than they do as objects!

This same technique can generate wisps of bubbles and dust, and swirls of water and fire, with any of the particle system Space Warps: Deflector, Displace, Gravity, and Wind. In this example, a Gravity Space Warp is used to pull particles toward it. Vary the strength of the Gravity Space Warp to see the effect it has on emitted particles. You can get quite a different effect when you stare straight into the particle emitter as well. Render the Camera02 viewport to get a *starburst* effect with any of the materials you map to the particle system.

In a similar way that sparkles can be generated with particle systems, you can also create flares and highlights. Open file 12FLARE1.MAX, move the frame slider to about 30, and select the particle emitter to see how a Gravity Space Warp is being used to create a bended flare.

Three materials are used in this scene: a self-illuminated material is used for the star; a speck material similar to the ones used in the previous spark example is used for the flare; and a gradient material is used for a projector Direct light that shines on the particle system. The appearance of the flare trail is partly controlled by the particle system drop size and the image mapped to each face of the particle system (see fig. 12.18).

FIGURE 12.18
The Direct light helps to control the color and boundary of the flare.

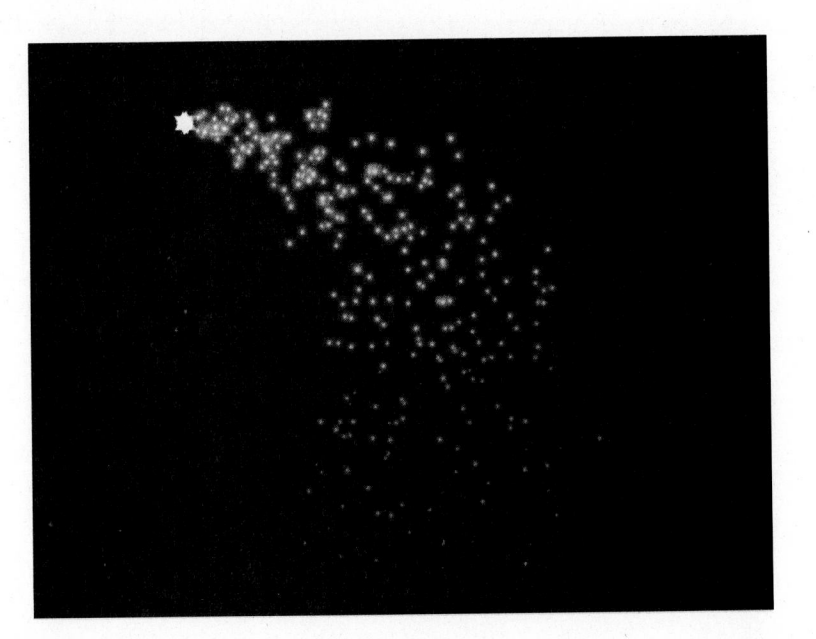

By using different light models, including projector spotlights, you can completely control which areas of a particle system are visible. Attenuated lights can also create a decaying effect on the visibility of particle systems. In the spark example, circular shapes were used as the foundation for most of the particle systems. You can create many different shapes of maps using the spectral profiles of simple geometric objects. Open file 12FLARE2.MAX and render the Front viewport. These are just a few examples of shapes that can be applied as particle system maps (see fig. 12.19).

FIGURE 12.19
The same spectral transparent material is used to create all these shapes.

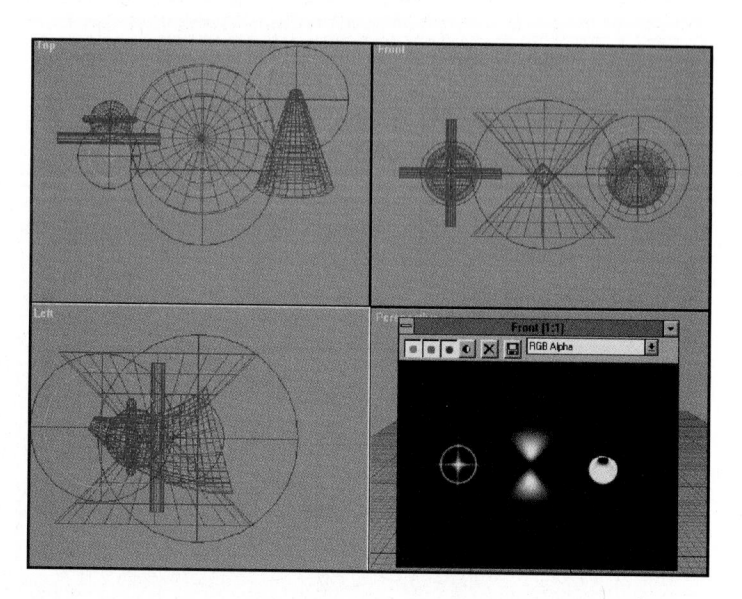

NOTE

These shapes can be used to create highlights, starry skies, starfields, and glares as seen through glass camera lenses. Particle systems use squares, so if you want these shapes to appear undistorted as they are mapped to the particle squares, be certain to render these map shapes by using a uniform resolution. Also, you can control the brightness the particles by changing the Output Amount in the Output Rollout menu of the Opacity and Diffuse Map.

Open file 12FLARE3.MAX and set the frame slider to about frame 30. In this scene, two particle systems that create two types of stars are being used. One uses the default snow capabilities, the other uses a starburst map material (see fig. 12.20).

TIP

Be certain to set a Shininess strength of 0.0 for these flare materials when using them with particle systems, so that the square edges of the particles do not reflect light sources. These kinds of scenes are also easy to animate so that the particles from both emitters rush at the camera. When white flare materials are used, they also accept colors from light sources effectively.

FIGURE 12.20
A night sky is generated.

Using Lights as Materials

The capability of spotlights to project images onto geometry can also be thought of as projecting *materials* onto geometry. By relying on lights as materials, objects can assume the materials of the lights in front of which they pass, or objects can assume materials based on their location in the scene. This gives rise to the bizarre but powerful concepts of *geometry-independent materials*, *attenuated materials*, and *non-axial–dependent materials*.

- **Geometry-independent materials.** Materials that can be applied to any object or group of objects in the same manner regardless of their shape.

- **Attentuated materials.** Materials that are a function of the distance from the objects to which they are applied.

- **Non-axial–dependent materials.** Materials that do not require mapping coordinates.

Open the file 12SPOT1.MAX and render the Perspective viewport. In this scene, direct lights are used to project four different materials onto the object word Spotlight. Open the Materials Editor to view the images being used by the lights. From the front view, you can see how the boundaries of three directional lights are *tiled* so that each letter receives whatever *material* it is in front of (see fig. 12.21).

FIGURE 12.21

Three directional spotlights project three different "materials" on to a single text object.

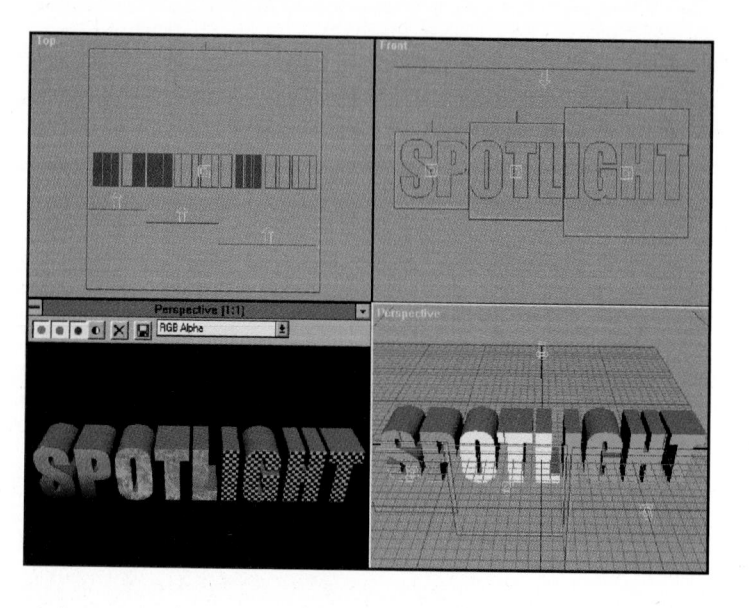

Enabling materials to become a function of an object's location opens up a world of possibilities in creating lighting special effects. Orthographic views provide an easy means of creating *tiles* of directional lights. Because directional spotlights cast the same amount of light on objects regardless of their distance from geometry, you can *cast* materials anywhere in the scene.

Open the file 12SPOT2.MAX and render the Perspective viewport (see fig. 12.22). The *materials* shine through all objects. As new objects move into line, they take on the next materials. Because lights are not limited to being projecting in the positive and negative X, Y, and Z axes, you can project any number of materials from any angle and blend them as desired.

NOTE

Using this technique can save a great deal of time when working with vast amounts of different objects that need the same types of materials.

TIP

If Omni lights or target spotlights are used rather than directional lights, attentuation with projected *materials* is also possible. As objects move closer to the light source, the material becomes more apparent.

FIGURE 12.22
Any new object may instantly acquire the "materials" of a specific location in the scene.

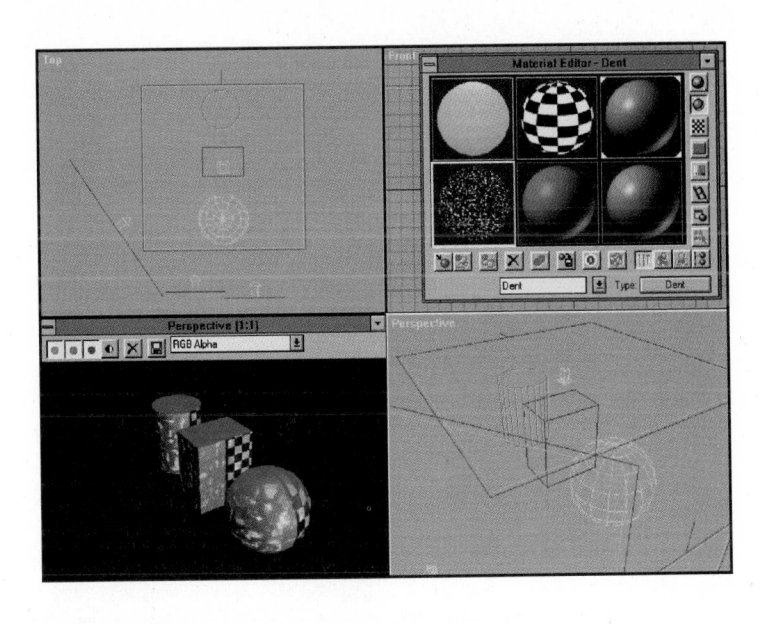

Psychedelic Materials

Through the use of exaggerated settings for geometry, modifiers, and effects, you can produce intentionally unrealistic and bizarre materials. These types of materials can be used stand-alone to create weird images or they can be used as components of other materials to add a touch of the unexpected or unexplainable.

In this first example, a simple box is transformed into a psychedelic materials generator through the uses of Noise Modifiers and a top down view. From globular mounds to skin-like streams, the steps show how different values set for the box and modifier can produce different types of effects materials.

In the second example, a single Combustion apparatus is viewed head-on through a camera, and the characteristics of the Combustion Atmosphere Effect are exaggerated to minimum and maximum values, producing visual effects from plasma and fibrous netting to wispy gasses and globular lava.

In the third example, a kaleidoscope object is created through which scenes, objects, and backdrops are viewed. The sides of the kaleidoscope all use flat mirrors so that anything viewed through the object's *opening* can be mirrored. This enhances a material's capability to be mirrored in more than just the U and V directions.

Noise Revisited

Open the file 12NOISE1.MAX. In this scene, a simple box is created with a Noise Modifier applied, but by rendering views in the Top viewport, a multitude of really strange patterns emerges as the Noise Modifier and box settings are exaggerated. Select the box, and click on the Modify panel so that you are able to change the settings of the box and Noise Modifier. Render the top viewport (see fig. 12.23).

FIGURE 12.23
Rectilinear seams resulting from unsmooth surfaces are not a nuisance with this material. They are the effect itself.

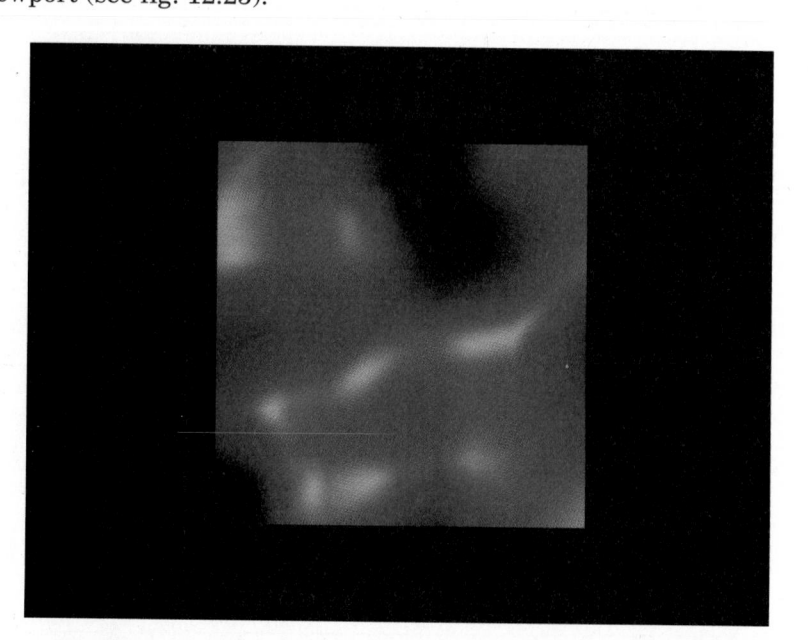

To give you a hint of the wide array of effects materials you can create by experimenting with geometry and modifier values, a series of images is shown here which you will generate in the tutorial that follows (see fig. 12.24).

FIGURE 12.24
Each of these materials can be used by itself or composited with other materials to add a touch of weirdness.

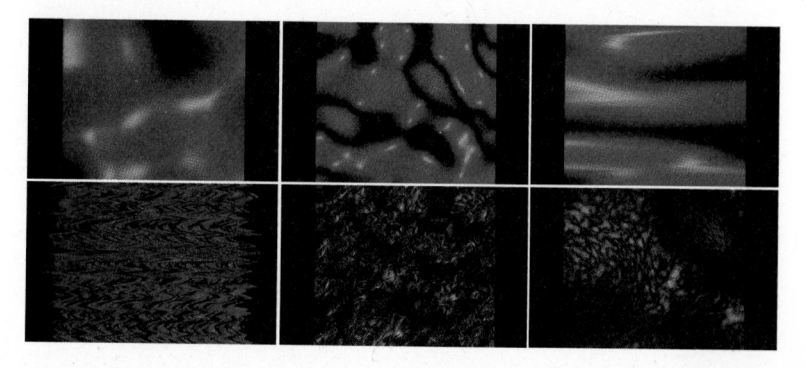

These types of images are difficult to describe. They may or may not occur in the natural world, and may look very awkward. But that's the point! These materials can be mirrored in the U and V directions when applied as a material so that they form strange but seamless tiles, or they can be used without tiling to intentionally produce abrupt and odd patterns. For each step outlined, the top viewport is rendered to see the effect. Some of the steps may not seem to make much of a difference, but the resulting *materials* are striking. An example of this technique is shown in the following steps:

1. Set the Noise Modifier seed value to 1 and render.

2. Click on the Noise Modifier Fractal toggle so that it is active and render.

3. Set the Noise Modifier Seed to 2, the Scale to 50, Roughness to 0, Iterations to 1, and render.

4. Set the Box Length Segments and Width Segments to a value of 30 and render.

5. Set the Box Width Segments to 1 and render.

6. Set the Box Width Segments to 2 and render.

7. Set the Box Length Segments to 50 and the Width Segments to 50. Set the Noise Modifier Scale to 4, Roughness to 0.5, Iterations to 1, X Strength to 50, Z Strength to 400, and render.

8. Set the Box Length and Width Segment values to 20 and render.

All these materials have been generated using the default material. By applying new materials of your own or existing materials with exaggerating settings, you can corrupt the same strange geometry in the preceding steps to create very different materials. An example of this technique is outlined in the following steps:

1. Toggle Generate Mapping Coord active in the Box's Parameters rollout menu. Click on the Materials Editor button from the main toolbar. Select the first (upper-left) sample slot and click on the Get Material button. Select Standard map type, and set the material's Diffuse map to a Noise map. Apply the material to the box by using the Assign Material to Selection button. In the Noise Parameters rollout menu, set the Size to 10 and the Noise type to Turbulence and render.

2. Set the Noise Modifier X Strength to 0, Y Strength to 0, Z Strength to 200, and render.

3. Set the Noise Modifier Scale to 100.0, Roughness to 0, Iterations to 1 and render.

4. Set the Noise Modifier Roughness to 1 and Iterations to 2. Click on the Materials Editor button and select the first sample slot material you created. Click on the Diffuse map to bring up the Noise map parameters. Set the Noise Type to Fractal, Size to 10, and in the Output rollout check the Invert toggle. Close the Material Editor and render (see fig. 12.25).

FIGURE 12.25
A simple box distorted with Noise Modifiers and an inverted Noise Material produces new possibilities for Diffuse, Bump, Opacity, and Shininess maps.

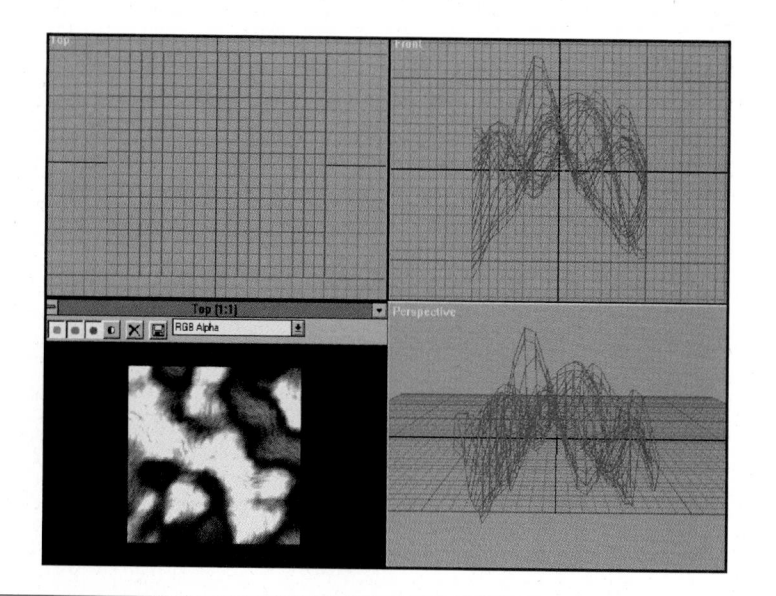

The possibilities are endless when other geometry is used. Experiment using other primitives with the same series of steps outlined for the box; apply materials to the box from the existing library. Use the resulting maps as bump maps or masks on existing materials.

Combustion Revisited

The Combustion Atmosphere Effect tool can also be tweaked to create materials that look nothing like flames or smoke. Through the use of different color schemes, odd flame sizes, and strange values for other characteristics, and through deformation of the Combustion apparatus, you can generate misty and gaseous materials unlike anything the fog tools can produce.

Open the file 12COMB1.MAX. In this scene, a spherical Combustion apparatus is viewed from a camera that uses a lens and FOV value to fill the entire camera viewport. Click on the Modify panel and select either the apparatus or the camera to view and modify its settings. Use the Rendering/Environment pull-down option to bring up the Environment dialog. View the settings for the Combustion Effect by selecting the Combustion item in the Effects list. Render the camera view (see fig. 12.26).

FIGURE 12.26
By using small values for flame size and density, a globular material unlike any flame is created.

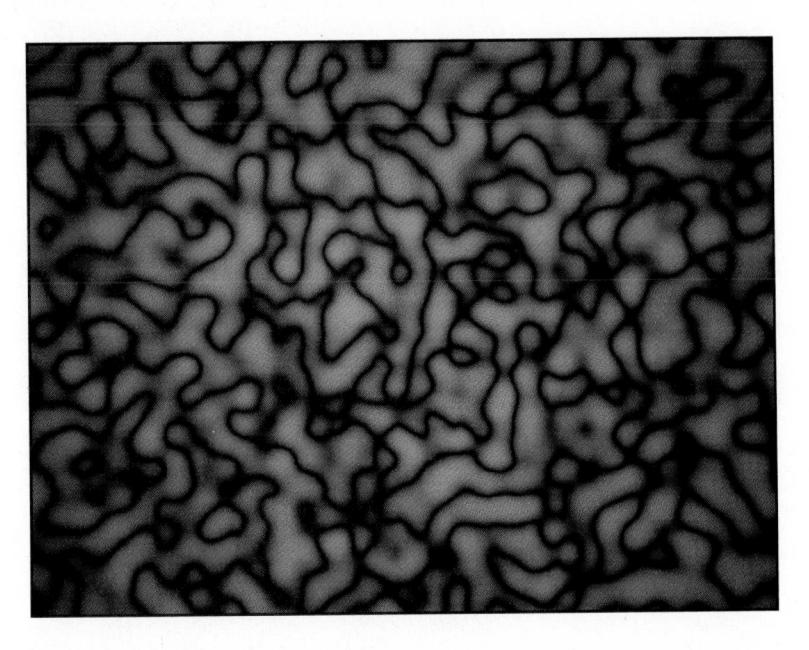

Globular, liquidy, fibrous, gaseous, netted, and spattered materials can all be generated by using the Combustion tool. Shown in the following series of images are a variety of example materials you will generate in the tutorial that follows (see fig. 12.27).

For each step outlined, the camera viewport is rendered to see the effect.

1. In the Combustion Parameters, set the Inner color to a bright green and the Outer color to black. In the Combustion parameters rollout menu for the apparatus, set the seed to 2, and render.

2. In the Combustion Parameters, set the Inner color to white. Set the flame size to 2 and render.

3. In the Combustion Parameters, set the Inner color to yellow. Set the flame size to 1, the Flame Detail to 1, the Density to 10, the Samples to 10 and render.

FIGURE 12.27

Each of these materials uses a single Combustion apparatus to be created.

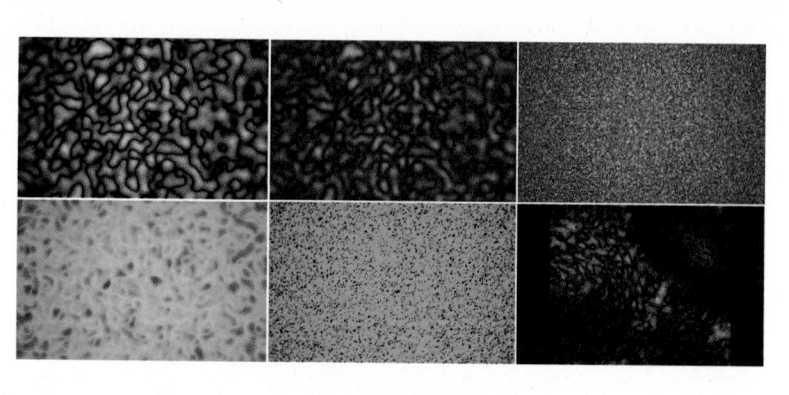

4. In the Combustion Parameters, set the Inner color to bright green and the Outer color to bright blue. Set the Flame Type to Tendril. Set the flame size to 5, the Flame Detail to 1, the Density to 5, the Samples to 3 and render.

5. In the Combustion Parameters, set the Outer color to black. Set the flame size to 1, the Flame Detail to 1, the Density to 5, the Samples to 2 and render.

6. In the Combustion Parameters, set the Inner color to cyan. Set the flame size to 20, the Flame Detail to 10, the Density to 5, the Samples to 2 and render.

By using more than one apparatus, you can create intertwining patterns of color and texture. Open the file 12COMB2.MAX and examine the two Combustion Atmosphere Effects in use. Notice that the size of the apparatuses has been varied. By combining the singular effects of each apparatus, you can create plasma, lightning, strange planetary terrains, and a wide assortment of gaseous materials for nebulae and novas (see fig. 12.8).

FIGURE 12.28

Two apparatuses are used to create multicolored plasma.

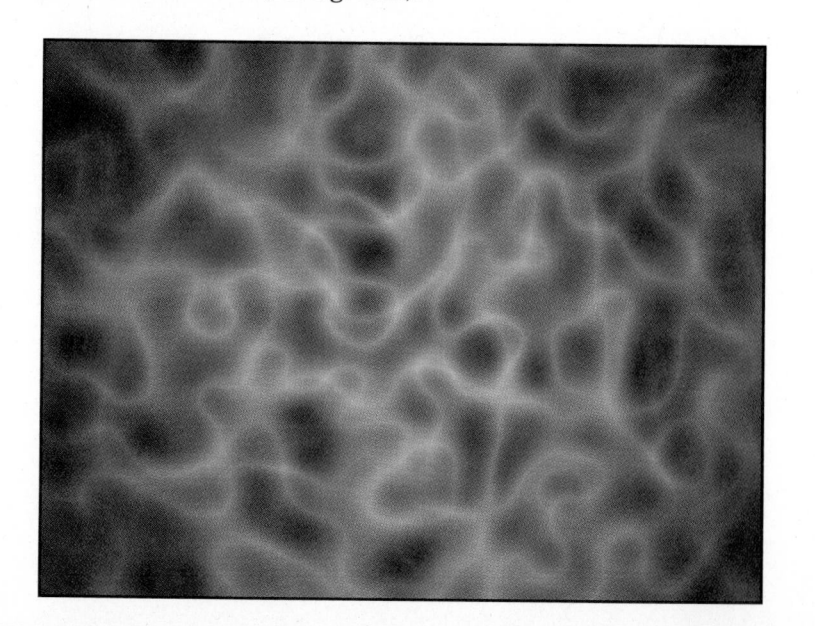

Mirror Tricks

You can extend the mirroring effect of materials from the U and V directions to any number of directions you desire by viewing your materials through kaleidoscope objects. Kaleidoscopes are tubes with three or more flat surfaces through which any scene, material, or object can be viewed.

Open the file 12MIRR1.MAX (see fig. 12.29). A camera is placed *inside* six arrayed flat surfaces which form the kaleidoscope tube. A flat mirror material is applied to each side of the tube so that any object, pattern, light, or effect that can be seen through the hole of the tube reflects on all sides, filling the screen.

FIGURE 12.29

The flat mirror material applied to each tube surface appears as a black area when viewed in the camera viewport.

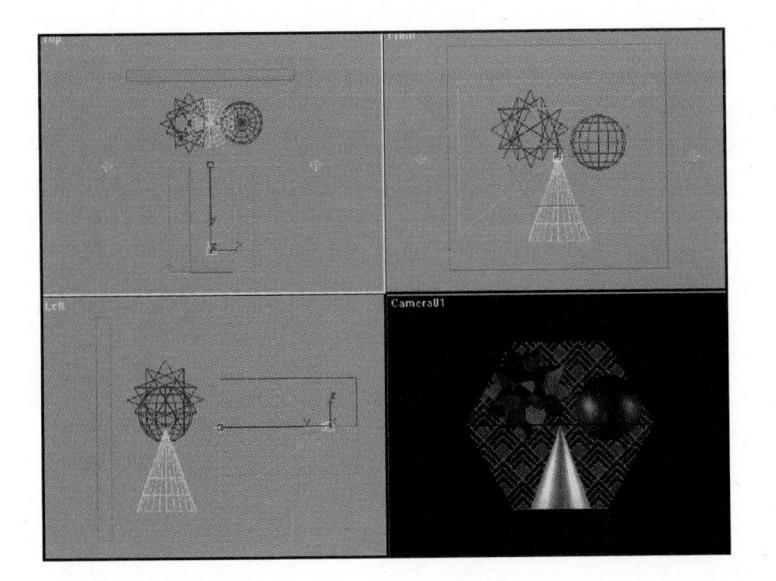

A backdrop with an elaborate pattern shows through the tube opening near the camera's target. If you wish to mirror any material in more than four directions, you can create a number of sides to the kaleidoscope equal to the number of mirroring directions you want and then place the material to be mirrored on the backdrop object. After you have your scene set, render the camera view (see fig. 12.30).

TIP

When using this technique to create new materials, in many cases it can help to set Self-Illumination of the material being mirrored to a high value. By the same token, using scene lights outside the kaleidoscope to highlight areas of the backdrop can also produce neat effects.

In Practice: Designing Special Effects Materials

- **Spinner and field values.** Try outrageous values for the spinners and field values when designing special effect materials. Many new effects can be achieved by using values of zero or very high positive or negative values. Revisit the techniques outlined in this chapter using unthinkable values.

- **Camera angles.** Special effects can often be achieved simply through a peculiar placement of the camera. Staring directly into lights, using odd camera lens settings, looking at your scenes through warped surfaces, or projecting your finalized scenes and animations onto warped "movie screens" can take your work one step beyond.

- **Recycling.** There will be times when you accidentally or experimentally create an unexpected effect. Even if you're under the gun, take the time to write down how the effect was accomplished so that it can be recreated if needed later. Don't waste neat accidents!

IMAGE BY LEE STEEL

Chapter 13

by Lee Steel

ANIMATED MATERIALS

It's common knowledge that carefully created materials and mapping far outweigh modeled geometry when the main concern is rendering time or face count. With this in mind, an animator with insight into the materials capabilities of MAX can create very believable scenes using very little geometry. Animated materials can take the place of a large number of applications where you once would have had to do a great deal of modeling to achieve similar effects such as rippling water or clouds in the sky. One aspect of 3D Studio MAX that sets it apart from all other animation packages is the fact that almost everything is animatable—including most parameters in MAX's Material Editor. This capability removes virtually all limitations when you're creating animated materials.

The Material Editor's Make Preview button (see fig. 13.1) is a very important feature. When you tweak animated materials, it is much easier to create material previews by using this function than it is to render the scene itself (even though final adjustments require that you render the geometry to adjust tiling and UVW scaling). The following sections give you greater insight into the capabilities at your fingertips in MAX. Along with the sample MAX files and rendered scene AVIs is a material library that includes all materials used in the exercises in this chapter.

Concepts covered in this chapter include the following:

- Animating color changes and controlling their transition

- Using Blend materials

- Creating the illusion of constant motion by using an AVI file as a map

- Simulating natural phenomena such as water and clouds by using noise

- Using sequential TGA files as an animated environment map

- Using third-party plug-ins to add control and a higher level of realism

FIGURE 13.1
Click on the Make Preview button to generate an AVI file of the current material slot.

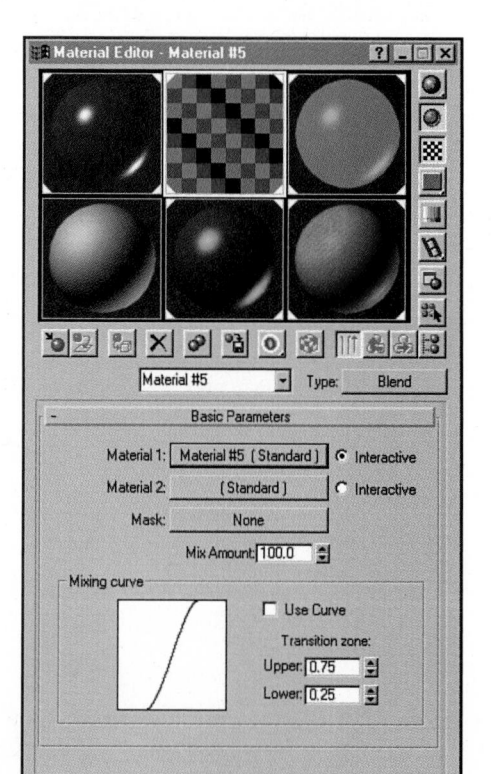

Animating Color Changes

To animate color changes, the level of opacity, the amount of shininess, and so forth, just set an initial color or value, turn on the animate button, drag the Time Slider to a new point in time, and change any of these values—and you have an animated material. The true power behind having so many animatable parameters, however, comes from using strategic combinations of material types and animated parameters, coupled with strategically adjusted key tangents to control how the changes take place. Virtually all limitations have been removed from material creation and, as with any software package, every user will find his or her own approach. The rule of thumb is: *If you can imagine it, you can do it.*

Although a host of new and exciting plug-ins have already begun to emerge, MAX's Material Editor is rich in features and has virtually unending depth and functionality. MAX's "shader-tree" topography offers the capability to embed several materials in another material. The tree structure used to map out a material, and the tree's accessibility through Track View give you, the user, absolute control over the way the individual parameters that make up the material are controlled over time.

After the material is mapped out and the timing is set for any changes that will take place, you must use some type of controller to dictate how the changes take place. Several types of controllers are available for this purpose. Brief descriptions of some useful ones follow:

- **Bézier Color controller.** Typically the default key controller, it interpolates how material changes take place from one key to the next. These key values are accessible through Track View. After the keys have been set, right-click on a key to display the Key Info dialog (see fig. 13.2) with controls for the way values are derived between keys, both coming into or going out of the selected key. The option of creating a custom tangent is available also. These trajectories add a great deal of control over the way a material's parameters change. Perhaps you need a nice smooth transition from one color or map to another, or perhaps you want a blinking effect where one color or map changes abruptly at each key with no transition. These are the types of effects associated with Bézier controllers. When you use this controller, the curve data displayed in Track View is clamped when color ranges fall below 0 or rise above 255.

FIGURE 13.2

*Bézier curves display
interpolated values
between keys.*

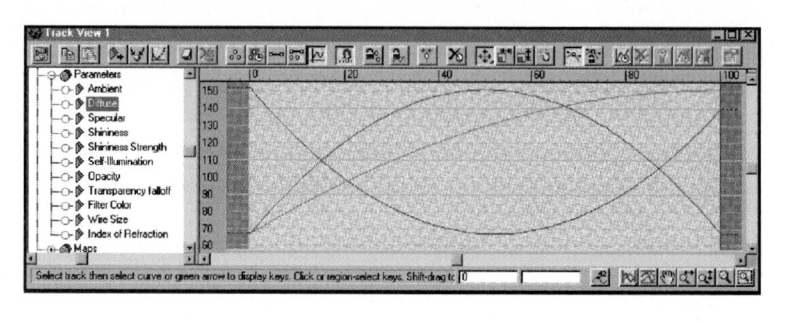

- **A Noise Float.** Applied to the Self-Illumination track, a noise float can be used to simulate random blinking similar to that of a neon light or open flame.

- **The Bézier Point3 controller.** This controller acts in much the same way as the Bézier Color controller. The RGB values are displayed as XYZ, however, and no color swatch is displayed. The curves, viewed in Track View, do not appear clamped when color ranges fall below 0 or rise above 255, even though these values are clamped by the color parameter.

- **The Noise Point3 controller.** This controller generates random color changes, and with the use of a Point3 List controller, can be combined with other color controllers.

Each controller is complete in and of itself but becomes increasingly powerful when used in conjunction with others to create complex shader-trees. In the following exercises, you see how to create some remarkable effects by combining certain material types and controllers.

Creating a Simple Color Change

In this section, you create a simple color change and use function curves to control how this change takes place over time. Start with a simple animated gradient.

1. Load the sample file 1301.max. The material in slot #1 changes from black at frame 0 to white at frame 20, yellow at frame 40, orange at frame 60, red at frame 80, and back to black at frame 100. In the case of colored particles, this gives you exact control of the particles' color throughout their life span.

2. Open Track View. Under Medit Materials, Colors (the name of the material), Diffused. Keys are associated with each individual color change.

3. Right-click on the key at frame 0 (see fig. 13.3). As you can see, the color swatch represents the color for this key. You also see the function curves for In and Out, which control how the transition is made between the keys. This is where the fun begins. By choosing one of the six preset curves, you have full control over how all the transitions take place.

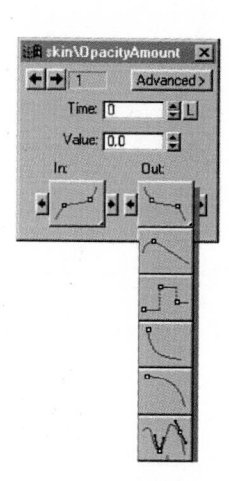

FIGURE 13.3

Left-click on the Key Tangent flyout for In and Out Bézier tangents to display the six preset curve styles.

4. Take a few minutes to experiment with the curve settings, and then render material previews by clicking on the Make Preview icon in the Material Editor panel.

5. Render an AVI file of this scene by using Video Post. Most settings have already been made, including a glow effect.

As you can see, you can control an object's color over time with a great deal of precision—a far cry from the R4 days of using an AXP to read a bitmap, pixel by pixel. Don't forget that you can animate other settings in the Material Editor—such as Shininess (Shin), Strength, Self-Illumination, and Opacity—as well. The same techniques of adjusting the keyframes' function curves apply here also. Your final scene should look something like the 1301.avi file located on the *Inside 3D Studio MAX Volume II* CD.

Blend Materials

Blend is a compound material type that actually enables you to control the way two separate maps are combined. These two maps can be of any map type, including Mix, that would enable you to combine two more maps into each of the Blend's map slots—and so on, and so on. The exercise in this section is a good example of animated opacity coupled with an animated Blend material. In this example, you animate this material mixing to create a dissolve from one material into another.

Load the sample file 1302.max from the accompanying CD. In this scene, you see the transporter room aboard an alien vessel. The task at hand is to create the effect of the alien being teleported into the room. You have been asked to simulate that sparkly *Star Trek* style effect that appears first as static noise and then transitions into the natural skin color. This is the perfect application for a Blend material.

---

1. Start by setting up the desired skin color for the alien. Name this material **Flesh**.

2. Pick the Type button in the Material Editor interface and select New. A list of material types appears.

3. Select Blend from the list. At the prompt, select Keep Old Material As Sub-Material and click on OK.

4. The original Flesh material is now listed in the Material 1: slot (see fig. 13.4). This is the main control dialog of the new Blend material; all controls that affect how the Blend takes place are located here. Set the initial Mix Amount to 100. In the Material Editor window, rename this material **Skin**.

5. To make any changes to the original skin color, click on the Material 1 button to display the parameter controls for Flesh.

6. Click on the Material 2 button. This is going to be the material that seems to sparkle as the transporter is initialized.

FIGURE 13.4

Main control dialog for Blend.

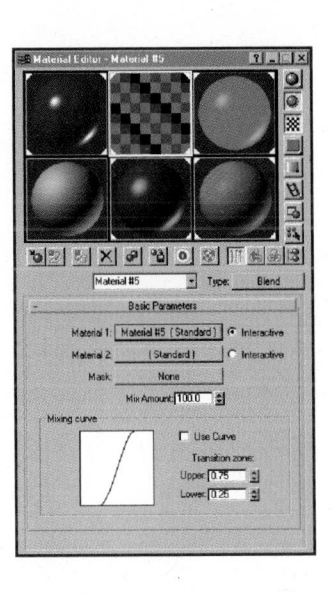

7. Change Shininess, Shin. Strength, and Opacity to 0. This ensures that the material is initially totally transparent.

8. Select Maps and click on the map slot for Diffuse. You are prompted to select a map type. Pick Noise from the list and click on OK.

9. Set the Noise Parameters as follows: Turbulence, High: .5, Low: 0; Size: .5, Levels: 1, and Phase 0. You might want to change some of these parameters later. (Having already gone through the experimentation process, however, the author believes that these parameters work best as a starting point.)

10. Click on the Go to Parent button in the Material Editor interface and drag a copy of the Diffuse Noise down to the Opacity slot. Pick Instance. This ensures that any changes made later to Diffuse Noise are made simultaneously to the Opacity Noise.

11. Set the Amount of Opacity to 0 for now. Add a background to the Material Preview window by clicking on the icon (see fig. 13.5). The material should be completely transparent at this point.

12. Pick Go to Parent, return to the main Blend control window, and change the Mix Amount to 0. The original skin material should now appear.

FIGURE 13.5

Click on the Background icon to add a checker pattern to the Material Preview window; this pattern is handy for controlling opacity.

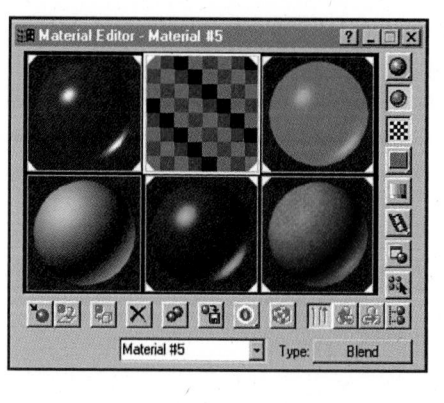

Change Mix Amount back to 100. You are now ready to animate the material.

Start the material animation process by creating some initial keys. You adjust these keys later, using Track View. You make the noise transition from transparent to sparkle take place over 30 frames, sparkle for 30 frames, and transition to the final skin color over 30 frames.

1. Pick the Animate button and move the Frame Slider to 30.

2. In the Material Editor, click on Material 2. Go to Maps, and set Opacity Amount to 100. This creates a fade-in of Noise from completely transparent to sparkle, over the first 30 frames.

3. While you set the parameters for Noise, click on the Diffuse slot. Move the Frame Slider to 100 and set Phase to 10. This causes the Noise to appear to twinkle.

4. Return to the Blend root and (at frame 90) set the Mix Amount to 0. This completes the basic key settings.

5. Now open Track View. Pick the Filters button (see fig. 13.6) and select Show Only: Animated Tracks. Now the keys for Mix Amount and Opacity Amount are visible (see fig. 13.7).

FIGURE 13.6

Click on the Filters icon to keep unnecessary tracks from being visible in Track View.

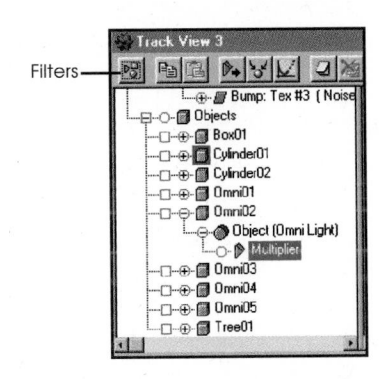

FIGURE 13.7

Mix Amount and Opacity Amount keys are now visible in Track View.

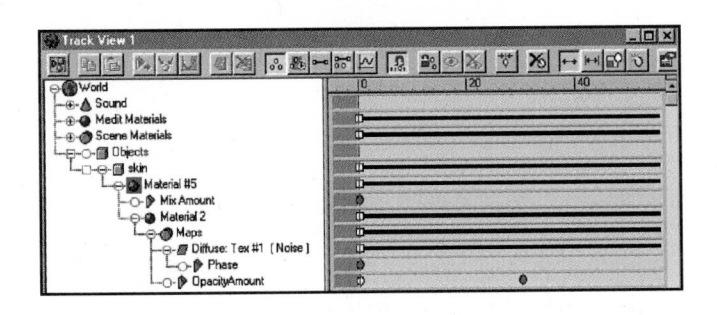

6. Because the transition from Noise to Skin is not scheduled to take place until frame 60, copy the key for Mix Amount at frame 0 and move it. Do this by holding down the Shift key, clicking on the key at frame 0, and dragging the copy over to frame 60. This holds the Mix Amount to a value of 100 from frame 0 through frame 60.

7. Edit these keys by right-clicking on the key at frame 0. Change the In and Out transition curves to Linear style curves. Move between keys by using the arrows in the upper-left corner (see fig. 13.8) of this window, and set all transitions in this manner.

8. Now create a Material Preview. Apply this material to the Skin of the alien (if you haven't already).

FIGURE 13.8
Click on the left- and right-arrow icons to move between keys.

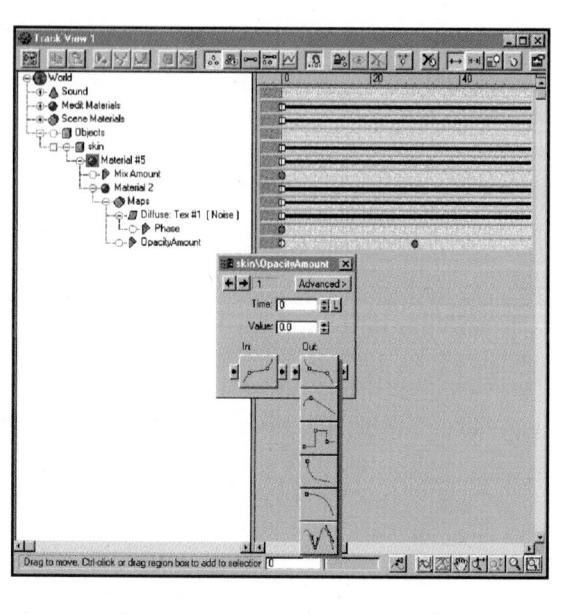

Finally, you need to re-create this process for all remaining mesh objects associated with the alien character. Then your task is complete. Your final scene should look something like the 1302.avi file on the accompanying CD.

Creating the Illusion of Constant Motion

An endless number of things in the world, from tank treads to conveyor belts, display constant motion. This type of motion can be quite easy to approximate in 3D Studio MAX with the use of carefully created animated materials.

An animated material that displays constant motion must loop at some point, and you can accomplish the task in several ways. In this exercise, you create an AVI file that appears to loop because the pattern is moved in such a way that when the next row in the pattern is about to appear, the AVI recycles to frame 1, where this row is visible.

In this next exercise, you create the effect of some clear glass tubes surrounding the transporter platform. Inside these tubes, bubbles rise in an endless flow from bottom to top.

1. Start a new file. Activate the Front view and create a box with the dimensions Length:200, Height:200, and Width:1. Check the Generate Mapping Coords box.

2. Open the Material Editor, create a new Standard material, and name it **Bubbles**.

3. In the Diffuse Map, load the bitmap file, BEEBEES.JPG (a bitmap that ships with 3DS MAX). Apply this material to the box. Click on the Show Map in Viewport icon.

4. From the MAX pull-down menus pick Views, Viewport Configuration, and in the Safe Frames tab, check the box under Application, next to Show Safe Frames in Active View. A series of boxes should appear in the Front viewport. Also make sure you have the viewport set for shaded mode.

5. In the Front viewport, zoom in and move the box until the first full row of beebees down to the second from the last row fills the viewport horizontally and touches the yellow safe frame box from side to side (see fig. 13.9).

FIGURE 13.9
Align the bitmap within the safe frame to ensure proper tiling.

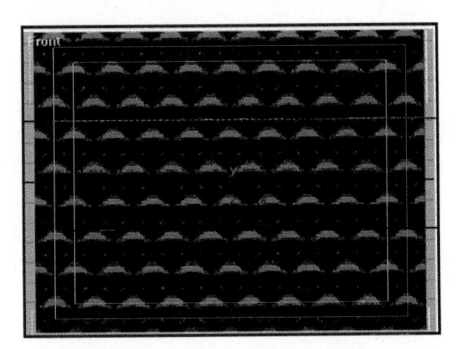

6. Set the animation length to 10 frames. Move the frame slider to frame 10, and click on the Animate button.

7. With the axis constrained to Y, move the box up a distance equal to two rows of beebees, until the row is just above the bottom line of the viewport.

8. Render an AVI of this file, named Bubbles.

Now to apply your newly created animated material to a scene. Open file 1302.max, the scene of the transporter room.

1. Create a new Standard material and name it Post. In the Diffuse map slot, load Bubbles.avi. Set V: Tiling to 2.0. Make an Instance copy of this map to the map slots of both Opacity and Bump. Set Self-Illumination to 100.

2. Apply this material to the four columns in the scene and render the scene. The final outcome should be the illusion of constantly flowing bubble-shaped highlights rising on each of the poles.

This technique can be applied to the creation of any material that needs to appear in constant motion. Your final scene should look something like the 1302.AVI file located on the accompanying CD.

Using Noise to Simulate Water and Sky

Look around the next time you venture into the great outdoors. Many things are always moving around us. Trees and leaves gently move as they are disturbed by wind, even on the calmest of days. A pool of water almost always has slight ripples or swells. Clouds gracefully pass by overhead. All these elements of nature are easily overlooked, yet required for our brain to truly believe that what we are seeing is real.

In 3D Studio MAX, these types of occurrences are easily recreated and help make a much more believable scene. Load the sample file 1303.max—an outdoor scene of a brick well filled with water and surrounded by torches. You enhance the final animated scene by using a Noise material to simulate the ripples in the water without having to model them (which would greatly increase the face count in the scene). You also use a Noise material to create soft puffy clouds as an animated environment map. Finally, you add animated flames to the torches.

Water

Water can be very tricky to simulate. Water is always changing, always moving, and in the real world is very unpredictable. Certain features, however, trigger intuition and assure you of the fact that, "Yes, this is water!"

1. In the Material Editor, pick Get Material, pick New and Standard. Name this material Water.

2. Because water is usually very shiny on the surface, set Shininess to 50, and Shin. Strength to 100. And because water has transparency, set Opacity to 80.

NOTE

By activating a material's Background button, you make it easier to visualize just how Opaque the material is.

3. Click on the Diffuse Map slot. Select Noise from the list and click on OK (see fig. 13.10). Under Noise Parameters are two color swatches labeled Color #1 and Color #2. The color of the water is a combination of these two colors.

FIGURE 13.10

The Noise Parameters dialog contains all settings for combining the colors that will be your water.

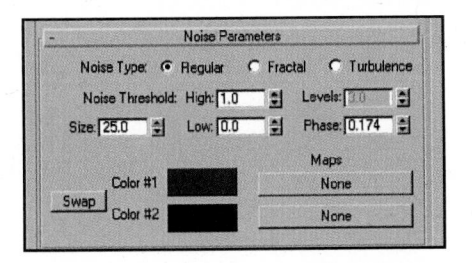

4. Pick the color swatch for Color #1 and make adjustments to create a dark green. A good starting point is Red:0, Green:67, and Blue:57. Now do the same for Color #2 but adjust RGB to create a navy blue. Start by setting Red:7, Green:29, and Blue:49.

5. Because the water's surface must appear to move, activate the Animate button in the main MAX screen, move the frame slider to 100, and change the Phase setting to .6. This animates the intermixing of the two colors throughout the animation. Note that the higher the Phase setting, the faster the colors change over time.

6. Use a similar technique to create the rolling, rippled surface of the water. Click on the Bump Map slot and again select Noise from the list.

7. Change the Angle so that the ripples move in a different direction from the changing color. Note that in nature the surface of water and the waves usually seems to move in opposite directions. To achieve this effect, turn off Animate, and under Coordinates, set X:90 and Y:90.

8. To simulate the water's "rolling" action, be certain that you are still at frame 100, activate MAX's Animate button, and change the Phase setting under Noise Parameters to 5.

9. The settings for your Water material should now be complete. Use the Make Preview button to test-render your material, and apply it to the Water object in the scene.

N OTE

To add one more level of realism to your scene, you can use the Environment Map material that you create in the next section as a reflection map for the water.

Set the Reflection Amount very low—around 10 to 15. Don't forget that because you want to simulate a realistic reflection, the reflection map coordinates need to be rotated 180 degrees.

Now that you have completed the main areas of interest in this scene, let's move on to create the environment these objects will reside in. Note that the tree included in this scene has an animated bend modifier applied to simulate blowing wind and was created with Digimation's Tree Factory Plug-in.

Sky and Space

In this section, you use animated Noise materials to simulate a day and night environment map. Creating photo-realistic environments with plug-ins alone can be anywhere from difficult to near-impossible. Plug-ins, however, can be used to create some very surrealistic effects. The best way to simulate accurate environments is to use time lapse sequences of real images. In the following exercises, you will experiment with both approaches.

1. In the Material Editor, click on Get Material, pick New, and then pick Noise. Name this material **Day Sky**.

2. Select Noise Type: Fractal and Set Size:15.

3. Click on the color swatch for Color #1 and set Red:62, Green:136, and Blue:192. This color represents the sky.

4. Click on the color swatch for Color #2 and set Red:205, Green:205, and Blue:205. This color represents the clouds.

5. Clouds usually appear to be stretched, parallel to the horizon. In the Coordinates section, set Tiling: X:0.2.

NOTE

Appropriate color is always in the eye of the beholder. None of the color values suggested here are set in stone. You, the user, the adventurer, are completely at liberty to experiment with color settings that you feel are most characteristic of sky and clouds.

By decreasing the Tiling:X amount, you make the clouds stretch more along the horizon. By increasing the amount, you make the clouds appear smaller and fluffy.

6. Because you want these clouds to move slightly throughout the animation, activate the Animate button and move the frame slider to frame 100. In the Coordinates section, set Angle X:0.5 and Angle Y:0.5. Now set Phase:0.3. The higher the number in the Phase setting, the faster the clouds move across the sky.

7. Finally, from the main MAX pull-down menu, pick Rendering and then pick Environment. In the Background section, pick Assign and choose Browse From: Material Editor. Select the material Day Sky from the list and pick OK.

8. Render an AVI of your scene. Water and clouds should both appear to be moving.

The sky in your scene should resemble the one in 1303c.avi located on the CD-ROM.

Next turn day into night.

1. In the Material Editor, click on Get Material, pick New, and then pick Noise. Name this material **Night Sky**.

2. Select Noise Type: Turbulence, and Set Size:0.02.

3. Set Noise Threshold: High:0.001, Levels:1.0, and click on the Swap button located next to the swatches for Colors #1 and #2.

This is the star field in your night sky. For one more level of realism, add some night clouds as well.

1. Click on the Maps box just to the right of the color swatch for Color #2, and choose Browse From: Material Editor. Select the material Day Sky from the list and pick OK.

2. Click on the color swatch for Color #1 and set Red:0, Green:0, and Blue:0. This color represents the sky.

3. Click on the color swatch for Color #2 and set Red:60, Green:60, and Blue:60. You want to diminish the whiteness of the clouds because they are not illuminated by the sun.

4. Because this material was a copy of the Day Sky material, all animated parameters are the same.

5. Finally, from the main MAX pull-down menu, pick Rendering and then pick Environment. In the Background section, pick Assign and choose Browse From: Material Editor. Select the material Day Sky from the list and pick OK.

6. Re-render an AVI of the scene. Now you should see a night sky and slowly moving clouds and water.

You can easily animate the transition from day to night by creating a new Blend material and using the material named Day Sky as a Diffuse map for Material 1. Then use Night Sky as a Diffuse map for Material 2. Set Shininess and Shin. Strength to 0 in both instances. Because the animated parameters for the clouds are the same for both day and night, the transition from one to the other should be very smooth. Your final scene should look something like the 1303b.avi file located on the accompanying CD.

Another way to create a realistic daytime environment for the sky is to use a sequence of time-lapse pictures of real clouds. The accompanying CD includes a low-resolution sequence of images from the Image Shoppe's "Colorado Altitudes" CD. Locate these sequential images on the CD-ROM and copy them to your Maps sub-directory.

1. From MAX's pull-down menu select Rendering, Environment, and Assign. From this list, pick Bitmap and click on OK. Now click on the Environment Map button and choose a slot number (see fig. 13.11).

FIGURE 13.11

Choose a slot number from this dialog to begin building your environment map.

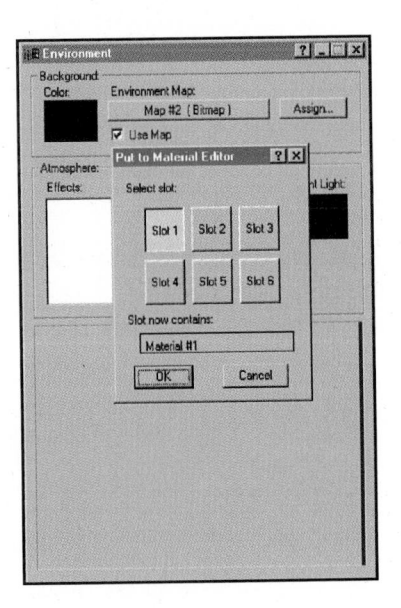

2. In the Material Editor, the slot you have chosen is now black and the controls for Spherical Environment are visible.

3. Because the camera is not moving, use the down-arrow key next to Spherical Environment and pick Screen from the list. This constrains the entire bitmap used as the environment to the viewport.

4. Click on the Bitmap button and locate the path to the Colorado Altitudes subdirectory on the accompanying CD. Under File Name, type **CLDG*.JPG** and click on OK.

5. Now the line next to Bitmap: reads `cldg000a.ifl`. MAX uses each of these images as the environment bitmap in numerical order.

6. If you render a single frame at this point, you can see that the background image is centered in the viewport and partially blocked by the geometry. To fix this problem, set Offset V: to 0.68. This setting raises the image so that the bottom of the bitmap is just below the simulated horizon of the geometry in the scene.

7. Render an AVI of the scene again. Now the moving image of clouds is visible as the animated environment.

With our environment complete, you can now move on to add one more level of realism.

Fire

As a finishing touch to this scene, you add fire to the stacks around the well. You can do this in several ways. One way is to use Combustion, an Atmospheric Effect that ships with 3D Studio MAX. Another method is to map a sequence of time-lapse images of real fire on geometry designed to approximate the shape of the flames. "Pyromania" is a collection of fire sequences created by VCE and available through Trinity Enterprises. The *Inside 3D Studio MAX Volume II* CD includes a low-resolution sequence of images from VCE's "Pyromania 1" CD.

1. Unhide Sphere01, 02, 03, and 04. Use the Display panel and click on Unhide by Name. These spheres have been deformed to approximate the size of the flames. Cylindrical UVW mapping has been applied. Note that in Sub-Object mode, the height of the mapping gizmo can be nonuniformly scaled to adjust the height of the flames. Locate the Pyromania files located on the CD-ROM and copy them to your Maps sub-directory.

2. In the Material Editor, pick Get Material, and then pick New and Standard. Name this material **Flames**.

3. Change the settings for Shininess and Shin. Strength to 0, and set Self-Illumination to 100.

4. Click on the Diffuse Map button and pick Bitmap from the list.

5. Under Bitmap Parameters, click on the Bitmap button and locate the path to the set of flame images provided on the accompanying CD. Type the name **FR51*.JPG** and click on OK.

6. The Bitmap slot now reads FR510000.ifl. Note that if the files were residing on your hard drive and no IFL file existed, MAX would automatically create an IFL file for you. An IFL file is an ASCII file that includes a list of all image names in the sequence you have specified.

7. Change U: Tiling to 0.8. This scales the image and widens the flames around the diameter of the Sphere object.

8. A total of 79 image files make up the Fire material, and the total animation length is 100 frames. How do you stretch the timing of the flames to match? Go to the Time roll-up at the very bottom of this window and change Playback Rate to 0.7 (see fig. 13.12). This stretches out the sequence over time. If you had entered a value of 2, the sequence would play twice as fast.

FIGURE 13.12

Whenever a sequence of frames is specified as a map, you can use the Time roll-up to scale the rate at which these frames are used to fit the space in which they are needed.

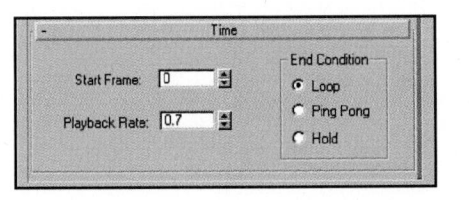

9. Click on the Go to Parent button and make an Instance copy of this map in the Opacity Map slot.

10. Click on the Show Map in Viewport button, select the four spheres, and apply the map.

11. As a final touch, four omni lights are added, one in the center of each flame sphere. Settings in Track View for each light have added Noise Float to the Multiple of each light (see fig. 13.13). Strength has been constrained to 1 and selected the >0 Value constraint to keep the light value from going into negative values.

NOTE

The color of the light could also be an animated color map. By adjusting the parameters of the Noise, you are able to simulate the flares of light given off by the flickering flames.

FIGURE 13.13

Noise Float Controller dialog, showing settings for flickering lights.

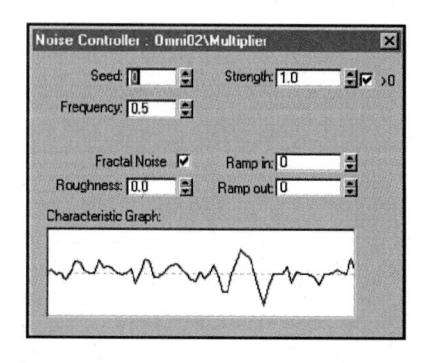

Your final scene should look something like the 1303a.avi file on the accompanying CD. AVI file 1303b demonstrates the night scene, and 1303c demonstrates the day scene, using the Noise settings for sky and Texture Lab (available from Digimation) for the fire.

Third-Party Plug-Ins

Several new routines that are about to hit the market will be a great help in the creation of exciting, realistic animated materials. Because Kinetix and the Yost Group have provided such an open architecture and an extremely user-friendly software development kit (SDK), software developers have begun to flood the market with useful plug-in routines to help speed up the creation of animated effects and, in some cases, create effects that would otherwise be impossible.

In their simplest form, these plug-ins might be nothing more than a programmed macro to help cut down on the time-consuming trial-and-error tweaking of values to achieve a particular task. At the other end of the spectrum is a class of exotic new material types; derived from complex mathematical algorithms, they create otherwise unobtainable material effects. Think of these plug-ins as programs in and of themselves, that are executed from within the MAX environment.

The following list describes four exceptional plug-ins for animating materials:

- **Fractal Flow MAX.** This Video Post plug-in filter, which functions just as its name suggests, is a port from 3D Studio R4 with some added features. The programmers at Digimation have developed elaborate, unique algorithms for creating the smoothest, most believable flowing pixel effects available (to date) for 3DS (see fig. 13.14). By using animated gradients as masks for virtually any or all parameters, gracefully flowing fractals can be used to create a wide variety of believable effects. A few examples are floating, puffy clouds; realistically flowing water; smoke and vapor that bubble up with that "dry ice" look; space dust; whirlpools; predator-style cloaking and uncloaking; heat rising from hot asphalt; and virtually any distortion effect. These effects can be used on an entire scene or masked to affect only a predefined area. Because the effects can be masked, animated maps such as ripples and waves can be used as masks to create the same type of effects previously available in R4 from Mirage. Fractal Flow effects are pixel based, not actual particles, which makes rendering much faster.

FIGURE 13.14

The Fractal Flow MAX interface, showing the Ripples tab. The real-time Preview window provides instant feedback as to how the ripple effect will appear.

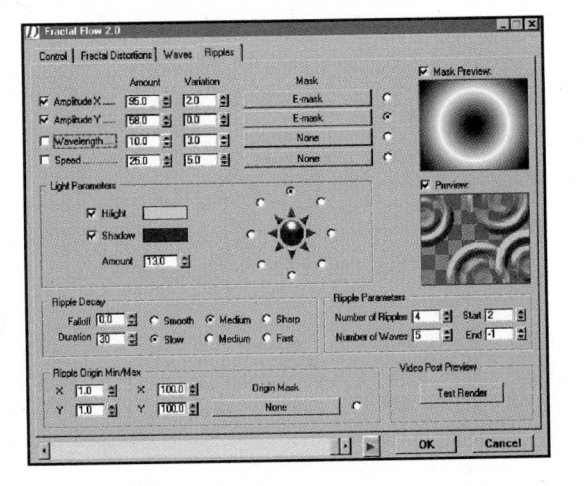

- **Texture Lab.** This plug-in, a collection of procedural textures, will be available soon from Digimation. *Procedural textures* are derived completely from formulas and require no bitmaps. These are very similar to the Marble, Wood, and Dent materials that ship with MAX. Texture Lab includes such materials as Fog, Strata, Electrics, Water, Advanced Noise, and Fire (see fig. 13.15). Also see AVI files 1303b and 1303c located on the *Inside 3D Studio MAX Volume II* CD. These animations show a good example of the Fire Procedural texture used as the flames.

FIGURE 13.15

*Procedural Fire is just
one of the new textures
in Digimation's Texture
Lab package.*

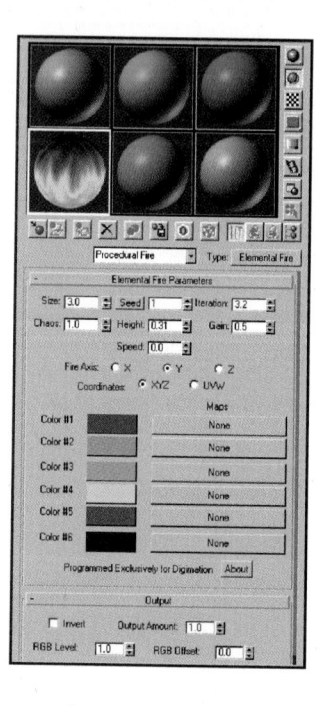

- **Electrolize.** This shareware plug-in, written by Harry Denholm, is included on the accompanying CD. Future upgrades and releases will be available in CompuServe's KINETIX forum. Electrolize creates animated noise barriers between two defined materials that act much like animated wipes. These type effects have been used recently in both the opening logo sequence for *Cable Guy* and the uncloaking effects in *Predator 2*. Electrolize and few other freeware plug-ins for MAX are included on the accompanying CD. Open file 1305.MAX for a closer look at Electrolize.

In this exercise, your alien friend from the earlier transporter room scene has to look down the barrel of what appears to be an ominous freeze-ray. The alien's arms were repositioned using Digimation's Bones Pro, after which a Snapshot was taken of the mesh.

1. Render the scene using Video Post. The result should look somewhat like the file 1305.avi located on the accompanying CD. Around frame 35, the alien's skin turns from tan to white and the edge that appears to grow and take over the mesh has a pixelated edge. This effect was created by using Electrolize.

2. Open the Material Editor and look at the material called Alien. As you can see, this Multi/Sub-Object material includes six different materials. Now click on the button for Material 1: skin (Standard), and click again on the Diffuse Map button. As you can see, Electrolize has been loaded as a material type for this slot (see fig. 13.16).

FIGURE 13.16

Electrolize is a freeware plug-in, written and distributed by Harry Denholm of Ishani Graphics.

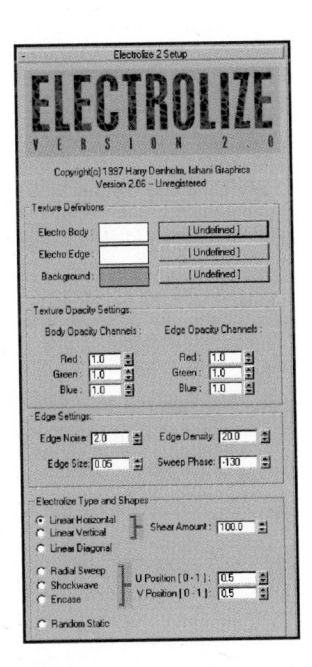

3. Before converting this material slot to Electrolize, the original material color was retained by using MAX's Color Clipboard (see fig. 13.17). Select Color Clipboard from the Utility tab and pick New Floater. A floating color pallet with 12 swatches appears on your desktop. You can now drag and drop the diffuse color from the swatch beside each material slot to the floating clipboard.

4. To add Electrolize, click on the Diffuse Map button and select Electrolize from the Material/Map Browser window.

5. Drag the appropriate color from the floating pallet and drop it on the swatch for Background in Electrolize. The colors for Electro Edge and Electro Body, which in this case are both white to simulate freezing, can be completely different colors.

FIGURE 13.17
*Select Color Clipboard
from the Utilities tab,
and pick New Floater
to utilize the floating
pallet.*

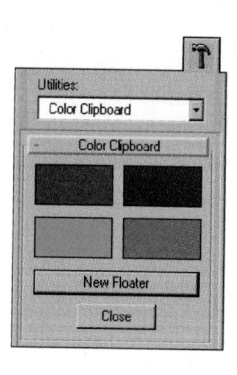

6. Experiment with Edge Size and Edge Density. These controls determine how much of a pixelated edge the wipe effect will have.

7. Sweep Phase is the parameter that causes the edge to move from one location to another. In this case, the effect is set to –130 at frame 0, holds until frame 35, and increases to 100 at frame 70. A few sample renders proved that with Sweep Phase set to –130, the effect is totally hidden from the camera's view until it is increased.

8. Finally, click the Apply WaveForms button. The SINE Waves settings (see fig. 13.18) control the twisted path the edge will have.

FIGURE 13.18
*Waveform controls
used by Electrolize to
bend the edge of the
wipe effect.*

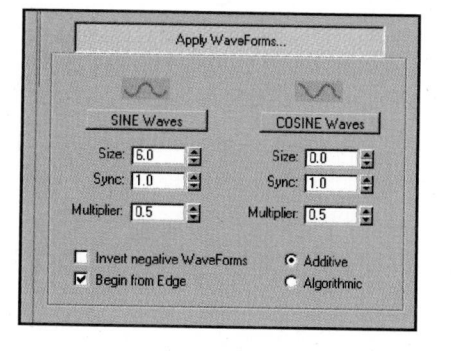

9. Take the time to go through the rest of the materials that make up the Alien and convert these materials to Electrolize.

The animated material features in 3D Studio MAX are among the strongest features that set this animation package apart from the others. With the techniques presented here and a little ingenuity, you should be well on your way to creating some very exciting animated effects.

In Practice: Animated Materials

- You have learned to animate color and use key tangents to control the rate at which colors can be cycled over time.

- You have a better understanding of how to use Blend materials to dissolve from one material to another.

- Creating carefully framed AVI files to create the illusion of constant motion can eliminate the use of unnecessary geometry.

- Using Noise to simulate water, fire, clouds, and stars can be quite effective is some applications.

- The use of sequential files as an IFL can be used to create more realistic scenes.

- You have gained an increased awareness of third-party plug-ins used to generate more appealing animated materials.

Part V

APPENDIX

Appendix A

INTEGRATING AUTOCAD WITH 3D STUDIO MAX

In the world of precise CAD data, the AutoCAD program and its .dwg format have become ubiquitous. Even if you are not a person that uses a CAD program, the chances of you encountering a .dwg file (or its .dxf cousin) are extremely high. CAD programs such as AutoCAD are used to define the majority of buildings and manufactured parts built today. Because of this, it is very common to have this data available when modeling such things as buildings, city streets, vehicles, machinery, furniture, or parts. To aid in this coordination of data, this appendix is dedicated to understanding:

- The various formats of exchange possible between AutoCAD and 3D Studio MAX

- The details of the various AutoCAD entities and their MAX equivalents

- The geometric conversion that occurs between the two programs' objects, and how that varies between the various methods of exchange

- The organizational strategies often used to coordinate data between the two programs

Why Is AutoCAD Used with 3D Studio MAX?

With all the modeling capabilities inherent to 3D Studio MAX, it may be an easy question to ask why coordinate with a CAD program. Several potential reasons exist, but the real decision on which to model with is based on the program's capabilities and strengths and your experience with it.

- **Already use AutoCAD.** If you are currently comfortable with AutoCAD, it is quite common to continue to use it for what it excels at—fast and accurate 2D drawing. Many modelers find that these drawings form excellent templates for extrusion and lofting within 3DS MAX. With some knowledge of AutoCAD's 3D capabilities, a significant synergy between the two modeling databases can often take place.

- **Wealth of information.** With so many structures and manufactured components detailed in AutoCAD, it is possible that useful information already exists for the model on which you are working. Many projects progress from design stages directly to preliminary CAD documentation. This is often the stage when visualization is required, and is where .dwg data can be used by 3D Studio MAX quite naturally. The amount of available data goes far beyond the project at hand however, because numerous manufactures and municipalities offer drawings and sometimes models for AutoCAD incorporation (many times free of charge).

- **Specialized AutoCAD applications.** The most striking similarity AutoCAD has to 3D Studio MAX is its own open architecture. Many specialized programs exist for performing complex tasks easily for various professions. When the similar tasks are required in 3DS MAX, it should be realized that the similar problem may have been already optimized for AutoCAD, and a result created there can be imported into 3DS MAX.

■ **Ease of accuracy.** Accuracy can mean many things. To most people, accuracy means being able to key enter specific coordinates or offsets, or use object snapping whenever needed. To others, it's the fact that AutoCAD maintains its data in double floating point precision, and 3DS MAX stores its in single. Although both situations can be overcome in MAX, the fact is that AutoCAD does excel in precision and many CAD-literate users find it faster to achieve an accuracy with it.

Exchanging Data Between AutoCAD and 3D Studio MAX

Three file formats currently enable AutoCAD and 3D Studio MAX to exchange geometric data: .dwg, .dxf, and .3ds. The correct format depends on how the information exists in AutoCAD, how you want it translated into MAX, or what type of information in 3DS MAX you want to export to AutoCAD. The primary differences between the three formats are:

■ **.dwg**   This is the native format of AutoCAD and affords the purest conversion of both AutoCAD and 3DS MAX geometries and organizational methods. Although it does not currently translate materials or mapping information, it maintains a high degree of parametric intelligence between the diverse geometries in the two programs.

■ **.dxf**   This was for many years the only documented file format available from AutoCAD. As such, it established a standard for the generic transfer of information between numerous CAD and modeling programs and can often be found as an export or import option in non-Autodesk products. In translation, its advantage is in providing the most direct method for converting CAD models to explicit 3DS MAX meshes.

■ **.3ds**   This is the native format for the 3D Studio DOS product, and is the only current method for transferring materials and mapping to and from AutoCAD. Although it primarily translates meshes, it is the superior method by which to export custom ARX object classes (such as Mechanical Desktop models) from AutoCAD to 3D Studio MAX.

N OTE

The .3ds format has also become a primary transfer mechanism between animation programs and in-house proprietary formats. This is because the .3ds format has been public for years and contains the basic information required for rendering and animation. Although .3ds is extremely important in this regard, this appendix is concerned with its connection to AutoCAD.

The translation characteristics of the three formats enable you to choose the best method of coordination based on what data you have and what data you need in the other program:

- You want the resulting geometry to be as parametric as possible within 3DS MAX or AutoCAD? *Use the .dwg format.*

- You want data to make a round trip from AutoCAD to MAX back to AutoCAD? *Use the .dwg format.*

- You have materials and/or mapping that you want to maintain to or from AutoCAD? *Use the .3ds format.*

- You want explicit meshes only to and from AutoCAD? *Use the .dxf format.*

- You want to bring AutoCAD Mechanical Desktop models into 3DS MAX? *Use 3DSOUT from AutoCAD.*

- You want to have the conversion control on the 3DS MAX side? *Use either the .dwg or .dxf format.*

You may want try converting some small representative models as tests of these three formats, especially those containing curved and closed entities, to ensure the file format you choose is the best for the job. When using the two programs side-by-side, you will probably find AutoCAD to be a very accurate modeler designed to handle organizations of great complexity, and that 3D Studio MAX is a very robust modeler capable of making complex forms quite easily and, of course, being capable of animating them. Together, they have considerable synergy.

AutoCAD Characteristics

This section is presented as an aid to those that need to communicate with AutoCAD but may not be completely familiar with the methods or terms used in that program.

The first important fact is that both AutoCAD and 3DS MAX maintain their data in relation to the world origin. This means that you can be confident of importing AutoCAD data time and time again and having it align perfectly with what was previously imported. It also means that 3DS MAX data can be exported back to AutoCAD in precise relationship to the originating drawing. This correlation is true regardless of the file format used to transfer between the two programs and is independent of any User Coordinate System that may be active in AutoCAD when writing the files. The two programs also use the same world axes labeling for X,Y,Z (a labeling often termed "left-hand rule"), so what was Z in AutoCAD is Z in 3D Studio MAX.

AutoCAD Organizations

The successful coordination of mutually evolving AutoCAD drawings and 3D Studio MAX scenes is usually a matter of modeling organization and using consistent procedures. Each firm or studio will develop their own methods for accomplishing this, but it usually entails a series of files in both formats that have varying levels of basic data, notation, 3D information, and final scenes with materials, lighting, and animation that correspond to the AutoCAD data of proposed, developing, or existing projects. Good communication and established processes are essential for any advanced project that evolves in two programs.

If the AutoCAD files are coming from a site unfamiliar with 3D modeling and rendering, some understanding of how typical drawings are organized can assist you in making the best translation into 3DS MAX. The typical AutoCAD organization tends to have very different goals than those in 3DS MAX. For most AutoCAD users, the eventual goal for the drawing is a two-dimensional, hard-copy plot. Organizational techniques have thus evolved to coordinate data according to the pen weights, fills, and colors required to produce quality plots. Organization in terms of a 3D database is often secondary to the needs of producing readable prints.

Plotting is coordinated within AutoCAD by assigning pen numbers to display color numbers (the same palette of 255 colors shown in the ACI color palette with 3DS MAX). Color assignment is either done by layer (where every entity receives the same color) or by entity property (where each entity can be given its own color regardless of the layer it is on). These two methods may coexist within the same drawing, so choosing to derive MAX objects by color should be done with some caution.

When coordinating with 3D Studio MAX, most modelers find that a layer-based approach provides the best opportunities for clear organization and future coordination. The layer names become the object names and can become a like-named layer again on return to AutoCAD. This usually proves much clearer than conversion to object names of abstract color numbers or entity types. Many modelers find further convenience in organizing entities into layers based on their eventual material assignment. This has the advantage of creating MAX objects that will share similar materials and mapping coordinates. Actually naming the layer the eventual material name is not necessary, but many find that doing so forces them to think in terms of materials within AutoCAD, and the subsequent 3DS MAX material assignment phase goes even faster.

If you are in control of how the AutoCAD drawing is organized, you will probably find that layer organization provides the most control. This enables you to give explicit names to the layers that are then shared when imported to 3DS MAX. If you inherit a drawing based on an organization that was never really meant for modeling conversion, you will probably find that the time spent changing it to a layered organization will be paid back several times over in efficiency and ease of use if you need to have an ongoing coordination of data between the two programs.

AutoCAD Entity Types

The remainder of this appendix will assume your understanding of AutoCAD entity types. With AutoCAD, you have numerous entity types, each having their own parameters (much like parametric objects begin in 3DS MAX). A line is a vector that connects two points, a circle has a center and a radius, and so on. It is common for these entities to maintain these parameters for the life of the drawing. When you perform a Render or Shade in AutoCAD, any 3DSolid or extruded line, arc, or circle is temporarily converted by AutoCAD's Renderer to its mesh equivalent. Entities unique to AutoCAD and common to 3DS MAX work are identified and explained in the following list:

NOTE

Until Release 13, AutoCAD termed everything created within it an *entity*. With Release 13 came an object-oriented approach and the desire to reflect that by changing the term from entity to *object*. For clarity, this appendix uses the term entity to mean something in AutoCAD, and the term object is reserved for things within 3D Studio MAX.

- **Polylines.** Polylines actually come in several varieties. A 2D Polyline is a continuous series of line and arc segments. 2D Polygons can be given widths to make them appear wider on-screen and plot bolder. They also can be given curve information with Curve-fit and Spline-fit options that actually create intermediate vertices to produce the curves. 3D Polylines are series of linear line segments unrestricted as to their placement. These cannot contain arcs, do not have width capabilities, and cannot be given thickness. In practice, closed polylines and those with thickness properties often prove extremely efficient for modeling basic geometry because the information stays light weight and parametric within both AutoCAD and 3DS MAX.

- **Meshes.** Entities that form a 3D skin are termed meshes within AutoCAD. Mesh entities include 3D Faces (a single rectilinear face equivalent to two 3D Studio MAX faces), polygon meshes, and polyface meshes. Polygon meshes are actually a form of polyline created with one of AutoCAD's 3D surface commands (such as RULSURF or REVSURF). Polyface meshes are arbitrary topology rarely created by the user directly but rather are the product of routines or import. When 3D Studio MAX exports a mesh to AutoCAD, the form is always that of a polyface mesh.

- **Blocks.** Blocks and Hatches (which are actually "anonymous" Blocks) are essentially drawings within drawings. These are used extensively within AutoCAD to conserve disk space by defining the block one time and using it repeatedly. In this manner, they are very similar to 3DS MAX instances. Another version of a Block is an XREF. These are externally referenced Blocks and are not actually present within the drawing but rather point to other .dwg files. Because 3D Studio MAX has no method to represent these external files, XREF blocks are not translated.

AutoCAD Entity Properties

Entities can be given certain *properties* that affect the way they are organized within the database and are treated in three dimensions. AutoCAD contains many properties that can be assigned, but only a few are relevant for export to 3D Studio MAX:

- **Layers.** All AutoCAD entities reside on *layers*, with all layer names being unique and in uppercase. A layer organizational method is required when you want names in AutoCAD to match names in 3DS MAX. Layers are the primary organization method within AutoCAD and can be placed in an Off or Frozen state for the purpose of display. Entities on a layer receive that layer's color and linetype definitions. Although linetypes are always ignored by 3DS MAX, the color can have an influence.

- **Color.** Knowledge of how color is defined is important when choosing to derive by color on conversion to 3DS MAX. Although entities are commonly given the By Layer color distinction, they can be assigned individual *color* integers from 1–255 that correspond to ACI color palette (just like layers do). This overrides any color from the layer on which the entities reside.

- **Thickness.** Many entities are allowed to have a defined *thickness*. Lines, arcs, circles, 2D polylines, traces, and solids are all eligible for a thickness property. The thickness makes the entity behave in AutoCAD as if it were a walled mesh. When an entity's thickness is zero or unassigned, it is considered to be flat. When an entity's thickness property is other than zero (any positive or negative value), the entity forms a wall perpendicular to its plane in a manner often called "extrusion."

- **Polyline width.** 2D Polylines can be given a width factor that forms a wider, bolder line when plotted. When converted to 3DS MAX, this property can be used to define meshes with any of the three formats. When combined with thickness, the width forms a cap on the top and bottom of the extruded height.

AutoCAD Versus 3DS MAX Precision

With precision as a paramount focus, AutoCAD stores its data in what is termed "double precision" (using two floating point numbers); 3DS MAX stores its data in single precision for greater speed. The primary capability gained with double precision is a larger *dynamic range*—capable of working at extremely large and small scales within the same drawing.

For actual data conversion, the issue of converting from double to single precision is usually a one-time affair with very little round off. The main issue is to define a 3DS MAX System Unit Scale in proper relation to the size of the AutoCAD model (this procedure is detailed in Chapter 5 of *Inside 3D Studio MAX Volume I*). Although not usually a problem when modeling in 3DS MAX itself, having the proper System Unit Scale can be vital when importing CAD models of vast or minute scales.

3D Studio MAX accuracy can also be degraded when the CAD model is located an enormous distance from the world origin. This can be a common situation when the model is in relation to specific data (for example, a land survey benchmark). Although increasing the System Unit Scale can adjust for this, it does so at the extent of smaller scale accuracy. Because of this unwanted tradeoff, the best alternative is usually to move the model in AutoCAD closer to the world origin before importing it into 3DS MAX.

AutoCAD's capability for exact and relative point placement is the real accuracy advantage it has. Object snap capabilities can ensure that all vertices are aligned and all faces meet at exact points. The capability to pick points and define command displacements to existing points can ensure exact entity locations. Even with these advantages, however, it is not nearly as efficient a 3D environment as 3DS MAX. It is thus not uncommon for modelers familiar in both programs to define fast, accurate 2D templates in AutoCAD for manipulation, lofting, and further manipulation in 3D Studio MAX.

Coordinating with DWG Files

The DWG format is commonly the preferred method of translation between AutoCAD and 3D Studio MAX because it maintains the highest degree of geometry possible between the two programs—it is a very "smart" translator. The DWGIO that ships with 3DS MAX R1.2 can read any version of .dwg while exporting to the R13 format.

N O T E

With the advent of AutoCAD R14, it is very likely that a more recent DWGIO will be available on the Kinetix web site that communicates with the R14 format.

Several sample .dwg files and their resulting .max scenes shipped with 3DS MAX R1.2 to demonstrate the possibilities with importing AutoCAD files for 3D modeling and visualization. Figures A.1 and A.2 show the imported files and eventual MAX model chairs. Figures A.3 and A.4 show what is possible when importing architectural data.

FIGURE A.1

The imported chair drawing.

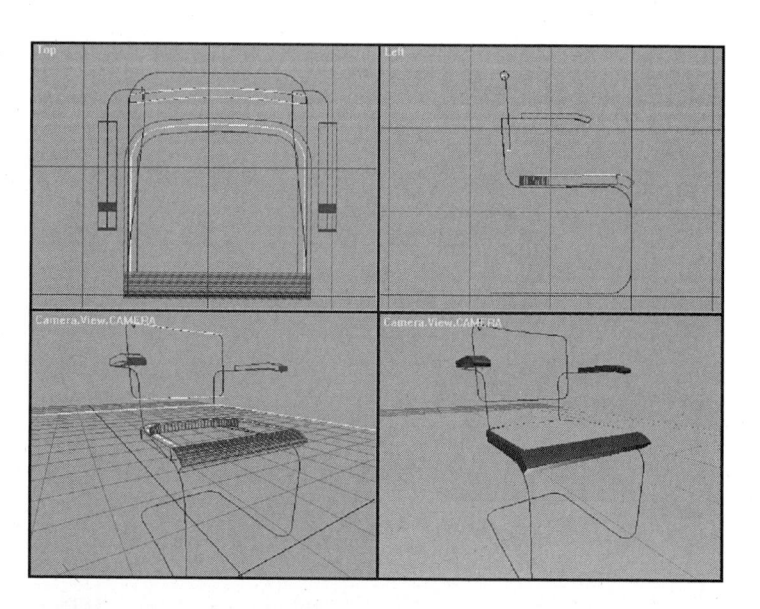

FIGURE A.2

The imported model with lofted elements on welded paths.

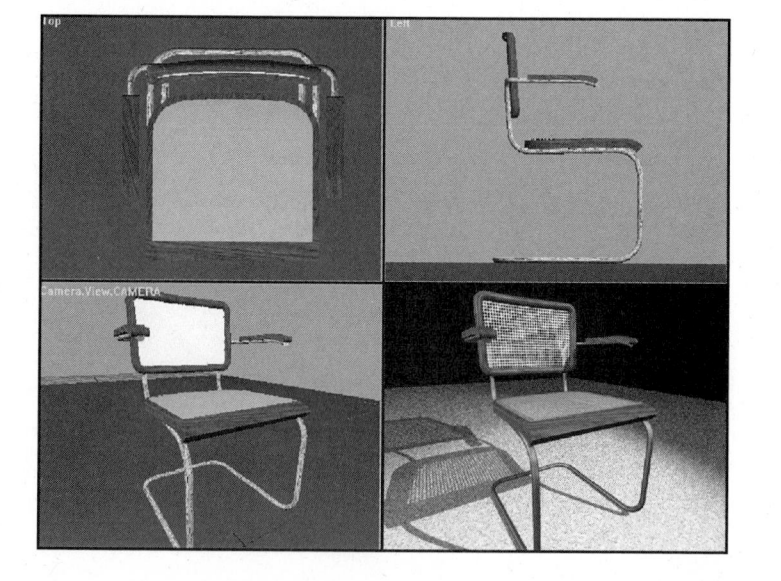

FIGURE A.3
The imported architectural drawing.

FIGURE A.4
The imported scene with lofted elements, materials, and lighting.

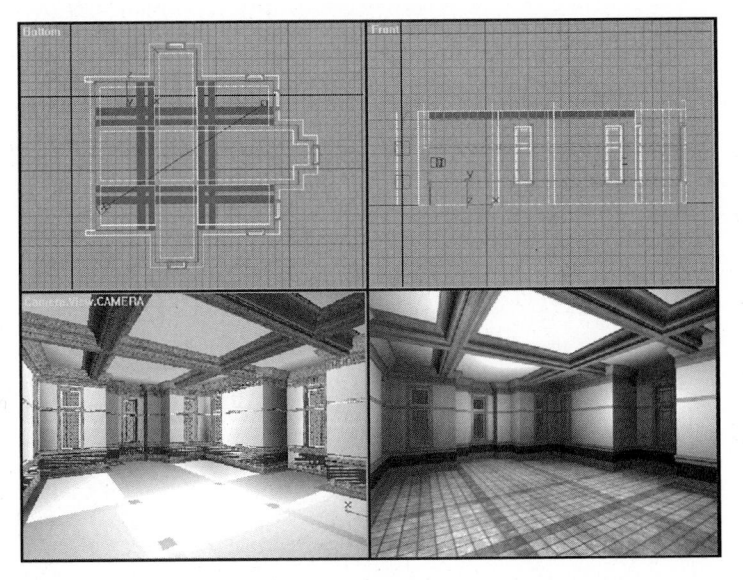

As both programs evolve, it is safe to assume that enhancements will continue to be made to the quality and extent of .dwg translation while the .3ds and .dxf translators will tend to evolve at a slower pace. The evolution of the DWGIO translator has been rapid. Three versions have been posted from just June to November of 1996, each with more capabilities than its predecessor. Each of these improvements has been available on the Kinetix web site at www.ktx.com, and the reader is strongly advised to check the web site for the very latest version, because translators such as DWGIO are often updated more often than 3DS MAX itself.

NOTE

The November 1996 version of DWGIO (version 1.11), which shipped with 3DS MAX R1.2, provided essential compatibility with Windows NT 4. All previous versions of DWGIO were incompatible with NT 4 and produced a "bad memory pointer" error on exiting 3DS MAX. It is essential that only the very latest version of DWGIO ever be used with the NT 4 operating system.

Throughout the conversion process, DWGIO strives to make the resulting geometry as parametric as possible. A circle with a thickness property, for example, will import as a Bézier Circle object with an Extrude modifier, and will export back to AutoCAD as a circle with a thickness property. The DWG Import makes several assumptions on the data translation and what you want to import into 3D Studio MAX. The defaults shown in figure A.5 involve having every check box active, and assume the following:

- The resulting geometry should be as close in nature as possible to its AutoCAD original.

- The .dwg layer organization and display status determine the resulting 3DS MAX object compositions.

- Block entities remain identifiable and easy to manipulate.

- The least number of objects should be created.

- Notational information intended for plotting (such as text, dimensions, symbols, hatches, and points) are not wanted.

- 3D objects should be made as render ready as possible.

For many users, the defaults shown in figure A.5 work quite well, but each option impacts how the AutoCAD data is translated into 3DS MAX. The DWG Import dialog is separated into four sections, discussed next.

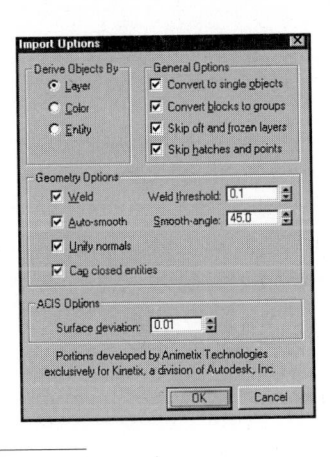

DWG Import Derive Options

The *Derive Objects By* section of DWG Import influences how the AutoCAD entities will be organized into 3DS MAX objects, and possibly groups. The Derive By options are actually just the first step in determining which MAX objects will result. You will see in the next section that the active Derive By option works very closely with the General Options. Depending on the General Options chosen, one or many MAX objects may be created per Derive By organization method. The particulars of the three Derive By options are as follows:

- **By Layer.** When translated, each object created per layer is given the AutoCAD layer name followed by a numeral. Entities that were on the Wall and Ceiling layers, for example, would become objects named WALL.01 and CEILING.01.

- **By Color.** When translated, each object created per layer is given a name based on the AutoCAD Color Index (ACI). Yellow entities (which is ACI 2), for example, will become objects named Color002.

- **By Entity.** When translated, each object created per AutoCAD entity type is given a name based on what the entity is termed in AutoCAD. Entities that were arcs and polylines, for example, will import as objects starting with Arc.01 and 2DPolyLine.01.

DWG Import General Options

The general options within DWG Import have a dramatic impact on the number of objects created in the MAX scene. These options are actually processed *first*, with the Derive By options organizing those results, and welding occurring on the contents of each object at the end. After everything is welded, the final objects are determined.

Convert to Single Objects

When active, this option combines all the entities qualified by the active Derive By option into one 3DS MAX object (note that differing AutoCAD thickness properties can affect how successful this reduction in objects actually is). If this option is not active, every individual entity within AutoCAD will become a unique 3DS MAX object. In this case, the only influence of the current Derive By method is for how each object will be named.

WARNING

Use extreme caution when making the *Convert to single objects* option inactive. It is common for .dwg files to have hundreds or thousands of entities, and converting to that many 3DS MAX objects is usually not desirable.

Convert Blocks to Groups

Blocks can contain numerous entities of any layer or color and are the only entities within AutoCAD that can be instanced in the 3D Studio MAX sense. AutoCAD blocks thus have a considerable similarity to a MAX group containing multiple objects. The *Convert blocks to groups* option completes this correlation by creating 3DS MAX groups of the AutoCAD block, with the group being given the block's name (objects within the group are named according to the Derive By option). If the block was inserted multiple times within AutoCAD, it is translated as instanced groups within 3D Studio MAX. If this option is not checked, the status of being within a block is ignored and all the entities within all blocks are imported as if the blocks had been "exploded" in AutoCAD.

Skip Off and Frozen Layers

Layer visibility is the primary method within AutoCAD for making the often vast amount of data manageable. Entities on either Off or Frozen layers are not displayed in AutoCAD in a manner similar to hidden objects in 3D Studio MAX (the only difference is that Freeze clears them from the AutoCAD display list for faster redraws; Off does not). When this option is active, entities not visible in AutoCAD will not import to 3DS MAX. This affords you a powerful and very clear sorting method for complex drawings: what you see in AutoCAD is what you get in 3DS MAX.

NOTE

The Off status of Block insertion layers does not affect the capability for those blocks to be imported by DWG Import. This is different than the method used by DXF Import, where blocks inserted on Off layers will not import.

Skip Hatches and Points

Hatches and points are AutoCAD entities nearly always intended for indicating material properties in plots in much the same way that textures are used in 3DS MAX. (This method of hatching or stippling is commonly termed pochè in drafting parlance.) When modeling, it is usually not desirable to deal with the multitude of geometry that these entities would nearly always produce. It is thus very common to have this option On. When this option is Off, the entities within hatches will convert to line segments as if they had been exploded in AutoCAD, and points will convert to Point Helper objects.

NOTE

A common need for having this option Off is when you have defined specific points in AutoCAD (possibly for camera matching) and want to import them as Point Helpers in 3DS MAX.

DWG Import Geometry Options

The actions controlled by the geometry options are performed after all entities have been organized into possible objects within the importer. The welding operation occurs next, with the resulting objects being named according to the Derive By options and the geometry being processed by the remainder of the Geometry Options.

Weld and Weld-Threshold

The Weld option looks for coincidental vertices and welds them together to form cohesive meshes or continuous splines. The question of which entity is welded to what is answered by the organization. Every entity of a given layer, color, or entity type will be tested with every other according to the respective Derive By option. Entities with different thickness properties will not be welded together because they will be receiving Extrude modifiers with different heights.

NOTE

DWG Import's Weld option affects splines as well as meshes, unlike the 3DS MAX DXF Import or AutoCAD 3DSOUT that only affect meshes.

The accompanying Weld-threshold value provides a "fudge factor" for which vertices should be considered coincidental with one another. The threshold value is in units, and a neighboring vertex is considered in range when the threshold exceeds the *absolute* distance between the two vertices. Obviously, the larger the threshold, the more vertices will be considered coincident to one another and thus welded. When vertices are welded, the location of the new vertex is the average location of the original vertices that contributed to the weld.

NOTE

The Weld options are grayed out when the Derive By Entity is chosen and Convert to single objects is Off. This is because the conversion will never combine entities, and welding cannot take place.

It is very common for 3D .dwg files to be composed of numerous 3D Faces, because they are the only real method for creating vertex-by-vertex face models in AutoCAD. Welding is essential to make these separate pairs of faces a cohesive mesh. Welding should be done with caution, however, when importing 3D models based on polyface meshes or ACIS Solids, because welding to neighboring meshes can often make the resulting normal determination inaccurate.

T I P

If you are not depending on the welding results, and are confident of the existing model's integrity, turning the Weld option Off can save noticeable time on Import because unnecessary calculations are not being performed.

DWG Import's capability to weld consecutive lines, arcs, and polylines is especially valuable because doing so is either time-consuming in AutoCAD (using the PEDIT command) or just not possible (because polylines must be coplanar and 3D polylines cannot contain arcs). This enables you to set up connections of lines, arcs, 2D polylines, 3D polylines, and splines that will become continuous Bézier splines in 3DS MAX that would be impossible to make continuous in AutoCAD. Splines with the same orientation and thickness property are also valid for welding if they will belong within the same 3DS MAX object.

N O T E

Earlier versions of DWG Import would only weld spline entities having a thickness property of zero. The latest version of DWG Import (from www.ktx.com) will weld all splines having the same thickness value and orientation.

Auto-Smooth and Smooth Angle

The Auto-smooth option performs the same function as the Auto-smooth function within either the Edit Mesh modifier or the Editable Mesh object. The angle between adjacent, welded faces is analyzed and smoothing groups are assigned based on the threshold. The higher the Smooth Angle, the sharper the angle of welded faces that is given the same smooth group (see *Inside 3D Studio MAX Volume I* for information on angle threshold calculations).

Unify Normals

The Unify Normals option orients the normals of any resulting mesh according to the standard rules within 3DS MAX. This calculation is done after all geometry has been organized and welded, so this option does not impact other results or extruded splines. This option should not generally be used when importing ACIS objects or meshes produced from other solid modelers (such as AME). This is because solids have an inherent understanding of face normal orientation due to their volume calculations, and the rules of thumb used by the program may easily undo the work already done.

Cap Closed Entities

Capping was a very valuable service that was historically provided by the 3D Studio DOS .dxf importer. With it, any closed entity was capped with a mesh, and closed entities with thickness were capped on both top and bottom. DWG Import improves on this capability by assigning an Extrude modifier to the same closed entities with the modifier's Cap Start and Cap End options On. This preserves the spline nature of the original geometry, while providing a parametric method of capping and extrusion distance. If the *Cap closed entities* option is Off, 2D closed entities will remain as splines, while closed entities with thickness are given an Extrusion modifier but with the capping options Off. DXF Import should be used if you desire an explicit mesh rather than a parametric object.

DWG Import ACIS Solids Options

ACIS is the solids engine within AutoCAD R13 and later, and many AutoCAD operations produce what AutoCAD terms 3DSolid entities. When these entities are translated, they use the ACIS engine to evaluate their surface and a mesh is formed with a density that relates to the accompanying Surface Deviation value. What must be understood is that Surface Deviation is calculated in units and not by angle. This means that a value that works for one model may not be appropriate for another of differing size. In general, the lower this value, the less adjacent faces can deviate from their parametric definition and the denser the resulting mesh becomes.

TIP

Although all Mechanical Desktop, Designer, and AutoSurf models are based on ACIS 3DSolids, they are organized in their own ARX object classes and are skipped on DWG Import because unique ARX classes are not translated by DWG Import. To import these models by DWG Import, any XREF Blocks must be made local with the XBIND command and then all ARX objects exploded into their 3DSolid components. A much easier and less destructive method is to just use 3DSOUT directly from AutoCAD and import the resulting .3ds file into 3DS MAX.

This conversion to an Editable Mesh is one of the few instances within the DWG Import where higher order geometry is being simplified. This is the only situation where the choice made on import will control how smooth curves within the resulting surfaces will be. Because of this, it is common to import the 3DSolids several times until the correct deviation can be determined for the desired smoothness and/or mesh density.

DWG Geometry Matching

AutoCAD creates much of the same geometry as found in 3D Studio, but being a different program it refers to them by different names. Knowing the basics of these names and how they relate to 3D Studio is important in extracting exactly what you need from the AutoCAD database.

Geometry Translation on DWG Import

Every piece of geometry in the AutoCAD environment that can be independently affected is termed an entity. This can be as basic as a simple Point or as complex as a Block. The basic modeling entities are *Points*, *Lines*, *Arcs*, *Circles*, and *3D Faces*. It is from these entities that more complex ones are formed (see table A.1).

TABLE A.1

DWG Format to 3D Studio MAX Conversion Mappings

General AutoCAD Entity Class	Resulting 3DS MAX Translation
Model Space Entities	All supported entities
Paper Space Entities	Not translated
AutoCAD Geometry	3D Studio MAX Objects
Line entities	Bézier Spline shapes
Arc entities	Arc shapes
Circle entities	Circle shapes
Ellipse entities	Ellipse shapes
Donut (Polyline) entities	Donut shapes
2D and 3D Polyline, Spline, Region, and MLine entities	Bézier Spline shapes
MLine intersections and caps	Not translated (explode them in AutoCAD for export instead)
Solid and Trace entities	Bézier Spline shapes with Extrude modifiers
Point entities	Point Helper objects
Text (TTF- or PFB-based) entities	Text shapes
Text (SHX-based), Shape (SHP-based), or Dimension entities	Not translated
Ray or Xline entities	Not translated
3Dfaces, Polyline Meshes, Polyface Meshes, or ACIS 3D Solids	Editable Mesh objects
Blocks	Groups or individual objects
Nested Blocks	Nested groups or individual objects
Block Instances	Instanced groups (if blocks to groups)

General AutoCAD Entity Class	Resulting 3DS MAX Translation
Anonymous Blocks (for example, Hatches), Non-Referenced Blocks, XREF Blocks, Custom ARX objects	Not translated
Non-Geometric Entities	3D Studio MAX Translation
Stored UCS	Grid Helper object
Perspective (DVIEW) Views	Free Camera objects
Point, Spot, and Directional lights	Omni, Free Spot, and Directional light objects
AutoVision Materials and Mapping	Not translated
ASE, ADE, AME data	Not translated
AutoCAD Entity Properties	3D Studio MAX Translation
Thickness properties	Extrusion modifier to Spline object
Elevation properties	Translated (not stored for return)
Polyline Fit and Spline options	Bézier Spline vertices
Polyline Width properties	Outlined Spline object
Linetype property	Not translated
Block attributes and entity X-Data	Not translated

DWG Export Options

The options shown in figure A.6 control how the 3DS MAX scene will be organized in the resulting AutoCAD drawing. Within it there are many correlations to DWG Import, and with the corresponding options chosen, a fairly reliable round trip can be made from AutoCAD to 3DS MAX back to AutoCAD.

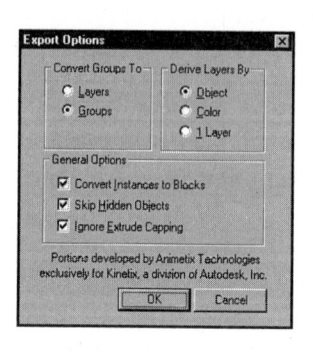

Convert Groups to Layers, Groups

3DS MAX groups are similar to AutoCAD layers in being a primary method for multi-object organizations, yet their behavior most closely parallels AutoCAD groups. There is thus a valid argument for converting 3DS MAX groups to either AutoCAD groups or layers. This option affords you that choice. Converting Groups to Layers will create layer names of the group name and supersede the Derive By options for layer organization.

Derive Layers By Object, Color, 1 Layer

As with DWG Import, the Derive By options determine the overall organization of the resulting drawing. Unlike DWG Import, the choice does *not* impact the geometry, but only the layer on which the geometry is placed. Unlike 3DS MAX objects, there is no restriction to what geometry may coexist on any given layer. With the *Object* option, a new layer will be created for every 3DS MAX object and the layer will have the color closest to the 3DS MAX object color. Objects with duplicate names (usually due to capitalization) will receive decimal suffixes. With the *Color* option, objects will be placed on layers having the color that they did in 3DS MAX and given the name MXCOLOR#. For this conversion, the 24-bit color options in 3DS MAX are converted to their closest equivalent in AutoCAD's 255-color index. With the *1 Layer* option, every MAX Object is placed on an AutoCAD layer named UNTITLED, and the resulting entities are given color properties that reflect the object colors they had in 3DS MAX.

Convert Instances to Blocks

When this option is active, a block definition will be created for any object that has been instanced at least one time. Once defined, block inserts are made for each instance. This does not affect references unless the references have themselves been instanced. Instanced groups will not be converted as blocks, although their contents will be.

Skip Hidden Objects

This option is the primary option for controlling what gets exported to the .dwg file. If left Off, the entire scene will be exported. If On, what is visible in the viewports will be exported.

Ignore Extrude Capping

When this option is On, the capping status of Extrude modifiers is ignored. This allows objects that began as AutoCAD entities with thickness to return to AutoCAD in the same state. If this option is Off, the extruded objects will convert to a mesh with the capping assigned in the Extrude modifiers. Circle shapes with Extrude modifiers are the exception to this rule; they will always import as circle entities with a thickness property.

Geometry Translation on DWG Export

With DWG Export, a sincere attempt is made to send geometry and organization back to AutoCAD in the same manner it was received, as shown in table A.2. With basic scenes, it is quite possible to perform a round trip from AutoCAD to MAX and back again that is nearly lossless.

TABLE A.2
3D Studio MAX to DWG Format Conversion Mappings

3D Studio MAX Object	AutoCAD Entity
Single Segment shapes*	Line entities
Circle shapes*	Circle entities
Donut shapes***	Polyline "Donut" entities
Ellipse shapes*	Ellipse entities
Text shapes*	Text entities (w/basic Style)
Rectangle and N-Gon shapes**	2D Polyline entities
Bézier Spline shapes (co-planar)**	2D Polyline entities
Bézier Spline shapes (3D)	3D Polyline entities
Objects with Surfaces (TriMesh and Patch)	Polyface Meshes (the current frame's validity mesh)
Grid Helper objects	Stored UCS (w/ Helper's name)
Camera Target and Free Cameras	Perspective Views (w/ Camera's name)
Omni, Spot, and Direct Light objects	Point, Spot, and Direct lights
Particle Systems and Helper objects	Not translated
3DS MAX Object Attributes	AutoCAD Results
Mesh Edge Visibility	Respected within Polyface Mesh
Animation	Current frame state is exported
Mapping coordinates and material assignments	Not translated
Hierarchy and Pivot Points	Not translated
Smoothing groups, AppData, and attributes	Not translated

Valid for Shapes with no modifiers or an Extrude modifier only. Further modifications will cause a conversion to a polyline, spline, or mesh.

**Valid for Shapes with no modifiers that cause the spline to be 3D. Further modifications will cause a conversion to a spline or mesh.*

***Valid if Ignore Extrude Capping is Off. Otherwise, it is considered as two circles.*

The DXF format is the oldest method AutoCAD has for communicating with other programs, and was the primary method available for communicating with the 3D Studio DOS series. Because of this tradition, many modelers may still rely on methods that have served them well over the years. DXF files are also used because they can communicate with a vast number of other programs. The format has been a documented standard for quite some time and many programs support it. DXF comes in four flavors: Release 13 and pre-R13 in both binary and ASCII. Although MAX reads all four, it writes only to the pre-R13, ASCII format (which is the most universally read by other programs).

Entities Incapable of 3DS MAX DXF Import

A primary issue in coordinating with .dxf files is to understand what cannot be translated from AutoCAD to 3D Studio MAX. Although 3D Studio MAX converts the majority of what a .dxf file can contain, there are entity types that it does not convert. Regardless of import options, the following AutoCAD entities can never be directly imported into 3DS MAX:

- **Entities introduced in AutoCAD Release 13 or later.** This includes Regions, Ellipses, Splines, and 3DSOLIDS. A workaround in R13 is to export these entities by the SaveAsR12 command and export the resulting conversion.

- **XREF entities.** These are externally referenced Blocks, and are files separate from the one that created the .dxf file. For 3DS MAX to read these, the XREFS must be inserted into the drawing with the XBIND command before being exported by DXFOUT.

- **Text, Shape, and Dimension entities.** If you absolutely need to import Text or Shapes into 3DS MAX, you can plot to a .dxb file and use the DXBIN command to import the file back into AutoCAD as straight line segments.

- **Point entities.** Although Points are the equivalent of isolated vertices, they cannot be translated. For raw vertex information, you need to create an open Polyline or Line and import those vertices instead.

DXF Import in 3D Studio MAX

While quickly taking a second seat to DWG Import in many studios, DXF Import is still widely used for fast mesh conversion. The DXF Import dialog shown in figure A.7 has many similarities to DWG Import.

FIGURE A.7

DXF Import for 3D Studio MAX.

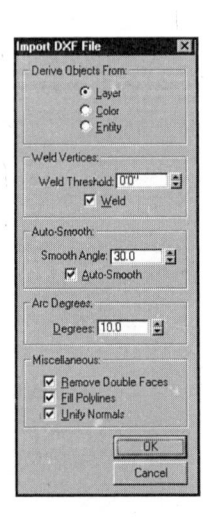

Derive Objects From: Layer, Color, Entity

The *Derive Objects From* methods of *Layer, Color*, and *Entity* work much the same as the *Derive Object By* section in DWG Import (see previous discussion). Unlike DWG Import, DXF Import will change everything into either a Mesh object or a Spline shape (there is no conversion to higher order geometries). When importing by Layer, for example, there is often a one-to-one correspondence in the number of AutoCAD layers and resulting MAX objects. If a layer were to include both splines and meshes, there would be an additional MAX object for the shape, so there is a maximum of two objects created per AutoCAD layer.

NOTE

DXF Import truncates layer names to their first eight characters and appends them with a numeral. If the layer name began with a trailing number, the original number is removed and replaced with numbers starting with 01. The truncating of numeric layer names can lead to organizational problems that should be kept in mind when naming layers for informational purposes (for example, the layers PANEL60, PANEL48, STREET42, and PANEL72 would be renamed by DXF Import as PANEL01, PANEL02, STREET01, and PANEL03).

The Derive From Entity option should only be used with the knowledge that every individual AutoCAD entity will become a separate object starting with the name Entity01. This can lead to an unmanageable amount of objects, especially if the model had been composed of 3DFaces or many lines.

Weld, Weld Threshold, Auto-Smooth, Smooth Angle

The Weld and Auto-Smooth options perform the identical functions as their DWG Import counterparts except they only affect meshes. AutoCAD arcs, lines, and polylines without thickness are never welded. The same 2D entities with thickness properties are converted to meshes on import, and the resulting meshes would then be welded if the Weld option was active.

Turning this option Off when welding is not needed will save on import conversion time.

Welding may seem like a given, but it should be used with some care. In AutoCAD models, it can be quite common for entities, such as extruded Polylines, to be stacked on top of one another. This stacking can produce many coincidental vertices within the converted object that will be welded together. This welding can destroy the original entity's integrity and will usually lead to erratic face normals when they would normally have been faced correctly. Unless you know that your model does not have such conditions (such as one composed entirely of 3D Faces) you should actually leave this option Off and weld the vertices with Edit Mesh or Editable Mesh after import.

Arc Degrees

As previously mentioned, all arc and circle entities with thickness are converted to meshes. The number of sides they are given is controlled by the Arc Degrees value. A circle with an Arc Degree setting of 5, for example, would import with 72 sides. Unlike AutoCAD's 3DSOUT, this value is used for every arc and circle entity in the imported file and gives you precise control over the resulting segmentation. Modelers that require varying segmentation levels will usually import separately exported .dxf files, or sometimes the same .dxf file, with differing Arc Degree settings.

Remove Double Faces

The Remove Double Faces option checks for coincidental faces in meshed objects. This can be a common problem for CAD-generated models, and having this option active will prevent rendering problems down the line. If your renderings are showing faces that come and go, or "flash" in an animation, it is likely that two faces are occupying the same spot.

Fill Polylines

This option has a somewhat misleading title because it actually "caps" closed polylines and circles with a mesh. Polylines and circles that have a thickness property will be capped on both the top and bottom. The exception is that polylines with a width will always be capped according to the width value and do not rely on the Fill option. If you have closed polylines and want to keep them as splines on input, you should leave this option Off.

NOTE

Nothing prevents a polyline from crossing itself and forming an illegal capping situation. In such a case, the polyline vertices will be imported as raw mesh vertices, but no capping mesh will be generated.

Entity Translation on DXF Import

Table A.3 shows how AutoCAD geometry is converted on DXF Import. Unlike DWG conversion, DXF conversion is to explicit geometry, which can make it fast when only raw meshes are required.

TABLE A.3

How AutoCAD Geometry is Converted on DXF Import

AutoCAD .DXF Entity	Translated 3D Studio MAX Object
3Dfaces, polygon meshes, polyface meshes	Mesh object (respecting AutoCAD edge visibility)
Lines, arcs, open 2D polylines, 3D polylines	Bézier Spline shape object
Lines, arcs, circles, and polylines with thickness.	Mesh object of thickness height (arcs segmented according to Arc Degree setting)

AutoCAD .DXF Entity	Translated 3D Studio MAX Object
Closed 2D polylines and circles	Coplanar Mesh object*
Closed 2D polylines and circles with thickness	Mesh object of thickness height, capped top and bottom (arcs segmented according to Arc Degree setting)*
Polylines with width factors	Coplanar Mesh object of polyline width**
Polylines with width factors and thickness	Mesh object of polyline width and thickness height, capped top and bottom (arcs segmented according to Arc Degree setting)**
Traces and Solids	Mesh object (with invisible center edge)**
Traces and Solids with thickness	Mesh object of thickness height capped top and bottom**
Blocks	Import as their separate components would
Text, Dimensions, Shapes, ACIS 3D Solids, Ellipses, Splines, XREF Blocks, AutoVision material properties	Not translated

*With the Cap Polylines option On
**Regardless of whether the Cap Polylines option is On or Off

Using AutoCAD's DXFOUT

AutoCAD writes a drawing's information to a .dxf file with its DXFOUT command. This file can be in either ASCII or compiled binary format. The ASCII format is often used because it can be edited manually or created externally by many third-party programs. The DXF file itself is broken into various *sections* entitled TABLES, BLOCKS, and OBJECTS (or ENTITIES in pre-R13 files).

After choosing the name of the .dxf file, the DXFOUT command produces the following prompt that needs some explanation because very different DXF files are produced depending on which option you select:

```
Enter decimal places of accuracy (0 to 16)/Objects/Binary <6>:
```

■ The *Objects* option prompts you to select which entities to write to a DXF file and then again for the precision of the written file (either binary or a number of decimal places). Doing this will create a file that contains *only* the OBJECTS section, and will list them in the order you selected them. Blocks *cannot* be exported with this option.

■ If you do *not* select Objects and only choose an accuracy option, AutoCAD will write *all* sections for all entities in the drawing regardless of whether their layers are frozen or turned Off. This method must be used if you want to export Block information. The OBJECTS section itself will list the entities in the order of their creation.

■ The *Decimal Places of Accuracy Option* parameter refers to how many decimal places are written for every point indication within the data base. This option will create an editable ASCII file.

■ The *Binary* option makes things much easier, because it will always write the DXF file to AutoCAD's full precision of 16 places. This file is smaller and can be read quicker, but cannot be conventionally edited.

For export to 3D Studio MAX, the only real question to ask yourself is whether you need Blocks to be exported. When you are *not* exporting Blocks, the optimum choice for DXFOUT is *Objects* followed by *Binary*. This will export only what you need and the file will be at its smallest and most accurate. If you need to export Blocks, the optimum choice is *Binary*. It is very unlikely that you will need to edit the DXF file, and you will find that the Binary option is quicker to write, faster to read, and takes much less disk space than the ASCII alternative.

When you need to export the entire drawing for Blocks, you can reduce the number of entities actually imported by turning unwanted layers Off before exporting. 3D Studio MAX ignores all entities that were on Frozen and Off layers at the time of the DXFOUT command, while the locked status of layers has no effect.

NOTE

It is possible for blocks, or parts of blocks, to display contents while the block itself is actually inserted on an Off layer. DXF Import will consider all the block's contents to be Off in this situation. Blocks on Off layers will thus not import, even though their contents may be visible in the AutoCAD session that exported them. For exporting to 3DS MAX, it is always safer to Freeze rather than turn Off layers, so you can see what 3DS MAX will convert.

Unifying Face Normals of DXF Imports

The face normals determined in the translation process are often considered the bane of using DXF files. They can be conquered, however, with a knowledge of how normals are determined and some forethought in the actual AutoCAD modeling process.

Face Normal Determination

For isolated 3DFaces, the direction of the two face normals is determined in the order in which the vertices were defined. Selecting the vertices clockwise will be opposite of a face built counter-clockwise. In actuality, there is very little need to ever consider this while modeling in AutoCAD because it is only valid for 3D Faces that do not share vertices with other faces. Whenever faces are welded to form a mesh, the determination of their normal direction is done by some rules of thumb. It is important to understand what these rules are and how you can construct models so that they weld and unify properly. Figure A.8, for example, shows the differences between a correct and incorrectly modeled opening.

Once welding has taken place, each element is analyzed and has its normals facing outward from its centroid. A properly constructed mesh is essential for this automatic process to determine what is "in" and "out." Erratic face normals will result if the mesh was built inconsistently, and only a correctly formed mesh will work properly with smoothing groups.

FIGURE A.8
*DXF correct and
incorrect ordering of
faces in a model.*

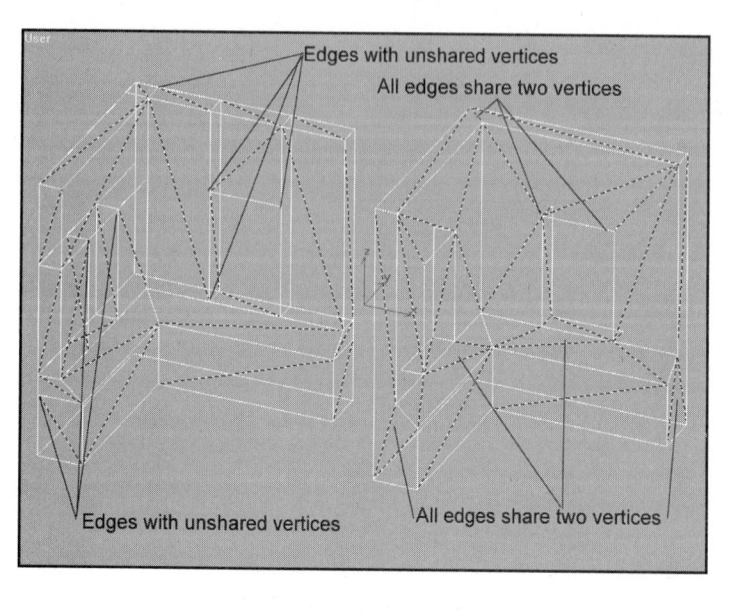

The primary rule of face building is that adjacent faces must share two vertices (that is, a complete edge) to be welded and have the faces consistently oriented. This matching of vertices must continue throughout the entire mesh. Even a few faces that do not obey this rule will usually produce errors. Another confusing situation arises when unifying normals are edges shared by more than two faces. Not only can this condition cause unpredictable normals, but it will also make the mesh invalid for use with Boolean operations and the MeshSmooth modifier.

Entities with Uniform Normal Translation

Several AutoCAD entities will consistently import with uniformly faced normals (assuming they do not self-intersect):

- Coplanar entities that are capped will have their mesh faced uniformly. The direction the element faces, however, is nearly random.

- Extruded entities will have their normals facing out in a box-like fashion as long as they do not weld with adjacent entities on import.

- Polygon mesh and polyface mesh entities will come in with uniform normals facing outward. Meshes created with the AutoCAD REVSURF may need to have their normals flipped.

The DXF entities that are troublesome tend to be 3DFaces and extruded lines and arcs. Unfortunately, these entities can make up the bulk of many models. Extruded arcs will have their normals facing away form their center, whereas extruded lines and 3DFaces are random. The only way to ensure that these entities' normals unify correctly is to build them accurately with aligned vertices following the ordering principals of shared vertices, as previously described.

TIP

Extruded lines and arcs can be formed into polylines within AutoCAD with the PEDIT command to ensure a more consistent result on DXF Import.

When using DXF files, the workhorse within AutoCAD often becomes the simple polyline. These are extremely versatile entities that efficiently define capped meshes and translate with consistent normals. Even when you do not need to cap a polyline, you should really consider closing the entity and allowing it to cap anyway. Doing so will ensure that its face normals are uniform and directed out. You will find it is much easier to select and delete capped faces than correct their normals.

Flipping Normals

The need to flip normals is almost inevitable when working with complex DXF files. As entities are translated from their layers or color, the direction and extent of the overall object become quite diverse and unfocused. This can result in objects having initially erratic normals. If the model was built correctly, these normals should be consistent on an entity-by-entity basis and are not too difficult to correct. When flat closed entities are imported as planar meshes, the direction that they face is nearly random. Objects composed of these elements will almost always need to be flipped at the element level.

DXF Export from 3D Studio MAX

When saving to the DXF format in 3DS MAX, you are presented with just one option that will control the resulting AutoCAD organization (see fig. A.9). The resulting .dxf file will contain only one AutoCAD entity type: the polyface mesh. The number of resulting layers and their names depend on which option you choose.

FIGURE A.9
*DXF Export from 3D
Studio MAX.*

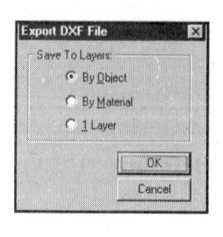

Choosing the *By Object* option will export a single mesh entity for each 3DS MAX object on a layer with the object's name. Choosing *By Material* will export a single entity composed of all the faces assigned the same material on a layer that uses the material's name. Although this option changes the object organization method considerably, it does break the scene into portions that can more easily be assigned AutoCAD-based materials. Choosing *1 Layer* exports the entire model as one entity on Layer 0.

WARNING

When exporting By Object or Material, you need to be careful that the 3DS MAX names do not contain characters that are illegal as AutoCAD layer names. DXF files with layer names that contain non-alphanumeric characters cannot be imported by DXFIN.

Each 3DS MAX object will export to a single polyface mesh on DXF Export. Objects composed of multiple mesh elements will still form a single polyface mesh entity connected by invisible edges. This may be a surprising characteristic for AutoCAD users, because an entity cannot normally be composed of unconnected portions.

Using AutoCAD's DXFIN

AutoCAD imports DXF files with its DXFIN command. When using DXFIN within an existing drawing, you will be prompted with the warning:

```
Not a new drawing — only ENTITIES section will be imported.
```

When working with 3D Studio MAX .dxf files, this is completely acceptable because only the ENTITY section was written to begin with. Objects will import as independent layers, named the object name, and will always have the color 0.

Coordinating with 3DS Files

Being the native format for 3D Studio DOS, and the original communication mechanism for AutoVision, the .3ds format command is currently the *only* method to translate materials and mapping information between 3D Studio MAX and AutoCAD/AutoVision. The AutoCAD equivalent of the 3DS MAX .3ds import and export is its 3DSOUT and 3DSIN commands. The 3DSOUT option first became available to AutoCAD users with Autodesk's companion products *Visual Link* and *AutoVision*. AutoCAD Release 13 brought the 3DSOUT capability into the core and is now available to anyone having Release 13 or later.

Using AutoCAD's 3DSOUT

In many ways, 3DSOUT is the simplest export option because what you see in an AutoCAD render or shade is what you will receive in the .3ds file. This means that to be exported to the 3DS format, the entity must define a surface. A line entity, for example, is not a surface, does not render, and will not be converted. The same line given a thickness property does have a surface and will be converted to a mesh composed of two faces. The dialog shown in figure A.10 controls the conversion from AutoCAD.

NOTE

AutoCAD's 3DSOUT command is of significant importance because it is the only method to export ARX data from AutoCAD to 3D Studio MAX without significant effort. The recent Autodesk Mechanical products are premier examples of using this custom ARX object architecture, and the easiest method to get these mechanical models to 3DS MAX is by using 3DSOUT.

The options you find in AutoCAD's 3DSOUT are nearly identical in operation to those in 3D Studio MAX's DWG Import and DXF Import. The only new option is the Override for Blocks that conveniently combines the mesh contents of each block into a single 3D Studio object, with multiple insertions of the same block being considered additional objects and not instances. Table A.4 shows the actual entity to mesh object conversion. You will probably find that the challenge in using 3DSOUT is not the dialog's options, but the critical variables not in the export dialog at all.

FIGURE A.10
*AutoCAD's 3D Studio
File Export Options
dialog.*

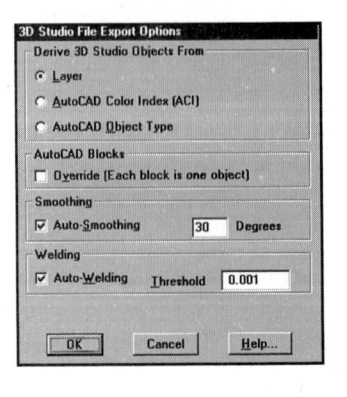

TABLE A.4

AutoCAD to 3DS Format to 3DS MAX Conversion Mappings

AutoCAD Entity	*3D Studio Conversion*
Circles*	Circular mesh
Lines, arcs*, and polylines with thickness	Mesh of thickness height (never capped)
Circles* with thickness	Circle of thickness height, capped top and bottom
Solids, Traces, and Polylines w/ width factors	The 2D mesh equivalents
Solids, Traces, and Polylines w/ width factors and thickness.	Mesh of thickness height, capped top and bottom
ACIS 3DSOLIDS**	Mesh (using unify normals is not recommended)
Saved views created with DVIEW	Target Cameras
Point, Spot, and Distant lights	Omni, Spot, and Spot lights
Material Assignments	3DS MAX Material equivalents
Mapping Assignments	3DS MAX Mapping equivalents

Segmentation is controlled by the AutoCAD VIEWRES variable.
**Tessellation density is controlled by the AutoCAD FACETRES variable.

Meshing Solids and Curves in 3DSOUT

Controlling the mesh created from 3DSOUT is unfortunately not a straight-forward procedure. Although the 3DSOUT dialog shown in figure A.10 contains controls for organization, blocks, smoothing, and welding, it does not contain anything about arc segmentation or ACIS conversion. Instead, these are controlled by AutoCAD variables that need to be set prior to using 3DSOUT.

It may help to understand AutoCAD's meshing procedures when you realize that it is the rendering portion of AutoCAD that is responsible for that program's mesh conversion and 3DS import/export. Because of this relationship to the renderer, the engine that converts arcs and surfaces to renderable meshes is concerned with producing the best result for the given, active view. Also known as *view-dependent tessellation*, this meshing technique enables the renderer to process meshes with a minimum of faces while trying to keep them relatively smooth. Unfortunately for 3D Studio MAX, this advantage can become a liability because it is not easy to predict or control what the resulting mesh resolution will be. It thus becomes very important to become familiar with the following two AutoCAD variables whenever using 3DSOUT:

- **AutoCAD's FACETRES variable.** This variable controls the mesh density of all ACIS 3DSolids (of which Mechanical models are also composed). FACETRES has a range of 0.01 to 10.0, but actually results in only 6 levels of tessellation (for a 90 degree curve, the resulting mesh will have either 1, 2, 4, 8, 16, or 32 sides). The higher the FACETRES variable is set, the larger the number of sides. The less prominent the ACIS entity is in the viewport, the fewer segments it is given.

- **AutoCAD's VIEWRES variable.** This variable was originally included to control the number of segments that arcs and circles were drawn with on the AutoCAD screen. Because arcs and circles need to be converted to meshes for rendering, the VIEWRES variable also controls their resulting segmentation. Although VIEWRES has a range of 1–20,000, the maximum segmentation is limited to 7.5 degrees for the minimum arc segment (a 48-sided circle). The less prominent the arc or circle is in the viewport, the fewer sides it is given.

Given these methods for mesh conversion, you should be aware of several situations that could cause problems in 3DS MAX. For ACIS Solids, it is very common to have different elements or features within the same model receive differing mesh densities. This means that adjacent surfaces meant to be smooth will have a seam where the vertices do not match (at fillets, for example). To correct for this, the models should either be imported with varying FACETRES settings and the elements with matching segmentation "pieced together," or use the DWG Import and see whether its tessellation is adequate. For arc segments, the maximum segmentation is often far too coarse. Broad gentle arcs may receive only one or two segments when they need to receive much more. This situation can be corrected by importing them by DXF Import (as a mesh) or DWG Import (as a parametric arc). In practice, most modelers find that these restrictions and unpredictabilities in mesh conversion make AutoCAD's 3DSOUT the choice of last resort.

NOTE

When a consistent mesh density is required, you may want to explore the option of using XBIND and EXPLODE on Mechanical Desktop models (or other ARX objects), and use 3DS MAX's DWG Import for its different tessellation method.

3DS Export from 3D Studio MAX and AutoCAD's 3DSIN

AutoCAD's 3DSIN command enables you to merge any or all of a .3ds file's contents into the current AutoCAD drawing. The dialog shown in figure A.11 includes a variation on how to organize the incoming data. Because AutoCAD cannot store information at the sub-entity level, there is no way to translate materials assigned at the sub-object level. The option to derive layers *By Material* and the *Multiple Material Objects* options give you the ability to split the incoming meshes so that AutoVision can render the materials in the way they were assigned in the .3ds file. It should be remembered, however, that AutoCAD has no method for splitting or combining mesh objects once in a drawing, so the option to split or maintain meshes on import is a significant one.

Although the 3DS format supports meshes, materials, mapping, smoothing, hierarchy, and object-level animation, AutoCAD has no way to store sub-object information. Therefore, smoothing groups and face-level mapping and materials are not retained by 3DSIN. AutoVision also has no concept of hierarchies or animation, so this information is discarded on import to AutoCAD as well. With regard to AutoCAD, the .3ds format is for meshes, materials, mapping, lights, and cameras. This loss of data does not impact the model's use in AutoCAD because that information cannot be used there. The only adverse impact of this loss is if you expect this information to be retained for a round trip back to 3D Studio or 3D Studio MAX. Table A.5 shows a summary of this conversion.

FIGURE A.11

AutoCAD's 3DSIN dialog.

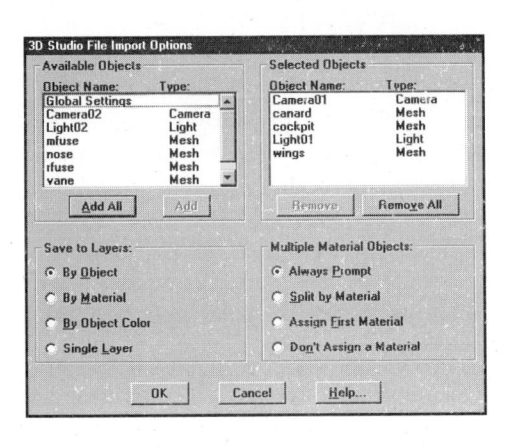

TABLE A.5

3D Studio MAX to 3DS Format to AutoCAD Conversion Mappings

3D Studio MAX Data	3DS Conversion in AutoCAD
Modifier stack	Collapsed to final mesh result
Any 3D Geometry	PolyFaceMesh
Bézier Splines and Helpers	Not translated
Material assignments*	AutoVision material equivalents**
Mapping assignments**	AutoVision mapping equivalents
Smoothing group assignments	Not translated
Cameras	Saved view with camera's name
Omni, Spot, and Distant lights	Point, Spot, and Spot lights
Pivot points, hierarchy, animation	Not translated

**Object level mapping assignments of planar, cylindrical, or spherical only
**Object level material assignments only

Note

There is currently no method to export 3DS MAX sub-object material or sub-object mapping information to AutoCAD.

In Practice: Integrating AutoCAD with 3D Studio MAX

- Most modelers that coordinate 3D data find the most effective method of AutoCAD organization is By Layer. Making the layers reflect the eventual 3D MAX material assignment makes their evolution to a finished scene even faster.

- The .dwg format preserves geometry to its highest degree. If you want your data to behave in as close to the same manner as possible between the two programs, then .dwg should be your primary choice of conversion.

- The .dxf format is ideal for when you want a complete conversion to explicit meshes. Its capability to cap closed entities with a mesh—and orient the normals of closed entities reliably—is especially valuable.

- The .3ds format is your method for exchanging material and mapping information between the AutoCAD and 3D Studio MAX.

- When exporting Mechanical Desktop models or other ARX objects, you should use AutoCAD's 3DSOUT command for converting these special objects to meshes.

- A valuable aspect of DWG Import is the ability to weld a continuous series of arcs, lines, 2D or 3D polylines, and splines into a single Bézier spline. This enables you to form shapes and paths that would otherwise not be possible in AutoCAD.

Index

Symbols

2D graphics versus real-time 3D graphics, 105

3D graphics

storage requirements, 105

see also real-time 3D graphics

3D paint packages

as materials plug-ins, 46-47

enhancing with character highlighting, 308

enhancing with character shadowing, 306

3ds files, 519

3DS MAX

AutoCAD conversion mappings, 552, 555

data exchange with AutoCAD, 519-520

geometry, matching to AutoCAD geometry, 535-541

justifying integration with AutoCAD, 518-519

porting to gaming platforms, 106

precision versus AutoCAD precision, 524-525

scenes

exporting to AutoCAD, 537-541, 554-556

saving to DXF format, 549-550

3DSIN command (AutoCAD), 554-556

3DSolid entities (AutoCAD), importing to 3DS MAX, 534-535

3DSOUT command (AutoCAD), 551-554

4D Paint plug-in, 46

applying texture maps to characters, 304-311

mapping materials to biped characters, 34

4D Vision web site, 47

A

adding

Anchor helper objects to VRML worlds, 161-162

AudioClip helper objects to VRML worlds, 163-165

Background helper objects to VRML worlds, 155-156

faces, 277

Inline helper objects to VRML worlds, 159

LOD helper objects to VRML worlds, 160

NavInfo helper objects to VRML worlds, 157

reflection to water (natural material), 367-368

Sound helper objects to VRML worlds, 163-165

TimeSensor helper objects to VRML worlds, 158

TouchSensor helper objects to VRML worlds, 162-163

VRMLOUT plug-in helper objects to VRML worlds, 155-165

Affect Region Edit Mesh modifier, 414

alignment

axes, in shapes, 122

faces with exterior frameworks, 210

loft shapes, 64

materials, 327-328

by bitmap traces, 333-337

by pixel/material ID, 328-333

by plug-ins, 343-346

by screen capture/ grids, 338-343

starting points, 328

objects in technical models, 196

scaled shapes with Path Parameter controls, 74-77

alpha channel data (images), displaying, 428

Anchor helper object (VRML plug-in), 161-162

animated materials, 491-492

blend, 496-500

color changes, 493-495

fire, 508-510

outer space, 504-508

perpetual motion simulation, 500-502

rendering as AVI files, 505

sky, 504-508

third-party plug-ins, 510-514

using time-lapse photography for, 507

water, 502-504

animation

models, 22-24

patch models, 244-246

VRML models, 148

controlling settings, 158

playing out of sequence, 158

sample rates, 150

starting with linked objects, 162

architectural modeling, 24-30

architectural models

building, 52-53

column basecap objects, lofting, 60-65

column objects, 77-83

cornice objects, 80-81

doorjamb objects, 99-101

doorway objects, 97-101

extruding from floor plans, 54-55

objects

lofting, 58-69

scaling, 59

teetering, 70-74

plinth objects, lofting, 66-67

procedures involved with, 101

real-world issues, 53

roof objects

adding moldings to, 92-97

applying treatments to, 89-91

mapping materials to, 85

modeling, 83-97

spanning, 86

scaled shapes, positioning with Path Parameter controls, 74-77

stringcourse objects, lofting, 67-69

structure, modeling, 53-101

walls

Boolean modeling, 56-57

cross-section lofting, 57

drawing as elevations, 55-56

modeling with 3DS MAX and CAD programs, 58

wireframes, 52

arcs (AutoCAD entities), importing from dxf files, 543

Atomizer plug-in, 46

attaching

spline frameworks, 263-265

vertices in spline objects, 259

AudioClip helper object (VRML plug-in), 163-165

auto-smoothing AutoCAD entities when importing to 3DS MAX, 533

AutoCAD

3DS conversion mappings, 552, 555

3DSIN command, 554-556

3DSOUT command, 551-554

blocks, converting to 3DS groups, 530

coordinating with 3DS files, 551

data exchange with 3DS MAX, 519-520

DXFIN command, 550

DXFOUT command, 545-547

entities

3DS translation from dxf files, 544-545

3DSolid, importing to 3DS MAX, 534-535

arcs, importing from dxf files, 543

auto-smoothing when importing to 3DS MAX, 533

closed, importing to 3DS MAX, 534

converting to single 3DS objects, 530

creating 3DS mesh objects from, 551-554

deriving 3DS objects from in dxf files, 542

double faces, removing during dxf imports, 544

faces, normalizing for dxf import to 3DS, 547-549

hidden, importing to 3DS MAX, 531

importing to 3DS MAX from dxf files, 541-545

mapping to 3DS mesh objects, 552

normalizing when importing to 3DS MAX, 534

organizing as 3DS MAX objects, 529

properties, 523-524

types, 522-523

welding during 3DS MAX dxf imports, 543

welding during 3DS MAX dwg imports, 532-533

files, exporting to 3DS MAX, 546

geometry, matching to 3DS MAX geometry, 535-537

hatches, importing to 3DS MAX, 531

justifying integration with 3DS MAX, 518-519

modeling organization, 521-522

plotting, 521

precision versus 3DS MAX precision, 524-525

program characteristics, 520-525

axes (shapes), alignment, 122

B

Background helper object (VRML plug-in), 155-156

bamboo (natural material)

color issues, 378

creating, 370-379

variation, 374-386

Bend modifiers, creating realistic man-made materials with, 418

Bézier Color controller, 493

Bézier handles, adjusting for accuracy/ sensitivity, 72

Bézier Point3 controller, 494

binary separation planes, 111, 116

biped characters

mapping materials to, 33

modeling, 30-34

bitmap browsers, 324, 350

bitmaps (materials)

blending with procedural textures, 373

resolution issues, 344

rotating, 332-333

troubleshooting

smearing, 402

tiling patterns, 357

blend materials, creating, 496-500

blending

bitmap materials with procedural textures, 373

dirt with mud (natural materials), 360-362

organic materials, 405

blocks (AutoCAD entity type), 523

converting to 3DS groups, 530

Blur Offset values, setting, 429

Bones Pro MAX plug-in, 298-304

Boolean operations, implementing

in architectural models, 56-57

in technical models, 200-201

browsers

bitmap browsers, 324, 350

VRML browsers, 141

Community Place, 167-168

controlling display, 157

controlling viewport colors, 156

Cosmo Player, 168

Live3D 2.0, 169

Topper, 165

updating, 166

World View, 166-167

BSPs (binary separation planes), 111, 116

Build face control (Edit Mesh modifier), 277

bump maps

faking in real-time 3D objects, 128

top value limits, 424

bursting meteor materials, creating, 455-458

bushes (natural material), creating, 387-389

C

camera views (VRML models), creating, 147-148

cardboard materials, creating, 434-435

CGI models, 16

character modeling, 223-224

creating a cartoon head, 283-289

creating a head with Bones Pro MAX plug-in, 299-304

creating a meta-
muscle superhero
arm, 291-298

mock-ups, 273

procedural overview,
238-239

seamless versus
segmented, 281-282

tools for, 276-281

via metaball modeling,
290-298

via patch modeling,
282-289

via skeletal deforma-
tion modeling,
298-304

with patch tools,
241-268

with plug-ins, 271-272

*guidelines for,
272-281*

*procedural
overview, 311*

characters

biped characters

*mapping materials
to, 33*

modeling, 30-34

building prototypes
for, 273

complex characters

*mapping materials
to, 36*

modeling, 34-36

defining, 226-229

detailing, 275

developing, 229-238

developing stories for,
230-234

emotions, establishing,
228

frogs

*blending all sides,
405*

creating, 399-408

*eyes, creating,
406-407*

sides, creating, 405

*topside, creating,
400-401*

*underside, creating,
403-404*

function of, 224-226

*as physical develop-
ment, 235-236*

*as plot development,
235*

*establishing,
235-236*

interaction between,
establishing, 234

mapping materials to
with 3D Paint,
304-311

mirroring, 275

organic, creating with
MeshSmooth
modifier, 279

personality, develop-
ing, 229, 234-235

references, 274-275

symmetrical issues,
275

thought processes,
establishing, 226-228

visual design, 236-238

*maquettes, 238-239,
274*

references, 237

sketching, 237-238

see also models; objects

**Chartres Cathedral
(architectural model-
ing example), 26-30**

Clay Studio plug-in, 42

cloning objects, 62

color

AutoCAD entity
property, 524

design issues

*in natural
materials, 378*

*in standard
materials, 505*

real-time 3D objects,
troubleshooting
limitations, 126

**color depth (real-time
3D objects), 113**

**colored light streak
materials, creating,
471-474**

**column basecap
objects (architectural
models), lofting, 60-65**

**column objects (archi-
tectural models),
modeling, 77-83**

combining
  Loft objects with primitives for technical models, 215-219
  texture maps to create blend materials, 496-500

Combustion Atmosphere Effect tool
  creating explosion materials with, 455-462
  creating psychedelic materials with, 484-486
  experimenting with, 458
  linking effects created with, 455

Community Place VRML browser, 167-168

complex characters
  mapping materials to, 36
  modeling, 34-36

conceptual sketches (object modeling), 15

concrete materials, creating, 432-433

concurrent engineering, 179

conscious lofting real-time 3D objects, 118-123

Construct's Stratus Gallery VRML site, 172-173

converting
  AutoCAD blocks to 3DS groups, 530

  AutoCAD entities to single 3DS objects, 530
  dwg files to/from AutoCAD and 3DS MAX, 525-550
  MLI files to MAT files, 352
  object instances to blocks in AutoCAD, 539
  primitive shapes to VRML primitive shapes, 150
  spline objects to smoothe/Bézier vertices, 263

convex modeling (real-time 3D gaming), 116

cornice objects (architectural models), modeling, 80-81

Cosmo Player VRML browser, 168

counting faces in VRML models, 149

Create panel (line tool), 61

cross-section lofting walls in architectural models, 57

cross-section patch models, creating, 265-268

curved surfaces, creating in real-time 3D models, 129-134

curved, transparent objects, creating in technical models, 202-215

curving mesh objects without affecting sub-objects, 279

cutouts, using in technical models for efficiency, 197

D

dancing alien (biped character modeling example), 31-34

defining characters, 226-229

Deform fit lofting, 120

deleting faces in VRML models, 143-144

Derive Objects By section (DWG Import dialog box), 529

Detailer (Paint package), 304

dialog boxes
  DWG Import
    Derive Objects By section, 529
    Import ACIS Solids section, 534-535
    Import General section, 530-531
    Import Geometry section, 532-534
  Export (VRMLOUT plug-in), 150
  Scale Deformation, 74
  Scale Transform Type-in, 62

Teeter Deformation, 72-74

digital cameras

acquiring materials from, 324-325

purchase considerations, 324

Digits of Precision option (VRMLOUT-5 plug-in Export dialog box), 150

dimensioning

technical models, 193

VRML models, 150

dirt (natural material)

blending

with grass, 359-360

with mud, 360-362

creating, 357-362

discoloring man-made materials for realism, 420-422

displaying

alpha channel data for images, 428

materials when applied to hidden objects, 383

dissolving seams, 455

doorjamb objects (architectural models), 99-101

doorway objects (architectural models), 97-101

dragons (complex character modeling example), 35-36

dwg files, 519

converting between AutoCAD and 3DS MAX, 525-550

DWG Import dialog box

Derive Objects By section, 529

Import ACIS Solids section, 534-535

Import General section, 530-531

Import Geometry section, 532-534

DWGIO translator (AutoCAD-to-3DS MAX), 528

dxf files, 519

importing AutoCAD entities from, 541-545

DXF Import, 542-545

DXFIN command (AutoCAD), 550

DXFOUT command (AutoCAD), 545-547

dynamic meta-muscles, 291

E

edge controls (Edit Mesh modifier), 278

Edge to Spline plug-in, 262-263

Edit Mesh modifier

Build face control, 277

edge controls, 278

Extrude face controls, 277

face controls, 276-277

Tessellate face control, 277

vertex controls, 278

Edit Spline 2 modifier, 288

editable meshes, creating from objects, 195

editing spline objects for cross-section patch models, 266-268

Electrolize plug-in, 512

EMBED HTML tag, reducing VRML model file size with, 151

entities (AutoCAD)

3DS translation from dxf files, 544-545

3DSolid, importing to 3DS MAX, 534-535

arcs, importing from dxf files, 543

auto-smoothing when importing to 3DS MAX, 533

closed, importing to 3DS MAX, 534

converting to single 3DS objects, 530

creating 3DS mesh objects from, 551-554

deriving 3DS objects from in dxf files, 542

double faces, removing during dxf imports to 3DS MAX, 544

faces, normalizing for dxf import to 3DS MAX, 547-549

hidden, importing to 3DS MAX, 531

importing to 3DS MAX from dxf files, 541-545

mapping to 3DS mesh objects, 552

normalizing when importing to 3DS MAX, 534

organizing as 3DS MAX objects, 529

properties, 523-524

types, 522-523

welding during 3DS MAX dwg imports, 532-533

welding during 3DS MAX dxf imports, 543

erupting volcano materials, creating, 458-460

explosion materials, creating, 454-462

Export dialog box (VRMLOUT plug-in), 150

exporting

3DS MAX scenes to AutoCAD, 537-541, 554-556

AutoCAD drawings to 3DS MAX, 546

hidden objects to AutoCAD, 539-541

object groups to AutoCAD, 538

objects to VRML, 152-153

Extrude face control (Edit Mesh modifier), 277

Extrude modifier, ignoring during export to AutoCAD, 539

extruding

architectural models from floor plans, 54-55

faces, 277

eyes (materials), creating, 406

F

fabric materials, creating, 446-448

face controls (Edit Mesh modifier), 276-277

Face Map 2 plug-in, 247

faces (3DS MAX objects)

adding, 277

alignment with exterior frameworks, 210

balancing complexity with overlap in technical models, 198

budgeting in VRML models, 142

counting, 149

deleting in VRML models, 143-144

extruding, 277

hiding

for detail enhancement, 125

in technical models, 198

in VRML models, 143-144

reducing segments in VRML models, 142-143

reducing with instances in VRML models, 145-146

reducing with Optimize Modifier in VRML models, 144-145

rounding, 278

smoothing to overcome Boolean operation results, 207

tessellating, 277

vertices, selecting, 277

faces (AutoCAD entities), normalizing for dxf import to 3DS, 547-549

far clipping planes (real-time 3D objects), 111

Ferrari (industrial modeling example), 38-40

Filter plug-in, creating Glow filters with, 465

filtering natural materials for realism, 388

finding Phase values for images, 462

fire (animated material), 508-510

flame materials, 455-458

flare materials, 475-478

flat shading real-time 3D objects, 113

fog materials, 461-462

Fractal Design Detailer plug-in, mapping materials to biped characters, 34

Fractal Flow MAX plug-in, 511

Free-form Deformation modifier, 279-281

frogs (characters)
blending all sides, 405
creating, 399-408
eyes, 406-407
sides, 405
topside, 400-401
underside, 403-404

G

gaseous materials, 484-486

Genesis Project VRML site, 170

glass materials, 440-442

Glow filter, 463
creating, 465
creating lightning bolts with, 466-467

glowing materials, 463-475

Gouraud shading, applying to real-time 3D objects, 113

gradient materials, creating a sky with, 362-365

graphics
2D versus real-time 3D graphics, 105
3D graphics
prerendered 3D graphics versus real-time 3D graphics, 110-113
storage requirements, 105
real-time 3D graphics
basics of, 106
geometry of, 106
versus prerendered 3D graphics, 110-113
Z-buffering, 111
rendering with anti-aliasing disabled, 131

grass (natural material)
blending with dirt, 359-360
creating, 357-362

Gravity Space Warp particle system, 476

grids, aiding in material alignment, 338-343

GZIP file compression, reducing VRML model file size, 152

H

half-modeling characters, 275

hatches (AutoCAD entity type), 523
importing to 3DS MAX, 531

helper objects (VRMLOUT plug-in)
adding to VRML worlds, 155-165
Anchor, 161-162
AudioClip, 163-165
Background, 155-156
Inline, 159
LOD, 160
NavInfo, 157
Sound, 163-165
TimeSensor, 158
TouchSensor, 162-163

hidden objects, exporting to AutoCAD, 539-541

hiding faces
for detail enhancement, 125
in technical models, 198
in VRML models, 143-144

highlight materials, creating, 475-478

highlighting, eliminating in natural materials, 397

I

identifying spline objects, 285

images

alpha channel data, displaying, 428

drawing on white backgrounds, for use with 3DS MAX, 251

libraries, acquiring materials from, 321-322

Phase values, finding, 462

Import ACIS Solids section (DWG Import dialog box), 534-535

Import General section (DWG Import dialog box), 530-531

Import Geometry section (DWG Import dialog box), 532-534

importing

AutoCAD 3DSolid entities from dwg files, 534-535

AutoCAD arc entities from dxf files, 543

AutoCAD closed entities from dwg files, 534

AutoCAD entities from dxf files, 541, 542-545

AutoCAD hatches from dwg files, 531

AutoCAD hidden entities from dwg files, 531

AutoCAD polyline entities from dxf files, 544

dwg files, 525-550

materials

into Material Editor, 352

into scenes, 352

MLI files with MLIIMP.DLI plug-in, 351-352

SXPs (procedural textures), 352

Indentation parameter (VRMLOUT plug-in Export dialog box), 150

industrial modeling, 38-40

industrial objects, 38-40

Inline helper object (VRML plug-in), adding to VRML worlds, 159

inserting VRML worlds in other worlds, 159

instances (objects)

converting to blocks in AutoCAD, 539

using to reduce faces in VRML models, 145-146

Intervista's VRML Circus VRML site, 171

isosurfaces, 290

K–L

kaleidoscopic materials, creating, 487

Kinetix's Character Studio software, 30

lava materials, creating, 458

layers (AutoCAD entity property), 524, 538

leaves (natural material), 396-398

light banding, troubleshooting, 469

light emission materials, 463-475

light materials, 474, 479-480

lightbulb materials, 467-469

lighting

applying to materials, 318

natural materials, 395

shadows, disabling, 474

simulating flares with, 510

special effects materials, 460

lightning bolt materials, 466-467

line tool (Create panel), 61

linking
Combustion Atmospheric Effects, 455
VRML models to other VRML worlds, 161

Live3D 2.0 VRML browser, 169

LOD (level of detail), real-time 3D objects, 111-112

LOD helper object (VRML plug-in), adding to VRML worlds, 160

LOD helper utility, 150

Loft objects, combining with primitives for technical models, 215-219

loft shapes
positioning, 64
scale factors, 60
teetering, 70-72

lofting
column basecap objects in architectural models, 60-65
conscious lofting (real-time 3D objects), 118
deform fit lofting, 120
objects
in architectural models, 58-69

in technical models, 203

plinth objects in architectural models, 66-67

real-time 3D objects, 121

stringcourse objects in architectural models, 67-69

M

man-made materials
aging, 429-431
cardboard, 434-435
concrete, 432-433
creating, 431-449
creating blurry puddles for realism, 422-425
creating dust and debris for realism, 427-429
creating oil slicks for realism, 425
creating scorch marks for realism, 426-427
denting surfaces for realism, 426-427
design guidelines, 449
design overview, 411-412
discoloring, 420-422
fabric, 446-448
glass, 440-442
imperfections, design issues, 412-413

mesh, 442-446
metal, 442-446
paper, 434-435
plastics, 438
rope, 446
rounding edges, 416-417
rubber, 439-440
smudging, 422-425
stone, 436-438
surfaces
bulging for realism, 418
chipping for realism, 415
creating seams for realism, 416
denting for realism, 416
folding for realism, 418-419
splitting for realism, 416
wrinkling for realism, 418-419
using photographs for reference, 419
vinyl, 439-440
warping edges for realism, 414-415
weathering, 429-431
wire, 442-446
wooden, 435-436

mapping
AutoCAD entities to 3DS mesh objects, 552

materials
- *to biped characters, 33*
- *to characters with 3D Paint, 304-311*
- *to complex characters, 36*
- *to industrial objects, 39-40*
- *to objects, 318*
- *to patch models, 257*
- *to roof objects in architectural models, 85*
- *to technical models, 38*
- *with non-mesh color, 340*
- objects after Boolean operations, 208

maquettes (character design), 238, 274

masking natural materials, 378

MAT (Material library) files, converting MLI files to, 352

matching
- 3DS MAX geometry to AutoCAD geometry, 539-541
- AutoCAD geometry to 3DS MAX geometry, 535-537

Material Library files, 351-352

materials
- acquiring
  - *from 3DS MAX, 324*
  - *from image libraries, 321-322*
  - *from paint programs, 322-324*
  - *from portable digital cameras, 324-325*
  - *from scanners, 320*
  - *from screen captures, 324*
  - *from surrounding resources, 326-328*
  - *from video cameras/recorders, 326*
- alignment, 327-328
  - *by bitmap traces, 333-337*
  - *by pixel/material ID, 328-333*
  - *by plug-ins, 343-346*
  - *by screen capture/grids, 338-343*
  - *starting points, 328*
- animated materials, 491-492
  - *blend, 496-500*
  - *color changes, 493-495*
  - *fire, 508-510*
  - *outer space, 504-508*
  - *perpetual motion simulation, 500-502*
  - *rendering as AVI files, 505*
  - *sky, 504-508*
  - *third-party plug-ins, 510-514*
  - *using time lapse photography for, 507*
  - *water, 502-504*

bitmap requirements, 317

bitmaps
- *blending with procedural textures, 373*
- *resolution issues, 344*
- *rotating, 332-333*
- *smearing, troubleshooting, 402*
- *tiling patterns, troubleshooting, 357*

camera distance issues, 318

color design issues, 505

design
- *considerations, 316-319*
- *efficiency, 353*

display time issues, 319

displaying when applied to hidden objects, 383

external resource files, organizing, 347

eyes, 406-407

geometrical issues, 318

gradient materials, creating a sky with, 362-365

impact on modeling, 21-22

importing
- *into Material Editor, 352*
- *into scenes, 352*

interaction with
models, 371
lab sessions, 316-319
levels, naming, 348
libraries, 321-322
lighting issues, 318
man-made materials
aging, 429-431
bulging surfaces for
realism, 418
cardboard, creating,
434-435
chipping surfaces
for realism, 415
concrete, 432-433
creating, 431-449
creating blurry
puddles for
realism, 422-425
creating dust and
debris for realism,
427-429
creating oil slicks
for realism, 425
creating scorch
marks for realism,
426-427
creating seamed
surfaces for
realism, 416
denting surfaces for
realism, 416,
426-427
design guidelines,
449
design overview,
411-412
discoloring, 420-422
fabric, 446-448
folding surfaces for
realism, 418-419

glass, 440-442
imperfections,
design issues,
412-413
mesh, 442-446
metal, 442-446
paper, 434-435
plastics, 438
rope, 446
rounding edges for
realism, 416-417
rubber, 439-440
smudging for
realism, 422-425
splitting surfaces for
realism, 416
stone, 436-438
using photographs
for reference, 419
vinyl, 439-440
warping edges,
414-415
weathering, 429-431
wire, 442-446
wooden, 435-436
wrinkling surfaces
for realism,
418-419
mapping
to biped characters,
33
to characters with
3D Paint, 304-311
to complex charac-
ters, 36
to industrial objects,
39-40
to objects, 318
to patch models, 257

to roof objects in
architectural
models, 85
to technical models,
38
with non-mesh
color, 340
naming, 348
natural materials
angle display issues,
370
bamboo, 370-379
bushes, 387-389
design overview, 408
designing, 355-356
dirt, 357-362
eliminating high-
lighting, 397
filtering for realism,
388
fine-tuning with
material IDs, 375
grass, 357-362
importance of
creating back-
ground imagery
first, 390
leaves, 396-398
lighting, 395
masking, 378
plants, 393-398
rocks, 379-385
shrubs, 389-390
sky, 362-365
tall grass, 391-392
test renderings, 356
trees, 370-379,
386-387

underwater, *384-385*

variation in, 389

vegetation, 386-392

water, 365-369

notation, 349

opacity-mapped

   creating, 392-398

   previewing, 503

organic materials, blending, 405

organizing/file management, 346-349

overview, 315-316

plug-ins, 46-47

previewing

   in bitmap browsers, 350

   in image files, 349-350

   in thumbnail images, 350

   on external CD-ROMs, 350

procedural materials, 47

realism

   design issues, 371

   through imperfection, 413-419

saving original/modified versions of, 347

special effects materials, 453-454

   bursting meteor, 455-458

colored light streaks, 471-474

erupting volcano, 458-460

explosions, 454-462

flames, 455-458

flares, 475-478

fog, 461-462

gaseous, 484-486

glowing, 463-475

highlights, 475-478

kaleidoscopic, 487

lava, 458

light emission, 463-475

lightbulbs, 467-469

lighting, 460, 474, 479-480

lightning bolts, 466-467

neon, 464-466

psychedelic, 481-487

radiant auras, 469-481

ray patterns, 469-471

shattering window, 460-462

smoke, 461-462

sparkles, 475-478

switching to Multi/Sub-Object materials, 398

using on architectural objects, 30

see also surfaces; texture maps

mesh materials, creating, 442-446

mesh modeling, 17

mesh models versus patch models, 243

mesh objects

   adjusting with edge controls, 278

   creating patch models from, 262-265

   curving without affecting sub-objects, 279

meshes (AutoCAD entity type), 523

meshes (3DS MAX), creating editable meshes from objects, 195

MeshSmooth modifier, 279

meta-muscles, 290

metaball modeling, 20-21

   creating characters with, 290-298

   plug-ins, 41-42

   using with biped characters, 33

metal materials, creating, 442-446

metamuscle feature (Metareyes Metaballs plug-in), 42

Metareyes Metaballs plug-in, 42, 290

Microsoft Foundation Class library, 272

mirroring

characters, 275

spline frameworks, 263-265

MLI (Material LIbrary) files, 351-352

MLIIMP.DLI plug-in, importing MLI files, 351-352

modeling (objects)

architectural modeling, 24-30

Boolean modeling, 56-57

character modeling, 223-224

creating a cartoon head, 283-289

creating a head with Bones Pro MAX plug-in, 299-304

creating a meta-muscle superhero arm, 291-298

mock-ups, 273

procedural overview, 238-239

seamless versus segmented, 281-282

tools for, 276-281

via metaball modeling, 290-298

via patch modeling, 282-289

via skeletal deformation modeling, 298-304

with patch tools, 241-268

with plug-ins, 271-281, 311

conceptual sketches, 15

fine-tuning

with attention to detail, 23-24

with real-world observation, 23

industrial modeling, 38-40

mesh modeling, 17

metaball modeling, 20-21

for characters, 290-298

plug-ins, 41-42

using with biped characters, 33

methods of, 14

NURBS modeling, 20, 38

plug-ins, 42-44

using in complex character modeling, 35

patch modeling, 19, 241-242

accuracy issues, 247

advantages of, 243-244

assigning keyboard shortcuts for efficiency, 246

creating a hand, 249-257

creating a head, 262-265

creating a torso, 257-261

creating an arm with cross-sections, 265-268

for characters, 282-289

plug-ins, 242-243

procedural overview, 248-249, 268

resource materials, 249, 258

using in 3DS MAX versus other programs, 242-243

using with biped characters, 33

plug-ins, 40-46

process of, 14-22

real-world implementation, 22-24

skeletal deformation modeling for characters, 298-304

solid modeling, 19

using in architectural objects, 28

versus wireframe modeling, 52

spline modeling, 18

plug-ins, 45-46

using in architectural objects, 28

technical modeling, 36, 175-183
animation issues, 186
common products created with, 187
for legal animation, 177-183
for technical documentation, 179
for technical promotion illustrations, 179-180
for technical proposal illustrations, 180-183, 187-220
plug-ins, 185
precision issues, 185-186
procedural overview, 219-220
scheduling requirement issues, 184-185
target audience, 183-184
visual accuracy issues, 186
techniques, 17-21
using with materials, 21-22
versus texture mapping in real-time 3D gaming, 114
VRML modeling, 141-152, 172-173
models (objects)
animation, 22-24

architectural
building, 52-53
column basecap objects, lofting, 60-65
column objects, 77-83
cornice objects, 80-81
doorjamb objects, 99-101
doorway objects, 97-101
extruding from floor plans, 54-55
objects, lofting, 58-69
objects, scaling, 59
objects, teetering, 70-74
plinth objects, lofting, 66-67
procedures involved with, 101
real-world issues, 53
roof objects, 83-97
scaled shapes, positioning with Path Parameter, 74-77
stringcourse objects, lofting, 67-69
walls, Boolean modeling, 56-57
walls, cross-section lofting, 57
walls, drawing as elevations, 55-56

walls, modeling with 3DS MAX and CAD programs, 58
wireframes, 52
architecural models, structuring, 53-101
CGI models, 16
character models
biped characters, 30-34
building prototypes for, 273
complex characters, 34-36
defining, 226-229
detailing, 275
developing, 229-238
developing stories for, 230-234
emotions, establishing, 228
frogs, 399-408
function of, 224-226, 235-236
interaction between, establishing, 234
mapping materials to with 3D Paint, 304-311
mirroring, 275
organic, creating with MeshSmooth modifier, 279
personality, developing, 229, 234-235
references, 274-275

symmetrical issues,
275

thought processes,
establishing,
226-228

visual design,
236-239, 274

interaction with
materials, 371

mesh models versus
patch models, 243

patch models

anatomical struc-
tures, 249-268

animation, 244-246

constructing from
extruded splines,
248

constructing from
mesh/primitive
objects, 248

creating from mesh
objects, 262-265

creating spline
frameworks for,
252-255, 258-259

limitations, 246-247

materials, mapping,
257

surfaces, control
problems, 246

surfaces, creating,
255-261

surfaces, creating
sharp edges for,
260-261

surfaces, fine-
tuning, 260

templates, creating
from images,
250-252, 258

texture map limita-
tions, 247

versus mesh models,
243

physical models, 16

polygonal models,
290-298

rough, 16

technical models

Boolean operations,
implementing,
200-201

combining Loft
objects with
primitives,
215-219

componets, build-
ing, 192-202

curved, transparent
objects, creating,
202-215

cutouts, using for
efficiency, 197

dimensioning, 193

environment,
establishing, 191

faces, balancing
complexity with
overlap, 198

faces, hiding, 198

object alignment,
196

object lofting, 203

preliminary render-
ings, 188-189

profiles, changing,
195

retaining object
history, 194

scene components,
189-192

symmetry, shortcuts
for, 199

VRML models

animation, 148,
150, 158, 162

camera views,
creating, 147-148

dimensioning, 150

faces, budgeting,
142

faces, deleting/
hiding, 143-144

faces, reducing
segments, 142-143

faces, reducing with
instances, 145-146

faces, reducing with
Optimize Modifier,
144-145

linking to other
VRML worlds, 161

performance issues,
141-148

previewing, 150

reducing file size
with EMBED
statement, 151

reducing file size
with GZIP file
compression, 152

reducing file size with texture maps, 146-147

size considerations, 141-148

see also objects

modifiers

Affect Region Edit Mesh, 414

Bend, creating realistic man-made materials with, 418

Edit Mesh, 276-281

Edit Spline 2, 288

Extrude, ignoring during export to AutoCAD, 539

Free-form Deformation, 279-281

MeshSmooth, 279

Noise

adding realism to man-made materials, 414

creating psychedelic materials with, 482-484

Relax, 278-279

Taper, creating realistic man-made materials with, 418

UVW Mapping, 402

mud (natural material), 360-362

N

naming

material levels, 348

materials, 348

natural materials

angle display issues, 370

bamboo

color issues, 378

creating, 370-379

variation, 374-386

bushes, 387-389

creating background imagery first, 390

designing, 355-356, 409

dirt

blending with mud, 360-362

creating, 357-362

eliminating highlighting, 397

filtering for realism, 388

fine-tuning with material IDs, 375

grass

blending with dirt, 359-360

creating, 357-362

leaves, 396-398

lighting, 395

masking, 378

mud, blending with dirt, 360-362

plants, 393-398

rocks, 379-385

shrubs, 389-390

sky

creating, 362-365

rendering, 363

tall grass, 391-392

test renderings, 356

trees, 370-379, 386-387

underwater, 384-385

variation in, 389

vegetation, 386-392

water

creating, 365-367

fine-tuning reflection in, 368-369

reflection, adding, 367-368

rendering, 366

special effects, 369

NavInfo helper object (VRML plug-in), adding to VRML worlds, 157

neon materials, 464-466

Noise Float, 494

Noise Modifier

adding realism to man-made materials, 414

creating psychedelic materials with, 482-484

Noise Point3 controller, 494

Non-uniform rational B-spline modeling, *see* **NURBS modeling**

normalizing

AutoCAD entities when importing to 3DS MAX, 534

AutoCAD entity faces for dxf import to 3DS MAX, 547-549

NURBS (Non-uniform rational B-spline) modeling, 20, 38

plug-ins, 42-44

third-party software requirements, 20

using in complex character modeling, 35

O

objects

alignment in technical models, 196

architectural models

lofting, 58-69

scaling, 59

teetering, 70-74

Bézier handles, adjusting for accuracy/sensitivity, 72

cloning, 62

curved, transparent, creating in technical models, 202-215

exporting to VRML, 152-153

faces

adding, 277

alignment with exterior frameworks, 210

balancing complexity with overlap in technical models, 198

budgeting in VRML models, 142

counting, 149

deleting in VRML models, 143-144

extruding, 277

hiding for detail enhancement, 125

hiding in technical models, 198

hiding in VRML models, 143-144

reducing segments in VRML models, 142-143

reducing with instances in VRML models, 145-146

reducing with Optimize Modifier in VRML models, 144-145

rounding, 278

smoothing to overcome Boolean operation results, 207

tessellating, 277

vertices, selecting, 277

groups, exporting to AutoCAD, 538

hidden, exporting to AutoCAD, 539-541

industrial objects

mapping materials to, 39-40

modeling, 38-40

instances

converting to blocks in AutoCAD, 539

using to reduce faces in VRML models, 145-146

layers, organizing when exporting to AutoCAD, 538

Loft objects, combining with primitives for technical models, 215-219

lofting in technical models, 203

materials, alignment, 326-327

mesh objects

adjusting with edge controls, 278

creating patch models from, 262-265

curving without affecting sub-objects, 279

modeling

conceptual sketches, 15

mesh modeling, 17

metaball modeling, 20-21

methods of, 14

NURBS modeling, 20

patch modeling, 19
process of, 14-22
solid modeling, 19
spline modeling, 18
techniques, 17-21
organic objects
creating, 399-408
planar mapping,
402
polygon counts,
reducing, 79
real-time 3D objects
bump maps, faking,
128
color depth, 113
color limitations,
troubleshooting,
126
conscious lofting,
118-123
curved surfaces,
creating, 129-134
detailing with
opacity mapping,
134-136
far clipping planes,
111
flat shading, 113
Gouraud shading,
113
LODs, 111-112
lofting, 121
modeling guide-
lines, 114
modeling low-res on
high-res templates,
117-118
shadows, 112

spot-light effects,
creating, 129
surface properties,
110
texture maps,
113-115, 126-136
transforms, 107-109
remapping after
Boolean operations,
208
scaling with non-
uniform scale trans-
form, 62
selecting by name, 62
spline objects
3DS MAX
workaround, 287
converting to
smooth / Bézier
vertices, 263
creating, 262
creating for cross-
section patch
models, 265-266
editing for cross-
section patch
models, 266-268
identifying, 285
vertices, attaching,
259
technical objects
mapping materials
to, 38
modeling, 36-38
Trim objects, creating
man-made materials
with, 415
vertices, validating,
125

VRMLOUT plug-in
helper objects
adding to VRML
worlds, 155-165
Anchor, 161-162
AudioClip, 163-165
Background,
155-156
Inline, 159
LOD, 160
NavInfo, 157
Sound, 163-165
TimeSensor, 158
TouchSensor,
162-163
see also characters;
models; shapes
**Omni lights, using to
create special effects
materials, 480**
**opacity-mapped
materials**
creating, 392-398
detailing real-time 3D
objects with, 134-136
previewing, 503
Optimize Modifier
reducing faces in
VRML models,
144-145
using for real-time 3D
gaming models, 118
**organic characters,
creating with
MeshSmooth modi-
fier, 279**
**organic materials,
blending, 405**

organic objects
    creating, 399-408
    planar mapping, 402
outer space (animated material), 504-508
Oz Inc. VRML site, 170

P

paint programs, acquiring materials from, 322-324
Paintbrush
    aiding in material alignment, 327-346
    transfering Clipboard contents to images, 339
paper materials, 434-435
Particle Systems
    display, controlling, 477
    using to create sparkle/flare/highlight materials, 475-478
Patch MatID plug-in, 247
patch modeling, 19, 241-242
    accuracy issues, 247
    advantages of, 243-244
    assigning keyboard shortcuts for efficiency, 246
    creating a hand, 249-257

creating a head, 262-265
creating a torso, 257-261
creating an arm with cross-sections, 265-268
for characters, 282-289
plug-ins, 242-243
procedural overview, 248-249, 268
resource materials, 249, 258
using in 3DS MAX versus other programs, 242-243
using with biped characters, 33
patch models
    anatomical structures, 249-268
    animation, 244-246
    creating
        from extruded splines, 248
        from mesh objects, 248, 262-265
        from primitive objects, 248
    creating spline frameworks for, 252-255, 258-259
    limitations, 246-247
    materials, mapping, 257

surfaces
    control problems, 246
    creating, 255-261
    fine-tuning, 260
    sharp edges, creating, 260-261
templates, creating from images, 250-252, 258
texture map limitations, 247
versus mesh models, 243
PatchOut plug-in, 247
Path Parameter controls, positioning scaled shapes, 74-77
Pesce, Mark, 140
Phase values (images), finding, 462
physical models, 16
planar mapping (organic objects), 402
plants (natural material), 393-398
plastic materials, 438
playing VRML model animation
    out of sequence, 158
    with linked objects, 162
plinth objects (architectural models), 66-67
plotting in AutoCAD, 521

plug-ins

4D Paint, mapping materials to biped characters, 34

aiding in material alignment, 343-346

Atomizer, 46

Bones Pro MAX, 298-304

character modeling with, 271-281

Clay Studio plug-in, 42

developing for technical modeling, 185

Edge to Spline, 262-263

Electrolize, 512

Face Map 2, 247

Filter, creating Glow filters with, 465

Fractal Design Detailer, mapping materials to biped characters, 34

Fractal Flow MAX, 511

importance of, 40

materials-related, 46-47

metaball modeling requirements, 20

metaball modeling-related, 41-42

Metareyes Metaballs plug-in, 42, 290

MLIIMP.DLI, importing MLI files, 351-352

modeling plug-ins, 40-46

NURBS modeling-related, 42-44

Patch MatID, 247

patch modeling-related, 242-243

PatchOut, 247

real-time 3D graphics-related, 106

Rhino, 42

Sculptor NT, 43

SnapShot Plus, 46

spline modeling-related, 45-46

Surface Tools, 45, 257, 282-289

Texture Lab, 47, 511

Tree Factory, 504

types of, 40

unwrap, mapping materials to biped characters, 33

UNWRAP.DLU, aligning materials with, 343-346

VRMLOUT, 149-150

   Export dialog box, 150

   helper objects, adding to VRML worlds, 155-165

   LOD helper utility, 150

   Polygon Counter utility, 149

   procedural overview, 154-155

see also third-party software

Polygon Counter utility, 142, 149

polygon counts (objects), reducing, 79

polygonal models, 290-298

polyline width (AutoCAD entity property), 524

polylines (AutoCAD entity type), 523, 544

prerendered 3D graphics versus real-time 3D graphics, 110-113

previewing

materials

   in bitmap browsers, 350

   in image files, 349-350

   in thumbnail images, 350

   on external CD-ROMs, 350

   opacity, 503

   when applied to hidden objects, 383

VRML models, 150

primitive shapes

combining with Loft objects for technical models, 215-219

converting to VRML primitive shapes, 150

modifying for use with real-time 3D gaming, 123-126

Primitives option (VRMLOUT plug-in Export dialog box), 150

procedural materials, 47

profiles (technical models), changing, 195

properties (AutoCAD entities), 523-524

psychedelic materials, 481-487

Pyromania **(animated material), 508**

R

radiant aura materials, 469-481

ray pattern materials, 469-471

real-time 3D gaming

  convex modeling for accurate display, 116

  efficiency in design, 115

  explosion of, 103-104

  future developments, 137

  modeling versus texture mapping, 114

  modifying primitives for use with, 123-126

  procedural guidelines, 137

real-time 3D graphics

  basics of, 106

  geometry of, 106

  versus

    2D graphics, 105

    prerendered 3D graphics, 110-113

  Z-buffering, 111

real-time 3D objects

  bump maps, faking, 128

  color

    depth, 113

    limitations, troubleshooting, 126

  conscious lofting, 118-123

  curved surfaces, creating, 129-134

  detailing with opacity mapping, 134-136

  far clipping planes, 111

  flat shading, 113

  Gouraud shading, 113

  LODs, 111-112

  lofting, 121

  modeling guidelines, 114

  modeling low-res on high-res templates, 117-118

  shadows, 112

  spot-light effects, creating, 129

  surface properties, 110

  texture maps, 113

    limitations, troubleshooting, 127

    versus meshes, 114-115

  transforms, 107-109

redraw time, speeding up in VRML worlds, 160

reducing

  faces

    in VRML models with Optimize Modifier, 144-145

    with instances in VRML models, 145-146

  polygon counts for objects, 79

  segments in VRML model faces, 142-143

  VRML model file size

    with EMBED statement, 151

    with GZIP file compression, 152

    with texture maps, 146-147

reflection, adding to water (natural material), 367-369

Relax modifier, 278-279

remapping objects after Boolean operations, 208

rendering

  animated materials as AVI files, 505

  graphics with anti-aliasing disabled, 131

  sky (natural material), 363

  speeding up, 381, 471

  water (natural material), 366

Rhino NURBS modeler plug-in, 36, 42

rocks (natural material), 379-385

roof objects (architectural models)

  adding moldings to, 92-97

  applying treatments to, 89-91

  mapping materials to, 85

  modeling, 83-97

  spanning, 86

rope materials, 446

rotating bitmaps in materials, 332-333

rough modeling, 16

rounding faces, 278

rubber materials, 439-440

S

Sample Rate parameter (VRMLOUT plug-in Export dialog box), 150

sample rates (VRML model animation), 150

saving

  3DS MAX scenes to DXF format, 549-550

  materials, original/ modified versions of, 347

Scale Deformation dialog box, 74

scale factors (loft shapes), 60

Scale Transform Type-in dialog box, 62

scaled shapes, positioning with Path Parameter controls, 74-77

scaling objects

  in architectural models, 59

  with non-uniform scale transform, 62

scanners, acquiring materials from, 320

screen captures, aiding in material alignment, 338-343

Sculptor NT plug-in, 43

seamless character modeling versus segmented, 281-282

seams, dissolving, 455

segmented character modeling versus seamless, 281-282

segments (VRML model faces), reducing, 142-143

Select by Name dialog box, 58

shadows

  disabling, 474

  real-time 3D objects, 112

shapes

  axes, alignment, 122

  loft shapes

    positioning, 64

    scale factors, 60

    teetering, 70-72

  primitives

    combining with Loft objects for technical models, 215-219

    converting to VRML primitive shapes, 150

    modifying for use with real-time 3D gaming, 123-126

  scaled shapes, positioning with Path Parameter controls, 74-77

  scaling

    in architectural models, 59

    with non-uniform scale transforms, 62

  teetering with vertex manipulation, 94

  see also objects

sharpening texture maps, 394

shattering window materials, 460-462

shrubs (natural material), 389-390

skeletal deformation modeling for characters, 298-304

sketching, *see* **conceptual sketches**

sky

animated material, 504-508

natural material, 362-365

rendering, 363

smoke materials, 461-462

Smooth modifier, locating bad faces created by Boolean operations, 207

smoothing faces to overcome Boolean operation results, 207

SnapShot Plus plug-in, 46

software (third-party)

Kinetix's Character Studio software, 30

NURBS modeling requirements, 20

Rhino NURBS modeler, 36

see also plug-ins

solid modeling, 19

using in architectural objects, 28

versus wireframe modeling, 52

Sound helper object (VRML plug-in), adding to VRML worlds, 163-165

space (animated material), 504-508

space station (technical modeling example), 37

spanning roof objects in architectural models, 86

sparkle materials, 475-478

special effects, using on water (natural materials), 369

special effects materials, 453-454

bursting meteor, 455-458

colored light streaks, 471-474

erupting volcano, 458-460

explosions, 454-462

flames, 455-458

flares, 475-478

fog, 461-462

gaseous, 484-486

glowing, 463-475

highlights, 475-478

kaleidoscopic, 487

lava, 458

light emission, 463-475

lightbulbs, 467-469

lighting, 460, 474, 479-480

lightning bolts, 466-467

neon, 464-466

psychedelic, 481-487

radiant auras, 469-481

ray patterns, 469-471

shattering window, 460-462

smoke, 461-462

sparkles, 475-478

speeding up rendering, 160, 381, 471

spline frameworks

attaching, 263-265

creating for patch models, 252-255, 258-259

creating with Edge to Spline plug-in, 262-263

mirroring, 263-265

spline modeling, 18

plug-ins, 45-46

using in architectural objects, 28

spline objects

3DS MAX workaround, 287

converting to smooth/Bézier vertices, 263

creating, 262

creating for cross-section patch models, 265-266

editing for cross-section patch models, 266-268

identifying, 285

vertices, attaching, 259

spot-light effects (real-time 3D objects), 129

static meta-muscles, 291

Steel Studio Landscape VRML site, 171

stone materials, 436-438

stories (character development), 230-234

stringcourse objects (architectural models), lofting, 67-69

surface properties (real-time 3D objects), 110

Surface Tools plug-in, 45, 257, 282-289

surfaces
creating for patch models, 255-257, 259-261
fine-tuning for patch models, 260
isosurfaces, 290
patch models, control problems, 246
sharp edges, creating for patch models, 260-261
see also materials; texture maps

SXPs (procedural textures), importing, 352

T

tall grass (natural material), 391-392

Taper modifier, creating realistic man-made materials with, 418

target spotlights, using to create special effects materials, 480

technical modeling, 36, 175-183
animation issues, 186
common products created with, 187
for legal animation, 177-183
for technical documentation, 179
for technical promotion illustrations, 179-180
for technical proposal illustrations, 180-183, 187-220
plug-ins, 185
precision issues, 185-186
procedural overview, 220
scheduling requirement issues, 184-185
target audience, 183-184
visual accuracy issues, 186

technical models
Boolean operations, implementing, 200, 201
combining Loft objects with primitives, 215-219
componets, building, 192-202
curved, transparent objects, creating, 202-215
cutouts, using for efficiency, 197
dimensioning, 193
environment, establishing, 191
faces
balancing complexity with overlap, 198
hiding, 198
objects
alignment, 196
lofting, 203
mapping materials to, 38
modeling, 36-38
preliminary renderings, 188-189
profiles, changing, 195
retaining object history, 194
scene components, 189-192
symmetry, shortcuts for, 199

Teeter Deformation dialog box, 72-74

teetering

loft shapes, 70-72

objects in architectural models, 70-74

shapes with vertex manipulation, 94

templates (patch models), creating from images, 250-252, 258

Tessellate face control (Edit Mesh modifier), 277

tessellating

faces, 277

man-made materials, 414

test rendering natural materials, 356

Texture Lab plug-in, 47, 511

texture mapping versus modeling in real-time 3D gaming, 114

texture maps

applying to characters with 3D Paint, 304-311

bump maps

faking in real-time 3D objects, 128

top value limits, 424

combining to create blend materials, 496-500

implementing in VRML models for file size reduction, 146-147

opacity maps, detailing real-time 3D objects with, 134-136

patch model limitations, 247

real-time 3D objects, 113, 126-136

sharpening, 394

see also materials; surfaces

thickness (AutoCAD entity property), 524

third-party software

animated material-related, 510-514

Kinetix's Character Studio software, 30

NURBS modeling requirements, 20

Rhino NURBS modeler, 36

Thumbnails Plus, 350

see also plug-ins

thumbnail images, previewing materials in, 350

Thumbnails Plus software, 350

time lapse photography, creating animated materials, 507

TimeSensor helper object (VRML plug-in), 158

Topper VRML browser, 165

TouchSensor helper object (VRML plug-in), 162-163

transforms (real-time 3D objects), 107-109

Tree Factory plug-in, 504

trees (natural materials), 370-379, 386-387

Trim objects, creating man-made materials with, 415

troubleshooting

light banding, 469

real-time 3D objects

color limitations, 126

texture limitations, 126-136

smearing in material bitmaps, 402

texture maps with patch models, 247

tiling patterns in material bitmaps, 357

U

underwater materials, 384-385

unwrap plug-in, mapping materials to biped characters, 33

UNWRAP.DLU plug-in, aligning materials with, 343-346

updating VRML browsers, 166

utilities

LOD helper, 150

Polygon Counter, 142, 149

see also modifiers; plug-ins

UVW Mapping modifier, 402

V

vegetation (natural material), 386-392

vertex controls (Edit Mesh modifier), 278

vertices

faces, selecting, 277

objects, double checking, 125

spline objects, attaching, 259

video cameras/recorders, acquiring materials from, 326

vinyl materials, 439-440

VRML (Virtual Reality Markup Language), 139

3DS MAX object support, 152-153

browsers, 141

Community Place, 167-168

controlling display, 157

controlling viewport colors, 156

Cosmo Player, 168

Live3D 2.0, 169

Topper, 165

updating, 166

World View, 166-167

sites, 140

Construct's Stratus Gallery, 172-173

Genesis Project, 170

Intervista's VRML Circus, 171

Oz Inc., 170

Steel Studio Landscape, 171

source code, disabling indentation for file size reduction, 150

specification, 140-141

version 1.0 versus 2.0, 165

worlds

adding Anchor helper objects, 161-162

adding AudioClip helper objects, 163-165

adding Background helper objects, 155-156

adding Inline helper objects, 159

adding LOD helper objects, 160

adding NavInfo helper objects, 157

adding Sound helper objects, 163-165

adding TimeSensor helper objects, 158

adding TouchSensor helper objects, 162-163

controlling browser viewport color, 156

controlling VRML browser display, 157

creating with 3DS MAX, 153

inserting in other worlds, 159

speeding redraw time, 160

VRML Consortium, 141

VRML modeling, 141-152, 172-173

VRML models

animation, 148

controlling settings, 158

playing out of sequence, 158

sample rates, 150

starting with linked objects, 162

camera views, creating, 147-148

dimensioning, 150

faces
  budgeting, 142
  deleting, 143-144
  hiding, 143-144
  *reducing segments,
    142-143*
  *reducing with
    instances, 145-146*
  *reducing with
    Optimize Modifier,
    144-145*
linking to other VRML
  worlds, 161
performance issues,
  141-148
previewing, 150
reducing file size
  *with EMBED
    statement, 151*
  *with GZIP file
    compression, 152*
  *with texture maps,
    146-147*
size issues, 141-148
**VRMLOUT plug-in,
  149-150**
creating VRML worlds
  with, 153-165
Export dialog box, 150
helper objects
  *adding to VRML
    worlds, 155-165*
  Anchor, 161-162
  AudioClip, 163-165
  *Background,
    155-156*

Inline, 159
LOD, 160
NavInfo, 157
Sound, 163-165
TimeSensor, 158
*TouchSensor,
  162-163*
LOD helper utility,
  150
Polygon Counter
  utility, 149
procedural overview,
  154-155

W

**walls (architectural
  models)**
  Boolean modeling,
    56-57
  cross-section lofting,
    57
  drawing as elevations,
    55-56
  modeling with 3DS
    MAX and CAD
    program, 58
water
  animated material
    creating, 502-504
    *reflection, adding,
      504*
  natural material
    creating, 365-367
    *fine-tuning reflec-
      tion in, 368-369*

  *reflection, adding,
    367-368*
  rendering, 366
  special effects, 369
**welding AutoCAD
  entities**
  during 3DS MAX dwg
    imports, 532-533
  during 3DS MAX dxf
    imports, 543
wire materials, 442-446
wireframes, 52
**wooden materials,
  435-436**
workcells, 187
**World View VRML
  browser, 166-167**
worlds (VRML)
  Anchor helper objects,
    adding, 161-162
  AudioClip helper
    objects, adding,
    163-165
  Background helper
    objects, adding,
    155-156
  controlling browser
    viewport color
    control, 156
  controlling VRML
    browser display, 157
  creating with 3DS
    MAX, 153
  Inline helper objects,
    adding, 159
  inserting in other
    worlds, 159

LOD helper objects,
  adding, 160

NavInfo helper objects,
  adding, 157

Sound helper objects,
  adding, 163-165

speeding redraw time,
  160

**TimeSensor helper
objects, adding, 158**

TouchSensor helper
  objects, adding,
  162-163

X–Y–Z

Z-buffering, 111